Programming by Design

A First Course in Structured Programming

Programming by Design

A First Course in Structured Programming

Special Edition

Philip L. Miller, PhD
Computer Science Department
Carnegie Mellon University

Lee W. Miller
Computer Science Department
Carnegie Mellon University

with Purvis M. Jackson
Software Engineering Institute
Carnegie Mellon University

Wadsworth Publishing Company
Belmont, California

Carnegie Publishing, Inc.
Pittsburgh, Pennsylvania

ISBN 0-534-08244-0

Printed in the United States of America
1 2 3 4 5 6 7 8 9 — 90 89 88 87

Dedicated to the students for whom this was written

in memory of my mother,
Martha E. Miller,
1921-1985

P.L.M.

to Bob Spies and Donna René,
without whom this book may never have been finished.

L.W.M.

Foreword

The driving force behind the creation, introduction, and refinement of the College Board's Advanced Placement (AP) Computer Science course has been Phil Miller. Far more than any other one person, Phil has shaped both the spirit and content of that course. He served first as a member of a College Board Task Force considering College Board offerings in computer science, then as a member of the initial AP Development Committee for the AP Computer Science examination, and finally as Chairman of that committee for the last 4 years. Now Phil, together with Lee Miller, has authored a textbook that displays the same principles of programming methodology that he has consistently advocated for the AP Computer Science course since its inception.

As an observer of the work of the AP Computer Science Development Committee and as a reviewer of *Programming by Design*, I see the same themes dominating the textbook that I have seen driving the AP course. The use of Karel the Robot in the textbook as a precursor to Pascal mirrors the influence of Phil on the AP course, where the earliest possible introduction of procedural abstraction as a dominant characteristic is one of the principles on which Phil's views prevailed within the AP Development Commmittee even before he became its chairman.

The exact course material in a first course varies from university to university. It is my observation through work with the AP Computer Science Committee and the GRE Computer Science Committee that this text is in line with what is being taught at leading computer science departments around the country, though I have made no systematic investigation of curricula. This text solidly covers the aspects of programming methods of the year-long AP Computer Science course, though teachers will want to supplement *Programming by Design* with a good algorithms/data-structures text for a year-long AP course.

The effervescence of Phil Miller's personal style so evident in earlier versions of this text has been toned down in this published edition. I personally preferred the "rough-cut," intimate approach, but appreciate the need for a more civilized touch. Reviewing this text is much like watching Phil in a three piece suit delivering a polished lecture on the AP program after having watched him make the same points in committee using much more colorful language while he was dressed in blue jeans. Nevertheless, his commitment to the teaching of programming methods by means of real communication with the student still comes through. *Programming by Design* is not a dry presentation of programming methodology nor is it a passive instrument in the teacher's hand. It is rich in pedagogical material and tries to teach by engaging the student, and I believe it succeeds.

J. R. Jefferson Wadkins, Senior Examiner
Test Specialist for the AP CS Examination
Educational Testing Service

Preface

When we set out to write this book, we had one simple goal in mind—to develop a text that would present the materials appropriate for a first course in computer science. We were motivated to take on the project by the fact that—even though there were numerous texts on the market—none of the available texts effectively supported the aims of the introductory courses offered at Carnegie Mellon University. No matter which of the available texts we tried, we found ourselves faced with two primary problems: (1) topics we hold to be important were not treated, and (2) far too much of our time in lectures had to be devoted to explaining to students the material they had read from the textbook. In attempts to overcome those two problems, we developed a significant stack of lecture notes and extended examples to explain further the concepts we found to be lacking or inadequately explained in each of the texts we had attempted to use. Increasingly, we found ourselves relying more on our notes and less on available texts. Eventually, we arrived at a point where we began distributing our materials to the students, which enabled us to follow the course we felt to be appropriate. Moreover, it enabled us to benefit from the feedback supplied by the students and other instructors—feedback that told us that although we had made significant progress toward solving our first problem, the second problem was still evident.

The feedback we received made poignant the need for a *thorough* text, one that would go beyond the ritual of *discussing* a topic to the unorthodox practice of *explaining* the topic. Toward that end, we have attempted to develop a book that incorporates the *teaching* we had been forced to add to texts we previously used. This meant adding hundreds of illustrations and hundreds more programming examples. Our experience with previous versions of this book suggests that we have gotten a great deal of the teacher into the text. This book is intended now for use at either the college level or in high schools that offer advanced courses. No background in computing or advanced mathematics is assumed. The only prerequisite is literacy in the English language.

To Teachers

Although we intend this book to be used to teach programming methodology, we realize that programming skills must be learned by writing programs in a particular language. Toward that end, our presentation includes the study of two programming languages, Karel and Pascal, both of which are used as vehicles for developing general programming and problem-solving skills. Pascal is given the more thorough treatment of the two.

There are numerous reasons for selecting Pascal as a teaching language. Most important is the prevalence of computer systems supporting Pascal, the pertinence of the high-level, block-structured features of the language, our own success with it at Carnegie Mellon University, and the strong endorsement it has received from the College Board's committee that designed the Advanced Placement Computer Science (APCS) course.

Having found that the initial segment of a programming course is crucial to students' perception of the subject, we have selected the language Karel as a precursor to Pascal. We have found that Karel enables them to grasp somewhat easily the concepts of structured programming, which we later look at in more detail when discussing Pascal. We use Karel as an overview of the subject; we use Pascal to provide the necessary detail and reinforcement. With Karel, the novice can plunge into programming and problem solving with a minimum of overhead. Further, Karel provides an interesting problem domain, within which students can learn to write increasingly complex, well-structured programs.

Karel is a robot simulator language, developed by Richard E. Pattis, that allows students to see their programs execute in the two-dimensional world of Karel the Robot. At Carnegie Mellon, we teach

Karel with the aid of the simulator software; however, others have reported success in using Karel without the simulator, i.e., by having students develop their programming solutions on paper. In our own experience, we have found that the time spent with Karel pays for itself many times over. It provides a very accurate overview of structured programming methodology. More importantly, it makes subsequent study of Pascal much easier for the student. Beyond this, thanks to the intuitive nature of Karel, it is superb in overcoming the "fear of computing" syndrome common to many students.

To Students

A common, and understandable, question many students ask is, "Why should I learn about computers and programming?" There are, of course, a number of ways that question might be answered. In general, however, there are four reasons why we think you should learn about computing.

Computers have become very prevalent in today's society. The computer has already changed, or is in the process of influencing, many aspects of our lives, ranging from the scientific exploration of space to the cash registers at the local supermarket. Every time we pick up the telephone or watch the evening news, we witness applications of computing. With computers so prevalent, it is important for you to understand the principles of computing and how they affect your life. Usually, people feel less annoyed and less threatened by things they understand. Thus, the first reason for understanding computing is to better understand the world around us.

Computing is thought of by many people to be the province of the scientifically inclined, the folks who love and live by numbers. Today, however, computers are no longer relegated to the laboratories and offices of engineering and science departments. In fact, they are used throughout the arts, business, and the humanities. In each of these areas, computing is allowing new approaches to long-standing problems. Thus, a second reason for learning about computing is to share in the intellectual stimulation it can foster—in any discipline.

Estimates by experts show that there were 100,000 available positions for software professionals in 1980 that simply could not be filled because the demand for software far exceeds our ability to produce software professionals. The shortage is expected to reach one million by 1990, if the current trend continues. Unlike people educated or trained in other professions, software professionals are virtually guaranteed well-paying job opportunities. Thus, the third reason for learning about computing is to gain the knowledge and experience that can lead to a lucrative career within the computing industry.

The old adage that states "Time is money" can be altered slightly to "Time is life" to more accurately reflect the importance of time. How we spend our time is how we spend our lives. All too often we literally waste time by doing the same things over and over that we could do more effectively in other ways. The average person spends a significant amount of time on relatively mundane tasks—such as record keeping and filing expenses—that can be handled more quickly and more accurately by computer. Thus, the fourth—and perhaps most important—reason for learning about computing is to gain more control over how we spend our time.

The material presented in this book will provide you with the principles and concepts necessary for you to create a whole range of programs capable of solving a number of important problems. But beyond that, you can apply many of the principles to problems other than those involving programming. In short, the concepts in this text provide methods that you may use to think about any complex problem or situation. Properly used, they will serve you well. Work the exercises and solve the problems at the end of each section to make sure you understand the principles.

Some of the sections and exercises are marked with asterisks (*) to indicate that you may wish to skip them on first reading. We suggest you skip all sections marked with three asterisks (***) on first reading. Some readers may wish to skip these items altogether.

To All

This book comprises 18 chapters, 8 appendices, and 4 indices. It contains nearly 500 illustrations and over 3,000 index entries. We utilized the computer to prepare every facet of this book. All page layout was done using the computer; all of the hundreds of illustrations were prepared by computer and merged electronically using custom-made software; and the thousands of index entries were processed completely automatically. We can not imagine preparing a document such as this without a computer.

Whatever success this book, or subsequent editions of it, may have will be due in large part to the good ideas and sound advice offered by our colleagues at Carnegie Mellon University and elsewhere in the Computer Science community. Were it not for their suggestions and continued encouragement, this book would not have reached its current state. For their support throughout this project, we wish to thank all of the people who read and commented on drafts of chapters, who suggested exercises or problems, and who gave to us the inspiration to continue. We especially thank the lecturers at Carnegie Mellon: Terry Gill, Nahid Capell, Dennis Goldenson, Jim Roberts, Jacobo Carrasquel, and particularly Mark Stehlik, whose genuine concern for students has found its way onto a great many pages of this book. We also thank Rob Chandhok, Harry Holland, Wanda Keppler, Becky Alden, Michelle Lurye, Eric Goodman, Amy McMurtry, and Nick Spies. We recognize the students who suffered with us through earlier drafts while we developed and refined this work. We would like to especially thank Bob Spies, who patiently provided many hours of technical and other assistance at a time when he was quite busy with many other projects.

Although the first draft of this book was written by a two-person author team, the final form was the result of three people. The extensive contributions of Purvis Jackson can be seen on nearly every page of this book. To recognize his contributions, we include his name in the appropriate place, on the front cover.

P.L.M.

L.W.M.

Pittsburgh, Pennsylvania

1986

Contents

UNIT I: Foundations of Computing   1

Chapter 1: An Historical Perspective   3

Chapter 2: Overview of Programming   21

UNIT II: Elements of Pascal   91

Chapter 3: Programming in Pascal   93

Chapter 4: Background Tools   117

Chapter 7: Repetition   199

UNIT III: Modular Programming   239

Chapter 8: Procedures   241

Chapter 9: Parameters   273

Chapter 10: Functions   301

UNIT I: Foundations of Computing

Chapter 1: An Historical Perspective

Chapter 2: Overview of Programming

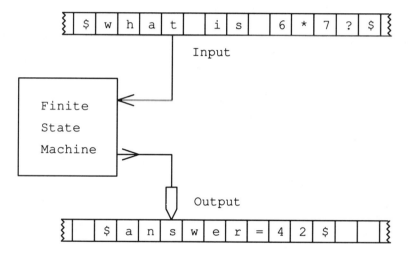

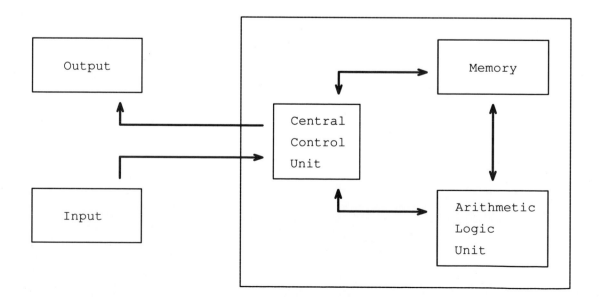

Chapter 1: An Historical Perspective

When we think of the modern computer, many of us picture in our minds those clever little devices with crisp color graphics and voice synthesizers on display in fashionable shops tucked between the pharmacies and the shoe stores at the local shopping mall. Some of us may associate that mental picture with curiously shy whiz kids who break into *secure* information systems that were built by the federal government, multinational corporations, or the military. Others may picture the solitary recluse who designs and develops sophisticated software packages to do everything from game playing to quantum mechanics. While that mental picture is not entirely accurate, it is not entirely false either. Computer whizzes can be young or old, shy or outspoken, loners or members of groups. Amazingly, children with little or no training can operate and program computers as they learn to read.[1] As a result of the efforts of scientists and engineers, according to the best estimates of experts, we are in the middle of a technological revolution of computing and robotics that may have a more profound impact than the Industrial Revolution.

While the computer may seem like a very recent invention, its roots reach back hundreds of years. Those compact machines in the shopping mall have resulted from ideas pondered for centuries by some of the finest minds the earth has known. But the modern computer can be used effectively by many of us who are not necessarily geniuses. In this chapter, we will trace some of the vital events and ideas that formed the foundation for the development of computers and computing as we know them today. In Chapter 2 we will begin to focus our attention on programming, learning to turn the modern computer into a tool that we can use to solve a wide range of problems. By the time we finish this course, you will be writing programs that you may view as impossible right now. Once you reach that point, you will be in a position to use the computer as an immensely powerful tool regardless of whether you pursue a career in computer science. But before digging in, let's take a quick look at the birth and growth of computing and get an idea of what computers are all about.

1.1. Automatic Computing

As recently as the seventeenth century the ability to perform ordinary arithmetic was not common, even among the educated classes. Yet the need for computations was well advanced. Therefore, many of the problems that we would find relatively easy to solve today were extremely difficult for our ancestors to solve. The more difficult the problems became, the greater the chance for errors. For example, sailors could determine their position and effectively navigate over great distances by using a set of tables that showed the positions of the sun, moon, and stars on each day of the year. Although the greatest mathematicians of that time, such as Newton, Euler, and Laplace, worked on such tables, their calculations to determine these locations had to be carried out by hand. Many a sailor went to Davy Jones's locker, due largely to the inaccuracies of human computation.

Another illustration of the need for accurate mathematical computation also involves navigation. The depth of water at a seaport varies with the tides, and some ports can be entered safely only during high tide. Tides are closely related to the location of the sun and the moon relative to the earth. Nevertheless, a relatively complex analysis is required to determine the water level in a port at any specific time. In the distant past such computations were carried out by hand, which proved entirely too inaccurate, and far too many vessels ran aground. What was both needed and sought was a means of *automatic computation* to bypass human errors.

Machines that automatically computed mathematical functions date back at least three centuries [4]. In 1642, at the age of 20, Blaise Pascal constructed a machine, called the *Pascal Engine*, that automatically performed addition and subtraction. In 1673, Leibniz, co-inventor of the calculus, developed a device known as the *Leibniz Wheel* that extended automatic computation to multiplication

---

[1]Seymour Papert points this out in *Mind-Storms* [10].

and division. A number of similar machines were reported during this same period of history. The important point is that some mathematical calculations were performed rapidly, accurately, and automatically by machines over 300 years ago.

1.1.1. Charles Babbage

The story of the computer begins with an eccentric genius from England, Charles Babbage, who lived from 1791 to 1871. Babbage appears to have foreseen the ideas that lie at the heart of the computer that we know today. In his day, it was possible to construct machines to perform predetermined calculations such as addition and subtraction. His new idea was to build machines to perform a computation based on the execution of a set of instructions, one instruction after another, each in its turn.

The importance of this insight cannot be overstated. Whereas the machines that Leibniz and Pascal had invented performed some basic operations of arithmetic, Babbage realized that a machine capable of performing an arbitrary sequence of such operations would be a much more powerful tool. The Pascal machine could perform arithmetic; the Babbage machine *used* arithmetic in computing geometry, trigonometry, and physics! The idea of performing a sequence of specified actions is a concept fundamental to computer science.

> **Definition 1-1:** An *algorithm* is a finite sequence of instructions that solves a specified problem.

Before we go on with the story of Babbage's algorithmic machines, let's think about the algorithm concept. Suppose we want to construct a dog house. We find plans for a sturdy dog house at the local library. The plans include a list of materials and instructions for using the materials. The materials list calls for a sheet of plywood, two framing studs, and nails. The instructions tell us to cut the plywood and studs to certain sizes, build a frame of the studs, and nail the plywood to the frame. These instructions are an algorithm for building the dog house. If the instructions are not followed properly, you will not get the dog house right. If you cut the boards the wrong lengths or nail them together before cutting them, your dog house will deviate from the plans. So, both the instructions and their order are important aspects of the algorithm. This is an important point that will be seen throughout our discussion of programming.

Now that we understand what an algorithm is, we can return to Charles Babbage and his contribution to the development of computing. Babbage actually planned and worked on several different classes of computing machines. The first was his *Difference Engine*, which worked on the principle that the value of an expression of the form $N^2 + N + C$ could be computed with no multiplications, by simply adding constants [4]. In the expression $N^2 + N + C$, the letter N is a symbol for a whole number, and the letter C is the symbol for some arbitrary constant. This proved to be a good machine for repeatedly cranking out a value given some polynomial. However, it was not a general purpose computer.

The concept of a general purpose computer is embodied in Babbage's *Analytical Engine*. Simply stated, the *Analytical Engine* is a machine that works on two kinds of information: a *set of data* and a *sequence of operations*. Interestingly, the automatic bank tellers that have become popular in the last decade operate the same way. The set of data to be operated on are the accounts of the bank customers, and the operations include, among other things, deposit, withdrawal, and interest calculations.

> **Definition 1-2:** A *computer* is a machine capable of executing an arbitrary sequence of instructions.

> **Definition 1-3:** A *computer program* is a sequence of instructions written in a specialized language to be executed by a computer.

While both a computer program and an algorithm are a finite sequence of instructions, only a computer program is written in a specialized language to be executed by a computer.

Successful people seem to have the ability to learn from and extend the good ideas that are around them. It appears that Babbage derived the idea for his general purpose computer from the Jacquard Loom, which Joseph Marie Jacquard developed at about the time of the French Revolution. Before the

Jacquard Loom, a weaver had to know the pattern to be woven. The weaver would follow a set of instructions that explained which thread to use as the fabric was created. Jacquard used metal cards with holes punched in them to encode the desired pattern. The holes allowed only certain threads to be engaged by the shuttle on a given pass. This may be a little hard to visualize, but the principle is essentially the same as that of a player piano. The program (sequence of instructions) of Babbage's machine is analogous to the coded pattern of Jacquard's Loom or the stored music of the player piano. Since these machines could execute a variety of programs rather than just one, they were truly programmable. While you may not think of your microwave oven or VCR as a computer, many of them are fully programmable machines.

Coming up with the idea for such a general purpose computing machine was a stroke of genius; making such an idea work required engineering skill and perseverance of equal rarity. Babbage designed a device that used a set of punched cards to describe the data and another set of cards to describe the operations on the data. For now, you can think of the data as the materials in the previous dog house algorithm, and the operations as the instructions that explain what to do to the materials. Babbage's machine was to inspect an operation card, complete the desired activity on the appropriate data, and then proceed to the next operation. In this way, a sequence of instructions (i.e. a program) was to be executed. The technology of his day did not provide for the construction of such a machine, and although Babbage's insight and energy were legendary, he died before completing work on this machine.

Babbage's work is known largely because of communications with The Royal Society of Science in London. Babbage traveled in excellent intellectual circles, counting among his acquaintances Dickens, Darwin, Bessel, Fourier, Mill, and Browning. One close friend was Augusta Ada Byron, the brilliant daughter of the British poet Lord Byron. She not only grasped the idea behind the Babbage Analytical Engine, but also wrote of it more effectively than Babbage himself. Her place in the history of computing was assured when the U.S. Department of Defense named its new and advanced language, Ada[2], in her honor.

1.1.2. Early American Computers

Some have suggested that Babbage did not receive support from the Royal Society of Science in building his Analytical Engine because the need for computing was not widely recognized. However, toward the end of the nineteenth century, a number of scientists recognized the need for rapid, accurate computations and attempted to satisfy that need. Much of this activity took place in America.

Whereas the developments discussed thus far arose from science's need for computing, the next arose from a much more practical need. John Billings, who was in charge of the work on vital statistics for both the tenth and eleventh U.S. censuses (1880 and 1890 respectively), was directly responsible for collecting and tabulating the census data. As the eleventh census approached, the results of the tenth were still unfinished.

An employee of the census office, Herman Hollerith, had designed an automatic tabulating system as part of his doctoral dissertation. One account states that Billings suggested to Hollerith that hand tallying of statistics could be replaced by a machine similar to the Jacquard Loom. Hollerith invented the *punch card* to represent data gathered for the census. The cards were the size of a dollar bill and had holes punched in them to represent the census items such as sex, age, occupation, and education. It greatly reduced tabulation times. By the time the eleventh census came around, Hollerith's system was so improved that he was able to determine the population of the entire country within one month after the return of all census data.

In 1896, Hollerith started the Tabulating Machine Company to make cards and the machines to process them. It was immediately very successful. The company went through several name changes until 1924, when it was renamed the International Business Machines Corporation (IBM), the name by which it is known today.

---

[2]Ada is a trademark of the U.S. Department of Defense

1.1.2.1. Harvard Mark I

In 1937, Professor Howard Aiken of Harvard University proposed a new type of high-speed automatic calculating machine controlled by a coded sequence of instructions. In 1939, under the direction of President Thomas J. Watson, Sr., IBM Corporation decided to design and build the machine. Professor Aiken and several IBM engineers established that the machine's requirements could be met through a combination of components from IBM's standard line of calculators and a number of specially made mechanisms.

The machine consisted of 78 adding machines linked together. Containing nearly 750,000 parts and more than 500 miles of wire, the massive machine was 51 feet long, 9 feet high and weighed 5 tons. Completed in 1943 and installed at Harvard in early 1944, the Automatic Sequence Controlled Calculator, named the "Mark I" at Harvard, brought Babbage's principles of the *Analytical Engine* to full realization.

The Harvard-IBM Mark I was the first automatic digital computer. At the time, it was also the largest electromechanical calculator ever built. It could perform table look up, much as you might look up a number in a table of squares or sines. It could also compute addition, subtraction, multiplication and division on numbers up to 23 digits long. Input to the Mark I consisted both of programs and data. Both input and output were performed through punched cards.

Although it took 6 seconds for one multiplication and nearly 12 seconds for one division, the Mark I's flexibility was demonstrated by its solutions to various defense problems, including logistics, ballistics tables, and a highly secret mathematical simulation of the first atomic bomb. Its suitability for computations insured its continued operation for over 15 years. Though this electromechanical machine was soon surpassed by completely electronic machines, it was the first completed and operational automatic, general-purpose, digital calculator. It fulfilled Babbage's dream.

1.1.2.2. ENIAC

The **E**lectronic **N**umerical **I**ntegrator **A**nd **C**omputer (ENIAC) were the first *completely electronic* digital computer. The Federal Government funded the development because the military desperately needed help to aim its artillery accurately. Accurate long range artillery fire demanded either precise tables or some means of computing the ballistics (the trajectory of the projectile). The technology for hurling projectiles had far outpaced the physics required to determine where they would come to earth. For example, Germany had built a powerful gun early in World War I. Much to the Germans' surprise, the gun's range was about twice what they expected. Automatic computation seemed to be a logical approach to solving such complex problems, since manual computation was clearly unsuitable.

The Ballistics Research Laboratory and the University of Pennsylvania was responsible for the development of ENIAC, which consisted of approximately 18,000 vacuum tubes, 1,500 relays, 70,000 resistors, 10,000 capacitors, and 6,000 switches. It was 100 feet long, 10 feet high, and 3 feet wide. The machine used pairs of vacuum tubes to form the basic units of memory. The machine operated on base 10 (decimal) arithmetic.

Work on ENIAC began in 1942 and was completed in June of 1946. However, ENIAC was extremely difficult to program, because it required circuit modifications to change its program. It was not until 1947 that ENIAC was modified to be a computer in which a program could be stored, like the Babbage machine or the Jacquard Loom.

1.2. Theoretical Underpinnings

Computers have always been designed to use recent advances in the engineering fields. This has tended to limit the field of computer science to people with backgrounds in engineering, mathematics, or the physical sciences. There is a more fundamental sense in which mathematics supports computing. It is the intellectual heritage of the foundations of computing that we look at now.

There are practical limits to what can be computed. In the early 1970s, it appeared to experts in the field that there was a practical limit that would prohibit machines from playing chess better than human Grand Masters [9]. Today, there are programs that run on special hardware and play chess at the expert level.

Though computers with a limited ability to speak are commonly used in arcade games and automobiles, it is still impractical to use computers conversationally. A computer that can speak and hear a vocabulary of 20,000 words is *possible*, but not *practical* for the time being. By comparison, the English language has on the order of 1,000,000 words, but no one person possesses more than 100,000.

Given examples such as these, we might be tempted to think that today's practical limit to computing is tomorrow's off-the-shelf technology. But the theory of computing has shown that there is a *real* limit to what can be computed! Enough mathematics was known prior to construction of the ENIAC and the Harvard Mark I to demonstrate the limits of computation. In the early 1900s, mathematicians from several apparently divergent areas of the field had come to the same conclusion.

1.2.1. David Hilbert

Around the turn of the century, it was believed that mathematics, and possibly formal science, could answer its questions unambiguously. This meant that *any* mathematically formulated statement could be proved to be either true or false. David Hilbert stated the position in his famous address of 1900 [6]:

> As an example of the way in which fundamental questions can be treated I would like to choose the thesis that every mathematical problem can be solved. We are all convinced of that. After all, one of the things that attracts us most when we apply ourselves to a mathematical problem is precisely that within us we always hear the call: here is the problem, search for the solution; you can find it by pure thought, for in mathematics there is no ignoramus.

What was really exciting about Hilbert's approach (called Hilbert's Program) was his conviction that truth was absolutely knowable. Hilbert maintained that *all* statements were either true or false and that mathematics was the means by which the truth could be established. To Hilbert, nothing was unknowable; there were only unanswered (but answerable) questions. The implication was that problems that had been around for decades, centuries, and even millennia could be solved! In fact, the real problem was to *find* and *state* problems: The proof, be it true or false, would follow logically.

1.2.2. Kurt Gödel

Hilbert's program was exciting to mathematicians of his day. Imagine how powerful you could be with an automatic theorem prover at your disposal. However, in 1931, Kurt Gödel showed that in the mathematics that underlies numbers, there exist propositions that are both true and unprovable! This was really a direct and complete contradiction of Hilbert's Program. Gödel's proof showed that there was a limit to what can be represented and proved logically. Some true statements simply cannot be proved within the system from which they are drawn. This not only showed that Hilbert's Program was not possible, it showed over a decade before the Mark I that all computers have their limits.

1.2.3. Alan Turing

Alan Turing characterized the computer in abstract terms. The most important of his abstractions, known as the *Turing Machine*, is a precisely defined, generalized conception of a computer. It is a rigorous formalism representing computation, an abstract machine rather than a physical device. The Turing Machine has three fundamental components: an input tape, an output tape, and a state machine (see Figure 1-1). Each tape is infinite in two directions, and it is divided into cells. The cells of the input tape may be read in either direction, and the cells on the output tape may be written in either direction. The state machine contains a finite number of internal states. The contents of the current cell on the input tape and the machine's internal state determine whether to write a symbol on the output tape, what symbol to write, which direction to move the read head, which direction to move the write head, and what the next state is.

Turing showed that given such a mathematical idealization, there is no way to determine whether an arbitrary program, once started, will halt. This is known as the *Halting Problem* and is, in a sense, equivalent to Gödel's result. Turing's representation underlies theoretical computer science and is still very much in use today. Unfortunately, the contributions of this genius were cut short by his sudden death at the age of 42. In recognition of the importance of Turing's contribution to the field, the Association for Computing Machinery (ACM) named its prestigious award after him. Annually, the ACM presents the Turing Award to the outstanding computer scientist of the year.

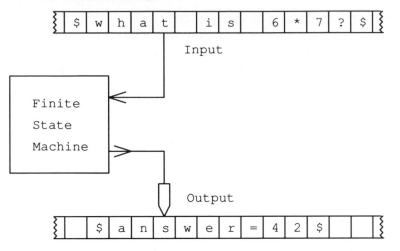

Figure 1-1: Turing Machine

The representation of computation that Turing used came more than a decade prior to the first electronic digital computer. It appears quite similar to the magnetic tape that is used in computing today and provides a convenient illustration for a number of concepts that will be used later in this text.

1.2.4. Alonzo Church

Alonzo Church also worked in the area of computability. Using a set of mathematical functions now known as the lambda-calculus, he established an equivalence of computing power between the lambda-calculus and the Turing Machine. Moreover, he also showed that the procedure for which Hilbert searched could not possibly exist. An interesting side note is that the lambda-calculus of Church was the starting point for the now popular programming language LISP.

Church attempted to make the Turing Machine more powerful by adding a variety of enhancements. Among other things, he tried an infinite number of tapes, an infinite alphabet of symbols, and random access of the read/write head. He found them all to be equivalent to the Turing Machine in terms of what could be computed. It is Church's Thesis that the Turing Machine (often referred to as the Universal Turing Machine) is the most powerful model of computation and cannot be made more powerful. Since Church, many others have tried unsuccessfully to make a more powerful abstract machine.

A number of other approaches to the representation of effective procedures have led to the same conclusion. Among those who have worked in this area are Raphael Robinson, Andrey Markov, Emil Post and S.C. Kleene. What is important for us to understand is that, even with an infinitely fast computer with an infinitely large memory, some problems simply do not allow a mechanical or logical solution. The *Halting Problem* described above is but one example.

1.3. Modern Computing

By modern standards, ENIAC, the Harvard Mark I, and other early electronic computers were very primitive. They were also very difficult to think about, program, and keep running. One of the people involved in the design and construction of ENIAC developed a good approach to the first two problems. His approach was so good that we still use it today.

1.3.1. The Von Neumann Machine

John von Neumann, an immigrant to America from Hungary, was one of the greatest intellects of the twentieth century. He made fundamental contributions to the Manhattan Project (which created the first atomic bomb), economic and game theory, the design and construction of computers, and other areas. In addition to his scholarly abilities, his memory startled those who worked with him; he could recite, at will, page after page of novels. He traveled widely to participate in numerous projects, but his base of operation was the Institute For Advanced Study at Princeton University. In 1945, von Neumann gave us his logical overview of computers [13]. The von Neumann machine consists of the following five parts:

Arithmetic Unit During von Neumann's time, computers were used to solve most numerical problems such as military ballistics. Many of the anticipated uses of computers were also numerical in nature. It seemed natural to von Neumann that the computer should have the basic operations of arithmetic built in as a primitive hardware function. Today this component of the computer is known as the arithmetic logic unit (ALU).

Control Unit ENIAC was a "three ring circus" with many different operations going on at the same time. While this made the ENIAC a little faster, it made the ENIAC extremely difficult to understand and program. Von Neumann believed it was better to sacrifice speed for the sake of conceptual clarity. Therefore, the von Neumann machine was a "one ring circus" with a single component controlling all actions. This component is called the central control and operates in a strictly sequential fashion, that is, one instruction at a time. The difference between the Arithmetic Logic Unit and the Control Unit is that the ALU performs arithmetic while the control unit controls the action of all the components. In most of today's computers, the ALU and control unit are combined as a single component referred to as the CPU (Central Processing Unit).

Memory Computers deal with information. This information or data must be represented and stored in the computer. Von Neumann's model provides a component, called memory, to store information. There is no inherent difference in the way that a computer stores data and programs. Even today, there is still a direct trade-off between the amount of memory available for storage of a program and the amount available for storage of data.

Input Von Neumann designed a general purpose machine. A general purpose machine operates on many different programs and on various sets of data. In order to get new information into the memory of the machine, there must be some sort of input device. Thus von Neumann provided input capability in his design.

Output Output is necessary if the computer is to communicate the results of its computations. Von Neumann also provided for output devices in his model of the computer.

The following illustration shows the components of the von Neumann machine. Arrow heads indicate the direction of the communication lines.

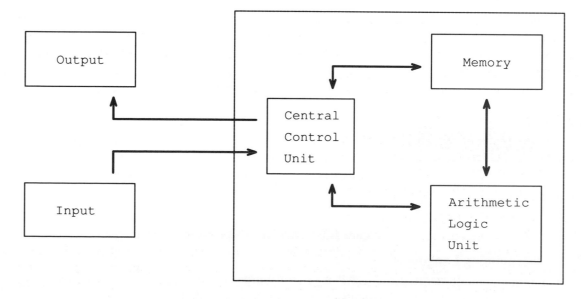

Figure 1-2: Von Neumann Machine

1.3.2. The Modern Computer

The von Neumann machine is realized in many ways today. The arithmetic logic unit is typically combined with the control unit and is referred as the central processing unit (CPU). Most CPUs consist of a single silicon chip. Some computers have more than one CPU, which allows them to process more than one instruction at a time. Computers with more than one CPU are referred to as parallel-processing machines.

There are a number of currently popular implementations of memory as well. Most machines distinguish between primary and secondary memory. Primary memory is fast but expensive, while secondary memory is slow but cheap. Primary memory has consisted of vacuum tubes, crystals and standing waves, ferrite doughnuts strung together in a lattice called *core*, semiconductors, as well as some other implementations. Secondary memory has been built using paper tape, punched cards, magnetic drums, and magnetic tape. Magnetic disks are very widely used now as secondary memory, but optical techniques are beginning to show promise.

Input devices are diverse and numerous. They include microphones for speech recognition systems, cameras for computer vision systems, light pens, the seemingly indestructible joy-stick associated with PacMan games, and of course the familiar keyboard of a computer terminal. In some places, input is on a punched card much like the original Hollerith Punch Card and read by a high-speed card reader. The keyboard is currently the most common input device.

Output devices are as numerous and varied as input devices. They include all printing devices such as dot-matrix, daisy wheel, laser, and line printers. They also include oscillators that synthesize sound similar to voices and musical instruments. The monitor or cathode ray tube (CRT) that creates a video display is the most common output device.

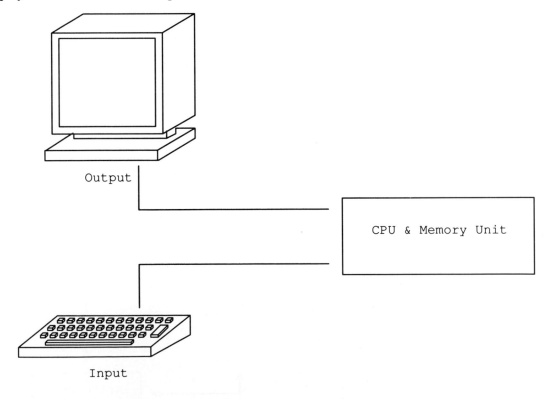

Figure 1-3: The Modern Computer

1.3.3. Programming Languages

Computer scientists discovered early that a general purpose computer was not very useful if it was extremely difficult to program. Difficulty in programming was definitely a problem with ENIAC. It took experts days to program the slightest changes to ENIAC. The task required the experts to essentially rewire the hardware for each new application. The ENIAC programming manual consisted of a thick volume of staggering complexity and detail. A better way was needed for users to communicate with ENIAC's hardware conveniently. The users needed a language for expressing algorithms that could be used instead of rewiring ENIAC. Von Neumann made the decision to build such a language, and the task of implementing it was given to Adele Goldstine. The result was a slower ENIAC, but one whose usefulness was dramatically improved.

Computing machines have a definite and very limited vocabulary commonly referred to as **machine language**.

> **Definition 1-4:** *Machine language* is a language whose statements can be executed directly by a computer.

But all instructions and data in machine language are typically represented in binary, which means machine language programs are long sequences of 0s and 1s. It is easy to see that machine language is very difficult for people to understand and use. Therefore, languages that are easier for people to use have been developed.

An **assembly language** uses symbolic names instead of the binary sequences of machine language. As an example, assembly language might use the symbol ADD instead of the machine language equivalent binary sequence 010. Although people find assembly language programs much easier to work with than machine language programs, assembly language is still *machine specific*. An assembly language program written for one computer will not execute on a computer with a different machine language.

Some programming languages are designed to operate on many different machines (not machine-specific); these are called **high-level languages**. They exist to provide humans with a more convenient and straightforward way to express a sequence of instructions to the machine. A program written in a high-level computer language can be executed on a variety of computers, each with a different machine language.

> **Definition 1-5:** *Assembly language* is a machine-specific language that uses symbolic instructions rather than the binary equivalents in the machine language for that machine.

> **Definition 1-6:** A *high-level computer language* is a machine-independent language designed for expressing computer programs in a way that is easier for people to understand than assembly or machine language.

The following illustration shows the same sequence of instructions in machine language, assembly language and a high-level programming language:

High-level Language	Assembly Language	Machine Language
GrossPay ← NetPay + Taxes	RETR A	100 001
	RETR B	100 010
	ADD A,B	111 001 010
	STORE C	011 011

Figure 1-4: Machine, Assembly, and High-Level Languages

The previous illustration should make it clear that high-level languages are much easier for people to understand. Unfortunately, the computer does not "understand" any language other than machine language. Therefore, we need a means of *translating* our programs into machine language. Originally this task was done manually by humans. It was then realized that the computer could do this task if given proper instructions. There are now special computer programs that do such translations automatically. A program that translates a high-level language into machine language is called a **compiler**; a program that translates assembly language into machine language is called an **assembler**.

> **Definition 1-7:** An *assembler* is a computer program that translates the symbolic instructions of an assembly language program to equivalent instructions in machine language.

> **Definition 1-8:** A *compiler* is a computer program that translates a program written in a high-level language into an equivalent program in machine language.

Although both assemblers and compilers are language translators that take a program in a particular language and yield an equivalent machine language program, compilers must do much more than assemblers. There is a one-to-one correspondence between every instruction in an assembly language program and its equivalent machine language program. This greatly facilitates the translation process since, for example, every ADD instruction in an assembly language program becomes, say, instruction 010 in machine language. Such a correspondence does not exist between high-level languages and machine languages. Figure 1-4 shows a single high-level language instruction that is equivalent to four machine language instructions. It should be obvious that no person would prefer writing programs in machine language. It should also be obvious that one should opt for programming in a high-level language over assembly language whenever possible.

1.3.3.1. Operating Systems, Time Sharing, and Environments

Before we go into detail about the development of high-level languages, it is important to realize that a fundamental change took place in the 1960s. The early computers served only one user at a time. If you needed to solve, say, a ballistics problem, you would write a computer program, enter the program into the computer, enter the data for the problem into the computer, and then get computer output. Everyone else who needed to use the computer would have waited while you typed in your program and data and got your output. The computer only computed between the input and output stages. The computer and all but one of its users waited while a single user worked. Hence, extremely expensive computers actually did very little of the work of which they were capable of doing.

At some point it was observed that most of what a computer did was sit around waiting for an incredibly slow human to enter a problem. Computers, extremely expensive computers, basically did nothing. Think of it this way. Suppose there was an enormously expensive and amazingly fast toaster with only one slot for bread to be toasted. And, at the same time, there were many people with slices of bread who wanted toast. The toaster could toast a slice of bread in about a second, but it took the bread carrier an hour to get the slice of bread into the toaster and another hour to get it out again. Mind you, there is no hope of speeding up this input/output process.

One solution would be to build lots of these very expensive toasters. Another would be to build toasters with more than one slot for toasting. It is this second approach that the computing industry took. Computers soon changed from single-user to multi-user machines, which permitted many people to share the computer's time.

> **Definition 1-9:** *Time sharing* is the use of a device by two or more people during the same time period. It is accomplished by giving each user exclusive use of the device for small periods of the overall time period.

Multi-user computers had many input and output devices to accommodate the users. It appeared as if each user's program were executing simultaneously, but it was not. The computer worked on one user's program for a while and then worked on another's program for a while, and so on. Since the computer worked on each program for only small periods and since computers work much faster than humans, most users noticed no delays. Because of the complexity involved in keeping track of all the users, a master control program was needed to control execution of each of the users' programs. Such a program is called an **operating system**.

> **Definition 1-10:** An *operating system* is the master program that controls all the computer's resources (memory, devices, processing time) and allocates them among all the computer's users and programs.

The operating system made sure that input from one user came from that user and not someone else. It placed output in the appropriate location. It kept track of where the data for each program was located. Operating systems tended to make computers seem larger than they were. They moved programs and pieces of programs from primary to secondary memory according to complicated scheduling schemes. They determined what should be printed first.

Operating systems manage the resources of a computer. In addition to keeping track of program execution, they usually contain programs of their own, including compilers to prepare high-level programs for execution.

Computers have been used for the preparation of documents as well as programs for a long time. It may be surprising, but in many places the same tool is used for preparing business letters as is used for preparing programs for compilation.

> **Definition 1-11:** An *editor* is a computer program used to write information into a computer.

Computerized units of information are sometimes called **files**, following the name used in offices. Sometimes they are called data-sets, following a more scientific name. Sometimes these units are letters and memos; sometimes they are collections of data like opinion polls or telephone directories; sometimes they are programs. These units of information are often created and modified using the editor of an operating system.

> **Definition 1-12:** A *file* is a computerized unit of information, stored in machine readable form.

We will refer to the computerized units of information as files in this text. A computer user's files are generally stored on secondary storage devices. Currently this means that files are stored on magnetic disks. In the earlier days, files were more often stored on magnetic tape. Soon files will be stored on optical disks. This suggests that the study of files and file structure is more important than the study of a particular medium for storage.

When a file contains a program, the operating system has a number of tools that are used to process and execute that program. We have already mentioned the compiler. A number of other tools are hidden from the user's view. These background tools make up the environment for that program. Sometimes we speak more generally of the **environment** of the computer.

> **Definition 1-13:** An *environment* is a collection of tools, managed by the operating system, that supports a computer user's activities.

1.3.3.2. Early High-level Languages

One of the first high-level languages was developed in the late 1950s. Its name, FORTRAN, is an acronym[3] for **FORmula-TRANslator**. Very important to the development of FORTRAN was John Backus. FORTRAN was designed to be of service to scientists and is still widely used today.

Another very early high-level language was ALGOL. This name, also an acronym, came from **ALGOrithmic-Language**. This language was designed by Alan Perlis. The principle that Perlis had in mind was to provide language constructs for expressing algorithms that conform to the way people think about problems, rather than forcing people to conform to constructs that are easy for computers to implement. ALGOL gained a good deal of popularity, especially in Europe, and served as the starting point for the development of the language we will use in our study of programming, Pascal.

In the 1950s and 1960s, a number of computer manufacturers, each wanting to attract as many customers as possible, rushed to provide a wide variety of programming languages. Unfortunately, this led to each manufacturer providing a somewhat different version of FORTRAN and other popular languages. This was a problem. Often a program was written on one brand of computer, and people with other computers wanted to use it too. The job of moving it from one class of machine to another turned out to be very difficult, even when both machines used the same language. The problem was that they used different versions of the same language.

In reaction to an ever increasing number of incompatible versions of the popular languages, attempts were made at standardization. International committees were formed to determine the *standard* for FORTRAN and ALGOL. Another language, PL/1, was designed by a committee. The American National Standards Institute (ANSI), the governmental agency charged with providing standards for weights and measures, published standards for programming languages as well. One mark of the purity of a programming language is to be able to claim that it conforms to the ANSI standard, that it is ANSI-FORTRAN, for example. Other standards organizations, including the International Standards

---

[3]An acronym is a word that is made up from the first letters or groups of letters from other words.

Organization (ISO) and the Institute of Electrical and Electronics Engineers (IEEE), also published standards. As you might guess, these standards were not always the same. There was no standard for standards.

A major problem of the times involved language features that enabled the programmer to jump around at will in a program. It seems that programmers of that era were bent on avoiding the sequential execution of instructions. Another problem was that languages tended to grow: Features from one language crept into and became a standard part of other languages.

In the mid-1960s, a number of academic computer scientists began to express the opinion that a leaner language was needed. About this same time, Edsgar Dijkstra began writing on the subject of the structure of programming languages and good programs [3].

> **Definition 1-14:** *Structured programming* is a the programming practice based on the use of sets of structural units developed to ensure well-designed programs.

Growing out of this school of thought was a reaction against jumping around in programs and a reaction against cumbersome languages designed by cumbersome committees. Niklaus Wirth designed a lean programming language that reinforced the best programming methods known at that time and named it Pascal in honor of Blaise Pascal.

> **Definition 1-15:** *Programming methods* are a collection of techniques used in writing programs.

Wirth's idea was that Pascal would be a language for teaching programming. By virtue of its lean design, the student programmer would be almost forced to use a good style of programming. It was hoped that the student would not forget these methods when the student became a programmer and used a *real* programming language. Pascal has not only provided the teaching tool that Wirth had hoped for, it has gained quite a following as a *real* programming language as well. It is now used in writing large programs that are used in research, education, and industry.

The development of programming languages by no means ended with the introduction of Pascal. Modula-2 was a direct descendant of Pascal. Ada went far beyond Pascal in incorporating the latest scholarly thought. The language C proved to be a useful marriage between ALGOL-like languages and low-level languages. In an entirely different vein, SmallTalk proved to be interesting and inspirational.

The goal of this text is to provide the information for teaching programming methodology, and we choose to use Pascal as the vehicle for discussing programming methodology. Pascal is not perfect, and it is not the latest development in computer programming languages. It is, however, a widely available language. And, if used properly, it can help you to develop the skills necessary to write good, clear, and reliable programs.

1.3.4. The Personal Computer

In the early days of computing, the size of computers was measured in cubic feet, the weight in tons, and the cost in millions of dollars. Today there are still computers that are rightly measured by such standards, cooled by liquid oxygen, and tended to by the high priests of technology. But there is another class of computer, the personal computer, with which we are vastly more familiar. These are the clever little machines in the shopping mall stores.

Beginning with the Apple II and the TRS-80 and continuing with the IBM-PC and its look-alikes, computers have become very much like an appliance, even a necessary tool, for doing business. Many people have a computer or two at home. These computers are the size of a portable television, light enough to carry in hand, and costs are measured in thousands, or even as little as hundreds, of dollars. They require no special heating or cooling equipment, and they pretty much take care of themselves, except for an occasional misaligned disk drive or power cable chewed by the family dog.

What happened to make all this possible? In 1947 a device called a transistor was developed. Almost a decade later its inventors shared the Nobel Prize in Physics for its invention. The transistor took the place of the mechanical relays of the Mark I and the vacuum tubes of ENIAC. Complex circuits could be built into one slice of semiconductor, and integrated circuitry was born. Radios dropped from the size of small refrigerators to the size of small wallets in just a few years.

A race began in the semiconductor industry, and ever denser circuits were packed into smaller and smaller areas. Integrated Circuitry (IC) led to Large Scale Integrated Circuitry (LSI), and that gave way to Very Large Scale Integrated Circuitry (VLSI). At the time of the writing of this book, circuits with hundreds of thousands of transistors on two or three square inches are commonly manufactured.

Circuits much smaller than the thickness of a human hair are commonplace on VLSI chips, and the physical limits of VLSI have not been reached, even though those limits are easy to figure out. The medium for the circuit must be large enough for electrons to move. So the diameter of an electron is a lower bound on the size of a single connection on a VLSI chip. This means that densities of ten to one-hundred times greater than we see today could be realized in the future.

Even with increased circuit densities, silicon chips are inexpensive to mass produce. So while the power of computer chips increases, the cost decreases. To get a perspective on the situation, imagine the auto industry had kept pace with the electronics industry. This would mean that a Rolls Royce would cost about three dollars and travel at nearly the speed of light.

At some point, engineers in the computer industry were bound to notice that chips could be used to make a very inexpensive computer. This was first noticed in the 1960s, when people of vision actually proposed inexpensive personal computers. However, no one chose to pursue the ideas. We speculate that this was so because the computer industry was busy making BIG COMPUTERS. They were also making BIG MONEY, so there was really no monetary incentive for an executive to commit a major company to making personal (then called micro) computers.

There is some disagreement as to what the first actual personal computer was, but there is no disagreement that the Altair MITS was among the first. The Altair MITS was announced in early 1975 as the cover story for *Popular Electronics* magazine. This computer came in kit form, used the Intel 8080 chip as its CPU, possessed almost no memory, and in the beginning had no hint of a programming language. So the story goes, Altair was immediately deluged with orders for the kits. There was enormous latent demand for hands-on computing. Priced at less than $400 a kit, the MITS was purchased by more than enough computer and electronics enthusiasts to launch the industry.

Languages were needed to program these personal machines. Initially, the languages had to be sufficiently small to fit into the very modest memory available. The well-known language BASIC (Beginners All-purpose Symbolic Instruction Code) had been around for a number of years. In addition to meeting the space requirements of the personal computer, it had a very immediate feedback and short learning time. It was brought to the world of personal computers by the founders of Microsoft, who were, at the time, eccentric, brash, and clever college students. Despite the fact that the language and the way it has been used have received justified and serious criticism, the contribution of BASIC to the personal computer revolution is not to be overlooked.

The personal computer (PC) brought a new way of doing business with a computer. Before the PC, computers were something few people ever saw. They were huge, and they had special airconditioning, and they always cost 8 million dollars. Computers were a precious resource, and they were to be found at universities, in government agencies, and in very big businesses. Tending these beasts were droves of professionals. They were much like any other engineer of their time, except, of course, that they had a tendency to work between the hours of 6 PM and 5 AM exclusively. In part because of the wide spread student riots of the late 1960s, computers were kept behind locked and guarded doors. A user submitted a program on carefully punched cards, and a printout came back in a few hours or a few days.

The personal computer changed the rules of the game. The extra bedroom became the computer room, and ordinary folks became programmers. The engineers, guards, locked doors, and long waits for computer output became history. Computer programs, better known as software, were produced at a staggering rate. Suddenly there were video games, document preparation systems, tax filing systems, music synthesis systems, and flight simulator systems.

None of this should be interpreted as meaning that either the computer hardware or software were uniformly very good. They were not. There were severe limitations imposed by the computers themselves. Their memory was modest at best, and the software usually contained errors, better known as bugs. But you could walk into a store and buy one. You could write your own programs, use them, and even sell them. It was and still is exciting, enjoyable, and economically rewarding.

Personal computers grew into the 1980s, making millionaires and paupers of inventors and entrepreneurs. But they seemed to stop short of full scale acceptance. There were *toy computers*, fun for eighth graders and hobbyists, but they weren't something everybody felt they had to own, and they certainly weren't to be found in the best universities or businesses. These places had real computers, the kind whose movement required assistance from Allied Van Lines and a forklift.

In 1981 IBM announced its first personal computer, and personal computing instantly became as respectable as using the telephone. Large, medium and small businesses began ordering IBM PCs by the dozen. Many other large corporations tried to keep pace by making IBM-compatible or competing personal computers. A PC, like a Chevy, belonged in every American home.

In 1984 Apple Computer introduced the Macintosh. This tiny and inexpensive computer used the very powerful Motorola-68000 processor. More importantly, the centerpiece of this system was very sophisticated software that enabled the user to replace long sequences of cryptic commands to an unforgiving operating system with a familiar desktop metaphor. The keyboard could be almost completely bypassed by using an input device called the *mouse*.

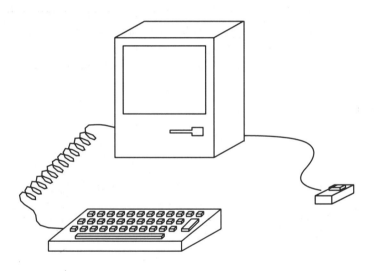

Figure 1-5: Personal Computer with Mouse

One exciting aspect of the personal computer revolution, from our point of view, is that PCs are now powerful enough to help train the next generation of computer scientists. We expect that most people who use this text will actually write their programs on one of the PCs mentioned in this chapter.

1.4. Areas of Computer Science

Computer science can be viewed as an academic discipline that is composed of four areas of study: computing systems, programming systems, artificial intelligence, and theory. A number of alternative taxonomies of the discipline exist, but we choose to develop this one. While the discipline can be divided into these areas, there are overlaps among these subfields.

1.4.1. Computing Systems

The purpose of computing-systems research is to investigate ways to improve the hardware aspects of computing. Most of the effort here is spent to make faster and more powerful computers. Research in this area focuses on such issues as the design and development of networks linking computers together, computers with more than one CPU, and the supercomputers of the future. The idea of executing more than one instruction at a time has been around for quite a while.

> **Definition 1-16:** *Parallel processing* is the use of more than one computer at a time to solve a problem.

Imagine that you are on a path in a deep woods. You are searching for a small child, believed to be on a path in the woods. After a while the path you are on splits into two paths. Which one do you take? You make a choice, knowing that the child might be just a short distance down the other path. The path that you are now on splits into two paths. You are again faced with a choice that you would rather not make. At each juncture, you are either getting closer to or farther away from the child.

What you would like to do is start at the beginning of the first path with lots of people and radio communication. At the first juncture you send half of them down one path and half down the other. At each new juncture, people again branch off down the new paths. When the child is found or you prove that the child is not in the woods, the process terminates.

Many problems that computers are used to solve are very much like the first situation described above. There is a problem to be solved and at some point several potential solutions arise. Down the path of these potential solutions there are more potential solutions competing for attention. A good example of this is a computerized game. The program tries to think ahead before selecting a move. If the program is to think very far ahead at all there are a very large number of possibilities to consider.

The Von Neumann computer can do exactly one thing at a time. If the wrong path is chosen, the solution may never be found or may be found only after an unacceptably long delay. This is analogous to wandering through the woods alone, tracing one path after another in search of the lost child.

In much the same way as we would use a group of people to search the woods for the child, computer scientists have tried to use groups of computers to work together on solving problems. By having many computers working in parallel on a problem, some problems can be solved more rapidly. Some famous parallel computers have been built, but we are still only beginning to realize the potential of these machines.

Computers, like most machines, fail on occasion. Computer failures may be devastating. Fault-tolerance research involves, in part, building redundant systems to automatically recover from computer failures, and is another area of computing systems.

1.4.2. Programming Systems

Research in the area of programming systems focuses on the software aspects of computing. The purpose of this research is to develop tools that will make computers easier to understand, use, and program. Classic examples of such tools include compilers, editors, and operating systems. More recent examples include electronic mail systems, computerized bulletin boards, and document preparation systems such as the one used to typeset this book. Due to years of research and development within this area, many people who were completely baffled by computers a few years ago now use them daily.

One recent development with which we are particularly familiar is syntax-directed programming environments. As you will soon learn, programming languages require instructions to be written according to very strict rules of grammar. Although human languages also follow rules of grammar, we often violate those rules when speaking without creating sentences that are difficult for others to understand. In general, compilers—unlike people— cannot understand what you might mean when you violate grammatical rules.

In the past, much of the effort in learning a programming language was devoted to learning the precise syntax of the programming language. A more modern approach to programming uses an editor that is based on the programming language syntax so that it interacts with the programmer. The programmer is therefore relieved of the burden of memorizing low-level details and can concentrate on problem solving. We expect that you do not have the advantage of using a syntax-directed editor in your study of programming and Pascal. However, these sorts of systems should become available in the coming years.

1.4.3. Artificial Intelligence

Artificial intelligence as a field dates to a meeting at Dartmouth University in 1956. Invited to this meeting was a distinguished group who wanted to have computers programmed to exhibit intelligent behavior, that is, behavior that would be considered intelligent behavior if it were being done by a human. Out of this meeting grew a field that has blossomed into the disciplines of expert systems and robotics.

Since there is no agreed-upon definition of intelligence, the notion of artificial intelligence cannot be clearly defined. However, Alan Turing proposed a test to determine if a computer exhibited intelligence [12]. In the Turing test, there are three participants: the machine to be tested, a human, and an interrogator. The object for the interrogator is to distinguish the human from the machine. The object for the machine is to foil the interrogator. If the machine can do so, it is considered to exhibit intelligence. A machine exhibiting intelligence in this fashion is said to possess artificial intelligence (AI), or machine intelligence (as opposed to human intelligence).

Artificial Intelligence is well illustrated by the subject matter with which it deals. The following topics have received considerable attention in AI:

Two-Person Games   There are now chess-playing programs that compete at the expert level. Recently, a backgammon program defeated the human world champion in Monte Carlo to win the $10,000 prize that was offered. The current world champion Othello player has declined to play the reigning world champion Othello program!

Problem Solving   One of the first areas to which attention was directed was the proof of theorems. The idea was not to simply check every possible answer but to use some heuristics (educated guesses) in the proof of interesting theorems. Other domains of problem solving include the composition of melodies and the extraction of plots from short stories.

Diagnosis   For some years now, medical diagnoses have been made by a program named MYCIN. It uses knowledge of bacteriological phenomena and is able to make expert-level inferences. Given a set of symptoms, MYCIN will attempt to determine the cause for the illness. The Digital Equipment Corporation has a similar expert program to configure its computing systems.

Perception   One goal of computer science is to enable the computer to hear, see, and speak. There exists some systems with vocabularies of over 10,000 words that can both hear sound and synthesize appropriate aural responses. Vision systems to interpret visual information are useful for a wide range of applications, including monitoring the military actions of unfriendly nations via satellites.

Robotics   No discussion of artificial intelligence would be complete without reference to the robotics effort. Dangerous, routine, and error-prone jobs are being turned over to robots. Not only is this area technologically important, but it is socially significant as well. Many jobs presently performed by people will be soon taken over by machines. However, it is not clear what should be done to ensure employment for the workers displaced by robots.

1.4.4. Theory

A number of areas make up theoretical computer science. We list only four of them here. Each of these four is a heavily researched area.

Computability Theory   The theory of computation studies the limits of computation, what is computable, and models of computation. Some taxonomies would include automata and the theory of formal languages here. Connections are, among other things, to the design of compilers.

Algorithm Analysis   Algorithm analysis is concerned primarily with the speed of algorithms, but it is also concerned with the amount of space algorithms require in computer memory. As will be shown later, there are very profound effects, depending on which of several algorithms is implemented.

Numerical Analysis   It is important to realize that we are dealing with a digital computer. It is a finite machine, but it is used to represent, among other things, the infinity of the real number system. The computer does not represent these numbers with complete accuracy. This area studies the precision of results and determines how to encode various types of information in the best ways.

Verification   The study of program verification addresses one of the fundamental questions of computer science: Given any program, how do we know that it computes what the programmer intends it to compute? This area investigates ways of verifying or proving programs to be correct. Some of the elementary techniques will be introduced later in this book.

1.5. Summary

This historical overview of computing describes some of the important developments that led to the modern computer and computing as it is known today. Each of these topics is discussed at length in many volumes written by many different authors. We hope this brief discussion has provided you with a broad understanding of the ideas behind computers and computing. We think you will find this information useful as we move on through the following chapters. We reiterate below some of the more important points from our overview:

- The need for automatic computations has existed for hundreds of years.

- The first automatic computation devices to add, subtract, multiply, and divide were built in the 1600s.

- Babbage came upon the idea to extend the programmable feature of the Jacquard Loom to automatic computation.

- An *algorithm* is a finite sequence of instructions that solves a specified problem.

- A *computer* is a machine capable of executing an arbitrary sequence of instructions.

- A *computer program* is a sequence of instructions written in a specialized language to be executed by a computer.

- There are theoretical limits in addition to the practical limits of what can be computed. This means that there will always be a class of problems that are not computable regardless of how fast or how powerful computers become.

- Most modern computers follow Von Neumann's original design with *memory*, *input*, *output*, *central control*, and *arithmetic logic unit*.

- *Machine language* is the language a computer "understands."

- *Assembly language* is a machine-specific language that uses symbolic instructions rather than the binary equivalents in the machine language for that machine.

- A *high-level computer language* is a machine-independent language designed for expressing computer programs in a way that is easier for people to understand than assembly or machine language.

- Computer programs written in any language other than machine language must be "translated" into machine language before the computer can execute them.

- An *assembler* is a computer program that translates the symbolic instructions of an assembly-language program to equivalent instructions in machine language.

- A *compiler* is a computer program that translates a program written in a high-level language into an equivalent program in machine language.

- Time sharing permits many people to use the same computer at the same time by giving each user small slices of the total processing time.

- An *operating system* is the master program that controls all the computer's resources (memory, devices, processing time) and allocates them among all the computer's users and programs.

Now that we have our bearings, let's move on to Chapter 2 and begin our exploration of programming methodology. You are about to become a computer programmer!

Chapter 2: Overview of Programming[1]

2.1. Programming

Modern computers are capable of executing a wide variety of highly complex programs. Though such programs are often designed for extremely sophisticated purposes, they are written in languages that contain relatively few *primitive instructions*. These primitive instructions may be sequentially combined to derive new, more complex instructions. The result is a language that is infinitely rich. This process is reflected somewhat in natural languages, such as English, which contain a finite number of words that may be used to produce an infinite number of sentences.

The idea of sequencing operations to extend a machine's computational capacity has been around since the days of Charles Babbage. The process of choosing the sequence of operations that results in a desired computation is exactly what is meant by programming a computer. Therefore, the people who punched cards for the Jacquard Loom, making it weave a desired pattern, were perhaps the earliest programmers. They were programmers in exactly the same sense that someone writing a video game program or a system to keep track of dental records is a programmer.

A sequence of instructions or operations that solves some well-defined problem is referred to as an algorithm. The study of algorithms, their complexity, and their correctness constitutes a significant subfield of computer science. Although the formal definition of an algorithm is precise, you can think of an algorithm as a finite sequence of operations that solves a specific problem.

2.2. Programming Languages

With the first electronic digital computers, programmers had to express algorithms in languages directly executable by the machine (machine language). However, such languages are very different from human languages. Thus, these machines were extremely difficult to program. The solution was to define a language (high-level language) that was adequate for expressing algorithms that could be translated into machine-executable instructions.

The nature of programming languages and what makes a good one is controversial. Some people believe that the arithmetic precision of FORTRAN is ideal. Others claim that APL is best because of its ability to express matrix algebra. A respected community of scholars finds function-theoretic LISP to be superior to all others. COBOL has many advocates in the world of business computing. Some systems programmers still use assembly language, a near cousin to machine language. The Department of Defense supported the development of the language Ada so that the best ideas of the programming-language community could be integrated in a standard way.

In this text, we will use two languages, Karel and Pascal, as vehicles for illustrating the concepts vital to a sound introduction to computer science. Karel is a simple language that is easy to learn. It introduces a number of concepts that are important to computer science, and it presents those concepts in a way that makes them easy to understand and apply. Just as important, Karel illustrates good programming methods, which will serve you well throughout your study of computer science. The principles stressed in the following sections of this chapter will provide a firm foundation for you to build on as we step through Pascal in the later chapters. Therefore, you should read this chapter carefully to be sure you understand each new concept and how those concepts can allow you to create increasingly powerful programs.

Our goal in presenting Karel is to provide you with an effective set of programming tools that are at the same time fun and easy to learn and use. Too often, people assume that programming is an extremely difficult skill that only comes after years of study and practice. While it is true that study and practice

---

[1]Portions of this chapter are from *Karel The Robot* by Richard E. Pattis, copyright (c) 1981, John Wiley & Sons, Inc. Reprinted with permission.

will make you an ever better programmer, you don't have to work long and hard before seeing the fruits of your efforts. After studying this chapter, you will be equipped with ideas that will make Pascal much easier to understand. Once you have learned Pascal, other programming languages will be relatively easy to understand. The point here is that all programming languages share certain characteristics, and each language has its own set of unique features. After you have learned the basic features of Karel, you can use them as a springboard to Pascal. Pascal can be, in turn, a springboard to other programming languages. Thus, our aim is to help you to learn to program properly, using Karel and Pascal as teaching languages. As you will discover later, Pascal is by no means limited to the classroom, and its range of application is growing wider every day. Let's learn Karel, the language of a fictitious robot who can, if you tell him how, do an amazing number of tasks. Crank up your powers of imagination, and let's zoom in on Karel in his 2D world.

2.3. The Robot World

This section introduces Karel[2] the robot and sketches the world he inhabits. In later sections, where a greater depth of understanding is necessary, we shall amplify this preliminary discussion.

2.3.1. Karel's World

Karel lives in a world that is unexciting by present-day standards (there are no volcanoes, Chinese restaurants, or symphony orchestras), but it does include enough variety to allow him to perform simply stated, yet interesting tasks. Informally, the world is a grid of streets that Karel can traverse. It also contains special objects that Karel can sense and manipulate.

Figure 2-1 is a map illustrating the structure of Karel's world, whose shape is a great flat plane with the standard north, south, east, and west compass points. The world is bounded on its west side by an infinitely long vertical wall extending northward. To the south, the world is bounded by an infinitely long horizontal wall extending eastward. These boundary walls are made of solid *neutronium*, an impenetrable metal that restrains Karel from falling over the edges of his world.

Crisscrossing Karel's world are horizontal <u>streets</u> (running east-west) and vertical <u>avenues</u> (running north-south) at regular, one-block intervals. A <u>corner</u>, sometimes referred to as a street corner, is located wherever a street and an avenue intersect. Karel can be positioned on any corner, facing one of the four compass points. Both streets and avenues are numbered; consequently, each corner is identified uniquely by its street and avenue numbers. The corner where 1st Street and 1st Avenue intersect is named the <u>origin</u>.

Besides Karel, there are two other types of objects that can occupy his world. The first type of object is a <u>wall section</u>. Wall sections are also fabricated from the impenetrable metal neutronium, and they can be manufactured in any desired length. They are positioned sideways between adjacent street corners, effectively blocking Karel's direct path from one corner to the next. Wall sections are used to represent obstacles that Karel must navigate around, such as hurdles and mountains. Enclosed rooms, mazes, and other barriers can also be constructed from wall sections.

The second type of object in Karel's world is a <u>beeper</u>. Beepers are small plastic cones that emit a quiet beeping noise. They are situated on street corners and can be picked up, carried, and put down by Karel. Some of Karel's tasks involve picking up or putting down patterns made from beepers, or finding and transporting beepers.

2.3.2. Karel's Capabilities

Let's now shift our attention away from Karel's world and concentrate on Karel himself. Karel is a mobile robot: he can move forward, in the direction he is facing, and he can turn in place. He can also perceive his immediate surroundings: Karel possesses a rudimentary sense of sight, sound, direction, and touch.

---

[2]Karel is named after the Czechoslovakian dramatist Karel Capek, who popularized the word "robot" in his play <u>R.U.R.</u> (Rossum's Universal Robots). The word "robot" was derived from the Czech word "robota," meaning "forced labor."

Karel sees by using any one of his three TV cameras, which point straight ahead, to his left, and to his right. These three cameras are focused to detect walls exactly one half of a block away from Karel. Karel also has the ability to hear a beeper, but only if he and the beeper are on the same corner; the beepers beep that quietly. By consulting his internal compass, Karel can determine which direction he is facing. Finally, Karel is equipped with a mechanical arm that he can use to pick up and put down beepers. To carry these beepers, Karel wears a soundproof beeper-bag around his waist. Karel can also determine if he is carrying any beepers in this bag by probing it with his arm.

Whenever we want Karel to accomplish a task in his world, we must supply him with a detailed set of instructions that explains how to perform the task. Karel is able to receive, memorize, and follow such a set of instructions, which is called a program.

What language do we use to program (here we use "program" to mean "write instructions for") Karel? Instead of programming Karel in English, a natural language for us, we program him in a special programming language, which was designed to be useful for writing robot programs. Karel's robot programming language -- like any natural language -- has a vocabulary, punctuation marks, and rules of grammar. But this language -- unlike English, for example -- is simple enough for Karel to understand; yet it is a powerful and concise language that allows us to write brief and unambiguous programs for Karel.

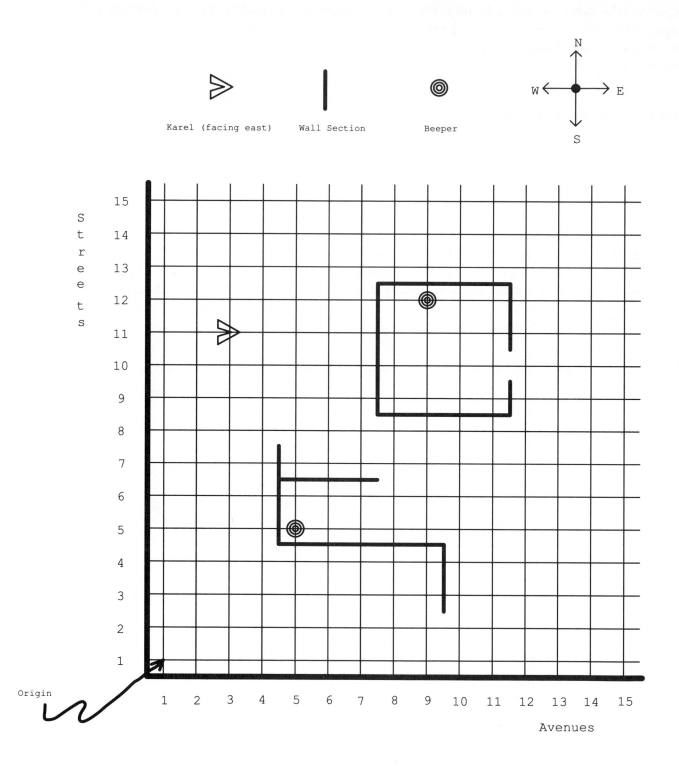

Figure 2-1: The Structure of Karel's World

2.3.3. Tasks and Situations

A <u>task</u> is just something that we want Karel to do. The following examples are tasks for Karel: move to the corner of 15th St. & 10th Ave., run a hurdle race (with wall sections representing hurdles), escape from an enclosed room that has a door, find a beeper and deposit it on the origin, and escape from a maze.

A <u>situation</u> is an exact description of what Karel's world looks like. Besides the basic structures of Karel's world, which are always present, wall sections and beepers can be added. To specify a situation completely, we must state the following information.

- What is Karel's current position? We must specify both Karel's location (which corner he is on) and what direction he is facing.

- What is the location and size of each wall section in the world?

- What is the location of each beeper in the world? This information includes specifying the number of beepers in Karel's beeper-bag.

Situations are specified in this book by a small map or brief written description. If we know the number of beepers that Karel has in his beeper-bag, then the map in Figure 2-1 completely specifies a situation. The <u>initial situation</u> for any task is defined to be the situation that Karel is placed in at the start of the task. The <u>final situation</u> is the situation that Karel is in when he turns himself off. Unless told otherwise, you may assume that Karel starts all his tasks with an empty beeper-bag.

2.4. Primitive Instructions and Simple Programs

This chapter begins our study of Karel's programming language. We shall start with a detailed explanation of the five primitive instructions that are built into Karel's vocabulary. Using these instructions, we can command Karel to move through his world and handle beepers. Section 2.4.4 demonstrates a complete robot program and discusses the elementary punctuation and grammar rules of Karel's programming language. By the end of this section, we shall be able to write programs that instruct Karel to perform simple obstacle avoidance and beeper transportation tasks.

Before explaining Karel's primitive instructions, we first must define the technical term *execute*: Karel *executes* an instruction by performing its associated action. Furthermore, Karel executes a program by executing each instruction in the program.

2.4.1. Changing Position

Karel understands two primitive instructions that change his position. The first of these instructions is move, which changes Karel's location.

move

When Karel executes a move instruction, he moves forward one block; he continues to face the same direction. To avoid damaging himself, Karel will not move forward if he sees a wall section or boundary wall between himself and the corner that he would move toward. Instead, Karel executes a move instruction in this situation by turning himself off. This action, called an *error shutoff*, will be explained further in Section 2.4.5.

From this definition, we see that Karel executes a move instruction by either moving forward (when his front is clear to the next corner) or performing an error shutoff (when his front is blocked). Both situations are illustrated in the next two sets of figures. Figure 2-2 shows the successful execution of a move instruction. The pictured wall section is beyond Karel's one-half-block range of vision and therefore cannot impede his movement. In contrast, Figure 2-3 shows a thwarted attempt to move. When Karel executes a move instruction in this situation, he sees a wall section directly in his path. Relying on his instinct for self-preservation, Karel executes this move instruction by performing an error shutoff.

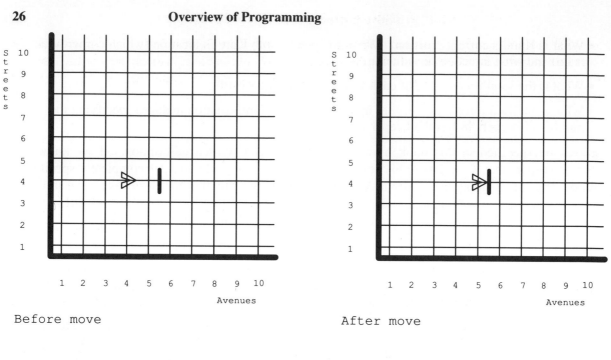

Before move   After move

Figure 2-2: Successful Execution of a move Instruction

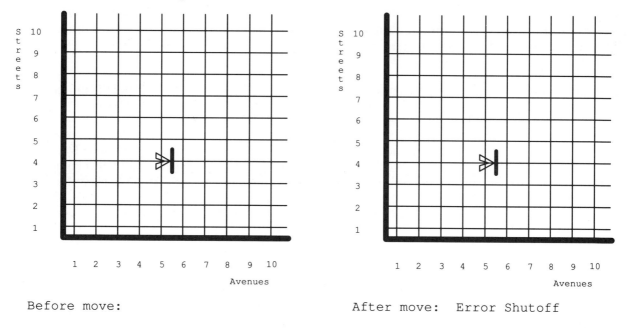

Before move: After move: Error Shutoff

Figure 2-3: Execution of this move Instruction Causes an Error Shutoff

The second primitive instruction that changes Karel's position is turnleft. This instruction changes the direction that Karel is facing, but does not alter his location.

turnleft   Karel executes a turnleft instruction by pivoting 90° to the left; thus, Karel remains on the same street corner while executing a turnleft instruction. Because it is impossible for a wall section to block Karel's turn, turnleft cannot cause an error shutoff.

Karel always starts his task on some corner, facing either north, south, east, or west. He cannot travel fractions of a block or turn at other than 90° angles. Therefore, although both move and turnleft change his position, after executing either of these instructions, Karel still is on some corner and still is facing one of the four compass points.

Karel's designer purposely did not provide him with a built-in turnright instruction. Would adding a turnright to Karel's list of primitive instructions allow him to perform any task he cannot accomplish without one? A moment's thought -- and the right flash of insight -- shows that the `turnright` instruction is dispensable; it does not permit Karel to accomplish any new tasks. The key observation for verifying this conclusion is that Karel can manage the equivalent of a `turnright` instruction by executing three `turnleft` instructions.

2.4.2. Handling Beepers

Karel understands two primitive instructions that permit him to handle beepers. These two instructions perform opposite actions.

`pickbeeper` — When Karel executes a `pickbeeper` instruction, he picks up a beeper from the corner he is standing on and then deposits it in his beeper-bag. If he executes a `pickbeeper` instruction on a beeperless corner, Karel performs an error shutoff. On a corner with more than one beeper, Karel randomly picks up one -- and only one -- of the beepers and then places it in his beeper-bag.

`putbeeper` — Karel executes a `putbeeper` instruction by extracting a beeper from his beeper-bag and placing it on his current street corner. If Karel tries to execute a `putbeeper` instruction with an empty beeper-bag, he performs an error shutoff.

Beepers are so small that Karel can move right by them; only wall sections and boundary walls can block his movement.

2.4.3. Finishing a Task

Finally, we need a way to tell Karel that he is finished with his task. The `turnoff` instruction fulfills this requirement.

`turnoff` — When Karel executes a `turnoff` instruction, he turns himself off and is incapable of executing any more instructions until he is restarted on another task. The last instruction in every robot program must be a `turnoff` instruction.

2.4.4. A Complete Program

In this section we pose a task for Karel and then exhibit a complete program that instructs him to perform the task correctly. Karel's task, illustrated in Figure 2-4 , is to transport the beeper from 2nd St. & 4th Ave. to 4th St. & 5th Ave. After he has put down the beeper, Karel must move one block farther north before turning himself off.

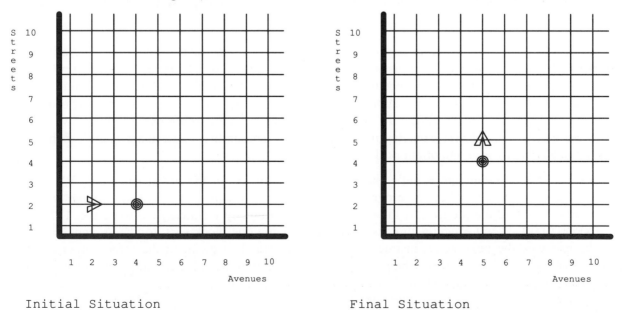

Initial Situation   Final Situation

Figure 2-4: A Beeper Transportation Task

The following robot program correctly instructs Karel to perform this task. The program is constructed from the five primitive instructions, a few new words from Karel's vocabulary, and the semicolon (";") punctuation mark. We'll discuss Karel's execution of this program first, and then we shall analyze the general structure of all robot programs.

```
BEGINNING-OF-PROGRAM
  BEGINNING-OF-EXECUTION
    move;
    move;
    pickbeeper;
    move;
    turnleft;
    move;
    move;
    putbeeper;
    move;
    turnoff
  END-OF-EXECUTION
END-OF-PROGRAM
```

2.4.4.1. Executing a Program

What must we do to make Karel execute this program? First, we activate Karel by pressing his Turn-On button. Once this is done, Karel's power is switched on, and he is then ready to receive and memorize a program. Next we read Karel the program, making sure to include each word and punctuation mark. In this example, we start by reading: "beginning-of-program beginning-of-execution move semicolon move semicolon pickbeeper semicolon move semicolon turnleft ...." Unfortunately, we cannot communicate the program's indentation to Karel; it is for our benefit only. While we read the program to Karel, he memorizes it, but does not yet start executing the instructions it contains.

When we finish reading the program to Karel, we first set up the initial situation by adding the required wall sections and beepers to the world. Next we press his Execute-Program button, which tells Karel to start executing the program. He is then completely under the control of the program, and we cannot affect his actions again until after he turns himself off. If our program is faulty, we must wait for the error to occur before correcting the program and re-reading it to Karel.

How does Karel execute a program? The rules are quite simple: He sequentially executes each instruction between the words BEGINNING-OF-EXECUTION and END-OF-EXECUTION. This is done, without omitting any instructions, in a strict top-to-bottom order. Karel continues executing instructions until he either executes a turnoff instruction or performs an error shutoff.

Of course, Karel is not a real robot, so we cannot read him a program and watch him execute it. To determine what a program does, we must *simulate* Karel's execution of it. Simulating a robot program means that we must systematically execute the program exactly as Karel would have, recording every action that takes place. We can hand-simulate a robot program by using markers on a sheet of paper (representing Karel and his world). In order to become proficient robot programmers, we must understand exactly how Karel executes robot programs. The ability to simulate Karel's behavior quickly and accurately is an important skill that we must acquire.

Now we are ready to simulate Karel's execution of our program in the initial situation. We press Karel's Turn-On button, read him the program, set up the world, and press his Execute-Program button. Karel starts executing the program at the move instruction directly following the word BEGINNING OF EXECUTION. Karel executes this instruction by moving one block east, to 2nd St. and 3rd Ave. Then he executes the next move instruction; this causes Karel to move to the same corner as the beeper. Karel successfully executes the pickbeeper instruction next. He continues by executing the subsequent move instruction, which brings him to the corner of 2nd St. & 5th Ave. Here Karel executes the turnleft instruction; this instruction faces him north. He executes the next two move instructions, after which he is on the corner of 4th St. and 5th Ave. -- where Karel then executes the putbeeper instruction. The last move instruction directs him one more block northward, to 5th St. & 5th Ave. Finally, karel executes the turnoff instruction, completing the program and accomplishing the required task. Thus, we have <u>verified</u> that our program is correct through simulation.

2.4.4.2. The Form of Robot Programs

Now that we have a good understanding of how Karel executes a program, let's explore the grammar rules of the robot programming language. Karel pays an inordinate amount of attention to grammar and punctuation rules -- a foolish consistency is the hobgoblin of small robot minds -- so our time is well spent studying these rules precisely. We start by dividing the symbols that Karel understands into three classes. The first class is punctuation marks, and its only member is the semicolon. All other symbols are in Karel's vocabulary, and they are classified as either instructions, which we have already seen examples of, or reserved words.

<u>Reserved words</u> are used to structure and organize the primitive instructions in Karel's language. Throughout this book, reserved words are printed in upper-case letters, while instructions are printed in lower-case letters. This distinction should help us keep these two word classes separate; only we, however, can benefit from this notation, because Karel only *hears* a program being read -- he cannot differentiate between upper-case and lower-case spoken words. In the following discussion, we explain the four reserved words and the punctuation rules used in this programming example. But before proceeding, let's review our program.

```
BEGINNING-OF-PROGRAM
  BEGINNING-OF-EXECUTION
    move;
    move;
    pickbeeper;
    move;
    turnleft;
    move;
    move;
    putbeeper;
    move;
    turnoff
  END-OF-EXECUTION
END-OF-PROGRAM
```

Every robot program must start with the reserved word BEGINNING-OF-PROGRAM. This word is followed by the reserved word BEGINNING-OF-EXECUTION[3], which in turn is followed by a sequence of instructions. After this instruction sequence comes the reserved word END-OF-EXECUTION, finally followed by the reserved word END-OF-PROGRAM. Matching pairs of BEGIN/END reserved words are called <u>delimiters</u>, because they delimit the beginning and end of some important entity.

The reserved word BEGINNING-OF-EXECUTION tells Karel where in the program to start executing instructions when his Execute-Program button has been pressed. The reserved word END-OF-EXECUTION does not tell Karel that he is finished executing a program; the turnoff instruction is used for this purpose. Instead, the word END-OF-EXECUTION delimits the end of the instructions that Karel will execute. If Karel is executing a program and reaches END-OF-EXECUTION, it means that a turnoff instruction has been omitted from the program, and Karel will perform an error shutoff. This is an incorrect way for Karel to finish executing a program.

Now let's scrutinize the semicolon punctuation of this program. The semicolon (";") serves to separate consecutive instructions. The rule we must follow is: "Each *instruction* is separated from the next *instruction* by a semicolon." We write each semicolon directly after the first of the two separated instructions. This simple punctuation rule is often misinterpreted as: "Each instruction is followed by a semicolon," but, as we shall see in the next paragraph, these two punctuation rules are slightly different.

---

[3]BEGINNING-OF-EXECUTION does not always directly follow BEGINNING-OF-PROGRAM. In the next chapter we shall learn what can be placed between these two reserved words.

The difference between these two punctuation rules can be detected by inspecting the `turnoff` instruction in the program. The `turnoff` instruction does not have a semicolon after it because it is followed by END-OF-EXECUTION, which is a reserved word, not another instruction. There is no rule requiring that reserved words be separated from instructions by semicolons. Consequently, whereas the "semicolon after each instruction" rule fails to punctuate this case correctly, the "semicolon between instructions" rule succeeds. Also, notice the two consecutive reserved words, such as BEGINNING-OF-PROGRAM and BEGINNING-OF-EXECUTION, are not separated by a semicolon.

This punctuation strategy is analogous to the way we write a set of numbers in mathematics. For example, we write the set consisting of the elements 1, 4, and 7 as {1,4,7}. In our analogy, the braces are delimiters, the numbers are instructions, and the commas between numbers take the places of semicolons. If we wrote this set as {1,4,7,} -- here we have put a comma after each number; notice the extraneous final comma -- it would look as if we had forgotten to write the final number in the set. Likewise, if we included a semicolon after `turnoff`, Karel would expect to hear another instruction, not the END-OF-EXECUTION reserved word. We must punctuate our programs carefully, as many grammatical errors are the result of incorrect semicolon punctuation.

Finally, notice how delimiters and the entity they delimit are indented. Observe that the entire program is nicely indented, clear, and pleasing to the eye. The importance of adopting a lucid programming style cannot be overemphasized. Embrace the habit not only of writing correct programs, but writing programs that are easy to read. When we discuss different facets of programming style, please pay close attention to these hints and examples, and try to emulate the style of programming presented herein.

Hurrah! You have made it through one of the most fact-packed sections in this book. Much of this material can be learned only through memorization. But take comfort; what appears at present to be a large number of arbitrary conventions and rules will soon seem natural and make logical sense. Programming languages share this arbitrariness with natural languages (why is the thing we sit on called a "chair," and why must a comma precede a conjunction introducing an independent clause?). Take a minute to rest and rejoice before continuing with the next section.

2.4.5. Error Shutoffs

When Karel is prevented from successfully completing the action associated with a primitive instruction, he executes the erroneous instruction by turning himself off. This action is known as an error shutoff, and its effect is equivalent to Karel's executing a `turnoff` instruction. But turning off is not the only way such a problem could be addressed: An alternative strategy might have Karel just ignore any instruction that he could not successfully execute. Using this rule he would continue executing the program as if he had never been required to execute the unsuccessful instruction. In the next paragraph, we discuss why Karel's designer chose the first, more conservative of these two options.

To justify this choice, we observe that an error shutoff results from an incorrect program that leads Karel astray. Once an unexpected situation arises -- one that prevents successful execution of an instruction -- Karel probably will be unable to make further progress toward accomplishing his task. Continuing to execute a program under these circumstances would lead to an even greater discrepancy between what the programmer had intended for Karel to do and what Karel is actually doing; consequently, the best strategy is to have Karel turn himself off as soon as the first inconsistency appears.

So far, we have seen three instructions that can cause error shutoffs: `move`, `pickbeeper`, and `putbeeper`. We must construct our programs carefully and ensure that the following conditions are always satisfied.

- Karel executes a `move` instruction only when his path is clear to the next corner.

- Karel executes a `pickbeeper` instruction only when he is on the same corner as at least one beeper.

- Karel executes a `putbeeper` instruction only when his beeper-bag is not empty.

These conditions are easily met if, before writing our program, we know the exact initial situation in which Karel will be placed. Also, to avoid an error shutoff when a program finishes, we must remember to include a `turnoff` instruction as the last instruction in our programs.

2.4.6. Programming Errors

In this section we classify all programming errors into four broad categories. These categories are discussed by an analogy that helps clarify the nature of each error type. You might ask, "Why spend so much time talking about errors when they should never occur?" The answer to this question is that programming requires an inhuman amount of precision, and although errors should not occur *in principle* they occur excessively *in practice*. Instead of expecting to write completely correct programs, we should expect to write 90%-correct programs. We must become adept at quickly finding and fixing errors by simulating our programs. Knowing the names of our enemies is the first step toward defeating them[4], so to this end we dedicate the following discussion.

A <u>lexical error</u> occurs whenever we read Karel a word that is not in his vocabulary. As an analogy, suppose that we are standing on a street in San Francisco, and we are asked by a lost motorist, "How can I get to Portland, Oregon?" If we tell him "fsdt jdhpy hqngrpz fgssj zgr ghhgh grmplhms," we would have committed a lexical error. The motorist is unable to follow our instructions because he is unable to decipher the words of which the instructions are composed. Similarly, Karel must understand each word in a program that he is asked to execute.

Even if Karel recognizes every word in a program, the program still might harbor a <u>syntactic error</u>. This type of error occurs whenever we use incorrect grammar or inaccurate punctuation. Going back to our lost motorist, we might reply, "for keep hundred just miles going eight." Although he recognizes each of these words individually, we have combined them in a senseless, convoluted manner: The parts of speech are not in their correct positions for English grammar. We discussed the grammar rules for basic robot programs in Section 2.4.4.2.

If our program contains either lexical or syntactic errors, Karel will discover the errors while we read him our program. In both cases, Karel has no conception of *what we meant to say*; therefore he does not try to correct our errors. Instead, he informs us of the detected errors and then turns himself off, because Karel is incapable of executing a program that he does not fully understand. This action is not an error shutoff, for in this case Karel has no program to execute.

While discussing the next two categories of errors, we shall assume that Karel has found no lexical or syntactic errors in our program. So, after we press Karel's Execute-Program button, he starts to execute the program.

The third error category is called an <u>execution error</u>. As with lexical and syntactic errors, Karel can also detect these errors when they occur. Execution errors occur whenever Karel is unable to execute an instruction successfully and is forced to perform an error shutoff. Returning to our motorist, who is trying to drive from San Francisco to Portland, we might tell him "Just keep going for eight hundred miles." But if he happens to be facing west at the time, and takes our directions literally, he would travel for only a few miles before reaching the Pacific Ocean. At this point he would stop, realizing that he cannot follow our instructions to completion. Likewise, Karel will turn himself off if he is asked to execute a primitive instruction that he is incapable of completing successfully.

The final error class is the most insidious, because Karel cannot detect this type of error when it occurs. We label this category of error an <u>intent error</u>. An intent error occurs whenever Karel successfully completes his program, but does not successfully complete his task. This means that the program is incorrect for the task, but not so incorrect that Karel can discover the error. Coming back to our motorist, we could again tell him, "Just keep going for eight hundred miles." If this time he happens to be facing south, he can successfully follow our instructions to completion, but he will end up in Tijuana, Mexico.

---

[4]In ancient days, a wizard could control an inanimate object by knowing its "true" name. Unfortunately, the true names for programming errors were lost in antiquity, but the "close" names discussed in this section should help us think about finding and fixing errors in our programs.

Remember that Karel does not *understand* the task for which we have programmed him; all Karel knows is how to execute the instructions we have given him in our program. Thus, there is no way for him to know that the program did not accomplish what we intended.

Frequently, intent errors occur early in a program and later lead to execution errors. Once Karel makes a wrong turn or moves incorrectly, it is only a matter of time before he tries to move through a wall or pick up a beeper that is not where he thinks it should be. Therefore, just because an instruction causes an error shutoff, it does not mean that the instruction is wrong; an earlier incorrect instruction might lead to an error that Karel discovers later in the program. In such cases, we must trace backward through the program from the instruction that caused the error shutoff, to discover which instruction started Karel on his errant path. This type of interaction, between intent and execution errors, is illustrated concretely in Problem 2.4.7-1.

2.4.6.1. Bugs and Debugging

In programming jargon, all types of errors are known as bugs. There are many apocryphal stories about the origin of this term. In one story the term "bug" is said to have been originated by telephone company engineers. They used the term to describe the source of random noises transmitted by their electronic communications circuits, saying that there were bugs in the circuits.

In another story, the Harvard Mark I computer was producing incorrect answers. When the engineers took it apart, trying to locate the problem, they found that a dead fly (which was caught between the contacts of a relay) was causing the malfunction; ergo, the first computer bug. Other stories abound, so perhaps we shall never know the true entomology of this word.

The term "bug" became popular in programming to save the egos of programmers who could not admit that their programs were full of errors. Instead, they preferred to say that their programs had bugs in them. Actually, the metaphor is apt: bugs are hard to find, and although a located bug is frequently easy to fix, it is difficult to ensure that all bugs have been found and removed from a program. Debugging is the name that programmers give to the activity of removing errors from a program.

2.4.7. Problem Set

The purpose of this problem set is to test your knowledge of the form and content of simple robot programs. The programs you are required to write are long, but not complicated. Concentrate on writing grammatically correct, pleasingly styled programs. Refer back to the program and discussion in Section 2.4.4 for rules and examples of correct grammar and punctuation. Verify that each program is correct by simulating Karel in the appropriate initial situation.

1. > Start Karel in the initial situation illustrated in Figure 2-5 and simulate his execution of the following program. Karel's task is to find the beeper, pick it up, and then turn himself off. Draw a map of the final situation, stating whether an error occurs. If an execution or intent error does occur, explain how you would correct the program. This program has no lexical or syntactic errors.

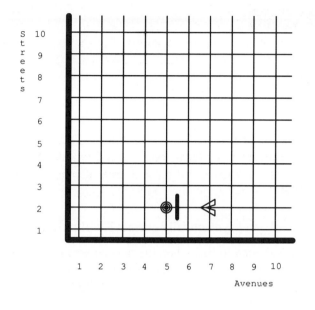

Figure 2-5: Initial Situation for Problem 1

```
BEGINNING-OF-PROGRAM
  BEGINNING-OF-EXECUTION
    move;
    turnleft;
    turnleft;
    move;
    turnleft;
    move;
    turnleft;
    move;
    pickbeeper;
    turnoff
  END-OF-EXECUTION
END-OF-PROGRAM
```

2. > Carefully inspect the following program and correct all lexical and syntactic errors. **Hint:** There are eight errors; five errors involve semicolons, one is grammatical, and the other two errors are lexical. Confirm that each word is in an appropriate place and that it is a correctly spelled instruction name or reserved word. You may use the program in Problem 2.4.7-1 as a model for a lexically and syntactically correct program.

```
BEGINNING-OF-EXECUTION;
  BEGINNING-OF-PROGRAM
    move;
    move
    pickbeeper;
    move;;
    turnleft;
    move;
    move;
    turnright;
    putbeeper;
    move;
    turnoff;
  END-OF-EXECUTON
END-OF-PROGRAM;
```

3. What is the smallest lexically and syntactically correct Karel program?

4. Every morning Karel is awakened in bed when his newspaper, represented by a beeper, is thrown onto the front porch of his house. Program Karel to retrieve his paper and bring it back to bed with him. The initial situation is given in Figure 2-6, and the final situation must have Karel back in bed (same corner, same direction) with the newspaper.

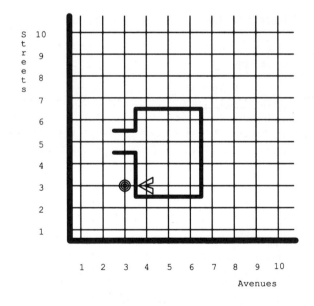

Figure 2-6: Initial Situation for the Newspaper Retrieval Task

5. > The wall sections in Figure 2-7 represent a mountain (north is up). Program Karel to climb the mountain and then plant a flag, represented by a beeper, on the summit; Karel then must descend the other side of the mountain. Assume that he starts with the flag-beeper in his bag. Remember that Karel is not a super-robot from the planet Krypton who can leap to the top of the mountain, plant the flag, and then jump down in a single bound (his name is Karel, not Kar-el). As illustrated, Karel must closely follow the mountain's face on his way up and down.

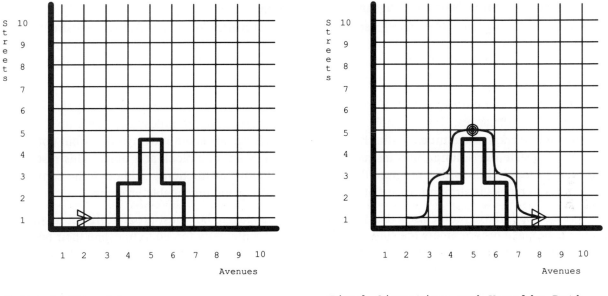

Initial Situation   Final Situation and Karel's Path

Figure 2-7: The Mountain Climbing Task

6. On the way home from the supermarket, Karel's shopping bag ripped slightly at the bottom, leaking a few expensive items. These groceries are represented by -- you guessed it -- beepers. The initial situation, when Karel discovered the leak, is represented in Figure 2-8. Program Karel to pick up all the dropped items and then return to his starting position.

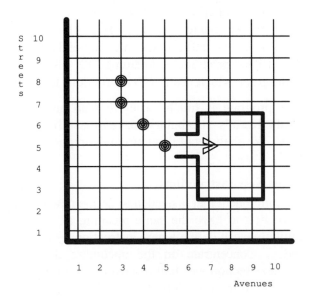

Figure 2-8: Initial Situation for the Grocery Pickup Task

2.5. Extending Karel's Vocabulary

This section explains the mechanics of extending Karel's vocabulary and, in the process, discusses the concept of *block structuring*. Besides its usefulness here, block structuring is integrally linked to the other complex instructions that Karel has been built to understand. We shall also demonstrate, in Section 2.5.8, a style of program construction that is known as *stepwise refinement*. The ability to extend Karel's vocabulary and the method of stepwise refinement complement each other, simplifying our programming problems.

2.5.1. Creating a More Natural Programming Language

In Section 2.4.1 we saw that Karel can perform the equivalent of a `turnright` instruction by executing a sequence of three `turnleft` instructions. But writing three `turnleft` instructions for the simple act of turning right is both unnatural and verbose. The robot programming language should contain a more concise way of conveying these instructions to Karel.

Let's look at another clumsy aspect of robot programming. Suppose that we need to program Karel to travel over vast distances. For example, assume that he must move ten miles[5] east, pick up a beeper, and then move another ten miles north. Because Karel understands about moving *blocks* but not *miles*, we must translate our solution into instructions that move Karel one block at a time. This restriction forces us to supply him with a program that contains 160 move instructions. Although the conversion from miles to blocks is straightforward, it results in a very long and unreadable program.

The crux of both these problems is that we think in one language, but must program Karel in another. Rather than make programmers the slaves of the machine, continually forced to translate their powerful ideas into Karel's primitive instructions, Karel's designer turned the tables and endowed Karel with a simple mechanism to *learn* the definitions of new instructions.

Karel's learning ability is actually quite limited. Our programs can furnish him with a *dictionary* of useful instruction names and their definitions, but each definition must be built from simpler instructions that Karel already understands; the simplest of these instructions are the primitive instructions that Karel intrinsically understands. By providing Karel with instructions that perform complex actions, we can build his vocabulary to correspond more closely to our own. Given this mechanism, we can solve our programming problems using whatever instructions are natural to our way of thinking, and then we can teach Karel the definitions of these instructions.

Returning to our first example, we can inform Karel that the definition of a `turnright` instruction is three `turnleft` instructions. Similarly, we can define a `move-mile` instruction as eight `move` instructions. When Karel must execute either of these new instructions in a program, he remembers the definition associated with the instruction name and executes it. Now our unwieldy beeper-moving program can be written with a `move-mile` definition, containing eight `move` instructions, and another 20 `move-mile` instructions. This program, containing 28 instructions, would be quite an improvement over the original program, which needs 160 instructions to accomplish the task.

More significantly, the smaller program is much easier to read and understand. In complicated problems, the ability to diversify Karel's vocabulary makes the difference between understandable programs and unintelligible ones. We shall detail this extremely important definition mechanism in the next two sections.

2.5.2. A Mechanism that Defines New Instructions

This section introduces the first component that is needed to define new instructions. Karel's <u>definition mechanism</u> defines a new instruction to have the same meaning as one other instruction. Yes, the learning mechanism is that simple; we can define a new instruction by using only one other instruction that Karel already understands. Concentrate on the upcoming details of this trivial definition mechanism for now, and in the next section we shall discover how to increase its power dramatically. Isolated from a program, the general form of the definition mechanism is as follows.

---

[5]In Karel's world there are eight blocks to the mile

```
DEFINE-NEW-INSTRUCTION <new-name> AS
    <instruction>
```

This mechanism uses the reserved words DEFINE-NEW-INSTRUCTION and AS. The DEFINE-NEW-INSTRUCTION signals Karel that a new instruction is being defined, and AS separates the new instruction name from its definition. When this mechanism is used in a program, we replace <new-name>[6] by any word consisting of lower-case letters and numbers. This word cannot already be the name of an instruction, and we are also prohibited from choosing a reserved word as the name of a new instruction. Despite these restrictions, Karel's language does allow hyphenated names when a multiple-word name is needed (for example, face-north and go-to-wall).

We can replace <instruction> by any single instruction that Karel understands; this instruction becomes the definition of <new-name>. Possible replacements include all of the primitive instructions and any new instructions previously defined by using DEFINE-NEW-INSTRUCTION. Karel executes a new instruction by remembering the definition associated with the instruction's name and then executing it.

The restriction of replacing <instruction> by a single instruction is extremely severe, and it will be rectified in the next section; however, even this simple form of DEFINE-NEW-INSTRUCTION can be useful. If Karel were ever sent to France, his French programmers might employ DEFINE-NEW-INSTRUCTION to create the following simple translations.

```
DEFINE-NEW-INSTRUCTION avance AS
move
```

and

```
DEFINE-NEW-INSTRUCTION tourne-a-gauche AS
turnleft
```

2.5.3. Block Structuring

When building complex commands such as turnright and move-mile, we frequently need to replace <instruction> by more than just one instruction. Karel's designer chose block structuring as the method to perform this replacement. Block structuring is simple enough for Karel to understand, and it is general enough to be used with other complex instructions in the robot programming language. Block structuring is accomplished by placing a sequence of instructions between the reserved words BEGIN and END, making one big instruction out of a sequence of smaller ones. We write a BEGIN/END block in the following way, using indentation to reinforce the idea that a BEGIN/END block represents one large, aggregate instruction.

```
BEGIN
    <instruction>;
    <instruction>;
        .        .
        .        .
        .        .
    <instruction>;
    <instruction>
END
```

Let's explore the properties of this new grammar rule in greater detail.

- The reserved words BEGIN and END delimit a block whose inside consists of a sequence of instructions separated by semicolons. The internal punctuation of a BEGIN/END block is the same as the internal punctuation of a BEGINNING-OF-EXECUTION/END-OF-EXECUTION block. Remember that a semicolon does not separate the last instruction in the sequence from the reserved word END.

---

[6]We use the bracket notation (<new-name> and <instruction>) to help describe Karel's language generally. The word inside the brackets indicates what the bracketed word can be replaced with. For example, we may replace the bracketed word <instruction> by a move in one instance and by a turnleft in another. **Appendix II** contains a complete list of bracketed words and the associated words in Karel's vocabulary by which they can be replaced.

- We can write any number of instructions within a BEGIN/END block -- if we want, we may even put in just one. Although a single instruction does not need to be enclosed in a BEGIN/END block, this construction does not violate any of Karel's grammar rules.

- Karel executes a BEGIN/END block by sequentially executing the instructions within the block. Once he starts to execute a BEGIN/END block, Karel eventually executes all of the instructions inside the block, unless he either executes a turnoff instruction or performs an error shutoff.

The fundamental property of a BEGIN/END block is that Karel understands the entire block to represent one instruction. This property permits us to replace <instruction> by a BEGIN/END block. Armed with the concept of block structuring, we can now completely solve the turnright problem by defining the following new instruction. (The move-mile instruction can be written similarly.)

```
DEFINE-NEW-INSTRUCTION turnright AS
BEGIN
  turnleft;
  turnleft;
  turnleft
END
```

So far, we have shown new instruction definitions only outside of a program. In Section 2.5.5, we shall exhibit a complete program that uses the instruction definition mechanism. But first, we present a slight digression to establish the boundaries of Karel's understanding of new instructions.

2.5.4. The Meaning and Correctness of New Instructions

Here is an old riddle: "If you call a thumb a finger, how many fingers do you have?" The correct answer is eight, because calling a thumb a finger does not make it one. This riddle is based on the distinction between what a thing *is* and what a thing *is called*. In this section we explore Karel's version of this distinction. In Karel's world, just because you define a new instruction named turnright, it doesn't necessarily mean that the instruction really turns Karel to the right. To demonstrate this point, there are no restrictions prohibiting the following instruction definition.

```
DEFINE-NEW-INSTRUCTION turnright AS
BEGIN
  turnleft;
  turnleft
END
```

According to Karel's rules of grammar, this example is a perfectly legal definition, for it contains neither lexical nor syntactic errors. But by defining turnright this way, we make Karel believe that executing a turnright instruction is equivalent to executing two turnleft instructions. Karel does not *understand* what a turnright instruction is supposed to accomplish; his only conception of a turnright instruction is the definition we give him. Consequently, any new instruction we define may contain an intent error, as the example in this section does.

Besides intent errors, a new instruction can also cause execution errors if it is defined by using primitive instructions that can cause error shutoffs. Can this incorrect definition of turnright ever cause an error shutoff? The answer is no, because turnleft instructions are immune to error shutoffs. As a result, it is impossible for Karel to detect that anything is wrong with this instruction.

This example is somewhat trivial because the error is blatant; but with a more complex defined instruction, we must take care to write a definition that really accomplishes what its name implies. The name specifies *what* the instruction is intended to do; the definition specifies *how* the instruction does what the name implies. The two had better match exactly; otherwise one or both should be changed.

We must also be careful when simulating Karel's execution of a defined instruction. We must adhere to the rule that Karel uses to execute these instructions: Karel executes a defined instruction by executing its definition. Do not try to shortcut this process by doing what the instruction *means*, because Karel does not know what a defined instruction means; he knows only how it is defined. We must recognize the significance of this distinction and learn to interpret Karel's programs as literally as he does.

2.5.5. Defining New Instructions in a Program

In this section we display a complete robot program that uses the instruction definition mechanism. As in our example of a complete program in the last chapter, we shall first see how the program is executed and then discuss the general form of programs that use this mechanism. Karel's task is shown on the next page in Figure 2-9: He must pick up each beeper in his world while climbing the stairs. Following these maps is a program that correctly instructs Karel to accomplish the task.

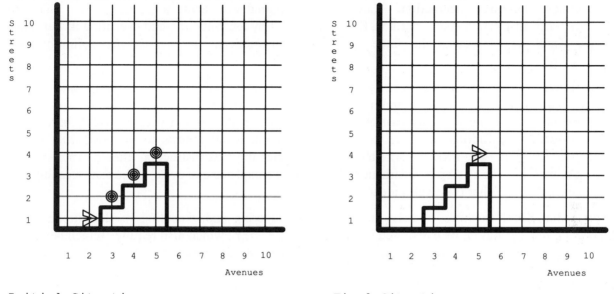

Initial Situation   Final Situation

Figure 2-9:   A Stair-Cleaning Task

```
BEGINNING-OF-PROGRAM
  DEFINE-NEW-INSTRUCTION turnright AS
  BEGIN
    turnleft;
    turnleft;
    turnleft
  END;

  DEFINE-NEW-INSTRUCTION climb-stair AS
  BEGIN
    turnleft;
    move;
    turnright;
    move
  END;


  BEGINNING-OF-EXECUTION
    climb-stair;
    pickbeeper;
    climb-stair;
    pickbeeper;
    climb-stair;
    pickbeeper;
    turnoff
  END-OF-EXECUTION
END-OF-PROGRAM
```

To verify that this program is correct, we simulate Karel's execution of it, emphasizing his execution of the defined instructions. First, we press Karel's Turn-On button and then read him the program. He memorizes the definitions of our two new instructions, `turnright` and `climb-stair`, and then he memorizes all of the instructions contained in the `BEGINNING-OF-EXECUTION`/`END-OF-EXECUTION` block. Karel finds no lexical or syntactic errors, so, after we have set up the initial situation and pressed his Execute-Program button, Karel starts executing the program at the instruction directly following BEGINNING-OF-EXECUTION.

The first instruction that Karel must execute is climb-stair and, because it is a defined instruction, Karel executes it by remembering and executing its definition. This definition is a BEGIN/END block, which Karel executes by sequentially executing each instruction within the block. He starts to execute this block by first executing the turnleft instruction. After he completes executing this instruction, he executes the move instruction. Karel is then required to execute a turnright. Since the turnright instruction is also defined, Karel executes it by remembering and executing its definition. Thus, Karel next executes the three turnleft instructions that are in the definition of a turnright.

After Karel finishes executing turnright, he returns to the climb-stair instruction and executes the final move in its definition. Karel has now completely executed climb-stair and successfully climbed one stair -- he is facing east on the same corner as the bottom beeper. Next, because the climb-stair definition has been completely executed, Karel returns to the BEGINNING OF EXECUTION/END-OF-EXECUTION block and executes the first instruction after climb-stair, which is the first pickbeeper instruction. This action completes one cycle of the stair cleaning task; Karel executes the other two cycles identically to this one.

Notice that Karel executes climb-stair by remembering and executing its definition. While executing this definition, he is required to execute turnright, which also requires remembering and executing a definition. Karel must temporarily interrupt his execution of the climb-stair instruction to start executing turnright, just as he temporarily interrupted his execution of the BEGINNING-OF-EXECUTION/END-OF-EXECUTION block to execute climb-stair. Karel resumes executing climb-stair after he finishes executing turnright.

It is important for us to understand that no complex rules are needed to execute a program containing defined instructions. Simulating Karel's execution of this program is a bit tedious, because each step is small and simple, but Karel is not equipped to understand anything more complicated. He is able to follow only a very simple, albeit dull, set of rules that tell him how to execute a program. Yet we can use these simple rules, coupled with Karel's willingness to follow them, to command him to perform non-trivial tasks.

We should now understand how Karel executes a program that includes the instruction definition mechanism. We next turn our attention toward program form, and we make the following observations about the stair-cleaning program.

- We briefly mentioned in the previous chapter that something could be written between the BEGINNING-OF-PROGRAM AND BEGINNING-OF-EXECUTION reserved words. In our programming example, we saw that the definitions of the two new instructions are placed here. We must always write our new instruction definitions in this area only. We call this portion of the program Karel's <u>dictionary</u>, and each definition is called a <u>dictionary entry</u>.

- The order of instruction definitions is important: Each instruction must be defined before it is used in either a subsequent definition or the BEGINNING-OF-EXECUTION/END-OF-EXECUTION block. In our example, the turnright instruction must be defined first, because turnright is used in the definition of climb-stair. Whenever this order is violated, Karel reports a lexical error -- because he will hear an instruction name before he has been told its definition.

- Now on to matters of punctuation, where we introduce two new semicolon punctuation rules. First, observe that dictionary entries are -- and must be -- separated from one another by a semicolon. Second, the semicolon separating the last dictionary entry from the BEGINNING-OF-EXECUTION/END-OF-EXECUTION block is also necessary.

Karel does not memorize forever the dictionary entries he learns. Each time he is turned on, his vocabulary reverts to the primitive instructions and reserved words that he was originally designed to understand; therefore, each program must contain a complete set of definitions for all new instructions that it uses.

2.5.6. Boxing: How Karel Understands a Program

In this section we explain how Karel can understand a program by isolating its constituents. The next section and subsequent chapters will demonstrate how we can use this information to help us recognize and avoid common pitfalls when writing and simulating programs. Specifically, in the next section we shall show how Karel can detect a syntactic error (a missing BEGIN/END block in the definition of a new instruction) in a robot program.

We start our study of *boxing* by defining a <u>unit</u> to be either: (1) a primitive or defined instruction name; (2) any type of BEGIN/END block; or (3) a complete dictionary entry. This third type of unit includes the reserved words DEFINE-NEW-INSTRUCTION and AS, the new instruction's name (which is already within its own box by rule 1), and the instruction's definition (which is the first instruction following the AS, and is also already in its own box). In the program on the next page, taken from the previous section, we have drawn <u>boxes</u> around every unit. We call such an operation <u>boxing</u>. By boxing the programs we read to him, Karel is able to check for syntax errors and determine exactly how to execute our programs.

Carefully study the following example to understand how boxing works. To help illustrate the process, the units have been numbered in the order Karel boxes them.

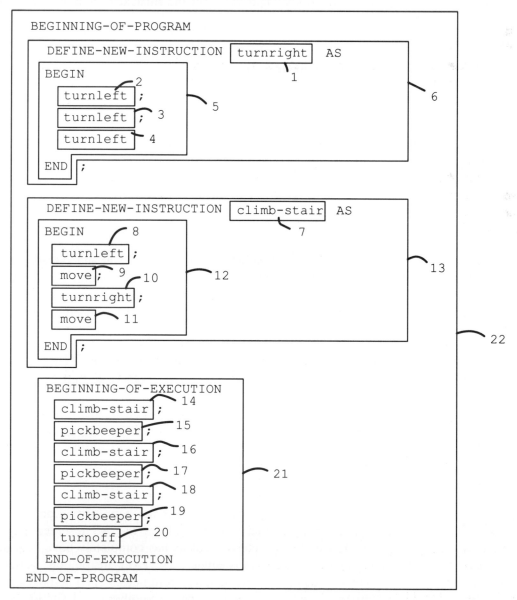

Karel starts boxing a program at its beginning. Generally, he builds units in a top-to-bottom order -- but he cannot box a unit until all of its constituents have been boxed. For example, he cannot box a

BEGIN/END block until he has boxed all the instructions it comprises. Numerically, each box contains only boxes with smaller numbers. Therefore, within this top-to-bottom order Karel boxes primitive instructions first and then works his way outward, building larger units out of smaller ones.

The main geometric property of boxing is that boxes are either <u>nested</u> (one inside another), or adjacent (one following another). As a rule, units can never overlap. Also notice that the entire program is itself one big unit. Furthermore, semicolons are placed between every pair of adjacent units. This simple punctuation rule is a more uniform restatement of all the semicolon punctuation rules we have learned in our previous discussions of syntax. From now on, we shall continue our analysis of Karel's grammar by using boxing.

2.5.7. An Ungrammatical Program

Before reading this section, quickly look at the small program in the immediately following example, and see if you can find a syntactic error.

This program illustrates a common programming mistake: the omission of a BEGIN/END block. The program is nicely indented, but the indentation is misleading. The DEFINE-NEW-INSTRUCTION appears to define turnright correctly, but we have omitted the BEGIN/END block that necessarily encloses the three turnleft instructions. Did you spot the mistake? It is not easy, because the indentation makes it look correct to us.

```
BEGINNING-OF-PROGRAM

    DEFINE-NEW-INSTRUCTION turnright AS
        turnleft;
        turnleft;
        turnleft


    BEGINNING-OF-EXECUTION
        move;
        turnright;
        turnoff
    END-OF-EXECUTION

END-OF-PROGRAM
```

While Karel is being read a program, he continuously checks it for lexical and syntactic errors. Karel discovers syntactic errors by boxing the program and checking for proper grammar and punctuation. In the following example, we illustrate how Karel finds the mistake in our program via boxing. Remember that he only *hears* the program being read and is unaware of our indentation.

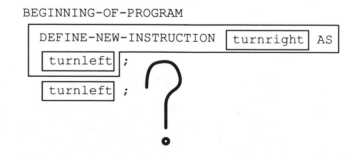

Karel successfully boxes the first unit, turnright, which is the new instruction name. Then he boxes the primitive instruction turnleft that directly follows the AS reserved word. By our omission of a BEGIN/END block, Karel now believes that he has completely boxed the definition of turnright. He also believes that this definition is single turnleft instruction. Karel next boxes the entire dictionary entry, notes the required semicolon, and continues. Then he boxes the next unit, which by the grammar rules must be another definition or the BEGINNING-OF-EXECUTION/END-OF-EXECUTION block. But he finds an inconsistency: this next unit is a turnleft instruction, which does not satisfy either of Karel's options, so he tells us that a syntactic error has occurred. In summary, forgetting to use a necessary BEGIN/END block can lead to syntactic errors.

We are rapidly becoming experts at analyzing programs. Given a robot program, we should now be able to detect grammar and punctuation errors quickly. We should also be able to simulate programs efficiently. But the other side of the programming coin, constructing programs, may still seem a little bit magical. The next section is a first step toward demystifying this process.

2.5.8. Programming by Stepwise Refinement

This section is a departure from our description of Karel's programming features, and it takes a more general view of programming and problem solving. We shall discuss *stepwise refinement*, a method we can use to construct robot programs. This method addresses the problem of how we can naturally write concise programs that are correct, simple to read, and easy to understand.

It may appear natural to define all the new dictionary entries that Karel will need for a task first, and then write the program using these instructions. But how can we know which new instructions are needed before we write the program? <u>Stepwise refinement</u> tells us first to write the program using any instruction names we desire, and then write the definitions of these instructions. That is, we write the sequence of instructions in the BEGINNING OF EXECUTION/END-OF-EXECUTION block first, and then we write the definitions of the new instruction names used within this block. Finally, we assemble all of these separate pieces into a complete program.

We shall explore this process more concretely by writing a program for the task shown in Figure 2-10. These maps represent a harvesting task that requires Karel to pick up a rectangular field of beepers.

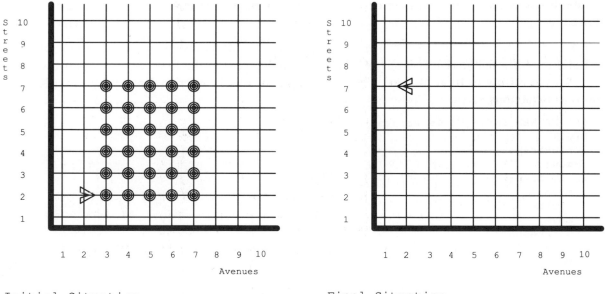

Initial Situation   Final Situation

Figure 2-10: The Harvest Task

We program Karel to accomplish this task by commanding him to harvest furrows horizontally, two at a time. Each time he executes the harvest-2-furrows instruction, Karel harvests five beepers going east and then comes back west, one block farther north, harvesting five more beepers. He then maneuvers into position for harvesting the next two furrows and repeats the entire process two more times. This solution is only one of the many ways we can plan this task; in Problem 2.5.10-4, you may try writing a program to accomplish this same task by using a different plan. We begin writing the program for this task by translating our basic plan into Karel's programming language.

```
BEGINNING-OF-EXECUTION
  move;
  harvest-2-furrows;
  position-for-next-2;
  harvest-2-furrows;
  position-for-next-2;
  harvest-2-furrows;
  move;
  turnoff
END-OF-EXECUTION
```

We have taken the original task and divided it into several smaller, easier-to-understand subtasks, where each subtask requires us to define a new instruction. Once these subtasks have been solved (all the new instructions have been defined) the original task will also have been solved. So, to continue writing our programs, we now must define the new instructions `harvest-2-furrows` and `position-for-next-2`. We write `harvest-2-furrows` first.

```
DEFINE-NEW-INSTRUCTION harvest-2-furrows AS
BEGIN
  harvest-a-furrow;
  go-to-next-furrow;
  harvest-a-furrow
END
```

While writing this definition, we invented two more new instructions to help structure our task, so we add `harvest-a-furrow` and `go-to-next-furrow` to the list of instructions that we must eventually define. From this example, we see that stepwise refinement allows our subtasks to generate sub-subtasks. Let's continue with our current train of thought and write `harvest-a-furrow` first, followed by `go-to-next-furrow`.

When Karel executes `harvest-a-furrow`, he must pick up all five beepers in the furrow. Observe that Karel executes this instruction only when he is standing next to the first beeper in a furrow, with the rest of the furrow in front of him. Thus, we can define this instruction directly by using Karel's primitive instructions.

```
DEFINE-NEW-INSTRUCTION harvest-a-furrow AS
BEGIN
  pickbeeper;
  move;
  pickbeeper;
  move;
  pickbeeper;
  move;
  pickbeeper;
  move;
  pickbeeper
END
```

Now we define `go-to-next-furrow`. Notice that Karel executes this instruction only after harvesting the first of two furrows; therefore, we can assume that he is facing east and wants to go one block farther north and then turn to face west. We also know that when Karel starts to execute this instruction, he is on the corner of the last harvested beeper in a furrow -- the easternmost corner.

```
DEFINE-NEW-INSTRUCTION go-to-next-furrow AS
BEGIN
  turnleft;
  move;
  turnleft
END
```

Now we can return to our original plan and write the `position-for-next-2` instruction. For reasons similar to those used to write the previous instruction, we know that Karel executes `position-for-next-2` only when he is facing west on the corner of the last harvested beeper in a furrow. After Karel executes `position-for-next-2`, he should be one block farther north and facing east.

```
DEFINE-NEW-INSTRUCTION position-for-next-2 AS
BEGIN
  turnright;
  move;
  turnright
END
```

This leads us back to our old friend the `turnright` instruction, whose definition is not written here, but must be included in the complete program.

Hey, we're finished! We have defined all the new instructions that we needed to write the program. Now we can assemble these instructions into a complete robot program. Remember that we must ensure that each instruction in the program is defined before it is used. Typically, instructions appear in a program in the reverse of the order in which they were written, with the BEGINNING-OF-EXECUTION/END-OF-EXECUTION block appearing last.

```
BEGINNING-OF-PROGRAM

    DEFINE-NEW-INSTRUCTION turnright AS
    BEGIN
      turnleft;
      turnleft;
      turnleft
    END;

    DEFINE-NEW-INSTRUCTION position-for-next-2 AS
    BEGIN
      turnright;
      move;
      turnright
    END;

    DEFINE-NEW-INSTRUCTION go-to-next-furrow AS
    BEGIN
      turnleft;
      move;
      turnleft
    END;

    DEFINE-NEW-INSTRUCTION harvest-a-furrow AS
    BEGIN
      pickbeeper;
      move;
      pickbeeper;
      move;
      pickbeeper;
      move;
      pickbeeper;
      move;
      pickbeeper
    END;

    DEFINE-NEW-INSTRUCTION harvest-2-furrows AS
    BEGIN
      harvest-a-furrow;
      go-to-next-furrow;
      harvest-a-furrow
    END;

    BEGINNING-OF-EXECUTION
      move;
      harvest-2-furrows;
      position-for-next-2;
      harvest-2-furrows;
      position-for-next-2;
      harvest-2-furrows;
      move;
      turnoff
    END-OF-EXECUTION
END-OF-PROGRAM
```

Of course, we should still simulate Karel's execution of this program in the initial situation to verify that it is correct. We may have relied on some invalid assumptions when writing the instructions that move Karel between furrows, or we may have made an error when copying our instructions into the final program. A skeptical attitude toward the correctness of our programs will put us in a good frame of mind for trying to verify them. Programs, unlike United States citizens, are assumed to be guilty of being wrong until they are proven correct.

It is useful to divide a program into many small instructions, even if these new instructions are only executed once. Instruction definitions nicely structure programs, and English words and phrases make programs more understandable; they help convey the intent of the program. As a quick example, we show the basic plan for one solution to Karel's paper-retrieving task, taken from Problem 2.4.7-4.

Although you might have forgotten the task, this program's solution plan is evident because of the instruction names it uses for subtasks.

```
BEGINNING-OF-EXECUTION
    go-to-door;
    exit-house;
    get-paper;
    return-to-door;
    enter-house;
    go-back-to-bed;
    turnoff
END-OF-EXECUTION
```

Finally, we should always start our stepwise refinements carefully. The early decisions we make are the most important, as they establish the structure of the rest of the program. Bad early decisions make it difficult to complete a program; a good plan, however, will allow the rest of the program refinement process to proceed smoothly. One way to write a program is to start a few different refinements, trying different approaches to solving the problem. We can then review these plans, selecting the best one to use for completing our stepwise refinement of the program.

This completes our discussion of stepwise refinement in this chapter. In Section 2.7.5, we shall construct a more complicated program by again using stepwise refinement.

2.5.9. Writing Understandable Programs

Writing understandable programs is as important as writing correct ones, some say that it is even more important. They argue that most programs initially have a few errors, and understandable programs are easiest to debug. Good programmers are distinguished from bad ones by their ability to write clear and concise programs: programs that someone else can read and quickly understand. What makes a program easy to understand? We present two criteria.

First, a good program is the simple composition of easily understandable parts. Each part in our harvesting program can be understood by itself. Even without a detailed understanding of the parts, the plan that the program uses to accomplish the complete task is also easy to understand.

Second, dividing a program (or large instruction definition) into small, easy-to-understand pieces is not enough. We must also make sure to name our new instructions properly; these names provide a description of how our program accomplishes its task (there are typically any different correct programs for any given task). Imagine what the previous program would look like, if for each meaningful instruction name we had used a name like `first-instruction` or `do-it-now`. Karel allows us to choose any instruction names we desire, but with this freedom comes the responsibility to select accurate and descriptive names.

It is much easier to verify or debug a program that contains defined instructions. The following two facts support this claim.

- Defined instructions can be independently tested. When writing a program, we should test each instruction immediately after it is written, until we are convinced that it is correct. Then we can forget how the instruction works and just remember what the instruction does. Remembering should be easy, if we name the instruction accurately.

- Defined instructions impose a structure on our programs, and we can use this structure to help us locate bugs. When debugging a program, we should first find which of the defined instructions is malfunctioning. Then we can concentrate on debugging that instruction, ignoring the other parts of our program, which are irrelevant to the bug.

Thus, we see that there is an interesting psychological phenomenon related to Karel's instruction definition mechanism. Because the human brain can focus on only a limited amount of information at any one time, the ability to ignore details that are no longer relevant is a great aid to program writing and debugging.

To help make our new instruction definitions understandable, we should also keep their lengths within a reasonable range. A good rule of thumb is that definitions should rarely exceed five to eight instructions. This limit leaves us enough room to write a meaningful instruction, but restrains us from cramming too much detail into any one definition. If an instruction's size exceeds this limit, we should divide it into a set of smaller instructions. This rule applies to the number of instructions written within the `BEGINNING-OF-EXECUTION/END-OF-EXECUTION` block too. Most novice programmers tend to write instruction definitions that are too large; resist this temptation. It is better to write many small, well-named instructions, rather than to have a small number of oversized definitions.

In summary, how can writing an understandable program help us? Imagine what the harvesting program would look like if it were written without any defined instructions, using only Karel's primitive instructions. Compare this expanded program with the compact one given in the last section. How easy would it be to convince someone that each is correct? If we made an error by leaving out some parts of the program -- some single instruction, for example -- how easy would it be to locate and correct the error in each case? Finally, if we want to change Karel's task slightly, such as by requiring him to harvest three more beepers per furrow, how difficult would it be to change each of the programs to accomplish this new task? These reasons are part of the overwhelming evidence suggesting that the best program for a task is the one that is the easiest to understand.

2.5.10. Problem Set

The problems in this section require defining new instructions for Karel, or writing complete programs that include dictionary entries. Concentrate on writing well-structured programs, built from naturally descriptive new instructions. Practice using stepwise refinement and freely define any new instructions that you need. If you find yourself continually writing the same sequence of instructions, it is a sure sign that you need to define that sequence as a new instruction. Carefully check for syntactic errors in your programs, and simulate Karel's execution of each program to verify that it is correct.

Paradoxically, the programs in this problem set will be among the largest you write. The instructions covered in the next chapters are so powerful that we shall find that complex tasks can be solved with programs comprising a small number of these potent instructions.

1. > Write appropriate definitions for the following four new instructions: (1) `turnaround`, which turns Karel around 180°; (2) `move-mile`, remembering that miles are 8 blocks long; (3) `move-backward`, which moves Karel one block backward but leaves him facing the same direction; and (4) `move-kilo-mile`, which moves Karel 1000 miles forward. This last problem is difficult, but a fairly short solution does exist. You may use the `move-mile` instruction in this problem without redefining it. Also, which of these four instructions might cause an error shutoff when it is executed?

2. Karel sometimes works as a pin-setter in a bowling alley. Write a program that instructs Karel to transform the initial situation in Figure 2-11 into the final situation. Karel starts this task with ten beepers in his beeper-bag.

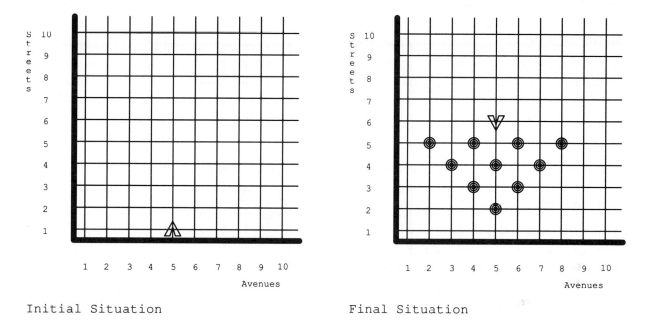

Initial Situation   Final Situation

Figure 2-11: A Pin-Setting Task

3. > Copy the complete program written in the stepwise-refinement section and box it. Make sure that your boxes do not overlap and that semicolons appear only between adjacent boxes.

4. Rewrite the harvesting program using a different stepwise refinement.

5. > Figure 2-12 illustrates a field of beepers that Karel planted one night when he was drunk after a baseball game. Write a program that harvests all these beepers. *Hint: This task is not too different from the harvesting example. If you see the correspondence between these two harvesting tasks, you should be able to develop a program for this task that is similar to the original harvesting program.*

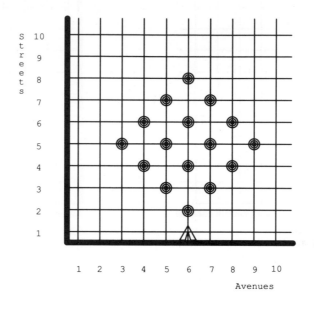

Figure 2-12: Another Harvesting Task

6. Karel wants to send his greetings to the other inhabitants of his universe, so he needs to plant a field of beepers that broadcasts his message to alien astronomers. Program Karel to plant the message of beepers shown in Figure 2-13. You may choose Karel's starting position.

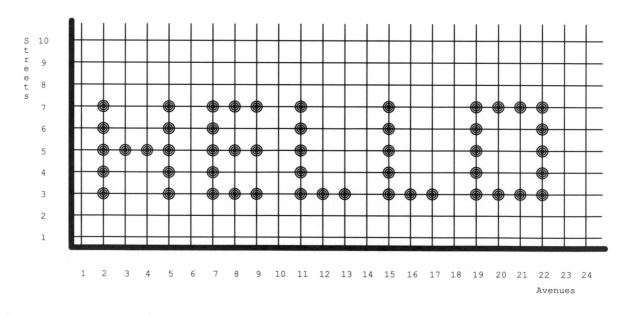

Figure 2-13: A Message for Alien Astronomers

2.6. Conditionally Executing Instructions

In the preceding chapters, we always were told exactly which initial situation Karel would be placed in at the start of his task. When we wrote our programs, this information easily allowed us to command Karel to find beepers and avoid running into walls. But these programs were not very general. If Karel tried to execute one in a slightly different initial situation, he would almost certainly be forced to perform an error shutoff. What Karel needs is the ability to survey his local environment and then decide, on the basis of the information he gleans, what to do next.

The `IF` instructions discussed in this chapter -- there are two versions, the `IF/THEN` and the `IF/THEN/ELSE` -- provide Karel with this decision ability. Both command Karel to test his environment and, depending on the result of the test, allow him to execute an appropriate instruction. These instructions enable us to write much more general programs for Karel -- programs that instruct him to accomplish tasks regardless of in which initial situation he is started.

2.6.1. The IF/THEN Instruction

The `IF/THEN` instruction is the simpler of the two `IF` variants, so we shall discuss it first, It has the following general form.

```
IF <test>
  THEN <instruction>
```

The `IF/THEN` instruction introduces the two new reserved words `IF` and `THEN`. The reserved word `IF` signals Karel that an `IF` instruction is present, and the reserved word `THEN` separates <test> from <instruction>. The <instruction> is known as the <u>THEN clause</u> of the `IF` instruction. We indent the `IF/THEN` instruction as shown, to highlight the fact that the `THEN` clause is a component of the `IF` instruction.

Karel executes the `IF/THEN` instruction by first checking whether <test> is true or false in his current situation. If <test> is true, Karel executes <instruction>; if <test> is false, Karel ignores <instruction>. In either case, he is then finished executing the entire `IF/THEN` instruction. For an example, let's look at the following <u>program fragment</u>[7], which consists of an `IF/THEN` instruction followed by a move instruction (notice the placement of the semicolon between the entire `IF` instruction and the `move` instruction.)

```
IF next-to a beeper
  THEN pickbeeper;
move
```

Karel executes this `IF/THEN` instruction by first checking whether he is next to (on the same corner as) a beeper. If Karel finds that `next-to-a-beeper` is true, he executes the `THEN` clause, which instructs him to execute `pickbeeper`. He is now finished executing the `IF/THEN` instruction, and he continues by executing the rest of the program starting at the `move` instruction.

Now suppose that there are no beepers on the corner when Karel executes this program fragment. In this case <test> is false, so Karel does not execute the `THEN` clause. Instead, he skips directly to the `move` instruction and continues executing the program from there. The result of this second case is that Karel executes the `IF/THEN` instruction by doing nothing more than checking whether he is next to a beeper.

An error shutoff cannot occur in either case, because Karel executes the `pickbeeper` instruction only if he confirms the presence of at least one beeper on his corner.

2.6.2. The Conditions Karel Can Test

In Chapter 1 we briefly discussed Karel's sensory modes. We learned that he can see, hear, discover which direction he is facing, and determine if there are any beepers in his beeper-bag. The conditions that Karel can test are divided according to these same four categories. What follows is a complete list

---

[7]To conserve space, we often demonstrate a programming idea without writing a complete robot program or defined instruction. Instead, we just write the necessary instructions, which are called a program fragment.

of the vocabulary words that can be substituted for the bracketed word <test> in the IF/THEN instruction.

For purposes of classification, Karel treats these words much like primitive instructions; hence, they are written using lowercase letters. Also notice that each condition is available in both its positive and negative form (for example, `front-is-clear` and `front-is-blocked`).

- `front-is-clear, front-is-blocked, left-is-clear, left-is-blocked, right-is-clear,` and `right-is-blocked.`

- `next-to-a-beeper` and `not-next-to-a-beeper.`

- `facing-north, not-facing-north, facing-south, not-facing-south, facing-east, not-facing-east, facing-west,` and `not-facing-west.`

- `any-beepers-in-beeper-bag` and `no-beepers-in-beeper-bag.`

Remember that Karel has three TV cameras for eyes, each focused to detect walls exactly one half of a block away. One camera is facing directly ahead, one is facing toward Karel's left, and the final camera is facing toward Karel's right. He tests `right-is-clear`, for example, by checking whether there is a wall between himself and the first corner over on his right.

The `next-to-a-beeper` test is true when Karel is on the same corner as one or more beepers. He cannot hear beepers any farther away, and he obviously cannot hear beepers that are in his soundproof beeper-bag.

Karel consults his internal compass when he must test whether or not he is facing a particular direction.

Finally, Karel can test whether he has any beepers in his beeper-bag by probing it with his mechanical arm.

2.6.3. Simple Examples of the IF/THEN Instruction

This section examines three instruction definitions that use the IF/THEN instruction. During our discussion of the second definition, we explain what happens when a necessary BEGIN/END block is omitted from a THEN clause. We shall also discuss how IF/THEN instructions are boxed, before concluding.

2.6.3.1. The harvest-a-furrow Instruction

Do you remember the harvesting task that was programmed in Section 2.5.8 by stepwise refinement? Karel's new task still requires him to harvest the same size field, but this time there is no guarantee that a beeper is on each corner of the field. Because Karel's original program for this task would cause an error shutoff when it tried to execute a `pickbeeper` on any barren corner, we must modify it to avoid executing illegal `pickbeeper` instructions. Karel must harvest a beeper only if he has determined that one is present.

Now that we know about Karel's IF/THEN instruction, we can write a program for this slightly more general task -- it is more general because any program that solves the modified harvesting task also solves the original harvesting task. One sample initial situation is illustrated in Figure 2-14.

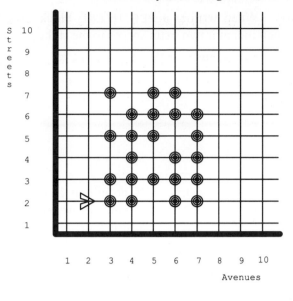

Figure 2-14: A Modified Harvest Task -- Not All Corners Have Beepers

Please notice that this is only one of many possible initial situations. Our program must be able to harvest this size field (six by five) regardless of which corners have beepers and which corners do not. Luckily for us, almost all of our previously written harvesting program can be reused -- another advantage of clear and clean programming. All we need to do is modify the `harvest-a-furrow` instruction by replacing `pickbeeper` with `pickbeeper-if-present`.

```
DEFINE-NEW-INSTRUCTION harvest-a-furrow AS
BEGIN
  pickbeeper-if-present;
  move;
  pickbeeper-if-present;
  move;
  pickbeeper-if-present;
  move;
  pickbeeper-if-present;
  move;
  pickbeeper-if-present
END
```

Of course, we must also write the `pickbeeper-if-present` instruction, but this is easily done by using the `IF/THEN` instruction.

```
DEFINE-NEW-INSTRUCTION pickbeeper-if-present AS
BEGIN
  IF next-to-a-beeper
    THEN pickbeeper
END
```

Astute grammarians and nitpickers will recognize that the BEGIN/END block surrounding the definition of `pickbeeper-if-present` is superfluous. This block is unnecessary because the definition contains only one instruction -- the `IF/THEN`. The `pickbeeper` instruction within the THEN clause of this `IF` is part of the encompassing `IF` instruction. We shall adopt the convention of always defining a new instruction by enclosing its definition in a BEGIN/END block. We recommend that you too follow this convention, but more importantly, you should know whether such a block is necessary or redundant.

2.6.3.2. The turnaround-only-if-blocked Instruction

Next we define an instruction that turns Karel around when his front is blocked, but does not change Karel's position when his front is clear. Notice that this definition has a THEN clause whose <instruction> is replaced by a BEGIN/END block. Indeed, Karel's concept of block structuring is useful in IF instructions too. When writing a BEGIN/END block in a THEN clause, we place it beneath the word THEN and then indent it two extra spaces to the right.

```
DEFINE-NEW-INSTRUCTION turnaround-only-if-blocked AS
BEGIN
  IF front-is-blocked
    THEN
      BEGIN
        turnleft;
        turnleft
      END
END
```

The BEGIN/END block enclosing this instruction's definition is redundant, because the complete definition is again only one large IF/THEN instruction. However, the BEGIN/END block in the THEN clause is necessary because both turnleft instructions are needed to turn Karel around when his front is blocked. Verify that this instruction is correct by simulating Karel's execution of it.

What happens in this instruction if we accidentally omit the BEGIN/END block in the THEN clause? Study the following *incorrect* definition.

```
DEFINE-NEW-INSTRUCTION incorrect-turnaround-only-if-blocked AS
BEGIN
  IF front-is-blocked
    THEN
      turnleft;
      turnleft
END
```

This instruction may look correct to us; unfortunately, we mere mortals are easily fooled by the instruction's written indentation. Karel is not so stupid -- or is it smart? When we read him this instruction, he hears it literally, without indentation information, and boxes it as follows:

How is this definition different from the correct one? Let's first look at the structural difference between these two instructions. The correct definition consists of one IF/THEN instruction, whose THEN clause is a BEGIN/END block containing two turnleft instructions. The incorrect definition comprises two instructions; the first is an IF/THEN with a turnleft in its THEN clause, and the second instruction is the second turnleft. In the incorrect instruction, the second turnleft is always executed after Karel has finished executing the IF/THEN instruction, regardless of whether his front was blocked or clear.

To show the difference in execution between these two instructions, we simulate Karel's execution of the incorrect definition in a blocked initial situation first and then in a clear one. Whenever Karel's front is blocked, the test will be true; accordingly, he will execute the turnleft instruction that is in the THEN clause. Now that he has finished with the IF/THEN instruction, he executes the second turnleft instruction, which results in Karel being turned around. It is surprising, but in this situation Karel does exactly what we want him to do; however, before assuming that the instruction is correct, we next simulate Karel in a situation where his front is clear. In this case, Karel discovers his front is not blocked when he performs the test, so he skips executing the THEN clause and proceeds to execute the second instruction in the definition - the turnleft. Therefore, when Karel's front is initially clear he does not stay facing the same direction; instead, he turns left.

This simulation demonstrates a subtle intent error. Although we omitted a necessary BEGIN/END block, the resulting instruction is still syntactically correct and, because Karel does not leave his corner during the instruction's execution, this instruction is also immune to execution errors. Furthermore, it even works correctly whenever Karel's front is blocked. But whenever Karel executes this instruction with his front clear, he does not perform the action we intended. What conclusion should we draw from this discussion? To verify that an IF instruction is correct, we must remember to test Karel in all situations that he may encounter while executing the instruction.

It should start to dawn on us that programming errors are indeed possible, and it requires a genuine effort on our behalf to understand the exact meaning of an instruction. Karel determines the meaning of an instruction by boxing it, and we too can use boxing as one way to help us understand an instruction. In addition, a healthy skepticism about the correctness of an instruction is beneficial when we develop test situations to verify that the instruction is correct. An adversary approach is even better suited to this testing phase. Do not passively test an instruction in various situations; instead, actively think of special situations where the instruction may fail to satisfy its intent. Then rigorously simulate Karel in these situations, and determine whether he executes the instruction as we had intended him to execute it.

We end this section with a discussion of one more programming phenomenon related to testing. What might happen if we inadequately test an instruction, assume that it is correct, and use it in a program that Karel executes frequently? Even if we fail to debug an instruction -- suppose it is similar to `incorrect-turnaround-only-if-blocked` in that it works correctly in some situations, but not in others -- it may still work correctly in the program for many days, as long as Karel is never asked to execute this instruction in a situation where it does not perform as intended. With each passing day, Karel's programmer will grow more confident that his or her program is correct. But sooner or later, Karel will be required to execute this instruction in an untested-for situation, and then the program may suddenly malfunction.

By this time Karel's programmer will probably have forgotten how the program works, and he or she will have quite a problem finding and fixing the error -- especially if the program was poorly written in the first place. From this discussion, we must conclude that there is no guarantee that an inadequately-tested working program will continue to work correctly in the future. This discussion shows why it is so important to verify instructions by testing them in all conceivable situations immediately after they are written.

2.6.3.3. The face-north Instruction

The final example of an `IF/THEN` instruction in this section uses Karel's directional abilities. We define `face-north`, a new instruction that executes by turning Karel to face north regardless of the direction he is initially facing. Observe that if Karel executes this instruction while he is already facing north, the instruction should not turn him at all. Otherwise, he can be turned north by executing at most three `turnleft` instructions. Below we show a defined instruction that accomplishes this task.

Surrounding the definition of this instruction is a mandatory `BEGIN/END` block, because the definition comprises a sequence of three `IF/THEN` instructions. In addition, while executing `face-north`, the only primitive instruction that Karel can execute is a `turnleft`; therefore, it is impossible for `face-north` to cause an error shutoff.

```
DEFINE-NEW-INSTRUCTION face-north AS
BEGIN
  IF not-facing-north
    THEN turnleft;
  IF not-facing-north
    THEN turnleft;
  IF not-facing-north
    THEN turnleft
END
```

To verify that `face-north` is correct, we must simulate Karel's execution of this instruction in each of four different situations: initially facing north, south, east, and west. We present a detailed simulation for the initial situation where Karel is facing south.

Assuming that Karel is initially facing south, he executes the first `IF/THEN` instruction by determining that the `not-facing-north` test is true. Because <test> is true, he executes the THEN clause of the IF, which instructs him to turn left. Karel next executes the second IF instruction in the sequence that defines `face-north`. He checks the `not-facing-north` test and again finds that it is true (since he is now facing east); therefore, Karel executes the THEN clause and again turns to his left. Although Karel is now facing north -- the correct direction -- he must continue to execute the IF/THEN instruction remaining in the `BEGIN/END` block. We shall see that this IF instruction does not alter Karel's position further. In the last IF, Karel finds that <test> is false and skips the THEN clause, completing the definition of `face-north`.

We have now verified that the `face-north` instruction is correct in the initial situation where Karel is facing south. Continue this analysis for the three other possible initial situations to verify that the instruction is completely correct. If we incorrectly wrote the `face-north` instruction by using only two of the three `IF` instructions, which situation(s) would cause the instruction to fail to achieve its intended purpose? If we accidentally included an extra `IF/THEN` instruction in this definition (bringing the total number to four), which situation(s) would cause the instruction to fail to achieve its intended purpose? Check your answers to these questions through simulation.

2.6.3.4. Boxing the IF/THEN Instruction

Boxing an `IF/THEN` instruction is similar to boxing a dictionary entry, because both use reserved words to separate their different components. Karel boxes an `IF/THEN` instruction by first boxing <test>, then boxing the instruction inside the `THEN` clause (which may be a single instruction or a `BEGIN/END` block), and finally boxing the entire `IF/THEN` instruction. This last big box includes the reserved words `IF` and `THEN`, the previously boxed test, and the previously boxed `THEN` clause. Study the following example (the numbers again indicate Karel's order of boxing) and the boxing of the `incorrect-turnaround-only-if-blocked` instruction. Also, study the punctuation in these examples, and try boxing the other instructions that were defined earlier in this chapter.

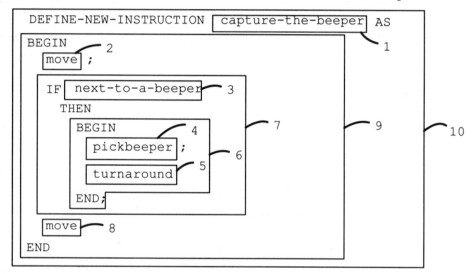

This definition contains three instructions: the first `move`, the `IF/THEN`, and the second `move`. Each of these instructions is separated from the next by a semicolon, and the two instructions inside the `BEGIN/END` block in the `THEN` clause are likewise separated by a semicolon.

2.6.4. The IF/THEN/ELSE Instruction

In this section we discuss the second type of `IF` instruction that is built into Karel's vocabulary. The `IF/THEN/ELSE` instruction is useful when, depending on the result of some test, Karel must execute one of two alternative instructions. The general form of the `IF/THEN/ELSE` is as follows.

```
IF <test>
   THEN <instruction-1>
   ELSE <instruction-2>
```

The form of the `IF/THEN/ELSE` is similar to the `IF/THEN` instruction, except that it also includes an <u>ELSE clause</u>. Furthermore, the `IF/THEN/ELSE` instruction can check the same tests as the `IF/THEN`. Both <instruction-1> and <instruction-2> may be replaced by the same vocabulary words that replace <instruction>. The most common `IF/THEN/ELSE` punctuation error has a semicolon separating <instruction-1> from the reserved word `ELSE`; there can be no semicolon placed here. Finally, observe that the `THEN` and `ELSE` clauses of this instruction are indented identically.

Karel executes this instruction in much the same manner as an `IF/THEN`: He first determines whether <test> is true or false in the current situation. If he finds that <test> is true, Karel executes <instruction-1>; otherwise, he finds that <test> is false and executes <instruction-2>. Thus, depending on his current situation, Karel executes either <instruction-1> or <instruction-2>, but not both.

Let's look at a new task that conveniently uses the IF/THEN/ELSE instruction. Suppose that we want to program Karel to run a one-mile-long hurdle race, where vertical wall sections represent hurdles. The hurdles are known to be only one block high, but they may be placed randomly between any two corners in the race course. One of the many possible race courses for this task is illustrated in Figure 2-15.

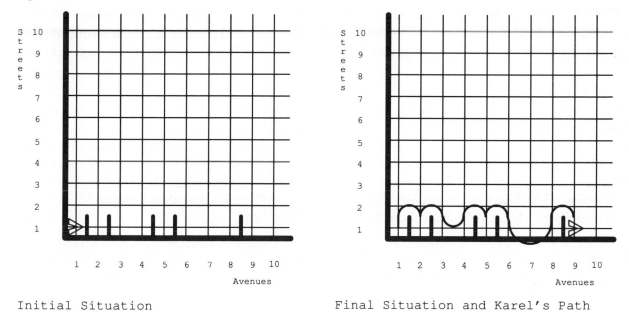

Initial Situation   Final Situation and Karel's Path

Figure 2-15: A Hurdle Jumping Race

Karel could easily run this race by jumping between every pair of corners, but although this strategy is simple to program, it would slow him down too much. Instead, we must program him to move straight ahead when he can, and jump over hurdles only when he must. The program implementing this strategy consists of a BEGINNING-OF-EXECUTION/END-OF-EXECUTION block that contains eight race-stride instructions followed by a turnoff. The definition of race-stride can be written using stepwise refinement.

```
DEFINE-NEW-INSTRUCTION race-stride AS
BEGIN
  IF front-is-clear
    THEN move
    ELSE jump-hurdle
END
```

We continue our refinement by writing jump-hurdle.

```
DEFINE-NEW-INSTRUCTION jump-hurdle AS
BEGIN
  jump-up;
  move;
  glide-down
END
```

Finally, we write jump-up and glide-down, the instructions needed to complete the definition of jump-hurdle.

```
DEFINE-NEW-INSTRUCTION jump-up AS
BEGIN
  turnleft;
  move;
  turnright
END
```

and

```
DEFINE-NEW-INSTRUCTION glide-down AS
BEGIN
  turnright;
  move;
  turnleft
END
```

Of course, the order of these instructions must be reversed in the complete program, and the definition of the omnipresent `turnright` instruction must also be included. To verify that these instructions are correct, complete and assemble the program, and then simulate Karel's running of the race in Figure 2-15.

2.6.5. Nested IF Instructions

Although we have seen a large number of IF instructions, we have ignored an entire class of complex IFs. These are known as <u>nested IF</u> instructions, because they are written with an IF instruction nested inside the THEN or ELSE clause of another IF. No new execution rules are needed to simulate nested IFs, but a close adherence to the established rules is required. Simulating nested IF instructions is sometimes difficult because it is easy for us to lose track of where we are in the instruction. The following discussion should be read carefully and understood completely, so that it can be imitated while testing instructions that include nested IFs.

To demonstrate a nested IF instruction, we propose a task that redistributes beepers in a field. This task requires that Karel traverse a field and leave exactly one beeper on each corner. He must plant a beeper on each barren corner and remove one beeper from every corner where two beepers coexist. All corners in this task are constrained to have zero, one, or two beepers on them. One sample initial and final situation is displayed in Figure 2-16. In these maps, multiple beepers on a corner are represented by a number. We can assume that Karel has enough beepers in his beeper-bag to replant the necessary number of corners.

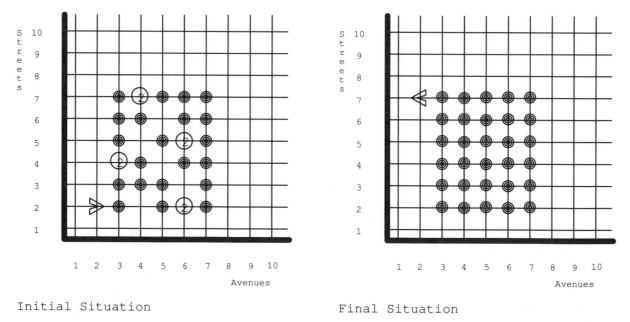

Initial Situation   Final Situation

Figure 2-16: A Beeper Replanting Task

The heart of the program that solves this task is an instruction that satisfies the one-beeper requirement for each corner. We conjecture that the following instruction leaves exactly one beeper on a corner.

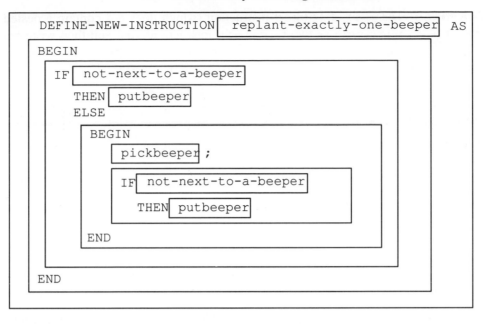

This definition has been boxed for easier reading and simulation. The *outside* IF in this definition is an IF/THEN/ELSE and the *nested* IF is an IF/THEN. The nested IF instruction is inside the ELSE clause of the outside IF. Next we simulate Karel in the three possible corner situations: on an empty corner, on a corner with one beeper, and on a corner with two beepers.

In the empty corner situation, Karel executes the outside IF and determines that he is not next to a beeper; therefore, he executes the putbeeper instruction in the THEN clause of the outside IF, placing one beeper on the corner. He has now completely executed the THEN clause of the outside IF instruction, so he is finished executing the outside IF. Because there is only one big IF instruction in this definition, Karel has finished executing replant-exactly-one-beeper, which we have now verified to work correctly in the no-beeper situation.

Next we assume that there is one beeper on Karel's corner. In this case Karel executes the outside IF and finds that the test is false, because he is next to a beeper, so he starts to execute the ELSE clause. This clause is a BEGIN/END block comprising two instructions. First, he executes pickbeeper, picking up the only beeper on the corner. Next Karel executes the nested IF instruction and finds that there are no more beepers on his corner; therefore, he executes the THEN clause of this IF instruction, which commands him to put a beeper back on the empty corner. Karel is now finished with the nested IF, the BEGIN/END block, the entire ELSE clause, the outer IF, and the entire replant-exactly-one-beeper instruction. Thus, Karel also handles the one-beeper situation correctly.

Finally, we assume that Karel is on a corner with two beepers. Here Karel executes the outside IF, finds the test is false, and then executes the ELSE clause. He starts the BEGIN/END block by executing pickbeeper first, picking up one of the two beepers on the corner. At this point Karel has duplicated his actions in the one-beeper situation, but now comes the difference in execution. He executes the nested IF instruction and finds that there still is one beeper on the corner, so he skips the nested IF's THEN clause. Once again Karel is finished with the nested IF, the BEGIN/END block, the entire ELSE clause, the outside IF, and the entire replant-exactly-one-beeper instruction definition. As before, the result is that he has left one beeper on the corner. We have now verified that the replant-exactly-one-beeper instruction is totally correct.

Another strategic point worth mentioning is that if nested IF instructions seem to intricate, we should try replacing the nested IF with a new instruction name. The definition of this auxiliary instruction must command Karel to perform the same actions as the nested IF, but the extra level of instruction names may help us better understand what Karel is doing. Because nesting also makes an instruction less readable, a good rule of thumb is to avoid nesting IF instructions more than one level deep. Even in the `turnaround-only-if-blocked` instruction (which does not contain a nested `IF`), it is a good idea to define `turnaround` as two `turnleft` instructions first and then write `turnaround` in the `THEN` clause of the `IF`. The `replant-exactly-one-beeper` instruction, which has one level of nesting, is rewritten as follows, by using an auxiliary instruction.

```
DEFINE-NEW-INSTRUCTION replant-exactly-one-beeper AS
BEGIN
  IF not-next-to-a-beeper
     THEN putbeeper
     ELSE next-to-one-replant-one
END
```

We write the next-to-one-replant-one instruction by copying the `ELSE` clause from our original definition of `replant-exactly-one-beeper`.

```
DEFINE-NEW-INSTRUCTION next-to-one-replant-one AS
BEGIN
  pickbeeper;
  IF not-next-to-a-beeper
     THEN putbeeper
END
```

Given the entire program from Section 2.5.8 along with either of these new definitions of the `replant-exactly-one-beeper` instruction, do we have a correct solution for the beeper replanting task? We may consider using our old method of verification and test the program with Karel in every possible initial situation, but there are over 200 trillion[8] different fields that this program must be able to replant correctly! It would be ludicrous to attempt verification by exhaustively testing Karel in every possible initial situation.

Instead, we shall settle for probable correctness based on the following informal argument: (1) we have verified that `replant-exactly-one-beeper` works correctly on any corner that is empty or contains one or two beepers, and (2) we can easily verify that our program commands Karel to execute this instruction on each corner of the field. Therefore, we can combine these two verifications and conclude that the program correctly replants the entire field.

This argument further enhances the claim that Karel's mechanism for instruction definition is a powerful aid to programming. In general, we can informally conclude that an entire program is correct by verifying that: (1) each defined instruction in the program works correctly in all possible situations in which it can execute, and (2) the program executes each defined instruction at the appropriate time. This method allows us to verify a program by splitting it into separate, simpler verifications -- just as stepwise refinement allows us to write a program by splitting it into separate, simpler instructions.

2.6.6. Transformations for Simplifying IF Instructions

This section discusses four useful transformations that help us simplify programs containing `IF` instructions. We start by observing that the following two `IF/THEN/ELSE` instructions, although different in form, execute equivalently. When two instructions result in Karel's performing exactly the same actions, we call this pair of instructions <u>execution equivalent</u>. (For a simple example, one `turnleft` instruction is execution equivalent to five `turnleft` instructions -- they both leave Karel turned 90° to the left from his original position.)

```
IF front-is-clear             IF front-is-blocked
   THEN move                     THEN jump-hurdle
   ELSE jump-hurdle              ELSE move
```

In general, we can create one execution equivalent `IF/THEN/ELSE` instruction from another by replacing <test> with its opposite and interchanging the `THEN` and `ELSE` clauses. We call this transformation <u>test reversal</u>. Notice that if we perform test reversal twice on the same instruction, we get back to the instruction with which we started.

---

[8]There are 3 different possibilities for each corner, and there are 30 corners in the field. The total number of different fields is thus 3^{30}, which is 3 multiplied by itself 30 times. For you mathemagicians, the exact number of different fields is 205,891,132,094,649.

Test reversal can be used to help novice programmers overcome the following difficulty. Suppose that we start to write an IF instruction and get ourselves into the dilemma illustrated below on the left. The problem is that we want Karel to do nothing special when his front is clear[9], but when his front is blocked we want him to execute <instruction>. We would like to remove the THEN clause, but doing so would cause a syntax error -- Karel does not understand an IF/ELSE instruction. The solution to our problem is illustrated on the right.

```
IF front-is-clear                IF front-is-blocked
   THEN do-nothing                   THEN <instruction>
   ELSE <instruction>
```

To transform the IF on the left into the IF on the right, we use test reversal. First we change <test> to its opposite, then switch the do-nothing instruction into the ELSE clause and bring <instruction> into the THEN clause. By the previous discussion of test reversal, execution equivalence is preserved. Finally, the new ELSE clause (which contains the do-nothing instruction) can be removed, resulting in the simpler IF/THEN instruction on the right.

The second transformation we discuss is <u>bottom factoring</u>. Bottom factoring is illustrated as follows , where we shall show that the IF/THEN/ELSE instruction on the left is execution equivalent to the program fragment on the right. We have kept the bracketed words in these instructions because their exact replacements do not affect this transformation.

```
IF <test>                        IF <test>
   THEN                             THEN <instruction-1>
     BEGIN                          ELSE <instruction-2>;
       <instruction-1>;          <instruction-3>
       <instruction-3>
     END
   ELSE
     BEGIN
       <instruction-2>;
       <instruction-3>
     END
```

In the program fragment on the right, we have *factored* <instruction-3> out of the bottom of each clause in the IF (after factoring, we can remove both redundant BEGIN/END blocks). We justify the correctness of this transformation as follows: If <test> is true, the instruction on the left has Karel execute <instruction-1> directly followed by <instruction-3>.

In the program fragment on the right, if <test> is true Karel executes <instruction-1> and then, having finished the IF, he executes <instruction-3>. Thus, when <test> is true, these forms are execution equivalent. A similar argument holds between the left and right sides whenever <test> is false.

In summary, <instruction-3> is executed in the IF on the left regardless of whether <test> is true or false, so we might as well remove it from each clause and put it directly after the entire IF/THEN/ELSE instruction.

Moreover, if the bottoms of each clause were larger, but still identical, we could bottom factor all of the common instructions and still preserve execution equivalence. Think of this process as bottom factoring one instruction at a time, until all common instructions have been factored. Since execution equivalence is preserved during each factoring step, the resulting program fragment is execution equivalent to the original instruction.

The third transformation we discuss in this section is <u>top factoring</u>. Although this transformation may seem as simple and easy to use as bottom factoring, we shall see that not all instructions can be top factored successfully. We divide our discussion of this transformation into three parts. First, we examine an instruction that can safely be top factored. Then we show an instruction that cannot be top factored successfully. Finally, we state a general rule that tells us which IF instructions can safely be top factored.

---

[9]We can define the instruction do-nothing as four left turns. Executing this instruction would leave Karel's position unchanged, and this instruction is also immune to error shutoffs.

Top factoring can safely be used in the following example to convert the instruction on the left into the simpler program fragment on the right. These two forms can be shown to be execution equivalent by a justification similar to the one used in our discussion of bottom factoring.

```
IF facing-north                    move;
   THEN                            IF facing-north
      BEGIN                           THEN turnleft
        move;                         ELSE turnright
        turnleft
      END
   ELSE
      BEGIN
        move;
        turnright
      END
```

In the next example, we have incorrectly used the top factoring transformation. We shall discover that the program fragment on the right is not execution equivalent to the instruction on the left.

```
IF next-to-a-beeper               move;
   THEN                           IF next-to-a-beeper
      BEGIN                          THEN turnleft
        move;                        ELSE turnright
        turnleft
      END
   ELSE
      BEGIN
        move;
        turnright
      END
```

To show that these forms execute differently, let's assume that Karel is on a corner containing one beeper, and that the corner in front of him is barren. If Karel executes the instruction on the left, he will first find that he is next to a beeper, and then he will execute the THEN clause of the IF by moving forward and turning to his left. The program fragment on the right will first move Karel forward to the next corner and then will instruct him to test for a beeper. Since this corner does not contain a beeper, Karel will execute the ELSE clause of the IF, which causes him to turn to his right. Thus, top factoring in this example does not preserve execution equivalence.

Why can we correctly use top factoring in the first example but not in the second? Our first instruction can be top factored safely because the test that determines which way Karel is facing is not changed by having him move forward. Therefore, whether he moves first or not, the test will remain the same. But in the second example, the move changes the corner on which Karel checks for a beeper, so he is not really checking the same test. The general rule is that we may top factor an instruction only when the test that Karel performs does not change between the original and factored version of the instruction. The fourth and final transformation is used to remove redundant tests in nested IF instructions. We call this transformation <u>redundant-test factoring</u> and show one application of this rule.

```
IF facing-west                    IF facing-west
   THEN                              THEN
      BEGIN                             BEGIN
        move;                             move;
        IF facing-west                    turnleft
           THEN turnleft               END
      END
```

In the instruction on the left, there is no need for the nested IF instruction to recheck the condition facing-west. The THEN clause of the outside IF is only executed if Karel is facing west, and the move inside this THEN clause does not change the direction that Karel is facing; therefore, facing-west is always true when Karel executes the nested IF instruction. This argument shows that Karel always executes the THEN clause of the nested IF. So, the entire nested IF instruction can be replaced by turnleft, as has been done in the instruction on the right. Once again, this transformation preserves execution equivalence. A similar transformation applies whenever we look for a redundant test in an ELSE clause, though in an ELSE clause we know <test> to be false.

This transformation is also a bit more subtle than bottom factoring, and we must be careful when trying to use it. The potential difficulty is that intervening instructions might change Karel's position in an unknown way. For example, if instead of the `move` instruction we had written a `turnaround-only-if-blocked` instruction, we could not have used redundant-test factoring. In this case we cannot be sure whether Karel would be facing west or east when he had to execute the nested `IF`.

These four transformations can help us make our programs smaller, simpler, more logical, and -- most important -- more readable.

2.6.7. The Dangling ELSE

This section examines a syntactic anomaly of nested `IF` instructions. Look at the following two nested `IF`s, and carefully study how each is boxed. We have kept the bracketed words in these instructions, because their exact replacements do not affect our discussion.

```
IF <test-1>
   THEN
      ┌──────────────────────────────┐
      │ IF <test-2>                  │
      │    THEN <instruction-1>      │
      │                              │
      │    ELSE <instruction-2>      │
      └──────────────────────────────┘
```

```
IF <test-1>
   THEN
      ┌──────────────────────────────┐
      │ IF <test-2>                  │
      │    THEN <instruction-1>      │
      └──────────────────────────────┘
   ELSE <instruction-2>
```

The difference between these two instructions is the boxing of the `ELSE` clause. In the first instruction, the `ELSE` is boxed with the nested `IF`, but in the second the `ELSE` is boxed with the outside `IF`. These are obviously two different instructions, yet Karel cannot tell them apart. To prove this to yourself, ignore the boxing and read each of the instructions. Both contain exactly the same words in exactly the same order.

We are therefore faced with two questions: First, if we read this instruction to Karel, which way would he box it? Second, if we want Karel to box the instruction the other way, how would we tell him to do so? This anomaly is known in programming jargon as the <u>dangling `ELSE`</u> problem.

The first question is answered by introducing a new grammar rule. This rule states that whenever Karel is read an `ELSE` clause, he boxes it with the most recently read `IF` instruction that it can be a part of. Therefore, if we read Karel the preceding instruction, he boxes it like the previous boxing on the left.

We next show two related solutions to the second question. Each of the following two instructions is interpreted by Karel in a manner similar to the previous boxing on the right.

```
IF <test-1>
   THEN
      ┌──────────────────────────────────┐
      │ BEGIN                            │
      │    ┌──────────────────────────┐  │
      │    │ IF <test-2>              │  │
      │    │    THEN <instruction-1>  │  │
      │    └──────────────────────────┘  │
      │ END                             │
      └──────────────────────────────────┘
   ELSE <instruction-2>
```

```
IF <opposite-of-test-1>
   THEN <instruction-2>
   ELSE
      ┌──────────────────────────────┐
      │ IF <test-2>                  │
      │    THEN <instruction-1>      │
      └──────────────────────────────┘
```

In the example on the left, we use a `BEGIN/END` block to inform Karel that the nested `IF` instruction is of the `IF/THEN` type. When Karel boxes this block, the `END` reserved word forces him to conclude that he has seen the entire nested `IF` instruction. He must treat the `BEGIN/END` block as a single instruction, and he must completely box all instructions within this block before reaching the `END` delimiter; thus, when the `ELSE` is finally read to Karel, there is only one `IF` instruction with which he can match it.

But we do not have to stop here. Now that we have the instruction on the left, we can simplify it by using test reversal. To perform test reversal, we replace <test-1> by its opposite and switch the THEN and ELSE clauses; now the BEGIN/END block in the ELSE clause is unnecessary, so it can be removed. These two steps result in the instruction on the right, which allows Karel to match the ELSE with the outside IF unambiguously.

2.6.8. Problem Set

The problems in this section require the use of the IF instruction in its two forms. Try using stepwise refinement on these problems, but no matter what method you use to obtain a solution, write a clear and understandable program. Keep the nesting level small for those problems requiring nested IF instructions. Use proper punctuation and grammar, especially within the THEN and ELSE clauses of the IF instructions. Carefully simulate each definition and program that you write to ensure that there are no execution or intent errors.

1. > Define face-south, a new instruction that executes by facing Karel south regardless of the direction he is initially facing. First, do this without using face-north as a known instruction. Experiment with different forms of the IF/THEN and IF/THEN/ELSE instructions. Next, write face-south assuming that the instruction face-north has already been defined. This second definition should be much simpler, and given that face-north is correct, it should be easy to convince anyone of the correctness of face-south.

2. Look at the following instruction. Is there a simpler, execution equivalent instruction? If so, write it down; if not, explain why not. *Hint: A simplifying transformation for the* IF *may prove useful. Common sense helps too.*

   ```
   IF not-next-to-a-beeper
      THEN move
      ELSE move
   ```

3. Assume that Karel is on a corner with either one or two beepers. Write a new instruction that commands him to face north if he is started on a corner with one beeper and to face south if he is started on a corner with two beepers. Besides facing him in the required direction, after Karel has executed this instruction there must be no beepers left on his corner. Name this instruction find-next-direction.

4. Write another version of find-next-direction (see the previous problem). In this version, Karel must eventually face the same directions, but he also must leave the same number of beepers on the corner as were there originally.

5. Write an instruction that turns Karel off if he is completely surrounded by walls, unable to move in any direction. If he is not completely surrounded, Karel should execute this instruction by leaving himself turned on, and by remaining on the same corner, facing the same direction in which he started. Name this instruction turnoff-if-surrounded. *Hint: To write this instruction correctly, you will need to include a* turnoff *inside it. This combination is perfectly legal, but it is the first time that you will have to use a* turnoff *instruction outside of the* BEGINNING-OF-EXECUTION/END-OF-EXECUTION *block.*

6. >Program Karel to run a mile-long steeplechase. The steeplechase course is similar to the hurdle race, but here the barriers can be one, two, or three blocks high. Figure 2-17 shows one sample initial situation, where Karel's final situation and path are indicated on the right.

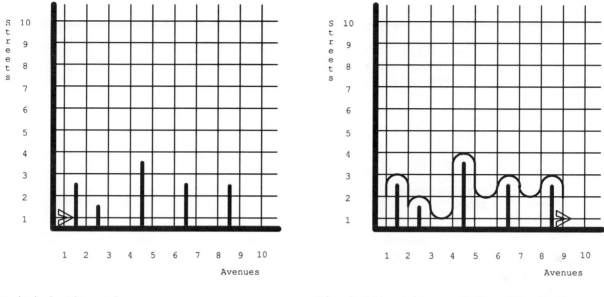

Initial Situation   Final Situation and Karel's Path

Figure 2-17: A Steeplechase Race Task

7. >Rewrite and box the following instruction, taking care to interpret all of Karel's grammar rules correctly. This instruction uses nested IFs to face Karel toward the east; verify that it is correct by simulation. **Hint:** When trying to box this instruction, put yourself in Karel's place and ignore the instruction's indentation. One way of doing this is to have someone read you the instruction. While they are reading the instruction, you should box it -- after all, this is exactly what Karel does.

```
DEFINE-NEW-INSTRUCTION face-east AS
BEGIN
  IF not-facing-east
    THEN
      IF facing-west
        THEN
          BEGIN
            turnleft;
            turnleft
          END
      ELSE
        IF facing-north
          THEN turnright
          ELSE turnleft
END
```

8. The current version of mystery-instruction is syntactically correct, but very difficult to read. Simplify it by using the IF transformations.

```
DEFINE-NEW-INSTRUCTION mystery-instruction AS
BEGIN
  IF facing-west
    THEN
      BEGIN
        move;
        turnright;
        IF facing-north
          THEN move;
        turnaround
      END
    ELSE
      BEGIN
        move;
        turnleft;
        move;
        turnaround
      END
END
```

9. Write an instruction named follow-wall-right, assuming that whenever Karel executes this instruction there is a wall directly to his right. Figure 2-18 shows all four of the different position changes that he must be able to make. This instruction is the cornerstone for a program that directs Karel escape from a maze (this maze-escape problem is Problem 2.7.6-11.

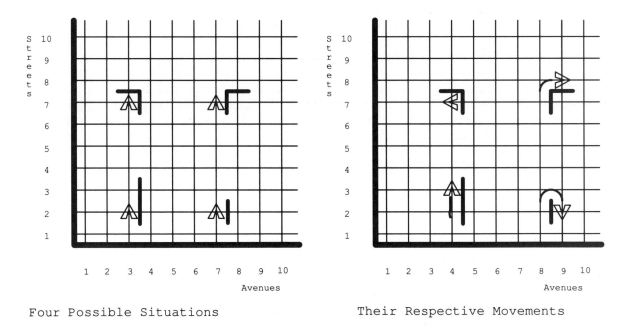

Four Possible Situations   Their Respective Movements

Figure 2-18: The follow-wall-right Specification

2.7. Instructions That Repeat

This chapter completes our discussion of the instructions that are built into Karel's vocabulary. The two new instructions we shall learn are ITERATE and WHILE. Both of these instructions can repeatedly execute any instruction that Karel understands, including nested ITERATE and WHILE instructions. These additions greatly enhance the conciseness and power of the robot programming language. Also, in Section 2.7.5 we shall construct a complex, room-escaping robot program by using stepwise refinement and all of the instructions we have learned.

2.7.1. The ITERATE Instruction

When we program Karel, it is sometimes necessary to have him repeat an instruction a fixed number of times. We previously handled this problem by writing the instruction as many times as needed. The ITERATE instruction provides us with a shorthand notation that instructs Karel to repeat another instruction a specified number of times. It has the following general form.

```
ITERATE <positive-number> TIMES
    <instruction>
```

This instruction introduces the reserved words ITERATE and TIMES. The bracketed word <positive-number> tells Karel how many times to execute the instruction that replaces <instruction>. We refer to <instruction> as the <u>body</u> of the ITERATE instruction, and we shall also use the term <u>ITERATE loop</u> to suggest verbally that this instruction loops back and executes itself (no, it does not commit suicide). Our first example of an ITERATE loop is another definition of turnright.

```
DEFINE-NEW-INSTRUCTION turnright AS
BEGIN
  ITERATE 3 TIMES
    turnleft
END
```

As a second example, we rewrite the harvest-a-furrow instruction that was written in Section 2.5.8. This definition originally comprised nine primitive instructions, but by using ITERATE we can define this instruction more concisely. With this new, more general version of harvest-a-furrow, we can also easily increase or decrease the number of beepers harvested per furrow; all we need to change is the number in the ITERATE instruction.

```
DEFINE-NEW-INSTRUCTION harvest-a-furrow AS
BEGIN
  pickbeeper;
  ITERATE 4 TIMES
    BEGIN
      move;
      pickbeeper
    END
END
```

Finally, we show an ITERATE instruction nested within another ITERATE instruction. Carefully observe the way that this instruction is boxed, for this is a strong clue to how Karel executes it.

```
DEFINE-NEW-INSTRUCTION make-square-of-length-6 AS
BEGIN
  ITERATE 4 TIMES
    BEGIN
      ITERATE 6 TIMES
        move ;
      turnleft
    END
END
```

If we assume no blocking walls, this instruction moves Karel around the perimeter of a square whose sides are 6-blocks long. The outside ITERATE instruction loops a total of 4 times, once for each side of the square. Each time the outside ITERATE loop's body is executed, Karel executes two instructions. He first executes the nested ITERATE, which makes one side of the 6 block square. Then Karel executes the turnleft, which prepares him to trace the next side. Thus, Karel executes a total of 24 moves and 4 left turns, which are arranged in an order that makes him travel in a square.

2.7.2. The WHILE Instruction

In this section we explain the WHILE instruction and analyze many of its interesting properties. It is the most powerful instruction that is built into Karel's vocabulary.

2.7.2.1. Why WHILE is Needed

To motivate the need for a WHILE instruction, we look at what should be a simple programming task. Assume that Karel is initially facing east on some street, and somewhere east of him on that same street is a beeper. Karel's task is to move forward until he is on the same corner as the beeper, and then pick it up. Despite its simple description, this program is impossible to write with our current repertoire of instructions. Two attempts at solving this problem might be written as follows.

```
IF not-next-to-a-beeper             ITERATE ? TIMES
   THEN move;                          move;
IF not-next-to-a-beeper             pickbeeper
   THEN move;
           .
           .
           .
IF not-next-to-a-beeper
   THEN move;
pickbeeper
```

We can interpret what is meant by these instructions, but Karel understands neither "..." nor "?". The difficulty is that we do not know in advance how many move instructions Karel must execute before he arrives at the same corner as the beeper; we do not even have a guaranteed upper limit. The beeper may be on Karel's starting street corner, or it may be a million blocks away. Karel must be able to accomplish this task without knowing in advance the number of corners that he will pass before reaching the beeper. We must program Karel to execute move instructions repeatedly, until he senses that he is next to a beeper. What we need is an instruction that combines the repetition ability of the ITERATE instruction with the testing ability of the IF instruction.

2.7.2.2. The WHILE Instruction

The WHILE instruction commands Karel to repeat another instruction as long as some test remains true. It is executed somewhat similarly to an IF/THEN instruction, except that the WHILE instruction repeatedly executes itself as long as <test> is true. The general form of the WHILE instruction is as follows.

```
WHILE <test> DO
   <instruction>
```

The new reserved word WHILE starts this instruction, and the word DO separates <test> from the body of the WHILE loop. The vocabulary words that can replace <test> are the same ones that are used in the IF instructions.

Karel executes a WHILE loop by first checking <test> in his current situation. If <test> is true, Karel executes <instruction> and then re-executes the entire WHILE loop; if <test> is false, Karel is finished with the WHILE instruction, and he continues by executing the instructions following the entire WHILE loop. Here is a sample WHILE instruction, which solves the problem that motivated this discussion.

```
DEFINE-NEW-INSTRUCTION go-to-beeper AS
BEGIN
   WHILE not-next-to-a-beeper DO
      move
END
```

This instruction moves Karel forward as long as not-next-to-a-beeper is true. When Karel is finally next to a beeper, he finishes executing the WHILE loop. The following instruction is another simple example of a WHILE loop, and we shall examine its behavior in detail.

```
DEFINE-NEW-INSTRUCTION clear-corner-of-beepers AS
BEGIN
    WHILE next-to-a-beeper DO
        pickbeeper
END
```

This instruction commands Karel to pick up all of the beepers on a corner. Let's simulate Karel's execution of this instruction on a corner containing two beepers. He first determines whether `next-to-a-beeper` is true or false. Finding it true, he executes the body of the WHILE, which is the `pickbeeper` instruction. Then he re-executes the entire WHILE loop. Karel again finds that he is next to a beeper (one is still left), so he again executes the body of the WHILE loop. After picking up the second beeper, Karel re-executes the entire WHILE instruction -- although we know that there are no beepers remaining, Karel is unaware of this fact until he rechecks the WHILE loop test. Now he rechecks the test and discovers that next-to-a-beeper is false, so he finishes executing the WHILE loop. Because the entire definition consists of one WHILE loop, he is finished executing `clear-corner-of-beepers`. It appears that no matter how many beepers are initially on the corner, Karel will eventually pick them all up when he executes this instruction.

But what happens if Karel executes `clear-corner-of-beepers` on a corner that has no beepers? In this special case, <test> is false the first time that the WHILE instruction is executed, so the WHILE body is not executed at all. Therefore, Karel also handles this situation correctly. The key fact to remember about a WHILE instruction is that until Karel discovers that <test> has become false -- and it may be false the first time -- Karel repeatedly checks <test> and executes the loop's body.

2.7.2.3. Infinite WHILE Loops

What happens if Karel executes the following curious WHILE loop? Observe that the body of this WHILE loop is a turnleft instruction; the body of this loop is not a `pickbeeper`.

```
DEFINE-NEW-INSTRUCTION incorrect-clear-corner-of-beepers AS
BEGIN
    WHILE next-to-a-beeper DO
        turnleft
END
```

First, let's assume that there are no beepers on the corner. In this case `next-to-a-beeper` is false, so Karel immediately finishes executing the WHILE instruction. This situation is handled correctly, but what happens if there is at least one beeper on the corner? In this case `next-to-a-beeper` is true, so Karel executes the `turnleft` in the body of the loop and re-executes the entire WHILE instruction. Do you see the impending problem? He rechecks the test, finds that he is still next to a beeper, turns left again, and re-executes the WHILE instruction. Karel will continue executing this WHILE instruction forever, spinning like a top.

This problem is known as getting Karel stuck in an <u>infinite loop</u>. Infinite looping is a kind of intent error, because Karel cannot determine when he is in an infinite loop. The possibility is the price that we must pay for allowing Karel the ability to execute an instruction an unknown number of times. The WHILE is the only instruction that can cause Karel to get stuck in an infinite loop; the only other repetitive instruction is ITERATE, which always finishes since we specify in the instruction itself how many times it will loop. We add infinite loops to our list of pitfalls to avoid, so we should carefully check each WHILE loop that we write to verify that it eventually terminates.

2.7.2.4. A Formal Property of the WHILE Instruction

So far, in this chapter we have discussed three definitions containing WHILE loops. The first WHILE loop tested `not-next-to-a-beeper`; when Karel finished executing this loop, he was next to a beeper. The next WHILE loop tested `next-to-a-beeper`; when Karel finished executing this loop, he was not next to any beepers. The third WHILE loop never terminated.

An important formal property of the WHILE instruction is that when it finishes executing, <test> is known to be false. This is proven by paraphrasing the execution rule for WHILE loops: "If <test> is true, then the loop continues executing." Therefore, if a WHILE loop finishes executing -- and we have seen that not all of them do -- <test> is guaranteed to be false. We can use this property to write instructions that are required to make a certain condition true. Whenever we must make <test> true, we write something similar to the following WHILE instruction into our program.

```
WHILE <opposite-of-test> DO
   <instruction>
```

This general form is possible because Karel's vocabulary includes both the positive and negative forms of each test. For example, if we want next-to-a-beeper to be true, we write a WHILE loop with <opposite-of-test> replaced by not-next-to-a-beeper. If we want front-is-blocked to be true, we write a WHILE loop with <opposite-of-test> replaced by front-is-clear. Whenever a WHILE loop terminates, the <opposite-of-test> is guaranteed to be false, which means that <test> is guaranteed to be true.

How do we ensure that a WHILE loop always terminates? We should write the loop body with the following thought: Each time the loop body executes, Karel should perform some action that brings him closer to finishing the loop. An infinite loop occurs whenever <instruction> does not cause Karel to progress toward making <test> false. In the incorrect-clear-corner-of-beepers instruction, for example, it is obvious that Karel's execution of turnleft does not bring him any closer to having picked up all the beepers. Unfortunately, infinite loops are not always so easy to spot in more complex instructions.

To demonstrate one more WHILE instruction, we show a second, elegant way to define the face-north instruction.

```
DEFINE-NEW-INSTRUCTION face-north AS
BEGIN
   WHILE not-facing-north DO
      turnleft
END
```

When this instruction finishes executing, <test> will be false according to the formal WHILE property. In this example, not-facing-north will become false -- or by removing the double negative, facing-north will be true. But we have shown only that this instruction is partially correct. We must also prove that by continually executing turnleft instructions, the WHILE loop will eventually terminate. Because each turnleft changes the direction that Karel faces by 90°, we can guarantee that he will be facing north after at most three left turns. This same argument allowed us to conclude in Section 2.6.3.3 that our first definition of the face-north instruction is correct.

2.7.2.5. Verifying WHILE Loops

We pause here for a minute and reflect on how we can verify programs that use WHILE loops. It was bad enough when we found in Section 2.6.5 that small programs with IF instructions sometimes need to execute correctly in trillions of different initial situations. Now we have introduced an instruction that must be capable of working correctly in an unbounded number of initial situations.

How can we possibly verify programs that use this type of instruction? In general, there is no useful, rigorous way to verify robot programs that use WHILE loops; instead, we settle for probable correctness based on the following argument. (We faced a similar problem and chose a similar solution when verifying complex programs that used IF instructions.)

To argue that a WHILE instruction is correct, we rely on the following informal method of reasoning.

- First, we must show that the instruction works correctly in a situation where <test> is false.

- Second, we must show that each time the loop body is executed, Karel's new situation (after executing the body) is a *simpler* and *similar* version of his old situation (before executing the body). By *simpler*, we mean that Karel now has less work to do before finishing the loop, and by *similar* we mean that Karel's situation has not changed radically during his execution of the loop body.

- From these two facts we can conclude that no matter how many times the loop body must be executed, the instruction performs correctly. We can also conclude that the WHILE instruction eventually terminates, because each time Karel executes the loop body he is performing some action that brings him closer to having <test> become false.

As an example, let's argue that the `clear-corner-of-beepers` instruction is correct by using this style of reasoning. First, if there are no beepers on Karel's corner in the initial situation, the `WHILE` instruction performs correctly by immediately finishing. Second, if there are any beepers on the corner before the loop body executes, there will be one less beeper there after the loop body executes. This is the desired simpler (one less beeper) and similar (Karel is still on the same corner ready to pick up beepers) situation.[10] Karel will continue executing the loop body and removing beepers from the corner until no beepers remain. He then correctly finishes executing the loop in this no-beeper situation, as shown in the first step of this argument. Thus, we have argued that `clear-corner-of-beepers` is correct.

Generally, even this style of reasoning is too difficult to apply to complicated `WHILE` instructions. Therefore, few complex robot programs are actually argued correct by this method. Instead, instructions are tested in many different initial situations. For the `clear-corner-of-beepers` instruction, a typical testing argument might be, "I simulated Karel's execution in initial situations with 0, 1, 2, 3, and 7 beepers on the corner, and in each case the instruction worked correctly. Because all other situations are similar to these, the instruction probably works correctly in all situations." (Can you write a `clear-corner-of-beepers` definition that works correctly in these situations but fails in others? It can be done; see Problem 2.7.6-12 for details.)

We hope that the test situations we use typify all possible situations that Karel may encounter, but being human, we are limited in our ability to discover obscure situations. Although arguments based on testing give us a certain measure of confidence that our `WHILE` instructions are correct, it is not the same thing as verifying them. The verifying versus testing dilemma can be boiled down to the aphorism: "Testing only shows the presence of bugs, not their absence."

Since we must test the instructions that we write, we should be aware of a rule of thumb that is useful for hand-simulating `WHILE` loops. Because the beginning and end of a loop's execution are prone toward errors, each `WHILE` loop should be closely observed during its first few and last few repetitions. We should also carefully simulate a few repetitions in the middle of the loop, just to ensure that it is correct too.

2.7.2.6. When the <test> of a WHILE is Checked

The rules in Section 2.7.2.2 that explained how Karel executes a `WHILE` instruction are correct, yet unless read carefully, they may leave room for some ambiguity. In this section we closely examine the execution rules for a `WHILE` instruction and point out a common misconception about when Karel checks <test>. Let's simulate the following instruction cautiously.

```
DEFINE-NEW-INSTRUCTION harvest-line AS
BEGIN
  WHILE next-to-a-beeper DO
    BEGIN
      pickbeeper;
      move
    END
END
```

This instruction correctly commands Karel to pick up a line of beepers. He finishes executing this instruction after moving one block beyond the final corner that has a beeper. Of course, a gap in the line would also cause Karel to believe that he is at the end of the beeper line.

This instruction's definition contains the first `WHILE` loop body we have seen that is a sequence of instructions; consequently, the loop body must be contained in a `BEGIN/END` block. First, let's correctly simulate this instruction in detail for a line of two beepers. Karel starts his task on the same corner as the first beeper. He executes the `WHILE` instruction and finds that the test is true, so he next executes the body of the loop. The loop body instructs him to pick up the beeper and then move to the

---

[10]Consider what would happen if, instead of instructing Karel to pick up a beeper, the body of the `WHILE` loop caused him to move to another corner. Karel's new situation may be simpler -- the new corner may contain no beepers at all -- but Karel cannot correctly finish his task because this situation is too unlike his original situation: Karel is no longer on the same corner.

next corner. Now he re-executes the loop; the test is checked again, and Karel again senses that he is next to a beeper. Therefore, Karel picks up the second beeper and moves forward. He then executes the loop again. Now when he checks the test, he finds that his corner is beeperless, so he is finished executing the WHILE loop. This definition of harvest-line contains only one instruction -- this WHILE loop -- so harvest-line is also finished.

The point demonstrated here is that Karel checks <test> only before he executes the body of the loop. He is totally insensitive to the <test> while executing instructions inside the loop body. To state this another way, once Karel starts executing the loop body, he does not recheck <test> until he starts to re-execute the entire WHILE instruction, which happens only after he has completely executed the loop body.

A common misconception among novice programmers is that Karel checks <test> after each instruction he executes inside the loop body. It is easy to arrive at this misconception when dealing with a WHILE loop that contains only one instruction in its body, for in this case the two rules yield identical results. But in multiple instruction loop bodies like the one in harvest-line, there is a distinguishable difference between these two rules.

Let's see what would happen if Karel used the incorrect rule to execute the harvest-line instruction in the two-beeper situation. This rule would force Karel to finish the WHILE loop as soon as he was not next to a beeper. Karel would start by testing whether he was next to a beeper. Finding the test true, he would execute the loop body. This is fine so far, but after executing the first instruction in the loop body, the pickbeeper, Karel would not be next to a beeper anymore - he has just put the one that he was next to into his beeper-bag. So, according to this second, incorrect execution rule, Karel would now be finished with the loop. This rule would limit Karel to picking up only one beeper, regardless of the length of the beeper line.

We emphasize that the first of these rules is the one that Karel uses; the second is incorrect.

2.7.3. Repeating Instructions and Block Structure

This section examines what can happen to a repeating instruction when a necessary BEGIN/END block is omitted. We discuss a WHILE instruction in our example, but the same type of argument holds for the ITERATE instruction as well. Karel's task in this section is again to harvest a line of beepers, except this time the end of the line is marked by a wall. We can assume that every corner between Karel's starting corner and the wall contains exactly one beeper. One of the many possible initial situations for this task is given in Figure 2-19.

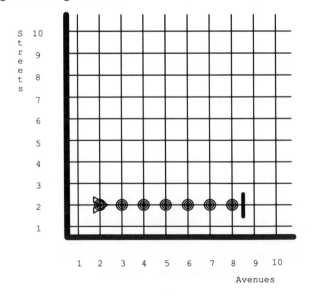

Figure 2-19: A Line-Harvesting Task

The following instruction correctly accomplishes the task.

```
DEFINE-NEW-INSTRUCTION harvest-to-wall AS
BEGIN
   pickbeeper;
   WHILE front-is-clear DO
     BEGIN
       move;
       pickbeeper
     END
END
```

Notice that without the first `pickbeeper`, Karel would `move` first, before picking up the beeper on his starting corner. If you think the situation can be remedied by removing the first `pickbeeper` and then switching the instructions in the body of the `WHILE` loop, think again. Although Karel would now pick up the first beeper, this instruction would leave the last beeper unharvested.

Generally, observe that the number of beepers that Karel must pick up is one greater than the number of moves that he must perform (in Figure 2-19, he must pick up seven beepers, but move only six times. Simple counting arguments such as this one can frequently help you determine which instructions must be inside of a loop and which instructions must be outside of a loop. It would be correct to remove the first `pickbeeper` and switch the two instructions in the loop body if we added an extra `pickbeeper` at the end of this definition, directly after the `WHILE` loop. But we prefer writing this special case first, to make it more visible.

What would Karel do if we read him the previous instruction without the `BEGIN` and `END` delimiters that surround the loop body? Karel would box and interpret the instruction as follows.

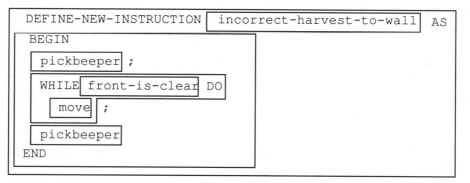

Box `harvest-to-wall` and then compare these two instructions. Both are syntactically correct, but notice that the boxing is different. The correct definition consists of two instructions: The `pickbeeper` and a `WHILE` loop whose body contains a sequence of two instructions. The incorrect definition consists of three instructions: the `pickbeeper`, the `WHILE` loop containing only the `move` within its body, and the final `pickbeeper` instruction. The results of Karel's execution of each of these instructions are shown in Figure 2-20.

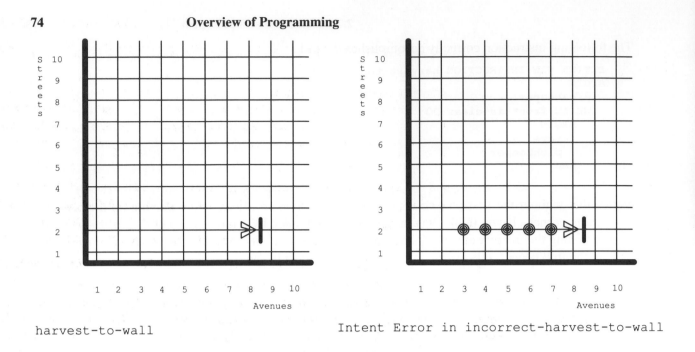

harvest-to-wall   Intent Error in incorrect-harvest-to-wall

Figure 2-20: Karel's Execution of Both Instructions

Karel executes the incorrect instruction by first picking up the beeper on his starting corner. The WHILE loop then moves Karel forward until his front becomes blocked, without commanding him to pick up any additional beepers. This happens because the faulty loop body contains only the move instruction. When Karel's front is finally blocked, he exits the WHILE loop and then executes the second pickbeeper instruction. The result of executing incorrect-harvest-to-wall is that Karel picks up only the first and last beepers in the line.

Can you think of an initial situation in which this incorrect instruction causes an error shutoff? How about an initial situation in which this instruction actually performs correctly? Both situations do exist. Here again we have an instruction that executes correctly in some situations and incorrectly in others; it sometimes causes an execution error and sometimes results in an intent error.

This discussion -- the last of its kind -- is similar to our previous boxing-error discussions. The central idea in all of the omitted-BEGIN/END-block errors is that we must be aware of exactly how Karel boxes and executes our programs. Incorrect use of BEGIN/END blocks is such a common error for novices, we wanted to show in detail, for each kind of instruction, what happens when such a mistake is made. Sometimes Karel recognizes the mistake as a syntactic error, but most of the time a subtle intent error results; consequently, we should check our programs carefully for missing BEGIN/END blocks.

2.7.4. IF Instructions in WHILE Loops

Before starting the big programming example in this chapter, we shall uncover another frequent cause of trouble and misunderstanding when we simulate Karel's programs. This problem involves IF instructions that are inside the body of a WHILE loop. Confusion might arise because both IFs and WHILEs perform tests that have similar execution rules. We summarize each execution rule before proceeding with our example. Karel executes a WHILE loop by repeatedly executing the loop body as long as <test> remains true. Karel executes an IF instruction by checking <test> once, and then executing the appropriate clause once (he is then finished executing the IF instruction).

The task in this section again requires Karel to harvest a line of beepers between his starting corner and a wall that marks the end of the beeper line. It is different from the last task in that we do not guarantee that every corner has a beeper on it. To avoid an execution error, Karel must not attempt to execute a pickbeeper instruction on any barren corner while he is harvesting the line. Although we leave unspecified how many corners have beepers on them, we do guarantee that each corner has either zero or one beeper on it. One example of this task is illustrated in Figure 2-21.

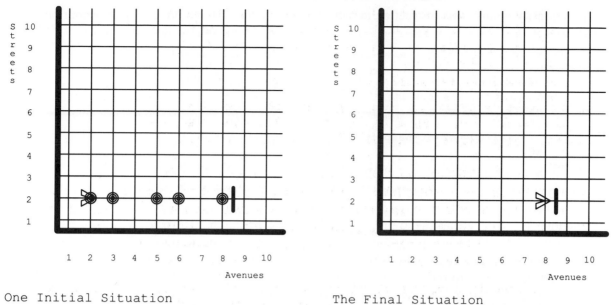

One Initial Situation   The Final Situation

Figure 2-21: A Sparse Line-Harvesting Task

The following instruction is a slight modification of the original `harvest-to-wall` instruction. As before, the purpose of the `WHILE` loop is to move Karel ahead until he reaches the wall. But in this definition, Karel uses the `IF` instruction in the body of the loop to decide whether he should execute a `pickbeeper`. He makes this decision once for each corner.

```
DEFINE-NEW-INSTRUCTION sparse-harvest-to-wall AS
BEGIN
   IF next-to-a-beeper
     THEN pickbeeper;
   WHILE front-is-clear DO
     BEGIN
       move;
       IF next-to-a-beeper
         THEN pickbeeper
     END
END
```

The execution of this definition in the initial situation of Figure 2-21 starts by having Karel execute the first `IF` instruction, which results in his picking up the first beeper. He then executes the second instruction in the definition -- the `WHILE` loop. Karel finds that his front is clear, so he moves ahead and then executes the `IF` instruction, checking for a beeper on his new corner. Because he is next to a beeper, he executes the `pickbeeper` in the `THEN` clause. Karel has now completely executed the loop body, and therefore he re-executes the `WHILE` loop. Once again he checks whether his front is clear. It is, so he executes the loop body by both moving ahead to the corner of 2nd St. and 4th Ave. and then executing the `IF` instruction. On this corner Karel is not next to a beeper, so he does not execute the `pickbeeper` in the `THEN` clause. Again he is finished with the `IF` instruction and the loop body, so he re-executes the `WHILE` loop.

Let's assume that Karel keeps up the good work and soon finds himself on 7th Avenue, about to re-execute the `WHILE` loop. His front is clear, so he moves forward and picks up the last beeper. Again he executes the `WHILE` loop, but this time finds that his front is now blocked, and thus finishes the instruction. Karel has correctly accomplished his task in this initial situation.

If we wanted to simplify `sparse-harvest-to-wall`, we could do so by replacing each `IF`/`THEN` instruction by the defined `pickbeeper-if-present` instruction. Not only would this substitution decrease the size of the definition, it would decrease the level of instruction nesting as well; the result would be a more readable instruction.

Can we easily modify this instruction to handle situations that have more than one beeper per corner? Yes, we can use `clear-corner-of-beepers` and write the following instruction.

```
DEFINE-NEW-INSTRUCTION many-beeper-sparse-harvest-to-wall AS
BEGIN
  clear-corner-of-beepers;
  WHILE front-is-clear DO
    BEGIN
      move;
      clear-corner-of-beepers
    END
END
```

We have now written four instructions that harvest lines of beepers. Each instruction was slightly more general then the previous one, and each was written by modifying an already written instruction. Sometimes it is too hard for us to immediately write a program that solves Karel's required task; there are too many details to keep in mind at one time. If we are unable to make any progress by using stepwise refinement, a good rule of thumb is to try solving a similar but simpler task. If the simpler task is similar enough to the original, it will be easy for us to modify the simple solution to solve the original task. Of course, finding the right "similar but simpler" task is frequently difficult. It is not easy to decide how to simplify the task -- to determine which details should be ignored because we can modify our program to account for them later. The more programming experience we acquire, the easier it is for us to decide correctly.

In general, we should always strive to re-use our previous work. Many programs are slight variations of previously written programs, or are similar enough to allow copying large portions of already written and tested instructions. We should accumulate a library of useful instructions and programs, which we can consult whenever we must write a new program.

2.7.4.1. A Syntax Error

Here is a syntax error that may be difficult to spot. Can you quickly determine what is syntactically wrong with the following instruction?

```
IF next-to-a-beeper
  DO pickbeeper
```

Either you do see the error or you do not; studying the instruction will probably do you no good. The error is that the reserved word DO does not belong before the THEN clause; the word THEN belongs there, of course. But this instruction reads so naturally that it is hard for our minds to interject, "Hey, wait a minute, that's not legal here." This is another example of an error that is hard for the human mind to discover, but is trivial for Karel's small-but-precise intellect to spot.

Often, programming errors are hard to find, but once discovered they are painfully obvious. Do not be too upset with yourself when you find these errors. If you find a "stupid" error, do not think "I'm really dumb"; instead, think "I must be a genius to locate such an obscure and hard-to-spot error!" Granted, both are overstatements, but the second is closer to the truth than the first.

2.7.5. A Large Program Written by Stepwise Refinement

In this section we shall write a complex program by using stepwise refinement. The program instructs Karel to escape from any rectangular room that has an open doorway exactly one block wide. After escaping from the room, the program commands Karel to turn himself off.

Instead of deftly avoiding mistakes and presenting a polished program, we shall develop the program in a logical manner, commit the mistakes, recognize that mistakes have been made, and rewrite the program until it correctly performs the task. We proceed in this way because it more accurately reflects how complicated programs are written. We should be aware that throughout the development of a complex program, we are increasing our knowledge of the task. During this time we should constantly be on guard for errors in the program or discrepancies between the program and the specification of the task.

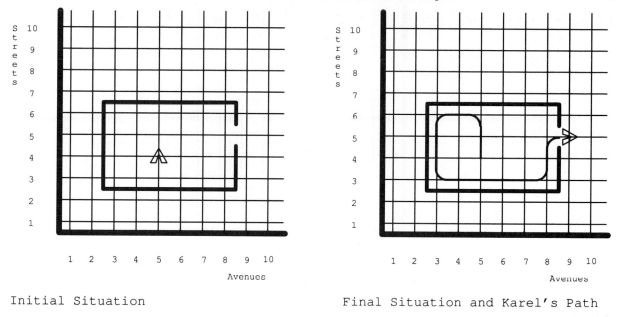

Initial Situation   Final Situation and Karel's Path

Figure 2-22: A Room-Escape Task

Figure 2-22 illustrates one possible initial situation for this task. We use this situation to create a general plan for escaping from rooms. Karel is initially somewhere in the room, facing some arbitrary direction. He starts the task by moving to the wall that he is initially facing. Karel then follows the inside perimeter of the room in a counter-clockwise direction, keeping his right side to the wall, until he senses the door on his right. He next exits through the door and finally turns himself off. Translating this informally stated escape plan, we obtain the following program.

```
BEGINNING-OF-EXECUTION
   go-to-wall;
   turnleft;
   follow-until-door-is-on-right;
   exit-door;
   turnoff
END-OF-EXECUTION
```

This program accomplishes the task, but in order to have Karel understand it, we must first define the instructions `go-to-wall`, `follow-until-door-is-on-right`, and `exit-door`. We begin by writing the `go-to-wall` instruction. This instruction must move Karel forward until he senses a wall directly in front of him. The test we eventually want to become true is `front-is-blocked`, so by using the formal WHILE property, we should be able to write this instruction as follows.

```
DEFINE-NEW-INSTRUCTION go-to-wall AS
BEGIN
   WHILE front-is-clear DO
      move;
END
```

But although this simple instruction works in Figure 2-22, and many other similar initial situations, it does not work correctly in all initial situations. Unfortunately, there are some initial situations in which the while instruction never terminates, leaving Karel stuck in an infinite loop. What is common among these situations is that Karel starts the task already facing toward the door, instead of toward one of the walls. When Karel executes this `go-to-wall` instruction in such a situation, he zooms out of the room without knowing that he has exited. One situation of this type is illustrated in Figure 2-23.

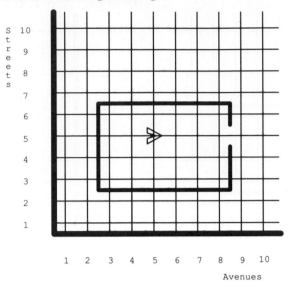

Figure 2-23:   A Beyond-The-Horizon Situation for the Room-Escape Task

We call this type of situation a <u>beyond-the-horizon situation</u>. Normally, we write a program guided by a few initial situations that seem to cover all interesting aspects of the task. Although we would like to prove that all other situations are not too different from these sample situations, frequently the best we can do is hope. As we explore the problem and learn more about the task, we may discover situations that are beyond our original horizons -- situations that are legal, but special trouble-causing cases. Once we have discovered a beyond-the-horizon situation, we should immediately simulate Karel's execution in it. If our suspicions are confirmed, and Karel does not perform as we intended, we must modify our program accordingly.

Let's construct a simple numerical argument that calculates the probability of finding a beyond-the-horizon situation by randomly testing Karel in legal initial situations. We restrict the following discussion to the room pictured in Figure 2-23. If we include all possible room sizes and door locations, the problems we encounter would become more severe.

In our example room, there are 24 possible corners on which Karel can start this task. Moreover, there are four ways that Karel can be placed on each corner (the four directions that he can face). Consequently, there are 96 different initial situations in which Karel can start this task. Out of this possible 96, there are only 6 placements of Karel that cause trouble for the `go-to-wall` instruction -- Karel facing east on any one of the 6 corners on 5th Street. Thus, Karel malfunctions in less than 7% of all his possible starting positions. This argument demonstrates that randomly testing Karel in different initial situations is most likely to be ineffective. We must use our intellect to try to uncover those few situations where Karel's program may malfunction.

We must think hard to discover these situations, because they are not in our intuitive field of view. But our time is profitably spent doing so, because looking for beyond-the-horizon situations can only benefit us: If we find situations that cause errors, we can correct our program to account for them; if we cannot find any situations that cause errors, we have made progress toward convincing ourselves that our program is correct. Good programmers become skilled at extending their horizons and finding dangerous situations that prevent a program from accomplishing its task.

Returning to Karel's task, what can we do to correct our program? The basic plan is still valid, but we must modify the `go-to-wall` instruction, making sure that Karel finds a wall before he accidentally exits the room. The fact that the door is only one block wide is the key to our next attempt at writing `go-to-wall`. Instead of moving Karel straight ahead, we shall program him to move forward in a sideways shuffling motion.

Karel starts by checking for a wall directly in front of himself; if he does not find one, he next checks for a wall in front of the corner on his right. If Karel finds walls in neither of these places, he returns to his original corner and then moves one block forward. He repeats this right-left shuffling motion until he finds a wall. In this way he is guaranteed not to pass through the unnoticed door, because the door is only one block wide. The path Karel takes in the beyond-the-horizon situation is displayed in Figure 2-24. This same type of path works correctly in Figure 2-22 too.

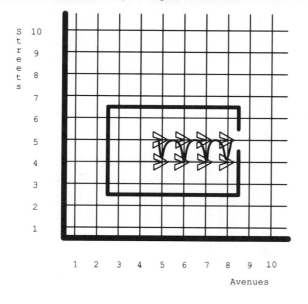

Figure 2-24: Karel's Shuffle Toward the Wall

So now let's rewrite `go-to-wall` to correspond to our new plan for moving Karel to a wall. We again use a WHILE loop with the same test, but in this instruction his forward motion is more complicated.

```
DEFINE-NEW-INSTRUCTION go-to-wall AS
BEGIN
   WHILE front-is-clear DO
     shuffle
END
```

We continue by using stepwise refinement to write `shuffle`.

```
DEFINE-NEW-INSTRUCTION shuffle AS
BEGIN
   sidestep-right;
   IF front-is-clear
     THEN
        BEGIN
          sidestep-back-left;
          move
        END
END
```

Finally, we write the simple sidestepping instructions directly in terms of Karel's primitive instructions and `turnright`.

```
DEFINE-NEW-INSTRUCTION sidestep-right AS
BEGIN
   turnright;
   move;
   turnleft
END
```

and

```
DEFINE-NEW-INSTRUCTION sidestep-back-left AS
BEGIN
   turnleft;
   move;
   turnright
END
```

Simulate these instructions in Figure 2-22 and Figure 2-24 to become better acquainted with this new `go-to-wall` instruction.

But even this plan has a small hidden wart on it; there are some initial situations in which Karel cannot perform a shuffle. For an example, look at the new beyond-the-horizon situation illustrated in Figure 2-25.

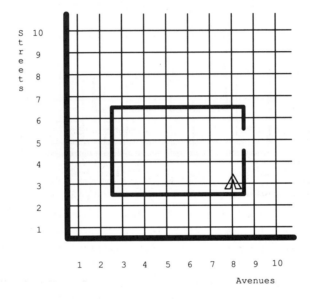

Figure 2-25: A Beyond-The-Horizon Situation That Prevents Shuffling

The wall on Karel's right prevents him from correctly performing the shuffle. Luckily, in situations like Figure 2-25, all we must do is turn Karel to the right; he will then be facing a wall, which easily satisfied the intent of `go-to-wall`. So, if Karel starts this task with his right side blocked by a wall, he merely turns to face this wall. Otherwise, his right is not blocked by a wall, and he can shuffle forward and to the right until his front becomes blocked. To accomplish this modification, we must rewrite only the definition of `go-to-wall`.

```
DEFINE-NEW-INSTRUCTION go-to-wall AS
BEGIN
   If right-is-blocked
      THEN turnright
      ELSE
         WHILE front-is-clear DO
            shuffle
END
```

Well, as you may have suspected, there is still a problem with `go-to-wall`. This problem is illustrated in Figure 2-26, one of the beyondest-the-horizon situations you may ever see; it is the single situation in which the present `go-to-wall` instructions fails. This is the last difficulty we shall see before completing a correct version of `go-to-wall`, so please don't get disgusted and stop reading.

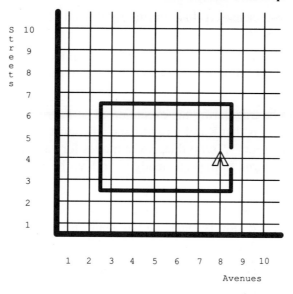

Figure 2-26: A Beyond-The-Horizon Situation That Causes an Error Shutoff

If Karel executes our current `go-to-wall` instruction in this initial situation, he will think that he can shuffle to the wall ahead -- because his right is clear. So Karel starts executing the WHILE loop in the ELSE clause of `go-to-wall`. He first finds that his front is clear, which means that he will execute `shuffle`. The `shuffle` instruction moves him out of the door, where his front is still clear, then it moves him back inside the room and one block forward. This instruction leaves him facing north on 5th St. & 8th Ave. Although Karel's actions look strange, nothing is terribly wrong -- after all, Karel is still looking in front of himself for a wall. He next rechecks `front-is-clear` in the while loop and finds it true again, so he again starts to execute `shuffle`. But this time he is stopped by an error shutoff in `sidestep-right`, which commands him to turn right and then move -- an impossibility in his current situation.

The problem is that we thought that Karel's right side could never become blocked if it was not originally blocked in his initial situation. Figure 2-26 showed us that this assumption is incorrect. We must modify `go-to-wall` so that Karel always checks to his right before executing a `shuffle`. This has been done in the following, finally correct definition of `go-to-wall`. Notice that the final definition consists of a WHILE loop that tests `front-is-clear`, so when this instruction finishes executing -- and now we know that it always will -- Karel's front is guaranteed to be blocked by one of the walls in the room.

```
DEFINE-NEW-INSTRUCTION go-to-wall AS
BEGIN
   WHILE front-is-clear DO
     IF right-is-blocked
       THEN turnright
       ELSE shuffle
END
```

The `go-to-wall` instruction now works correctly in any room. After executing `go-to-wall`, Karel will always have his front blocked by one of the four walls in the room. Because this instruction is so complicated and crucial to the task, you should immediately simulate Karel's execution of it in the initial situations illustrated in Figures 2-22 through 2-26. Do not proceed until you are familiar with exactly how Karel executes each instruction and what part each instruction plays in moving Karel to a wall.

Next we shall write the `follow-until-door-is-on-right` instruction. Recall that in the initial plan, Karel executes a `turnleft` instruction after `go-to-wall`; therefore, we can safely assume that just before Karel executes `follow-until-door-is-on-right`, his right is blocked by one wall of the room. This new instruction must satisfy two criteria.

- It must finish when Karel senses a door on his right-hand side. Karel senses this door when his right becomes clear.

- If a door has not been found, the instruction must keep Karel's right side adjacent to a wall while commanding him to follow the perimeter of the room in a counter-clockwise direction

A condition that must always be true during the execution of an instruction is called an <u>invariant</u>. The invariant for the second criterion is that Karel's right-hand side must be adjacent to a wall (blocked) as he follows the perimeter of the room. To do this, Karel moves forward along a wall until he reaches a corner; when this happens, he turns to the left, ready to follow the next wall with his right side still blocked.

We begin by using the first criterion to write the instruction that finds the door. Karel must maneuver into a situation in which his right side is clear, so we again use the formal property of the WHILE instruction to write our definition.

```
DEFINE-NEW-INSTRUCTION follow-until-door-is-on-right AS
BEGIN
  WHILE right-is-blocked DO
    follow-perimeter
END
```

By the formal property of the WHILE instruction -- again, provided that this loop terminates -- Karel's right-hand side will be clear when Karel finishes executing follow-until-door-is-on-right. We now use the second criterion to write the follow-perimeter instruction.

```
DEFINE-NEW-INSTRUCTION follow-perimeter AS
BEGIN
  IF front-is-clear
    THEN move
    ELSE turnleft
END
```

This instruction moves Karel forward along a wall until he reaches a corner. Whenever he reaches a corner, Karel performs a left turn and is ready to continue following the perimeter with his right-hand side next to the new wall. The invariant that his right side is always next to a wall remains true, until he finally senses that the door is on his right-hand side.

Finally we write the exit-door instruction. This is easy to do because it contains no complicated subparts. We can safely assume that Karel's right side is clear, since this instruction is executed directly after follow-until-door-is-on-right. The exit-door instruction can be written by using only Karel's primitive instructions and turnright.

```
DEFINE-NEW-INSTRUCTION exit-door AS
BEGIN
  turnright;
  move
END
```

We have now specified every instruction that Karel needs to accomplish his task. Although we cannot verify correctness, we should at least be able to verify that execution errors cannot occur. We can do this by showing that Karel never tries to execute a move instruction -- the only primitive in this program capable of causing an error shutoff -- when his front is blocked. We hope that this section has demonstrated how a difficult task can be programmed successfully by using the stepwise-refinement programming method. The entire program for this task is listed starting on page 84.

Before leaving this example, what would Karel do in the beyond-the-horizon situations illustrated in Figure 2-27? In both of these situations, he successfully escapes from the room and turns himself off, but not quite in the manner we may expect. Which instruction(s) must we change to remove the slight flaw from karel's performance in the "unexpected door" situation? In this initial situation, Karel should exit the room and then turn himself off when he reaches the corner of 8th St. and 6th Ave.

Although we believe that this program is correct, there still may be other, undiscovered beyond-the-horizon situations that force it to fail. Our minds are still open on the subject. This attitude is not false modesty; in earlier versions of this book, I incorrectly wrote the `go-to-wall` instruction by not discovering the beyond-the-horizon situation illustrated in Figure 2-26. Writing a completely, no doubts about it, 100% correct program, even for a seemingly simple task like this one, is a very difficult endeavor.

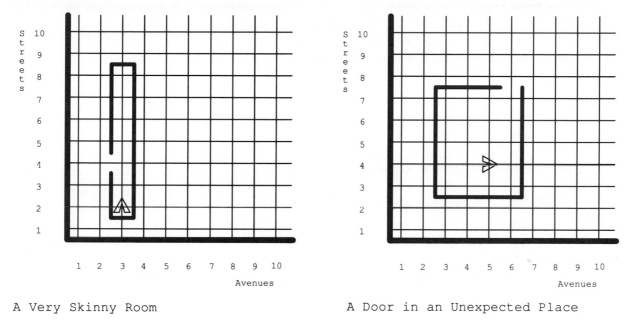

A Very Skinny Room   A Door in an Unexpected Place

Figure 2-27: Two Beyond-The-Horizon Situations

When attempting to write a large program, do not succumb to the "I've got to get it perfect the first time" syndrome. This leads to programmer's block: the inability to begin writing a program. You cannot foresee all of the difficulties that you will encounter while writing a program and, as already mentioned, it is impossible to try to plan an entire program in your head.

The most important step toward writing a program is putting something concrete down on paper. Once this is done, you can test the program by simulation, spot errors, and revise the program to remedy the errors. But with nothing written down, progress will be slow -- and frustration will be high. Do not forget that a correct program is only half a solution; make sure that your program is also easily understandable.

Finally, if you revise your program to the point of losing the original thread of reasoning, you might want to rewrite the entire program. Rewriting a program is not as time consuming as you may think, because you can use all the knowledge that you gained while writing the previous version.

```
BEGINNING-OF-PROGRAM


    DEFINE-NEW-INSTRUCTION turnright AS
    BEGIN
      ITERATE 3 times
        turnleft
    END;


    DEFINE-NEW-INSTRUCTION sidestep-right AS
    BEGIN
      turnright;
      move;
      turnleft
    END;


    DEFINE-NEW-INSTRUCTION sidestep-back-left AS
    BEGIN
      turnleft;
      move;
      turnright
    END;


    DEFINE-NEW-INSTRUCTION shuffle AS
    BEGIN
      sidestep-right;
      IF front-is-clear
        THEN
          BEGIN
            sidestep-back-left;
            move
          END
    END;

    DEFINE-NEW-INSTRUCTION go-to-wall AS
    BEGIN
      WHILE front-is-clear DO
        IF right-is-blocked
          THEN turnright
          ELSE shuffle
    END;
```

```
DEFINE-NEW-INSTRUCTION follow-perimeter AS
BEGIN
  IF front-is-clear
    THEN move
    ELSE turnleft
END;


DEFINE-NEW-INSTRUCTION follow-until-door-is-on-right AS
BEGIN
  WHILE right-is-blocked DO
    follow-perimeter
END;


DEFINE-NEW-INSTRUCTION exit-door AS
BEGIN
  turnright;
  move
END;



BEGINNING-OF-EXECUTION
  go-to-wall;
  turnleft;
  follow-until-door-is-on-right;
  exit-door;
  turnoff
END-OF-EXECUTION


END-OF-PROGRAM
```

2.7.6. Problem Set

The problems in this section require writing definitions and programs that use WHILE instructions. Try using stepwise refinement and the formal WHILE property discussed in Section 2.7.2.4 while writing these definitions and programs. Test your solutions by simulating them in various initial situations, and try to find beyond-the-horizon situations too. Take care to write programs that avoid error shutoffs and infinite loops.

A common mistake among beginning programmers is trying to have each execution of a WHILE loop's body make too much progress. As a rule of thumb, try to have each execution of a WHILE loop's body make as little progress as possible (while still making some progress toward terminating the loop).

1. Write a new instruction for Karel named empty-beeper-bag. After Karel executes this instruction, his beeper-bag should be empty.

2. >Write a new instruction called go-to-origin that positions Karel on 1st St. and 1st Ave. facing east, regardless of his initial location or the direction he is initially facing. Assume that there are no wall sections present. *Hint: Use the south and west boundary walls as guides.*

3. >Study both of the following program fragments separately. What does each do? For each one, is there a simpler program fragment that is execution equivalent? If so, write it down; if not, explain why not. *Hint: the formal* WHILE *property is useful.*

```
WHILE not-next-to-a-beeper DO          WHILE not-next-to-a-beeper DO
  move;                                  IF next-to-a-beeper
IF next-to-a-beeper                          THEN pickbeeper
  THEN pickbeeper                          ELSE move
  ELSE move
```

Describe the difference between the following two program fragments.

```
     WHILE front-is-clear DO            IF front-is-clear
         move                               THEN move
```

4. Write an instruction that faces Karel east if he is on a corner with an even number of beepers, and faces him west if he is on a corner with an odd number of beepers (zero is considered an even number for this task). Karel can clear the corner of beepers while he is determining which direction to face. *Hint: See Problem 2.6.8-3 for a more restricted version of this problem.*

5. Program Karel to escape from a rectangular room if he can find a doorway. If there is no doorway, he must turn himself off. We cannot use the program written in Section 2.7.5 for this task, because executing this program in a doorless room would cause Karel to run around inside the room forever; can you identify the instruction that will never finish executing? *Hint: There is a slightly messy way to solve this problem without resorting to beepers. You can write the program this way, or you can assume that Karel has one beeper in his bag, which he can use to remember if he has circumnavigated the room. This program may require a separate* turnoff *instruction for the completely enclosed situation in addition to a* turnoff *instruction for the situation with a door.*

6. Program Karel to run a super steeplechase. In this race the hurdles are arbitrarily high and the course has no fixed finish corner. The finish of each race course is marked by a beeper, which Karel must pick up before turning himself off. Figure 2-28 illustrates one possible course. Other courses may be longer and have higher hurdles.

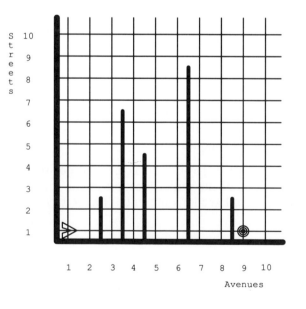

Figure 2-28: A Super Steeplechase

7. Program Karel to run a super-duper steeplechase. In this race the hurdles are arbitrarily high and arbitrarily wide. In each race course the finish is marked by a beeper, which Karel must pick up before turning himself off. Figure 2-29 illustrates one possible course.

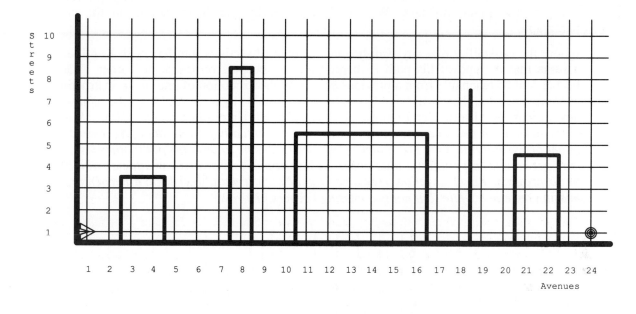
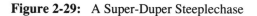

Figure 2-29:   A Super-Duper Steeplechase

8. Write an instruction that harvests a rectangular field of any size. The field is guaranteed to be bordered by beeperless corners. Also, assume that every corner within the field has a beeper on it and that Karel starts out facing east on the lower left hand corner of the field.

9. >Karel likes to take long meandering walks in the woods on his world, and even though he has a built-in compass, he sometimes cannot find his way back home. To alleviate this problem, before Karel walks in the woods he fills his beeper-bag and then he leaves a trail of beepers behind him (Karel obviously has not heard the story of Hansel and Gretel). Program Karel to follow this kind of path back home. There are many questions one can ask about this task. We shall try to clarify the specifications in the next paragraph.

Ignore the possibility that any wall boundaries or wall sections interfere with Karel, and assume that the end of his path is marked by two beepers on the same corner. Each beeper will be reachable from a previous beeper by the execution of one move instruction in some direction; there will be only one beeper reachable by a move. Also, the path will never cross over itself. See Figure 2-30 for a path that Karel must follow. *Hint: Karel must probe each possible next corner in his path, eventually finding the correct one. It might prove useful to have Karel pick up the beepers as he follows the path; otherwise, he may get caught in an infinite loop going backward and forward. How difficult would it be to program Karel to follow the same type of path if we allowed for a beeper to be missing once in a while (but not two missing beepers in a row)?*

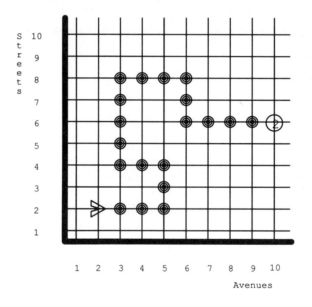

Figure 2-30: A Path of Beepers

10. Assume that Karel is somewhere in a completely enclosed rectangular room that contains one beeper. Program Karel to find the beeper, pick it up, and turn himself off.

11. Program Karel to escape from a maze that contains no islands. The exit of the maze is marked by placing a beeper on the first corner that is outside the maze, next to the right wall. This task can be accomplished by commanding Karel to move through the maze, with the invariant that his right side is always next to a wall. See Problem 2.6.8-9 for hints on the type of movements for which Karel must be programmed. Figure 2-31 shows one example of a maze.

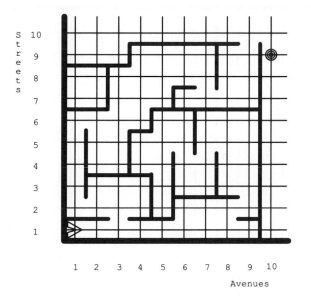

Figure 2-31: A Maze

There is a simpler way to program this task without using the instructions written in Problem 2.6.8-9. Try to write a shorter version of the maze-escaping program. *Hint: Program Karel to make the minimal amount of progress toward his goal at each corner in the maze.*

Finally, compare the maze escape problem with Problem 2.7.6-7, the Super-Duper Steeplechase. Do you see any similarities?

12. This problem is inspired by the discussion on the verification of WHILE loops (pages 70-71). Simulate Karel's execution of the following instruction in initial situations where he is on a corner with 0, 1, 2, 3, and 7 beepers.

```
DEFINE-NEW-INSTRUCTION will-this-clear-corner-of-beepers AS
BEGIN
    ITERATE 10 TIMES
      IF next-to-a-beeper
        THEN pickbeeper
END
```

State in exactly which initial situations this instruction works correctly. What happens in the other situations?

13. Program Karel to go on a treasure hunt. The treasure is marked by a corner containing 5 beepers. Other corners (including the corner on which Karel starts) contain clues, with each clue indicating in which direction Karel should next proceed. The clues are as follows: 1 beeper means Karel should next go north, 2 means west, 3 means south, and 4 means east. Karel should follow the clues until he reaches the treasure corner, where he should turn himself off. Figure 2-32 shows one possible treasure hunt.

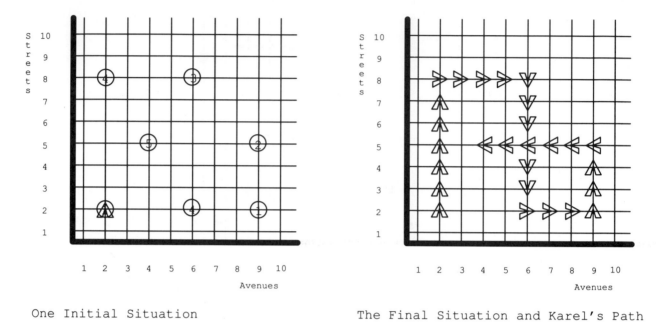

One Initial Situation   The Final Situation and Karel's Path

Figure 2-32: A Treasure Hunt

14. Program Karel to arrange vertical piles of beepers into ascending order. Each avenue, starting at the origin, will contain a vertical pile of one or more beepers. The first empty avenue will mark the end of the piles that need to be sorted. Figure 2-33 illustrates one of the many possible initial and final situations. (How difficult would it be to modify your program to arrange the piles of beepers into descending order?)

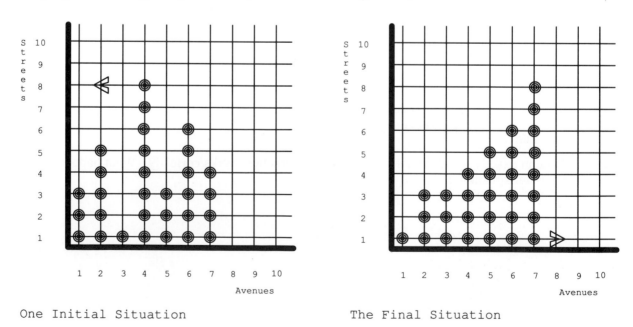

One Initial Situation   The Final Situation

Figure 2-33: A Sorting Task

UNIT II: Elements of Pascal

Chapter 3: Programming in Pascal

Chapter 4: Background Tools

Chapter 5: Details of Input, Output, and Variables

Chapter 6: Conditional Execution

Chapter 7: Repetition

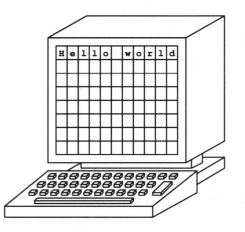

```
PROGRAM OutputExample (INPUT, OUTPUT);
BEGIN
    WRITELN(OUTPUT, 'Hello world')
END.
```

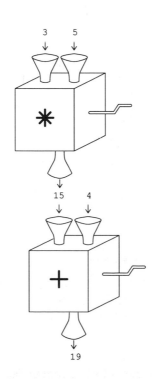

Chapter 3: Programming in Pascal

In the last chapter we used the programming language Karel to illustrate many of the elements of computer programming. With this overview of programming behind you, you are ready to begin programming in Pascal. We will be drawing on your understanding of Karel in this and the following chapters. In this chapter, we will introduce many of the elements of the Pascal programming language quickly, and we will examine the details in later chapters. This chapter also will provide the groundwork for later chapters that are designed to teach programming methods. You will be able to write your first Pascal program after just a few pages, and by the end of this chapter you will be able to write many small but useful programs that will lead into the more advanced programs to come in the later chapters.

Since we will be using the programming language *Pascal* to teach *programming methods*, it is appropriate that we discuss the origins of Pascal. Pascal is a very popular programming language that was created in the late 1960s by Professor Niklaus Wirth [7]. Most programming languages of the 1960s tended to be more elaborate versions of already existing programming languages, which meant they were excessively complicated. Pascal represents a programming language designed to be useful yet relatively simple. Professor Wirth wanted to design a simple programming language that could be used as a teaching language. He wanted a language that would provide a sound introduction to programming methodology that could be reliably and efficiently implemented on the computers popular in the 1960s.

The minor ambiguities in Wirth's design of Pascal originally presented no problem for either its users or implementors. Since its creation, Pascal has been accepted far beyond the classroom. It has been accepted by business, government, and hobbyists, in addition to educators. The acceptance of Pascal has outstripped all expectations and dreams of its creator. Yet this broad acceptance has made the ambiguities of the original design unacceptable.

The process of determining an unambiguous standard for Pascal was undertaken by the International Standards Organization (ISO). Achieving agreement on such a standard was not easily accomplished. After years of disagreement and discussion, agreement was finally reached, and the resulting standard is now referred to as *ISO Standard Pascal*. The ISO standard has also been accepted by the American National Standards Institute (ANSI) and the International Organization of Electrical and Electronics Engineers (IEEE) and is commonly referred to as *Standard Pascal*. We use Standard Pascal as our vehicle in teaching programming methods, and we mean ISO Standard Pascal whenever we say Pascal. Since you may be using a version of Pascal that differs from Standard Pascal, it is important for you to learn the differences as you go along.

3.1. Comparing Pascal with Karel

The form of a Karel program is remarkably similar to the form of a Pascal program. Many of Karel's other features also have counterparts in Pascal. The forms of the Karel and Pascal programs appear in Example 3-1, side by side. Angle brackets (<>) designate portions of the program to be supplied by the programmer. Words in capital letters, such as PROGRAM, BEGINNING-OF-EXECUTION, and END, indicate the **reserved words** that must be present for the program to work.

> **Definition 3-1:** *Reserved words* are a collection of words that have special meaning for a programming language's compiler and interpreter. They must be used by the programmer.

```
            Karel                                    Pascal

    BEGINNING-OF-PROGRAM                  PROGRAM  <program-name> (INPUT, OUTPUT);


    <new-instruction-definitions>         <new-statement-definitions>


        BEGINNING-OF-EXECUTION            BEGIN
            <instruction-1>;                  <statement-1>;
            <instruction-2>;                  <statement-2>;
            <instruction-3>;                  <statement-3>;
                  .                                 .
                  .                                 .
                  .                                 .
            <instruction-n>                   <statement-n>
        END-OF-EXECUTION                  END.
    END-OF-PROGRAM
```

Programming Example 3-1: Comparison of Karel Program and Pascal Program

The first line of the Pascal program skeleton shown in example 3-1 is known as the *program heading*. The reserved word **PROGRAM** is used to indicate the start of the program and is followed by the program's name. A Pascal program's name is supplied by the user, and, like the names selected for Karel's new instructions, it should accurately reflect what the program does. What you put between the parentheses that follow the program name will be discussed in detail at a later point, but for now let's say that it sets up the standard way for your Pascal program to communicate with its user (the standard input/output capability).

The program heading is followed by *new-statement definitions*, which correspond directly to the new-instruction definitions of Karel. The statements of a Pascal program are written between the reserved words **BEGIN** and **END** and correspond directly to the instructions of a Karel program that are written between **BEGINNING-OF-EXECUTION** and **END-OF-EXECUTION**. The termination of the Pascal program is signified by the **END.**, that is, **END** followed by a period. The **END.** is equivalent to the **END-OF-EXECUTION** and **END-OF-PROGRAM** combination in Karel. The end of a Pascal program is the only time the reserved **END** will be followed by a period in a Pascal program. The **END** followed by a period tells the Pascal compiler or interpreter that the program has been completed. Anything following the **END.** is typically ignored.

Pascal programs are composed of *statements* in the same fashion that Karel programs are composed of *instructions*. Like Karel instructions, Pascal statements are *separated* by a semicolon (;) rather than being *terminated* by one. This means semicolons are placed between two statements rather than following every statement, just as in Karel. Note that there is no semicolon after the last statement, since there is no following statement from which it must be separated. Consider the following Karel example:

```
BEGINNING-OF-PROGRAM

DEFINE-NEW-INSTRUCTION turnright AS
BEGIN
    turnleft;
    turnleft;
    turnleft
END;

    BEGINNING-OF-EXECUTION
        turnleft;
        move;
        turnright;
        move;
        putbeeper;
        turnoff
    END-OF-EXECUTION
END-OF-PROGRAM
```

Programming Example 3-2: Semicolon as a Separator Rather Than as a Terminator

Note that there is no semicolon after the last instruction in the program, `turnoff`, in the previous program. Note also that there is no semicolon after the last instruction in the definition of the new instruction `turnright` (the third turnleft). This is the case since **END** is a reserved word and not a statement.

3.2. Generating Output

It is quite natural to want programs to generate output. In fact, a program's output is typically the primary reason for having the program! A program computes something, and the program's output communicates the results of such computations. A program that computes something yet gives no output might just as well have not computed anything. Every useful program generates some output.

Recall how we had to write messages in the language Karel. We instructed the robot to move about in his world dropping beepers on particular corners to form letters, thereby creating a message. Also recall how tedious it was to make Karel write simple messages like **HELLO** (problem 6 on page 50). Fortunately, Pascal provides a much simpler way to output messages than Karel. If we want to write the message *Hello world*, the following simple Pascal program works fine:

```
PROGRAM HelloExample (INPUT, OUTPUT);

BEGIN
    WRITELN(OUTPUT, 'Hello world')
END.
```

Programming Example 3-3: Hello world

Recall that the first line of a Pascal program is the *program heading*. We named the above program **HelloExample** in the program heading. The actual program consists of only one *statement*. The statement used is *WRITELN*, a predefined Pascal statement just like **move** and **turnleft** are predefined Karel instructions. We need not define Pascal's predefined statements in order to use them in the same way we need not define Karel's predefined instructions. We use Pascal's predefined statement WRITELN when we want to *write* information. *What* is to be written as well as *where* it is to be written is specified between the matching parentheses following WRITELN. In the above program, the message to be written is *Hello world*, and the word *OUTPUT* specifies that the message is to be written to the standard output device, presumably the display screen. Note that the message to be written appears between matching single quotes ('). Such a message between single quotes is called a **literal string**.

> **Definition 3-2:** A *literal string* in Pascal is a sequence of characters enclosed in matching single quotes (').

Similarly, if we wanted to write a program that displays the message *Good morning America!*, the following Pascal program does the trick:

```
PROGRAM Example (INPUT, OUTPUT);

BEGIN
    WRITELN(OUTPUT, 'Good morning America!')
END.
```

Programming Example 3-4: Single Statement Program

The following Pascal program displays the three messages: *Computer programming is fun.*, *Computer programming is challenging.*, *Computer programming is rewarding!*, three statements we think you will find to be true.

```
PROGRAM Example (INPUT, OUTPUT);

BEGIN
    WRITELN(OUTPUT, 'Computer programming is fun.');
    WRITELN(OUTPUT, 'Computer programming is challenging.');
    WRITELN(OUTPUT, 'Computer programming is rewarding!')
END.
```

Programming Example 3-5: Multiple Statement Program

Note that the program has *three* statements that are separated by *two* semicolons. Pascal uses the semicolon as a statement *separator* rather than *terminator*, just like Karel.

At this point you should have a firm enough grasp on the Pascal WRITELN statement to create your first Pascal program to write a message of your choice. The Pascal program to write a message is much simpler than the Karel program to write the same message.

Like Karel, Pascal has other predefined statements. We will introduce each of them as the need arises. We can define new statements in Pascal just like we can define new instructions in Karel.

3.3. Defining New Statements

Consider again the problem of writing the message HELLO. Recall how we solved it in Karel. In order to write the whole message, we wrote each one of the letters one at a time. In order to accomplish that we defined a new instruction for each distinct letter of the message. In this case, that means four new instructions: **DisplayH**, **DisplayE**, **DisplayL**, **DisplayO**. Suppose we wanted to write the message "HELLO" in large letters, say five lines high and five characters wide. A solution in Pascal would be very much like one in Karel. We would write the whole message by writing one letter at a time. We would define a new statement for each distinct letter of the message and create the whole message by writing each letter in the appropriate order. This type of problem solution is general and therefore useful, regardless of the particular programming language being used. The following program illustrates such a solution in Pascal:

```
PROGRAM Example (INPUT, OUTPUT);


PROCEDURE DisplayH;

BEGIN
    WRITELN(OUTPUT, '*   *');
    WRITELN(OUTPUT, '*   *');
    WRITELN(OUTPUT, '*****');
    WRITELN(OUTPUT, '*   *');
    WRITELN(OUTPUT, '*   *')
END;    (* DisplayH *)



PROCEDURE DisplayE;

BEGIN
    WRITELN(OUTPUT, '*****');
    WRITELN(OUTPUT, '*    ');
    WRITELN(OUTPUT, '***  ');
    WRITELN(OUTPUT, '*    ');
    WRITELN(OUTPUT, '*****')
END;    (* DisplayE *)



PROCEDURE DisplayL;

BEGIN
    WRITELN(OUTPUT, '*    ');
    WRITELN(OUTPUT, '*    ');
    WRITELN(OUTPUT, '*    ');
    WRITELN(OUTPUT, '*    ');
    WRITELN(OUTPUT, '*****')
END;    (* DisplayL *)



PROCEDURE DisplayO;

BEGIN
    WRITELN(OUTPUT, ' *** ');
    WRITELN(OUTPUT, '*   *');
    WRITELN(OUTPUT, '*   *');
    WRITELN(OUTPUT, '*   *');
    WRITELN(OUTPUT, ' *** ')
END;    (* DisplayO *)



BEGIN
    DisplayH;
    DisplayE;
    DisplayL;
    DisplayL;
    DisplayO
END.
```

Programming Example 3-6: Defining New Statements with Procedures

The program in example 3-6 writes the message HELLO in large letters. It has only five statements, each of which is a *call* to one of the user-defined statements. Each of the four user-defined statements is composed of calls to the predefined statement WRITELN.

When writing Karel programs to solve problems, we *decomposed* the original problem into smaller problems (subproblems) and defined new instructions to solve each of the smaller subproblems. Often, in writing the definition of a new instruction, we needed another instruction to solve an even smaller problem and therefore defined other new instructions. We do precisely the same thing in Pascal by defining new statements. New statements in Pascal are called **procedures**. This is an extremely useful technique for solving programming problems. It is a general programming method that can be used regardless of the programming language being used.

Definition 3-3: A Pascal *procedure* is a user-defined statement.

3.3.1. Questions

1. What version of Pascal is taught in this textbook?

2. What version of Pascal will you be using on your computer system?

3. Pascal is strikingly similar to Karel. What in Pascal is the counterpart of the *instruction* in Karel?

4. What is a reserved word?

5. Name two reserved words from Karel. Name two reserved words from Pascal.

6. What is the first line of a Pascal program called?

7. What is the difference between a separator and a terminator?

8. Is the semicolon used as a separator or terminator for Pascal statements?

9. Is there a semicolon *after* the last statement in a PASCAL program?

10. What in Pascal is analogous to Karel's predefined instruction **putbeeper**?

11. What Pascal statement is used to write information? Is it predefined?

12. What two things must be specified to the WRITELN statement?

13. What is a literal string?

14. What are new statement definitions in Pascal called?

3.3.2. Exercises

1. What output does the following program display?

```
PROGRAM Patty (INPUT, OUTPUT);

BEGIN
    WRITELN(OUTPUT, 'Patty had a little lamb.')
END.
```

2. What output does the following program display?

```
PROGRAM Squares (INPUT, OUTPUT);


PROCEDURE DisplaySquare;

BEGIN
    WRITELN(OUTPUT, '*****');
    WRITELN(OUTPUT, '*   *');
    WRITELN(OUTPUT, '*   *');
    WRITELN(OUTPUT, '*****')
END;    (* DisplaySquare *)


BEGIN
    DisplaySquare;
    DisplaySquare;
    DisplaySquare
END.
```

3.3.3. Problems

1. Enter the very first program presented in this chapter (Programming Example 3-3) into your computer and run it.

2. Modify the program from the previous problem so it writes *Hello world. Your wish is my command!*

3. Write a Pascal program to display the message "Jack and Jill went up the hill."

4. Write a Pascal program that displays the following four-line message.

   Trains of thought
   Run through dark tunnels.
   --Theodor Reik
   from, "Listening with the Third Ear"

5. Extend the example program that writes HELLO in large 5 by 5 letters to write HELLO WORLD in large letters. *Hint: You don't need to define five new procedures. Three are enough.*

3.4. Naming Constants

The predefined statement WRITELN has been used in every Pascal program up to this point. The messages appear between matching single quotes in the program and are called *literal strings*. Often, we wish to use the same literal string more than once in a program. Rather than retyping the same literal string over again every time we wish to use it, we can give the literal string a name and then reuse it by simply referring to it by name. Recall our first program, which wrote *Hello world*. The following Pascal program generates the same output as our original:

```
PROGRAM Example (INPUT, OUTPUT);

CONST
    message = 'Hello world';

BEGIN
    WRITELN(OUTPUT, message)
END.
```

Programming Example 3-7: Named Constants

The program still has only one statement, a call to the predefined procedure WRITELN. Note, however, that what is to be written is *message*. This is different from writing 'message', which puts the characters *m e s s a g e* on the output device. In the previous program, we write the *value* of message, since message is the name for a value. In this case, *message* is a name that refers to the literal string 'Hello world' and is commonly called a **named constant**.

Definition 3-4: A *named constant* in Pascal is a constant that has been given a name in the constant definition section of the program.

Named constants are most useful when we wish to use the constant more than once. Recall our third Pascal program (programming example 3-5) of this chapter, which made three statements about computer programming. It can be rewritten as follows:

```
PROGRAM Example (INPUT, OUTPUT);

CONST
    message = 'Computer programming is ';

BEGIN
    WRITELN(OUTPUT, message, 'fun.');
    WRITELN(OUTPUT, message, 'challenging.');
    WRITELN(OUTPUT, message, 'rewarding!')
END.
```

Programming Example 3-8: Rewriting with a Named Constant

Recall the Pascal program that wrote HELLO in large 5 by 5 letters. The same patterns were used over many times in making the procedures that wrote the individual letters. Let's define named constants for the three most common patterns from that program: one * in the left-most position followed by four spaces; one * at each end separated by three spaces; and five * symbols ('*   ', '*   *', and '*****' respectively). The program can be rewritten as follows:

```
PROGRAM Example (INPUT, OUTPUT);


CONST
    left = '*    ';
    ends = '*    *';
    all = '*****';


PROCEDURE DisplayH;

BEGIN
    WRITELN(OUTPUT, ends);
    WRITELN(OUTPUT, ends);
    WRITELN(OUTPUT, all);
    WRITELN(OUTPUT, ends);
    WRITELN(OUTPUT, ends)
END;    (* DisplayH *)


PROCEDURE DisplayE;

BEGIN
    WRITELN(OUTPUT, all);
    WRITELN(OUTPUT, left);
    WRITELN(OUTPUT, all);
    WRITELN(OUTPUT, left);
    WRITELN(OUTPUT, all)
END;    (* DisplayE *)


PROCEDURE DisplayL;

BEGIN
    WRITELN(OUTPUT, left);
    WRITELN(OUTPUT, left);
    WRITELN(OUTPUT, left);
    WRITELN(OUTPUT, left);
    WRITELN(OUTPUT, all)
END;    (* DisplayL *)


PROCEDURE DisplayO;

BEGIN
    WRITELN(OUTPUT, all);
    WRITELN(OUTPUT, ends);
    WRITELN(OUTPUT, ends);
    WRITELN(OUTPUT, ends);
    WRITELN(OUTPUT, all)
END;    (* DisplayO *)



BEGIN
    DisplayH;
    DisplayE;
    DisplayL;
    DisplayL;
    DisplayO
END.
```

Programming Example 3-9: Rewriting with Multiple Named Constants

Note that once we have defined a name for a pattern, we may refer to that pattern by name only. This makes modifying programs much easier. Say, for example, we decided to make all letters of the message six columns wide instead of five. We would need to change every pattern of the program. In the first example (without named constants), we would have to change every WRITELN statement in the program! In the second example, we could refer to the patterns by name only. Therefore, we would need to change only the definitions of the three named constants. We would not need to change any of the WRITELN statements.

Using named constants makes modifying programs much easier. Most programs get modified many times over their lifetime. Therefore, you should get into the habit of using named constants liberally.

Constant definitions appear in what is called the *constant definition section*. It is headed by the reserved word **CONST**. Each constant definition is *terminated* with a semicolon, regardless of how many constants are defined in the constant definition section. This is different than for statements, which are *separated* by semicolons rather than terminated by them. Below we show the skeleton of a Pascal program including the constant definition section:

```
PROGRAM  <program-name> (INPUT, OUTPUT);

CONST
    <constant definitions>


<new-statement definitions>


BEGIN
    <statement-1>;
    <statement-2>;
    <statement-3>;
           .
           .
           .
    <statement-N>
END.
```

Programming Example 3-10: Pascal Skeleton with Constant Definitions

Not every program has a constant definition, so the constant definition section is an optional part of a Pascal program. The constant definition section is required only if the program has at least one named constant.

3.5. Writing Expressions

Up to this point every call to the Pascal predefined procedure WRITELN has either been with a literal string containing letters or to a named constant that is a literal string containing letters. However, we may use any characters on the keyboard in the literal string, such as numbers or special characters. Consider the following program:

```
PROGRAM Example (INPUT, OUTPUT);

BEGIN
    WRITELN(OUTPUT, '5 + 1')
END.
```

Programming Example 3-11: Output a Literal String Expression

What output does the previous program generate? Do you think the output is *6*? Do you think the output is *5 + 1*? The output from the previous program is *5 + 1*.

Now consider the following program:

```
PROGRAM Example (INPUT, OUTPUT);

BEGIN
    WRITELN(OUTPUT, 5 + 1)
END.
```

Programming Example 3-12: Output an Arithmetic Expression

What do you think the output from this program is? It is *6*, the value of the expression *5 + 1*.

The two previous program examples are very similar but have one subtle difference. One has parentheses and one does not. This small difference causes the difference in output.

The procedure WRITELN writes *expressions*. If the expression to be written is in quotes, it is called a literal string and is output literally as it was typed. If the expression is not in quotes, it is evaluated, and the *value* of the result is output instead of the original expression. The following example contains one of each to illustrate the difference:

```
PROGRAM Example (INPUT, OUTPUT);

BEGIN
    WRITELN(OUTPUT, '5 + 1');
    WRITELN(OUTPUT, 5 + 1)
END.
```

Programming Example 3-13:   Literal String and Arithmetic Expression

The output from the previous program is *5 + 1* on the first line and *6* on the second line.

3.6. Storing Expressions

Just as we find it useful to refer to a literal string by name, we find it useful to store the value of an expression and refer to it by name. The following Pascal statement stores the value of the expression 5 + 1 in **sum**.

```
sum := 5 + 1
```

This Pascal statement is called the *assignment statement* . The symbol := is called the *assignment operator* . The assignment statement assigns the value of the expression to the right of the assignment operator to the name on the left of the assignment operator. The name on the left of the assignment operator is called a **variable**.

Definition 3-5: A *variable* is a named piece of computer memory that holds a value.

Definition 3-6: *Assignment* is the process of giving a variable a value explicitly.

Just as we need to define named constants at the top of the program, we must declare variables. Variables are declared in what is called the *variable declaration section*, which is headed by the reserved word **VAR** and follows the constant definition section in a Pascal program. The following program illustrates the declaration of, assignment to, and output of a variable.

```
PROGRAM Example (INPUT, OUTPUT);

VAR
    sum: INTEGER;

BEGIN
    sum := 5 + 1;
    WRITELN(OUTPUT, '5 + 1 = ', sum)
END.
```

Programming Example 3-14:   Output a Variables Value

The expression *5 + 1* is evaluated, and its value is assigned to the variable named **sum**. The value held by the variable **sum** (6) is written to the output device. The output of the previous program is *5 + 1 = 6*.

A variable may be one of four primitive types: INTEGER, REAL, CHAR, and BOOLEAN. INTEGER and REAL are for numeric information; CHAR is for character information; and BOOLEAN is for logical information. We will discuss these in detail in the following chapter.

Consider as an example a program to compute the area of a rectangular surface. The following program illustrates such a computation:

```
PROGRAM ComputeArea (INPUT, OUTPUT);

VAR
    length: INTEGER;
    width: INTEGER;
    area: INTEGER;

BEGIN
    length := 5;
    width := 4;
    area := length * width;
    WRITELN(OUTPUT, 'area = ', area)
END.
```

Programming Example 3-15:   Using Variables

Note that each variable declaration in the variable declaration section is *terminated* with a semicolon just like constant definitions. Pascal provides a shorthand technique for declaring several variables of the same type. The following program illustrates the shorthand technique:

```
PROGRAM ComputeArea (INPUT, OUTPUT);

VAR
    length, width, area: INTEGER;

BEGIN
    length := 5;
    width := 4;
    area := length * width;
    WRITELN(OUTPUT, 'area = ', area)
END.
```

Programming Example 3-16: Combining Variable Declarations

Several variables of the same type may be declared in one variable declaration by *separating* the variable names with commas. Consider as yet another example a program that computes the taxes and resulting net pay for a particular gross pay. The following program illustrates a Pascal program that does such computations:

```
PROGRAM Payroll (INPUT, OUTPUT);

CONST
    TaxRate = 0.35;                                   (* tax rate is 35% *)

VAR
    GrossPay, NetPay, Taxes: REAL;

BEGIN
    GrossPay := 30000.0;
    Taxes := GrossPay * TaxRate;
    NetPay := GrossPay - Taxes;
    WRITELN(OUTPUT, 'Your net pay is $', NetPay)
END.
```

Programming Example 3-17: Payroll

Note that we used a named constant for the tax rate. Named constants do not have to be names for literal strings; they may also be names for any value of the four primitive types.

The following skeleton of a Pascal program illustrates the variable declaration section:

```
PROGRAM  <program-name> (INPUT, OUTPUT);

CONST
    <constant definitions>

VAR
    <variable declarations>


<new-statement definitions>


BEGIN
    <statement-1>;
    <statement-2>;
    <statement-3>;
        .
        .
        .
    <statement-N>
END.
```

Programming Example 3-18: Skeleton with Variable Declarations

3.6.1. Questions

1. What is a named constant?

2. What is the reserved word used to head the constant definition section of a Pascal program?

3. Are constant definitions separated or terminated with a semicolon?

4. What effect do quotes have on an expression in a WRITELN statement?

5. What is a variable?

6. What is the reserved word used to head the variable declaration section of a Pascal program?

7. Are variable declarations separated or terminated with a semicolon?

8. What is an assignment statement?

9. What is an assignment operator?

10. What does Pascal use for an assignment operator?

11. What are Pascal's four primitive types?

3.6.2. Exercises

1. What output does the following program display?

```
PROGRAM Example (INPUT, OUTPUT);

CONST
    answer = 'The answer is 42.';

BEGIN
    WRITELN(OUTPUT, 'answer');
    WRITELN(OUTPUT, answer)
END.
```

2. What output does the following program display?

```
PROGRAM Example (INPUT, OUTPUT);

VAR
    total: INTEGER;

BEGIN
    total := 13 + 8 - 3;
    WRITELN(OUTPUT, total)
END.
```

3. What output does the following program display?

```
PROGRAM Example (INPUT, OUTPUT);

CONST
    expression = '27 - 3';
    result = 24;

VAR
    difference: INTEGER;

BEGIN
    difference := 27 - 3;
    WRITELN(OUTPUT, '27 - 3');
    WRITELN(OUTPUT, 27 - 3);
    WRITELN(OUTPUT, expression);
    WRITELN(OUTPUT, difference);
    WRITELN(OUTPUT, result)
END.
```

4. Define Pascal constants for degrees in a circle and centimeters in an inch.

5. Give valid Pascal constant definitions for the number of feet per mile, the number of pints per gallon, and the number of grams per pound.

3.6.3. Problems

1. Extend the program that computes the area for a given length and width to also compute the perimeter and display it. *Hint: The perimeter for a rectangle = length + length + width + width.*

2. Write a Pascal program that computes and displays the diameter and circumference of a circle given the circle's radius. *Hint: diameter = 2 * radius, circumference = π * diameter*

3. Extend the previous program to also compute the area of a circle given the circle's radius. *Hint: The area of a circle = π * r².*

3.7. Commenting Programs

High-level languages were created to make it easier for humans to communicate instructions to computers. However, programs written in a high-level language can still be difficult for humans to read. For this reason, most high-level languages permit the programmer to include descriptions in the program to explain how the program works for others who may have to read the program. These are called *comments*. Comments in Pascal are delimited by (* and *) or { and }, if available on your input device. They are solely for human readers since the compiler throws them away in translating the program into machine language. We used a comment in Programming Example 3-17 to document the assumed tax rate. We will discuss comments in more detail later, but in the meantime you should get into the habit of liberally commenting your computer programs.

3.8. Formatting Output

Consider again Programming Example 3-17, which we named **Payroll**. What output would that program generate? It would generate output resembling the following:

Your net pay is $ 1.95 E+4

However, it is not immediately obvious to everyone what the net pay is because of the way the output is formatted. We can fix this with a small change to the program **Payroll**, as indicated in the following example:

```
PROGRAM Payroll (INPUT, OUTPUT);

CONST
    TaxRate = 0.35;                                (* tax rate is 35% *)

VAR
    GrossPay, NetPay, Taxes: REAL;

BEGIN
    GrossPay := 30000.0;
    Taxes := GrossPay * TaxRate;
    NetPay := GrossPay - Taxes;
    WRITELN(OUTPUT, 'Your net pay is $', NetPay:9:2)
END.
```

Programming Example 3-19: Payroll with Formatting

Notice the *:9:2* after the variable **NetPay** in the WRITELN statement. These notations are known as *format specifications*. The format specifications state that the REAL variable **NetPay** is to be output in 9 spaces, with 2 decimal places to the right of the decimal point. The output of the revised payroll program would look like the following:

Your net pay is $ 19500.00

If a program does not specify how to format output (as in our first payroll example), the compiler uses the default formatting specification given by the people who wrote the compiler. Most default formatting typically uses much larger formatting than is necessary and uses exponential notation for expressions of type REAL. Most programmers find default formatting unacceptable and choose to give their own format specification for all output.

Specifying format permits you to align output in columns, tables, and other readable forms. There is a detailed discussion of formatting output in the following chapter, where we discuss many of the details of the topics introduced in this chapter. For now you need only understand that for types INTEGER, CHAR, and BOOLEAN you can specify the total fieldwidth, but for expressions of type REAL you can specify the number of decimal places in addition to the total fieldwidth.

Most programmers naturally want to specify format for output rather than rely on default formatting specifications. Formatted output is usually always more readable. You should get into the habit of always explicitly formatting all output.

3.9. Labeling Output

Consider again the WRITELN statement in the program **Payroll**. There was a literal string preceding the variable **NetPay** that explained the value to be printed. Without that string, anyone seeing the value wouldn't know for sure if it was net pay, taxes, gross pay, or something else. Similarly, the unit of the value is given. Otherwise, we wouldn't know if the result was in dollars, pounds, marks, or yen.

When writing programs, it is a good idea to include English descriptions to keep the user informed. Such descriptions are known as *output labels*. Unlabeled output provides no context and forces the user to guess what it means. Labeled output combined with well-designed formatting makes using a computer an easier, more enjoyable experience. Consider the difference between the following two possible messages generated by a program.

```
4.2182E+1 2.62E+1
```

```
42.182 kilometers is 26.2 miles.
```

The first message is not meaningful because it is not properly labeled. The second message is immediately meaningful. The second output example above is produced by the following WRITELN statement:

```
WRITELN(OUTPUT, 42.182:6:3, ' kilometers is ', 26.2:4:1, ' miles.')
```

It is important to realize that the blank space preceding the word *kilometers* and following the word *is* must be present to separate the message from the number of kilometers. The following WRITELN statement produces the confusing output that follows it:

```
WRITELN(OUTPUT, 42.182:6:3, 'kilometers is', 26.2:4:1, 'miles.')
```

```
42.182kilometers is26.2miles.
```

Again, notice that a literal string is another form of an expression (remember, Pascal writes expressions). We did not specify a fieldwidth for the literal strings since the default fieldwidth for them is typically the same as the number of characters they contain. The programmer may also specify the overall fieldwidth for literal strings. You should always say what output is as well as what the units are (ounces, liters, miles, cubic inches, millimeters).

3.10. Solving Bigger Programming Problems

Assume we want to write a payroll program. It should do two major things: *give instructions* on how the program works and *compute net pay*. Therefore, to solve our problem we could define two procedures to solve these two smaller problems. Let's name the procedures **GiveInstructions** and **ComputeNetPay**. The Pascal program for this problem would be structured as illustrated in the following partially-completed program:

```
PROGRAM Payroll (INPUT, OUTPUT);


PROCEDURE GiveInstructions;

BEGIN

END;    (* GiveInstructions *)



PROCEDURE ComputeNetPay;

BEGIN

END;    (* ComputeNetPay *)



BEGIN
    GiveInstructions;
    ComputeNetPay
END.
```

Programming Example 3-20: Payroll Outline

The procedure **GiveInstructions** can be simply a sequence of WRITELN statements. The procedure **ComputeNetPay** is more complicated; it needs to compute taxes, compute net pay, and then display both taxes and net pay. The following example illustrates the program with the procedures filled out:

```
PROGRAM Payroll (INPUT, OUTPUT);



PROCEDURE GiveInstructions;

BEGIN
    WRITELN(OUTPUT, 'Hello, I am Figuro Payroll, an instant accountant.');
    WRITELN(OUTPUT, 'My lot in life is to figure your payroll for you.');
    WRITELN(OUTPUT, 'To do that, I use your gross pay to determine taxes.');
    WRITELN(OUTPUT, 'I then deduct the taxes to derive your net pay.')
END;    (* GiveInstructions *)



PROCEDURE ComputeNetPay;

CONST
    TaxRate = 0.35;                           (* tax rate is 35% *)

VAR
    GrossPay, NetPay, Taxes: REAL;

BEGIN
    GrossPay := 30000.0;
    Taxes := GrossPay * TaxRate;
    NetPay := GrossPay - Taxes;
    WRITELN(OUTPUT, 'Your tax due is $', Taxes:9:2);
    WRITELN(OUTPUT, 'Your net pay is $', NetPay:9:2)
END;    (* ComputeNetPay *)



BEGIN
    GiveInstructions;
    ComputeNetPay
END.
```

Programming Example 3-21: Payroll Filled Out

Note that in the previous program we defined a constant and declared variables in the procedure **ComputeNetPay** rather than at the top of the program as we've done in the past. Pascal allows both constant definitions and variable declarations within each procedure as well as at the top of the program. However, a declaration within a procedure can be used only within that procedure, whereas a declaration at the top of the program may be used throughout the entire program.

3.11. Reading Input

The program **Payroll** above will give instructions and compute and display the net pay. The values that are used are said to be *hard-wired* into the program. In other words, the program uses the same values every execution (every time it's run) and therefore generates the exact same result and same output for every execution. A more interesting and useful program would allow the user to type in gross pay for it to use to compute net pay. To modify the program to do this, we have to understand how Pascal input works.

Just as Pascal has the predefined procedure WRITELN to write expressions, Pascal has a predefined procedure called READLN to read information. The procedure READLN requires two things: the name of the variable to read the information into and where to read the information from. If we wanted to read a value into the variable **GrossPay** from the standard input device, presumably the keyboard, we would use the following Pascal statement.

```
READLN(INPUT, GrossPay)
```

For the payroll program, we want to replace the assignment statement that assigns a constant to **GrossPay** with the procedure READLN. The following example is the modified program **Payroll**:

```
PROGRAM Payroll (INPUT, OUTPUT);



PROCEDURE GiveInstructions;

BEGIN
    WRITELN(OUTPUT, 'Hello, I am Figuro Payroll, an instant accountant.');
    WRITELN(OUTPUT, 'My lot in life is to figure your payroll for you.');
    WRITELN(OUTPUT, 'To do that, I use your gross pay to determine taxes.');
    WRITELN(OUTPUT, 'I then deduct the taxes to derive your net pay.')
END;    (* GiveInstructions *)



PROCEDURE ComputeNetPay;

CONST
    TaxRate = 0.35;                              (* tax rate is 35% *)

VAR
    GrossPay, NetPay, Taxes: REAL;

BEGIN
    READLN(INPUT, GrossPay);
    Taxes := GrossPay * TaxRate;
    NetPay := GrossPay - Taxes;
    WRITELN(OUTPUT, 'Your tax due is $', Taxes:9:2);
    WRITELN(OUTPUT, 'Your net pay is $', NetPay:9:2)
END;    (* ComputeNetPay *)


BEGIN
    GiveInstructions;
    ComputeNetPay
END.
```

Programming Example 3-22: Payroll with Input

3.12. Prompting for Input

The previous program is valid Pascal, but something is wrong with it. Should it ever come to pass that the user happens to type in a number that represents gross pay, the program will compute and attractively write out the net pay. The problem is that the user is forced to guess first that user input is needed, and second that it should be a gross pay. **READLN of user input should always be prefaced**

by a graceful prompt for the desired information. This is accomplished by writing a message to the user. In the following example we show the program **Payroll** with such a **prompt** added:

```
PROGRAM Payroll (INPUT, OUTPUT);


    PROCEDURE GiveInstructions;

    BEGIN
        WRITELN(OUTPUT, 'Hello, I am Figuro Payroll, an instant accountant.');
        WRITELN(OUTPUT, 'My lot in life is to figure your payroll for you.');
        WRITELN(OUTPUT, 'To do that, I use your gross pay to determine taxes.');
        WRITELN(OUTPUT, 'I then deduct the taxes to derive your net pay.')
    END;    (* GiveInstructions *)


    PROCEDURE ComputeNetPay;

    CONST
        TaxRate = 0.35;                                (* tax rate is 35% *)
        prompt = 'Please type in your gross pay => ';  (* prompt for user input *)

    VAR
        GrossPay, NetPay, Taxes: REAL;

    BEGIN
        WRITELN(OUTPUT, prompt);
        READLN(INPUT, GrossPay);
        Taxes := GrossPay * TaxRate;
        NetPay := GrossPay - Taxes;
        WRITELN(OUTPUT, 'Your tax due is $', Taxes:9:2);
        WRITELN(OUTPUT, 'Your net pay is $', NetPay:9:2)
    END;    (* ComputeNetPay *)


BEGIN
    GiveInstructions;
    ComputeNetPay
END.
```

Programming Example 3-23: Payroll with Prompt

The idea is to make the program interact with the user as gracefully as possible. A prompt is really nothing more than a message written to the output device to tell the user what the program wants.

> **Definition 3-7:** A *prompt* is a message written to the user of a program asking for an input value.

3.13. Naming All Constants

A named constant is very similar to a variable in that both have a name, a type, and a value. However, the value of a variable may change during the course of a program, whereas the value of a named constant cannot. The value of a constant is determined at *compile time* (when the program is compiled), but the value of a variable is determined at *run time* (when the program executes). The type of the named constant is deduced from its definition.

The prompt for user input in the previous program employs a named constant. The labeled output uses a literal string. We could have used literal strings for both, named constants for both, or one of each. You will probably develop your own style for including text for your software to display to the user.

Note that we used a named constant for the input prompt. We use this technique throughout the text, and it has several advantages. Literal strings tend to clutter up the program. Gathering all prompts in the constant definition block reduces clutter and increases program readability. Often, we wish to use the same prompt several times. With this technique, we need only refer to the prompt by name rather than retyping the entire prompt. Should we want to change the prompt, we need only change it once at the definition site since all uses are by name only. This eliminates the need to search through the entire program for each occurrence. Hence, if we use an input prompt more than once, we always use a named constant for it.

If we are using the mathematical quantity π many times in a program, we might define the named constant **Pi** with a value of 3.141592654. Every time we need the value of π in an expression, we simply use **Pi**. You should use named constants very liberally in Pascal programs. There are several advantages to this:

1. We are sure that every use of the named constant has the same value. If we were required to retype a constant's value for every use, we might mistype it at least once.

2. If we need to change the value being used, we simply change the initial definition of the named constant. All the individual occurrences need no modification, since the references to it are by name only.

3. Use of named constants removes "mystery constants" from populating the entire program. This results in a more readable program.

4. Finally, less typing is required since **Pi** is only two characters, whereas 3.141592654 is eleven.

Numeric constants tend to be the most confusing to the reader of a program. It is for this reason that we virtually always define a named constant for every numeric constant. Normally, our only exceptions are 0, 1, and -1. Sometimes we do not define a named constant for the integers used in output format specification.

3.14. Picking Good Names

We have been picking names in this chapter for variables, procedures, and named constants. The programmer has a lot of choice in naming things. Pascal has only two requirements: (1) All names are one of the 26 letters followed by zero or more letters and digits, and (2) Pascal's reserved words may not be used as names. Therefore, **sum**, **radius**, and **area2** are valid Pascal names, but **2ndArea**, **employee#**, and **BEGIN** are not.

Since there are no other language requirements on the names for things, the programmer has a lot of freedom in naming. The programmer should exercise some discretion over this freedom. The names, also known as *identifiers*, should be picked to reflect what is being named. The more meaningful, or mnemonic, the name is, the better the name is. Although more mnemonic identifiers tend to be longer, longer identifiers are not always better identifiers; however, shorter identifiers are not always better: More meaningful identifiers are always better.

3.14.1. Questions

1. What does output formatting mean?

2. Why would a programmer want to specify the output format?

3. What happens to output if its format is not specified by the programmer?

4. What does it mean to label output?

5. Why would a programmer want to label output?

6. Why would we want input to programs?

7. What predefined statement in Pascal permits input?

8. What does it mean to prompt for input?

9. Why do we need to prompt for input to a program?

10. What is the primary criterion of a good identifier?

3.14.2. Exercises

1. Describe briefly the action of the following program.

```
PROGRAM SquareMaker (INPUT, OUTPUT);

VAR
    value, square: INTEGER;

BEGIN
    WRITELN(OUTPUT, 'Enter value to be squared');
    READLN(INPUT, value);
    square := value * value;
    WRITELN(OUTPUT, value, 'squared = ', square)
END.
```

What output is generated for each of the following inputs: 3, −2, 1?

3.14.3. Problems

1. Modify the **Payroll** program so that **TaxRate** is a variable that is read into the program rather than a named constant. Be sure that you prompt the user gracefully for this input.

2. Extend the **Payroll** program to deduct social security. Assume a deduction of 7%.

3. Extend the previous program to deduct for health insurance. Assume $20 per pay period.

3.15. Putting It All Together

Gas mileage is a subject of interest to auto makers, auto owners, the Federal Government, and oil companies. Suppose we need a Pascal program to calculate gas mileage. Assume we want to give our users some help on the program, calculate their gas mileage, and then offer some advice on the result. Knowing this much, we can write the main execution block (or main program) of our solution. It would have three procedures, one for each component of our solution. It would look something like the following:

```
BEGIN    (* Main Program *)
    GiveHelp;
    ComputeMPG;
    OfferAdvice
END.     (* Main Program *)
```

Programming Example 3-24:   GasMileage Main Program

Having written our solution at the highest level, we would then complete the lower levels. Let's work on the procedure **GiveHelp**. It should describe what the program does, the input it requires, the computations it performs, and the output it provides. Therefore, our **GiveHelp** procedure might look something like the following:

```
PROCEDURE GiveHelp;

BEGIN
    WRITELN(OUTPUT,'This program helps you determine your gas mileage.');
    WRITELN(OUTPUT,'It requires the distance traveled in miles and the');
    WRITELN(OUTPUT,'amount of gas consumed in gallons.  The gas mileage');
    WRITELN(OUTPUT,'is computed in miles per gallon.  Finally some');
    WRITELN(OUTPUT,'advice is offered for the result.')
END;     (* GiveHelp *)
```

Programming Example 3-25:   GiveHelp Procedure

The next procedure is the most complex of the three. It must get the input for the miles traveled and the gallons of gasoline used before calculating and displaying the gas mileage. The user is prompted for both of the necessary values.

```
PROCEDURE ComputeMpg;

CONST
    DistancePrompt = 'How many miles have you traveled? => ';
    FuelPrompt = 'How many gallons of gas did you use? => ';

VAR
    miles,                          (* miles traveled *)
    gallons,                        (* gallons of fuel used *)
    result: REAL;                   (* computed gas mileage *)

BEGIN
    WRITE(OUTPUT,DistancePrompt);
    READLN(INPUT,miles);
    WRITE(OUTPUT,FuelPrompt);
    READLN(INPUT,gallons);
    result := miles / gallons;
    WRITELN(OUTPUT,' Your vehicle gets ', result:8:2, ' miles per gallon.')
END;     (* ComputeMPG *)
```

Programming Example 3-26:   ComputeMPG Procedure

Note that each of the variables are declared on a separate line. We do this for two reasons. The first is to increase readability. The second is to permit a side comment for each variable declaration.

The last procedure to create is simple. Assume we simply wish to offer some advice on how to interpret the computed result. It might look something like the following:

```
PROCEDURE OfferAdvice;

BEGIN
    WRITELN(OUTPUT,'If your gas mileage is:');
    WRITELN(OUTPUT,'   above 30: you drive a fuel efficient vehicle');
    WRITELN(OUTPUT,'   10 - 30:  you get mediocre to average gas mileage');
    WRITELN(OUTPUT,'   below 10: you drive a gas guzzler. Consider a trade.');
    WRITELN(OUTPUT);
    WRITELN(OUTPUT,'Gas is one of our finite resources.  Conserve while');
    WRITELN(OUTPUT,'there is still some left.')
END;     (* OfferAdvice *)
```

Programming Example 3-27:   OfferAdvice Procedure

We have defined all three procedures. Therefore, we have finished writing the program. Putting it all together, we have the following Pascal program:

```
PROGRAM GasMileage (INPUT, OUTPUT);

    (******************************************************************)
    (*                                                                *)
    (*  This program interacts with the user to compute gas mileage.  *)
    (*  It also comments on fuel efficiency for various automobiles.   *)
    (*                                                                *)
    (******************************************************************)


PROCEDURE GiveHelp;

BEGIN
    WRITELN(OUTPUT,'This program helps you determine your gas mileage.');
    WRITELN(OUTPUT,'It requires the distance traveled in miles and the');
    WRITELN(OUTPUT,'amount of gas consumed in gallons.  The gas mileage');
    WRITELN(OUTPUT,'is computed in miles per gallon.  Finally some');
    WRITELN(OUTPUT,'advice is offered for the result.')
END;     (* GiveHelp *)


PROCEDURE ComputeMpg;

CONST
    DistancePrompt = 'How many miles have you traveled? => ';
    FuelPrompt = 'How many gallons of gas did you use? => ';

VAR
    miles,                      (* miles traveled *)
    gallons,                    (* gallons of fuel used *)
    result: REAL;               (* computed gas mileage *)

BEGIN
    WRITE(OUTPUT,DistancePrompt);
    READLN(INPUT,miles);
    WRITE(OUTPUT,FuelPrompt);
    READLN(INPUT,gallons);
    result := miles / gallons;
    WRITELN(OUTPUT,' Your vehicle gets ', result:8:2, ' miles per gallon.')
END;     (* ComputeMPG *)


PROCEDURE OfferAdvice;

BEGIN
    WRITELN(OUTPUT,'If your gas mileage is:');
    WRITELN(OUTPUT,'   above 30: you drive a fuel efficient vehicle');
    WRITELN(OUTPUT,'   10 - 30:  you get mediocre to average gas mileage');
    WRITELN(OUTPUT,'   below 10: you drive a gas guzzler. Consider a trade.');
    WRITELN(OUTPUT);
    WRITELN(OUTPUT,'Gas is one of our finite resources.  Conserve while');
    WRITELN(OUTPUT,'there is still some left.')
END;     (* OfferAdvice *)


BEGIN           (* Main Program *)
    GiveHelp;
    ComputeMPG;
    OfferAdvice
END.            (* Main Program *)
```

Programming Example 3-28: GasMileage Program

3.16. Chapter Summary

- There are many different dialects of the language Pascal. We have selected ISO Standard Pascal as our standard. Whenever we refer to Standard Pascal or just Pascal we mean ISO Standard Pascal unless we specifically indicate otherwise. You should know which dialect of Pascal you are using, and you should keep in mind any differences between your version and the Standard.

- Below is the skeleton of a Pascal program with all of the components presented thus far:

```
PROGRAM  <program-name> (INPUT, OUTPUT);

CONST
    <constant definitions>

VAR
    <variable declarations>



PROCEDURE  <procedure-name>;

CONST
    <constant definitions>

VAR
    <variable declarations>

BEGIN
    <statement-1>;
    <statement-2>;
    <statement-3>;
        .
        .
        .
    <statement-N>
END;



BEGIN
    <statement-1>;
    <statement-2>;
    <statement-3>;
        .
        .
        .
    <statement-N>
END.
```

Programming Example 3-29:   Pascal Skeleton with Constants, Variables, and Procedures

- *Reserved words* are a collection of words that have special meaning for a programming language's compiler and interpreter. They must be used by the programmer.

- A Pascal *procedure* is a user-defined statement.

- A *literal string* in Pascal is a sequence of characters enclosed in matching single quotes (').

- A *named constant* in Pascal is a constant that has been given a name in the constant definition section of the program.

- A *variable* is a named piece of computer memory that holds a value.

- *Assignment* is the process of giving a variable a value explicitly.

- Output is the information generated by a program.

- Pascal's predefined procedure WRITELN writes output.

- Input is the information required by a program.

- Pascal's predefined procedure READLN reads input.

- The three properties of Pascal variables are name, type, and value.

- The four primitive Pascal types are INTEGER, REAL, BOOLEAN, and CHAR.

- CHARacter values are always delimited with single quotes in Pascal to distinguish the value from the name of a variable.

- The semicolon is used to separate rather than terminate statements.

- The semicolon is used to terminate variable declarations.

- The semicolon is used to terminate constant definitions.

- Pascal has only two requirements on picking identifiers or names: (1) All identifiers are one of the 26 letters followed by zero or more letters and digits, and (2) Pascal's reserved words may not be used as identifiers.

3.17. Summary of Style

- The programmer has the choice of names for variables and constants. The names selected should be as mnemonic (meaningful) as is reasonably possible. Although that means names are more descriptive and usually require more characters, it is not the case that longer is always better. It is certainly not the case that shorter is always better. However, more mnemonic is always better.

- Named constants make a program easier to read and easier to modify. In general, all numeric constants used in the expressions of the program should be named constants. The only exceptions are 0, 1, and − 1. You should use named constants liberally.

- Always prompt for input. Specify the units (such as miles, gallons, or dollars) of the input quantities.

- Always label output. Specify the units of the output quantities.

- Always format output. Never rely on default formatting.

- It is a good idea to echo all input entered through the keyboard back to the user.

- Comments are essential for readable and well-documented programs. Use comments liberally throughout your program. If you are unsure whether to add a comment, the answer is probably to add it. Very few programs are overdocumented.

- A person shouldn't be forced to read a program's comments. They should be readily available but not be in the way.

3.18. Summary of Terms

- Pascal
- Standard Pascal
- reserved words
- program heading
- separator
- terminator
- primitive type
- CHAR
- INTEGER
- REAL

- BOOLEAN
- expression
- literal string
- output
- formatted output
- labeled output
- WRITELN
- variable
- variable declaration
- assignment

- assignment statement
- assignment operator
- named constant
- input
- READLN
- prompt
- subprogram
- procedure
- comments

3.19. Chapter Problems

1. Modify the gas mileage program (Program Example 3-24 on page 111) to take input in terms of kilometers instead of miles and fuel in liters instead of gallons. Also modify the help and advice procedures appropriately.

2. Extend the gas mileage program to take starting and final odometer readings and determine the distance traveled instead of requiring it to be entered. Modify the help procedure as needed.

3. Write a program that takes as input three REAL values, computes their average, and displays the result.

4. Write a program that balances a checkbook. It takes as input the starting balance, the total amount of withdrawals, and any deposits, then computes the current balance in the account. Print a suitable message if the account is overdrawn.

5. Some people like to build their own homes. Write a program to allow a user to enter the length, width, and number of stories for the proposed house. The program, using a constant cost per square foot, should compute the total cost of building the home. Assume all the stories have the same rectangular dimensions. Use a cost per square foot of $40.

6. Suppose you have been given the task of grading for a course. Write a Pascal program that calculates and displays a student's course grade by prompting the user for necessary information (exam grades, project grade, final exam grade) and computing the overall grade. Assume there are two exams, each worth 15%, a project worth 40%, and a final exam worth 30%. Also assume that each score is between 0 and 100, inclusive.

7. Resistances in electric circuits may be wired in series or in parallel. The formulas for their equivalent resistance are :

$$R(series) = R_1 + R_2 + R_3 + ... + R_n$$

$$1/R(parallel) = 1/R_1 + 1/R_2 + 1/R_3 + ... + 1/R_n$$

Write a program that takes as input three resistance measures and determines the equivalent resistance for both series and parallel circuits.

8. Compute distance traveled (d), given acceleration (a), time traveled (t), and initial velocity (v), according to the following formula: $d = 1/2\ a * t^2 + v * t$

9. Compute the total number of pages in a chapter, given a starting page and an ending page. *The answer is not what you probably first think it is.*

10. Write a program to determine the sales tax and total charge for a given purchase price. It should have a variable for purchase price and sales tax, while using a named constant for the sales tax rate. (Use 6% for the sales tax rate and $75 for the selling price.)

11. Modify the previous program so that the purchase price is input by the user.

12. Write a program to determine the total amount of money taken in at the gate for a baseball game. Assume there are three different ticket prices, and tickets are numbered incrementally for each price. Use named constants for the seat rates: regular ($6), economy ($4), and VIP ($12).

Chapter 4: Background Tools

The last chapter presented a quick introduction to Pascal, without worrying about details. It was fun. This approach is a good way to get started in programming, but it must be balanced with a solid understanding of the principles that underlie programming languages if you are to become a good programmer. In this chapter, we will focus exclusively on abstract tools rather than on programs. The material in this chapter will enable you to work out increasingly more difficult programming problems.

4.1. A Tool for Describing Pascal and Other Languages

Pascal is a language, just as English, French, and Karel are languages. There are rules that describe Pascal, just as there are rules that describe other languages. We need a language to express these rules that describe the structure of a language. One might be tempted to suggest English as a good language to describe the structure of a language. For an informal description, English is satisfactory, but for a precise description English proves to be too ambiguous and too wordy. To formally describe the rules of a language, we need another, special-purpose language called a **meta-language**.

> **Definition 4-1:** A *meta-language* is a language used to describe another language.

The particular meta-language we will use is known as BNF,[1] for Backus-Naur Form, which is named after John Backus and Peter Naur, who adopted this notation in the late 1950s to describe the programming language ALGOL. BNF is the usual tool used to describe programming languages in computer science. We use BNF in Appendix II to describe Karel and in Appendix V to describe Pascal. We will also use BNF throughout this text to formally describe new language features as they are introduced.

Assume we wish to describe precisely a valid integer. A valid Pascal integer is a valid digit followed by zero or more valid digits. In BNF, a valid integer is described as follows:

```
<integer> ::= <digit> { <digit> }
```

This states "An integer is defined as a digit followed by zero or more digits." The curly braces ({}) enclose objects that may be repeated zero or more times.

Similarly, a valid digit may be described in BNF as follows:

```
<digit> ::= 0 | 1 | 2 | 3 | 4 | 5 | 6 | 7 | 8 | 9
```

This states "A digit is a 0 or a 1 or a 2 or a 3 or a 4 or a 5 or a 6 or a 7 or an 8 or a 9." The vertical bar (|) separates objects that may be chosen between. In other words, a valid digit may be chosen from the 0 through 9 series. However, a valid digit cannot be more than one of the choices. Thus, a digit may be one or another of the choices.

BNF gives us a precise yet concise way to describe objects of a language. Each BNF definition defines exactly one object. Therefore, to formally define a programming language, we need a BNF definition for each object of the language being defined. Each BNF definition is known as a *production*. Each production has two components, the object being defined and the object's definition. The two components of a production are separated by the symbol *::=* (i.e. two colons followed by an equals sign), which is referred to as the *production symbol*. The name of the object being defined is enclosed in angle brackets (<>) and appears to the left of the production symbol. The object's definition appears on the right of the production symbol and is composed of special symbols called *meta-symbols*. Meta-symbols are simply symbols of the meta-language. In the following table we list all the meta-symbols in BNF:

---

[1]Actually, we will be using what is referred to as extended BNF, which contains some features not in the original Backus-Naur Form.

Symbol	Meaning
::=	production symbol—separates object from its definition
< >	encloses names of objects of language being defined
|	alternation—separates two valid choices, may choose either but not both
{ }	repetition—enclosed object repeated zero or more times
[ ]	option—enclosed object may exist zero or one times

Table 4-1: BNF Meta-Symbols

In our previous definition of integer we didn't mention a sign. A valid Pascal integer may optionally have either a + or − sign. Therefore, the modified BNF definition for a valid Pascal integer is as follows:

```
<signed-integer> ::= [ <sign> ] <digit> { <digit> }

where a valid sign is defined as:

<sign> ::= + | -
```

The BNF tells us that sequences of characters that have nondigits embedded are not integers in Pascal. It also tells us that integers can begin only with digits or + or -. The following table illustrates valid and invalid Pascal INTEGERs:

valid	invalid	reason
3	3.	decimal point not allowed
+42	++42	only a single sign allowed
−1286	1,286	no comma allowed
15	$15	no $ allowed
08	4.08	decimal point not allowed

Table 4-2: Pascal INTEGERs

The name for a variable or named constant is called an *identifier*. The BNF definition for a valid Pascal identifier is as follows:

```
<identifier> ::= <letter> { <letter> | <digit> }
```

An identifier is a letter followed by zero or more letters or digits.

A letter is defined in BNF as follows:

```
<letter> ::= A | B | C | D | E | F | G | H | I | J | K | L | M |
             N | O | P | Q | R | S | T | U | V | W | X | Y | Z
```

The BNF for identifiers allows sequences of characters that begin with a letter and are followed by letters and/or digits. It also tells us that no identifier begins with a digit or has other characters (such as a decimal point, a comma, or a dollar sign) embedded within. Here are some examples.

valid	invalid	reason
red	~red	~ not a letter
RedHats	Red Hats	blanks not allowed
num1000	num1,000	no comma allowed
dollars	$	no $ allowed

Table 4-3: Pascal Identifiers

Let's consider a few more examples. Suppose you were teaching a class, and you wanted to design a coding system to organize student records. Further assume that you decide to use two letters and a single digit as your scheme. You could formally describe valid codes with the following BNF:

> **<code> ::= <letter> <letter> <digit>**

This states "a *code* is defined as a *letter* followed by another *letter* followed by a *digit*. Assume *letter* and *digit* are defined as before. Examples of valid codes are AB6 and JT4. Examples of invalid codes are 4C and 6XY.

Suppose we wanted to formally describe a person's first name. If we assume a name is composed of one or more letters, we can specify the form of valid names with the following BNF description:

> **<name> ::= <letter> { <letter> }**

This states, "a *name* is a *letter* followed by zero or more *letter*s." We use a BNF description similar to this one any time we wish to define an object whose definition contains an item that is repeated at least once.

Suppose we want to give everyone enrolled in the programming course a computer id based on his or her initials. Since two people can have the same initials, we would permit an optional digit after the initials. Thus, Harry Jay Smith could be HJS1, and Heather Jane Stevens could be HJS2. The following BNF description specifies such valid *ids*.

> **<ids> ::= <initials> [<digit>]**
>
> **<initials> ::= <letter> <letter> <letter>**

This reads, "*ids* are *initials* optionally followed by a *digit*." *Initials* are defined as a sequence of three *letter*s. *Letter* and *digit* are defined as we did previously.

4.1.1. Questions

1. What is a meta-language?

2. What is the most commonly used meta-language for programming languages?

3. What is a meta-symbol?

4. What is the production symbol used in BNF?

5. What is the alternation symbol used in BNF?

6. What is the repetition (0 or more times) symbol used in BNF?

7. What is the optional (0 or 1 times) symbol used in BNF?

4.1.2. Exercises

1. Complete the following formal BNF description for birth dates. Assume birth dates are of the form March 21, 1960.

   > **<birthdate> ::= <month> <date> , <year>**
   >
   > **<date> ::= <digit> <digit>**
   >
   > **<year> ::=**
   >
   > **<month> ::=**
   >
   > **<digit> ::=**

2. Modify the answer to the previous exercise so that <date> can have one or two digits rather than exactly two digits.

3. Modify the answer to the previous exercise so that <year> can have two or four digits.

4. Give a BNF description for telephone numbers of the form 268-3783.

5. Modify the previous BNF description to permit area codes like (412) 268-3783.

6. Give the BNF for a person's full name (first, middle, and last).

7. Modify the previous solution to allow for hyphenated last names.

8. Give the BNF for license plates. Assume it is three letters followed by three digits.

9. Modify your answer to the previous problem to allow digits, letters, or a hyphen as every character except the first of the six.

10. Provide a BNF description for radio call letters. Stations east of the Mississippi River have a W followed by three letters, and stations west of the Mississippi River have a K followed by three letters.

11. Provide a BNF description for aircraft call letters. A valid aircraft call letter is a sequence beginning with the letter N, followed by five digits or by four digits and one letter.

4.2. Operators and Expressions

The term integers immediately brings to mind adding, subtracting, and the whole range of arithmetic. In the last chapter, we saw integer combinations such as `5 + 1` and `GrossPay - taxes`. The ability to combine values plays a big part in programming. Such combinations are technically called **expressions**.

Consider combining two integers by addition. This process is illustrated in Figure 4-1 with what we will call the *addition machine*:

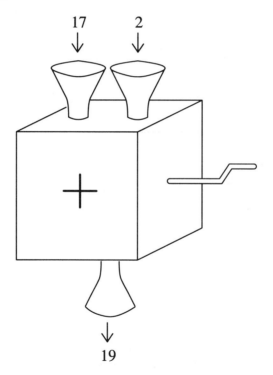

Figure 4-1: Addition Machine

The addition machine illustrates the process of addition applied to the two integers 17 and 2. The addition machine takes two integer values as input and, with a turn of the crank, produces an integer output. The machine itself is called an **operator**, and the input values, 17 and 2, are known as **operands**. The turn of the crank and production of output is known as **evaluation**. These are the three salient features of an *expression*: an *operator*, the *operands*, and *evaluation*.

Definition 4-2: An *operator* takes a specific number of values as input and evaluates to a single value as output.

Definition 4-3: An *operand* is an input value to an operator.

Definition 4-4: *Evaluation* refers to the process of determining the resultant value of applying an operator to its operands.

Though a graphic depiction (like the addition machine) is very useful for illustrating what an operation is, it isn't a very convenient notation. The standard form of notation for an operation is called an *expression*. An expression usually is formed by embedding the symbol for an *operator* between a pair of *operands*. Therefore, we would write the preceding expression as 17 + 2; + represents the addition operator, and 17 and 2 are the operands. Addition is only one of many well-known operators used in integer expressions.

> **Definition 4-5:** An *expression* consists of one or more operands joined by allowable operators.

Operators need not take numbers as operands nor evaluate to numbers. For example, there is an *equality operator* that takes a pair of CHARacters as operands and evaluates to a BOOLEAN value. The equality operator evaluates to TRUE if the operands are the same and evaluates to FALSE otherwise. For example, the expression `'a' = 'd'` evaluates to FALSE. Figure 4-2 depicts the equality operator.

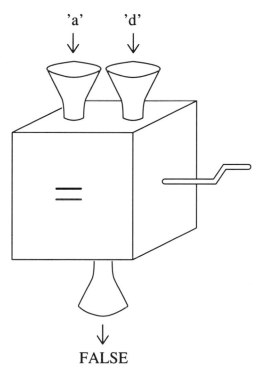

Figure 4-2: Equality Machine

When the expression is evaluated, the characters are found to be either equal or unequal. If they are equal, the expression evaluates to TRUE. If they are unequal, the expression evaluates to FALSE. Thus, `'a' = 'd'` evaluates to FALSE, and `'a' = 'a'` evaluates to TRUE. There is also an equality operator that takes two REAL numbers and evaluates to a BOOLEAN. Similarly, there is one for type INTEGER and one for type BOOLEAN. In Pascal, the = symbol is used to denote all four of the equality operators.

An operator takes operands of some type, be they INTEGER, REAL, BOOLEAN, or CHAR. We say that an operator is *defined over* a type when it can take any values of that same type as operands. For example, the addition operator is defined for values of types REAL and INTEGER but not for values of type BOOLEAN or CHAR. Therefore, the addition operator is defined over the type INTEGER and the type REAL but not over the type BOOLEAN or CHAR. The equality operator, denoted by =, is defined over all four of Pascal's primitive types.

4.2.1. Questions

1. What is an operator?

2. Name three operators in Pascal.

3. What is an operand?

4. What is an expression?

5. Write three Pascal expressions.

6. What does expression evaluation mean?

7. Evaluate and give the result for each of the three Pascal expressions you made up in the previous question.

8. What does it mean for an operator to be defined over a type?

9. Draw a *subtraction machine* that represents the expression `27-4`. Label the parts and briefly describe how it works.

4.3. Pascal's Four Primitive Types

The second chapter of this book developed Karel's programming language. Though there are many similarities between Karel and Pascal, there are also important differences between the two languages. Perhaps the principal difference is the way the two languages solve problems. A Karel program manipulates a robot and beepers in a world of corners, beepers, and walls. It is very visual, physical, and immediate. A Pascal program works quite differently. It manipulates symbolic representations of information called **data**. In Pascal, these data are grouped into meaningful classes, with each class called a **type**.

> **Definition 4-6:** *Data* are the collection of values that are used to symbolically represent information.

> **Definition 4-7:** A *type* is a collection of values grouped into a meaningful class or set.

In the last chapter you saw Pascal's four primitive types: INTEGER and REAL to represent numeric information, CHAR for character information, and BOOLEAN for logical information. This section discusses values and operators for each of the four primitive types.

4.3.1. INTEGER

4.3.1.1. INTEGER Values

Numeric values that can be represented as integers are members of the Pascal type **INTEGER**. The type INTEGER is for integral quantities, which may be either positive or negative. Informally, we may say that a Pascal INTEGER is one or more digits (0 through 9) with an optional sign. To formally specify the syntax, or grammar, of a Pascal INTEGER we use the BNF description seen earlier:

```
<integer> ::=  [ <sign> ] <digit> { <digit> }
```

We may think of the values of type INTEGER as an ordered continuum, as illustrated in the following way:

INTEGER:

$$-\infty \ldots -3 \; -2 \; -1 \; 0 \; 1 \; 2 \; 3 \ldots \infty$$

An INTEGER value is one element from this continuum.

Though we usually think of a continuum as infinite, in reality a computer can represent only a finite number of integers. Therefore, the proper way to think of the computer's representation of the type INTEGER is as follows:

INTEGER:

$$\text{MININT} \ldots -3 \; -2 \; -1 \; 0 \; 1 \; 2 \; 3 \ldots \text{MAXINT}$$

MININT and MAXINT are established by the computer manufacturer and the implementation of Pascal that is being used. You should determine these values for your system.

4.3.1.2. INTEGER Operators

The type INTEGER has five operators. Three of those are for addition, subtraction, and multiplication, which use the symbols +, −, and *, respectively. The other two allowable integer operators are *integer division* and *modular division*, which use the symbols **DIV** and **MOD**, respectively.

The **DIV** operator is simply the value yielded by division (the quotient) truncated to an INTEGER result. It tells us in whole numbers how many times one number goes into another. For example, 7 **DIV** 2 evaluates to 3. The **MOD** operator yields the remainder after dividing two integers. For example, 7 **MOD** 2 yields 1 since there is a remainder of 1 after 7 is divided by 2. **DIV** is kind of like a "keep the change" division, since the remainder is always forgotten. **MOD** is only interested in what the "change" is since it isn't concerned with how many times the divisor goes into the dividend. The following table shows the Pascal INTEGER operations, their operator symbols, and example expressions.

Operation	Operator Symbol	Expression
addition	+	8 + 5
subtraction	−	5 − 2
multiplication	*	12 * 5
integer division	DIV	9 DIV 2
modular division (remainder)	MOD	14 MOD 3

Table 4-4: INTEGER Operations

Note that the MOD operator is not strictly necessary since the result may be obtained using the DIV operator. To determine the the value of modular division for **a** and **b** (**a** MOD **b**), you could take the value from integer division (**a** DIV **b**) and multiply it by the divisor (**b**). The difference between this product ((**a** DIV **b**) * **b**) and **a** would be the result of modular division. In fact, **MOD** is formally defined as follows: **a** MOD **b** = **a** − ((**a** DIV **b**) * **b**). In Standard Pascal, it is an error for **b** to be zero in the expressions **a** DIV **b** or **a** MOD **b**. Additionally, it is an error in Standard Pascal for **b** to be any negative value in the expression **a** MOD **b**. Although addition, subtraction, and multiplication of integers needs little elaboration here, the operators for modular and integer division warrant additional elaboration. The following extensive table illustrates these operators:

Expression	Value
7 DIV 2	3
7 MOD 2	1
7.0 DIV 2	invalid because 7.0 is not a valid INTEGER
6 DIV 2	3
6 MOD 2	0
7 DIV 0	invalid because second operand is 0
7 DIV −2	−3
7 MOD −2	invalid because second operand is negative
−7 MOD 2	−1
−7 DIV 2	−3
−7 DIV −2	3
(7 DIV 2) * 2	6
7 − ((7 DIV 2) * 2)	1
(−7 DIV 2) * 2	−6
−7 − ((7 DIV 2) * 2)	−13
(7 DIV −2) * −2	6
7 − ((7 DIV −2) * −2)	1

Table 4-5: Expressions Using the MOD and DIV Operators

Another integer operator that is often used for math equations is the exponent. Exponentiation is normally indicated by the position of the exponent. For example, 4 raised to the third power is denoted by 4^3. Most programming languages provide an operator for exponentiation, known as the *exponentiation operator* . It is either commonly ^ or **. For the previous example, it would be written as 4^3 or 4 ** 3. Unfortunately, *Standard Pascal has no exponentiation operator*. Therefore, to specify 4^3 in Pascal, you have to write out 4 * 4 * 4. In other words, you have to write out each step of the multiplication.

4.3.1.3. Questions

1. How do you informally describe what constitutes a valid Pascal INTEGER?

2. How do you describe formally (via BNF) what constitutes a valid Pascal INTEGER?

3. What are MININT and MAXINT on your system?

4. How many INTEGER operators does Pascal have? Name each. What symbol denotes each?

5. Does your implementation of Pascal have an exponential operator? If so, what is its symbol?

4.3.1.4. Exercises

1. Which of the following are valid digits, which are valid Pascal integers, which are both, and which are neither?

a. 10	f. '−1'	j. −0	n. 1+
b. −10	g. '10'	k. +0	o. '2'
c. −1	h. +1	l. 0+	p. 1−
d. 1	i. 0	m. 3.14	q. 5,280
e. '1'			

2. Which of the following are valid Pascal expressions? Evaluate those that are valid.

a. 23 + 5	c. 35 − 24	e. 3 ** 4	g. 9 MOD 2
b. −23	d. 3 * 4	f. 9 DIV 2	h. 9 DIV −2

    i. 9 MOD −2   k. −9 MOD 2   m. −9 MOD −2

    j. −9 DIV 2   l. −9 DIV −2   n. 3 ↑ 4

4.3.1.5. Problems

1. Enter and run the following Pascal program.

```
PROGRAM IntegerRange (INPUT, OUTPUT);

BEGIN
    WRITELN(OUTPUT, 'MaxInt = ', MaxInt);
    WRITELN(OUTPUT, 'MinInt = ', MinInt)
END.
```

What does this program illustrate about the implementation of Pascal you are using?

2. Enter and run the following Pascal program.

```
PROGRAM IntegerOverflow (INPUT, OUTPUT);

BEGIN
    WRITELN(OUTPUT, 'MaxInt + 1 = ', MaxInt+1);
    WRITELN(OUTPUT, 'MinInt + 1 = ', MinInt-1)
END.
```

What does this program illustrate about the implementation of Pascal you are using?

3. Write a Pascal program that computes the value of each of the previous expressions in exercise 2. The output should include both the expressions and their results.

4. Write a Pascal program that prompts for and reads two integers, **a** and **b**, and then displays **a DIV b** and **a MOD b**.

4.3.2. REAL

4.3.2.1. REAL Values

In Pascal, if a numeric value has a *decimal point* or an *exponent* (or both), it is of type REAL rather than INTEGER. Therefore, there are three forms that REAL numbers can take in Pascal. They can be written in *decimal notation* and two different forms of *exponential notation*.

Exponential notation (or scientific notation) is a representation designed for very large and very small numbers. For example, the number 602,000,000,000,000,000,000,000 may be written as 6.02×10^{23} in exponential notation (i.e. 6.02 times 10 to the 23rd power). Exponential notation is written as a floating point number (a number between 1 and 10 with a decimal point) times 10 to a given power. A similar notation in Pascal denotes the exponent with the letter E. Therefore, the previous number would be written as 6.02 E 23 in Pascal.

REAL values are formally specified as:

```
<real> ::= <integer> . <unsigned-integer> |
           <integer> E <integer> |
           <integer> . <unsigned-integer> E <integer>
```

where we define <integer> and <unsigned integer> as follows:

```
<integer> ::= [ <sign> ] <unsigned integer>

<unsigned integer> ::= <digit> { <digit> }
```

The following table illustrates both syntactically valid and invalid Pascal REAL numbers.

Valid	Invalid	Reason
0.3	.3	digit must precede decimal point
2.0	2.	digit must follow decimal point
41 E −1	41^−1	^ is an invalid character
−12.3 E 2	−12.2 E 2.8	exponent must be an integer

Table 4-6: Pascal REAL Numbers

We have suggested thinking of a type as a sequence of values. This was easy to do in the case of INTEGER, although in the implementation of INTEGER we had to settle for only those values that fell between some minimum and maximum values. The real numbers are more difficult to represent.

Not only do real numbers extend to positive and negative infinity like the integers, but between any two integers there are infinitely many real numbers! In fact, *between any two real numbers there are infinitely many real numbers*!! For example, between 1 and 2 there are infinitely many real numbers. If we select two numbers from that interval, say 1.5 and 1.6, we realize that there are infinitely many more real numbers between these two. If we then select two more from within this new interval, say 1.52 and 1.53, there are infinitely many more real numbers between these. No matter how close two real numbers are, there are always infinitely more real numbers between them. We use ellipsis notation (...) to indicate this infinity.

REAL:

$$... 1 ... 1.4 ... 1.5 ... 1.6 ... 2 ...$$

$$... 1.5 ... 1.51 ... 1.52 ... 1.53 ... 1.57 ... 1.58 ... 1.59 ... 1.6 ...$$

$$... 1.52 ... 1.521 ... 1.522 ... 1.523 ... 1.527 ... 1.528 ... 1.529 ... 1.53 ...$$

Real numbers represent infinite infinity, but a computer has only a finite memory, so it is easy to see that we need a special type if we are to represent real numbers very well. This helps us to understand why real numbers have their own type and are treated separately from the integers, rather than having a single type called, say, *numeric*.

4.3.2.2. REAL Operators

The type REAL has four operators. Each takes two REAL operands as input and evaluates to a value of type REAL. The following table shows the REAL operations, the operator symbols, and example expressions.

Operation	Operator Symbol	Expression
addition	+	3.2 + 4.1
subtraction	−	6.2 − 2.3
multiplication	*	3.14 * 9.9
division	/	4.35 / 2.718

Table 4-7: REAL Operations

4.3.2.3. Questions

1. Informally described, what constitutes a valid Pascal REAL?

2. Described formally (via BNF), what constitutes a valid Pascal REAL?

3. In how many forms can REAL values be written? Name them and give an example of each.

4. Why are there distinct types for REAL and INTEGER?

5. How many REAL operators does Pascal have? Name each. What symbol is used for each?

4.3.2.4. Exercises

1. Which of the following are valid Pascal values and which are invalid? Explain why each invalid one is not valid.

a. 3.14	d. 3.	g. 0.0	j. 22 E 3
b. −.98	e. 3.00	h. +0.0	k. 22 E −3
c. .98	f. 0.98	i. −0.0	l. 22 ↑ 3

m. 22 ** 3   p. −22 E −3.14   r. −22.7 E −3   t. −22.7 E 17.2

n. −22 E 3   q. −22.7 E 3   s. −22.7 E +17   u. −22.7 E −17.2

o. −22 E 3.14

2. Convert the following into exponential notation (both scientific and Pascal).

a. −34.761   d. 42.181

b. 0.00000000000012   e. +26.2

c. 0.0   f. 0.000000000000000000016

3. Convert the following real numbers to decimal notation.

a. 5.280E3   c. −14E−9   e. 14.53E0

b. 6.624E−27   d. 1E6   f. 0.0E+23

4. Which of the following are valid Pascal expressions? Evaluate the valid ones. Explain why the invalid ones are invalid.

a. 3.14 + 2.24   c. 1.1 * 2.0   e. 9.6 MOD 3.2

b. 9.8 − 3.1   d. 9.6 / 3.2   f. 9.6 DIV 3.2

4.3.2.5. Problems

1. Write a Pascal program that prompts for two REAL numbers and then displays their sum, difference, product, and quotient.

2. Execute the previous program with zero as the first number, then the second number, and also as both numbers.

4.3.3. CHAR

4.3.3.1. CHAR Values

Each computer has a fixed character set, just as each typewriter has a limited set of characters. The type CHAR is this character set, so named because it represents CHARacters. The type CHAR includes all the English lowercase characters, all the English uppercase characters, the ten digits (0 through 9), most familiar punctuation symbols (for example, ? . , : ; !), and many special characters ($ & * #).

Several different character sets are commonly used on computers. Again, this is similar to the typewriter and, like typewriters, these differences are not very important. The exact character set that you will be using depends on the kind of computer you use. Chances are you will be using a character set called the American Standard Code for Information Interchange, or ASCII (pronounced ass'-key) . ASCII is by far the most commonly used character set, and the others are similar to it. We will not cover any other character sets in the body of this text, but some of the more common alternatives appear in Appendix VIII.[2]

There are exactly 128 characters in the ASCII character set, and each has a decimal (base 10) value associated with it in the range 0 through 127. You can determine the decimal value of any particular character in the ASCII character set from the following table by adding the numbers associated with its row and column. For example, the capital letter K is in row 64 and column 11. So the capital letter K is represented by character number 75. Likewise, the lowercase k is represented by character number 107, and the character 2 is represented by character number 50.

---

[2]Another common character set is known as EBCDIC and is used by many IBM computers.

	0	1	2	3	4	5	6	7	8	9	10	11	12	13	14	15
0	^@	^A	^B	^C	^D	^E	^F	^G	^H	^I	^J	^K	^L	^M	^N	^O
16	^P	^Q	^R	^S	^T	^U	^V	^W	^X	^Y	^Z	^[	^\	^]	^^	^_
32		!	"	#	$	%	&	'	(	)	*	+	,	-	.	/
48	0	1	2	3	4	5	6	7	8	9	:	;	<	=	>	?
64	@	A	B	C	D	E	F	G	H	I	J	K	L	M	N	O
80	P	Q	R	S	T	U	V	W	X	Y	Z	[	\	]	^	_
96	`	a	b	c	d	e	f	g	h	i	j	k	l	m	n	o
112	p	q	r	s	t	u	v	w	x	y	z	{	|	}	~

Table 4-8: ASCII Character Set

You may notice that two characters seem to be missing from the previous table because there are *holes* at positions 32 and 127. Actually, these holes are associated with characters, too. ASCII 32 is the space character, which works like the space bar on a typewriter. ASCII 127 is the DEL key, which deletes a single character. ASCII characters 33 through 126 print exactly the character that is associated with that number in the table. These 94 characters (ASCII 33 through ASCII 126) are, not surprisingly, known as the *printing characters* .

You may be wondering about the purpose the first 32 ASCII characters (ASCII 0 through ASCII 31). They are known as *control characters* . There were big plans for these characters back in 1963 when the ASCII standard was proposed. Some of the control characters have names like "End of Transmission" and "Unit Separator" associated with them. But these big ideas never were implemented, so the control characters are used today very sparingly or not at all. For the purposes of this book, we need not concern ourselves with the control characters.

One way to think of the character set is as a finite sequence of values, as illustrated in the following way.

CHAR:

... 0 1 2 ... 7 8 9 ... A B C ... X Y Z ... a b c ... x y z ... | } ~

A character value is then one item selected from this sequence. Every value of the type CHAR appears in Pascal programs between matching single quotes. Note that double quotes will not work. Also note that only one character may be between the single quotes of a value of type CHAR. Therefore, 'a', 'b', and 'c' are valid CHAR values, but 'ab', 'bc', and 'ac' are invalid as values of type CHAR.

You may have noticed that some values seem to be both of type CHAR and type INTEGER. An example is the character 5 (ASCII character 53). It is of type CHAR, but we know that 5 is also an INTEGER. So the question becomes, how do we tell the Pascal INTEGER 5 from the Pascal CHARacter 5? You might wonder if we want to differentiate between the two. The answer is yes. Pascal is a *strongly typed* programming language. This means a value of the language can only be of one type. If we didn't distinguish between CHARs and INTEGERs, the Pascal compiler would not know how to handle data properly. In Pascal programs, the distinction between these two is clarified by enclosing the CHARacter 5 in a pair of single quotes (i.e. '5'). Pascal INTEGERs are are not enclosed in single quotes. Therefore, the compiler treats the CHAR '5' and the INTEGER 5 differently.

There is a special character referred to as the *null character*. This character normally prints nothing, rather than printing as a blank space like the space character. You should determine and make a mental note of what the null character is for the character set you will be using. In the ASCII character set, the first character (ASCII 0) is the null character.

There are no operators that yield output of type CHAR since we do not add or divide characters; in short, there are no operations for characters that are similar to arithmetic operations performed on integers and reals.

4.3.3.2. Questions

1. What character set does your computer use? Use the answer to this question to answer questions 2 through 8. (Appendix VIII on page 547 may provide additional assistance.)

2. What are the decimal values associated with the character 1, the lowercase letter L, and the uppercase letter I?

3. What is the decimal value of the space character?

4. What is the decimal value of the null character?

5. What are the decimal values associated with the uppercase letter A and the lowercase letter a?

6. What are the decimal values associated with the uppercase letter Z and the lowercase letter z?

7. Is there a numerical constant difference from uppercase letters to lowercase letters? (In ASCII there is.) If so, what is it?

8. How many operators does Pascal provide that return values of type CHAR?

9. * Why is 128 a natural choice for the number of characters in a computer's character set? What are the next smaller and next larger natural choices?

4.3.3.3. Exercises

1. What type is '8'?

2. What is the difference between 7 and '7'? What is the type of each?

3. Which of the following are valid Pascal values? For the valid ones, indicate their type. For the invalid ones, indicate why they are not valid.

a. 8	h. '17'	o. "r"	v. '−8'
b. −8	i. 'T'	p. "4"	w. 12
c. 18	j. 'g'	q. "1"	x. "true"
d. '4'	k. 'su'	r. ''''	y. "A"
e. 4	l. 'r	s. 'true'	z. "3"
f. '1'	m. r'	t. '8'	aa. "'"
g. '7'	n. 'r'	u. "−8"	bb. ''''

4.3.4. BOOLEAN

4.3.4.1. BOOLEAN Values

The type BOOLEAN is used to represent logical information and has only two values: FALSE and TRUE. This type is named in honor of George Boole, who first formalized the mathematics of logic.

A formal specification of the type BOOLEAN is:

```
<boolean> ::= FALSE | TRUE
```

Any value other than the two listed above is not a valid Pascal BOOLEAN value. As we will see a little later, the type BOOLEAN is used when we need to know if the result of a computation is TRUE or FALSE. For now, the important point for you to remember is that the type BOOLEAN may be thought of as a list of possible values containing exactly two elements.

4.3.4.2. Relational Operators

A type with only two possible values might seem uninteresting and of little importance. However, there are as many operators that return values of type BOOLEAN as all the other types combined. Moreover, almost all larger programs perform different actions based on different conditions. The conditions are always a form of a BOOLEAN expression. Therefore, understanding BOOLEAN expressions is essential to successful programming.

There is a class of operators that takes a pair of objects from any single Pascal type and evaluates to a BOOLEAN value. They take any two INTEGERs, two REALs, two BOOLEANs, or two CHARacters and evaluate to TRUE or FALSE. These operators are known as **relational operators**.

> **Definition 4-8:** A *relational operator* is an operator that requires exactly two operands of a Pascal primitive type and evaluates to a BOOLEAN value.

The following Table illustrates Pascal's six relational operators.

Symbol	Meaning	Illustration	Evaluation
<	less than	3 < 4	TRUE
>	greater than	3 > 4	FALSE
=	equals	3 = 4	FALSE
<=	less or equal	3 <= 4	TRUE
>=	greater or equal	3 >= 4	FALSE
<>	not equal	3 <> 4	TRUE

Table 4-9: Relational Operators

4.3.4.3. BOOLEAN Operators

Pascal has three operators that take only BOOLEAN expressions as operands and evaluate to a BOOLEAN value: **NOT**, **AND**, and **OR**. **NOT**, commonly referred to as the *negation operator* , returns the opposite of its operand. **AND** yields TRUE if and only if both operands are TRUE. **OR** yields TRUE if either (or both) operands are TRUE. The truth tables in table 4-10 demonstrate these three logical operations.

a	NOT(a)		a	b	a AND b	a OR b
TRUE	FALSE		TRUE	TRUE	TRUE	TRUE
FALSE	TRUE		TRUE	FALSE	FALSE	TRUE
			FALSE	TRUE	FALSE	TRUE
			FALSE	FALSE	FALSE	FALSE

Table 4-10: Truth Tables for **AND**, **OR**, and **NOT**

The following table shows examples for these logical operations.

a	NOT(a)		a	b	a AND b	a OR b
2 = 2	FALSE		2 = 2	3 = 3	TRUE	TRUE
2 < 3	FALSE		2 < 3	9 = 6	FALSE	TRUE
3 < 2	TRUE		3 < 2	5 = 5	FALSE	TRUE
3 > 2	FALSE		2 > 3	8 = 3	FALSE	FALSE

Table 4-11: Truth Table Examples for **AND**, **OR**, and **NOT**

The last three tables have illustrated relational and BOOLEAN operators, but the BOOLEAN expressions you will be putting in your programs will be a bit different. The difference arises because when you write your programs, the exact values will be unknown. You will be using such BOOLEAN expressions as `GasMileage < 10` and `HoursWorked > NormalWorkWeek` rather than `2 < 3` and `3 = 3`. We chose the BOOLEAN expressions in the previous tables because they are easy to understand and evaluate.

4.3.4.4. Questions

1. How many BOOLEAN values are there? What are they in Pascal?

2. What are all of Pascal's relational operators and their symbols?

3. What are all of Pascal's Boolean operators and their symbols?

4. Which of the following are valid Pascal values? For the valid ones, indicate their type. For the invalid ones, indicate why they are not valid.

a. 13	g. 17.4	m. 824	s. −8.24 E 3
b. −.4	h. 'FALSE'	n. 8.24	t. 8.24 E −3
c. TRUE	i. 743	o. −8.24	u. 8 E 24
d. 17.8	j. "TRUE"	p. +8.24	v. 8 E −24
e. +	k. 0.4	q. 'TRUE'	w. −8 E 24
f. −431	l. 008	r. 8.24 E 3	

4.4. Some Finer Points of Operators, Types, and Evaluation

4.4.1. Binary and Unary Operators

One way that operators are classified is by the number of operands they have. Recall the little machines with cranks we used to graphically indicate operations. Each operand is indicated by an input funnel on top of the operation machine. Its number of operands is simply the number of input funnels. Note that operation machines always have exactly one output funnel.

Operators requiring two operands are known as **binary operators**, and operators requiring one operand are known as **unary operators**. All the operators we have seen thus far have been binary operators except NOT. NOT is the only unary operator we have seen. The NOT operator precedes its operand. The following figure graphically depicts the negation operator, NOT.

Figure 4-3: Negation Operator

Definition 4-9: A *binary operator* is an operator that requires exactly two operands.

Definition 4-10: A *unary operator* is an operator that requires exactly one operand.

Up to this point, we have mentioned only one unary operator, **NOT**. However, Pascal has a *unary minus operator* for both INTEGERs and REALs to represent negative values. The symbol used for both is − , and it precedes its operand. The following table shows examples of Pascal's unary operators.

Expression	Value
−3 + 4	1
3 − − 4	7
−(3 + 4)	−7
−(−3 − − 4)	−1
−3.14 − − 2.07	−1.07
−total *where total = 7*	−7
NOT(3 < 4)	FALSE

Table 4-12:   Examples of Unary Operators

4.4.2. Precedence Rules

Consider the arithmetic expression `3 + 4 * 6`. Does it have the same value as `7 * 6` (i.e. 42) or `3 + 24` (i.e. 27)? The value of the expression depends on the order in which the operators of the expression are applied. If you have studied algebra you may recall that multiplication has *precedence* over addition. Therefore, the multiplication is performed first; the addition is performed last. Hence, the expression evaluates to 27.

Likewise, the value of a Pascal expression depends on the order in which the operators are applied. The rules that describe which operators precede the others in evaluation of expressions are known as *operator precedence rules* . For Pascal, the precedence from highest to lowest is shown in the following table.

```
NOT unary-minus

AND  *  /  DIV  MOD

OR  +  −

<  >  <=  >=  =  <>
```

Table 4-13:   Pascal Precedence Rules

The unary operators have the highest precedence, so **NOT** and unary-minus are evaluated first. **AND**, *, /, **DIV**, and **MOD** have second highest precedence; **OR**, +, and − are third. The relational operators have the lowest precedence. When several operators of the same precedence are to be evaluated, the evaluation is done from left to right.

To alter the order of evaluation, we may use *parentheses*, which have precedence over all operators. Parts of an expression enclosed in parentheses are called subexpressions, and they are evaluated first. The precedence rules listed above apply to expressions within parentheses. Consider again the previous expression

```
3 + 4 * 6
```

The multiplication will be performed first and then the addition. If we wanted the addition to be performed first, we would enclose the addition subexpression in parentheses.

```
(3 + 4) * 6
```

This expression evaluates to 42 rather than 27.

Recall the little machines introduced earlier in this chapter as a model for operators. We can extend that model for more complicated expressions. The extension permits the output (result) of one operator to be input (operand) to another operator. Figure 4-4 illustrates this idea for the expression 3 * 5 + 4:

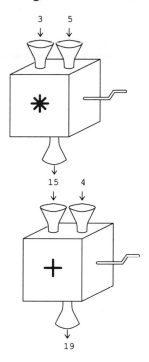

Figure 4-4: Graphic Depiction of 3 * 5 + 4

This model may be used for very complicated expressions. Figure 4-5 illustrates the model for the expression 3 - (2 * 3 + 4 * 5):

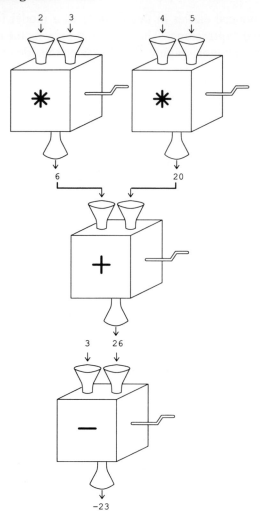

Figure 4-5: Graphic Depiction of `3 - (2 * 3 + 4 * 5)`

Consider the following Pascal expression.

`3 < 4 AND 4 < 7`

Since the AND operator has higher precedence than the relational operators, it is evaluated first. Essentially, the compiler tries to do the following:

`3 < (4 AND 4) < 7`

Since AND requires two BOOLEAN values rather than two INTEGER values, we would get a compiler error. For such expressions, we must parenthesize the expression to alter the order of evaluation:

`(3 < 4) AND (4 < 7)`

We often parenthesize complicated expressions just to clarify the evaluation for someone else who may have to read the program. It is a good idea to parenthesize expressions liberally because redundant parentheses enhance readability without affecting evaluation. Whenever we have *nested parentheses* (one pair of parentheses enclosed in another pair), the innermost pair is always evaluated first.

The following table demonstrates some expressions, their types, and values.

Expression	Type	Value
314	INTEGER	314
3.14	REAL	3.14
11 + 2	INTEGER	13
14 DIV 5	INTEGER	2
14 MOD 5	INTEGER	4
14.0 / 5.0	REAL	2.8
'B'	CHAR	'B'
2 < 4	BOOLEAN	TRUE
7 >= 8	BOOLEAN	FALSE
FALSE	BOOLEAN	FALSE
TRUE AND (7 < 8)	BOOLEAN	TRUE
(2 < 4) OR (7 >= 8)	BOOLEAN	TRUE
NOT(2 < 4)	BOOLEAN	FALSE
(2 < 4) AND (7 >= 8)	BOOLEAN	FALSE
NOT((2 < 4) OR (7 < 8))	BOOLEAN	FALSE

Table 4-14: Example Pascal Expressions

Consider the last expression in the previous table. Since the negation operator is the outermost operator, we know the entire expression is of type BOOLEAN. First, the two parenthesized subexpressions (operands of the **OR** operator) are evaluated. (2 < 4) evaluates to TRUE, and (7 < 8) evaluates to TRUE. So the expression is equivalent to NOT(TRUE OR TRUE), which is equivalent to NOT(TRUE). Therefore, the expression evaluates to FALSE.

4.4.3. Type Coercion

When we discussed type earlier in this chapter, we said a type not only specifies a set of possible values but also a set of allowable operators. Every operator required all its operands to be of the same type. This prevented such things as adding integers and characters. What about adding an integer and a real? Intuitively, we know that they are both numbers and therefore we should be able to add them together. However, they are of different types and therefore are not technically combinable.

To facilitate combining INTEGERs and REALs, the four primitive arithmetic operators are exceptions to the rule that all operands must be of the same type. The operators +, −, and * will all take two integers, two reals, or one of each. If either operand is a REAL value, the other operand is automatically converted to a REAL before the operation is performed, and the result will be a REAL. The / operator converts all operands to REAL values, and always returns a REAL result. Hence 6 / 2 returns 3.0. This automatic conversion of values from one type to another is called *type coercion*.

4.4.4. Type Cardinality

Cardinality is the mathematical term that captures the notion of "how many." You might be thinking that the term *number* captures the notion of "how many" perfectly well (How many players are on a basketball team? How many plus 2 makes 3?). It turns out that a number is insufficient to satisfactorily describe how many values exist for a type, although for types with a finite number of values a number is quite fine. The deficiency arises when we consider those types with infinitely many values. Consider the difference between integer and real: Both have an infinite number of possible values, but there are more real values than integer values (because between each two integers there are infinitely many real values). We wish to avoid a discussion on the orders of infinity. However, integers are said to be *countably infinite* and reals are *uncountably infinite* . This separation is maintained for computer language types also. If a type has no more values than that of type integer (countably infinite), then it is said to be an *ordinal type* . In Pascal, that means INTEGER, BOOLEAN, and CHAR are all ordinal types, but REAL is not.

4.5. Chapter Summary

- A **meta-language** is a language used to describe another language.

- **Meta-symbols** are simply symbols of the meta-language.

- The BNF production symbol ::= separates the object being defined from its definition.

- The meta-symbols < > enclose names of objects of the language being defined.

- The BNF alternation symbol | separates two valid choices, which means either may be chosen but not both.

- The BNF repetition symbols { } enclose objects that may be repeated zero or more times.

- The meta-symbols [ ] enclose objects that may exist zero or one times.

- An **operator** takes a specific number of values as input and evaluates to a single value as output.

- An **operand** is an input value to an operator.

- **Evaluation** refers to the process of determining the resultant value of applying an operator to its operands.

- An **expression** consists of one or more operands joined by allowable operators.

- Pascal has four primitive types: INTEGER, REAL, BOOLEAN, and CHAR.

- Pascal has four binary REAL operators: addition (+), subtraction (−), multiplication (*), and division (/).

- Pascal has five binary INTEGER operators: addition (+), subtraction (−), multiplication (*), integer division (DIV), and modular division (MOD).

- Pascal has six *relational operators*: less than (<), greater than (>), equal to (=), less than or equal (<=), greater than or equal (>=), and not equal (<>).

- Pascal has three BOOLEAN operators: NOT, AND, and OR.

- Standard Pascal has no operators defined over the type CHAR.

- A **binary operator** is an operator that requires exactly two operands.

- A **unary operator** is an operator that requires exactly one operand.

- Pascal has two unary operators: NOT and *unary minus*.

- Pascal expressions are evaluated according to the *rules of precedence*.

- *Type coercion* is the automatic conversion of a value from one type to another type. Pascal's REAL operators coerce INTEGER operands into REAL operands.

- If a type has no more possible values than the type integer, then it is considered to be an *ordinal type*. In Pascal, types INTEGER, BOOLEAN, and CHAR are ordinal types, but REAL is not.

- CHARacter values are always delimited with single quotes in Pascal. This is done to distinguish the value from an identifier.

4.6. Summary of Terms

• meta-language	• alternation	• INTEGER
• Backus-Naur Form (BNF)	• repetition	• REAL
• meta-symbol	• data	• BOOLEAN
• production	• type	• ASCII
• production symbol	• CHAR	• printing characters

- control characters
- exponent
- exponential notation
- scientific notation
- identifier
- operator
- operand
- expression

- evaluation
- MOD
- DIV
- NOT
- AND
- OR
- binary operator

- unary operator
- unary minus
- relational operator
- operator precedence
- type coercion
- type cardinality
- ordinal type

4.7. Chapter Questions

1. What are Pascal's four primitive types?

2. What is an operator?

3. What is an operand?

4. What are the four Pascal binary operators defined for REAL expressions? What are their symbols in Pascal?

5. What are the five Pascal binary operators defined for INTEGER expressions? What are their symbols in Pascal?

6. Name and give the symbols for all of Pascal's relational operators.

7. What are the three Pascal operators defined for BOOLEAN expressions? What are their symbols in Pascal?

8. What is a binary operator?

9. What is a unary operator?

10. What are the Pascal unary operators?

11. What are the rules of precedence in expression evaluation?

12. What is type coercion? Give an example in Pascal.

13. What is an ordinal type?

14. Which of Pascal's primitive types are ordinal types? Which are not?

15. What is the type and value of each of the following expressions?

a. 14 * 3

b. 29 MOD 4

c. (3 + 7) < (4063 DIV 2)

d. true OR false

e. true AND false

f. false OR false OR false OR true

g. TRUE > FALSE

h. 17 DIV 3

i. 17 MOD 3

j. 17.0 DIV 3

k. 16 DIV 2

l. 16 MOD 2

m. 9 / 3

n. 10 / 2

o. 10 / 1

p. 4*5 + 3

q. 3+4 * 5

r. 17 MOD −3

s. 17 DIV −3

t. −17 MOD 3

u. −17 DIV 3

v. −17 MOD −3

w. −17 DIV −3

x. (17 DIV 3) * 3

y. 17 − ((17 DIV 3) * 3)

z. (−17 DIV 3) * 3

aa. −17 − ((17 DIV 3) * 3)

bb. (17 DIV −3) * −3

cc. 17 − ((17 DIV −3) * −3)

dd. 1<2 AND 2<3

ee. NOT (3 >= 1) AND ((14 MOD 2) <> 6)

ff. NOT ((3>=1) AND ((14 MOD 2) <> 6))

gg. 5 / 1

hh. (1<2) OR NOT((sum>min) AND (sum<max) AND (max>min))

ii. 6 / 3.0

jj. 6.0 / 3

kk. (1=2) AND ((value>0) OR (value<0))

16. Draw an operation machine for each of Pascal's five binary INTEGER operators. Illustrate them with the operands 5 and 2.

17. Draw an operation machine for the exponentiation operator.

18. Using the expression **5 * 4 + 8 − 3**, illustrate the various ways it could be evaluated through changes in precedence.

Chapter 5: Details of Input, Output, and Variables

Chapter 3 provided a quick tour through some of the features of programming, without focusing on fundamentals or details. Chapter 4 provided the fundamentals, and in this chapter we will look at the details to better understand how Pascal works.

5.1. The Details of Output

The ability to generate output is an essential feature of any programming language. After a program computes a result, output communicates the result to the user. A program that never tells the user the result would not be very useful. *Every useful program generates output.*

5.1.1. The Output Display

Recall our description of the Turing Machine in Chapter 1 (page 8). The notion is that output is written one symbol at a time to the cells of the output tape. The Turing Machine is a useful model for describing Pascal's output. It is customary for output devices to be arranged in rows and columns of cells. You can think of this as a Turing tape that is torn at regular intervals and stuck onto a display device, forming a grid. There is some variation as to the number of cells in each row and the number of rows on each screen. The most common displays consist of 24 rows, each consisting of 80 cells. In this and following chapters, we assume that output is written to the standard output device, which is the display screen on the user's terminal. A good way to think of this display screen is to imagine that it is overlaid with a sheet of graph paper as illustrated below:

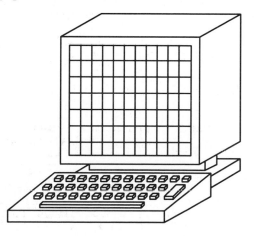

Figure 5-1: Computer Terminal with Graph Paper Screen

The output is written to the screen one symbol at a time until all the cells of the first row are filled, and then output starts on the next row. Our illustration has only 7 rows with 11 cells per row, but it illustrates the important points of output. Recall our first Pascal program, which wrote *Hello world*. The following illustration shows graphically that simple program and its output according to our model:

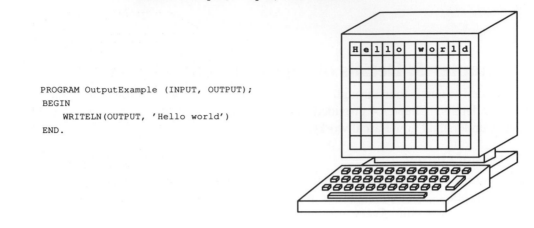

```
PROGRAM OutputExample (INPUT, OUTPUT);
BEGIN
     WRITELN(OUTPUT, 'Hello world')
END.
```

5.1.2. The Literal String and the Single Quote

The previous illustration shows the predefined procedure WRITELN with the literal string 'Hello world'. Recall that a literal string is just a sequence of characters enclosed in matching single quotes. Suppose we wanted to output a literal string that included a single quote or apostrophe. If we wanted to write *Jim's dog*, we might be tempted to try:

WRITELN(OUTPUT, 'Jim's dog')

However, the Pascal compiler interprets *'Jim's dog'* as the literal string *'Jim'* followed by the characters *s dog'*, which is altogether different. Since the single quote ' is used as the delimiter for a literal string, it cannot be used to print a single quote. To write a single quote, we use '', two single quotes. Note this is *not* the same as a double quote, ". The following example illustrates this point:

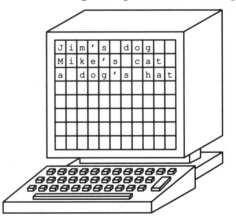

```
PROGRAM QuoteExample (INPUT, OUTPUT);
BEGIN
     WRITELN(OUTPUT, 'Jim''s dog');
     WRITELN(OUTPUT, 'Mike''s cat');
     WRITELN(OUTPUT, 'a dog''s hat')
END.
```

Note that each of the three literal strings contained two single quotes within their matching single quotes. Though apostrophes are indicated in literal strings with two single quotes, the output only contains one apostrophe.

5.1.3. Writing Output

In addition to **WRITELN**, Pascal has a second predefined statement to write expressions, called **WRITE**. The difference between WRITELN and WRITE is that WRITELN advances to the next line *after* it writes output, whereas WRITE remains on the same line. The effect is that WRITELN always leaves the write head (terminal's cursor) at the beginning of the next line, whereas **WRITE** leaves the write head immediately after the last character written. The following two examples illustrate this difference:

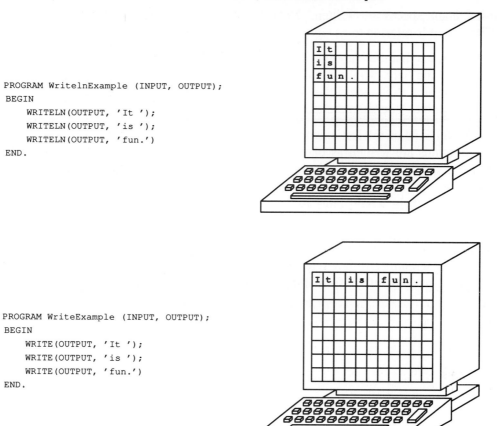

```
PROGRAM WritelnExample (INPUT, OUTPUT);
BEGIN
    WRITELN(OUTPUT, 'It ');
    WRITELN(OUTPUT, 'is ');
    WRITELN(OUTPUT, 'fun.')
END.
```

```
PROGRAM WriteExample (INPUT, OUTPUT);
BEGIN
    WRITE(OUTPUT, 'It ');
    WRITE(OUTPUT, 'is ');
    WRITE(OUTPUT, 'fun.')
END.
```

The forms of these two statements are as follows:

WRITE(OUTPUT, expression)

WRITELN(OUTPUT, expression)

5.1.4. Output Format Specification

Each expression written to the output screen occupies some number of cells or columns on the screen. We mentioned briefly in Chapter 3 that it is possible to format output. A programmer formats output by specifying in how many cells the output is to be written. For all expressions, it is possible to specify the *total fieldwidth* (total number of columns). For expressions of type REAL, it is possible to specify the number of *decimal places* in addition to the total fieldwidth. Below we illustrate formatting for expressions of various types:

```
PROGRAM FormatExample (INPUT, OUTPUT);
BEGIN
    WRITELN(OUTPUT, 5 + 7:4);
    WRITELN(OUTPUT, '*':3);
    WRITELN(OUTPUT, 'The End.':9);
    WRITELN(OUTPUT, FALSE:7);
    WRITELN(OUTPUT, 528.2:10:1)
END.
```

The INTEGER expression, *5 + 7*, is evaluated, and the result, *12*, is written on the first row in a field 4 columns wide. The **:4** denotes a total fieldwidth of 4 columns. Since the output requires only 2 of the

4 columns, 2 blank spaces are written. Note that the output comes after (to the right of) the 2 blank spaces. The output is referred to as *right justified*.

Right justified means that there are no blank spaces in the right portion of the field; any extra spaces go on the left side of the field. Right justified is also referred to as *right aligned* or sometimes *flush right*. Compilers conforming to Standard Pascal right justify all output. Many compilers do not adhere to the standard on this point. You should check to see if the compiler you are using does.

The second WRITELN of the last example writes the character value '*' in a fieldwidth of 3 columns. The 2 extra columns are written as blank spaces to the left of the *. Similarly, the third WRITELN writes the literal string *'The End.'* in a field 9 columns wide, with the first columns blank. The fourth WRITELN writes the BOOLEAN value *FALSE*[1] in a field of 7 columns. Note that had we written the BOOLEAN *TRUE*, there would have been 3 initial blank spaces instead of 2. The last WRITELN writes the REAL value 528.2 in a total field of 10 columns with exactly 1 decimal place. The extra columns are filled with blank spaces as usual.

Recall that the programmer is not required to format output and may use default formatting. The following table shows the default formatting for each of the types of expressions shown thus far:

Expression Type	Default Fieldwidth
characters	1
literal strings	same as number of characters in literal string
integers	implementation defined
reals	implementation defined
booleans	implementation defined

Table 5-1:   Default Formatting Fieldwidth

Including the use of default formatting, there are a total of three forms of output statements:

1. Free format: No specification of fieldwidth—the system *default fieldwidth* is used.

```
WRITE(OUTPUT, expression )
WRITELN(OUTPUT, expression )
```

2. Single format: Specification of overall fieldwidth (usually used with INTEGERS, CHARacters, BOOLEANS, and literal strings).

```
WRITE(OUTPUT, expression:fieldwidth )
WRITELN(OUTPUT, expression:fieldwidth )
```

3. Double format: Specification of fieldwidth and number of decimal places (used solely with expressions of type REAL).

```
WRITE(OUTPUT, realexpression:fieldwidth:decimalplaces )
WRITELN(OUTPUT, realexpression:fieldwidth:decimalplaces )
```

Fieldwidth and *decimalplaces* are both INTEGER expressions.

You might be wondering what happens if only one width is specified for an expression of type REAL. If only one width is specified, the value of the REAL expression is written in *exponential notation* using the specified width as a total fieldwidth. In fact, that is how exponential output is achieved. Although most implementations of Pascal use exponential notation as the default format for REAL expressions, you should use single formatting if you want exponential notation. Exponential notation is also called *floating point notation*, and nonexponential notation is called *fixed point notation*. The following example shows both fixed and floating point output:

---

[1]Standard Pascal does not specify uppercase or lowercase for BOOLEAN output. Therefore, your implementation might write FALSE, false, or perhaps False.

```
PROGRAM FixedFloatingExample (INPUT, OUTPUT);
BEGIN
     WRITELN(OUTPUT, 528.2:10);
     WRITELN(OUTPUT, 528.2:10:1)
END.
```

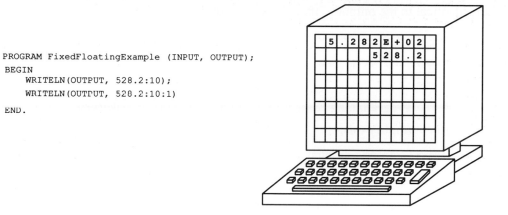

The following table summarizes expression formatting for WRITE and WRITELN.

Expression <u>T</u>ype	Fieldwidth <u>D</u>esignator
characters, booleans, and literal strings	Take a single designator for fieldwidth.
integers	Take a single designator for fieldwidth; allow one for sign.
reals (fixed)	Print with a decimal point and require both a total fieldwidth and the number of digits following the decimal point. The decimal point occupies one column of the total fieldwidth. Allow one column for sign also.
reals (floating)	Take a single designator for fieldwidth; allow one for sign and one for decimal point.

Table 5-2: Formatting Output

You may be wondering what happens if you specify a fieldwidth that is too small. Suppose you have an INTEGER expression of four digits and try to write it in a field specified to be three columns (e.g. **WRITELN(OUTPUT, 5280:3)**). Commonly, Pascal will fill the specified fieldwidth and truncate the remaining output. Other, less common, solutions are to print a field of asterisks (***) or use the default fieldwidth. Standard Pascal does not dictate how the compiler should act in this case, so the handling of this situation is implementation defined.

If no format specification is given, the default fieldwidth is used, and it may be different for each type of expression. The only advantage to using the default fieldwidth is that you can be sure that the fieldwidth will never be too small. We strongly suggest you determine the default output formatting for all the primitive types and literal strings and determine how your system justifies. Since default formatting changes from one compiler to the next, we discourage the use of default formatting; the programmer should always specify the format of all output.

5.1.5. Writing Multiple Expressions
Consider the following program:

```
PROGRAM WriteStars (INPUT, OUTPUT);
BEGIN
    WRITE(OUTPUT, '*');
    WRITE(OUTPUT, 6+2);
    WRITE(OUTPUT, '*');
    WRITELN(OUTPUT)
END.
```

Programming Example 5-1: Writing Multiple Expressions

The output is identical to the output of the following, simpler program.

```
PROGRAM WriteStars (INPUT, OUTPUT);
BEGIN
    WRITE(OUTPUT, '*', 6+2, '*');
    WRITELN(OUTPUT)
END.
```

Programming Example 5-2:   Combining WRITE Statements

In fact we can further simplify this:

```
PROGRAM WriteStars (INPUT, OUTPUT);
BEGIN
    WRITELN(OUTPUT, '*', 6+2, '*')
END.
```

Programming Example 5-3:   Combining WRITE and WRITELN Statements

WRITE and WRITELN display arbitrarily many expressions. Therefore, they may be combined into fewer statements with each expression separated by a comma.

Recall that the difference between WRITE and WRITELN is that WRITELN always finishes by placing the write head (cursor) at the beginning of a new line. This means that WRITELN(OUTPUT) executed when the write head is at the beginning of a blank line has the effect of writing a blank line.

5.1.6. When Expressions Are Actually Written

WRITE and WRITELN do not always cause output to be displayed on the terminal screen. Oftentimes, systems will print on the display device only after a carriage-return—supplied either by a WRITELN or the user pressing the return key—is encountered. This is called **buffered output**. The idea is that a computer's resources are most efficiently used when it outputs a line of information at a time, rather than a character at a time.

> **Definition 5-1:** A system with *buffered output* writes whole lines. In such systems, WRITE collects output, and WRITELN actually displays it.

The implication of this may be realized with the following example that simply prompts the user for a value and then reads it.

```
    WRITE(OUTPUT, 'Enter value: ')
    READLN(INPUT, value)
```

Note that the prompt is written with a WRITE statement and not a WRITELN. If the output is buffered, the prompt will not be written to the user's screen until *after* the user enters a value and a carriage return. A system with buffered output can clearly create subtle problems. Once again, beware that output may be buffered on the system that you are using. We suggest you determine how your system works.

5.1.7. Questions

1. What delimits literal strings in Pascal?

2. How do you get an apostrophe or single quote in output?

3. Name Pascal's two predefined output statements. How do they differ?

4. There are three forms of each output statement. Name and describe each.

5. What does WRITELN(OUTPUT) do?   What does WRITELN(OUTPUT); WRITELN(OUTPUT) do?

6. How many field designators do REAL, INTEGER, CHARacter, and BOOLEAN expressions require? How about literal strings?

7. How do you get expressions of type REAL written in exponential, or floating-point, notation?

8. How do you get expressions of type REAL written in nonexponential, or fixed-point, notation?

9. What happens if output is not formatted by the programmer?

5.1.8. Exercises

1. What is the default fieldwidth on your system for each of the following?

    a. INTEGER   d. BOOLEAN

    b. REAL   e. literal string

    c. CHAR

2. Does your system left or right justify each of the following?

    a. INTEGER   d. BOOLEAN

    b. REAL   e. literal string

    c. CHAR

3. What happens on your system if the programmer-specified width is too small?

    a. INTEGER   d. BOOLEAN

    b. REAL   e. literal string

    c. CHAR

4. Does your system buffer output? Determine this empirically.

5. What do each of the following statements write to the terminal?

a.	`WRITELN(OUTPUT, 43:3)`	n.	`WRITELN(OUTPUT, 'computer':8)`
b.	`WRITELN(OUTPUT, -387:7)`	o.	`WRITELN(OUTPUT, 'computer':4)`
c.	`WRITELN(OUTPUT, 813:2)`	p.	`WRITELN(OUTPUT, 'computer')`
d.	`WRITELN(OUTPUT, 18)`	q.	`WRITELN(OUTPUT, 'computer''s screen')`
e.	`WRITELN(OUTPUT, 25.916:8:3)`		
f.	`WRITELN(OUTPUT, 25.916:8:1)`	r.	`WRITELN(OUTPUT, '''')`
g.	`WRITELN(OUTPUT, 25.916:8:0)`	s.	`WRITELN(OUTPUT, '"')`
h.	`WRITELN(OUTPUT, 25.916:10)`	t.	`WRITELN(OUTPUT, '''')`
i.	`WRITELN(OUTPUT, 25.916:5)`	u.	`WRITELN(OUTPUT, 'TRUE')`
j.	`WRITELN(OUTPUT, 25.916)`	v.	`WRITELN(OUTPUT, TRUE)`
k.	`WRITELN(OUTPUT, 'B':2)`	w.	`WRITELN(OUTPUT, TRUE AND FALSE)`
l.	`WRITELN(OUTPUT, 'B':3)`	x.	`WRITELN(OUTPUT, 'TRUE AND FALSE')`
m.	`WRITELN(OUTPUT, 'B')`	y.	`WRITELN(OUTPUT, '''TRUE AND FALSE''')`

5.1.9. Problems

1. Write a Pascal program to display the following message: *I've a notion to sail the world's oceans to see the Queen's lands.*

2. Write a Pascal program that displays one apostrophe and skips to a new line.

3. Modify the previous program to write two apostrophes and skip to a new line.

4. Modify the previous program to write three apostrophes and skip to a new line.

5. Write a program that displays '5 + 7 = 12' on one line.

6. Modify the previous program to display each number on a new line, with the 5, 7, and 12 formatted as you would write them with a pencil and paper.

7. Write a Pascal program that displays all of the expression from Exercise 5 of the last section.

5.2. Variables and Assignment

Suppose we are planning to take up the game of tennis and wish to buy ourselves rackets. A friend has suggested a particular make and model racket. We decide on this model but want to get it for a good price. We call the local sporting goods stores and a few tennis shops. As we call, we write the name of each store and its price for the racket. After we have called all the likely retailers, we select the least expensive.

This example is meant to point out that people are accustomed to using paper to record and recall values. When we wish to record values in a computer program, we store the values in pieces of computer memory called **variables**. We saw variables briefly in Chapter 3. In this section, we will consider variables and their use in more detail.

> **Definition 5-2:** A *variable* is a piece of computer memory used to store a value of a given type.

5.2.1. The Variable

Most people are familiar with rectangles. A rectangle is described by its length and width. A rectangle's area is the product of its length and width (**length * width**), and its perimeter is the sum of its four sides (**2*length + 2*width**). The following program example illustrates the use of variables in calculating the perimeter and area of a rectangle.

```
PROGRAM Rectangle (INPUT, OUTPUT);

VAR
    length, width, area, perimeter: INTEGER;

BEGIN
    length := 4;
    width := 3;
    area := length * width;
    perimeter := 2 * length + 2 * width;
    WRITELN(OUTPUT, 'AREA = ', area);
    WRITELN(OUTPUT, 'PERIMETER = ', perimeter)
END.
```

Programming Example 5-4:   Storing and Recalling Values

We will use the example to illustrate the use of variables to store and recall values. The left portion of the illustration is for the program and the right portion is for the program's output. We used a simplified version of this scheme previously in this chapter. Although we no longer include the graph paper grid on the output display screen, we do include a cursor (denoted by _) to indicate the write position. Variables are represented by named boxes. The currently executing instruction is indicated by enclosing it in a rectangle. There is one such illustration for each instruction in the program plus one for the initial situation. The first illustration demonstrates the initial situation.

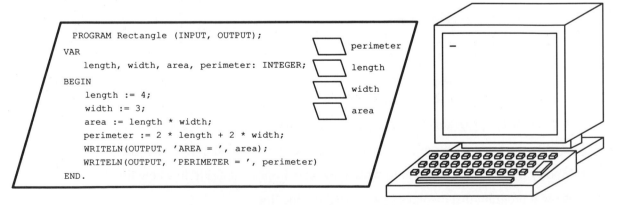

The second illustration demonstrates assignment to the variable **length**. Note that the corresponding box now has a value.

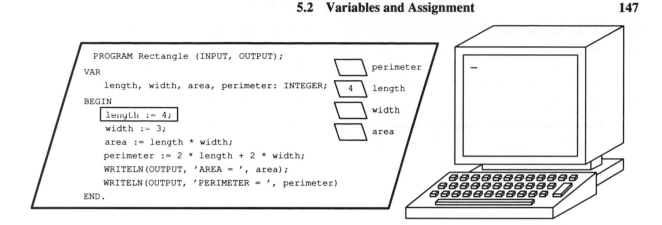

Similarly, the third illustration demonstrates assignment to the variable **width**.

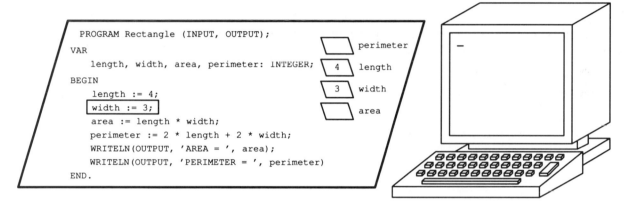

The next illustration demonstrates assignment to the variable **area**. Note that the values of the variables **length** and **width** are recalled to compute a value for **area**.

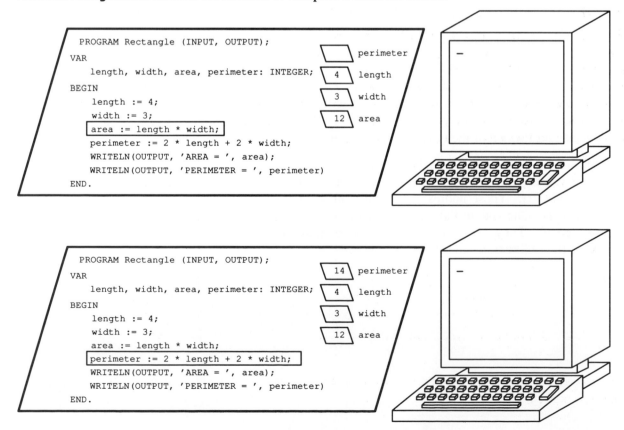

The next two illustrations demonstrate the use of variables in output statements. Note the changes on the display screen.

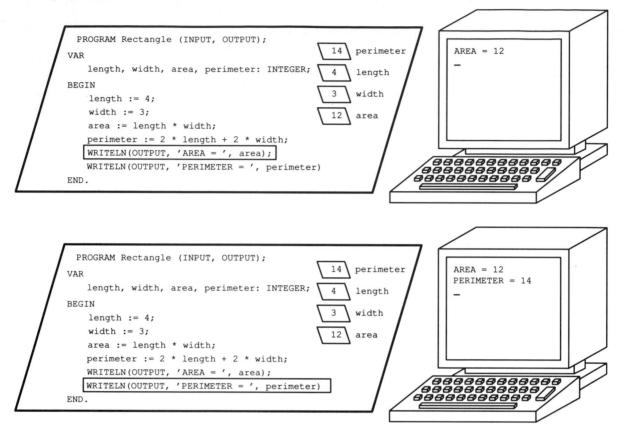

The previous series of illustrations demonstrates storing values in and recalling values from variables. We have developed this type of illustration series to demonstrate these and other programming concepts. We will use it extensively throughout this text. Be sure you understand both the simulation series and the concepts they demonstrate.

5.2.1.1. Properties of a Variable

Variables in Pascal have three properties: *name*, *type*, and *value*. A variable's *name* provides us with a way of referring to it. The *type* of a variable specifies its set of possible values. The *value* of a variable is the specific element of the possible set of values that it currently holds. For example, if we have a variable named **valid** of the type BOOLEAN, its value could be either TRUE or FALSE.

Variables may be thought of as boxes in a computer's memory where the programmer may store particular values. A computer associates a unique number with each cell of memory; each number is called an *address*. These addresses typically are expressed as numbers in base 8 (octal) or base 16 (hexadecimal). One way to think of memory is as a vast array of boxes, each with a number (address) stamped on it. They are similar to the wall of mail boxes found in your local post office. The following figure illustrates this view.

01	02	03	04
05	06	07	08
09	10	11	12
13	14	15	16

Figure 5-2: Computer Memory as an Array of Mail Boxes

The four variables of our last example program all had numeric addresses. Although a computer refers to its memory cells by their addresses, most people prefer to think in terms other than base 16 addresses. Therefore, programming languages routinely provide the programmer with a means for naming the memory locations. The programmer chooses the names for the variables of the program, and a compiler sets up the association between the symbolic identifiers (names convenient for programmers) and the machine addresses (memory locations used by the computer).

You should observe rules of syntax and style when picking variable names. Stylistic considerations include picking names that match the values they hold. Syntactic rules must be followed if a Pascal system is to recognize a variable name. These points are covered in the next section.

5.2.1.2. Details of Variable Names

Variable names must be valid Pascal *identifiers*. Identifiers in Pascal consist of at least one letter, which may be followed by any number of letters or digits. The BNF definition for a Pascal identifier is as follows:

```
<identifier> ::= <letter> { <letter> | <digit> }
```

This definition says that "an <identifier> is defined as a <letter> followed by zero or more <letter>s or <digit>s." Therefore, the following are valid Pascal identifiers: **total**, **sum**, **result**, **GetData**, **operand2**. The following are invalid Standard Pascal identifiers: **get-data**, **%correct**, **#wrong**, **2operand**. The first character must be a letter, and all other characters must be either letters or digits.

The formal specification of <letter> and <digit> follow:

```
<letter> ::= A | B | C | D | E | F | G | H | I | J | K | L | M |
             N | O | P | Q | R | S | T | U | V | W | X | Y | Z |
             a | b | c | d | e | f | g | h | i | j | k | l | m |
             n | o | p | q | r | s | t | u | v | w | x | y | z
```

```
<digit> ::= 0 | 1 | 2 | 3 | 4 | 5 | 6 | 7 | 8 | 9
```

Since every computer has a finite capacity, each implementation of Pascal has some maximum number of characters that may be in an identifier. The maximum varies from one implementation to the next. Environments supporting Standard Pascal must recognize as unique at least the first eight characters of an identifier. Many implementations of Pascal will uniquely recognize longer sequences of characters. Identifiers differing in some character occurring after the maximum length recognized by your system will be considered the same. Therefore, you should determine the maximum recognized by your implementation of Pascal, and you should always make sure no two variables appear the same beyond that limit. For example, if your implementation recognizes the first eight characters, you must be sure your variable names can be distinguished by the first eight characters.

You can choose names that you like for your program's variables, but you should try to use names that best describe the values the variables store. You could name variables v1, v2, v3, and so on, but that would tell us nothing about the values of the variables. Consider, for example, a program that read the following way: `v1 = v2 - v3`. Would you find that the least bit meaningful? What if the program instead read: `age = TodaysDate - BirthDate`? Obviously, the second is more meaningful. You should try to use the most meaningful names for variables that your system will permit. We can often make variables more descriptive by giving them longer names, but we must be sure each is unique within the length checked.

Once a name has been selected for a variable, it is fixed and may not change during program execution. However, the value of a variable can (and typically does) change. The ability of the value to *vary* is what gives it the name *variable*.

We discussed *reserved words* in the first chapter of this unit. As you can see by looking at Appendix IV, the reserved words are all valid Pascal identifiers. These, however, may NOT be redefined by the programmer. Therefore, they may not be used to name a variable. For example, you cannot name a variable "BEGIN" or "END" because they are reserved words in Pascal.

5.2.1.3. Some Details of Variable Type

All Pascal variables have a type. At this point we know of only the four primitive types. Later on, we will learn about other types, but for now all our variables will be of type INTEGER, REAL, BOOLEAN, or CHAR. No variable can be a literal string, because there is no such primitive type in Standard Pascal. However, many implementations of Pascal support a primitive type for *strings*, even though they are not part of Standard Pascal.

In our simulation of Programming Example 5-4, we used parallelograms to represent storage for the four variables. We will illustrate type by associating a shape with each box of memory. In the illustrations involving variables, a CHARacter variable will be a square, an INTEGER variable will be an angled rectangle (parallelogram), a REAL variable will be a pointed rectangle, and a BOOLEAN variable will be a rounded rectangle. The following table summarizes the scheme we have adopted to illustrate different types:

TYPE	SHAPE
Integer	▱
Real	⬡
Boolean	▭
Char	□

Table 5-3: Convention for Differentiating Types with Shapes

The type of a variable is determined by the programmer when the variable is declared.

5.2.1.4. Variable Declarations

For a program to have variables, they must be *declared*. A declaration tells the compiler how many storage cells to reserve, what to name them, and the type of values they may hold. An optional, but often-used, section of the Pascal program form is used just for this purpose. It is known as the *variable declaration section*. The variable declaration section is optional in the sense that it is not required in every Pascal program. It is, however, required for every program that contains variables. Pascal is unlike some other programming languages that do not require explicit variable declaration. The following figure shows a skeleton Pascal program including the variable declaration section.

```
PROGRAM  <program-name> (INPUT, OUTPUT);

VAR
    <any variable declarations>

BEGIN
    <statement 1>;
    <statement 2>;
    <statement 3>;
        .
        .
        .
    <statement N>
END.
```

Programming Example 5-5: Pascal Skeleton with Variable Declaration

The variable declaration section is headed with the reserved word **VAR**. Variable declarations are of the following form: variable name followed by a colon, followed by the variable's type. Hence, we might declare a variable named *number* as an INTEGER in the following way:

```
VAR
    number: INTEGER;
```

Programming Example 5-6: A Variable Declaration

Suppose we are writing a payroll program and we need several variables to represent gross pay, net pay, tax rate, and age. Three of these variables are of type REAL and one is of type INTEGER. One way to declare these is to place one variable per line as follows:

```
VAR
    GrossPay: REAL;
     NetPay: REAL;
    TaxRate: REAL;
        age: INTEGER;
```

Programming Example 5-7: Multiple Variable Declarations

You may have noticed that variable declarations seem to be *terminated* by a semicolon. This is indeed the case. Unlike statements in a Pascal program that are *separated* by a semicolon, Pascal variable declarations are *terminated* by a semicolon.

In addition to declaring one variable per declaration, variables of the same type may be combined in a multiple declaration. Thus, the previous example may be shortened:

```
VAR
    GrossPay, NetPay, TaxRate: REAL;
    age: INTEGER;
```

Programming Example 5-8: Combining Multiple Declarations

Notice in this example that each variable name in the multiple declaration is *separated* by a comma. The BNF defining Pascal's variable declaration follows:

```
<variable declaration part> ::=
    [ VAR <variable declaration> ; { <variable declaration> ; } ]

<variable declaration> ::= <identifier list> : <type>

<identifier list> ::= <identifier> { , <identifier> }

    <type> ::= INTEGER | REAL | BOOLEAN | CHAR
```

A variable declaration can contain any number of identifiers, separated by commas. The final identifier must be followed by a colon and a valid type. The type must be followed by a semicolon, which terminates the declaration.

5.2.1.5. Variable Values

Every variable has exactly one value at any specific point during the execution of the program. The specific value is one of the values in the set of possible values that forms the type of the variable. Thus a variable of type INTEGER cannot have the value TRUE or the value 0.4 or the value '5'. It can only have INTEGER values.

Variables must be represented in a computer's memory. Typically a *computer word*, some number of *bits*[2] (usually a multiple of 8) of memory, is allocated for each variable. Since there is a bit pattern associated with each variable, each variable has a definite value at all times. The interpretation associated with the type determines the variable's value.

Consider a tiny computer with words of memory that consist of two bits each. Such a word could represent the integers from 0 to 3, and it could just as well represent the characters a through d. In general, a single two-bit word of memory can represent any set of four elements, as the following figure shows.

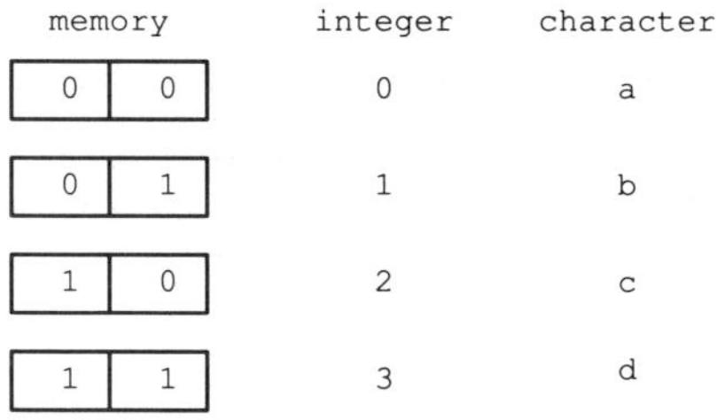

```
memory        integer      character

 0 | 0            0             a

 0 | 1            1             b

 1 | 0            2             c

 1 | 1            3             d
```

Figure 5-3: Representation with a Word of Two Bits

Primary memory in a computer consists of a large number of words, somewhat like the 2-bit words of our tiny example. By way of contrast, ENIAC, which we described on page 6, had just 20 words of memory, whereas personal computers popular over the past few years often have between 48,000 and 64,000 words of primary memory. Some personal computers currently available have 1,000,000 or more words of primary memory. Larger computers may have many millions of words of primary memory.

Consider the example of the tiny machine we just described. Words of that computer were adequate for representing four digits, four letters, or any four values. The problem is, how will the computer interpret a given bit pattern of a word of memory? For example, suppose a variable on the tiny machine holds this value:

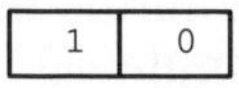

```
 1 | 0
```

Should this be interpreted as a **2** or a **c** (from the previous figure), or should it be interpreted as something else? The answer is that by associating a specific set of possible values (the type) with each

---

[2]Recall that a bit is a BInary digiT, specifically, 0 or 1.

variable, the computer can interpret each memory value. For example, if the variable were of type CHAR, then it would be interpreted as a **c**. Likewise, if it were of type INTEGER, it would be interpreted as a **2**. Thus, type declarations specify how to interpret values in memory.

There are three ways that variables obtain their values:

1. *Explicit assignment* by the program itself (assignment statement).

2. *Implicit assignment* by the program user (reading from input).

3. *Neglect by the programmer.* Even if a variable is not assigned a value by the program, the variable still has some value. Each declared variable has some bit pattern associated with it and therefore some value. Values that are arrived at through neglect are commonly thought of as *garbage*. Some compilers always give variables a specific value upon creation, even if the programmer neglects to do so. Since not all compilers do this, and the ones that do it use different values, we strongly suggest you always give variables a value and never rely on some other value being there.

You should always initialize a variable by explicit assignment or implicit assignment (reading from input) before using the value of the variable. However, it is not necessary to *clear* a variable before reading a value into it. Thus, you never need the following two statements together:

```
variable := SomeInitialValue;
READ(INPUT, variable)
```

5.2.2. The Assignment Statement

We have established that variables are storage cells in the computer's memory. Each variable has a name, a set of allowable values, and exactly one value. One way of giving a variable a value is the *assignment statement*. Let us look a little closer at this statement.

The purpose of the assignment statement is to explicitly assign a value to a variable. We have seen valid assignment statements in this chapter already. A few other examples of valid assignment statements follow:

```
age := 23;
NetPay   := GrossPay - Taxes;
sentinel := MaxLength;
response := 'Y';
index := index + 1;
```

The := (i.e. one colon followed by the = sign) is the *assignment symbol*. Note that two characters are used for the assignment symbol, that is := rather than just =. The symbol = is used for the equality operator in Pascal. The assignment symbol separates two operands. The operand on the left is the name of a variable. The operand on the right is an expression. First, the expression is evaluated. The result of this evaluation is the value assigned to the variable on the left of the assignment symbol. The types of the variable and the expression must be the same.

Consider the assignment statement **age := 23**. The statement is read *"age gets the value 23"* or simply *"age gets 23."* Here, the variable is named **age**, the assignment symbol is :=, and the value of the expression is **23**. The effect is that after execution of this statement, the memory cell referred to by **age** contains the value 23, regardless of the value it may have had previously. The value 23 is of type INTEGER, so assume **age** is declared an INTEGER. What if we declared **age** of type INTEGER but tried to use either of the following assignment statements? **age := 23.88** or **age := 'b'**. Both assignment statements are invalid due to reasons of type. Going back to shapes representing types, the box of memory known as **age** expects an INTEGER (parallelogram) value. The value 'b' is of type CHAR (square), and the value 23.68 is of type REAL (pointed rectangle). Neither value may be assigned to **age**, since they are not of type INTEGER. The old adage "You can't fit a square peg into a round hole" applies to typed languages, such as Pascal. In the model of computation we have created, two variables are of the same type if they have the same shape. Two variables are equal if they have the same shape and the same value.

To demonstrate assignments of more complex expressions to variables of several types, consider the following series of simulations. The first illustration shows the initial state.

```
PROGRAM AssignExample (INPUT, OUTPUT);

VAR
    sum: REAL;
    product, result: INTEGER;
    greater, less, equal: BOOLEAN;

BEGIN
    sum := 3.6 + 2.1;
    greater := sum > 5.5;

    product := 3 * 2 * 4;
    result := product;

    greater := product > result;
    less := product < result;
    equal := NOT(greater) AND NOT(less)
END.
```

sum
product
result
greater
equal
less

The second illustration demonstrates assignment of an expression containing a binary operator. Note that the box representing the variable named **sum** gets the value of **3.6 + 2.1**.

```
PROGRAM AssignExample (INPUT, OUTPUT);

VAR
    sum: REAL;
    product, result: INTEGER;
    greater, less, equal: BOOLEAN;

BEGIN
    sum := 3.6 + 2.1;
    greater := sum > 5.5;

    product := 3 * 2 * 4;
    result := product;

    greater := product > result;
    less := product < result;
    equal := NOT(greater) AND NOT(less)
END.
```

5.7 sum
product
result
greater
equal
less

Since the value of the variable **sum** is currently 5.7, the value of the expression **sum > 5.5** is TRUE.

```
PROGRAM AssignExample (INPUT, OUTPUT);

VAR
    sum: REAL;
    product, result: INTEGER;
    greater, less, equal: BOOLEAN;

BEGIN
    sum := 3.6 + 2.1;
    greater := sum > 5.5;

    product := 3 * 2 * 4;
    result := product;

    greater := product > result;
    less := product < result;
    equal := NOT(greater) AND NOT(less)
END.
```

5.7 sum
product
result
TRUE greater
equal
less

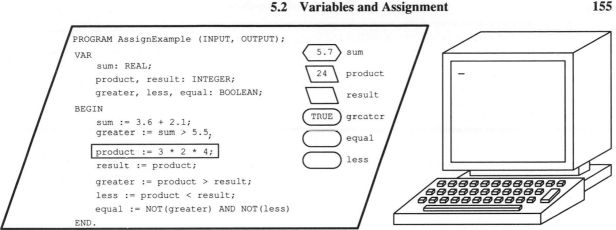

```
PROGRAM AssignExample (INPUT, OUTPUT);

VAR
    sum: REAL;
    product, result: INTEGER;
    greater, less, equal: BOOLEAN;
BEGIN
    sum := 3.6 + 2.1;
    greater := sum > 5.5;
    product := 3 * 2 * 4;
    result := product;

    greater := product > result;
    less := product < result;
    equal := NOT(greater) AND NOT(less)
END.
```

The next illustration demonstrates copying a value from one variable to another. Notice the nondestructive nature of the assignment statement. The variable named **product** is unchanged. Only the variable on the left of the assignment symbol changes.

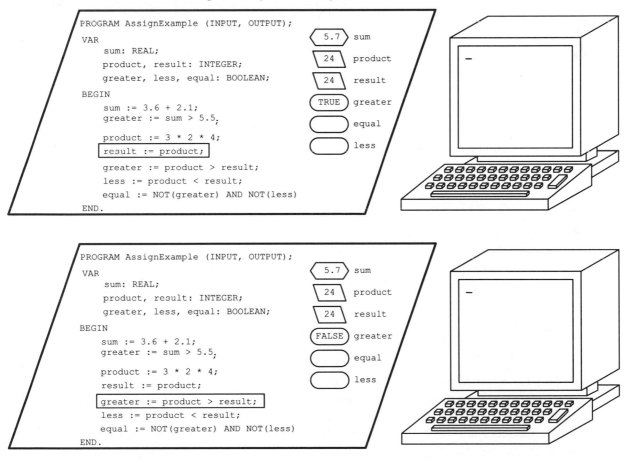

```
PROGRAM AssignExample (INPUT, OUTPUT);

VAR
    sum: REAL;
    product, result: INTEGER;
    greater, less, equal: BOOLEAN;
BEGIN
    sum := 3.6 + 2.1;
    greater := sum > 5.5;

    product := 3 * 2 * 4;
    result := product;

    greater := product > result;
    less := product < result;
    equal := NOT(greater) AND NOT(less)
END.
```

```
PROGRAM AssignExample (INPUT, OUTPUT);

VAR
    sum: REAL;
    product, result: INTEGER;
    greater, less, equal: BOOLEAN;
BEGIN
    sum := 3.6 + 2.1;
    greater := sum > 5.5;

    product := 3 * 2 * 4;
    result := product;

    greater := product > result;
    less := product < result;
    equal := NOT(greater) AND NOT(less)
END.
```

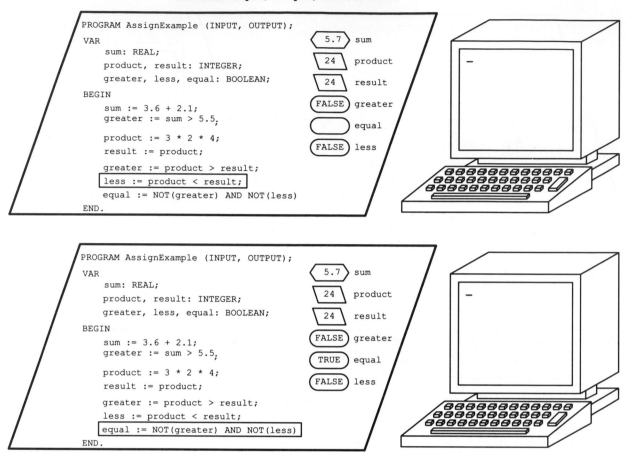

```
PROGRAM AssignExample (INPUT, OUTPUT);
    VAR
        sum: REAL;
        product, result: INTEGER;
        greater, less, equal: BOOLEAN;
    BEGIN
        sum := 3.6 + 2.1;
        greater := sum > 5.5;

        product := 3 * 2 * 4;
        result := product;

        greater := product > result;
        less := product < result;
        equal := NOT(greater) AND NOT(less)
    END.
```

5.7	sum
24	product
24	result
FALSE	greater
	equal
FALSE	less

```
PROGRAM AssignExample (INPUT, OUTPUT);
    VAR
        sum: REAL;
        product, result: INTEGER;
        greater, less, equal: BOOLEAN;
    BEGIN
        sum := 3.6 + 2.1;
        greater := sum > 5.5;

        product := 3 * 2 * 4;
        result := product;

        greater := product > result;
        less := product < result;
        equal := NOT(greater) AND NOT(less)
    END.
```

5.7	sum
24	product
24	result
FALSE	greater
TRUE	equal
FALSE	less

The expression on the right side of an assignment statement always evaluates first, and then the value is placed in the memory cell with the name specified on the left side of the assignment symbol. Only the value of the variable on the left side of the assignment symbol changes.

5.2.2.1. The Range and Accuracy of Variables

We have already mentioned that there are infinitely many integers and that computers are finite and may only represent some finite number of integers. The largest integer representable in your Pascal implementation is known as **MaxInt**. The important point is that the type INTEGER has some specific range of values that is only a subset of all integers. The range is implementation dependent. The range is adequate on many systems, but surprisingly small on others.

In a similar vein, computers can represent only a specific number of decimal places for floating point numbers. This has a few implications that at first sight might appear quite surprising. The expression **10 / 3 * 3** may yield a result of 9.9999999 rather than 10. Similarly, the assignment **total := 10.0** may result in 9.9999999 being stored as the value for the REAL variable **total**. It is important that floating point numbers are only approximately represented by computers and therefore somewhat imprecise. Although most implementations are "precise enough" for many applications, some are too imprecise for certain applications, and still others are too imprecise for most applications.

It is important for you to remember that both INTEGER and REAL have a limited range of allowable values and that REAL represents numbers only approximately.

5.2.2.2. Case Sensitivity—a Note

A computer distinguishes between uppercase and lowercase letters by giving them different representations in computer memory. Therefore, if we have the following constant definitions:

```
CONST
    CapA = 'A';
    LittleA = 'a';
```

Programming Example 5-9: CHARacter Values Differing in Case

then **CapA** is not equal to **LittleA**, because each holds a different value. Now consider the following declarations:

```
VAR
    letter: CHAR;
    LETTER: CHAR;
    Letter: CHAR;
```

Programming Example 5-10: Variable Names Differing in Case

The only difference in the three identifiers is their case. One is all lowercase; one is all uppercase; and one is mixed. Whether these are considered distinct or equivalent identifiers depends on the implementation of Pascal you are using. Usually, they are considered to be the same. The English language works pretty much like this. There are rules that describe when a word should be capitalized and when it should be in lowercase. It is very rare for capitalization to change the meaning of a word. In fact, the only example of this that we can think of is *Polish* (as in Polish sausage or the country located in eastern Europe) and *polish* (as in what you do to make your shoes shine). In computer science, when the capitalization of letters does not alter the meaning of an identifier, identifiers are said to be *case folded*. This means case is not distinguished, as opposed to *case sensitive* (e.g. Polish/polish).

If an implementation is case sensitive for identifiers, the previous variable names are considered three distinct identifiers and could be declared as three different types. If you use this difference to distinguish among identifiers, it may lead to bizarre results from your program. We propose that no two identifiers in a program should differ in case only. Writing a program with such subtle distinctions will, at the very least, diminish its readability.

5.2.3. Questions

1. What is a variable?

2. Why are variables used in programs?

3. Is it possible to write a Pascal program with no variables? Why?

4. What is the purpose of a variable declaration?

5. What are the three properties of a Pascal variable?

6. How do variables get values?

7. Discuss the notion of variables getting values by *programmer neglect*. Is it a bad idea to depend on values always being specific values?

8. Are there different uppercase and lowercase CHARacters? Do they have different values?

9. What is the difference between case-sensitive and case-folded identifiers?

5.2.4. Exercises

1. Give valid Pascal variable declarations for **answer** (CHAR), **age** (INTEGER), **QPA** (REAL), **correct** (BOOLEAN), and **StudentNumber** (INTEGER).

2. If necessary, rewrite the previous declarations so that there are no more than four declarations for the five variables. (Use multiple declarations.)

3. Given the following declarations, tell whether or not each assignment is valid. If it is invalid, explain why.

```
VAR
    count, total: REAL;
    sum, number, change: INTEGER;
    letter: CHAR;
    finished, flag: BOOLEAN;
```

a.	count := '5'	o.	finished := flag
b.	total := sum + count	p.	finished := true
c.	change := 4.0	q.	flag := 5 < 9
d.	number := 'i'	r.	finished := finished AND flag
e.	change := 56.0 DIV 4	s.	finished := true OR false
f.	total := 16 * count + 3	t.	number := 8.0 / 2.0
g.	number := total	u.	flag := 13 > 2 OR number = 18
h.	change := 1 + * 2	v.	flag := NOT(count >= total)
i.	letter := '3'	w.	total:= 104
j.	letter := 'number'	x.	flag := 'TRUE'
k.	letter := 'A' + 'B'	y.	flag := 1
l.	letter := letter * 2	z.	finished:= (letter = 'n') OR (letter = 'm')
m.	letter := letter		
n.	number := 8 / 2	aa.	sum := number + 1.0

4. Describe the effect of the execution of each of the statements in the following program.

```
PROGRAM Assign (INPUT, OUTPUT);

VAR
    sum: REAL;
    test: BOOLEAN;
    sentinel: CHAR;

BEGIN
    sum := 3.46 + 2.1;
    test := sum > (3.46 + 2.1);
    sentinel := 's';
    test := sentinel = 'c'
END.
```

5.2.5. Problems

1. What is the maximum length of identifiers recognized by your system? Determine this empirically.

2. Enter and run Programming Example 5-4 on your system.

3. Modify the previous program so that **length** and **width** are different values. Run the program again.

4. Write a program that has one variable of each of the four primitive types. Have the program output the value of each of the four variables using the WRITELN statement. Be sure to label the output. (Note that each variable has a value, even though you did not give it one.)

5. Can Pascal identifiers use both uppercase and lowercase characters? Do they result in different or equivalent identifiers on your system? Is the implementation of Pascal you are using case-sensitive or case-folded? Determine this empirically.

6. Write a program that compares the ages of two people (Bill and Bob) and returns a BOOLEAN value for the expression "Bill > Bob" at the end. The program should prompt the user for both people's ages. It should write 3 lines on the terminal screen after prompting for input: "Bill is x years old. Bob is z years old. Bill is older than Bob: BOOLEAN VALUE."

7. Suppose you worked at a bank and someone brought in a barrel filled with pennies that they wanted to exchange for bills. Write a program to determine how much the pennies total. For this program, you need to know the total weight of the pennies (*hint: subtract barrel weight*), and the weight for one penny (*hint: use 3 grams per penny*).

5.3. The Details of Input

Without input from the user, a program will do the same computations with the same data and always compute and display the same results every time it is run. User input provides a way to give a program different data to use in its computations. Although some programs do not require user input, every program that is normally expected to be run more than once accepts input.

5.3.0.1. The Input Tape

By using the Turing Machine (originally introduced on page 8), we can build a model of how input works. Our description of the Turing Machine provides for more than one tape. One of the tapes contains input information and is referred to as the *input tape*. The Turing Machine's *read head* scans the input tape one cell at a time from left to right without ever backing up. This provides a good model for how program languages in general and Pascal in particular actually handle program input.

In Pascal, all but one special symbol of the input tape have a value of type CHAR. The special symbol denotes an *end-of-line*, which is entered by the user depressing the 'ENTER' or 'RETURN' key. Assume you enter the date *3/21/1960*, followed by a carriage return, followed by *23*, followed by another carriage return. The input for this situation can be represented as follows:

We indicate end-of-line with a cent sign (¢). We indicate end-of-input (also referred to as end-of-file) by the end of the input tape.

5.3.1. READ and READLN

Pascal provides two output statements: WRITE and WRITELN. The difference between the two is that WRITELN always writes an end-of-line marker after writing its expression, but WRITE does not. In a similar way, Pascal provides two input statements: READ and READLN. Both of these statements read the next value from the input tape and assign the value to the specified variable. The difference between READ and READLN is that READ leaves the read head just after the value it reads, but READLN continues to read values on the tape until an end-of-line symbol is encountered. READLN always positions the read head after an end-of-line marker.

Assume the input tape is the one we previously described, two lines of input both terminated with an end-of-line marker (denoted with a cent sign):

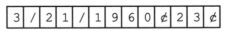

Consider the following Pascal program:

```
PROGRAM ReadExample (INPUT, OUTPUT);

VAR
    first, second: CHAR;

BEGIN
    READ(INPUT, first);
    READ(INPUT, second)
END.
```

Programming Example 5-11: READ Example

This program reads the value '3' into the variable **first** and '/' into the variable **second**. Consider now the same Pascal program with READ replaced with READLN as indicated in the following example:

```
PROGRAM ReadLnExample (INPUT, OUTPUT);

VAR
    first, second: CHAR;

BEGIN
    READLN(INPUT, first);
    READLN(INPUT, second)
END.
```

Programming Example 5-12: READLN Example

This program reads in '3' into the variable **first** and '2' into the variable **second**. In the second example, the read head also starts before the first symbol, namely, *3*. The symbol *3* is scanned and assigned to the variable **first**. Then the read head skips past all other symbols until it finds an end-of-line marker (*¢*). The read head stops after the end-of-line marker and before the *2* of *23*. Next, the *2* is scanned and assigned to the variable **second**. The read head then continues past the next end-of-line symbol, which puts it at the end of the input tape.

5.3.1.1. Detailed Simulation of READ and READLN

An understanding of the subtleties of READ and READLN is essential. We employ a specialized series of illustrations in the immediately following pages to help you gain such an understanding. You may be tempted to skip over the detail, presented here. We advise that you resist such temptations. We have found that careful attention to a few short examples can help you avoid major problems later.

Consider the following Pascal program:

```
PROGRAM ReadAssign (INPUT, OUTPUT);

VAR
    month, day, year, age: INTEGER;
    letter: CHAR;

BEGIN
    READ(INPUT, month);
    READ(INPUT, letter);
    READ(INPUT, day);
    READ(INPUT, letter);
    READ(INPUT, year);
    READLN(INPUT);
    READ(INPUT, age);
    READLN(INPUT)
END.
```

Programming Example 5-13: READ and READLN

In our illustrations the input tape is denoted as a sequence of joined cells. The read head is denoted with a vertical arrow pointing to its position on the tape.

The first illustration shows the initial situation before any statement has executed. INTEGER variables (parallelograms) are set up for **month, day, year**, and **age**, and a CHARacter variable (square) is set up for **letter**. The read head has not read any values and is therefore positioned before the first cell.

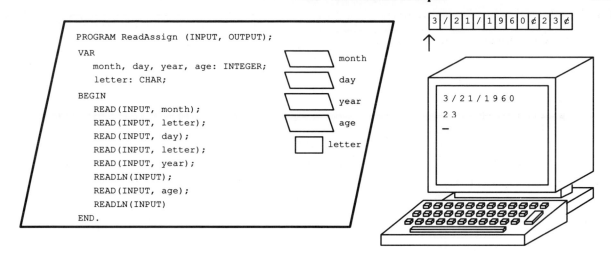

Almost every system echoes the user's input on the display. We reflect this fact by indicating the user's input on the display screen in addition to the input tape. It is a good idea for a program to echo back to its user input values provided by the user.

The next illustration shows the state after execution of the first statement. The contents of the first cell on the input tape (3) are read into the variable **month**. The read head advances to the next cell on the input tape. All other variables still have unknown values at this point.

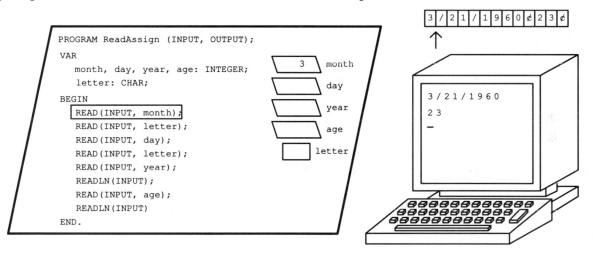

The next illustration shows the execution of the second READ statement. The contents of the next cell of the input tape (/) are read into the variable **letter**, and the read head is advanced to the next cell. The value of **month** is unchanged. The values of the remaining variables are still unknown.

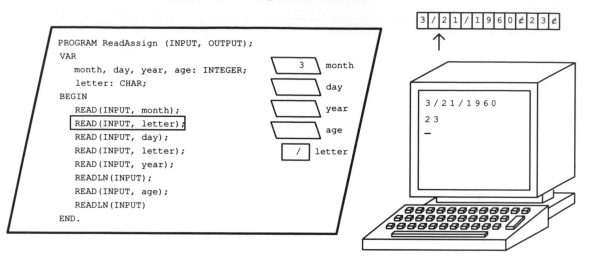

The next illustration shows the execution of the third READ statement. It says read the next value on the input tape into the variable **day**. The value 21 is read into **day**. The read head moves to the next cell after 21. **Month** and **letter** have their previously read values; other variables still have unknown values.

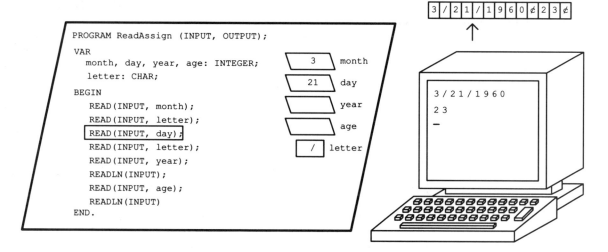

You are probably wondering why 21 was read into the variable **day** rather than just 2, which is the value in the next cell of the input tape. The action of READ (and READLN) depends on the type of the variable it is to read. If the type is CHAR, it simply reads the next character off the input tape of characters. If the variable is of type INTEGER or REAL, the action is different. Say that it is to read an INTEGER. READ knows that a valid Pascal INTEGER is an optional sign followed by one or more digits. Knowing this, READ reads as many cells as possible, as long as it is still a valid Pascal INTEGER. READ stops when it finds a cell that contains something not of type INTEGER. In the previous case, it stopped when it saw the / following the 21. Therefore, the read head stopped after the 21. If READ and READLN did not work this way, we would have to read one digit at a time and build these digits into an integer every time we wanted to read an integer from the input. The action for Pascal REAL values is similar.

The next illustration shows the execution of the fourth READ statement. The map of memory does not appear differently than it did in the previous plate. However, a new value has been read into **letter**; it just happens to be the same value that was already there. Notice that the read head has passed beyond the second / on the input tape.

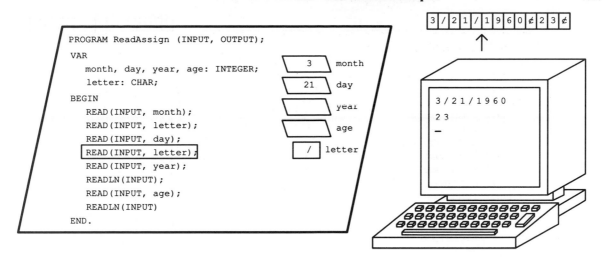

The next illustration shows the execution of the fifth READ statement. The value 1960 has been read into the variable **year**, with the read head advancing appropriately beyond this value. Note that 4 cells of the input tape were read in the INTEGER variable **year**. There is an end-of-line marker at the next position on the input tape.

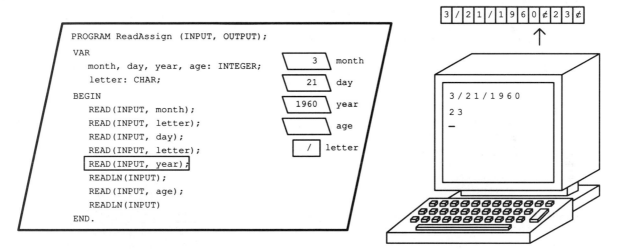

The next illustration shows the effect of the statement **READLN(INPUT)**. The read head advances beyond the next end-of-line marker found on the tape. There is no change to memory.

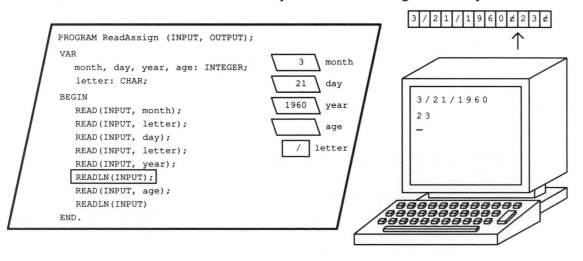

The next illustration demonstrates the next-to-last statement. The value 23 is read into the variable **age**. The read head advances and encounters an end-of-line marker.

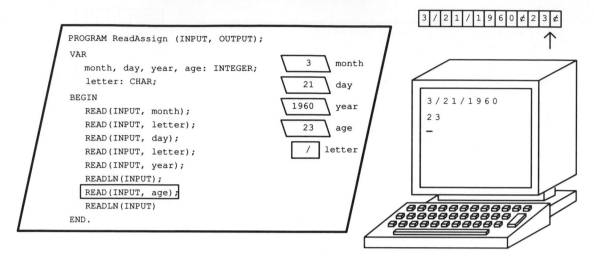

The last illustration shows the execution of the last statement, **READLN(INPUT)**. The read head advances past the next end-of-line marker to the end of the input tape. The program execution is now complete.

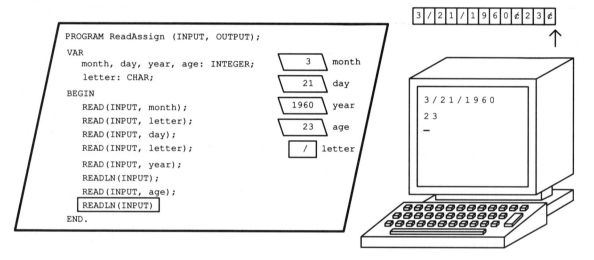

If you followed the previous series of detailed illustrations, you should have a good understanding of how both READ and READLN work. Do not proceed any further unless you have such an understanding.

5.3.2. Reading Multiple Values

The first five READs in the last example could have been combined. We can replace the five statements with one.

```
READ(INPUT, month);
READ(INPUT, letter);
READ(INPUT, day);
READ(INPUT, letter);
READ(INPUT, year);

READ(INPUT, month, letter, day, letter, year);
```

The program is now simplified:

```
PROGRAM ReadAssign (INPUT, OUTPUT);

VAR
    month, day, year, age: INTEGER;
    letter: CHAR;

BEGIN
    READ(INPUT, month, letter, day, letter, year);
    READLN(INPUT);
    READ(INPUT, age);
    READLN(INPUT)
END.
```

Programming Example 5-14: READ with More Than One Variable

Execution of this program would look the following way. The first illustration shows the initial situation:

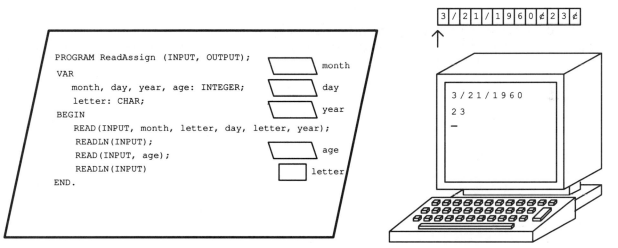

The second illustration shows the execution of the first statement. Note that **month**, **day**, **year**, and **letter** all get a new value from the one statement.

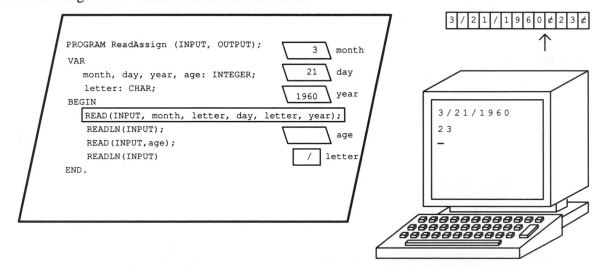

The remaining illustrations are pretty much the same as before. The third illustration shows advancing the read head past the end-of-line marker.

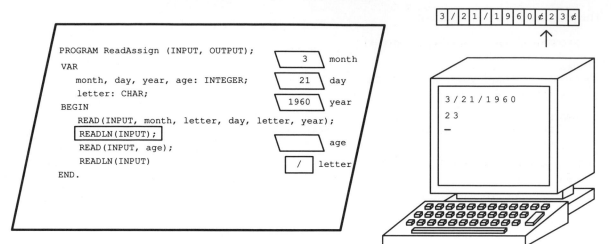

The fourth illustration shows the value being read into **age**.

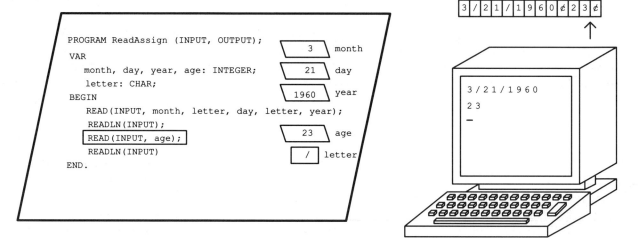

The last illustration shows the execution of the final READLN.

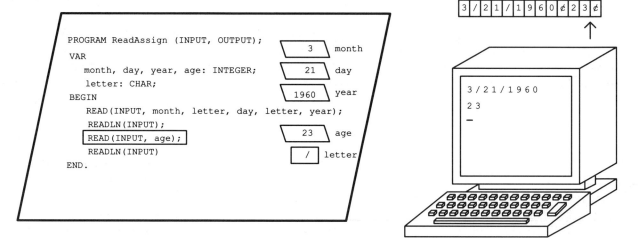

At this point, you might be wondering if the previous program's input statements can be combined any further. Specifically, can a READ and READLN be combined in a fashion similar to the way READs were combined? The answer is yes. The program that follows is an even simpler way to perform the same reads to the variables:

```
PROGRAM ReadAssign (INPUT, OUTPUT);

VAR
    month, day, year, age: INTEGER;
    letter: CHAR;

BEGIN
    READLN(INPUT, month, letter, day, letter, year);
    READLN(INPUT, age)
END.
```

Programming Example 5-15: Combining READ and READLN

Memory appears just as it did in our previous program, but the read head has traveled beyond the first end-of-line marker because we used a READLN. The effect of the READLN should be apparent. It performs READs for all its variables and then travels beyond the end-of-line marker. You might find it quite useful to remember such an equivalence for the READLN procedure. If the action of READLN appears strange, you might replace READLN with its long form equivalent (one READ for each variable followed by one READLN with no variables) to understand better what is actually going on.

5.3.3. When Values Are Actually Read

In our simulations of READ and READLN, we treated the input tape as a basic unit being read. However, we made no mention of when the symbols actually get added to the input tape. There are at least two distinct possibilities. The first is as they are typed. Each character is added to the input tape as the corresponding keys are pressed by the user one character at a time. The other possibility is to add a whole line at a time. In the second way, no pressed keys are actually added to the input tape until the user presses the 'RETURN' key. The first way is done on some microcomputers, and the second way predominates on all other systems. The second way is by far the most popular. You should determine which way your system does it.

5.3.4. Common Problems with Reading Input

What happens when there are more variables to be read than there are values to be read? The answer depends on whether there are not enough values on the input tape or too few values on a line but enough on the input tape. In the first case, there are enough values on the tape, but there is an end-of-line marker on the input tape before we expect it. In this case *the end-of-line marker is treated as a space character.* For example, suppose we prompt the user for three integers and then attempt to read them with the statement **READLN(INPUT, first, second, third).** Also assume that the user enters the following sequence: 11, space, 39, return, 16, return. Using our previous conventions, this may be represented as follows:

$$\boxed{1}\boxed{1}\boxed{}\boxed{3}\boxed{9}\boxed{¢}\boxed{1}\boxed{6}\boxed{¢}$$

Notice that there is an end-of-line marker where we are expecting a space character. Before continuing, recall that the example READLN is equivalent to the following:

```
READ(INPUT, first);
READ(INPUT, second);
READ(INPUT, third);
READLN(INPUT)
```

This equivalence will help us understand what is happening. First, *11* is read into the variable **first**. Next, the space is skipped and *39* is read into the variable **second**. Recall that *Pascal uses spaces to separate numeric values in the input.* Next, the end-of-line marker is treated as a space character and therefore skipped, so the integer value 17 is read into the variable **third**. Finally, READLN reads the remaining end-of-line marker. Standard Pascal specifies that the end-of-line marker is read as a space character. This provides greater flexibility in entering numeric values, since they are separated by spaces.

If, on the other hand, there are not enough values on the input tape, the situation is different. Variables being read from INPUT must have values supplied by the user. The system will not make up default values, and no values from INPUT are recycled. If a program requests three values and only two are supplied, there will be a pause (*input wait*) until the user supplies the third value.

What happens when there are more values on the input tape than we wish to read? For example, what happens if your program prompts the user for one integer, but the user enters two or more integers? The answer depends on whether the extra values are entered on one line or more than one line of input. If the extra values exist on one line, then by using READLN our program ignores any values remaining on the list. If we want to read one value from a line and then ignore all remaining values on that line we would use `READLN(INPUT, value)`. If there are more lines of input than are needed, the extra lines can be skipped over using READLN as `READLN(INPUT)`. READLN always advances the read head past the next end-of-line marker regardless of what input is on the line. READLN is useful in ignoring unwanted input. We should point out that since user input through the keyboard is commonly terminated with a carriage return, the end-of-line marker must always be read in addition to the values on the line. Use READLN to read the accompanying end-of-line markers.

What happens when the values on the input tape are of a different type than are needed for the variables to be read? Suppose, for example, the program is attempting to read into a variable of type INTEGER and a letter, say "z", is encountered on INPUT. This is a type conflict, because the INTEGER variable cannot take a CHAR value. You should determine what your system does in such a case. Some systems are very forgiving, printing a helpful message and prompting for valid input: **"I'm terribly sorry, an integer value was expected and the value encountered is not one of these. Could you please try again?"** Other implementations are rude, cryptic, and abrupt, printing a curt insult just prior to taking control away from the program: **"Type mismatch of operands."** You will, no doubt, become familiar with the peculiarities of your system. Good prompts can help prevent the user from entering values of the wrong type.

5.3.5. Questions

1. What are Pascal's two input statements?

2. What are the differences between READ and READLN?

3. What happens when READ does not read all the values on the INPUT tape?

4. What happens when READLN does not use (read) all the values on the INPUT tape?

5. What happens when a READ or a READLN attempts to read a value of one type into a variable of another type?

6. What happens when READ or READLN attempts to read values that are not present on the INPUT tape?

7. Standard Pascal specifies that the end-of-line marker is to be read as a character. What character is it?

8. Standard Pascal uses two characters as separators for numeric values. What are they?

5.3.6. Exercises

1. Does your system support input of BOOLEAN values? If so, how is this handled?

2. Suppose the following data are given as input

```
24 43
35    12
18 41
84
```

to a program with the following variable declarations:

```
VAR
    a, b, c, d: INTEGER;
```

What are the values of a, b, c, and d for each of the following code fragments?

FRAGMENT 1	FRAGMENT 2	FRAGMENT 3
`READ(INPUT, a, b, c)`	`READLN(INPUT, a, b, c);`	`READLN(INPUT, a);`
`READLN(INPUT, d)`	`READLN(INPUT, d);`	`READLN(INPUT, b, c);`
		`READLN(INPUT, d);`

3. Assume the following data is given to a program without any regard for what the program actually wants. There are five lines of input data, each terminated with a carriage return.

```
30 25    12 10 18
13
33 98 2
21 5 27 74 11
43 29 09
```

Assume the receiving program has the following variable declaration:

```
VAR
      a, b, c, d, e, f, g: INTEGER;
```

Given the previous test data, state the value of each variable after each of the following three program fragments.

FRAGMENT 1	FRAGMENT 2	FRAGMENT 3
`READ(INPUT, a, b, c);`	`READLN(INPUT, a, b);`	`READ(INPUT, a);`
`READLN(INPUT, d, e);`	`READLN(INPUT, c);`	`READLN(INPUT, b);`
`READLN(INPUT, f);`	`READ(INPUT, d, e);`	`READLN(INPUT, c);`
`READLN(INPUT, g)`	`READLN(INPUT, f);`	`READLN(INPUT, d, e);`
	`READLN(INPUT, g)`	`READLN(INPUT, f, g)`

4. Suppose the following input is given to the program

```
A B
C D E
F
G
```

with the following variable declarations:

```
VAR
     c1, c2, c3, c4, c5,: CHAR;
```

What is the value of each of the five variables after each fragment of code is executed?

FRAGMENT 1

```
READLN(INPUT,c1,c2,c3);
READLN(INPUT,c4);
READLN(INPUT,c5)
```

FRAGMENT 2

```
READ(INPUT,c1);
READLN(INPUT,c2);
READLN(INPUT,c3,c4);
READLN(INPUT,c5)
```

FRAGMENT 3

```
READ(INPUT,c1,c2,c3);
READLN(INPUT,c4);
READLN(INPUT,c5)
```

FRAGMENT 4

```
READLN(INPUT,c1,c2,c3,c4);
READLN(INPUT,c5)
```

5.3.7. Problems

1. It is important that you get to know how your system behaves with a wide variety of input. Here is some sample input that should exercise your system. By entering it and reading it as suggested, you will learn how your system interprets values on INPUT. Not all of the examples are guaranteed to execute on all systems. Assume the following declarations:

```
VAR
    intVar: INTEGER;
    realVar: REAL;
    charVar: CHAR;
```

   a. Input sequence: **1 2 3**

```
BEGIN                          BEGIN                          BEGIN
READ(INPUT, intVar);           READ(INPUT, realVar);          READ(INPUT, charVar);
WRITELN(OUTPUT, intVar);       WRITELN(OUTPUT, realVar);      WRITELN(OUTPUT, charVar);
READ(INPUT, intVar);           READ(INPUT, realVar);          READ(INPUT, charVar);
WRITELN(OUTPUT, intVar);       WRITELN(OUTPUT, realVar);      WRITELN(OUTPUT, charVar);
READ(INPUT, intVar);           READ(INPUT, realVar);          READ(INPUT, charVar);
WRITELN(OUTPUT, intVar)        WRITELN(OUTPUT, realVar);      WRITELN(OUTPUT, charVar);
END.                           END.                           END.
```

   b. Input sequence: **a123**

```
        BEGIN
            READLN(INPUT, charVar, intVar);
            WRITELN(OUTPUT, charVar, intVar)
        END.
```

   c. Input sequence: **123a**

```
        BEGIN
            READLN(INPUT, intVar, charVar);
            WRITELN(OUTPUT, intVar, charVar)
        END.
```

   d. Input sequence: **123.456**

```
        BEGIN
            READLN(INPUT, intVar, realVar);
            WRITELN(OUTPUT, intVar, realVar)
        END.
```

   e. Input sequence: **123.456**

```
        BEGIN
            READLN(INPUT, realVar, intVar);
            WRITELN(OUTPUT, realVar, intVar)
        END.
```

2. When are input values added to the input tape of your system character by character or a whole line at a time? Determine this empirically.

3. Does your system read the end-of-line marker as a space character? If not, how is it treated?

5.4. Chapter Summary

- Every useful program generates some output.

- It is useful to think of the output display overlaid with a piece of graph paper organizing the screen into rows and columns of cells.

- A literal string is a sequence of characters enclosed in matching single quotes.

- An apostrophe is indicated in a literal string with two single quotes (not one double quote).

- Pascal has two output statements, WRITE and WRITELN.

- The difference between WRITE and WRITELN is that WRITELN moves the write head (cursor) to the start of a new line *after* writing its expression.

- Standard Pascal right justifies all output.

- If no fieldwidth is specified by the programmer, a default fieldwidth is used. The default fieldwidth is normally 1 for CHARacter values, the length of the literal string for literal strings, and defined by the system implementation for INTEGER, BOOLEAN, and REAL.

- Pascal's output statements may take three forms: (1) free format—no specification of fieldwidth, system default is used; (2) single format—specification of overall fieldwidth (used with INTEGER, CHARacters, BOOLEANS, literal strings, and REAL exponential notation; (3) double format—specify both total fieldwidth and number of decimal places, used solely for REAL expressions in nonexponential notation.

- You should not specify a fieldwidth too small for the output. This error is commonly made when a sign or decimal point is forgotten. How the system reacts to this error is implementation defined.

- Some systems buffer output. You should be aware of whether your system does or does not because of the subtle problems buffering may cause.

- Both WRITE and WRITELN can write more than one expression. If more than one expression is to be written, they are to be separated with commas.

- A variable is a piece of computer memory used to store a value of a given type.

- Variables in Pascal have three properties: *name*, *type*, and *value*. A variable's *name* provides a way of referring to it. The *type* specifies its set of possible values. The *value* is the specific element of the possible set of values that it currently holds.

- A computer refers to its memory cell with numbers called *addresses*, but a programmer may name variables and refer to them by name.

- Pascal's reserved words may not be used as identifiers.

- Every implementation recognizes identifiers as unique to a certain number of characters. Standard Pascal expects at least 8 characters.

- Pascal programs are not required to have variables. For a program to use variables, each one must be appropriately declared.

- Every declared variable has exactly one value at any time.

- Every declared variable has a value whether the programmer gave it one or not.

- A variable may get its value in one of three ways: explicit assignment with the assignment statement; implicit assignment by reading it through input; or neglect of the programmer.

- Pascal's assignment symbol is :=.

- The character values 'A' and 'a' are different, as are all other uppercase and lowercase character pairs.

- Whether the variables **sum** and **SUM** are different depends on whether or not the system implementation is case sensitive.

- Pascal has two input statements: READ and READLN.

- READ always leaves the read head position immediately after the the last value read. READLN skips over all remaining values until an end-of-line symbol is encountered and then positions the read head *after* the end-of-line marker.

- Both READ and READLN can read more than one value. If more than one value is to be read, the corresponding variables must be separated by commas.

- **`READLN(INPUT, v1, v2, v3)`** is equivalent to

```
READ(INPUT, v1);
READ(INPUT, v2);
READ(INPUT, v3);
READLN(INPUT)
```

- Extra values on the input tape may be skipped over by using READLN.

- Numeric values are normally separated by spaces.

- Standard Pascal specifies that the end-of-line marker is treated as a space character if it is treated as a value instead of being read by READLN.

- The end-of-line marker may be used to separate numeric values.

- Although output of BOOLEAN values is part of Standard Pascal, input of BOOLEAN values is not.

- User input through the keyboard is commonly terminated with a carriage return. It is a common error to forget to read the end-of-line marker in addition to the desired value. Use READLN to correct this error.

5.5. Summary of Style

- If no format is specified, default formatting is used. But default formatting is different from one system to the next. We discourage the use of default formatting; the programmer should always explicitly specify the format for all output.

- The programmer has the choice of names for variables. The names selected should be as mnemonic as possible.

- Some implementations differentiate identifiers based on case (case sensitive). It is not a good idea to write programs based on case sensitivity. A program that requires case sensitivity to work properly will at the very least be difficult to read, modify, and port to other implementations, if not impossible.

- You should always initialize a variable by explicit assignment or implicit assignment (reading from input) before using the value of the variable.

- It is a good idea for a program to echo input values back to the user.

5.6. Summary of Terms

• output	• floating point notation	• assignment statement
• literal string	• buffered output	• case sensitive
• single quote (apostrophe)	• variable	• case folded
• double quote	• variable declaration	• input
• fieldwidth	• reserved word	• input tape
• decimal places	• computer word	• READ
• formatting	• bit	• READLN
• default formatting	• bit pattern	• INPUT
• free format	• address	• end-of-line
• single format	• variable name	• end-of-line marker
• double format	• variable type	• end-of-input
• exponential notation	• assignment	• end-of-file
• fixed point notation	• assignment symbol	

5.7. Chapter Problems

1. Write a Pascal program that converts inches to centimeters. Prompt the user for input. Assume one inch equals 2.54 centimeters.

2. Extend the previous program to accept both feet and inches as input.

3. Credit cards have become a very big business. Write a program to determine the monthly finance charge for a credit card, given the month's outstanding balance and interest rate. Prompt for both the balance and the rate.

4. The cost of postage continues to spiral upward. Write a Pascal program to determine the postage cost for an item. Assume the cost is 22¢ for the first ounce and 17¢ for each additional ounce.

5. When bought in bulk, beer is normally measured in kegs. The two most popular sizes are the half-keg (15.5 gallons) and the quarter-keg (7.75 gallons). Write a Pascal program that takes as input the cost of these two quantities and determines the cost per serving of each. Assume there are 12 servings per gallon.

6. Write a program to determine the total revenue for an airplane trip. Assume there are two classes: coach and first class. The price and number of tickets sold for each class is to be user input. Be sure to give appropriate prompts.

Chapter 6: Conditional Execution

All of the Pascal programs presented up to this point have been sequences of statements, such as READ, WRITE, and assignment. Each statement is executed in the same order as it appears in the sequence: The first statement is executed first, the second statement is executed second, and so on. If the name of a procedure is used as a statement (procedure call), the sequence of statements in that procedure is executed before continuing with the statement following the procedure call. This type of program execution is referred to as **sequential execution**.

> **Definition 6-1:** *Sequential execution* refers to executing a sequence of instructions in the same order as they appear in the sequence.

We have already pointed out that without the capability of input to computer programs, the data for a program is exactly the same every execution of the program. Without input, a program uses the same data, computes the same results, and displays the same output. Every execution of such a program is identical. User input permits more general programs in which computations and output depend on the input values. The program still performs sequential execution, but with different data.

For some programs, we want to determine which statements to execute depending on the input data. As an example, consider a program to compute net pay. If we consider 40 hours to be a normal work week, overtime is the time worked in excess of 40 hours. The portion of the program that computes overtime pay should execute only if the person worked overtime. Rather than relying on strictly sequential execution, we want to control the program so that statements execute only when necessary and in the correct order. The parts of a programming language that allow such control are called **control structures**.

> **Definition 6-2:** *Control structures* are the elements of a programming language that determine the flow of program execution. In Pascal, the control structures are all statements.

All high-level programming languages have control structures. Pascal's control structures allow the programmer to express computer instructions in a very natural way. Pascal's six control structures fall into two distinct classes: **conditional execution** and **repetition**. In this and the following chapter, we will examine Pascal's control structures, techniques for understanding them, and the tools for writing them. We will study conditional execution in this chapter and repetition in the next chapter. With control structures, you will be able to write more powerful and interesting programs.

Conditional execution means that an instruction executes when a specified condition occurs. In studying Karel we learned two conditional control structures: the **IF-THEN** and **IF-THEN-ELSE** instructions. Pascal has both of these control statements as well as a much more generalized selection statement, the **CASE** statement, which gives Pascal three conditional-execution control structures. Whereas Karel has eighteen primitive conditions to use with **IF-THEN** and **IF-THEN-ELSE**, Pascal allows any BOOLEAN expression to be used as a condition. This chapter discusses Pascal's **IF-THEN, IF-THEN-ELSE**, and **CASE** statements.

> **Definition 6-3:** The *conditional execution* control structures allow the programmer to control the execution of a statement according to specified conditions.

6.1. IF-THEN Statement

The **IF-THEN** statement is the simplest of Pascal's three conditional statements. For the previous gas mileage program (Programming Example 3-24, page 111), we included a procedure to offer advice on the computed result. The example said that if the automobile got less than 10 miles per gallon, the car was a "gas guzzler" and the owner should consider a trade. Suppose we only wanted to print out this message if the owner had really achieved such poor gas mileage. To do so, we could use the IF-THEN statement.

For the gas mileage example, you could use the following:

```
IF (result < 10)
    THEN WRITELN(OUTPUT, 'You drive a gas guzzler.  I''d consider a trade')
```

Programming Example 6-1: If-THEN Statement

One way to think of the IF-THEN construct in Pascal is as a condition-action pair.

condition → action

When the *condition* (IF clause) evaluates to TRUE, the specified *action* (THEN clause) executes. When the condition evaluates to FALSE, the action does NOT execute. The condition *guards* the action. For the previous example, the *condition* would be less than ten miles per gallon; the *action* would be a message to the user.

condition → action
result is less than 10 mpg → display message

With this conditional, the message will be displayed only if the mileage is less than 10 miles per gallon. Note that the parentheses around the expression *result < 10* are not necessary. Such redundant parentheses have no effect on the meaning or execution of the program; but, like comments, the parentheses usually improve program readability by reducing ambiguity.

In Pascal, any valid statement can serve as the *action* for the condition-action pair. Thus, the assignment statement, the READ and WRITE statements, and the names of procedures (procedure calls), all introduced in Unit II, can serve as the action. Additionally, there are a variety of other statements, which you will learn in later chapters. In Pascal, the *condition* may be any BOOLEAN expression. The form of the IF-THEN statement is as follows:

IF <boolean-expression>

THEN <statement>

Suppose, for example, we are writing a program that needs positive numbers as input. We would want a statement that checks the input and provides a message if it is a negative number. The condition is a negative value, and the action is a message. The following code fragment illustrates how this statement would look in Pascal:

```
WRITE(OUTPUT, prompt);
READLN(INPUT, value);
IF (value < 0)
    THEN WRITELN(OUTPUT, 'Unacceptable input.', value, ' is negative.')
```

Programming Example 6-2: Checking for Negative Values with IF-THEN

6.1.1. Formal Definition

The formal definition of the **IF-THEN** statement is given by its BNF.

```
<if-statement> ::= IF <boolean-expression> THEN <statement>
```

The IF-THEN syntax is simple. The reserved words **IF** and **THEN** enclose an expression of type BOOLEAN. The word **THEN** is followed by any valid Pascal statement.

6.1.2. Compound Statements

Any statement may serve as the action for a Pascal conditional statement. Often, it is useful to have more than one statement as the action clause. For example, suppose we wanted to have the "gas guzzler" message surrounded by a few blank lines. We might be tempted to write something like the following:

```
IF (result < 10)
    THEN
        WRITELN(OUTPUT);
        WRITELN(OUTPUT);
        WRITELN(OUTPUT, 'You drive a gas guzzler.  I''d consider a trade');
        WRITELN(OUTPUT);
        WRITELN(OUTPUT)
```

Programming Example 6-3: Erroneous Multi-Statement Action Clause

Although the indentation of the code suggests that the five WRITELN statements are triggered as a group by the condition, (result < 10), they are not, as indentation is ignored by the compiler. Only the first statement following the IF-THEN is guarded; the rest will always execute regardless of the value of the condition!

To accomplish execution of the five WRITELN statements as a group, we could use a **compound statement**, which is simply a list of statements treated as a single statement. In Pascal, enclose all the desired statements between a BEGIN-END pair, and separate the statements by semicolons. The entire BEGIN-END block is a valid Pascal statement (compound statement).   The following program fragment illustrates the corrected example from before:

```
IF (result < 10)
    THEN
        BEGIN
            WRITELN(OUTPUT);
            WRITELN(OUTPUT);
            WRITELN(OUTPUT, 'You drive a gas guzzler.  I''d consider a trade');
            WRITELN(OUTPUT);
            WRITELN(OUTPUT)
        END
```

Programming Example 6-4: Use of a Compound Statement

> **Definition 6-4:** A *compound statement* is a collection of statements enclosed in a BEGIN-END block.

Another way to achieve the same effect is to define the compound statement as a procedure and call the procedure as the statement part of the IF-THEN.

```
PROCEDURE GuzzlerQuip;

BEGIN
    WRITELN(OUTPUT);
    WRITELN(OUTPUT);
    WRITELN(OUTPUT, 'You drive a gas guzzler.  I''d consider a trade');
    WRITELN(OUTPUT);
    WRITELN(OUTPUT)
END;   (* GuzzlerQuip *)

    :
    :
    :

IF (result < 10)
    THEN  GuzzlerQuip
```

Programming Example 6-5: A Procedure Call as Action Clause

As a final note on the Pascal compound statement, the BEGIN-END blocks in Pascal are analogous to those in Karel (page 37). Five of Pascal's six control structures have a single statement as the action, and the compound statement is used often.

6.1.3. Pascal's Conditions

In Chapter 2 we learned that Karel has a fixed set of 18 predefined tests or conditions, and no other conditions can be tested, nor can any of the existing ones be combined into more complicated conditions. In Chapter 4 we learned about Pascal's relational operators (<, >, =, <=, >=, <>), which always result in BOOLEAN values. Pascal's control structures make extensive use of BOOLEAN expressions. Any valid BOOLEAN expression may be used as a Pascal condition. We have already seen the relational operator used with the conditional statement IF-THEN in our example concerning the gas mileage quip (`result < 10`). Since any BOOLEAN expression may be used as a Pascal condition, we may combine expressions with the BOOLEAN operators AND and OR to get a virtually endless variety of conditions.

Let us look at a few other BOOLEAN expressions as conditions for the IF-THEN statement. Consider the portion of a payroll program that handles input. It prompts for number of hours worked, reads the input value, and checks the input value for errors. The following program fragment does these three tasks. No one can work less than 0 hours in a week or more than 168 hours.

```
WRITE(OUTPUT, HoursPrompt);
READLN(INPUT, HoursWorked);
IF HoursWorked < 0.0
    THEN WRITELN(OUTPUT, 'Invalid data.');
IF HoursWorked > 168.0
    THEN WRITELN(OUTPUT, 'Invalid data.')
```

Programming Example 6-6: Relational Operators in Conditions

With the Pascal OR operator, this code can be simplified into a more compact form.

```
WRITE(OUTPUT, HoursPrompt);
READLN(INPUT, HoursWorked);
IF (HoursWorked < 0.0) OR (HoursWorked > 168.0)
    THEN WRITELN(OUTPUT, 'Invalid data.')
```

Programming Example 6-7: Boolean Operators in Conditions

In a similar way, we can use the AND operator to join BOOLEAN expressions. Perhaps we need input values to be within a certain range of values, between a low bound and a high bound. The following Pascal statement performs the necessary range check and writes an appropriate message.

```
WRITE(OUTPUT, prompt);
READLN(INPUT, value);
IF ( (value >= lowbound) AND (value <= highbound) )
    THEN WRITELN(OUTPUT, 'Acceptable input.', value, ' is in the range [',
                    lowbound, ',', highbound, '].')
```

Programming Example 6-8: Condition for Range Check

The third BOOLEAN operator, NOT, is often used in expressions that control the execution of a program. For example, we might use the following expression to check for user input within specified bounds.

```
WRITE(OUTPUT, prompt);
READLN(INPUT, value);
IF NOT ( (value >= lowbound) AND (value <= highbound) )
    THEN WRITELN(OUTPUT, 'Unacceptable input.', value, ' is not in range [',
                    lowbound, ',', highbound, '].')
```

Programming Example 6-9: NOT Operator in Condition

The use of BOOLEAN expressions as conditions rather than some small set of predefined conditions is one of the many ways Pascal is more general and more useful than Karel. A Pascal programmer may construct a BOOLEAN expression for any desired condition of the programming problem at hand.

6.1.4. Questions

1. What is conditional execution?

2. What are control structures?

3. What are the two reasons for using control structures?

4. How many conditional execution control structures does Karel have? Name each.

5. How many classes of control structures does Pascal have? Name each.

6. How many conditional execution control structures does Pascal have? Name each.

7. What is Pascal's IF-THEN statement.

8. What is a compound statement? Why is it useful?

9. What Pascal statements can serve as the action for an IF-THEN statement?

10. What may serve as conditions in Pascal?

6.1.5. Exercises

1. What output is produced by the following program fragment for input of *17*? For *30*? For *−30*?

```
READLN(INPUT, number);
IF number < 25
    THEN number := 25;
WRITELN(OUTPUT, number)
```

2. What output is produced by the following program fragment for input of *g*? For *G*?

```
READLN(INPUT, ch);
IF (ch >= 'a') AND (ch <= 'z')
    THEN WRITELN(OUTPUT, ch, ' is a lowercase letter.')
```

3. What output is produced by the following program fragment for input of *17*? For *30*? For *−30*?

```
READLN(INPUT, number);
IF number < 25
    THEN number := 25;
number := 33;
WRITELN(OUTPUT, number)
```

4. Simplify the following code so that there is a single IF-THEN statement rather than three statements.

```
IF (number MOD 2) <> 0 THEN
    IF number > 15 THEN
        IF  number < 32  THEN
            WRITELN(OUTPUT, number, ' is a special number.')
```

5. What is the output produced by the following program for the input *17*? For *1024*? For *−17*? For *−1024*?

```
IF ( (1 <= number) AND (number <= MaxInt) AND ((number MOD 2) = 0) )
    THEN WRITELN(OUTPUT, number, ' is an acceptable number.')
```

6.1.6. Problems

1. Write a Pascal program that reads one character and displays YES if it is a 'y' or a 'Y'.

2. Write a program that reads a CHARacter and displays CAPITAL if the entered character is a capital letter.

3. Write a program that reads a CHARacter and displays DIGIT if the character is in the range '0' through '9'.

4. Write a program that reads an integer and says whether it is negative or nonnegative.

5. Write a program that reads a CHARacter and displays LETTER if the entered character is either an uppercase letter or a lowercase letter. *Hint: There are 52 possible letters.*

6. Write a program that reads two integers and prints out the larger.

7. Write a program that reads three integers and prints out the largest.

8. Write a program that will advise the user about which income tax form to use when filing for tax returns. For this program, use the following fictional guidelines. If the user earned less than $15,000 for the year, he or she can use one of two short forms: 1040A if married or 1040-EZ if single. If the user earned $15,000 or more, a long form (1040) should be used. *Hint: The program should always ask at least one question. It should ask a second question if the user earned less than $15,000.*

6.2. IF-THEN-ELSE Statement

Recall the earlier example concerning the "gas guzzler" quip. Suppose we wanted to congratulate the user for NOT driving a "gas guzzler" while still advising a trade if the car guzzles. This is another case requiring two condition-action pairs. We can simplify the code by using the IF-THEN-ELSE statement. The condition is the result being less than 10 miles per gallon, the THEN action is displaying a message to trade the car, and the ELSE action is a message commending the user for NOT driving a gas guzzler.

```
IF (result < 10)
    THEN WRITELN(OUTPUT, 'You drive a gas guzzler.  I''d consider a trade')
    ELSE WRITELN(OUTPUT, 'You don''t drive a gas guzzler.  Good Job.')
```

Programming Example 6-10: IF-THEN-ELSE Statement

The **IF-THEN-ELSE** statement, as in Karel (page 56), provides guarded alternation. When the guard evaluates to TRUE, the first of two statements (THEN clause) executes. When the guard evaluates to FALSE, the second statement (ELSE clause) executes.

The IF-THEN-ELSE statement can be viewed as two condition-action pairs. The conditions are mutually exclusive and exhaustive. With mutually exclusive and exhaustive conditions, both can never be TRUE. Likewise, both can never be FALSE. Hence, one must be TRUE and the other must be FALSE.

$$\text{condition} \quad \rightarrow \quad \text{action-1}$$

$$\text{NOT(condition)} \quad \rightarrow \quad \text{action-2}$$

Definition 6-5: A set of *exhaustive* conditions means all possible conditions are considered.

An implication of this is that at least one condition must be TRUE.

Definition 6-6: A set of *exclusive* conditions means each condition is unique and no two can be TRUE at the same time.

When all possible conditions are considered, at least one condition will be TRUE. When each condition is unique, no more than one condition will be TRUE. In such a set of conditions, exactly one condition is always TRUE.

Definition 6-7: A pair of conditions are ***mutually exclusive and exhaustive*** if and only if each condition is the *negation* of the other.

In the automobile example, either the condition is true and you are driving a gas guzzler, or it is not. When the former is true, a trade is suggested. When the latter is true, the user is commended.

Similarly, the range check example can be modified to give a confirmation message if acceptable input is entered. The following Pascal code fragment illustrates this:

```
WRITE(OUTPUT, prompt);
READLN(INPUT, value);
IF ( (value < lowbound) OR (value > highbound) )
    THEN WRITELN(OUTPUT, 'Unacceptable input.', value, ' is not in range [',
                 lowbound, ',', highbound, '].')
    ELSE WRITELN(OUTPUT, 'Acceptable input')
```

Programming Example 6-11: Input Range Check Using IF-THEN-ELSE

Note the three pairs of parentheses in the condition. The two inner pairs are required, but the outer pair is not required. The outer pair is redundant to enhance readability.

The general form of the IF-THEN-ELSE statement is as follows:

```
IF <boolean-expression>

THEN <statement-1>

ELSE <statement-2>
```

If the BOOLEAN expression evaluates to TRUE, the THEN clause (statement-1) is executed; otherwise, the BOOLEAN expression evaluates to FALSE, and the ELSE clause (statement-2) is executed.

As with the IF-THEN, a single statement serves as the statement part of the conditional. When more than one statement is needed, they can be blocked together with the BEGIN-END pair, or procedures can be defined and called.

Another common use of the IF-THEN-ELSE statement occurs when we want to assign the larger of two values to another variable. Assume the two values are assigned to the variables named **first** and **second** and that the variable to receive the larger value is named **larger**. A statement to accomplish this would look like the following:

```
WRITE(OUTPUT, prompt);
READLN(INPUT, first, second);
IF (first > second)
    THEN larger := first
    ELSE larger := second
```

Programming Example 6-12:   Determining Larger with IF-THEN-ELSE

Both IF-THEN and IF-THEN-ELSE statements may serve as an action of either an IF-THEN or IF-THEN-ELSE statement. This is known as a *nested IF-THEN* statement. For example, suppose the previous example was modified so **larger** received the larger of **first** and **second** or the value of zero (0) if they have the same value.

```
WRITE(OUTPUT, prompt);
READLN(INPUT, first, second);
IF (first > second)
    THEN larger := first
    ELSE IF (second > first)
            THEN larger := second
            ELSE larger := 0
```

Programming Example 6-13:   Nested IF-THEN-ELSE

6.2.1. Formal Definition

The BNF for the Pascal IF statement follows:

```
<if-statement> ::= IF <boolean-expression> THEN <statement> |
                   IF <boolean-expression> THEN <statement>
                         ELSE <statement>
```

Notice that there is technically one IF statement in Pascal. The IF may take one of two forms. These forms are the IF-THEN and the IF-THEN-ELSE.

6.2.2. Dangling ELSE

Recall the *dangling else* problem introduced in Karel (page 63). The same problem occurs in Pascal. Say we were interested in some variable named **value**. Consider the following two fragments of code.

```
IF value <> 0                            IF value <> 0
  THEN IF value > 0                        THEN IF value > 0
        THEN WRITELN(OUTPUT,'value > 0')       THEN WRITELN(OUTPUT,'value > 0')
        ELSE WRITELN(OUTPUT,message)       ELSE WRITELN(OUTPUT,message)
```

Programming Example 6-14:   Dangling Else

At first glance, these appear to be two very similar but different constructions. The first appears to be an IF-THEN-ELSE statement with an IF-THEN statement as its action. The second appears to be an IF-THEN statement with an IF-THEN-ELSE as the THEN clause. What do we know about **value** when the statement WRITELN(OUTPUT, message) executes? It seems that (**value** < 0) for the first example, and (**value** = 0) for the second example. However, recall that indentation and spacing are ignored by the compiler. They are only aids to programmers. Here that fact can be particularly deceiving since both of the two fragments yield the same construction, an IF-THEN with an IF-THEN-ELSE as its action! Both of the previous code fragments are equivalent to the following fragment:

```
IF value<>0 THEN IF value>0 THEN WRITELN(OUTPUT, 'value > 0') ELSE WRITELN(OUTPUT,message)
```

Programming Example 6-15: Dangling Else Without Indentation

Pascal, like Karel, resolves this situation according to the following rule:

The "dangling else" is associated with the "closest elseless" IF-THEN statement.

This means the dangling else clause from the previous examples (WRITELN(OUTPUT, message)) is associated with the second IF-THEN statement (IF value > 0 THEN WRITELN(OUTPUT, 'value > 0')). This means the dangling ELSE clause executes when **value** is <> 0 AND not > 0, hence when **value** < 0.

To achieve the opposite effect (associate the ELSE with the first IF-THEN), we need to use a *compound statement*, as the following code fragment illustrates.

```
IF value <> 0
    THEN BEGIN
            IF value > 0
                THEN WRITELN(OUTPUT, 'value > 0')
         END
    ELSE WRITELN(OUTPUT, message)
```

Programming Example 6-16: Using BEGIN-END to Alter Dangling Else

Although the dangling else is automatically associated with the last elseless IF-THEN statement in Pascal, often we want to make it clear for someone else who might have to read our program. If we wanted the previous example to have the ELSE associated with the second IF-THEN, we might clearly show it the following way:

```
IF value <> 0
    THEN BEGIN
            IF value > 0
                THEN WRITELN(OUTPUT, 'value > 0')
                ELSE WRITELN(OUTPUT, message)
         END
```

Programming Example 6-17: Using BEGIN-END to Clarify Dangling Else

This BEGIN-END pair is not strictly necessary because it does not alter the program's meaning or order of execution. The extra BEGIN-END block, like redundant parentheses, makes the program more readable by eliminating ambiguity.

6.2.3. Questions

1. Describe the difference between Pascal's IF-THEN and IF-THEN-ELSE statements.

2. What are exclusive conditions?

3. What are exhaustive conditions?

4. What are mutually exclusive and exhaustive conditions?

5. What is the *dangling else* problem? What is Pascal's interpretation associated with such a construction?

6.2.4. Exercises

1. Consider the following code fragment. What output will be displayed for **value** = 1, 0 and −1.

```
IF value <> 0
    THEN IF value > 0
            THEN WRITELN(OUTPUT, 'value > 0')
    ELSE WRITELN(OUTPUT, 'value = 0')
```

2. Modify the previous program fragment so the output is not contradictory.

3. What is the output of the following program fragment for each of the following inputs: *0, 3, −3*?

```
READLN(INPUT, number);
IF number = 0
    THEN WRITELN(OUTPUT, 'number is zero.')
    ELSE IF number > 0
            THEN WRITELN(OUTPUT, 'number is positive.')
            ELSE WRITELN(OUTPUT, 'number is negative.')
```

6.2.5. Problems

1. Write a Pascal program that reads one character and displays YES if the character is one of the three characters (&, #, %) and displays NO otherwise. Be sure to prompt the user for the input.

2. Write a program that reads an integer and displays its absolute value. *Hint: The absolute value of a number has no sign.*

3. Write a program to determine if a given number is even or odd, and display an appropriate message in either case.

4. Write a program that prompts for and reads an integer and displays 1 if the value is positive, −1 if the value is negative, and 0 otherwise.

5. Write a program that reads two integers and determines and displays the smaller of the two.

6. Write a program that reads three integers and determines and displays the smaller of the three.

7. Write a simple payroll program. It should prompt for the number of hours and the hourly rate, and it should compute and display the amount earned. If any of the hours are in excess of 40, they should be computed at 1.5 times the normal hourly rate.

8. Modify the program for the tax advice problem from the previous section (problem 8 on page 179) so that it uses IF-THEN-ELSE statements. Also, extend this program so it will reduce the taxable income for dependents. The program should ask the user for total number of dependents, multiply the number of dependents by $1000, and subtract the result from the total earnings. This will yield the taxable income.

6.3. CASE Statement

We modeled the IF-THEN statement with one condition-action pair. We modeled the IF-THEN-ELSE with two condition-action pairs in which the two conditions were negations of each other. Therefore, up to this point we have been interested in only one condition or a condition and its negation. However, there are many situations in which we will be interested in more than two conditions. Suppose, for example, we were concerned with a variable named **day** with a value in the range 1 through 7, and we wanted to display the associated day of the week: Sunday through Saturday, respectively. Logically, we have seven condition-action pairs as follows:

```
(day = 1)   →    display Sunday
(day = 2)   →    display Monday
(day = 3)   →    display Tuesday
(day = 4)   →    display Wednesday
(day = 5)   →    display Thursday
(day = 6)   →    display Friday
(day = 7)   →    display Saturday
```

If we tried to implement this in Pascal using the IF-THEN statement, we would end up with something like the following:

```
IF (day = 1) THEN WRITELN(OUTPUT, 'Sunday');
IF (day = 2) THEN WRITELN(OUTPUT, 'Monday');
IF (day = 3) THEN WRITELN(OUTPUT, 'Tuesday');
IF (day = 4) THEN WRITELN(OUTPUT, 'Wednesday');
IF (day = 5) THEN WRITELN(OUTPUT, 'Thursday');
IF (day = 6) THEN WRITELN(OUTPUT, 'Friday');
IF (day = 7) THEN WRITELN(OUTPUT, 'Saturday')
```

Programming Example 6-18: Handling 7 Conditions with the IF-THEN

However, a little more careful consideration reveals that each of the seven conditions are exclusive (unique). Therefore, only one condition is TRUE and only one action will be executed. Knowing this, we can rewrite the previous series of IF-THEN statements as a nested series of IF-THEN-ELSE statements as follows:

```
        IF (day = 1) THEN WRITELN(OUTPUT, 'Sunday')
ELSE IF (day = 2) THEN WRITELN(OUTPUT, 'Monday')
ELSE IF (day = 3) THEN WRITELN(OUTPUT, 'Tuesday')
ELSE IF (day = 4) THEN WRITELN(OUTPUT, 'Wednesday')
ELSE IF (day = 5) THEN WRITELN(OUTPUT, 'Thursday')
ELSE IF (day = 6) THEN WRITELN(OUTPUT, 'Friday')
ELSE IF (day = 7) THEN WRITELN(OUTPUT, 'Saturday')
```

Programming Example 6-19: Handling 7 Conditions with the IF-THEN-ELSE

The second example stops evaluating the conditions as soon as a TRUE one is found, but the earlier example always evaluates all 7 conditions. Although the second example saves evaluations, it is somewhat harder to read and follow. While both of these solutions work, it should be clear that neither the IF-THEN or IF-THEN-ELSE statements were designed to handle this particular type of situation. For problems such as this, we can use Pascal's generalized selection mechanism, which is called the **CASE** statement. The previous program fragment rewritten with a single CASE statement looks like the following:

```
CASE day OF
    1: WRITELN(OUTPUT, 'Sunday');
    2: WRITELN(OUTPUT, 'Monday');
    3: WRITELN(OUTPUT, 'Tuesday');
    4: WRITELN(OUTPUT, 'Wednesday');
    5: WRITELN(OUTPUT, 'Thursday');
    6: WRITELN(OUTPUT, 'Friday');
    7: WRITELN(OUTPUT, 'Saturday')
END;     (* CASE *)
```

Programming Example 6-20: Handling 7 Conditions with the CASE

The value of the variable **day** is determined. Then the matching value is determined. The statement corresponding to the matching value is then executed.

Recall that we thought of the IF-THEN as a single condition-action pair:

condition → **action**

We thought of the IF-THEN-ELSE as two condition action pairs in which the two conditions were the negations of each other:

condition-1 → **action-1**
condition-2 → **action-2**

The CASE statement may be thought of as a collection of condition-action pairs:

condition-1 → **action-1**
condition-2 → **action-2**
condition-3 → **action-3**
     ⋮   ⋮
     ⋮   ⋮
     ⋮   ⋮
condition-N → **action-N**

The form of the CASE statement is as follows:

```
CASE <selector> OF
    <value1>: <statement1>;
    <value2>: <statement2>;
    <value3>: <statement3>;
           :              :
           :              :
           :              :
    <valueN>: <statementN>
END
```

The <selector> is any *ordinal expression*, which includes INTEGER, BOOLEAN, or CHAR expressions but not expressions of type REAL (ordinal types were discussed on page 135). Most commonly, they are expressions of type CHAR or a subset of the type INTEGER. The <value>s of the CASE statement are constants of the same type as the <selector>. The <statement>s are any valid Pascal statements.

The way the CASE statement works is very intuitive. The selector expression is evaluated. The enumerated value equal to the selector is then determined. The statement associated with the matching value is then executed. Program execution then continues after the END of the CASE statement.

As another example, suppose we were writing a program that tallies the number of people in each political party. Assume for this example that there are three political parties: Republican, Democrat, and Independent. There would be a portion of the program that prompts the user for his political party (say, R, D, or I) and then increments the appropriate total. It would look something like the following in Pascal:

```
WRITE(OUTPUT, prompt);
READLN(INPUT, party);

CASE party OF
    'R': Republicans := Republicans + 1;
    'D': Democrats := Democrats + 1;
    'I': Independents := Independents + 1
END;     (* CASE *)
```

Programming Example 6-21:   Political Party Counter

Another example arises from considering the computer that you are using. You type a command at the keyboard. The computer's operating system reads this command and then executes the appropriate system program. We do not know enough yet to write an entire operating system, but we can begin work on a simple command interpreter. Consider an example that uses only four commands: 'h' (to get help), 't' (to get the time), 'u' (to list all the current users), and 'q' (to quit). Using what we have learned, we might write a program fragment somewhat like the following:

```
WRITE(OUTPUT, CommandPrompt);
READLN(INPUT, command);

CASE command OF
    'h': GiveHelp;
    't': GiveTime;
    'u': ListUsers;
    'q': Quit
END;     (* CASE *)
```

Programming Example 6-22:   Simple Command Interpreter

The WRITE statement prompts the user for a command. The READLN statement takes the response from the input and gives it to the variable **command**. The variable **command**, which is of type CHAR, is then used as the selector expression of a CASE statement. The command entered determines which procedure is selected to execute.

This program fragment illustrates another very important point. Notice that we have not written the procedures for **GiveHelp**, **GiveTime**, **ListUsers**, or **Quit**. It is not important for the details of these procedures to be filled out when they are first used in the CASE statement. It is important for the CASE statement to work properly first; then you can fill in the details of the procedures. This point follows the programming design principle known as *top-down design*. This notion is called **programming with stubs**.

> **Definition 6-8:** *Programming with stubs* is the practice of writing small, place-holding or shell procedures as the first pass in writing a large program. The body of the stub procedure is filled out at a later time.

We will go into detail about top-down design and programming with stubs later in the text. However, the following example stub of **GiveHelp** illustrates the practice.

```
PROCEDURE GiveHelp;

BEGIN
    WRITELN(OUTPUT, 'Entering procedure GiveHelp.');
    WRITELN(OUTPUT, 'Procedure is not yet complete.');
    WRITELN(OUTPUT, 'Exiting procedure GiveHelp.')
END; (* GiveHelp *)
```

Programming Example 6-23: Stub Procedure

Allowing more than one or two condition-action pairs can complicate things a bit. We are faced with questions such as: Can two actions have the same condition? Can two conditions have the same action? Can some conditions have no action?

If several conditions have the same action, we may combine all the associated clauses into a single clause of the CASE statement. We enumerate all the conditions separated by commas and associate them with the common action. For example, we can replace the following fragment with the second abbreviated version:

```
CASE command OF
    'h': GiveHelp;
    't': GiveTime;
    'u': ListUsers;
    'q': Quit;
    'a': IllegalCommand;
    'b': IllegalCommand;
    'c': IllegalCommand;
    'd': IllegalCommand;
    'e': IllegalCommand
END;    (* CASE *)
```

Programming Example 6-24: Duplicated Action

```
CASE command OF
    'h': GiveHelp;
    't': GiveTime;
    'u': ListUsers;
    'q': Quit;
    'a', 'b', 'c', 'd', 'e': IllegalCommand
END;    (* CASE *)
```

Programming Example 6-25: Combining Conditions with Common Action

Similarly, if we wanted to permit the use of uppercase or lowercase letters for the political party counter, the following fragments would work:

```
WRITE(OUTPUT, prompt);
READLN(INPUT, party);

CASE party OF
    'R': Republicans := Republicans + 1;
    'r': Republicans := Republicans + 1;
    'D': Democrats := Democrats + 1;
    'd': Democrats := Democrats + 1;
    'I': Independents := Independents + 1;
    'i': Independents := Independents + 1
END;    (* CASE *)
```

Programming Example 6-26: Same Action for Uppercase and Lowercase Value

```
WRITE(OUTPUT, prompt);
READLN(INPUT, party);

CASE party OF
    'R','r': Republicans := Republicans + 1;
    'D','d': Democrats := Democrats + 1;
    'I','i': Independents := Independents + 1
END;    (* CASE *)
```

Programming Example 6-27: Combining Uppercase and Lowercase Values

These examples illustrate that conditions with a common action may be combined in Pascal's CASE statement. However, the conditions must still be *exclusive*. Therefore, all values in a CASE statement must be unique; none may be repeated.

Besides being exclusive, the values must also be *exhaustive*. *All possible values of the selector expression must be enumerated in the CASE statement.* This requirement can be a bit of a problem for selector expressions that may have many possible values, such as expressions of the type INTEGER. It is an error for a CASE statement selector expression to evaluate to a value that is not listed in the CASE statement. There are three ways to meet this requirement: (1) enumerate all possible values of the selector expression type, (2) test the selector expression with an IF-THEN statement before executing the CASE statement, or (3) exploit a nonstandard extension known as an "otherwise" clause.

The first of these three methods needs no further explanation. However, the first may be impractical in some cases; for example, the expression may be any possible INTEGER. The second is illustrated by the following program fragment:

```
IF (day >= 1) AND (day <= 7)
    THEN CASE day OF
            1: WRITELN(OUTPUT, 'Sunday');
            2: WRITELN(OUTPUT, 'Monday');
            3: WRITELN(OUTPUT, 'Tuesday');
            4: WRITELN(OUTPUT, 'Wednesday');
            5: WRITELN(OUTPUT, 'Thursday');
            6: WRITELN(OUTPUT, 'Friday');
            7: WRITELN(OUTPUT, 'Saturday')
        END;    (* CASE *)
```

Programming Example 6-28: Testing BEFORE a CASE Statement

Note that the IF test ensures that the CASE statement will not be executed with **day** having a value other than the 7 values listed in the CASE statement.

Although we do not propose using nonstandard features, we recognize that Standard Pascal places a requirement on its CASE statement that is not easy to comply with. This is a deficiency on the part of Standard Pascal. A "default" or "otherwise" clause would have eliminated such a deficiency. Many implementations have added an otherwise clause as an extension. In the event your implementation has an otherwise clause, we know you will find it extremely useful. However, you should remember that such a feature is nonstandard. This may cause problems if you wish to move any of your programs to another implementation.

There are a few final points you should know about Pascal's CASE statement. The first is that the order of the values and their actions does not affect the result of the CASE statement. Which condition-action pair is first and which is last has no effect on which one gets executed. Secondly, the action clauses (statements) of Pascal's CASE statement are technically optional. One or more values may have an *empty statement*, also known as the **null statement**.

>   **Definition 6-9:** The ***null statement*** is a statement that causes no action. It is also known as the ***empty statement***.

In the CASE statement, for example, the null statement is indicated by following the colon that separates the value and its associated statement with a semicolon. One does this only when no action is to be taken for a value of the selector expression. As an example, say we wanted our political party counter to ignore all the Democrats: The following program fragment illustrates this:

```
WRITE(OUTPUT, prompt);
READLN(INPUT, party);

CASE party OF
    'R','r': Republicans := Republicans + 1;
    'D','d': ;  (* no action *)
    'I','i': Independents := Independents + 1
END;    (* CASE *)
```

> **Programming Example 6-29:**   Null Statement as Action

The null statement indicates that no action is to be taken. It is a very good idea to include a comment in your program noting that no action is to be taken. Such a comment will prevent others from thinking you accidentally forgot to include the action.

There is one more thing to keep in mind about the CASE statement. You may recall that the CASE selector must be an expression of ordinal type. All our examples have used variables of ordinal type. The following example illustrates the use of an expression as the CASE selector. If you wanted to simulate the toss of a single die and **number** was indeed a random number, the following program fragment would do the job:

```
CASE (number MOD 6) + 1 OF
    1: WRITELN(OUTPUT, 'The die is a one');
    2: WRITELN(OUTPUT, 'The die is a two');
    3: WRITELN(OUTPUT, 'The die is a three');
    4: WRITELN(OUTPUT, 'The die is a four');
    5: WRITELN(OUTPUT, 'The die is a five');
    6: WRITELN(OUTPUT, 'The die is a six')
END;    (* CASE *)
```

> **Programming Example 6-30:**   Complicated Selector Expression

6.3.1. Formal Definition

The BNF for the full conditional statement is as follows.

```
<conditional-statement> ::= <if-statement> | <case-statement>

<if-statement> ::= IF <boolean-expression> THEN <statement> |
                   IF <boolean-expression> THEN <statement>
                        ELSE <statement>

<case-statement> ::=  CASE <case-index> OF <case-list-element>
          { ; <case-list-element> } [ ; ] END

<case-index> ::=  <expression>

<case-list-element> ::=  <case-constant-list> : <statement>

<case-constant-list> ::=  <case-constant> { , <case-constant> }

<case-constant> ::=  <constant>
```

Note that there is no matching BEGIN for the END of a CASE statement. Note also that a compound statement may be used as an action clause for the CASE statement. We do not advocate using the compound statement as the action clause because lengthy action clauses obscure the meaning of CASE. In general, if an action requires a compound statement it should be written as a procedure. A well-chosen procedure name will make the intent of the CASE statement clear.

6.3.2. Questions

1. What is conditional execution? When do we want to use it? What does it add to programs?

2. How many conditional execution control structures does Pascal have? Name each of them.

3. How many abstract condition action pairs are necessary to describe each of Pascal's conditional execution constructions?

4. Describe briefly how Pascal's CASE statement works.

5. What is programming with stubs?

6. Explain how condition-action pairs with the same action can be combined in Pascal's CASE statement.

7. What is an otherwise clause?

8. Does Standard Pascal have an otherwise clause?

9. Does your Pascal system implement the otherwise clause? What is it called?

10. Must all possible values of the selector expression be enumerated in the CASE statement? If so, in what ways may this requirement be met?

11. What is a null or empty statement? What action does it do? What purpose does it serve?

6.3.3. Exercises

1. Modify Programming Example 6-21 so that the selector expression may not have a value that is not enumerated in the case statement.

2. Make the same type of modification to Programming Example 6-22.

3. Does Programming Example 6-30 on page 188 need an IF-THEN test before the CASE statement? Justify your answer.

6.3.4. Problems

1. Write a program that converts the integers in the range 1 through 10 to their ordinal equivalents (first, second, third, etc.).

2. Write a program that takes the following characters as input and displays the corresponding output.

```
d        doe
r        ray
m        me
f        fah
s        so
l        lah
t        tea
```

3. Extend the previous program so it works for both uppercase and lowercase characters.

4. Write a program that takes the following characters as input and prints the corresponding day of the week.

```
m        monday
tu       tuesday
w        wednesday
th       thursday
f        friday
sa       saturday
su       sunday
```

5. Modify the program for the tax advice problem from the previous section to include the

CASE statement for determining amount of taxes. Use the following rates to determine the tax based on taxable earnings: Less than \$10,000 = 5% ; \$10,000 to \$15,000 = 10% ; \$15,001 to \$20,000 = 15% ; \$20,001 to \$25,000 = 20% . Although these rates are fictional, you should be able to use this approach to write a program using the correct information.

6.4. A Debugging Aid

After we get our program into the computer, we must get the errors or bugs out of our program. This process is known as *debugging* and is a natural step of programming computers. It is a good idea for the programmer to create test cases for the program as it is constructed. In this way the programmer can exercise a program making sure that the program's essential features are performed correctly. Good test cases provide a systematic way of uncovering a program's bugs.

A critical step in determining the correctness of a program or portion thereof usually involves knowing the values of certain variables. Some systems have elaborate debuggers built in to aid the programmer in a variety of ways. Unfortunately, many systems provide little or no debugging assistance to the programmer. Therefore, most programmers find themselves inserting a WRITELN statment here and there to determine the values of important variables. There is, however, a problem with this technique. Normally the problem arises when we believe the program or a portion thereof is debugged. We don't want this debugging information forever displayed (it is only to help in debugging) so there comes a time to remove the debugging WRITELNs. Inevitably, as soon as we remove the WRITELNs, another bug is found. We are then faced with the wasteful task of reinserting the statements we just finished removing. What we need is a way to turn debugging statements on and off in a simple way. The IF-THEN statement can provide a neat way to do just that. The following code fragment illustrates using the IF-THEN statement for this purpose:

```
CONST
    debugging = TRUE;     (* debugging is a switch, set before compilation *)
        .
        .
        .

    IF debugging           (* These occur at various places in the program *)
        THEN WRITELN(OUTPUT, variable)
```

Programming Example 6-31: Debugging Aid

Debugging is a constant of type BOOLEAN. During the debugging phase, the constant is set to TRUE. Once the debugging stage is thought to be over, the constant is set to FALSE. Should you discover another bug at some later time, you need only change the value of the constant **debugging** back to TRUE to activate the debugging features. Recall our simple command interpreter from earlier in the chapter. If we were debugging that program, one of the variables that probably would have interested us was the command being interpreted. The following programming fragment shows that code with this debugging aid.

```
CONST
    debugging = TRUE;
        .
        .
        .

    IF debugging THEN WRITELN(OUTPUT, 'DEBUG: command = ', command);

CASE command OF
    'h': GiveHelp;
    't': GiveTime;
    'u': ListUsers;
    'q': Quit;
    'a', 'b', 'c', 'd', 'e': IllegalCommand
END;     (* CASE *)
```

Programming Example 6-32: Debugging

Over the years, we have found this simple debugging aid, along with a few extensions to it, to be unbelievably useful. We hope it is equally useful to you.

6.5. Simplifying the Condition

With the ability to create arbitrary BOOLEAN expressions comes the possibility of creating expressions that are difficult to understand.   The mathematics of BOOLEAN operators is well understood, and a brief overview of some of the better known findings is helpful for writing accurate programs.   In this section we will consider the laws that govern simplification and evaluation of Boolean expressions.

6.5.1. Commutative Law

A binary operator is said to be *commutative* if exchanging the order of its two operands does not affect the result.   The addition and multiplication operators are commutative, but subtraction and division are not.   Both the operators **AND** and **OR** are commutative.   This means that the following equivalences hold logically.   We give both a specific example and the general form for each.   The ≡ symbol signifies equivalence.

$$(index < max) \text{ AND } (data <> sentinel) \equiv (data <> sentinel) \text{ AND } (index < max)$$

$$exp1 \text{ AND } exp2 \equiv exp2 \text{ AND } exp1$$

$$(index < max) \text{ OR } (data <> sentinel) \equiv (data <> sentinel) \text{ OR } (index < max)$$

$$exp1 \text{ OR } exp2 \equiv exp2 \text{ OR } exp1$$

Table 6-1: Commutativity of AND and OR

Commutativity of **AND** and **OR** means that for expressions consisting of BOOLEANs joined by these operators, operands may be exchanged without changing the truth value of the expression.   You might think that this is obvious and hardly worth mentioning, but problems can arise due to the differing ways that Pascal systems interpret the condition.   Here is an example.

A system can be speeded up if it stops evaluating a BOOLEAN condition as soon as the value of the expression is known.   Thus, an expression consisting of an **AND** operator can stop evaluating when one of its terms is found to be false because the entire expression is then FALSE.   Similarly, a BOOLEAN expression formed by an **OR** operator can safely terminate evaluation when one operand is found to be true because this fixes the truth value of the entire expression to TRUE.   Some systems actually perform evaluation of BOOLEAN expressions in exactly this way.

Here is how a programmer can get into trouble with this.   Suppose you have the following code:

```
IF (n/m) > (1.0) THEN statement
```

With **n** and **m** both of type REAL, this is a sensible condition that might have some mathematical use. What happens if **m** = 0.0? If **m** = 0.0, our condition asks for division by 0.0, which results in a runtime error in virtually any system.   Now let's suppose the Pascal system stops evaluation as soon as the truth value of the BOOLEAN expression is established.   Some programmers write the following:

```
IF (m <> 0.0)  AND  (n/m > 1.0) THEN statement
```

Whenever **m** is zero, the expression stops its evaluation before getting to the second clause of the AND, thereby avoiding the problem of division by zero.   Notice that the commutative law does not hold on such systems!

```
IF  (n/m > 1.0) AND (m <> 0.0) THEN statement
```

This is a different statement from its predecessor.   Programmers who exploit this sort of system feature tend to think of themselves as quite clever.   But the truth is that this style of programming is very bad. Code such as this is not transportable between systems.   One of the goals of programming is to write transportable, robust code.   *Transportable* means the code is not limited to only a particular machine or particular implementation.   *Robust* means it is not fragile by virtue of exploiting subtle or nonstandard language features.   The correct way to deal with the situation used in this illustration is to nest the IF.

```
IF   (m <> 0.0)
     THEN IF (n/m > 1.0)
              THEN statement
```

The rule by which you should program is to assume that BOOLEAN expressions are fully evaluated. Assume that the Commutative Law holds.

6.5.2. Associative Law

A binary operator is said to be *associative* if, when it is used several times, parentheses are irrelevant to the result. The addition and multiplication operators are associative, but the subtraction and division operators are not. Both the **AND** operator and **OR** operator are associative. The following table shows a specific example and the general form for each operator.

((*index* < *max*) AND (*data* <> *sentinel*)) AND (*command* = *quit*)
is equivalent to
(*index* < *max*) AND ((*data* <> *sentinel*) AND (*command* = *quit*))

(*exp1* AND *exp2*) AND *exp3* $\equiv$ *exp1* AND (*exp2* AND *exp3*)

((*index* < *max*) OR (*data* <> *sentinel*)) OR (*command* = *quit*)
is equivalent to
(*index* < *max*) OR ((*data* <> *sentinel*) OR (*command* = *quit*))

(*exp1* OR *exp2*) OR *exp3* $\equiv$ *exp1* OR (*exp2* OR *exp3*)

Table 6-2: Associativity of AND and OR

Operator associativity is fairly intuitive and, like commutativity, easily understood.

6.5.3. Distributive Laws

Most people are familiar with the Distributive Law of multiplication over addition. Specifically, (a * b) + (a * c) is equivalent to a * (b + c). Similarly, it holds for both **AND** over **OR** and **OR** over **AND**. The Distributive Laws for **AND** and **OR** help the programmer to simplify the condition for the guarded statement. In the following table, we give both a specific example and the general form of the Distributive Law.

((*index* < *max*) OR (*data* <> *sentinel*)) AND ((*index* < *max*) OR (*command* = *quit*))
is equivalent to
(*index* < *max*) OR ((*data* <> *sentinel*) AND (*command* = *quit*))

(*exp1* OR *exp2*) AND (*exp1* OR *exp3*) $\equiv$ *exp1* OR (*exp2* AND *exp3*)

((*index* < *max*) AND (*data* <> *sentinel*)) OR ((*index* < *max*) AND (*command* = *quit*))
is equivalent to
(*index* < *max*) AND ((*data* <> *sentinel*) OR (*command* = *quit*))

(*exp1* AND *exp2*) OR (*exp1* AND *exp3*) $\equiv$ *exp1* AND (*exp2* OR *exp3*)

Table 6-3: Distributive Law for AND and OR

The Distributive Law is useful in simplifying conditions that you create for your programs.

6.5.4. DeMorgan's Laws

Often in programming we need to negate a Boolean expression. There exists a pair of laws, known as DeMorgan's Laws, that give us an easy way to transform a negated expression into an equivalent expression. In the following table, we give both a specific example and the general form for both of DeMorgan's Laws.

NOT((*index* < *max*) AND (*data* <> *sentinel*))
which is equivalent to
NOT(*index* < *max*) OR NOT(*data* <> *sentinel*)
which reduces to
(*index* >= *max*) OR (*data* = *sentinel*)

NOT(*exp1* AND *exp2*) ≡ NOT(*exp1*) OR NOT(*exp2*)

NOT((*index* < *max*) OR (*data* <> *sentinel*))
which is equivalent to
NOT(*index* < *max*) AND NOT(*data* <> *sentinel*)
which reduces to
(*index* >= *max*) AND (*data* = *sentinel*)

NOT(*exp1* OR *exp2*) ≡ NOT(*exp1*) AND NOT(*exp2*)

Table 6-4:   DeMorgan's Laws

DeMorgan's Laws are quite useful in dealing with the negations of Boolean expressions.

6.5.5. Other Laws

There are many other laws that deal with Boolean expressions. We will look at five of the most useful ones from a programming standpoint. The name of each law, a specific example, and its general form appear in the following table:

Negation
NOT(NOT(command = quit)) ≡ (command = quit)
NOT(NOT(*exp*)) ≡ *exp*

Excluded Middle
(*command* = quit) OR (*command* <> quit) ≡ TRUE
exp OR NOT*exp* ≡ TRUE

Contradiction
(*command* = quit) AND (*command* <> quit) ≡ FALSE
exp AND NOT*exp* ≡ FALSE

OR Simplification
(*index* < *max*) OR ((*index* < *max*) AND (*data* <> *sentinel*)) ≡ (*index* < *max*)
exp1 OR (*exp1* AND *exp2*) ≡ *exp1*

AND Simplification
(*index* < *max*) AND ((*index* < *max*) OR (*data* <> *sentinel*)) ≡ (*index* < *max*)
exp1 AND (*exp1* OR *exp2*) ≡ *exp1*

Table 6-5:   Other BOOLEAN Laws

The laws of negation, the excluded middle, and contradiction are relatively easy to keep in mind and quite useful since they can be used to simplify expressions. However, the laws governing OR and AND simplification are surprising at first glance. They are equally useful. We summarize all of the laws presented in this section in the following table:

For this table assume a, b, and c are any valid BOOLEAN expressions.

Commutative	a AND $b \equiv b$ AND a a OR $b \equiv b$ OR a
Associative	$(a$ AND $b)$ AND $c \equiv a$ AND $(b$ AND $c)$ $(a$ OR $b)$ OR $c \equiv a$ OR $(b$ OR $c)$
Distributive	$(a$ OR $b)$ AND $(a$ OR $c) \equiv a$ OR $(b$ AND $c)$ $(a$ AND $b)$ OR $(a$ AND $c) \equiv a$ AND $(b$ OR $c)$
DeMorgan	NOT$(a$ AND $b) \equiv$ NOT(a) OR NOT(b) NOT$(a$ OR $b) \equiv$ NOT(a) AND NOT(b)
Negation	NOT(NOT$(a)) \equiv a$
Excluded Middle	a OR NOT$(a) \equiv$ TRUE
Contradiction	a AND NOT$(a) \equiv$ FALSE
OR Simplification	a OR $(a$ AND $b) \equiv a$
AND Simplification	a AND $(a$ OR $b) \equiv a$

Table 6-6: Summary of Simplification Laws

There are two main reasons for concerning ourselves with laws governing Boolean expressions. First, they allow us to determine if two Boolean expressions are equivalent. This is particularly useful when reading another person's program or when later reading your own program. You can tell if the expression you are currently thinking of is equivalent to one in another program. Second, often an expression is much simpler than an equivalent. Simpler expressions make a program easier to read. An equivalent program that is easier to read by humans usually requires fewer evaluations by the computer.

The following might illustrate this point:

```
IF  (index < max)  AND  ((index < max)  OR  (data <> sentinel))
    THEN SomeStatement

can be simplified to

IF  (index < max)
    THEN SomeStatement
```

The second form is simpler to read and simpler for the computer to evaluate.

6.5.6. Questions

1. Describe how the IF-THEN statement can be used in conjunction with a named constant as a simple debugging aid.

2. Name each of the four major laws presented in this section.

3. Give an example of each law named in the previous question.

4. State the general form of each of the four major laws.

5. Name each of the five minor laws presented in this section.

6. Give an example of each law named in the previous question.

7. State the general form of each of the five minor laws.

8. Some implementations of Pascal do not *completely* support the commutative law since exchanging the two operands to the AND operator can lead to different program action for what should be the same AND expression.

    a. Describe why this comes about.

    b. State how and why some programmers exploit such noncommutativity.

    c. Are such exploits a good or bad programming practice? Justify your answer with at least one reason.

    d. Does your system completely support commutativity?   Determine this empirically.

6.5.7. Exercises

Let a, b, c, d, and e all be expressions of type BOOLEAN. Using the laws defined in this section, simplify the following expressions. Be sure to state which law you used for each step of a simplification.

1. `(a OR b) AND (b OR c)`

2. `((a OR b) OR c) AND NOT (d and e)`

3. `(NOT a AND NOT b) OR NOT(c OR (d AND e))`

4. `(NOT a AND b) AND NOT(a AND NOT b)`

5. `IF NOT (a OR (b AND (b OR c)))`
      `THEN WRITELN(OUTPUT, sum)`

6. `IF a OR NOT a THEN`
      `THEN WRITELN(OUTPUT, total)`

7. `IF a THEN`
    `IF b   THEN`
        `IF c THEN WRITELN(OUTPUT, sum)`

8. `IF a AND (NOT a OR (NOT a AND b))`
      `THEN WRITELN(OUTPUT, count)`
      `ELSE WRITELN(OUTPUT, '****')`

6.6. Chapter Summary

- *Sequential execution* refers to executing a sequence of instructions in the same order as they appear in the sequence.

- *Control structures* are the elements of a programming language that determine the flow of program execution. In Pascal, the control structures are all statements.

- Pascal's six control structure statements fall into two distinct classes: conditional execution and repetition.

- The ***conditional execution*** control structures allow the programmer to control the execution of a statement depending on some condition.

- A set of *exhaustive* conditions means all possible conditions are considered.

- A set of *exclusive* conditions means each condition is unique and no two can be TRUE at the same time.

- A pair of conditions are ***mutually exclusive and exhaustive*** if and only if each condition is the *negation* of the other.

- The IF-THEN statement is the simplest of Pascal's three conditional execution control structures. When the *condition* evaluates to TRUE, the *action* executes. When the *condition* evaluates to FALSE, the *action* does not execute.

- Any BOOLEAN expression may serve as a condition for the IF-THEN and IF-THEN-ELSE statements.

- If the condition of an IF-THEN-ELSE statement is TRUE, the THEN clause is executed; otherwise the ELSE clause is executed.

- A dangling-else clause is an ELSE clause that can syntactically be associated with more than one IF-THEN statement.

- Pascal, like Karel, associates the dangling else with the "closest elseless IF-THEN statement".

- If the programmer wants an ELSE clause to be associated with other than the closest IF-THEN statement, a compound statement (BEGIN-END block) can be used to achieve the desired result.

- Neither the IF-THEN nor IF-THEN-ELSE statements were designed to handle more than two condition-action pairs. The CASE statement was created specifically for that purpose.

- The way the CASE statement works is very intuitive. The selector expression is evaluated. The enumerated value equal to the selector is then determined. The statement associated with the matching value is then executed. Program execution then continues after the END of the CASE statement.

- *Programming with stubs* is the practice of writing small, place-holding or shell procedures as the first pass in writing a large program. The body of the stub procedure is filled out at a later time.

- Pascal's CASE statement permits combining values with the same action into one clause.

- All values in a CASE statement must be *exclusive* (unique). None may be repeated in more than one clause.

- All possible values of the selector expression must be enumerated in the CASE statement. It is an error for a CASE statement selector expression to evaluate to a value that is not listed in the CASE statement. There are three ways to meet this requirement: (1) enumerate all possible values of the selector expression type, (2) test the selector expression with an IF-THEN statement before executing the CASE statement, or (3) exploit a nonstandard extension known as an "otherwise" clause. However, use of an "otherwise" clause, like the use of any other nonstandard feature, may cause problems if you later try to move the program to another implementation.

- The CASE selector may be any ordinal expression, rather than just a variable. Expressions of type REAL may not be used as CASE statement selectors.

- A bug is a program error.

- Debugging refers to the process of removing bugs from a program.

- The IF-THEN statement can be used in conjunction with a named constant to make a quite useful debugging aid.

- A *compound statement* in Pascal is simply a sequence of statements enclosed in a BEGIN-END pair and considered to be a single statement.

- A compound statement may be used as the action clause for either the IF-THEN, IF-THEN-ELSE, or CASE statements.

- Laws governing Boolean expressions allow us to determine if two Boolean expressions are equivalent.

- Simpler expressions make a program easier to read.

- An equivalent program that is easier to read by humans usually requires fewer evaluations by the computer.

- There are a variety of laws for creating simpler or equivalent Boolean expressions. The most common ones are summarized in Table 6-6 on page 194.

6.7. Summary of Style

- Redundant parentheses have no effect on how a Pascal program executes. The use of redundant parentheses is like that of comments. They are solely for those persons who read the program. They increase a program's readability.

- Indentation and spacing are ignored by the compiler. Reasonable usage in formatting programs can dramatically increase a program's readability.

- Although we must use a BEGIN-END block to alter how Pascal normally interprets which IF-THEN to associate with a dangling-else clause, it is a reasonable programming practice to use a BEGIN-END block to clarify how a dangling else is treated.

- The null statment can introduce confusion. We strongly recommend including a comment indicating that a null statement is being employed so the reader of a program will not incorrectly assume that a statement was simply forgotten.

- We do not advocate the use of lengthy action clauses in CASE statements with the compound statement. By replacing the sequence of statements with a single procedure call to a procedure that does the required actions, a program's readability is usually enhanced.

- One of the goals of programming is to write transportable, robust code. *Transportable* means the code is not limited only to a particular machine or particular implementation. *Robust* means it is not fragile by virtue of exploiting subtle or nonstandard language features.

- Some implementations of Pascal do not *completely* support the Commutative Law since exchanging the two operands to the AND operator can lead to different program actions for what should be the same AND expression. It is poor programming style to depend on the exploitation of such features in order for a program to work as expected.

6.8. Summary of Terms

- sequential execution
- control structures
- conditional execution
- repetition
- condition
- action
- condition-action pair
- IF-THEN statement
- compound statement
- IF-THEN-ELSE statement
- exclusive
- exhaustive

- mutually exclusive and exhaustive
- nested statement
- dangling else
- CASE statement
- empty statement
- null statement
- programming with stubs
- otherwise clause
- bug
- debugging

- Commutative Law
- Associative Law
- Distributive Law
- DeMorgan's Law
- Law of Negation
- Law of Contradiction
- Law of Excluded Middle
- OR Simplification Law
- AND Simplification Law
- transportable code
- robust code

6.9. Chapter Problems

1. Write a Pascal program that prompts for a letter and then determines and displays if the entered letter is a vowel.

2. Extend the previous program to also display if the entered letter is a consonant.

3. Extend the previous program to display an appropriate message if the character entered is not a letter.

4. The VHF television band covers channels 2 through 13. Write a Pascal program that prompts for a channel number and displays the call letters for the local station with that number.

5. Most television cable systems carry more than 12 channels. Extend the previous program to cover channels 2 through 36.

6. Write a program that prompts the user for a year and determines and displays whether that year is an Olympic year. Olympic years are evenly divisible by 4. For example, 1988 is an Olympic year, but 1990 is not.

7. Write a program that prompts the user for a year and determines and displays whether that year is a leap year. Leap years are evenly divisible by 4 but not by 400. For example, 1900 is a leap year, but 2000 is not.

8. Write a program that takes as input a date in numeric form (i.e. mmddyy) and translates it into a textual form. For example, input of 102857 becomes October 28, 1957.

Chapter 7: Repetition

The last chapter was devoted to *conditional control structures*. You should now have a firm grasp on Pascal's IF-THEN, IF-THEN-ELSE, and CASE statements. They will enable you to write numerous useful programs. In addition to the conditional control structures, there is another class of control structures best known as the *repetition control structures*. While conditional control structures use conditions to determine which action to execute, repetition control structures use conditions to determine how many times to repeat execution of an action.

Definition 7-1: The *repetition* control structures allow for repeated execution of statements.

As you will see later, there is a whole class of programs that we would be unable to write without repetition. Let us look at an example to help illustrate the need for repetition. Suppose you are to write a procedure that prints a histogram[1] to graphically represent running distances. The procedure must print some symbol, say an asterisk (*), for each mile that a marathon runner completes in a year's time. Initially, one solution to the problem seems straightforward. We could prompt the user for the number of miles run, read the value into a variable (call it **MilesRun**), and then write one * for each mile. The following procedure illustrates this:

```
PROCEDURE Histogram;

CONST
    MilesPrompt = 'How many miles have been run this year? ';
    PrintSymbol = '*';              (* symbol used to print histogram *)

VAR
    MilesRun: INTEGER;

BEGIN
    WRITE(OUTPUT, MilesPrompt);
    READLN(INPUT, MilesRun);
    IF MilesRun > 0
        THEN BEGIN
                WRITE(OUTPUT, PrintSymbol);
                MilesRun := MilesRun - 1
             END;
    IF MilesRun > 0
        THEN BEGIN
                WRITE(OUTPUT, PrintSymbol);
                MilesRun := MilesRun - 1
             END;
        :
        :
        :
    IF MilesRun > 0
        THEN BEGIN
                WRITE(OUTPUT, PrintSymbol);
                MilesRun := MilesRun - 1
             END

END;  (* Histogram *)
```

Programming Example 7-1: Need for Repetition

For this procedure to work properly, we must have as many IF-THEN statements as there are miles run. Since top distance runners frequently average more than twenty miles per day, this procedure would be a cumbersome way to represent the distance a marathon runner logs in a month. You might assume that—since the number of miles that a human runner logs is finite—you can write a program that will accommodate all human runners. While this may be true in principle, it is not true in practice. This example should help you to see the need for some simple way of repeating particular actions.

---

[1]A histogram is a graphic representation of one or more values. A bar graph is a histogram.

7.1. The WHILE Statement

The previous procedure does not provide a good solution because it forces us to use an IF-THEN statement for each mile the runner logs. However, we only need to repeat two of the actions to achieve our goal:

```
BEGIN
    WRITE(OUTPUT, PrintSymbol);
    MilesRun := MilesRun - 1
END
```

While the variable **MilesRun** has a value greater than 0, the procedure should repeat the two actions. Pascal provides a repetition statement to repeat a statement *while* some condition is TRUE. This repetition statement is known as the WHILE statement. The following example shows the previous procedure rewritten to include a WHILE statement:

```
PROCEDURE Histogram;

CONST
    MilesPrompt = 'How many miles have been run this year? ';
    PrintSymbol = '*';                (* symbol used to print histogram *)

VAR
    MilesRun: INTEGER;

BEGIN
    WRITE(OUTPUT, MilesPrompt);
    READLN(INPUT, MilesRun);
    WHILE (MilesRun > 0) DO
        BEGIN
            WRITE(OUTPUT, PrintSymbol);
            MilesRun := MilesRun - 1
        END
END;   (* Histogram *)
```

Programming Example 7-2:   WHILE Loop

It is important for you to understand how the WHILE loop works. Although you may understand the previous example, we will illustrate its execution in detail. The first illustration shows the initial situation, prior to execution.

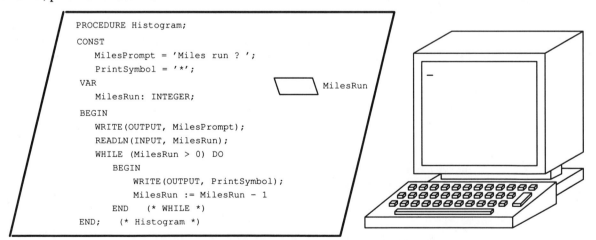

The second illustration shows the situation after the prompt is written. You may have noticed that we shortened the prompt. We did this so it would fit on our display screen.

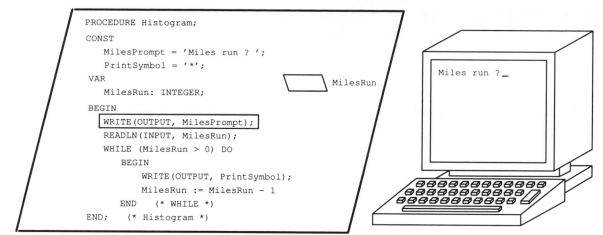

The user responds to the prompt by entering the number 2. The third illustration shows the situation after the input has been entered and read into the variable **MilesRun**.

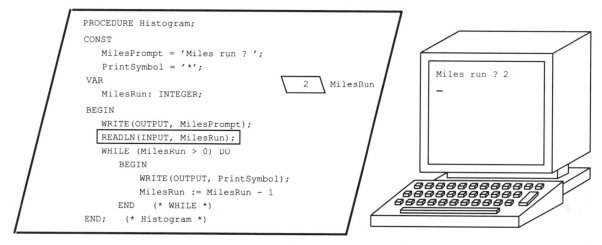

The remaining illustrations detail the execution of the WHILE loop. There is a box (or highlight) around the entire WHILE statement during its entire execution. We use a second box, enclosed in the outer box, to denote whether the WHILE's condition is being tested or its action is being executed. The next illustration demonstrates the testing of the WHILE loop condition.

```
PROCEDURE Histogram;
CONST
    MilesPrompt = 'Miles run ? ';
    PrintSymbol = '*';
VAR                                              2    MilesRun
    MilesRun: INTEGER;
BEGIN
    WRITE(OUTPUT, MilesPrompt);
    READLN(INPUT, MilesRun);
    WHILE  (MilesRun > 0)  DO
        BEGIN
            WRITE(OUTPUT, PrintSymbol);
            MilesRun := MilesRun - 1
        END    (* WHILE *)
END;    (* Histogram *)
```

Miles run ? 2

Since **MilesRun** has the value 2, the expression **(MilesRun > 0)** evaluates to TRUE. With a TRUE condition, the WHILE loop executes its action. This brings up two important points: The WHILE loop condition is tested *before* executing its action, and the WHILE loop condition must be TRUE for its action to be executed. The action is not executed if the condition is not TRUE. Hence, the action of the WHILE loop is said to be *guarded*. The following two illustrations demonstrate execution of the loop action.

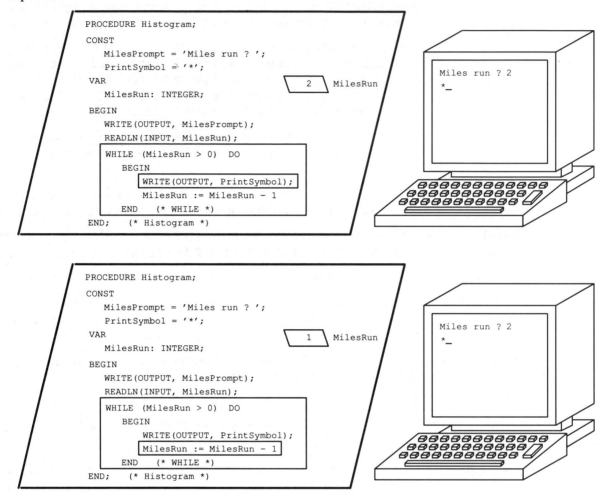

Having executed the loop action, the loop condition must be tested again. The following illustration denotes this.

Since the variable **MilesRun** has the value 1, the expression **(MilesRun > 0)** is still TRUE. Therefore, we must execute the loop guarded statements again, as indicated in the two following illustrations.

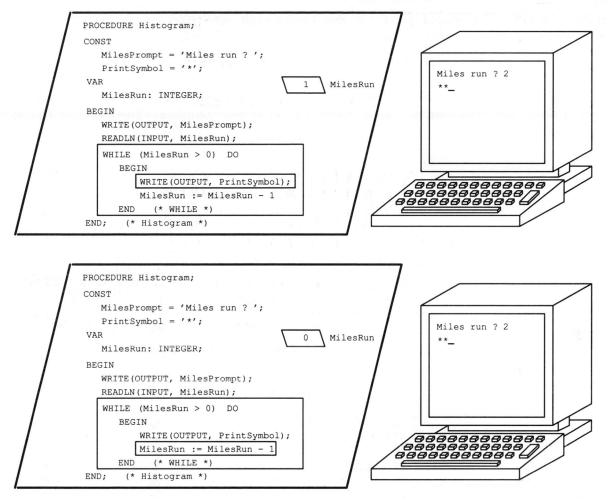

Having executed the loop action, the loop condition must be tested again, as indicated in the following illustration:

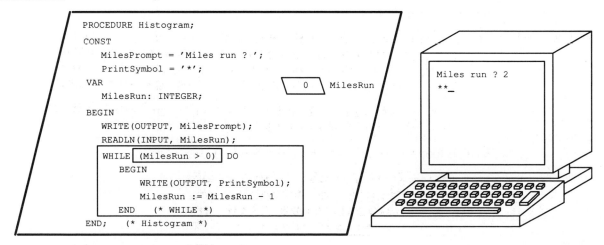

Since the variable **MilesRun** now has the value 0, the expression (**MilesRun > 0**) evaluates to FALSE. Therefore, the loop action will not be executed. Control passes to the next statement after the WHILE loop. However, there are no statements after the WHILE loop in this procedure. Hence, the procedure, **Histogram**, terminates.

Note that the number of miles run was unknown at the time the program was written. The number of miles run was an input value supplied by the user rather than the programmer. The programmer knew some action was to be repeated but had no way of determining at *compile time* how many times it was to be repeated.   We should point out that the example also works for input of 0, thereby accommodating those who do little or no running.

Pascal's WHILE statement is very similar to Karel's WHILE instruction, which we learned about in Chapter 2. A situation analogous to the previous one would be to have Karel clear a corner of all its beepers. We need to repeat some action as long as a particular condition is TRUE. Specifically, we wish to repeat **pickbeeper** as long as Karel is **next-to-a-beeper**. The following fragment illustrates this:

```
WHILE next-to-a-beeper DO
    pickbeeper
```

We do not know when we write the program how many times the action will be repeated. We know only that the action will be repeated. The number of repetitions will be determined when the program is executed. The program will work whether the corner contains two, fifty, or any other number of beepers. It also works if the corner contains no beepers.

The form of Pascal's WHILE statement is the same as that of Karel's WHILE instruction:

WHILE <boolean-expression> DO

<statement>

Pascal's WHILE statement can be used also when we know the number of iterations when writing the program. For example, suppose we have a procedure **WriteBlankLine** to write one blank line to the output display. Assume that we need a procedure to write ten blank lines. One solution is to enumerate all ten calls to the procedure **WriteBlankLine**, as in the following procedure declaration:

```
PROCEDURE Write10BlankLines;

BEGIN
    WriteBlankLine;
    WriteBlankLine;
    WriteBlankLine;
    WriteBlankLine;
    WriteBlankLine;
    WriteBlankLine;
    WriteBlankLine;
    WriteBlankLine;
    WriteBlankLine;
    WriteBlankLine
END;    (* Write10BlankLines *)
```

Programming Example 7-3: Repetition by Enumeration

Obviously, we want to repeat an action. Specifically, we want to repeatedly write a blank line while the number of lines already written is less than ten. The following code illustrates a Pascal procedure to do this using the WHILE loop:

```
PROCEDURE Write10BlankLines;

VAR
    NumberOfLines: INTEGER;

BEGIN
    NumberOfLines := 0;
    WHILE (NumberOfLines < 10) DO
        BEGIN
            WriteBlankLine;
            NumberOfLines := NumberOfLines + 1
        END
END;    (* Write10BlankLines *)
```

Programming Example 7-4: Repetition using WHILE

The variable **NumberOfLines** is used to count the number of lines written. First, the variable is initialized to 0 (no lines written). Since we want ten blank lines at the loop termination, we use the

BOOLEAN expression (`NumberOfLines < 10`) as the condition for the WHILE loop. For each iteration of the loop, we want to write a blank line and increment the value of **NumberOfLines**. Our two examples of Pascal's WHILE loop differed, in that in one we knew the number of repetitions at compile time (**Write10BlankLines**), but in the other we did not know the number until runtime (**Histogram**). However, the two procedures had something else in common. The number of repetitions was known *before* execution of the WHILE loop. In the one example we knew it would be ten repetitions; in the other we knew it would be whatever number the user entered (2, if 2 was entered). There are also situations in which the number of repetitions is unknown when the loop starts to execute.

Recall our earlier discussion of representing values in a computer's memory. Computer memory is organized into units called *words*. A computer word, in turn, is composed of *bits*. A bit is a Binary digIT in one of two possible states. Therefore, one bit can represent two values. Two bits can represent four values. Three bits can represent eight values. Each additional bit doubles the number of values that can be represented.[2]

As a more challenging example of the WHILE statement, assume we need to represent some group of values and would like to write a program to compute how many bits are needed to represent the values. The first thing the program should do is prompt the user for the number of values to be represented. It should then read this number from the input. The number of bits necessary to represent the desired number of values should be computed and displayed to the user.

We know that the number of possible values that can be represented depends on the number of bits used. Therein lies the basis of our solution. We start with one bit (which can represent two values), and while the number of bits is insufficient (number of possible values is less than the desired number of values), we repeatedly increase the number of bits by one. The following Pascal program illustrates such a solution:

```
PROGRAM ComputeBits (INPUT, OUTPUT);

CONST
    prompt = 'How many distinct values do you need to represent? ';

VAR
    DesiredValues,
    PossibleValues,
    NumberOfBits: INTEGER;

BEGIN
    WRITE(OUTPUT, prompt);
    READLN(INPUT, DesiredValues);

    NumberOfBits := 1;
    PossibleValues := 2;
    WHILE (PossibleValues < DesiredValues) DO
        BEGIN
            NumberOfBits:= NumberOfBits + 1;
            PossibleValues := PossibleValues * 2
        END;
    WRITELN(OUTPUT, DesiredValues,  ' values may be represented with ',
                    NumberOfBits, ' bits.')
END.
```

Programming Example 7-5: Compute Bits

Note that if the WHILE condition never evaluates to TRUE, the loop action never executes. Thus, in the previous example, if the user types in any number less than 3 to the prompt for **DesiredValues**, the WHILE action will never execute.

---

[2]In general, N bits can represent 2^N values.

7.1.1. Formal Definition

Pascal's WHILE statement is syntactically simple. Its BNF definition follows:

```
<while-statement> ::= WHILE <boolean-expression> DO <statement>
```

7.1.2. Infinite and Nonexecuting Loops

There are two points about the WHILE loop that are not necessarily obvious. The Boolean expression serving as the WHILE loop condition is always evaluated *before* the guarded statement is executed. If the condition initially evaluates to FALSE, the guarded statement will never be executed. However, it is possible to create loops with conditions that always evaluate to FALSE and, therefore, never execute the action. The following is an example of this:

```
WHILE FALSE DO
    WRITELN(OUTPUT, 'You''ll never see this printed.')
```

Programming Example 7-6: Simple Nonexecuting Loop

There are other, less obvious conditions that always evaluate to FALSE, causing this same type of loop problem. The following is one such example:

```
WHILE (sum < total) AND (total < max) AND (sum >= max) DO
    WRITELN(OUTPUT, 'You''ll never see this printed.')
```

Programming Example 7-7: Nonexecuting Loop

You should be careful not to write loops that will never execute because the loop condition can never be TRUE.

The second point has to do with loop conditions that always evaluate to TRUE. If a loop condition always evaluates to TRUE, the loop will never end. This is known as an *endless loop* or *infinite loop*. The following program fragment illustrates such a loop:

```
WHILE TRUE DO
    WRITELN(OUTPUT, 'Help me.  I can''t stop!')
```

Programming Example 7-8: Simple Infinite Loop

Infinite loops also can be less obvious, as indicated in the following example:

```
WHILE (sum < total) OR (total <= sum) DO
    WRITELN(OUTPUT, 'Help me.  I can''t stop!')
```

Programming Example 7-9: Infinite Loop

For loops to terminate, the loop action must do something to make the loop condition FALSE. In our procedure **Histogram**, we wrote the assignment statement such that it kept decreasing the value of the variable **MilesRun** until it was no longer greater than zero. In the procedure **Write10BlankLines**, the variable **NumberOfLines** increased by one until it equaled ten.

Later in this chapter, we will focus on the construction and verification of loops. For now, you should remember that you should be able to demonstrate that every WHILE loop you write has an action that does something that will eventually make the loop condition FALSE. In short, you should be able to demonstrate that the loops you write will terminate rather than looping infinitely.

7.1.3. Questions

1. What are Pascal's two types of control structures?

2. What is repetition?

3. Why do we need repetition in programming? Give one example of a need for repetition.

4. Is the WHILE loop condition evaluated before or after executing the loop action?

5. To what BOOLEAN value must the WHILE loop condition evaluate for its action to be executed?

6. What statement executes after the WHILE loop condition evaluates to FALSE?

7. What is the BNF of the WHILE statement?

8. How do we repeat more than one statement with the WHILE statement?

9. Can a WHILE loop be written such that it never executes its action? If so, what are the conditions?

10. Can a WHILE loop be written such that it never stops executing its action? If so, what are the conditions?

11. What is an infinite loop?

12. How can one demonstrate that a loop is not an infinite loop?

7.1.4. Exercises

1. What output is given by the following program fragment for inputs of 1, 9, 10, 11, 17?

```
READLN(INPUT, I);
WHILE I < 10 DO
    BEGIN
        WRITELN(OUTPUT, I);
        I := I + 1
    END;
```

2. What output is given by the following program fragment for inputs of 1, 9, 10, 11, 17?

```
count := 1;
WRITE(OUTPUT, 'Enter number ');
READLN(INPUT, I);
WHILE I < 100 DO
    BEGIN
        WRITELN(OUTPUT, I);
        count := count + 1
    END
```

3. Give an example of a Pascal WHILE loop that will never execute.

4. Give an example of a Pascal WHILE loop that is an infinite loop.

7.1.5. Problems

1. Enter the two programs you made in the previous exercises to demonstrate infinite and nonexecuting loops. Run them on your computer.

2. Enter the program ComputeBits (Program Example 7-5) into your computer. Run the program so that you understand how it works.

3. Modify the program in Chapter 3 that computes the cost of building a home (page 116) so that it also takes as input the amount of money available to spend and indicates if there is enough to build the home and how much is left for cost overruns.

4. Extend the previous program to allow the user to choose among a minimum-cost, standard, energy-efficient, or custom-built style of house with costs of $30, $40, $50, and $75 per square foot, respectively. The four values should be stored in the program as named constants.

7.2. The FOR Statement

Recall the procedure **Write10BlankLines** from the last section. It demonstrated repeating an action. However, we knew how many times the action was to be repeated *before* the loop started. This is a special case of repetition known as **iteration**.

> **Definition 7-2:** *Iteration* is a special case of *repetition* where the number of repetitions is known before the first repetition.

Iteration is so common that most high-level languages provide a construct to perform this for you. In Pascal the construct is the FOR statement. Following is the procedure **Write10BlankLines**, rewritten using the Pascal FOR statement.

```
PROCEDURE Write10BlankLines;

VAR
    NumberOfLines: INTEGER;

BEGIN
    FOR NumberOfLines := 1 TO 10 DO
        WriteBlankLine

END;    (* Write10BlankLines *)
```

Programming Example 7-10: FOR Loop

This version of **Write10BlankLines** performs the same action as it did previously. The variable **NumberOfLines** is assigned each of the 10 values 1 through 10. After each assignment, the procedure **WriteBlankLine** is executed.

Pascal's iteration construct in very similar to the Karel iteration construct. In Karel, it is called the ITERATE instruction. When we know the exact number of iterations prior to the execution of a block of Karel code, the ITERATE instruction is appropriate. The prototypical example of this is the definition of **turnright** as three turnlefts.

```
DEFINE-NEW-INSTRUCTION turnright AS
BEGIN
    ITERATE 3 TIMES
        turnleft
END;
```

Pascal's iteration is a little more complicated than Karel's. In Karel, we simply specified the number of iterations and the instruction to be iterated. The Pascal FOR statement requires more. It needs an initial value, a final value, a variable to count with, a direction in which to count, and the statement to repeat. With this information, the FOR loop will execute the statement the appropriate number of times. The form of the FOR statement is as follows:

FOR <index-variable> := <initial-value> <direction> <final-value> DO

      <statement>

The index-variable must be of *ordinal type*. Therefore, it may not be of type REAL. The initial value and the final value must be of the same type as the index variable. The direction is either **TO** (for counting upward) or **DOWNTO** (for counting downward). The statement to be repeated may be any valid Pascal statement. You may repeat more than one statement with a FOR loop by using a compound statement (BEGIN-END block). The following programming example shows the procedure **Write10BlankLines** rewritten to count down rather than up, illustrating the use of DOWNTO rather than TO.

```
PROCEDURE Write10BlankLines;

VAR
    NumberOfLines: INTEGER;

BEGIN
    FOR NumberOfLines := 10 DOWNTO 1 DO
        WriteBlankLine

END;    (* Write10BlankLines *)
```

Programming Example 7-11: FOR Loop with DOWNTO

Recall the procedure **Histogram** from the last section. How would you rewrite it to use a FOR loop instead of a WHILE loop? The following example is a common first rewrite:

```
PROCEDURE Histogram;

CONST
    MilesPrompt = 'How many miles have been run this year? ';
    PrintSymbol = '*';             (* symbol used to print histogram *)

VAR
    count, MilesRun: INTEGER;

BEGIN
    WRITE(OUTPUT, MilesPrompt);
    READLN(INPUT, MilesRun);

    FOR count := MilesRun DOWNTO 1 DO
        BEGIN
            WRITE(OUTPUT, PrintSymbol);
            count := count - 1
        END
END;   (* Histogram *)
```

Programming Example 7-12: FOR Loop with an Error

What is wrong with the rewrite of **Histogram**? The FOR loop contains an error. Note that the loop index variable is assigned a value inside the loop body by the statement **count := count - 1**. The FOR loop index variable is incremented or decremented automatically, depending on whether TO or DOWNTO is used for the direction. In this case, the variable **count** is automatically decreased by 1 after each iteration. Therefore, it is never necessary to alter the value of a FOR loop index variable. In fact, it is an error in Standard Pascal to make any assignment to a FOR loop index variable. The FOR loop always increments the index variable by 1 when TO is used to specify the direction and decrements it by 1 when DOWNTO is used. It can never use any value other than 1. Hence, we cannot specify a "step size" to the FOR loop. Since assignment to a loop index variable within a FOR loop body is not permitted in Standard Pascal, we can never achieve a step size other than 1 with a FOR loop. If you should need a step size larger than 1, then you must use a different loop, such as the WHILE loop. The following example illustrates the procedure **Histogram** correctly rewritten with a FOR loop:

```
PROCEDURE Histogram;

CONST
    MilesPrompt = 'How many miles have been run this year? ';
    PrintSymbol = '*';             (* symbol used to print histogram *)

VAR
    count, MilesRun: INTEGER;

BEGIN
    WRITE(OUTPUT, MilesPrompt);
    READLN(INPUT, MilesRun);

    FOR count := MilesRun DOWNTO 1 DO
        WRITE(OUTPUT, PrintSymbol)

END;   (* Histogram *)
```

Programming Example 7-13: Histogram with FOR Loop Using

This rewritten procedure seems simpler. In general, we should use an iteration construct whenever we know the number of iterations before the first iteration. The other repetition control structures, such as the WHILE statement, should be used when the FOR loop cannot be used.

In the previous programming example, we could have counted upward instead of downward. The following procedure demonstrates **Histogram** rewritten using TO instead of DOWNTO:

```
PROCEDURE Histogram;

CONST
    MilesPrompt = 'How many miles have been run this year? ';
    PrintSymbol = '*';              (* symbol used to print histogram *)

VAR
    count, MilesRun: INTEGER;

BEGIN
    WRITE(OUTPUT, MilesPrompt);
    READLN(INPUT, MilesRun);

    FOR count := 1 TO MilesRun DO
        WRITE(OUTPUT, PrintSymbol)

END;   (* Histogram *)
```

Programming Example 7-14: Histogram with FOR Loop

At the start of the FOR loop, the expressions for initial and final values are evaluated—but they are not evaluated at the start of each iteration. The initial value is assigned to the index variable. If the direction is upward, while the index variable is less than or equal to the final value, the statement is repeated. *After* each iteration of an upward loop, the index variable is increased. If the direction is downward, while the index variable is greater than or equal to the final value, the statement is repeated. After each iteration of a downward loop, the loop index variable is decreased.

Any variable of an ordinal type may be used as an index variable. The initial and final values must be expressions of the same type as the index variable. Since the index variable must be of ordinal type, neither the index variable, initial value, nor final value may be of type REAL. Most commonly they are of type INTEGER. If we wanted to create a procedure to write all the lowercase letters of the character set—call it **WriteLittleLetters**—we might use a loop index variable of type CHAR.

The initial value and the final value are not reevaluated before each iteration (although loop index var is incremented or decremented). Therefore, changing any variables that are part of expressions for initial value and final value within a FOR loop body will not affect the number of loop iterations.

```
PROCEDURE WriteLittleLetters;

VAR
    letter: CHAR;

BEGIN
    FOR letter := 'a' TO 'z' DO
        WRITE(OUTPUT, letter:3)
END;     (* WriteLittleLetters *)
```

Programming Example 7-15: Loop Index Variable of Type CHAR

7.2.1. Formal Definition

Pascal's FOR loop may be defined formally as follows:

```
<for-statement> ::=  FOR <loop-index-variable> := <initial-value>
          TO | DOWNTO <final-value> DO <statement>

<loop-index-variable> ::= <identifier>

<initial-value> ::= <ordinal-expression>

<final-value> ::= <ordinal-expression>
```

The statement in a FOR loop may be any valid Pascal statement. This includes, among other things, READ, READLN, WRITE, WRITELN, assignment, IF-THEN, CASE, procedure calls, and FOR.

The **FOR** statement initializes the start value and performs needed loop increments or decrements. No program should depend on a loop index variable having a particular value outside the body of the loop, such as the final value or one greater than the final value. The value of the loop index variable should be considered undefined upon loop termination. Writing programs that depend on loop index variables having some particular value outside the loop is as poor a practice as failing to initialize variables. Writing programs that depend on such nonstandard assumptions will only lead to trouble.

If the initial and final values are integers, the loop will execute (| final-value - initial-value | + 1) times, which means 1 plus the absolute value of the difference between the initial and final values. This is true if the loop iterates at least once. It is not true otherwise. For example, the following loop does not execute at all because the TO should be DOWNTO.

```
FOR index := 5 TO 1 DO
    somestatement
```

The reason the FOR loop uses a user-named variable to count with is because such a variable holds a value that is often needed for calculations within the loop. For example, the following program uses the value of the loop-index variable in generating a table of numbers and their squares:

```
PROCEDURE WriteTableOfSquares;

CONST
    header = 'Number    Number Squared';
    MaxNumber = 25;                  (* Maximum number of entries in table *)

VAR
    count: INTEGER;

BEGIN
    WRITELN(OUTPUT, header);

    FOR count := 1 TO MaxNumber DO
        WRITELN(OUTPUT, count:10, count*count:10)

END;    (* WriteTableOfSquares *)
```

Programming Example 7-16:   Using the Loop-index Variable' Value

If we wanted the table displayed in decreasing order rather than increasing order, we would exchange the initial and final values and change the direction from TO to DOWNTO.

7.2.2. Nested Loops

There are many interesting programs that can be written using loops. Among these uses are the computations of prime numbers, perfect numbers, permutations, combinations, and factorials. One interesting and clever use of loops is in the construction of a special triangle of numbers. The triangle has 1 in the first row, 2 and 3 in the second row, 4, 5, and 6 in the third row, 7, 8, 9, and 10 in the fourth row, etc. This special triangle, known as Floyd's Triangle[3] , is depicted in the following figure:

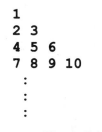

Figure 7-1:   Floyd's Triangle

Note that the number of columns in any given row equals the row number; that is, row 1 has 1 column, row 2 has 2 columns, row 3 has 3 columns, etc. Also note that we use consecutive integers as the print symbols; first 1, then 2, then 3, etc.

Consider the task of writing a Pascal program to print Floyd's Triangle. Given the information presented thus far, you should be able to write such a program. We want to repeatedly write numbers for each column in the row. We can use a loop to do this. But we want to repeat this process for each row of the triangle. Hence, we need another loop. The loop that runs from 1 to the number of columns

---

[3]This is called Floyd's Triangle after Robert Floyd, who is credited with its invention.

is part of the action of the loop that runs from the first row to the last row. When one loop occurs within another loop, it is called a *nested loop*. The following Pascal program uses a nested FOR loop to print Floyd's Triangle:

```
PROGRAM Triangle (INPUT, OUTPUT);

CONST
    MaxRows = 4;                      (* total rows in triangle *)

VAR
    row,                             (* determines the row we are writing *)
    column,                          (* determines the column we are writing *)
    PrintNumber: INTEGER;            (* determines the print symbol *)

BEGIN
    PrintNumber := 0;                (* initialize the number to be printed *)

    FOR row := 1 TO MaxRows DO
        BEGIN
            FOR column := 1 TO row DO
                BEGIN
                    PrintNumber := PrintNumber + 1;
                    WRITE(OUTPUT, PrintNumber)
                END;      (* FOR column *)
            WRITELN(OUTPUT)           (* position to WRITE a new row *)
        END      (* FOR row *)
END.    (* triangle *)
```

Programming Example 7-17: Floyd's Triangle

While the other examples of the FOR loop have not required our specialized series of simulations, we believe this example warrants such a detailed explanation. Nested loops can be tricky. As usual, the program is on the left, the output is on the right, and the variables are indicated as named boxes toward the center. Note that we use the value 2 for **MaxRows** for purposes of illustration.

The first illustration shows the situation before execution of the first statement. The three variables have unknown values, so there is no output yet.

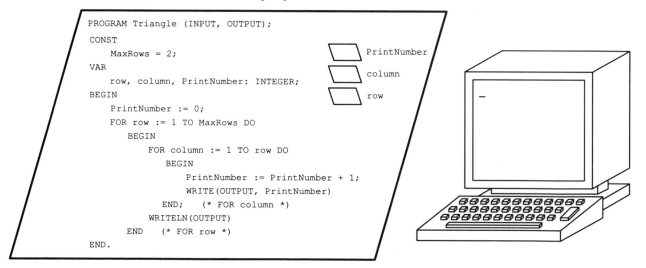

The assignment statement has been executed, and the variable **PrintNumber** has the value 0. The other variables still have unknown values. The outer FOR loop is about to start execution.

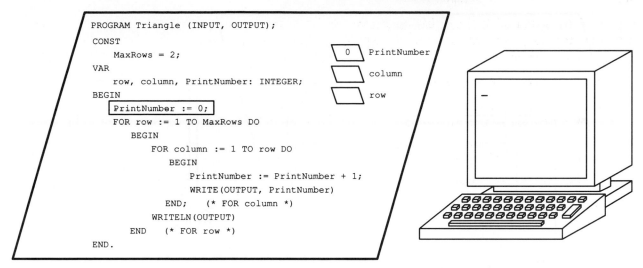

The loop index variable **row** gets the initial value of 1. Since the value of the index variable is less than or equal to the final value (**MaxRows** = 2), the FOR loop statement will be executed. The assignment to the index variable and the test against the final value are indicated by the inner box.

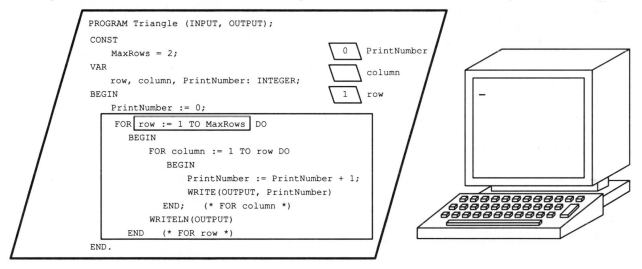

The loop body is a compound statement. First the inner FOR loop will be executed. The inner loop index variable, **column**, gets the initial value of 1. Since it is less than or equal to the final value (**row** = 1), the inner loop body will be executed. Assignment to the inner-loop index variable is indicated by the innermost box.

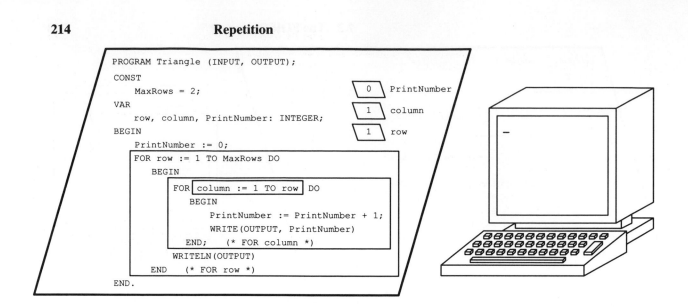

```
PROGRAM Triangle (INPUT, OUTPUT);
CONST
    MaxRows = 2;                                    0    PrintNumber
VAR
    row, column, PrintNumber: INTEGER;              1    column
BEGIN                                               1    row
    PrintNumber := 0;
    FOR row := 1 TO MaxRows DO
        BEGIN
            FOR column := 1 TO row DO
                BEGIN
                    PrintNumber := PrintNumber + 1;
                    WRITE(OUTPUT, PrintNumber)
                END;    (* FOR column *)
            WRITELN(OUTPUT)
        END    (* FOR row *)
END.
```

The inner loop also has a compound statement; therefore, its first statement is executed next. The value of **PrintNumber** is increased from 0 to 1. Nothing has been written to the screen yet.

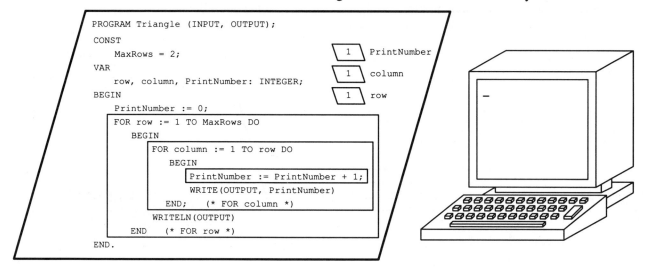

```
PROGRAM Triangle (INPUT, OUTPUT);
CONST
    MaxRows = 2;                                    1    PrintNumber
VAR
    row, column, PrintNumber: INTEGER;              1    column
BEGIN                                               1    row
    PrintNumber := 0;
    FOR row := 1 TO MaxRows DO
        BEGIN
            FOR column := 1 TO row DO
                BEGIN
                    PrintNumber := PrintNumber + 1;
                    WRITE(OUTPUT, PrintNumber)
                END;    (* FOR column *)
            WRITELN(OUTPUT)
        END    (* FOR row *)
END.
```

The value of **PrintNumber** is written to the output screen.

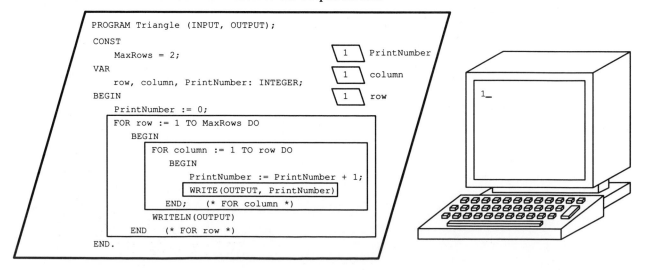

```
PROGRAM Triangle (INPUT, OUTPUT);
CONST
    MaxRows = 2;                                    1    PrintNumber
VAR
    row, column, PrintNumber: INTEGER;              1    column
BEGIN                                               1    row
    PrintNumber := 0;
    FOR row := 1 TO MaxRows DO
        BEGIN
            FOR column := 1 TO row DO
                BEGIN
                    PrintNumber := PrintNumber + 1;
                    WRITE(OUTPUT, PrintNumber)
                END;    (* FOR column *)
            WRITELN(OUTPUT)
        END    (* FOR row *)
END.
```

The inner loop index variable is increased by 1 to 2, which is greater than its final value (**row** = 1). The inner loop terminates.

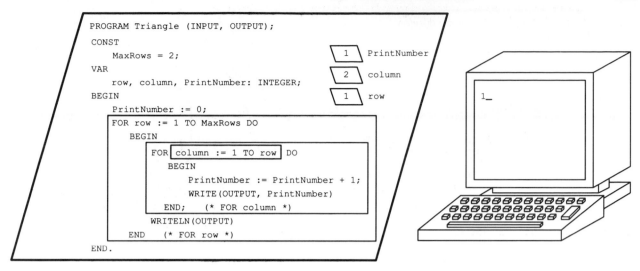

```
PROGRAM Triangle (INPUT, OUTPUT);
CONST
    MaxRows = 2;                                1   PrintNumber
VAR
    row, column, PrintNumber: INTEGER;          2   column
BEGIN
    PrintNumber := 0;                           1   row

    FOR row := 1 TO MaxRows DO
        BEGIN
            FOR column := 1 TO row  DO
                BEGIN
                    PrintNumber := PrintNumber + 1;
                    WRITE(OUTPUT, PrintNumber)
                END;    (* FOR column *)
            WRITELN(OUTPUT)
        END    (* FOR row *)
END.
```

The next statement to be executed is the statement following the inner loop. The output cursor advances to the next line.

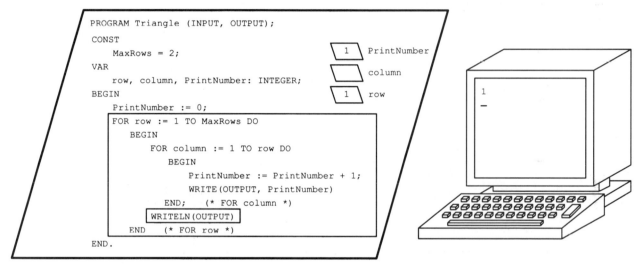

```
PROGRAM Triangle (INPUT, OUTPUT);
CONST
    MaxRows = 2;                                1   PrintNumber
VAR
    row, column, PrintNumber: INTEGER;              column
BEGIN
    PrintNumber := 0;                           1   row

    FOR row := 1 TO MaxRows DO
        BEGIN
            FOR column := 1 TO row DO
                BEGIN
                    PrintNumber := PrintNumber + 1;
                    WRITE(OUTPUT, PrintNumber)
                END;    (* FOR column *)
            WRITELN(OUTPUT)
        END    (* FOR row *)
END.
```

Having completed the loop action, the outer loop index variable **row** is incremented by 1 to 2. Its value is compared to determine if it is less than or equal to **MaxRows**.

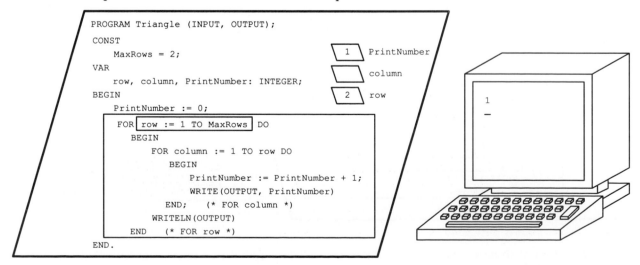

```
PROGRAM Triangle (INPUT, OUTPUT);
CONST
    MaxRows = 2;                                1   PrintNumber
VAR
    row, column, PrintNumber: INTEGER;              column
BEGIN
    PrintNumber := 0;                           2   row

    FOR row := 1 TO MaxRows  DO
        BEGIN
            FOR column := 1 TO row DO
                BEGIN
                    PrintNumber := PrintNumber + 1;
                    WRITE(OUTPUT, PrintNumber)
                END;    (* FOR column *)
            WRITELN(OUTPUT)
        END    (* FOR row *)
END.
```

Since **row** is less than or equal to **MaxRows**, the loop body is repeated. Therefore, the inner FOR loop is repeated.

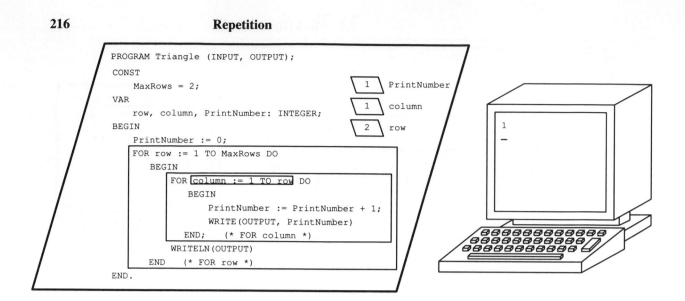

The variable **column** gets the value 1 prior to execution of the first statement.

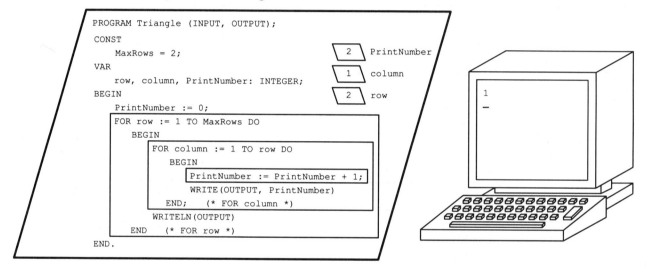

The variable **PrintNumber** is increased to 2.

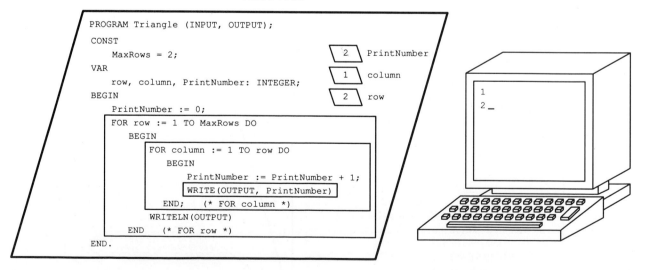

The value of **PrintNumber** is written to the screen. The variable **column** is incremented prior to the next iteration of the loop.

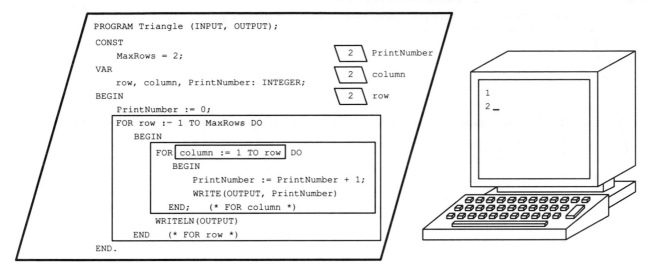

PrintNumber is increased to 3.

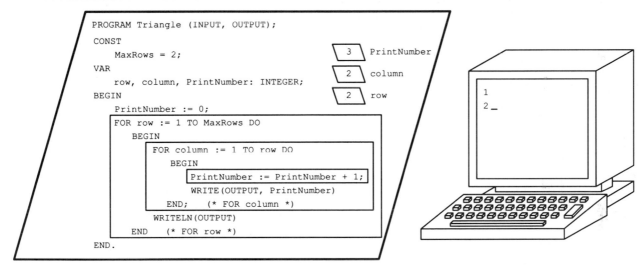

The value of **PrintNumber** is written to the screen.

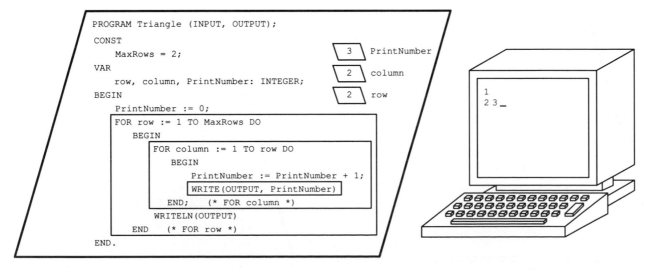

The variable **column** is increased to 3. Since 3 > row, the inner loop terminates.

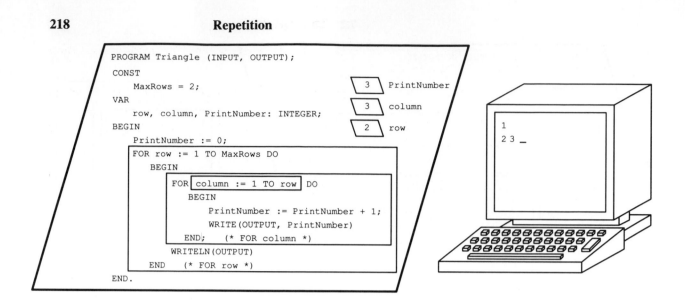

Next the WRITELN is executed.

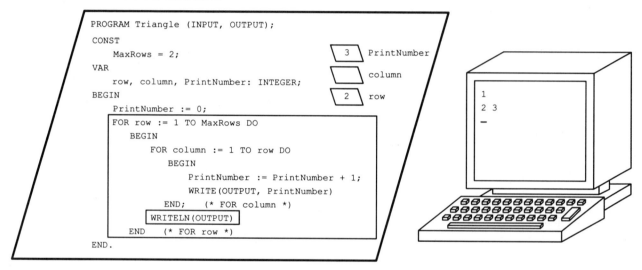

The loop variable **row** is increased to 3. Since 3 > **MaxRows**, the outer loop terminates.

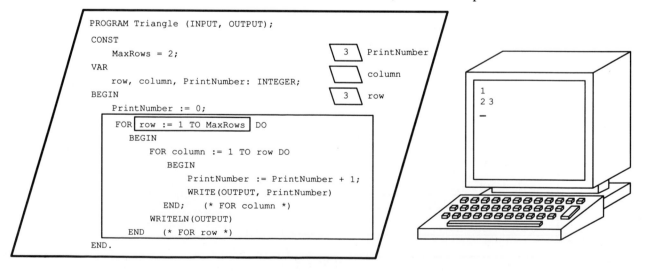

Having terminated the outer loop, the program is finished.

It often is not immediately obvious what a particular END matches. It can be END of program, END of procedure, END of CASE statement, or END of a compound statement. As we mentioned earlier, it is a good idea to put a brief comment after every END to identify what it ends. This leads to comments such as `(* CASE *)`, `(* THEN *)`, and `(* FOR *)`.

This notion is particularly useful when we are using nested statements such as nested loops. In our example of Floyd's Triangle, we used nested FOR loops, each with a compound statement. We identified the ENDs with the word FOR and the name of the FOR loop index variable, such as `(* FOR row *)` and `(* FOR column *)`.

7.2.3. Questions

1. What is the difference between iteration and repetition?

2. Does Pascal have an iteration control structure? If so, what is it called?

3. What is the general form of Pascal's FOR statement?

4. How does a FOR loop work?

5. Does the programmer need to increment the FOR loop index variable?

6. What is the effect of using DOWNTO with the FOR loop instead of using TO?

7. When should an iteration construct be used?

8. Can a FOR loop index variable be of type REAL?

9. What value should a programmer expect the FOR loop index variable to have after a loop has terminated?

10. How can more than one statement be repeated with a FOR loop?

7.2.4. Exercises

1. What is the output of the following fragment?

```
FOR i := 10 TO 1 DO
    WRITELN(OUTPUT, I:3)
```

2. What is the output of the following fragment?

```
FOR i := 15 DOWNTO 7 DO
    WRITELN(OUTPUT, I:3)
```

3. What is the output of the following fragment?

```
term := 10;
FOR i := 1 TO term DO
    BEGIN
        WRITELN(OUTPUT, I:3);
        term := 25
    END;
```

4. What is the output of the following fragment?

```
CONST
    first = 2;
    last = 8;

VAR
    count: INTEGER;
    :
    :
    :
count := 10;
WRITELN(OUTPUT, count:3, first:3, last:3);
FOR count := first TO last DO
    BEGIN
        WRITELN(OUTPUT, count:3, first:3, last:3);
        last := first;
        WRITELN(OUTPUT, count:3, first:3, last:3)
    END
```

5. What is the output of the following fragment?

```
FOR i := 1 TO 10 DO
    BEGIN
        i := i*2;
        WRITELN(OUTPUT, I:3)
    END
```

6. Assuming that the procedure **WriteBlankLine** is already declared, write a Pascal program called **ClearScreen** that writes enough blank lines to clear your display screen. Use the FOR loop.

7.2.5. Problems

1. Extend Programming Example 7-16 given on page 211 so that it generates both a table of squares and and a table of cubes.

2. Modify the program from the previous problem so that the table is written in decreasing order rather than in increasing order.

3. Write a Pascal program that writes the numbers 0 through 9 on the same line. Use a FOR loop.

4. Write a Pascal program that writes the letters '0' through '9' on the same line. Use a FOR loop.

5. At the end of Chapter 3 we suggested the following problem: Suppose you have been given the task of grading for a course. Write a Pascal program that calculates and displays a student's course grade by prompting the user for necessary information (exam grades, project grade, final exam grade) and computing the overall grade. Assume there are two exams, each worth 15%, a project worth 40%, and a final exam worth 30%. Also assume that each score is between 0 and 100 inclusive. Modify this program using the FOR statement to calculate and display the grades for all students in a class. Prompt the user for the number of students.

6. Write a program that writes a "Floyd's Triangle" using only one print symbol. The program should prompt for the height and the print symbol. Allow the print symbol to be any of the printing characters. The following example illustrates the output for a height of 3 and '*' as the print symbol.

```
*
**
***
****
```

7. Modern banks use computers extensively for record keeping and many mundane computations. Write a program that takes an amount of principal, rate of interest, and number of time periods, and generates a compound interest table showing the following information.

```
PRINCIPAL = $1000.00
INTEREST RATE = 9.00 %
PERIODS = 10

PERIOD          INTEREST          ACCUMULATED INTEREST
   1             90.00                    90.00
   2             98.10                   188.10
   3            106.93                   295.03
   4              :                        :
   5              :                        :
```

7.3. The REPEAT Statement

We have already pointed out that if we do not know the number of repetitions in advance of the first repetition, we cannot use the FOR loop. Such situations leave us with the WHILE loop. However, there are times when the WHILE loop just does not seem to be the right construct either. For example, consider this situation: We want our program to prompt users to ask them whether they wish to continue or quit the program. If the user enters an inappropriate response, we must repeatedly prompt for and read responses until an acceptable one is entered. The following program fragment illustrates how this might be done with the WHILE loop:

```
WRITE(OUTPUT, 'Please type c to continue or q to quit [c/q]: ');
READLN(INPUT, response);

WHILE NOT((response = 'c') OR (response = 'q'))
    BEGIN
        WRITE(OUTPUT, 'Please type c to continue or q to quit [c/q]: ');
        READLN(INPUT, response)
    END;          (* WHILE *)
```

Programming Example 7-18: The Need for an Alternative to the WHILE Loop

Note that we must always prompt for and read a response at least one time. We would like to test the loop condition *after* executing the loop body once. Pascal has a third loop, known as the REPEAT-UNTIL loop, which does precisely that. The previous program fragment is rewritten in the following example with the REPEAT-UNTIL loop:

```
REPEAT
    WRITE(OUTPUT, 'Please type c to continue or q to quit [c/q]: ');
    READLN(INPUT, response)
UNTIL ((response = 'c') OR (response = 'q'))
```

Programming Example 7-19: A REPEAT-UNTIL Loop

Note that, although the WHILE loop will work, the REPEAT-UNTIL loop is a more natural solution.

Many programming languages offer a variety of loop constructs. The three most common types are one for iteration only, one that tests the condition *before* the loop body, and one that tests the condition *after* the loop body. Pascal has all three of these: the FOR loop, the WHILE loop, and the REPEAT loop, respectively. The general form of Pascal's REPEAT-UNTIL loop is as follows:

```
REPEAT
    <statement1>;
    <statement2>;
    <statement3>;
         :
         :
         :
    <statementN>
UNTIL <boolean-expression>
```

Pascal's REPEAT-UNTIL loop works intuitively. The list of statements is repeated until the Boolean condition evaluates to TRUE. The REPEAT loop differs from the WHILE loop in two important ways: First, the REPEAT loop tests its condition *after* executing the loop body, whereas the WHILE loop tests its condition *before* executing the loop body. A consequence of this is that the REPEAT loop always executes at least one time, whereas the WHILE loop may execute zero times. Additionally, the REPEAT-UNTIL loop repeats a sequence of statements rather than one statement. Therefore, a compound statement (BEGIN-END block) is never needed with the REPEAT-UNTIL loop.

We saw in the last chapter how a CASE statment can be used in creating a simple command interpreter. However, we normally wish to handle more than one command. A common use of the REPEAT loop is in conjunction with the CASE statement to form a command interpreter loop. Below we illustrate such a combination:

```
REPEAT
    WRITE(OUTPUT, CommandPrompt);
    READLN(INPUT, command);
    CASE command OF
        'h' : GiveHelp;
        't' : GiveTime;
        'u' : ListUsers;
        'q' : Quit
    END     (* CASE *)
UNTIL (command = 'q')
```

Programming Example 7-20:   A REPEAT Loop As the Command Interpreter Loop

The previous program fragment makes no attempt to ensure that the command supplied by the user is one of the possible values of the CASE statement. We can use the idea from our first REPEAT-UNTIL example to reprompt if necessary, thereby ensuring that the user has entered a valid command.

```
REPEAT
    REPEAT
        WRITE(OUTPUT, CommandPrompt);
        READLN(INPUT, command)
    UNTIL (command = 'h') OR (command = 't') OR (command = 'u') OR (command = 'q');
    CASE command OF
        'h' : GiveHelp;
        't' : GiveTime;
        'u' : ListUsers;
        'q' : quit
    END     (* CASE *)
UNTIL (command = 'q')
```

Programming Example 7-21:   Nested REPEAT Loops for Prompting and Interpreting Commands

The previous code fragment illustrates the two most common uses of a REPEAT-UNTIL loop. Note that both cases are more naturally suited to a REPEAT loop than to a WHILE loop.

7.3.1. Loop Equivalence

The past few examples illustrated a need for repetition that we said could be solved using either the WHILE or REPEAT-UNTIL loop. At this point, you might be wondering if either type of loop can always be used.

Recall that a WHILE loop may execute its body zero times, but the REPEAT-UNTIL loop always executes its body at least once. It is because of this that in general a WHILE loop cannot always be replaced with a REPEAT-UNTIL loop. However, a REPEAT-UNTIL loop can always be replaced with a WHILE loop. If we call the action to be repeated S, and the condition BOOL, the following illustrates the WHILE loop equivalent of a REPEAT-UNTIL loop:

```
REPEAT                          S;
    S                           WHILE NOT(BOOL) DO
UNTIL (BOOL)                        S
```

Programming Example 7-22:   Equivalence of REPEAT and WHILE Loops

Note that the WHILE loop condition is the negation of the REPEAT-UNTIL loop condition. A REPEAT-UNTIL loop always can be replaced with an equivalent WHILE loop.

7.3.2. Formal Definition

The BNF definition for the REPEAT-UNTIL loop is as follows.

```
<repeat-statement> ::=
        REPEAT <statement> { ; <statement> } UNTIL <expression>
```

7.3.3. Questions

1. What are Pascal's three loop constructs?

2. What is the difference between iteration and repetition?

3. Which of Standard Pascal's loop constructs is an iteration construct?

4. When can Pascal's FOR loop not be used?

5. Does Pascal's WHILE loop test its condition before or after executing the body?

6. Does Pascal's REPEAT-UNTIL loop test its condition before or after executing the body?

7. What is the minimum number of repetitions a WHILE loop can repeat?

8. What is the minimum number of repetitions a REPEAT-UNTIL loop can repeat?

9. Under what circumstances is a REPEAT-UNTIL loop a more natural loop than a WHILE loop? Give at least one particular example of such a case.

7.3.4. Exercises

1. Can a WHILE loop always be replaced with an equivalent REPEAT-UNTIL loop? If so, explain how. If not, explain why not.

2. Can a REPEAT-UNTIL loop always be replaced with an equivalent WHILE loop? If so, explain how. If not, explain why not.

3. Can a FOR loop always be replaced with an equivalent WHILE loop? If so, explain how. If not, explain why not.

4. Can a FOR loop always be replaced with an equivalent REPEAT-UNTIL loop? If so, explain how. If not, explain why not.

5. Can a FOR loop *ever* be replaced with an equivalent REPEAT-UNTIL loop? If so, explain when and how. If not, explain why not.

6. Can either a WHILE or REPEAT loop always be replaced with an equivalent FOR loop? If so, explain how. If not, explain why not.

7. If you could use only one of Pascal's three loops for all programming, which loop would you pick? Justify why you would pick one over the other two.

8. Write an equivalent program fragment using the WHILE loop for the following code:

```
REPEAT
    WRITE(OUTPUT, prompt);
    READLN(INPUT, value)
UNTIL (value <> 0)
```

9. Write an equivalent program fragment using the WHILE loop for the following code:

```
FOR index := low TO high DO
    WRITE(OUTPUT, index, index MOD 2);
```

7.3.5. Problems

1. Write a program that prompts for a nonnegative integer and computes and displays if the number is odd or even. The program should reprompt the user until a nonnegative integer is entered.

2. Many cash registers now help the clerk by calculating a shopper's change. Write a program that will do the computations of such a cash register. The program should accept as input the prices of various items purchased until the user indicates to add them up. The user should be able to enter the amount tendered, so the program can display the change back in addition to the total price of the purchase.

3. Extend the last program so that sales tax is added to the total. If your state has no sales tax, use 6%.

4. Modify the previous program so that after it prints the change, it also prints the number of each monetary denomination. Use the following example to guide you:

```
Total purchase price:     $ 72.61

Amount tendered:          $100.00
Change:                   $ 27.39

          Twenties:    1
          Fives:       1
          Ones:        2
          Quarters:    1
          Dimes:       1
          Pennies:     4
```

If a particular denomination is not needed, don't display it (such as tens and nickels above). The change should always use the largest denomination possible. It is unacceptable to have all dollars returned in all ones and all fractional dollars returned in all pennies, unless it is unavoidable, as with the amount $4.04

7.4. Loop Construction and the Loop Invariant

Most programming textbooks provide a general form for the looping constructs available in the programming language at hand. Most textbooks also provide some examples of these looping constructs. However, virtually no programming textbooks explain how to actually create loops, nor do they discuss how to demonstrate that a loop will do what it was intended to do. These two topics are uniformly left to the readers' imagination. Although this is unfortunate, it is not by accident.

In the past, writing loops correctly was something that good programmers just seemed to do. When asked why they chose a particular loop construct or how they determined the loop condition, or from where they divined the loop body, most of these programmers were at a loss to provide an explanation. If further asked to verify that a loop works, most of these same programmers suggested watching the loop in action. After all, why should a good programmer have to verify that his already working loop is correct? And so, creating programming loops correctly tended to be a bit magical and for many novices part of a magic they seemed destined never to possess.

7.4.1. Method Not Magic

We believe computer science is a science rather than an art. Therefore, creating and verifying programming loops should have a method rather than magic. In this final section of this chapter, we hope to remove enough of the magic associated with loops so that most programmers feel comfortable creating and verifying loops rather than just a select few "magicians".

7.4.2. A Method of Determining Which Loop Construct to Use

Most programming languages have more than one type of loop to choose from. We have seen that Standard Pascal has three different loop constructs. Therefore, we need some method of determining which type of loop to use. We suggest using the following heuristics in making this decision:

1. Is the loop iteration? Recall that iteration is a special type of repetition where the number of repetitions is known before starting the loop. It might be known at compile time (as seen in the procedure **Write10BlankLines**). It might be entered by the user (as seen in the procedure **Histogram**). Sometimes, the number may be computed from other values in the program. The important point is that the number of iterations is known in advance of the first iteration rather than how the number of iterations is determined. When we have the special case of iteration, we should use an iterative loop if possible. Standard Pascal has an iterative loop known as the FOR loop. The only time we have iteration and might not be able to use a FOR loop is if we want a step size of other than 1. Recall that Pascal's FOR loop always increments (or decrements) the loop index variable by 1.

2. Will the loop always execute at least once? A loop can test its condition *before* executing its body or *after* executing its body. Many programming languages provide a loop

construct for each type. Standard Pascal provides two different loops: WHILE for testing *before* and REPEAT-UNTIL for testing *after*. If the loop condition is tested after executing the loop body, the loop body will always be executed at least one time. If you are programming in Pascal and wish always to execute the loop at least once, you should be using the REPEAT-UNTIL construct.

In all other cases, you should use Pascal's WHILE loop. You never have to worry that the WHILE loop is the wrong loop. Pascal's other loops (FOR and REPEAT-UNTIL) are not theoretically necessary. All repetition can be written using only the WHILE loop. If you are unable to decide which loop to use, pick the WHILE loop.

7.4.3. A Method of Selecting the Loop Condition

Once we have chosen the type of loop to use, we must determine the loop condition. Sometimes the right loop condition just stands out in our minds. Without further thought we have the right condition. However, we are not always so fortunate. Usually, the best way to get a handle on the right loop condition is by first determining what is supposed to be true *after* the loop has executed. This *after loop condition* is a statment of what the loop is to accomplish. To illustrate this, let us consider the following example:

You become involved in the local little league. The league's field has a new wall in left field, and the teams think that the new wall is too close to home plate. Having some computer programming background, you quickly find yourself on the "left-field wall" committee. One consideration in determining whether the new wall is too close is the number of home runs being hit by the players. It is your responsibility to compute the total number of home runs for each team in the league.

You are to write a program to compute the total number of home runs for a team, given the home run totals for each of the individual players. Assume that the number of players is unknown. Assume that the home run totals are entered into the keyboard, each separated by a space. Also assume that a negative number is entered to denote that all the home run totals have been entered. This is safe since the lowest number of home runs any player can have is 0. Some sample input is shown in Figure 7-2.

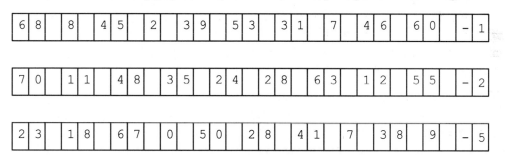

Figure 7-2: Example Input Tapes of Home Run Totals

To solve this problem, we want to read and sum integers repeatedly until we read a negative value. Since we are going to be repeating an action, we will need a loop. What type of loop do we want to use? Do we have iteration? Since we are assuming that the number of input values is not known in advance, we cannot use iteration. Hence, the FOR loop is wrong. Will we always have at least one repetition? Since the answer is yes, we want a REPEAT-UNTIL loop.

What should be true after the loop has finished? Recall that the last input value is negative. Special values in the data that are not really data but instead denote something else, in this case the end of data, are referred to as sentinel values, or simply sentinels. After the loop, it should be true that the sentinel was the last value read. Knowing what should be true after the loop, we can determine the loop condition. **If we are using a WHILE loop, the loop condition is the negation of the** *after loop condition.* **If we are using the REPEAT-UNTIL loop, the loop condition is the same as the** *after loop condition.* In our example, the *after loop condition* is that the *last value read is less than zero,* which can be written in Pascal as (`LastValueRead < 0`). This will be true because the last value read will be the sentinel, which is less than 0 (negative). Since we are using REPEAT-UNTIL in this example, we have the loop condition as illustrated in the following program fragment:

```
REPEAT


UNTIL (LastValueRead < 0)
```
Programming Example 7-23: Loop with Condition

Recall that the WHILE loop will always work. If we decided to use the WHILE loop instead of the REPEAT-UNTIL loop, we would have the following loop shell or its equivalent. Note that the WHILE loop condition is the negation of the REPEAT loop condition.

```
WHILE NOT(LastValueRead < 0)          WHILE (LastValueRead >= 0)
   BEGIN                                 BEGIN

   END                                   END
```
Programming Example 7-24: WHILE Loop with Condition

Determining the loop condition is easy once you know what type of loop you are using and what is supposed to be true *after the loop*. The *after loop condition* can be taken directly from the problem statement. In this example, we knew that the input values were to be *terminated* by some negative value or sentinel.

Often there are several possible ways to phrase the same condition. The conditions, although different in phrasing, are equivalent and any of them will suffice. To understand this point, consider the (after loop condition) from the home-run-total program. We phrased it as `LastValueRead < 0`; however, it could have been phrased as `LastValueRead <= -1` or `NOT(LastValueRead >= 0)` since the input values were to be integers. You can use any of the equivalent phrasings of conditions safely; however, we suggest that you use the simplest, easiest to read, or most natural condition.

7.4.4. A Method of Completing the Loop Body

Once we have chosen the type of loop to use and the loop condition, we can complete the loop body. A loop body must do something that will cause the loop to terminate eventually. Therefore, a loop body must contain at least one action. Often, a loop body consists of several actions, depending on what the loop is to accomplish. In the example we are considering, the loop will terminate when a negative value is read from INPUT. Therefore, we can add a READ statement to the loop body, as indicated in the following program fragment:

```
REPEAT
    READ(INPUT, LastValueRead)

UNTIL (LastValueRead < 0)
```
Programming Example 7-25: Loop with Body

Should the loop body contain any other action? What about the total of home runs? Each home run value must be added to the running total of home runs. Hence, we must add another action to the loop body, as illustrated in the following fragment.

```
REPEAT
    READ(INPUT, LastValueRead);
    HomeRunTotal := HomeRunTotal + LastValueRead
UNTIL (LastValueRead < 0)
```
Programming Example 7-26: Loop with Complete Body

7.4.5. Adding Requirements Outside the Loop

Things look pretty good. Must we add anything more to the loop? Think for a moment. The answer is yes. What is missing? The variable **HomeRunTotal** gets incremented within the loop body. However, remember that variables should be initialized before they are used. The following fragment includes the required initialization:

```
HomeRunTotal := 0;
REPEAT
    READ(INPUT, LastValueRead);
    HomeRunTotal := HomeRunTotal + LastValueRead
UNTIL (LastValueRead < 0)
```

Programming Example 7-27: Loop with Body and Initialization

Everything seems to be in order. Are we finished? Not yet. What is missing? The way the loop is currently written, the sentinel value is also added to **HomeRunTotal**. But the sentinel is just a marker rather than data to be processed like the other values. The easy way to fix this problem is by subtracting the last value read from **HomeRunTotal** after the loop has terminated. The following program fragment illustrates the entire loop. It is now complete.

```
HomeRunTotal := 0;
REPEAT
    READ(INPUT, LastValueRead);
    HomeRunTotal := HomeRunTotal + LastValueRead
UNTIL (LastValueRead < 0);
HomeRunTotal := HomeRunTotal - LastValueRead
```

Programming Example 7-28: Complete Loop

Often we must add statements outside the loop for the loop to work properly. To identify these required statements, consider the variables involved in a loop. What actions must be done to the involved variables before and after the loop executes?

7.4.6. A Method of Verifying Loop Termination

We have selected a type of loop, written the loop condition, and completed the loop body as well as the other required actions outside of the loop. Everything seems to be fine. Will the loop ever terminate? Will it always terminate? A loop that does not terminate is an *infinite loop*. You should be able to demonstrate that every loop you write can and will always terminate. This can be demonstrated informally or formally.

Informally, we must be able to show that every repetition of the loop body brings the loop termination one step closer. In the example we have been working with, we know that each repetition of the loop body reads another input value. Since the number of input values is finite, we will eventually read them all, regardless of how many there are.

To formally demonstrate that a loop terminates, we must show that there is an expression, call it e, such that:

1. Every repetition of the loop reduces the value of e.

2. There is a minimum value below which e cannot go.

For the previous example, the expression e is the number of still unread numbers. Initially, the expression is the total number of input values to be read. After each repetition, the expression is reduced by 1. Eventually, the expression will be 0 (no unread values; they have all been read). The expression can go no lower than 0. Therefore, the loop will always terminate.

7.4.7. A Method of Verifying That a Loop Works

At this point, you are probably pretty convinced that the loop we have developed here will work just fine. However, there will be times when you get to this stage of completion of your loop and still have questions about whether the loop you have written is working.

There are two cases to be studied: the case where the fewest possible repetitions happens and the case were some arbitrarily assumed number of repetitions, say n, happens. The first case is zero repetitions for a WHILE loop and one repetition for a REPEAT-UNTIL loop.

In the previous example, the minimum number of repetitions possible is one. In that case, the only input value is the sentinel. The total starts at 0, gets the sentinel added to it, exits the loop, subtracts the sentinel back from the total, and ends. Therefore, it works in the simplest case. When there are n repetitions, there are $n - 1$ input values before the sentinel value. The total starts at 0. Each of the $n - 1$ data values gets added to the total. Then the nth value, which is the sentinel value, is added to the total.

Having read the sentinel, the loop terminates. The last value read, which happens to be the sentinel, gets subtracted back from the total. The variable **HomeRunTotal** contains the desired result. Therefore, the loop works for some arbitrary number of repetitions.

7.4.8. A Method of Verifying That a Loop Always Works

There is another tool in the programmer's toolbox to aid in making sure loops do what they are supposed to. The key idea is to look at a loop in terms of what we know to be true of its variables before, during, and after execution. We begin by determining what is to be true when the loop terminates. For the example at hand, we might state the final condition in the following way: *"A variable, called **HomeRunTotal**, contains the sum of all the home run values read from INPUT."* The trick is to phrase this in terms of what is true not only after the loop terminates but also at the beginning of each trip through the loop. Thus, we need to modify our description to read as follows: *"A variable, **HomeRunTotal**, contains the sum of all the home run values read from INPUT so far."*

Before the loop starts, the variable **HomeRunTotal** has the value 0; therefore, this assertion is true *before* the loop. Each execution of the loop body reads one value and adds it to the variable **HomeRunTotal**; therefore, this assertion is true *during*, the loop execution. After the loop has finished, the variable **HomeRunTotal** contains the desired value; therefore, the assertion is true *after* the loop. You can see that this assertion is true *before*, *during* and *after* the loop execution. The assertion's truth is preserved by the loop. Hence, this phrase is called an ***invariant assertion***, or simply an ***invariant*** of the loop.

If you write the invariant assertion for a loop and demonstrate that the invariant is true before, during, and after the loop, you will be rewarded with a loop that always works. Always consider the loop invariant.

7.4.9. Method for Building Loops

Constructing a loop that executes correctly becomes a matter of science when we follow the systematic approach presented in this chapter. We summarize these methods in the following table:

1. Determine which type of loop to use.

   a. Is there iteration? Is the number of repetitions known in advance of the first repetition? If we have iteration, we should use an iterative loop wherever possible, such as Pascal's FOR loop.

   b. Should the loop always execute at least once? If so, the loop condition should probably be tested *after* executing the loop body, as with Pascal's REPEAT-UNTIL loop.

   c. If the answer was no to the other loop types, or if you are unable to determine which loop to use, use the most general loop type, a loop that tests its condition before executing its loop, such as Pascal's WHILE loop.

2. Determine the *after loop condition*. This usually follows directly from the problem statement.

3. Determine the loop condition. Pascal's WHILE loop condition is the negation of the *after loop condition*, and the REPEAT-UNTIL loop condition is the same as the *after loop condition*.

4. Complete the loop body. There must be at least one action in the loop body to cause loop termination. Other actions may be necessary also.

5. Add any actions required outside the loop. This refers to action both before and after the loop. Such action normally can be determined by considering all the variables involved in the loop. The most common example is initializing variables before the loop.

6. Demonstrate that the loop always terminates. This should be done, at least informally. The programmer should be able to do it formally also.

7. Verify that the loop does what it is supposed to do.

   a. Demonstrate that the loop works for the minimum possible number of repetitions.

   b. Demonstrate that the loop works for some arbitrary number of repetitions.

8. Write an invariant assertion. Show that it is true:

   a. prior to loop execution

   b. after executing the loop body

   c. after the loop has terminated

Table 7-1: A Systematic Method of Building and Verifying Loops

7.4.10. Applying the Systematic Approach to a Familiar Problem

Recall the ComputeBits program presented earlier in this chapter. We needed to represent some number of values and wrote a program to compute how many bits would be necessary to represent those values.

We know that one bit can represent two values. By adding another bit, we can represent twice as many values. Therefore, we wish to repeatedly add one bit at a time until we have just enough bits to represent the desired number of values. We can develop a solution to this problem by using our methods of loop creation and verification.

Step 1. Select which type of loop to use.

Do we have iteration? No, so the FOR loop is out. Should the loop always execute at least one time? Two or fewer values can be represented with one bit. Hence, it may not be necessary to always add more bits. Therefore, the REPEAT-UNTIL loop cannot be used. We will use the WHILE loop.

Step 2. Determine the *after loop condition*.

We know that the number of possible values represented by the bits must be at least as large as the number of desired values. If we name these quantities **PossibleValues** and **DesiredValues**, we know that the *after loop condition* is (**PossibleValues >= DesiredValues**).

Step 3. Write the loop condition.

Since we are using the WHILE loop, the loop condition is the negation of the *after loop condition*. Therefore, we can write the loop shell as indicated below:

```
WHILE (PossibleValues < DesiredValues)
    BEGIN

    END;          (* WHILE *)
```

Programming Example 7-29: Loop with Condition

Step 4. Complete the loop body.

Each repetition must increase the number of bits by 1. Since the value of **DesiredValues** is fixed, we must increase the value of the variable **PossibleValues** if the loop is to terminate. Each additional bit doubles the number of possible values. Hence, we need two actions in the loop body: one to increase the number of bits by 1 and another to double the number of possible values. Therefore, we can complete the loop body:

```
WHILE (PossibleValues < DesiredValues)
    BEGIN
        NumberOfBits:= NumberOfBits + 1;
        PossibleValues := PossibleValues * 2
    END;          (* WHILE *)
```

Programming Example 7-30: Loop with Body

Step 5. Add any actions required outside the loop.

Both variables **NumberOfBits** and **PossibleValues** must be initialized before the loop starts. We initially start with 1 bit that can represent 2 possible values, as indicated below:

```
NumberOfBits:=  1;
PossibleValues :=  2;

WHILE (PossibleValues < DesiredValues)
    BEGIN
        NumberOfBits:= NumberOfBits + 1;
        PossibleValues := PossibleValues * 2
    END;          (* WHILE *)
```

Programming Example 7-31: Loop with Initialization

Step 6. Show that the loop terminates.

Informally: We know that every repetition doubles the value of **PossibleValues**. Since the initial value is 2, and since **DesiredValues** does not change, eventually **PossibleValues** will become greater than or equal to **DesiredValues**, and the loop will terminate.

Formally: Consider the value of the expression **DesiredValues - PossibleValues**. Each repetition reduces this expression. If **PossibleValues** reached twice **DesiredValues**, that would indicate one too many bits. Therefore, the largest **PossibleValues** could be is one less than twice the value of **DesiredValues**. Hence, the expression **DesiredValues - PossibleValues** can be no smaller than **DesiredValues - (2*DesiredValues - 1)**, which is equivalent to **-DesiredValues+1**. With a well-defined lower bound on this expression, the loop is known to always terminate.

Step 7. Show that the loop normally does what it is supposed to do.

Minimum Repetition Case: The minimum number of repetitions is 0. In this case, the value of **DesiredValues** is 2 or fewer. The value of **NumberOfBits** is 1, and the value of **PossibleValues** is 2. Therefore, it works in the minimum repetition case.

Arbitrary Repetition Case: If the loop iterates n times, the value of **NumberOfBits** will be n, and the value of **PossibleValues** will be 2^n. Therefore, it works in the arbitrary case of n repetitions.

Step 8. Write the invariant assertion.

The invariant for this loop is that the value of **PossibleValues** is $2^{NumberOfBits}$.

Before the loop starts: Since **NumberOfBits** and **PossibleValues** are initialized to 1 and 2, respectively, and since 2^1 equals 2, the invariant assertion is true before the loop commences.

After the loop body executes: Since **NumberOfBits** is increased by one and **PossibleValues** is doubled each repetition, the invariant assertion is preserved by executing the loop body.

After the loop terminates: If the loop iterates n times, the value of **NumberOfBits** will be n, and the value of **PossibleValues** will be 2^n. Therefore, the invariant assertion is true after the loop terminates. We have demonstrated conclusively that the loop we constructed will perform as intended.

7.4.11. Systematic Approach to Another Problem: The Marble Bag

The use of invariant assertions may seem like overkill. The best way to think of them is as just one tool in the programmer's toolbox. Like other tools, not every programming tool must be used in every programming task. However, it is a useful and powerful tool to possess. The following puzzle should help you to see the power of invariants.[4] Although we are not interested in writing a Pascal program for this problem, we want to solve and understand this puzzle. Let us systematically apply the methods learned in this chapter. A tough-looking problem becomes simple when seen from the invariance point of view.

> A marble bag contains some white marbles and some black marbles and no other marbles. Without looking, take two marbles from the bag. If they are the same color, set them aside and place a single black marble into the bag. (There are enough extra black marbles to do this.) If the marbles are of different colors, put the white marble back into the bag and set the black marble aside. Continue this process until there is just one marble in the bag. What is known about the color of this marble, given the number of white marbles and the number of black marbles initially in the bag?

To solve this puzzle, we will set up a stylized program. We will skip two of steps in this example intentionally, because we want to focus on the invariant rather than write a real Pascal program.

Select which type of loop to use.
Assume we select the WHILE loop since it will always work.

Determine the *after loop condition.*
We start with some number of white and black marbles. We wish to stop when we have fewer than two marbles left. Therefore, the *after loop condition* is **NumberOfMarbles < 2.**

Write the loop condition.
Since we are using a WHILE loop, we know the loop condition is the negation of the after loop condition. Therefore, our loop is as follows:

```
WHILE (NumberOfMarbles >= 2) DO
    BEGIN

    END    (* WHILE *)
```

Complete the loop body.
The first loop action is to select two marbles, and the second action depends on the color of the two marbles selected. Since there are only three possible combinations of colors, it is easy to think in terms of a CASE statement. The CASE selector is ColorsSelected, and there are exactly three cases.

The loop body is illustrated in the following fragment:

```
WHILE (NumberOfMarbles >= 2) DO
    BEGIN
        SelectTwoMarbles;
        CASE ColorsSelected OF
            <2 white>: <replace one black>;
            <2 black>: <replace one black>;
            <1 of each color>: <replace one white>
        END    (* CASE *)
    END    (* WHILE *)
```

---

[4] Adapted from The Science of Programming [5].

Show the loop terminates.
Every repetition of the loop causes two marbles to be selected from the bag and one marble to be replaced. Therefore, every repetition reduces the number of marbles by exactly one. Since the number of marbles in the bag is finite, eventually all the marbles will be taken from the bag, terminating the loop.

Write the invariant assertion.
Notice that the only information that we have in the problem concerns the number and color of marbles. We are looking for an invariant, so what does not vary about the number of marbles left after each pass through the loop? The total number of marbles decreases by one with each trip through the loop, so that cannot be our invariant. The proportion of black marbles to white marbles might change, since we pull pairs of marbles out at random, so that cannot be the invariant, either. Consider the oddness or evenness of the number of marbles. The oddness of the blacks alternates each time we select two marbles of the same color, so that cannot be an invariant. But look, the oddness of the whites never changes! This is because, whenever a white marble is removed, two white marbles are removed. (Look at the **CASE** statement again to be sure.) Thus, the loop invariant is: *The oddness or evenness of the white marbles is fixed by the oddness or evenness of the number of white marbles at the start of the loop.* Oddness of the white marbles does not change.

If we begin with an odd number of white marbles, we will always have an odd number of white. If the number of white marbles is initially odd, the number of the white marbles always lies in the sequence {1,3,5,7,9...}. If the number of white marbles is even initially, then the number of white marbles always lies in the sequence {0,2,4,6,8...}.

The answer to the puzzle is now revealed. If the number of white marbles begins as an even number, there will never be an odd number of white marbles in the bag. In this case, the last marble in the bag is black since 1 is odd! If the number of white marbles at the start of the loop is odd, then there will always be an odd number of white marbles. In this case, the last marble in the bag must be white!

By applying the methods presented thus far, we were rewarded with a solution to what may have seemed like a quite difficult problem. You will find that these same methods will reward you with solutions you might not have otherwise been able to create. We strongly suggest you use the methods presented here.

7.4.12. Questions

1. What is one method of determining which loop construct to use?

2. What is one method of determining a condition for a loop?

3. Does every loop have a single correct loop condition, or may there be more than one correct condition for the same loop? Give an example to support your answer.

4. Often, certain actions must be added outside a loop for the loop to accomplish the desired result. Give an example of such an action required outside the loop. Which variables should be considered for requiring such outside actions? Should the programmer complete the loop body or the actions required outside the loop first? Give a reason why one should be done before the other.

5. Should a loop always terminate?

6. What are two methods of demonstrating that a loop terminates?

7. What are two cases to be considered in showing that a loop does what it is intended to do?

8. What is an invariant assertion?

9. How can loop invariants be used to demonstrate that a loop works correctly?

10. What steps are involved in a systematic approach to constructing loops?

11. What steps are involved in a systematic approach to verifying loops?

7.4.13. Exercises

1. Consider the following problem: We have a sequence of numbers. We need to determine which position (e.g. first, fourth, fifteenth) in the sequence a particular number occupies. You may assume that each number is an unique integer and that the desired number is always in the sequence of numbers. The desired number must be prompted for; and each value of the input sequence is separated with a space.

   a. Write a Pascal loop to solve this programming problem.

   b. Verify that this loop both terminates and works.

   c. What is this loop invariant?

2. Solve the previous problem again, but this time you may not assume that the desired value is always in the sequence. If the value is not present, return a position of 0. Assume the sequence of numbers contains nonnegative integers terminated with a negative sentinel.

   a. Write a Pascal loop to solve this programming problem.

   b. Verify that this loop both terminates and works.

   c. What is this loop invariant?

3. Consider the following problem. We have a sequence of numbers. We need to determine how many times a particular number occurs in the sequence. You may assume that the sequence of numbers are non-unique integers, each separated by a space and terminated with a negative sentinel. Assume the data values are randomly ordered.

   a. Write a Pascal loop to solve this programming problem.

   b. Verify that this loop both terminates and works.

   c. What is this loop invariant?

4. Assume we have a sequence of non-unique integers ordered from smallest to largest. We need to write a program to determine which integer occurs the most times in the sequence. You may assume that each number in the sequence is separated by a space and that exactly one value is the most frequent in the sequence.

   a. Write a Pascal loop to solve this programming problem.

   b. Verify that this loop both terminates and works.

   c. What is this loop invariant?

7.4.14. Problems

1. Make each of the loops you wrote in the last set of exercises into a Pascal program. Enter the programs into your system and show that they run properly.

2. Write a program to sum a sequence of integers. Assume the input sequence is terminated by a sentinel value of -9999. Write a Pascal program to solve this problem. Develop your solution with the systematic approach presented in this chapter.

3. Modify the previous program so that the user selects the sentinel value. Prompt the user for the sentinel value as the first step.

7.5. Chapter Summary

- Pascal has two types of control structures: conditional execution and repetition.

- The need for repetition is evidenced by the desire to repeat one or more statements.

- The *repetition* control structures allow for repeated execution of statements.

- Pascal's three repetition constructs are WHILE loop, FOR loop, and REPEAT-UNTIL loop.

- The WHILE loop condition is evaluated *before* executing the loop action.

- The WHILE loop condition must evaluate to TRUE for its action to be executed.

- Control passes to the first statement after the WHILE loop if the loop condition evaluates to FALSE.

- The general form of the WHILE statement is:

        WHILE `<boolean-expression>` DO

           `<statement>`

- Pascal's WHILE loop repeats exactly one statement. To repeat more than one statement with the WHILE loop, use a compound statement (BEGIN-END block).

- If a WHILE loop condition initially evaluates to FALSE, the loop will never execute.

- If a WHILE loop condition always evaluates to TRUE, the loop will never stop executing. This is known as an infinite loop.

- *Iteration* is a special case of *repetition* where the number of repetitions is known in advance of the first repetition.

- Pascal has a control structure for iteration. It is known as the FOR loop.

- The general form of Pascal's FOR statement is:

FOR `<index-variable>` := `<initial-value>` `<direction>` `<final-value>` DO

       `<statement>`

- The Pascal FOR loop works in the following way. The expressions for initial and final values are evaluated. The initial value is assigned to the index variable. If the direction is upward, while the index variable is less than or equal to the final value, the statement is repeated. *After* each iteration of an upward loop, the index variable is increased. If the direction is downward, while the index variable is greater than or equal to the final value, the statement is repeated. After each iteration of a downward loop, the loop index variable is decreased.

- The FOR loop index variable never needs to be incremented or decremented by the programmer because it is done automatically. It is an error in Standard Pascal to assign a value to a FOR loop index variable within the loop body. DOWNTO causes the FOR loop index variable to be decreased; TO causes the FOR loop index variable to be increased.

- An iteration control structure (Pascal's FOR loop) should be used whenever the number of repetitions is known in advance of the first repetition.

- A FOR loop index variable must be of *ordinal type*. Therefore, it cannot be of type REAL.

- A FOR loop initial value and final value are evaluated only once, at loop startup, rather than once every iteration. Therefore, changing any variables within a FOR loop body that are used in either the initial value or the final value expression has no effect on the number of iterations of the FOR loop.

- The FOR loop always increments or decrements the FOR loop index variable by 1. Since it is an error in Standard Pascal to assign a value to any FOR loop index variable, a FOR loop can never be used where a "step size" other than 1 is needed. Another type of loop must be used in these situations.

- A compound statement (BEGIN-END block) can be used with a FOR loop or a WHILE loop to repeat more than one statement. A compound statement is unnecessary with the REPEAT-UNTIL loop.

- The WHILE loop tests its condition before the loop body, and the REPEAT-UNTIL loop tests its condition after the loop body. A consequence of this is that a REPEAT-UNTIL loop must execute at least once, whereas a WHILE loop may execute zero times.

- A WHILE loop can always be used in place of a FOR loop or a REPEAT-UNTIL loop.

- The general form of the Pascal REPEAT-UNTIL loop is:

```
REPEAT
    <statement1>;
    <statement2>;
    <statement3>;
         :
         :
         :
    <statementN>
UNTIL <boolean-expression>
```

- A sentinel is a special data value that indicates some condition, such as the end of data, that is not treated like the other data values.

- We reviewed systematic methods of constructing and verifying programming loops. These methods are summarized in Table 7-1 on page 229.

- A loop should always terminate, and the programmer always should be able to demonstrate that every loop will always terminate.

- A loop invariant is an assertion that is supposed to be preserved by a loop. To be invariant, the assertion must be true before the loop, after executing the loop body, and after the loop has terminated. It can be used to demonstrate that a loop works correctly if part of the invariant states what the loop is to accomplish.

7.6. Summary of Style

- A FOR loop index variable should be considered undefined outside the body of the loop. It is very poor programming practice to expect a FOR loop index variable to be a particular value after the loop has terminated.

- Boolean conditions often can be phrased in several different but equivalent forms. Any of the equivalent forms can be used interchangeably. We suggest using the simplest, easiest to read, or most natural phrasing of the condition.

- It is often less than obvious what a particular END matches. It could be the END of a CASE statement, the END of a procedure, the END of the program, or one of many other BEGIN-END pairs. We have found that putting a brief comment after each END to identify what it matches alleviates the problem. For example, note the following code fragments:

```
CASE selector OF
    :
    :
    :
END;    (* CASE *)

WHILE expression DO
    BEGIN
        :
        :
        :
    END;    (* WHILE *)
```

Such comments are particularly important for identifying the boundaries of nested compound statements. In such cases, we normally identify what construct is ending and something unique about the particular structure, such as (* FOR column *) to denote the end of the FOR loop used to determine the columns in our triangle example.

7.7. Summary of Terms

- repetition
- WHILE statement
- loop condition
- loop action
- infinite loop
- endless loop

- nonexecuting loop
- iteration
- FOR statement
- TO
- DOWNTO
- nested loop

- REPEAT statement
- sentinel
- loop construction
- loop termination
- invariant assertion
- loop invariant

7.8. Chapter Problems

1. Write a Pascal program to compute the average (or arithmetic mean) of a sequence of integers. Assume the user knows the number of integers at the start of the program execution. *Hint: The mean of a sequence of numbers is their sum divided by the number of values in the sequence.*

2. All equipment, including computer equipment, has a limited useful life. The usefulness is reduced with usage. Depreciation refers to the useful value of equipment that has been used. There are a variety of methods to determine depreciation. They all need two pieces of data: the cost of the equipment to be depreciated and the expected useful life (usually in years) of the equipment. The method of depreciation known as *straight-line depreciation* allocates the usefulness equally among the years of the equipment's expected life. Write a Pascal program that computes and displays the depreciation and cumulative depreciation for each year of some equipment's life according to the straight-line depreciation method. The program will need to prompt the user for both the equipment's cost and its expected useful life.

3. Most people had to "learn" multiplication tables during elementary school. Write a Pascal program to compute and display the multiplication table up through 12 * 12. *Hint: This table will have 12 rows and 12 columns.*

4. Extend the previous program so an *n* * *n* table is displayed. Prompt the user for the value of *n*.

5. Write a program to compute factorials. *Note: The factorial of n (n!) is defined as n multiplied by the factorial of n-1 and the factorial of 1 is 1. Symbolically, n! = n * (n-1)! and 1! = 1.*

6. *** Write a program to compute Fibonacci numbers. *Hint: A Fibonacci number is defined as the sum of the two previous Fibonacci numbers, and the first two Fibonacci numbers are both 1. Symbolically, the nth Fibonacci number may be defined as: F(n) = F(n-1) + F(n-2) and F(1) = 1 and F(2) = 1. We illustrate this in the following table:*

```
n          Fibonacci(n)
1          1
2          1
3          2
4          3
5          5
6          8
:          :
:          :
n          Fibonacci(n-1) + Fibonacci(n-2)
```

7. Write a Pascal program that converts an integer number of seconds into an equivalent number of hours, minutes, and seconds. The result should not include more than 59 minutes or 59 seconds.

8. Write a program to determine the greatest common divisor of two positive integers. Use Euclid's greatest common divisor (GCD) algorithm. *Hint: Euclid's GCD algorithm*

starts with two unequal positive integers, call them `larger` *and* `smaller`. *The difference between the two values is determined. The* `larger` *then becomes the larger of the difference and the* `smaller`. *The* `smaller` *becomes the smaller of the difference and the* `smaller`. *The process continues until* `smaller` *equals 1, in which case the value of* `larger` *is the greatest common divisor, or until* `smaller` *and* `larger` *are equal, in which case there is no common divisor.*

9. Individual Retirement Accounts, better known as IRAs, provide an easy way to build a large retirement fund. Essentially, IRAs are special savings accounts that are not taxed while they grow. Write a Pascal program to compute the total in an IRA, given the current amount in the IRA and the annual interest rate it earns. The program should prompt for the user's age today and the age at which the user plans to retire to determine how many years the IRA will grow.

10. Extend the previous program so that in addition to the current amount, a yearly deposit amount can be supplied by the user. You may assume the deposits are the same amount every year; however, the maximum deposit cannot exceed $2,000 per year.

11. Write a Pascal program that reads two positive integers from the user and computes and displays the largest common prefix of the two. If there is no common prefix, the program should return NIL. Some examples of the input and corresponding output follow:

```
INPUT            OUTPUT
335 337          33
123 1234         123
27 27            27
123 23           NIL
```

UNIT III: Modular Programming

Chapter 8: Procedures

Chapter 9: Parameters

Chapter 10: Functions

Chapter 11: Recursive Subprograms

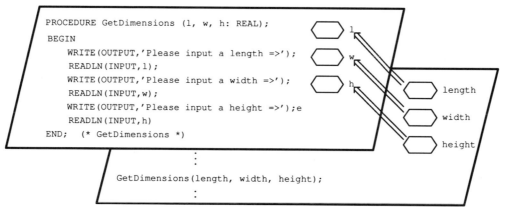

```
PROCEDURE GetDimensions (l, w, h: REAL);
BEGIN
    WRITE(OUTPUT,'Please input a length =>');
    READLN(INPUT,l);
    WRITE(OUTPUT,'Please input a width =>');
    READLN(INPUT,w);
    WRITE(OUTPUT,'Please input a height =>');e
    READLN(INPUT,h)
END;   (* GetDimensions *)

            :
            :
    GetDimensions(length, width, height);
            :
```

```
PROCEDURE GetDimensions (VAR l, w, h: REAL);
BEGIN
    WRITE(OUTPUT,'Please input a length =>');
    READLN(INPUT,l);
    WRITE(OUTPUT,'Please input a width =>');
    READLN(INPUT,w);
    WRITE(OUTPUT,'Please input a height =>');
    READLN(INPUT,h)
END;   (* GetDimensions *)

            :
            :
    GetDimensions(length, width, height);
            :
```

Chapter 8: Procedures

We introduced procedures in Chapter 3 and have used them ever since. You probably feel relatively comfortable writing Pascal procedures, even though we have not yet discussed them in depth. In this chapter we consider in detail procedures and the principles for writing them. Once you have mastered this material, you will be capable of solving an entire range of problems that may have seemed unsolvable to you previously. The programs you will be able to create will be interesting and useful, and they can be fun as well. As our first step, we will explore a method of creating computer programs by using procedures as building blocks.

8.1. Modular Programming

Computer programming refers to the process of creating a program to *solve a problem* on a computer. The heart of this process is *solving a problem*, generally referred to as **problem solving**. Therefore, it is essential that we understand *problem solving* as it relates to computer programming.

8.1.1. Problem Solving

Problem solving is defined as the act of generating a **solution** to a **problem**. The two abstract terms *problem* and *solution* may be defined as follows:

> **Definition 8-1:** A *problem* exists when there is some difference between the current state of affairs and some desired, or goal, state of affairs.

> **Definition 8-2:** A *solution* is a series of actions that alters the current state of affairs to equal the desired, or goal, state of affairs.

> **Definition 8-3:** *Problem solving* is the act of generating a *solution* to a *problem*.

Say John is at the school fieldhouse after football practice thinking about his birthday dinner waiting at home for him. The current state has John still at the team's fieldhouse, but the goal state has John at home enjoying his birthday dinner. The difference between these two states is the *problem*. John needs to *solve* the *problem* by generating a *solution*. Possible solutions may include walking, hitchhiking, riding a bus, hotwiring the coach's car, or some combination of these. Note that there may be more than one solution for a single problem. Choosing from possible solutions is a problem in itself. Although hotwiring the coach's car may get John home the quickest, it is probably not the best solution. As the number of possible solutions increases, picking the "best" solution becomes more difficult. We have defined and illustrated these notions so that we have a framework within which we can relate problem solving to computer programming.

8.1.2. Modular Problem Solving

Modular problem solving is based on a person's ability to a solve a *problem* in broad brush strokes before attempting to fill in the details of the *solution*. Modular problem solving divides the original problem into several smaller problems, or *subproblems*. We then solve each of the subproblems, thereby solving the original problem.

Modular problem solving employs the notion of "divide and conquer." A problem is decomposed ("divided") into several smaller problems. Each of the smaller problems (subproblems) are solved ("conquered"), thereby solving ("conquering") the original larger problem.

The real power of this technique is seen when we consider solving the subproblems. Each subproblem is solved in precisely the same fashion as the original problem, namely, by dividing it into several smaller problems (*sub-subproblems*) and then solving the smaller problems. Of course, the sub-subproblems may then be solved in the same fashion as the subproblems and the original problem. The process of decomposition is repeated as many times as necessary.

Solutions generated in this fashion are referred to as *modules*. Each module is an independent, self-contained solution to a particular problem whether, it is the original problem, a subproblem, or some yet smaller problem. Solutions to subproblems are often referred to as *submodules*, and so on.

We should point out that there is usually more than one acceptable *problem decomposition* to a single problem. Also note that the more complex the problem, the more times the decomposition process needs to be applied. Each repetition of the "divide and conquer" process yields another level of decomposition.

8.1.3. Top-Down Design and Solution Trees

The method of problem solving just described is known in computer science as **top-down design**. Each step of this process specifies the solution in finer detail. In computer science, the design is refined one step at a time and is said to be **step-wise refined**.

> **Definition 8-4:** *Top-down design* is a systematic strategy for solving problems by decomposing large problems into smaller subproblems. It works from the general to the specific, considering the major decisions first and the details last.

> **Definition 8-5:** *Step-wise refinement* refers to the process of repeatedly *refining* a solution one step at a time. Each additional step provides additional details not provided in prior steps.

To illustrate these ideas, consider the following situation. One Friday evening, John and Betty get a phone call from several friends who are in town for the weekend, and John invites the friends to come over for dinner. Much to his dismay, he realizes the grocery supply is low. John's problem is probably one that we are all familiar with in one way or another. In the current state of affairs, the grocery supply is low; in the desired state of affairs, the cupboards would be well stocked. "Well," says Betty, "I guess you'll have to go shopping." At the highest level, the problem can be solved through the task of *grocery shopping*, which can be divided into smaller tasks (subtasks) in many ways. John decides to decompose it into two subtasks: *generating a shopping list* and *buying the items on the list*. John's problem decomposition can be represented graphically by the following illustration:

Figure 8-1: Graphic Representation of Problem Decomposition

The subtask of *generating a shopping list* may be decomposed in a variety of ways. Assume John's solution is to *get a pencil and paper, examine the kitchen cupboards* to decide what they need, and *consult the spouse* for her contributions to the list. Once his shopping list is firmly in hand, John can consider the subtask of *generating the shopping list* completed. He can then turn his attention to the other major subtask, *buying the items on the list*. This, of course, could also be done in a variety of ways. John does it the following way: *go to the grocery store*; *collect the items on the list*; *pay the cashier*; and *return home with the groceries*. This additional level of decomposition may be represented graphically as follows:

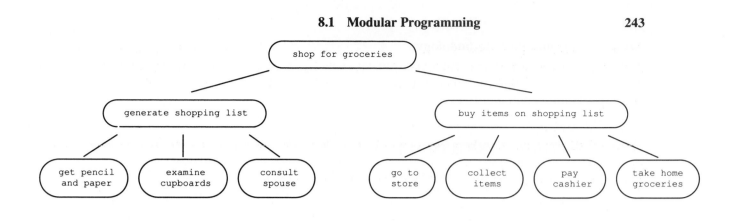

Figure 8-2: The Hierarchical Structure of Problem Decomposition

Note that the problem decomposition has a structure associated with it; it forms a hierarchy. Solutions generated by this method are called *hierarchically structured problem decompositions*. We call these hierarchically structured problem decompositions **solution trees**, primarily because the structure is similar to upside down trees. The root is at the top and branches reach down.

> **Definition 8-6:** A *solution tree* is a graphic description of the decomposition of a particular problem that reveals its hierarchical structure.

Note that our solution tree neglects many of the low-level details. For example, when making the list, we didn't say how to physically create it. The paper is to be placed on a solid surface. The pencil is to be grasped between the thumb and forefinger. Is the list to be printed or written in cursive? What language is to be used for the list? Are the items to be numbered, abbreviated, or grouped by category? We also left out many details of the acquisition phase. For example, we named a subtask *collect items on list*; however, we have said nothing about how this is to be accomplished. How is John going to search the store for the items on the list? Will he use a shopping cart, or perhaps, just a shopping basket? We named another subtask *paying the cashier*. This might be done with cash, a personal check, manufacturers' coupons, a credit card, or some combination of these methods. But since we are using top-down design, we need not worry about these details until later.

A **bottom-up design** would start with the most primitive tasks (such as grasping the pencil) and try to build them into an overall solution. Even for the modest task of grocery shopping, if John were to start by worrying about details such as how to hold the pencil, what abbreviations to use in the shopping list, or whether to use a shopping cart once he gets to the store, etc., he might never get to the store, much less get any shopping done!

> **Definition 8-7:** *Bottom-up design* is a problem-solving strategy opposite to *top-down design*. Bottom-up design seeks to compose solutions of smaller problems into a solution for a larger problem. The solution is thereby created from more elemental and specific solutions. The method works from the specific to the general.

Without the top-down design technique, we may become overwhelmed by the low-level details of a problem. The top-down design technique focuses our attention on the highest level of decision making, postponing decisions about the details until the very end. With this technique, if it turns out that any task requires modification (which quite frequently happens with formidable problems), we need only modify that particular module and perhaps some of the submodules below it. We never need to modify other parts of the solution tree above the task in question. Hence we may change the way we pay the cashier without affecting the way we generate the shopping list, get to the store, or collect the items. This is true because each module is an independent solution to a particular problem. Independent solutions may be modified independently. Modular solutions are a very powerful feature of top-down design.

8.1.4. A Programming Methodology

We have discussed problems, solutions, problem solving, modular problem solving, top-down design, and solution trees. But computer programming is more than problem solving; we must end up with instructions for a computer to execute. A *programming methodology* is the system of rules, principles, and methods people use when creating computer programs. The methodology that we advocate is called *modular programming*. Modular programming utilizes modular problem solving to design computer programs in a top-down fashion.

Programming problems get decomposed into modular solutions. When all of the problems have been fully decomposed, each of the solutions is coded into the desired programming language. Note that what we have described is a general programming methodology rather than a trick of some particular programming language. Therefore, this method may be used with most any programming language you decide to use. In fact, the programmer may create an abstract solution to a particular programming problem without having selected the programming solution. Moreover, the same abstract solution may be implemented in a variety of different programming languages.

Very small problems may require only one level of decomposition. Many medium-sized programs may be coded after a few levels of decomposition. Very large and complex software systems require many levels of decomposition. The complete program is composed of *modules*, each designed to solve a particular subproblem.

The approach we refer to as modular programming will help you to *plan* your program before you actually sit down to write it in a particular programming language. This approach will also help you to locate and correct bugs in your programs because each module can be compared to your program plan to make sure it works properly.

We first introduced top-down design in Chapter 2 when discussing Karel. Recall the problem of writing HELLO with beepers (page 50). The problem of writing HELLO decomposes into the four subproblems of write-H, write-E, write-L, and write-O. The four subproblems are small enough that they need no more decomposition. In writing an actual Karel program for this problem, we define a new instruction for each of the four subproblems. Each of the four new instructions, in turn, is completed with Karel's primitive instructions, such as **move** and **putbeeper**.

We revisited top-down design in Chapter 3 in introducing Pascal. Recall the problem of writing HELLO in large 5 by 5 letters (page 96). The problem of writing HELLO again decomposes into the four subproblems of write-H, write-E, write-L, and write-O. In writing an actual Pascal program for this problem, we define a new statement (procedure) for each of the four subproblems. Each of the four procedures are in turn completed with Pascal's primitive statement WRITELN.

Recalling these two programming problems should illustrate that the programming techniques advanced here are general and not tied to any particular programming language. The programming problem was decomposed into the same four modules, namely, write-H, write-E, write-L, and write-O. There are three important points to remember. The abstract solution could be implemented in any of a variety of programming languages, making it a *language-independent* solution. Modular programming is a general programming method independent of programming language. If we are writing a Karel program, we define new instructions. If we are writing a Pascal program, we define new statements (procedures). Second, each of the modules is an independent, self-contained solution to a particular problem. This means we can modify the module *write-O* without having to modify the module *write-H*. Third, although writing the word HELLO entails writing five separate letters, our solution requires only four distinct modules. A solution to a single subproblem may be reused as many times as desired in the overall solution. This reduces wasteful duplication of effort.

Recall that a computer program is a finite sequence of instructions that solves some problem. Both Pascal's procedures and Karel's new instructions fulfill this definition but only refer to part of an overall program. It is for this reason that they are known as **subprograms**. Modular programming is achieved using *subprograms*.

> **Definition 8-8:** A *subprogram* is a subset of the sequence of instructions of a program considered as a unit. Pascal's procedures are subprograms.

The abstract modules discussed in this chapter are normally implemented as subprograms. However, an abstract module may constitute more than a single subprogram. There exist programming languages, such as Ada and Modula-2, that provide a language construct specifically for a collection or unit of logically related procedures. Such logical units are known as *modules* or units. Neither Karel nor Standard Pascal have modules. In programming languages without modules, the abstract modules must be implemented solely with subprograms. In Karel, that means implementing abstract modules as new instructions. In Pascal, that means implementing abstract modules as procedures.

8.1.5. Questions

1. What is a problem?

2. What is a solution?

3. What is problem solving?

4. What is modular problem solving?

5. Briefly describe the top-down design approach.

6. Contrast the bottom-up approach with the top-down approach.

7. What are the two primary benefits of the top-down design strategy?

8. What is a solution tree?

9. What is step-wise refinement?

10. What is modular programming?

11. What is an abstract module?

12. What is a subprogram?

13. What language features of Karel are used to accomplish modular programming?

14. What in Pascal are used to accomplish modular programming?

8.1.6. Exercises

1. Extend the example solution tree for the task of grocery shopping to one more level of detail.

2. Write a solution tree for the task of going to the movies.

3. Write a solution tree for the task of buying a bike. Do not include too many details; expand the solution far enough to display the overall solution.

4. Design a solution tree for getting to school in the morning.

5. Design a solution tree for getting a pizza as a snack.

8.2. Subprogram Concepts

Using modular programming, we can view a problem as a series of subproblems, a task as a series of subtasks, and a program as a series of subprograms. For each subproblem, we need to create a subprogram capable of solving it. *Subprograms are the single most powerful component of modern programming languages.* They aid in top-down design, simplify program implementation, and make programs easier to extend. To use the power of subprograms properly, we need to understand both how to use them and when it is appropriate to use a particular kind of subprogram. Some of the illustrations that we use are abstract, focusing on exactly how Pascal works. In other cases the examples are drawn from common experience, using your intuition as an aid to understanding Pascal and sound programming methodology. To understand what happens when subprograms are called, we need a model of how subprograms execute. We develop such a model in the following section.

8.2.1. A Model of Subprogram Execution

Say, your uncle gives you a used stereo that needs a few minor repairs. You want to figure out how much those repairs will cost. You know that it needs a new speaker, several connectors, and a new stylus for the turntable. You check the prices for these items in a stereo parts catalog that you have on hand. You find the prices for the speaker and the connectors, but there is no listing for the stylus. You decide to call your local record shop to ask them about the price of the stylus. The saleswoman at the record shop puts you on hold while she checks her catalog. Unfortunately, she has the same catalog that you have already used, so her catalog doesn't list the stylus either. So, she uses another phone line to call her supplier at a nearby warehouse. The supplier puts her on hold while he checks his price catalog and examines his inventory. He locates the stylus and determines its price, reconnects to the saleswoman, and tells her the price. She reconnects to you and tells you the price.

Now think of a program, *Compute Repair Cost*, that performs all of this. The program is composed of four modules: *Check Catalog, Consult Record Shop, Call Warehouse*, and *Examine Inventory*.

To help build a model to understand how subprograms interact, we will suppose that each module, including the main program (*Compute Repair Cost*), is written on a separate sheet of paper. Our model begins by laying down the sheet of paper on which the main program, *Compute Repair Cost*, is written. This is seen in the first illustration. We know the first thing *Compute Repair Cost* must do is check the catalog. Therefore, the module *Compute Repair Cost* invokes the *Check Catalog* module. This is denoted by placing the paper containing *Check Catalog* on top of the paper containing *Compute Repair Cost*. This is demonstrated in the second illustration.

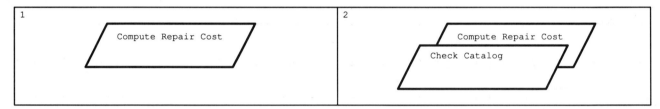

Note that the *module being called* (or invoked) is *stacked* on top of the *calling module*. Also note that the module on top of the stack is the *currently executing module* while action in all other modules on the stack is suspended.

The completion of *Check Catalog* is indicated by removing (*unstacking*) it from *Compute Repair Cost*, as indicated in the third illustration. Since we still need to determine the cost of a new stylus, we must call a record store. Therefore, the module *Compute Repair Cost* calls or invokes the module *Call Record Store*. Again, the module being called is stacked on top of the calling module, as indicated in the fourth illustration.

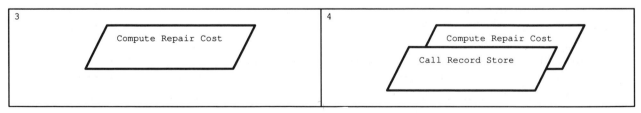

The first thing the woman at the record store does is check the catalog. Therefore, the module *Call Record Store* invokes the module *Check Catalog*. The sheet denoting *Check Catalog* is stacked on top of *Call Record Store*, which is stacked on top of *Compute Repair Cost*. The fifth illustration demonstrates this.

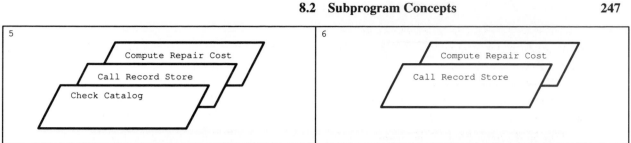

After completion of the module *Check Catalog*, it is removed from the stack of modules, as indicated in the sixth illustration. Next the woman calls the warehouse. Invoking the module *Call Warehouse* is indicated in the seventh illustration. The first thing the man at the warehouse does is check the catalog. The eighth illustration shows the call to *Check Catalog* made by *Call Warehouse*. The stack now contains four modules.

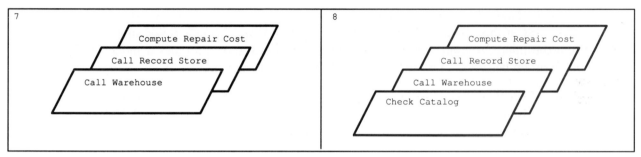

After *Check Catalog* is completed, control is passed back to *Call Warehouse* (illustration 9), after which *Examine Inventory* is called (illustration 10).

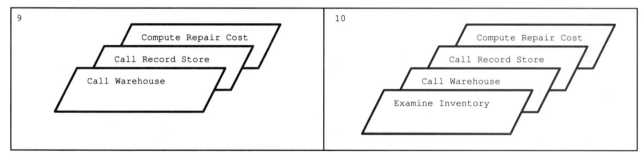

The inspection of the inventory successfully determines the price of the stylus. Once this is completed, *Inspect Inventory* is unstacked from *Call Warehouse* (illustration 11). The supplier then reports back to the saleswoman, which is indicated by unstacking *Call Warehouse* from *Call Record Store* (illustration 12).

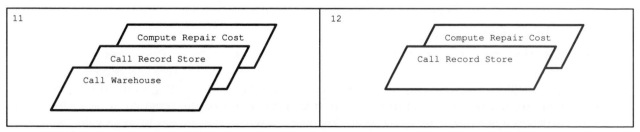

The saleswoman tells you the price of the stylus, and *Call Record Store* is completed (illustration 13). Finally, you have computed the repair costs and the program is completed!

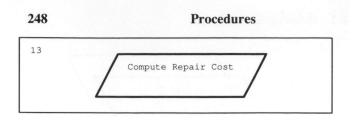

This *stacking* and *unstacking* of program modules is very much like what happens during the execution of a program. When a subprogram is called, it is stacked on top of the module from which it was called. When a subprogram terminates, it is removed from the top of this stack. This leads to the definition of the **call stack**, which is sometimes known as the *runtime stack* because it occurs when the program runs.

> **Definition 8-9:** The *call stack* is the stack of subprogram calls that are active at a given point in the execution of a program.

There are many details that this illustration does not address. These details indeed form the subject matter of the rest of this chapter. However, insofar as a program is made up of subprograms that are called from the main program and from each other, the illustration provides a model that faithfully represents program behavior. You should understand fully this stack model of subprogram calls.

8.2.2. Subprogram Declarations and Calls

It is important to distinguish and know the difference between the *definition* and the *use* of a subprogram.

> **Definition 8-10:** The *definition* of a subprogram is its *declaration*.

> **Definition 8-11:** The *use* of a subprogram is its *call*.

Think of these definitions in terms of Karel's new-instructions created by the programmer. Consider the following Karel program containing the programmer-defined instruction **turnright**. The block that *defines* **turnright** (larger box), is the **declaration** of **turnright**. The instruction, **turnright** (smaller box), that *uses* the new-instruction is a **call** to **turnright**.

```
BEGINING-OF-PROGRAM
  DEFINE-NEW-INSTRUCTION turnright AS
  BEGIN
      turnleft;
      turnleft;
      turnleft
  END;
  BEGINING-OF-EXECUTION
      turnright;
      turnoff
  END-OF-EXECUTION
END-OF-PROGRAM
```

Figure 8-3: Declaration and Call of a Subprogram

8.2.3. Procedures and Functions

Although Karel has only one type of subprogram, namely new-instructions, Pascal has two classes of subprograms: *procedures* and *functions*. While the difference between the two will become very clear in the coming chapters, we wish you to have at least an intuitive understanding of the difference now. Although both are a sequence of instructions considered as a unit of the program, a *procedure is a statement*, whereas a *function is an expression*. Therefore, a function evaluates to some value, whereas a procedure does not.

8.2.4. Questions

1. What model of subprogram execution do we use?

2. What is a call stack?

3. What is a subprogram declaration?

4. What is a subprogram call?

5. How many classes of subprograms does Pascal have? Name each.

6. What is a procedure?

7. What is a function?

8. What is the primary difference between procedures and functions?

8.3. Simple Procedures

The simplest of Pascal's subprograms is known as a *simple procedure*. You have already seen and written simple procedures. A very common use of the simple procedure is to provide information to the user of a program. Typically, these are seen at the beginning and end of programs to provide information that tells the user what the program does and how to use it. We illustrate such a procedure for a checkbook balancing program in the following example:

```
PROCEDURE Hello;

    (* ****************************************************************

     * DESCRIPTION:
            Procedure Hello says hello to the user and gives instructions
            on how to use the check book balance program.

     * METHOD:
            This procedure is simply a sequence of WRITELN statements.

     **************************************************************** *)


BEGIN
    WRITELN(OUTPUT);
    WRITELN(OUTPUT, 'Welcome to the Check Book Balance program.');
    WRITELN(OUTPUT, 'I will help you keep your records straight.');
    WRITELN(OUTPUT, 'Type "d" to record a deposit to your account.');
    WRITELN(OUTPUT, 'Type "w" to record a withdrawal from your account.');
    WRITELN(OUTPUT, 'If you wish to terminate the program type "q".');
    WRITELN(OUTPUT)
END;     (* Hello *)
```

Programming Example 8-1: A Simple Procedure

Although most simple procedures are fairly straightforward, not all simple procedures are just a series of WRITELN statements like the procedure **Hello**. A subprogram to clear the user's screen is another example of a simple procedure. An easy way to clear the user's screen is to call **WRITELN(OUTPUT)** as many times as there are rows on the screen. The code in Example 8-2 is an example of a procedure to clear the screen.

```
PROCEDURE ClearScreen;

    (* ***********************************************************************

     * DESCRIPTION:
             Procedure ClearScreen clear the user's display screen.

     * METHOD:
             WRITELN is used to write blank lines on the output device.
             Enough blank lines are written so that the resulting screen
             is completely blank.  A FOR loop is used to control
             the iteration.

    *********************************************************************** *)


    CONST
        ScreenLength = 24;              (* the number of lines on an output screen *)

    VAR
        count: INTEGER;

    BEGIN
        FOR count := 1 TO ScreenLength
            WRITELN(OUTPUT)
    END;      (* ClearScreen *)
```

Programming Example 8-2: A Nontrivial Simple Procedure

Although the procedure **ClearScreen** is nontrivial, it is pretty straightforward. It is really just WRITELN coupled with one FOR loop. Therefore, the action of this procedure could easily be written "in line" in a program rather than writing a separate procedure to do it. Indeed, a programmer never *has to* write procedures. You can write every program as one long sequence of instructions without a single subprogram. Some people like to follow this approach. Others tend to view subprograms as simply an arbitrary division of a program. Such people like to write a program first as a long sequence of instructions and then "chop up" the working program into subprograms. They will chop up their working 100-line program (without any subprograms) into two 50-line subprograms, five 20-line subprograms, one-hundred 1-line subprograms, or whatever size subprograms they like. Note that this approach will yield subprograms that will be executed exactly once each. Both of these approaches ignore the real benefits of using subprograms.

Without subprograms, every time the same sequence of actions needs to be executed, the same sequence of instructions must be duplicated. Besides having to type in the same keystrokes again, there is a good chance they will not be duplicated identically, thereby providing a good chance of introducing errors into the program. This becomes more apparent the more times a sequence of actions needs to be duplicated. By forming a subprogram out of a sequence of actions, the programmer can have the desired actions repeated by simply calling the sequence by name. The use of subprograms, like the use of named constants, saves the programmer keystrokes and makes programs more readable and easier to modify.

While the benefits of using subprograms may be apparent, knowing when to create another subprogram, as well as how big it should be, is not as obvious. Normally, we want a subprogram to accomplish a well-defined and named action. If the action in question is expected to be repeated, certainly we want to use a subprogram. By following the techniques of modular programming, you will decompose the programming problem into a collection of abstract modules that can be implemented as Pascal subprograms. It is for this reason that not every subprogram is expected to have the same number of lines of program code. It is ridiculous to say, for example, that every subprogram must have exactly 17 lines of code. The question often arises as to whether there is a range for the number of lines a subprogram should have. In general, the answer is no. We have already seen a one-statement procedure when we considered procedure **ClearScreen**. Although it is a small subprogram, it does a well-defined action and is likely to be repeated. Therefore, it is not too small to be a subprogram. Although it is impossible to pick a limit for the number of lines in a subprogram, a subprogram can be too big. In general, a subprogram should accomplish a single well-defined action. Thus, a subprogram that contains a variety of different actions is too big.

Although there are no strict rules governing subprogram size, our experience shows that nearly all of the subprograms we write are 1 to 10 statements long, and most of them are about 5 or 6 statements long. We have one rule of thumb about the size of subprograms. If the subprogram does not fit on a single output screen, it is probably too long.

8.3.1. Subprogram Comments and Declarations

We said as early as Chapter 3 that subprograms (procedures), like programs, can have their own constant definitions and variable declarations. Our last example, procedure **ClearScreen**, demonstrated the use of both. The syntax of the simple procedure in Pascal is as follows:

```
PROCEDURE <name>;

    (* ***********************************************

     * DESCRIPTION:

     * METHOD:

     ************************************************ *)


<constant definitions>

<variable declarations>

<subprogram declarations>

BEGIN
    <statements>
END;
```

Programming Example 8-3: Procedure Skeleton

Although you have seen this subprogram skeleton before, note the subprogram comments. They should not be idle chat. We advocate what we term *structured comments*. The *structured subprogram comments* we use have five components. At this point we are only interested in two of them, **Description** and **Method**, for a brief description of *what* the subprogram does and and *how* the subprogram does it, respectively. It is good practice to write a subprogram comment for every subprogram. We have found structured comments to provide a certain unformity that makes creating useful comments easier and reading them similarly easy. It is best to work on a subprogram's comment when working on the subprogram, rather than trying to "fill in" comments later for subprograms written in the past.

We have already pointed out that procedures are subprograms and that, as such, they have essentially the same characteristics as programs. Subprograms may have constant definitions, variable declarations, and even other subprogram declarations. The next section discusses the interaction of these different declarations.

8.4. Scope of Identifiers

Recall that the only user-definable objects (identifiers) in Karel are subprograms (or new-instructions). However, we have learned that Pascal programmers may define variables and named constants in addition to subprograms. Although this is an important difference between the two programming languages, there is an even more important difference.

Although user-defined identifiers can be defined only at one point in a Karel program, user-defined identifiers can be defined at more than one place in Pascal programs. Identifiers can be defined only at the top of a Karel program, but identifiers can be defined at the top of the program or within any subprogram in Pascal.

The difference in where identifiers can be defined gives rise to a difference in where the identifiers can be used. User-defined identifiers in Karel programs can be used anywhere in the Karel program in which they are defined. In general, not every identifier in a Pascal program can be used in every subprogram of the program. A natural question, then, is in what portion of a program may a particular identifier be used?

The portion of a program in which the identifier can be used is known as the identifier's **scope**. An identifier's scope is determined by where an identifier is defined. In general, the smallest subprogram that contains the declaration of an identifier is the scope of the identifier.

> **Definition 8-12:** The *scope* of an identifier is the portion of a program in which it is valid to use an identifier. In general, the smallest subprogram that contains the declaration of an identifier is the scope of the identifier.

This implies that identifiers declared at the top of a program can be used anywhere in the program, whereas identifiers declared within a subprogram may be used only in that subprogram.

8.4.1. Local and Global Declarations

When an identifier is declared at the top of a program, the declaration is known as a **global declaration**. The declaration of an identifier within a subprogram is known as a **local declaration**.

> **Definition 8-13:** A *global declaration* refers to the declaration of an identifier at the top of the program. Globally declared identifiers can be used throughout the entire program, including in all of its subprograms.

> **Definition 8-14:** A *local declaration* refers to the declaration of an identifier within a subprogram. Locally declared identifiers can be used only within the subprogram in which they are declared.

A consequence of all this is that a single Pascal identifier may be declared in more than one scope. For example, it is valid to declare two variables (one globally and one locally) with the same name. The normal reaction to this is to think that local declarations greatly complicate matters. You might be wondering why we do not just use all global declarations, since every identifier declared globally can be used anywhere throughout the entire program. It is precisely this huge freedom with global declarations that makes them unsuitable to be used exclusively. By the end of this chapter, you will come to realize this fully.

8.4.2. Boxing Programs

We have pointed out the importance of subprograms. Subprograms provide a modular, or block, structure for programs. In Chapter 2 we indicated the block structure of Karel programs graphically by boxing Karel's subprograms (new-instruction definitions). Pascal has the same type of block structure. Each of Pascal's subprograms (procedures) is an important block. Boxing Pascal subprograms in the same fashion that we boxed Karel instructions can be very illuminating. We have made up a short Pascal program to illustrate the two types of declarations, the scope of identifiers, and the use of boxing. The example is purposely abstract so your attention is focused on the principles involved rather than any specific example.

```
PROGRAM Scope (INPUT, OUTPUT);

VAR
     v: CHAR;


PROCEDURE Simple;
VAR
     v: INTEGER;

BEGIN
     v := 23;
     WRITELN(OUTPUT, v)
END;      (* Simple *)


BEGIN     (* Main Program *)
     v := 'F';
     WRITELN(OUTPUT, v);
     Simple;
     WRITELN(OUTPUT, v);
     v := 'W';
     WRITELN(OUTPUT, v);
     Simple;
     WRITELN(OUTPUT, v)
END.      (* Main Program *)
```

Programming Example 8-4: Global and Local Variable Declaration

In the previous program, there are two variable declarations, one global to the program and one local to the procedure **Simple**. Note that the same variable name **v** is used in both declarations. Also note that, in spite of using the same name, different types are used. A first glance provokes the thought that something is very wrong with the program. How can a variable be of two different types? The answer is that it cannot. What we have here are two different variables, one of type CHAR and one of type INTEGER; they both just happen to have the same name. The question then becomes how to distinguish between two variables with the same name. The variables' scopes determine the answer. Boxing graphically illustrates scope.

Draw a separate box around every subprogram declaration. In our example there is only one user-defined subprogram. Draw a box just around the procedure **Simple**. The box should enclose the procedure header and the BEGIN-END block. Normally, we also draw a box around the entire program. The boxed program looks as follows:

```
┌─────────────────────────────────────────┐
│ PROGRAM Scope (INPUT, OUTPUT);           │
│                                          │
│ VAR                                      │
│      v: CHAR;                            │
│ ┌──────────────────────────────┐        │
│ │ PROCEDURE Simple;             │        │
│ │ VAR                           │        │
│ │      v: INTEGER;              │        │
│ │ BEGIN                         │        │
│ │      v := 23;                 │        │
│ │      WRITELN(OUTPUT, v)       │        │
│ │ END;    (* Simple *)          │        │
│ └──────────────────────────────┘        │
│ BEGIN    (* Main Program *)              │
│      v := 'F';                           │
│      WRITELN(OUTPUT, v);                 │
│      Simple;                             │
│      WRITELN(OUTPUT, v);                 │
│      v := 'W';                           │
│      WRITELN(OUTPUT, v);                 │
│      Simple;                             │
│      WRITELN(OUTPUT, v)                  │
│ END.    (* Main Program *)               │
└─────────────────────────────────────────┘
```

Note that the local variable declaration falls within the inner box for the subprogram **Simple**, whereas the global variable declaration falls within the outer box around the entire program. The outer box denotes the scope of the globally declared variable, whereas the inner box denotes the scope of the locally declared variable. The two references to the variable **v** within the inner box refer to the locally declared INTEGER variable **v**, whereas all references to the variable **v** outside the inner box refer to the globally declared CHAR variable **v**. Although two variables in one program can have the same name, they must be declared in different scopes; **they cannot have the same name and the same scope.** Now consider the following slightly different example:

```
PROGRAM Scope (INPUT, OUTPUT);

VAR
     v: CHAR;


PROCEDURE Simple;
BEGIN
     v := 'P';
     WRITELN(OUTPUT, v)
END;     (* Simple *)


BEGIN     (* Main Program *)
     v := 'F';
     WRITELN(OUTPUT, v);
     Simple;
     WRITELN(OUTPUT, v);
     v := 'W';
     WRITELN(OUTPUT, v);
     Simple;
     WRITELN(OUTPUT, v)
END.      (* Main Program *)
```

Programming Example 8-5: Global Variable Declaration

The second example is only subtly different. The primary difference is that the second example has only one variable declaration, namely, the global variable declaration. Again, we box the program to aid understanding, as demonstrated in the following illustration:

```
PROGRAM Scope (INPUT, OUTPUT);

VAR
     v: CHAR;
 ┌─────────────────────────────────┐
 │ PROCEDURE Simple;               │
 │ BEGIN                           │
 │      v := 'P';                  │
 │      WRITELN(OUTPUT, v)         │
 │ END;     (* Simple *)           │
 └─────────────────────────────────┘
BEGIN     (* Main Program *)
     v := 'F';
     WRITELN(OUTPUT, v);
     Simple;
     WRITELN(OUTPUT, v);
     v := 'W';
     WRITELN(OUTPUT, v);
     Simple;
     WRITELN(OUTPUT, v)
END.     (* Main Program *)
```

Since the program has only one variable declaration all references to the variable **v** refer to the globally declared variable. This seemingly small difference has important effects on how the program executes. We illustrate both examples in detail in the following section.

8.4.3. Simulating Programs

We have designed a specialized sequence of illustrations to graphically represent execution of programs. We have utilized such tailormade illustrations in earlier chapters and will use them again here. Each subprogram is indicated by a boxed program segment. Variables are indicated along the right side of the subprogram box in which they are declared. The name of the variable is indicated next to the variable to which it corresponds. We use a different shape for different variable types. The currently executing instruction is highlighted with a rectangular enclosure. The program's state corresponds to the state *after* the instruction's execution. The terminal shows the output from the program. We have expended a good deal of effort to simulate both programs in detail. It is important that you understand what the simulations represent and the points they illustrate.

The first illustration shows the program prior to execution of any statements: The output screen is clear and the variable boxes are empty. This means the variable has an unknown value.

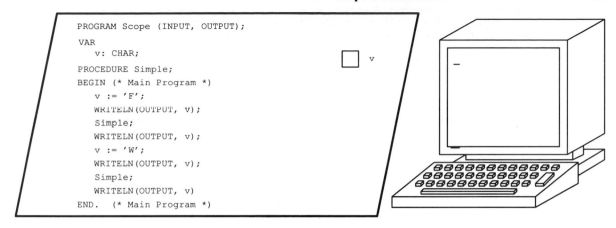

```
PROGRAM Scope (INPUT, OUTPUT);

VAR
    v: CHAR;                              ☐ v

PROCEDURE Simple;
BEGIN (* Main Program *)
    v := 'F';
    WRITELN(OUTPUT, v);
    Simple;
    WRITELN(OUTPUT, v);
    v := 'W';
    WRITELN(OUTPUT, v);
    Simple;
    WRITELN(OUTPUT, v)
END.  (* Main Program *)
```

Note that we show only the header for the procedure **Simple**. To save space and focus the reader's attention, we will show the procedure's body only when necessary to clarify the example.

The next two illustrations show the execution of the first two statements of the main program. The first statement assigns the character value 'F' to the the character variable named **v**. The second statement sends output to the terminal.

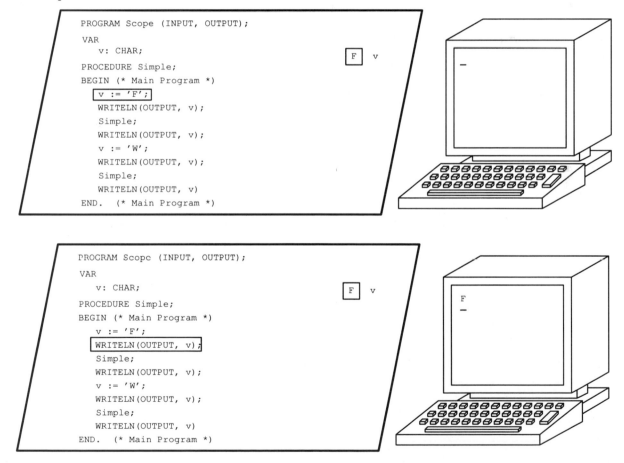

```
PROGRAM Scope (INPUT, OUTPUT);

VAR
    v: CHAR;                              F  v

PROCEDURE Simple;
BEGIN (* Main Program *)
    v := 'F';
    WRITELN(OUTPUT, v);
    Simple;
    WRITELN(OUTPUT, v);
    v := 'W';
    WRITELN(OUTPUT, v);
    Simple;
    WRITELN(OUTPUT, v)
END.  (* Main Program *)
```

```
PROGRAM Scope (INPUT, OUTPUT);

VAR
    v: CHAR;                              F  v

PROCEDURE Simple;
BEGIN (* Main Program *)
    v := 'F';
    WRITELN(OUTPUT, v);
    Simple;
    WRITELN(OUTPUT, v);
    v := 'W';
    WRITELN(OUTPUT, v);
    Simple;
    WRITELN(OUTPUT, v)
END.  (* Main Program *)
```

Now the subprogram **Simple** is called. The box for the subprogram **Simple** is *stacked on top of* the main program. Execution in the main program is suspended while the subprogram executes. The next three illustrations show the actual execution of the procedure **Simple**.

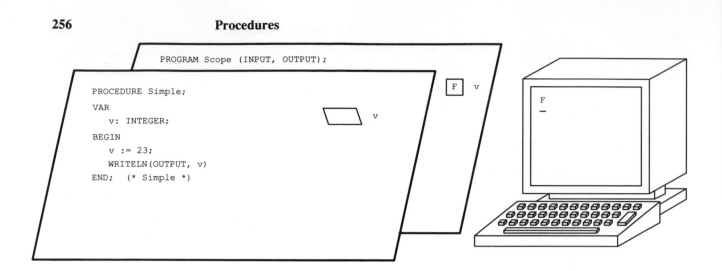

Note that the procedure **Simple** has a local variable also with the name **v**. The different shapes of variables indicate different types. The empty box indicates that the variable has an unknown value.

Procedure **Simple** is now completed. Control returns to the main program, and execution continues with the next instruction after the procedure call to the procedure **Simple**.

When the procedure **Simple** is finished executing, it is removed from the top of the stack. When this is done, the memory for its local variable **v** is *deallocated*. Therefore, any value held in that memory is lost. If the procedure is called again, new memory for the local variable is allocated. Since it can be an entirely different space in memory, it will not contain the same value held by the local variable the previous time the procedure was called. This is why we assume that variables declared in a procedure have an unknown value when that procedure is called, rather than having some particular value.

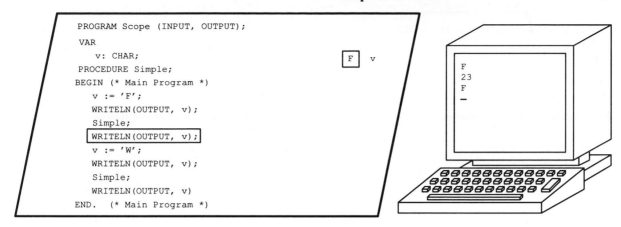

```
PROGRAM Scope (INPUT, OUTPUT);
VAR
    v: CHAR;
PROCEDURE Simple;
BEGIN (* Main Program *)
    v := 'F';
    WRITELN(OUTPUT, v);
    Simple;
    WRITELN(OUTPUT, v);
    v := 'W';
    WRITELN(OUTPUT, v);
    Simple;
    WRITELN(OUTPUT, v)
END.  (* Main Program *)
```

The value of **v** is written to the output. Next, **v** is assigned a new value.

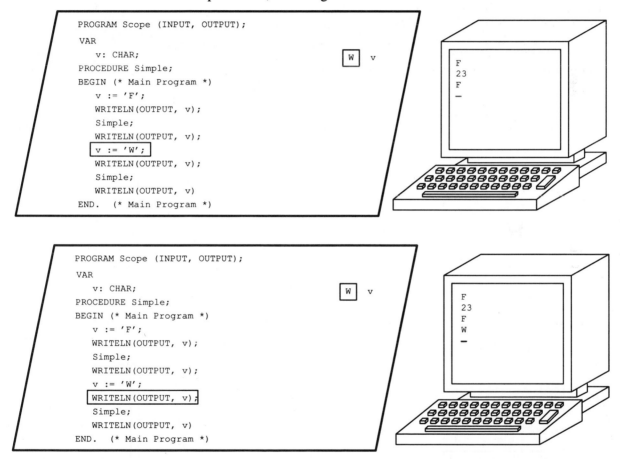

```
PROGRAM Scope (INPUT, OUTPUT);
VAR
    v: CHAR;
PROCEDURE Simple;
BEGIN (* Main Program *)
    v := 'F';
    WRITELN(OUTPUT, v);
    Simple;
    WRITELN(OUTPUT, v);
    v := 'W';
    WRITELN(OUTPUT, v);
    Simple;
    WRITELN(OUTPUT, v)
END.  (* Main Program *)
```

```
PROGRAM Scope (INPUT, OUTPUT);
VAR
    v: CHAR;
PROCEDURE Simple;
BEGIN (* Main Program *)
    v := 'F';
    WRITELN(OUTPUT, v);
    Simple;
    WRITELN(OUTPUT, v);
    v := 'W';
    WRITELN(OUTPUT, v);
    Simple;
    WRITELN(OUTPUT, v)
END.  (* Main Program *)
```

The procedure **Simple** is again invoked. The box for subprogram is again stacked on top of the box for the main program. Execution of the main program is suspended while the procedure **Simple** executes.

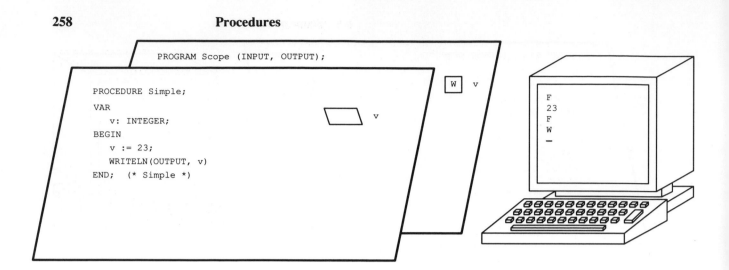

Note that the local variable **v** has an unknown value, which we indicate with an empty memory box. Specifically, it does not contain the value 23 from the previous call. The global variable **v** is inaccessible within the procedure **Simple** since they have the same name. A global declaration may be referenced only when there is no local declaration for the referenced identifier.

Procedure **Simple** is completed, and control returns to the main program. The global variable **v** is again accessible. The local variable **v** is deallocated and its value lost.

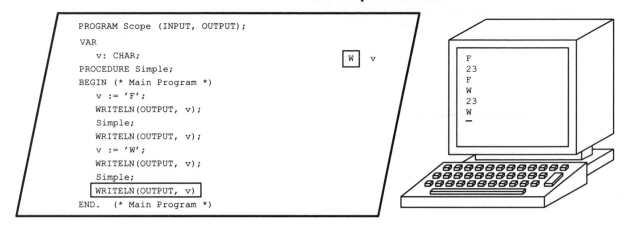

The simulation of the program **Scope** is now completed. It is very important that you understand this material. Do not go on until you understand the program's execution. You should feel confident that you can draw plates like those you have just seen if given an example program to illustrate.

What would have happened had the variable **v** not been declared locally in the procedure **Simple**? All references to the variable **v** would then refer to the globally declared variable **v** of type CHAR. The assignment of 23 to **v** within the procedure **Simple** would cause a type conflict and prohibit compilation. To further illustrate the concept of scope, we simulate the second example. You should be able to spot the crucial difference between these illustrations and the illustrations for the first example. Again, the first illustration depicts the situation before the program executes.

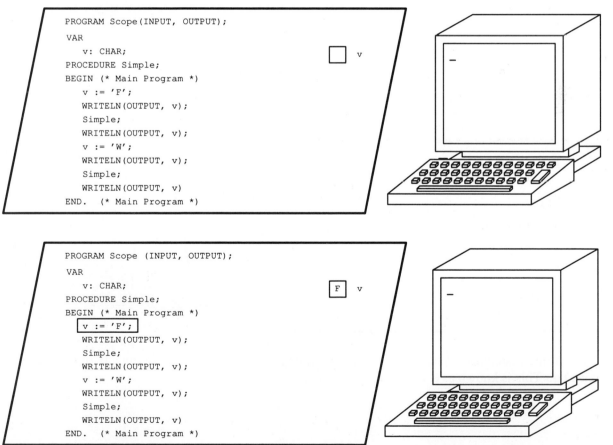

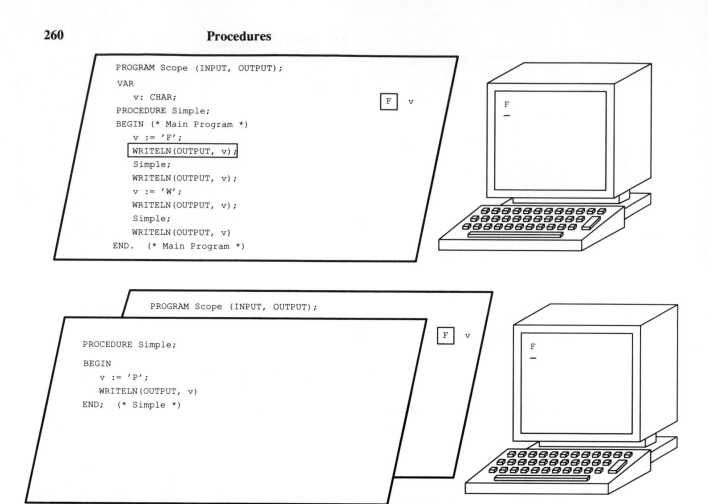

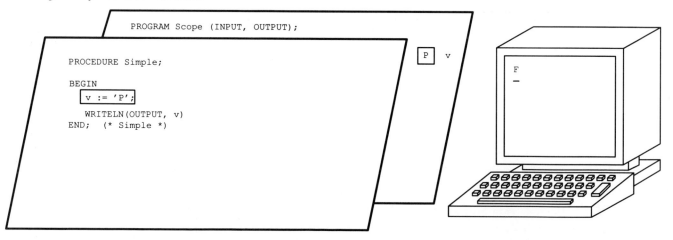

Note that there is no local variable in the previous illustration. Hence, all variable references refer to the globally declared variable.

Note that the assignment statement in procedure **Simple** modifies a variable outside of the procedure **Simple**. This is known as a **side effect**.

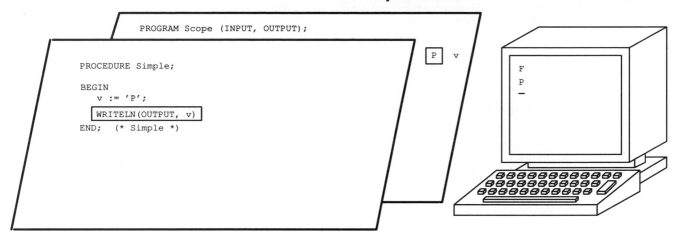

```
            PROGRAM Scope (INPUT, OUTPUT);


   PROCEDURE Simple;

   BEGIN
      v := 'P';
      WRITELN(OUTPUT, v)
   END;  (* Simple *)
```

Note that the variable has a different value after the procedure **Simple** executed than it had before. This is why the procedure is said to have a *side effect*.

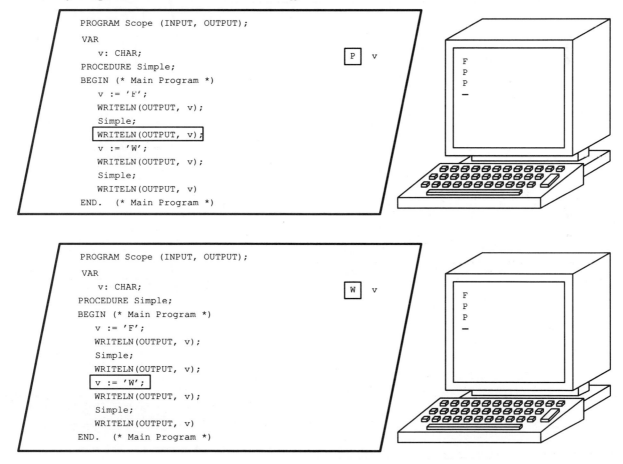

```
   PROGRAM Scope (INPUT, OUTPUT);
   VAR
      v: CHAR;
   PROCEDURE Simple;
   BEGIN (* Main Program *)
      v := 'F';
      WRITELN(OUTPUT, v);
      Simple;
      WRITELN(OUTPUT, v);
      v := 'W';
      WRITELN(OUTPUT, v);
      Simple;
      WRITELN(OUTPUT, v)
   END.  (* Main Program *)
```

```
   PROGRAM Scope (INPUT, OUTPUT);
   VAR
      v: CHAR;
   PROCEDURE Simple;
   BEGIN (* Main Program *)
      v := 'F';
      WRITELN(OUTPUT, v);
      Simple;
      WRITELN(OUTPUT, v);
      v := 'W';
      WRITELN(OUTPUT, v);
      Simple;
      WRITELN(OUTPUT, v)
   END.  (* Main Program *)
```

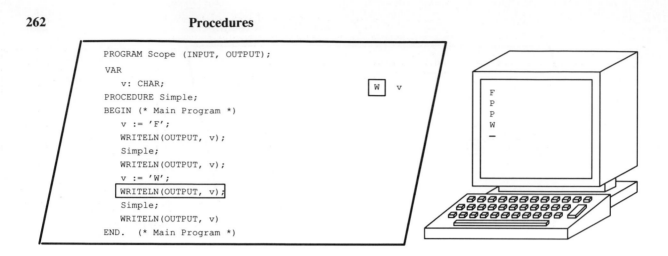

```
PROGRAM Scope (INPUT, OUTPUT);
VAR
    v: CHAR;
PROCEDURE Simple;
BEGIN (* Main Program *)
    v := 'F';
    WRITELN(OUTPUT, v);
    Simple;
    WRITELN(OUTPUT, v);
    v := 'W';
    WRITELN(OUTPUT, v);
    Simple;
    WRITELN(OUTPUT, v)
END.   (* Main Program *)
```

The subprogram box is stacked on top of the main program box when the procedure is called.

```
PROGRAM Scope (INPUT, OUTPUT);

PROCEDURE Simple;

BEGIN
    v := 'P';
    WRITELN(OUTPUT, v)
END;  (* Simple *)
```

Again the procedure **Simple** modifies the value of a variable outside of the procedure **Simple**.

```
PROGRAM Scope (INPUT, OUTPUT);

PROCEDURE Simple;

BEGIN
    v := 'P';
    WRITELN(OUTPUT, v)
END;  (* Simple *)
```

The value of the globally declared variable **v** is accessed and written to the output.

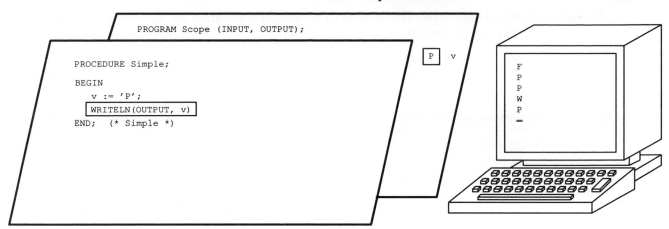

Note that the procedure's side effect is evidenced by the variable **v** containing a different value than it had before the procedure **Simple** started.

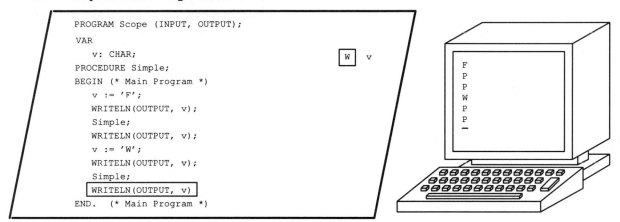

In the second example, we have called the assignment of 'P' to the variable **v** in the procedure **Simple** a *side effect*. This is an subject that warrants further discussion, which we provide in the following section.

8.4.4. Up-Level Addressing and Side Effects

Recall our discussion of *scope of identifiers*. Where an identifier is declared determines where an identifier can be used (otherwise known as the identifier's scope). A variable declared within a subprogram may only be used within that subprogram. Therefore, the boxes we draw around subprograms to illustrate scope are like *impenetrable walls*. An identifier declared locally within a subprogram's walls cannot be accessed by any portion of the program outside the subprogram's walls. Note, however, that such walls are solid only in one direction. A subprogram may use identifiers declared outside of the subprogram. The only requirement is that the subprogram be completely contained in the scope of the identifier it wishes to reference. When a subprogram references an identifier that is not declared locally within the subprogram, the referencing is referred to as **up-level addressing**.

> **Definition 8-15:** *Up-level addressing* refers to when a subprogram references an identifier declared outside the subprogram. The identifier being referenced is not declared local to the subprogram but in some enclosing scope.

In the last series of illustrations, the subprogram named **Simple** had no variable declarations. Therefore, when it modified the value of the variable **v**, the globally declared variable was modified. The subprogram **Simple** performed up-level addressing of the variable **v**. Whenever a subprogram changes the value of a variable declared in another scope by up-level addressing, we call this a *side effect*.

Definition 8-16: A *side effect* occurs when a subprogram modifies the value of a variable declared in another scope through up-level addressing.

Up-level addressing of variables and *side effects* are to be avoided. To help understand why side effects are a bad practice, consider the last example again. By looking only at the main program, there is no way to know that the procedure **Simple** modifies the value of any variables outside the subprogram. You might be thinking that all we have to do is take a look at the subprogram **Simple**. That is true. By looking at the procedure **Simple** we could determine easily enough that it has a side effect. However, the example has only one subprogram. A program with 20 or 30 subprograms would take a good deal more effort to determine if any of the subprograms have any side effects. You need to look at every statement in the program. When you realize that it is not uncommon for commercially available programs to contain many thousands of instructions, you quickly understand that having to be able to locate, much less understand, all side effects in a program is nearly impossible. There exist computer programs that were written by thousands of programmers over a period of years and contain over a million instructions. The only way to ensure that every programmer understands every side effect of every subprogram in such a program is to have no side effects. We advocate never writing subprograms with side effects. If you were forced to write a subprogram with a side effect (say, at gunpoint), the least you could do would be add to the subprogram a comment explicitly stating that the subprogram caused a side effect and what it did, and provide a comment with the call to the subprogram.

8.4.5. Nested Declarations

We have said that subprograms (procedures) have essentially the same characteristics as programs. We have examined local declarations for constants and variables. However, we may also declare subprograms within a subprogram. This is known as a *nested subprogram*. Pascal permits nesting subprograms to an arbitrary level of depth.

The complete program (8-6, page 265) illustrates all the aspects of scope and nested scope that you will need in Pascal programming. Although it requires effort on the part of the reader, an understanding of this example will be very well worth that effort.

```
PROGRAM Scope (INPUT, OUTPUT);

CONST  width = 22;               (* print width for write statements *)

VAR    v: REAL;


PROCEDURE Simple;
VAR    v: CHAR;

BEGIN    (* Simple *)
    v := 'W';
    WRITELN(OUTPUT, 'Simple':width, v)
END;     (* Simple *)


PROCEDURE NestedSimple;
VAR    v: INTEGER;


    PROCEDURE Simple;
    VAR    v: BOOLEAN;

    BEGIN    (* Simple *)
        v := TRUE;
        WRITELN(OUTPUT, 'NestedSimple/Simple':width, v)
    END;     (* Simple *)


BEGIN    (* NestedSimple *)
    v := 106;
    WRITELN(OUTPUT, 'NestedSimple':width, v);
    Simple;
    WRITELN(OUTPUT, 'NestedSimple':width, v)
END;     (* NestedSimple *)


PROCEDURE Bad;

BEGIN    (* Bad *)
    v := -19.3;
    WRITELN(OUTPUT, 'Bad':width, v:5:1)
END;     (* Bad *)


BEGIN    (* Main Program *)
    v := 3.7;
    WRITELN(OUTPUT, 'Scope':width, v:5:1);
    Simple;
    WRITELN(OUTPUT, 'Scope':width, v:5:1);
    NestedSimple;
    WRITELN(OUTPUT, 'Scope':width, v:5:1);
    Bad;
    WRITELN(OUTPUT, 'Scope':width, v:5:1);
    Simple;
    WRITELN(OUTPUT, 'Scope':width, v:5:1);
    NestedSimple;
    WRITELN(OUTPUT, 'Scope':width, v:5:1);
END.     (* Main Program *)
```

Programming Example 8-6: Multiple and Nested Declarations

The program has four procedures. Three are declared globally to the program, and one is local to (nested within) a particular procedure. There are four variables, all of which have the same name but are of different types. Draw boxes around the procedure declarations to better understand the scoping employed here.

There should be one box around each of the four subprograms as well as one around the entire program, making five boxes in all. The boxes should look like the following:

```
PROGRAM Scope (INPUT,OUTPUT);

CONST width = 22;    (* print width for write statements *)
VAR   v : REAL;

    PROCEDURE Simple;
    VAR   v : CHAR;
    BEGIN
        v := 'W';
        WRITELN(OUTPUT,'Simple':width,v)
    END;   (* Simple *)

    PROCEDURE NestedSimple;
    VAR   v : INTEGER;

        PROCEDURE Simple;
        VAR v : BOOLEAN;
        BEGIN   (* Simple *)
            v := TRUE;
            WRITELN(OUTPUT,'NestedSimple/Simple':width,v)
        END;    (* Simple *)

    BEGIN   (* NestedSimple *)
        v := 106;
        WRITELN(OUTPUT,'NestedSimple':width,v);
        Simple;
        WRITELN(OUTPUT,'NestedSimple':width,v);
    END;   (* NestedSimple *)

    PROCEDURE Bad;
    BEGIN   (* Bad *)
        v := -19.3;
        WRITELN(OUTPUT,'Bad':width,v:5:1);
    END;   (* Bad *)

BEGIN   (* Main Program *)
    v := 3.7;
    WRITELN(OUTPUT,'Scope':width,v:5:1);
    Simple;
    WRITELN(OUTPUT,'Scope':width,v:5:1);
    NestedSimple;
    WRITELN(OUTPUT,'Scope':width,v:5:1);
    Bad;
    WRITELN(OUTPUT,'Scope':width,v:5:1);
    Simple;
    WRITELN(OUTPUT,'Scope':width,v:5:1);
    NestedSimple;
    WRITELN(OUTPUT,'Scope':width,v:5:1);
END.   (* Main Program *)
```

Recall our specialized series of illustrations used to simulate a program's execution. You should be able to make such a set of illustrations. In the interest of brevity, we have omitted the illustrations for this example. We have, however, included the complete output for this example. Be sure you understand why the following output results from this program.

Scope	3.7
Simple	W
Scope	3.7
NestedSimple	106
NestedSimple/Simple	TRUE
NestedSimple	106
Scope	3.7
Bad	-19.3
Scope	-19.3
Simple	W
Scope	-19.3
NestedSimple	106
NestedSimple/Simple	TRUE
NestedSimple	106
Scope	-19.3

Figure 8-4: Example Program Output

In the last example, we named one procedure **Bad** for a reason. It is a subprogram that modifies the value of a nonlocal variable through up-level addressing. It has a *side effect*. We strongly believe it is a bad practice to write subprograms with side effects.

Programming Example 8-6 illustrated nesting a procedure declaration within another procedure declaration. We do not advocate nested subprogram declarations. A declaration within a subprogram cannot be used outside of the subprogram in which it is declared. Therefore, nested subprogram declarations can never be used outside of the subprogram in which it is declared. But recall that one of the reasons for writing subprograms is so they can be used as many times as necessary. In general, we believe all subprograms should be declared at the highest level to permit maximum use. The only use we have found for nested subprograms is when the subprogram of interest performs a very specialized task and is never needed outside of the subprogram in which it is declared. This exception is extremely rare.

8.4.6. A Style of Declaration

We have demonstrated that Pascal provides a choice about where to declare variables, constants, and subprograms. The choice should be made rationally rather than arbitrarily. We have adopted a style of declarations that has been useful for many programmers. This style, which we use throughout this text, is summarized in the following table:

- Define all named constants at the global level.

- Declare all subprograms at the global level.

- **Declare all variables local to the scope in which they are used.**

Table 8-1: Style of Declarations

You might be wondering why we advocate globally-defined constants and globally declared subprograms while adamantly promoting declaring all variables local to the subprogram in which they are used. The reason is that subprograms and named constants remain constant. A named constant does not change its value. Similarly, the declaration of a procedure is unchanged by use. Only variables can have their values change. Declaring all variables local to the scope in which they are used prevents up-level addressing of variables, thereby eliminating any side effects.

If we go to the effort of naming a constant or declaring a subprogram, we generally want to be able to use it by name. Therefore, declaring each globally provides such access. Since neither one can be altered by referencing, we preserve its integrity. The only time we define named constants or declare subprograms local to a subprogram is when we want to use it in only the subprogram in which it is declared.

A subprogram should be viewed as a complete and independent unit. It should not be necessary to understand an entire program to be able to understand a procedure in that program.

A deep understanding of why up-level addressing of variables is to be discouraged comes with experience. Often, this experience can be bitter. We hope you will adopt a good style of variable declaration and bypass the pains many programmers in the past have felt.

8.4.7. Questions

1. Are subprograms arbitrary divisions of a program?

2. What are two benefits of using subprograms?

3. What is a reasonable technique for determining how to partition a programming problem into subprograms?

4. Should every subprogram have the same number of instructions? Justify your answer.

5. Is there a definite range of sizes within which all subprograms must fall? Justify your answer.

6. What is at least one benefit of using *structured comments*?

7. When should a subprogram's comments be written?

8. What is meant by the *scope* of an identifier?

9. What is meant by global and local declaration? Contrast the two.

10. What technique can be used to illustrate the scope of an identifier?

11. Can a user-defined identifier be declared more than once in a single program? Justify your answer. Give an example if possible.

12. Can an identifier declared locally to a subprogram be referenced outside the subprogram in which it is declared? Explain your answer.

13. Can an identifier declared outside of a subprogram be referenced inside the subprogram? If so, explain under what conditions. If not, explain why not.

14. What happens to the value of a variable declared local to a subprogram once the subprogram terminates?

15. What is up-level addressing?

16. What is meant by the term *side effect*?

17. What is at least one bad point about subprograms with side effects?

18. What is a *nested subprogram*?

19. What is the style of declarations advocated in this text?

20. What are two reasons why variables should be declared differently from subprograms and named constants?

21. Can two different procedures use the same identifier as a local variable name? If so, must they have the same type? If they are the same type, are they really the same variable (refer to the same memory)? Justify your answer.

22. Can one subprogram have two variables with the same name? If so, must they be of the same type?

8.4.8. Exercises

1. What is the output of the following program?

```
PROGRAM Test (INPUT, OUTPUT)

VAR
    x: INTEGER;


PROCEDURE Double;

VAR
    x: INTEGER;

BEGIN
    x := x * 2;
    WRITELN(OUTPUT, x)
END;      (* Double *)


BEGIN
    x := 27;
    WRITELN(OUTPUT, x);
    Double;
    WRITELN(OUTPUT, x)
END.
```

2. Suppose the statement **x := 5** is placed before the statement **x := x * 2**. What is the output from the modified program?

3. Suppose the declaration of **x** inside the procedure **double** is eliminated from the previous two programs. What is the output of each?

8.5. Chapter Summary

- A *programming methodology* is the system of rules, principles, and methods people use when creating computer programs.

- *Top-down design* is a systematic strategy for solving problems by decomposing large problems into smaller subproblems. It works from the general to the specific, considering the major decisions first and the details last.

- *Bottom-up design* is a problem-solving strategy opposite to *top-down design*. Bottom-up design seeks to compose solutions of smaller problems into a solution for a larger problem. The method works from the specific to the general.

- *Step-wise refinement* refers to the process of repeatedly *refining* a solution one step at a time. Each additional step provides additional details not provided in prior steps.

- A *solution tree* is a graphic description of the decomposition of a particular problem to reveal its hierarchical structure.

- The two primary benefits of modular programming are *language independence*, which permits the technique to be used with a variety of different programming languages, and *modular independence*, which permits a solution (module) to a particular subproblem to modified without needing to modify other independent modules.

- A *subprogram* is a subset of the sequence of instructions of a program and is considered to be a unit.

- Execution of a subprogram may be modeled as a stack. The subprogram being called is stacked on top of the calling subprogram and is unstacked upon its completion. The subprogram on top of the stack is the currently executing subprogram, while all other subprograms on the stack are suspended. This stack is referred to as the *call stack* or runtime stack.

- The definition of a subprogram is termed its ***declaration***.

- The use of a subprogram is termed its ***call***.

- Pascal has two types of subprograms, procedures and functions. Procedures are a means of defining new statements, and functions are a means of defining new expressions. A function evaluates to a value, but a procedure does not.

- The use of subprograms, like the use of named constants, saves the programmer keystrokes, helps prevent programming bugs, and makes programs easier to read and modify.

- The *scope* of an identifier is the portion of a program in which it is valid to use an identifier. In general, the smallest subprogram that contains the declaration of an identifier is the scope of the identifier.

- A *global declaration* refers to the declaration of an identifier at the top of the program. Globally declared identifiers can be used throughout the entire program, including in all of its subprograms.

- A *local declaration* refers to the declaration of an identifier within a subprogram. Locally declared identifiers can be used only within the subprogram in which they are declared.

- Boxing subprograms may be used to illustrate scope.

- The memory for a locally declared variable is deallocated when the subprogram in which it is declared terminates. Therefore, the value of a local variable is lost upon subprogram termination.

- Any identifier declared locally to a subprogram cannot be referenced outside the subprogram in which it is declared.

- A subprogram may reference identifiers declared outside of the subprogram.

- *Up-level addressing* refers to when a subprogram references an identifier declared outside the subprogram. The identifier being referenced is not declared local to the subprogram but in some enclosing scope.

- A *side effect* occurs when a subprogram modifies the value of a variable declared in another scope through up-level addressing.

- If subprograms have side effects, the programmer must be aware of every side effect of every subprogram in order to understand the program.

- A *nested subprogram* is a subprogram declared within another subprogram.

- An identifier can be declared more than once in a single Pascal program. Each declaration must have a different scope.

- Two different subprograms can use the same identifier for a local variable. The result is two completely separate variables (except for their name) that refer to completely different memory spaces. The declarations may be of the same type or of different types.

- A single subprogram cannot declare two identifiers locally with the same name since that would result in two identifiers with the exact same name and the exact same scope.

8.6. Summary of Style

- There is more to the use of subprograms than simply "chopping up" a working program into smaller, arbitrarily determined pieces. Normally, a programmer wants a subprogram to accomplish a well-defined and named action. Actions that are likely to be repeated usually constitute a subprogram.

- The top-down design method yields abstract modules that may be implemented as subprograms.

- There is no justifiable size or range of sizes governing subprograms. We suggest that subprograms be limited to the size of the display screen to allow you to read them easily.

- Every subprogram should have a program comment describing it.

- We have found comments with structure to be better than their unstructured counterparts for subprogram and entire program comments. Structured comments provide a uniformity that makes it easier to create and read useful comments.

- Two of the components we normally include in structured subprogram comments are **Description** and **Method** for a brief description of *what* the subprogram does and *how* the subprogram does it, respectively.

- It is best to work on a subprogram's comments when working on the subprogram rather than attempting to fill in the missing comments later.

- The style of declarations advocated in this text is:
    - Define all named constants at the global level.
    - Declare all subprograms at the global level.
    - **Declare all variables local to the scope in which they are used.**

- The only use we have found for nested subprograms is when the subprogram of interest performs a very specialized task and is never needed outside of the subprogram in which it is declared. This exception is extremely rare.

- Similarly, we only use local constants when we do not want the named constant used outside of the subprogram in which it is declared.

- Declaring subprograms and named constants globally enables maximum use of them. Declaring all variables local to the scope in which the are used prevents up-level addressing of variables, thereby avoiding side effects.

8.7. Summary of Terms

- programming methodology
- problem
- solution
- problem solving
- modular problem solving
- top-down design
- bottom-up design
- step-wise refinement
- solution tree

- modular programming
- module
- subprogram
- call stack
- runtime stack
- subprogram declaration
- subprogram call
- procedure
- function

- simple procedure
- subprogram comments
- structured comments
- structured subprogram
- scope
- global declaration
- local declaration
- up-level addressing
- side effects

8.8. Chapter Problems

1. Write a simple procedure that draws a 5 by 5 box of exclamation points on the user's display.

2. Use the procedure from the previous problem to draw a box on a blank display.

3. Write a program to call a simple procedure that prints a long welcoming message to the user.

4. Write a program that calls three simple procedures: the first prints a long welcoming message; the second prompts the user for a list of numbers and computes and prints the larger; the third informs the user that the program has finished.

5. Sometimes, an analogy of program scope is built on the geographic division of the continental United States. The entire program represents the United States, each subprogram represents a state, and nested subprograms represent counties. Explain how this analogy can be built. Explain how having two different states with counties of the same name is possible and in agreement with the model of scope Pascal uses.

Chapter 9: Parameters

In the last chapter, we learned about the top-down design method and how it can be used to design and implement programs. We learned to decompose a programming problem into a collection of subprograms. Quite often, information computed in one subprogram is needed by another subprogram in the same program. In such cases, we want to communicate the information out of one subprogram and into another subprogram. In the last chapter, we also gave an argument against up-level addressing of variables (e.g. global variables) to communicate information between subprograms. Therefore, another mechanism for such subprogram communication is required. The mechanism is called the **parameter**.

> **Definition 9-1:** *Parameters* permit communication between subprograms.

Pascal has two types of parameters: *value parameters* and *variable parameters*. There are three cases of information flow into and out of subprograms:

1. No information coming into or going out (no parameters)

2. Information coming into a subprogram (value parameters)

3. Information going out of a subprogram (variable parameters)

We mentioned in the last chapter that Pascal subprograms can be either procedures or functions. Pascal subprograms can have value parameters, variable parameters, or no parameters. The following figure shows the six kinds of subprograms.

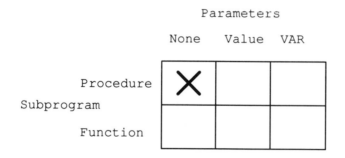

Figure 9-1: Parameterless Procedures

In the last chapter, we studied the simplest type of subprogram, procedures without parameters, which are otherwise known as *parameterless procedures*. They are indicated in the previous figure in the upper left cell.

Having already seen parameterless procedures, we turn our attention to procedures with parameters. Understanding parameters will enable you to design and build programs to solve larger and more interesting programming problems.

9.1. Value Parameters

Parameters that permit communication *into* but not *out of* a subprogram are referred to as **value parameters**. They are indicated in the following figure.

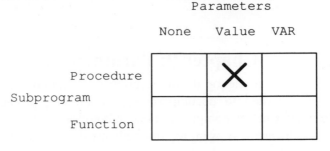

Figure 9-2: Procedures with Value Parameters

Definition 9-2: A *value parameter* communicates information *into* a subprogram.

Assume that we are writing a computer program to do the thankless job of keeping track of students' grades. Let's say that we wish to represent grades graphically with lines of asterisks. Therefore, we need a procedure to print a line of asterisks. Consider the procedure **PrintLine**:

```
PROCEDURE PrintLine;

    (* ******************************************************************

     * DESCRIPTION:
            Procedure PrintLine prints a horizontal line.

     * METHOD:
            The horizontal line is written one symbol at a time from left to
            right.  The length of the line is specified by "length", while
            the print symbol used is specified by "symbol".  A single FOR
            loop is used to control printing.

     ****************************************************************** *)

CONST
    length = 10;
    symbol = '*';
    fieldwidth = 1;

VAR
    count: INTEGER;

BEGIN
    FOR count := 1 TO length DO
        WRITE(OUTPUT, symbol:fieldwidth);
    WRITELN(OUTPUT)
END;     (* PrintLine *)
```

Programming Example 9-1: Procedure **PrintLine**

The procedure **PrintLine** executes the FOR loop from 1 to the number held by the named constant **length**. In this case that means 10 iterations. The body of the FOR loop is simply a call to the WRITE statement with the character constant **symbol**, which has the value '*'. The WRITELN following the FOR loop forces the write head to skip to a new line. Output from the procedure **PrintLine** looks like the following:

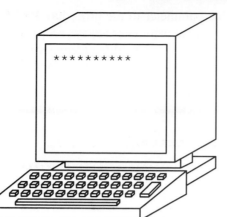

If we only want to print lines of exactly 10 asterisks, the procedure **PrintLine** is fine. However, recall that this is for our student grade management program. Since different students earn different grades, we will need to print lines of different lengths. One solution is to write a print line procedure for every possible line length. However, if scores range from 0 to 100, we will need 101 print line procedures. This is obviously not a very attractive solution. What we want is to *generalize* our procedure **PrintLine** to print lines of any desired length. Thus we need in **PrintLine** a variable "length" rather than a constant "length." A *value parameter* accomplishes this.

9.1.1. Declaring Procedures with Value Parameters

Value parameters are very similar to local variables. Declaring a procedure with a value parameter is very similar to declaring a procedure with a local variable. Value parameters must be declared within a procedure declaration. A value parameter declaration, like a local variable declaration, is simply a variable name followed by a colon followed by the variable's type. The difference in the declarations is that the parameter declaration is part of the procedure heading and is delimited by matching parentheses. Below is the procedure **PrintLine** with the constant **length** changed to a *value parameter*.

```
PROCEDURE PrintLine ( length: INTEGER );

    (* ********************************************************************

     * DESCRIPTION:
            Procedure PrintLine prints a horizontal line.

     * METHOD:
            The horizontal line is written one symbol at a time from left to
            right.  The length of the line is specified by "length", while
            the print symbol used is specified by "symbol".  A single FOR
            loop is used to control printing.

     * INPUT:
            length: the length of the line

    ******************************************************************** *)


CONST
    symbol = '*';
    fieldwidth = 1;

VAR
    count: INTEGER;

BEGIN
    FOR count := 1 TO length DO
        WRITE(OUTPUT, symbol:fieldwidth);
    WRITELN(OUTPUT)
END;      (* PrintLine *)
```

Programming Example 9-2: Procedure **PrintLine** with a Value Parameter

The variable **length** is a value parameter to the procedure **PrintLine**. **Length** receives a value when **PrintLine** is called. A value parameter always receives a value when the procedure in which it is declared gets called. A procedure with a value parameter must always be called with a value. The following program illustrates both the *declaration* and *call* of the procedure **PrintLine**:

```
PROGRAM Grader (INPUT, OUTPUT);


PROCEDURE PrintLine ( length: INTEGER );

    (* *********************************************************************

     * DESCRIPTION:
             Procedure PrintLine prints a horizontal line.

     * METHOD:
             The horizontal line is written one symbol at a time from left to
             right.  The length of the line is specified by "length", while
             the print symbol used is specified by "symbol".  A single FOR
             loop is used to control printing.

     * INPUT:
             length: the length of the line

    ********************************************************************* *)


CONST
    fieldwidth = 1;
    symbol = '*';

VAR
    count: INTEGER;

BEGIN
    FOR count := 1 TO length DO
        WRITE(OUTPUT, symbol:fieldwidth);
    WRITELN(OUTPUT)
END;      (* PrintLine *)



BEGIN    (* Main Program *)

    PrintLine(10)

END.      (* Main Program *)
```

Programming Example 9-3:   Declaration and Call of **PrintLine**

Recall our specialized illustrations designed to simulate a program's execution. When a subprogram is called, we stack a plate on top of the calling scope. Each of the subprogram's local variables are indicated as named boxes. The following illustration shows what happens when the procedure **PrintLine** is called with a value parameter.

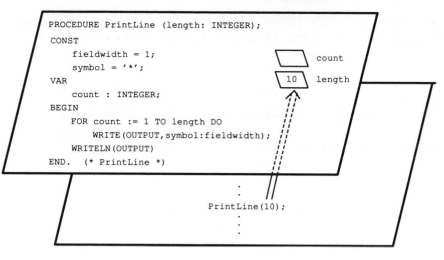

```
PROCEDURE PrintLine (length: INTEGER);
CONST
     fieldwidth = 1;
     symbol = '*';
VAR
     count : INTEGER;
BEGIN
     FOR count := 1 TO length DO
          WRITE(OUTPUT,symbol:fieldwidth);
     WRITELN(OUTPUT)
END.   (* PrintLine *)

                                    PrintLine(10);
```

Figure 9-3: Subprogram Call with a Value Parameter

Note that we represent the value parameter **length** just like the local variable **count**. This is because value parameters behave just like local variables within the subprogram in which they are declared. The arrow indicates how the parameter **length** gets its value. The constant expression 10 is evaluated and assigned as the value of **length**. Note that the arrow goes in only one direction; this points out the fact that information is communicated *into* a subprogram with a value parameter and not *out of* it. Changing the value of the value parameter **length** within the procedure **PrintLine** has no effect outside the procedure (again, this is just as a local variable acts). **Unlike a global variable, modifying the value of a value parameter will cause no side effects outside the scope of the subprogram in which it is declared.**

Recall that we advocate *structured subprogram comments*. You may have noticed that we added another section to the subprogram comment in the declaration of the procedure **PrintLine**. Glance back at Programming Example 9-2 for a moment, and notice the addition to the comment. Parameters provide a means to communicate information into a subprogram. We denote the input information in the section labeled **INPUT**. Our structured subprogram comment now has three components: **DESCRIPTION, METHOD**, and **INPUT**. Normally we do not specify input received through READ or READLN in this new section. We reserve this section for input via parameters.

9.1.2. Formal Parameters, Actual Parameters, and Parameter Binding

There is some additional terminology required for understanding parameters. Most important is the distinction between **formal parameters** and **actual parameters**. The formal parameter refers to the parameter declaration in the heading of the subprogram, whereas the actual parameter refers to the parameter of the subprogram call. In the last example, **length** is the formal parameter and 10 is the actual parameter. The formal value parameter gets its initial value from the actual parameter of the subprogram call. In the previous example, the formal value parameter **length** gets the initial value 10.

> **Definition 9-3:** A *formal parameter* is declared in the subprogram heading and behaves as a local variable in the scope of that subprogram.

> **Definition 9-4:** An *actual parameter* appears in the call to a subprogram containing corresponding formal parameters. Actual parameters set the initial value of formal value parameters.

Setting of the value of a formal parameter by an actual parameter is called **parameter binding**.

> **Definition 9-5:** *Parameter binding* is the association of *actual parameters* with *formal parameters* during a subprogram call.

Calls to procedures that have formal parameters that are *value* parameters are referred to as *call-by-value* parameter bindings. The folowing table summarizes the rules for binding actual parameters and formal value parameters.

1. There must be the same number of actual parameters in a subprogram call as there are in the formal parameter list of the subprogram declaration.

2. The first actual parameter is bound to the first formal parameter, the second actual parameter is bound to the second formal parameter, and in general the nth actual parameter is bound to the nth formal parameter.

3. Actual parameters must be an expression of compatible type with the corresponding formal parameter. (Mentally place an assignment statement between them, *formal :=actual*; if it works, the binding is OK.)

Table 9-1: Rules for Binding of Actual Parameters and Formal Value Parameters

With the rules for binding parameters in mind, here are some *valid* calls of the procedure **PrintLine** and the corresponding output:

Call	Output
`PrintLine(10)`	`**********`
`PrintLine(2 + 3)`	`*****`
`howLong := 7;` `PrintLine(howLong)`	`*******`
`PrintLine(howLong + 2)`	`*********`

Table 9-2: Valid Calls to **PrintLine**

We say that the actual parameter is *bound* to the formal parameter at the time of procedure call. With value parameters, here is what happens. The statement **PrintLine** informs the system that the procedure **PrintLine** is to be executed. Since **PrintLine** has a formal parameter, there must be an actual parameter to set its initial value. Inside the parentheses of the call to **PrintLine** is an expression. The expression is *evaluated*, just as we learned before, and the result is the value of **length** for the current call to **PrintLine**. So in the four calls to **PrintLine**, the values of the parameter **length** are 10, 5, 7, and 9, respectively.

There is no more than one formal parameter list for a subprogram since a subprogram is declared exactly once. There are as many actual parameter lists as there are subprogram calls. Getting each actual parameter list to be in agreement with the corresponding formal parameter list is more easily said than done. In Table 9-3, we illustrate some of the common mistakes with parameter lists with calls to the procedure **PrintLine**.

Call	Error
`PrintLine`	`(* too few parameters *)`
`PrintLine(12.3)`	`(* parameter of wrong type *)`
`PrintLine(12,3)`	`(* too many parameters *)`
`PrintLine('a')`	`(* parameter of wrong type *)`
`Printline(TRUE)`	`(* parameter of wrong type *)`
`DesiredLength := 98.6;` `PrintLine(DesiredLength)`	`(* parameter of wrong type *)`

Table 9-3: Invalid Calls to `PrintLine`

Two additional points need to be made: **Modifying the value of a formal value parameter has no effect on the corresponding actual parameter.** This point is easy to believe if the actual parameter is a constant or some other expression. It is also true even if the actual parameter is a variable. To understand why this is so, we must consider how value parameters actually work.

Formal value parameters are like local variables. Memory is allocated for them when the procedure in which they are declared is called, and their memory is deallocated when the procedure terminates. The only difference between the two is that value parameters get values copied into them upon procedure invocation, and local variables do not. Since the formal value parameter is different from the actual parameter, changes made to the formal value parameter change the new memory associated with the formal parameter and not the memory associated with the variable that happens to be the actual value parameter.

It is also important to realize that **the name of the formal and actual parameters have no effect on the parameter binding.** They may be the same or different names. The variables are entirely different variables and are stored in completely different memory cells. The names for the cells may be the same or different. We typically pick different names to illustrate that naming has no effect on parameter binding.

9.1.3. Expressions as Actual Value Parameters
Recall the example to write Floyd's Triangle that we first presented when discussing loops. The following program example is that procedure:

```
PROCEDURE Triangle;

    (* *********************************************************************

     * DESCRIPTION:
             Procedure Triangle prints Floyd's Triangle.

     * METHOD:
             Floyd's Triangle is written one row at a time, left to right.
             Nested FOR loops are used to control the printing.

    ********************************************************************* *)

CONST
    MaxRows = 4;                  (* total rows in triangle *)

VAR
    row,                          (* determines the row we are writing *)
    column,                       (* determines the column we are writing *)
    PrintNumber: INTEGER;         (* determines the print symbol *)

BEGIN
    PrintNumber := 0;             (* initialize the number to be printed *)

    FOR row := 1 TO MaxRows DO
        BEGIN
            FOR column := 1 TO row DO
                BEGIN
                    PrintNumber := PrintNumber + 1;
                    WRITE(OUTPUT, PrintNumber)
                END;     (* column *)
            WRITELN     (* position to WRITE a new row *)
        END     (* row *)
END;     (* Triangle *)
```

Programming Example 9-4: Procedure `Triangle`

This procedure will print Floyd's Triangle with four rows. But what if we want to print Floyd's Triangle of any size? This procedure can be *generalized* by using a value parameter to set the size of the triangle. We do this by using a value parameter in place of the constant **MaxRows**, as shown in the the following programming example:

```
PROCEDURE Triangle ( MaxRows: INTEGER );

    (* ***************************************************************

     * DESCRIPTION:
            Procedure Triangle prints Floyd's Triangle.

     * METHOD:
            Floyd's Triangle is written one row at a time, left to right.
            Nested FOR loops are used to control the printing.

     * INPUT:
            MaxRows: maximum number of rows to be printed of triangle

     ************************************************************* *)


VAR
    row,                        (* determines the row we are writing *)
    column,                     (* determines the column we are writing *)
    PrintNumber: INTEGER;       (* determines the print symbol *)

BEGIN
    PrintNumber := 0;           (* initialize the number to be printed *)

    FOR row := 1 TO MaxRows DO
        BEGIN
            FOR column := 1 TO row DO
                BEGIN
                    PrintNumber := PrintNumber + 1;
                    WRITE(OUTPUT, PrintNumber)
                END;    (* column *)
            WRITELN     (* position to WRITE a new row *)
        END     (* row *)
END.    (* Triangle *)
```

Programming Example 9-5: Procedure **Triangle** Declared with a Value Parameter

Note that we added this input information under the section INPUT of our structured comment. The following main program illustrates valid calls to the procedure **Triangle**.

```
BEGIN    (* Main Program *)
    Triangle(2);
    Triangle(3 + 1);
    FOR count := 2 TO 4 DO
        Triangle(count)
END.    (* Main Program *)
```

Programming Example 9-6: Procedure **Triangle** Called with a Value Parameter

Note that there are a total of five calls to the procedure **Triangle**. The first call is with the constant value *2*. The second call is with the expression *3 + 1*. The remaining 3 calls are with the INTEGER variable **count** (2, 3, and 4). Remember, any expression of the correct type may be used as a value parameter.

The following table illustrates the five calls to the procedure **Triangle**, with the corresponding output.

Call	Output
Triangle(2)	1 2 3
Triangle(3 + 1)	1 2 3 4 5 6 7 8 9 10
FOR count := 2 TO 4 DO Triangle(count)	
Triangle(2)	1 2 3
Triangle(3)	1 2 3 4 5 6
Triangle(4)	1 2 3 4 5 6 7 8 9 10

Table 9-4: Valid Calls to **Triangle**

9.1.4. Procedures with More Than One Value Parameter

Recall the procedure **PrintLine**. We made that procedure more general—capable of printing lines of arbitrary length—with a parameter. Say that we wanted to print lines of some arbitrary symbol rather than lines of asterisks. Since a subprogram may have any number of parameters, we can again *generalize* the **PrintLine** procedure by passing the print symbol into the procedure with another value parameter. Programming Example 9-7 is a modified version of **PrintLine**.

```
PROCEDURE PrintLine ( length: INTEGER;  symbol: CHAR );

    (* *********************************************************************

     * DESCRIPTION:
            Procedure PrintLine prints a horizontal line.

     * METHOD:
            The horizontal line is written one symbol at a time from left to
            right.  The length of the line is specified by "length", while
            the print symbol used is specified by "symbol".  A single FOR
            loop is used to control printing.

     * INPUT:
            length: the length of the line
            symbol: the symbol used to print the line

     ********************************************************************* *)


CONST
    fieldwidth = 1;

VAR
    count: INTEGER;

BEGIN
    FOR count := 1 TO length DO
        WRITE(OUTPUT, symbol:fieldwidth);
    WRITELN(OUTPUT, output)
END;     (* PrintLine *)
```

Programming Example 9-7: Procedure **PrintLine** with Two Value Parameters

Notice that this version of **PrintLine** has two value parameters: one for the line length and one for the print symbol, named **length** and **symbol**, respectively. Now consider the procedure call **PrintLine(10,'+')**.

The parameter binding for this call may be illustrated in the following way:

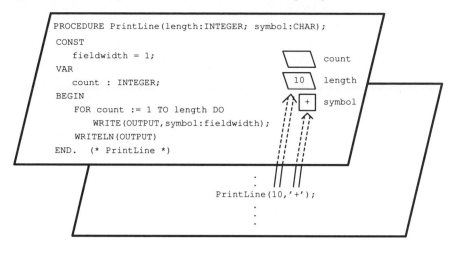

```
PROCEDURE PrintLine(length:INTEGER; symbol:CHAR);
CONST
    fieldwidth = 1;                          count
VAR
    count : INTEGER;                    10   length
BEGIN
    FOR count := 1 TO length DO         +    symbol
        WRITE(OUTPUT,symbol:fieldwidth);
    WRITELN(OUTPUT)
END.  (* PrintLine *)


                             PrintLine(10,'+');
```

Figure 9-4: Subprogram Call with Two Value Parameters

Parameter bindings follow the rules specified in table 9-1 on page 278. The first actual parameter is bound to the first formal parameter. The second actual parameter is bound to the second formal parameter. In general, the nth actual parameter is bound to the nth formal parameter. This correspondence requires actual parameters to agree with formal parameters in number, type, and order. In the previous example, there are only constants for actual parameters. Remember that any expression of the correct type is allowable as an actual parameter. The following table illustrates some examples of valid calls to the new **PrintLine** and the corresponding output:

Call	Output
`PrintLine(5, '-')`	`-----`
`PrintLine(2, '$')`	`$$`
`PrintLine(2 + 2, '?')`	`????`
`howlong := 3` `PrintLine(howlong+2, '=')`	`=====`
`PrintLine(5, '6')`	`66666`

Table 9-5: Valid Calls to Modified **PrintLine**

The following are examples of invalid calls to the new **PrintLine**:

Call	Error
`PrintLine('+',5)`	`(* type conflict, parameters in wrong order *)`
`PrintLine(5)`	`(* too few parameters *)`
`PrintLine(5,'*',3)`	`(* too many parameters *)`
`PrintLine('*')`	`(* too few parameters *)`
`PrintLine(5, 6)`	`(* type conflict, 6 is not of type CHAR *)`

Table 9-6: Invalid Calls to Modified **PrintLine**

It is our experience that the two most common errors with parameters are putting them in the wrong order or forgetting one altogether.

9.1.5. Up-Level Addressing of Variables: A Practice To Be Avoided

Recall the rules governing the scope of identifiers that we presented in the last chapter. The scope of a value parameter is exactly the same as the scope of a local variable. A value parameter gets an initial value when the procedure in which it is declared gets called. If a box is drawn around the procedure in which the value parameter is declared, the box denotes the scope of the parameter. The value parameter can be accessed only within this box. A value parameter cannot be accessed outside of the subprogram in which it is declared. Changing the value held in a value parameter is like changing the value held in a local variable. Such a change has no effect outside the subprogram in which it is declared.

Recall that it is possible to refer to global variables anywhere in a program. Therefore, we can communicate information into a subprogram by up-level addressing of global variables instead of using value parameters. The following program example illustrates the procedure **PrintLine** rewritten using up-level addressing of global variables rather than value parameters.

```
PROGRAM Bad (INPUT, OUTPUT);

VAR
    length: INTEGER;
    symbol: CHAR;



PROCEDURE PrintLine;

CONST
    fieldwidth = 1;

VAR
    count: INTEGER;

BEGIN
    FOR count := 1 TO length DO
        WRITE(output, symbol:fieldwidth);
    WRITELN(OUTPUT)
END;    (* PrintLine *)



BEGIN
    length := 10;
    symbol := '+';
    PrintLine
END.
```

Programming Example 9-8:   Using Global Variables Instead of Value Parameters

Programming Example 9-8 accomplishes exactly the same result as the previous call with parameters, **PrintLine(10,'+')**. Instead of declaring **PrintLine** with two value parameters, we declare two global variables, set the appropriate variables to the desired values, then call the procedure without parameters. This may seem to imply that up-level addressing of global variables eliminates the need for parameters. However, this is not the case. **Communication into and out of subprograms by up-level addressing rather than using parameters is extremely poor programming practice.**

There are at least three strong reasons why up-level addressing is inferior to using parameters. The first reason is the burden it places on all of the calling procedures (and the programmer who must write them). Instead of simply calling the procedure with the appropriate values (e.g. PrintLine(10, '+')), one must know the exact variable names used within the procedure to be called since there must be an explicit assignment to those variables if the procedure is to work as desired. Moreover, if we want to change the name of one of the variables accessed through up-level addressing, we must change every single procedure call so that the corresponding assignments to the variable all refer to the correct name. Thus, using value parameters simplifies communicating information into a subprogram.

A second reason against the use of up-level addressing is the potential for unwanted side effects. Changing the value of a value parameter within the subprogram in which it is defined is just like changing the value of a local variable. The change has no effect outside of the subprogram in which it is declared. Changing the value of global variable does have an effect outside the subprogram in which it is changed—an effect that can be both unexpected and unwanted. Since every place the procedure is called must modify the particular variables, a relatively large number of places can be changing a single variable or group of variables. Each assignment to one of these variables effectively undoes all other assignments to the variable. This situation can lead to very bizarre results.

A third reason against using up-level addressing arises from debugging considerations. When all necessary information is communicated into a subprogram by value parameters, we can confine our debugging of a subprogram to only that subprogram. If some information is communicated to a subprogram by up-level addressing a global variable, we must search the entire program for every assignment to the variable. With parameters, all inter-subprogram communication is clearly specified, which allows us to treat a subprogram as an independent unit and concentrate on only that subprogram. For larger programs this is particularly helpful since we need only look at one procedure rather than at all of them. Up-level addressing greatly complicates the task of debugging, and the use of parameters simplifies debugging.

Careful parameter passing to well-constructed subprograms is one of the hallmarks of good programming. It is an extremely important aspect of a methodology that will serve you well in programming projects from classroom exercises to large programming systems. The beginning programmer should not fall into the trap of sloppy design and style. **No programmer should ever rely on the use of up-level addressing of variables (e.g. global variables) for communication between subprograms; use parameters.** The use of parameters rather than up-level addressing simplifies calling subprograms, eliminates the potential of side effects, and simplifies the task of debugging. Later in this chapter we will review a technique we use to ensure parameter passing rather than up-level addressing of global variables.

9.1.6. Questions

1. What purposes do parameters serve?

2. How many types of parameters does Pascal have? Name them.

3. What purpose do value parameters serve?

4. Value parameters are like what type of variables?

5. What is the difference between a local variable and a value parameter?

6. How is a value parameter like a local variable?

7. How are formal and actual parameters alike? How do they differ?

8. Will changing the value of a parameter within the subprogram in which it is formally declared change the value of the actual parameter? Justify your answer.

9. Can a constant be an actual parameter to a formal value parameter?

10. Can a variable be an actual parameter to a formal value parameter?

11. Can an expression be an actual parameter to a formal value parameter?

12. What is parameter binding? When does it take place?

13. What are the rules of binding formal value parameters and actual parameters?

14. What effect does assigning a value to a formal parameter have on the corresponding actual parameter?

15. What effect does naming have on the process of parameter binding?

16. Can a subprogram have more than one formal value parameter? If so, how many can it have?

17. Under what component of our structured subprogram comment do we include value parameters?

18. Describe the scope of a value parameter in terms of boxing subprograms.

19. Some people are under the misconception that up-level addressing of variables (e.g. global variables) is a reasonable alternative to using parameters. Give at least three reasons why parameters are a superior means of communicating information to subprograms.

9.1.7. Exercises

1. What output does the following program produce?

```
PROGRAM Test (INPUT, OUTPUT);


PROCEDURE Switch (a, b: INTEGER);

BEGIN
    a := b;
    b := 27;
    WRITELN(OUTPUT, a, b)
END;    (* Switch *)


PROCEDURE Start;

VAR
    a, b: INTEGER;

BEGIN
    a := 5;
    b:= 10;
    WRITELN(OUTPUT, a, b);
    Switch(a, b);
    WRITELN(OUTPUT, a, b)
END;    (* Start *)


BEGIN
    Start
END.
```

2. What output does the following program produce?

```
PROGRAM TryIt (INPUT, OUTPUT);


PROCEDURE Square (a, b: INTEGER);

BEGIN
    a := a * a;
    b := b * b;
    WRITELN(OUTPUT, a, b)
END;    (* Square *)


PROCEDURE Start;

VAR
    a, b: INTEGER;

BEGIN
    a := 5;
    b := 10;
    WRITELN(OUTPUT, a, b);
    Square(b, a);
    WRITELN(OUTPUT, a, b)
END;    (* Start *)


BEGIN
    Start
END.
```

9.1.8. Problems

1. Write a procedure that prints an arbitrary number of blank lines. It should take one parameter.

2. In the last problem set, you wrote a simple procedure to draw a box of exclamation points with the length of a side equal to 5. Modify that procedure so that the length of the side can vary from 2 to 15.

3. Extend the previous procedure so that the print symbol is a value parameter as well as the length of a side.

4. Write a procedure that has as parameters a beginning checking balance and the amount of a check. It should print the new balance to the screen.

5. Write a procedure that has value parameters for a baseball player's at bats and hits. The procedure should compute and display the player's batting average.

6. Write a procedure that takes two real numbers and prints out all the integers between them (e.g. when given input of 4.1 and 7.9, it should print 5, 6, 7)

7. Write a procedure that takes two integers as parameters: One will represent the length of a word, the others the width of a line. The procedure is to calculate how many spaces to leave on the left and right sides of the word so that the word is centered on the line. The procedure should print out the resulting numbers.

8. Write a Pascal procedure to write a BOOLEAN expression. It should take a single parameter of type BOOLEAN.

9. Write a Pascal procedure to write an INTEGER expression. It should take a single parameter of type INTEGER. Assume for this problem that the predefined procedure WRITE only writes one CHAR at a time.

10. Extend the procedure in the previous question so that it also takes a parameter for the fieldwidth and writes the integer expression right-justified in the same fieldwidth.

11. *Write a procedure that takes an Arabic numeral from 1 through 1000 and converts it to a Roman numeral and prints it.

9.2. Variable Parameters

Suppose we need to write a computer program to determine the volume of a rectangular solid. Such a program can be decomposed into two subproblems: *getting the dimensions of the solid* and *computing the volume of the solid*. Both of these subproblems can be coded directly as Pascal procedures without further decomposition. Therefore, our program will have two subprograms, which we call **GetDimensions** and **ComputeVolume**, respectively.

Let us focus our attention on the procedure **GetDimensions**. A rectangular solid has three dimensions: length, width, and height. The procedure **GetDimensions** needs to prompt and read from the user each of the three dimensions. A first attempt at this will probably yield a procedure looking something like the following:

```
PROCEDURE GetDimensions ( l, w, h: REAL );

BEGIN
    WRITE(OUTPUT, 'Please input a length => ');
    READLN(INPUT, l);
    WRITE(OUTPUT, 'Please input a width => ');
    READLN(INPUT, w);
    WRITE(OUTPUT, 'Please input a height => ');
    READLN(INPUT, h)
END;     (* GetDimensions *)
```

Programming Example 9-9: **GetDimensions** with Value Parameters

Procedure **GetDimensions** has three parameters, one for each of the three dimensions to be read. Each dimension is prompted for and read into the corresponding parameter.

If we want the three dimensions in the variables **length**, **width**, and **height**, we would call the procedure as: **GetDimensions(length, width, height)**. This procedure call can be depicted as follows:

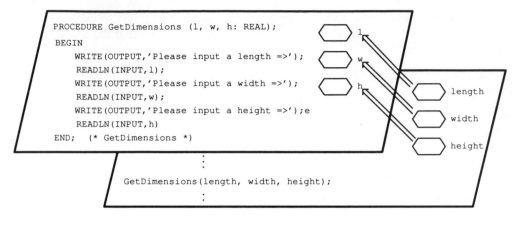

Figure 9-5: **GetDimensions** with Value Parameters

The three variables **length**, **width**, and **height** are denoted by the three boxes with those names. Since these three variables initially have unknown values, the boxes are empty. When **GetDimensions** is called, storage for the three parameters **l**, **w**, and **h** is allocated, and the values of the variables **length**, **width**, and **height** are copied to **l**, **w**, and **h**, respectively. This type of binding is indicated by an arrow from the actual parameters to the formal parameters.

Each of the three dimensions are prompted for and read into the formal parameters **l**, **w**, and **h**. Note that this does not change the values of the variables **length**, **width**, and **height**. Changing the values of value parameters has no effect outside of the subprogram in which they are declared. When the procedure **GetDimensions** terminates, the memory for the formal parameters **l**, **w**, and **h** is deallocated, and their values are lost. The values of the variables **length**, **width**, and **height** still have not changed.

The procedure **GetDimensions** prompts for the three desired values, reads them into the three formal parameters **l**, **w**, **h**, and then terminates without having changed the variables **length**, **width**, and **height**. Therefore, we need another kind of parameter in addition to value parameters. We need a type of parameter for passing information back out of a subprogram. Information is passed *out of* a subprogram with a *variable parameter* or *VAR parameter*. Calls to subprograms with VAR parameters are known as *Call-by-Reference* or *Call-by-VAR* parameter bindings.

Procedures with VAR parameters, the third type of Pascal procedure, are indicated in the following figure:

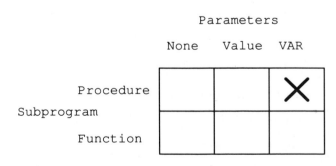

Figure 9-6: Procedures with Variable Parameters

9.2.1. Declaring Procedures with VAR Parameters

VAR Parameters are declared just like value parameters, except that VAR parameters are preceded by the reserved word VAR in the formal parameter list. The following programming example illustrates the procedure **GetDimensions** with VAR parameters:

```
PROCEDURE GetDimensions ( VAR l, w, h: REAL );

BEGIN
    WRITE(OUTPUT, 'Please input a length => ');
    READLN(INPUT, l);
    WRITE(OUTPUT, 'Please input a width => ');
    READLN(INPUT, w);
    WRITE(OUTPUT, 'Please input a height => ');
    READLN(INPUT, h)
END;    (* GetDimensions *)
```

Programming Example 9-10: GetDimensions with Variable Parameters

Upon first seeing VAR parameters, many people think they work in the following way: New memory cells are allocated for the formal parameter on the subprogram's call, the value of the actual parameter is copied to the new storage as an initial value, and upon subprogram termination, the resulting value of the formal parameter is copied back to the actual parameter. This accurately describes a well-known type of parameter passing, but it is not VAR parameters. This type of parameter passing is referred to as *call-by-value-result* and is different from *call-by-reference* or *call-by-VAR*. While there are many conceivable types of parameter passing, Pascal has just two types of parameter passing, *call-by-value* and *call-by-reference*.

Although VAR parameters are declared much like value parameters, they behave quite differently. A value parameter creates a new variable with a new name. A VAR parameter creates a new name for an already existing variable but does not create a new variable. This is a very important distinction. The following illustration depicts a call to **GetDimensions** with VAR parameters.

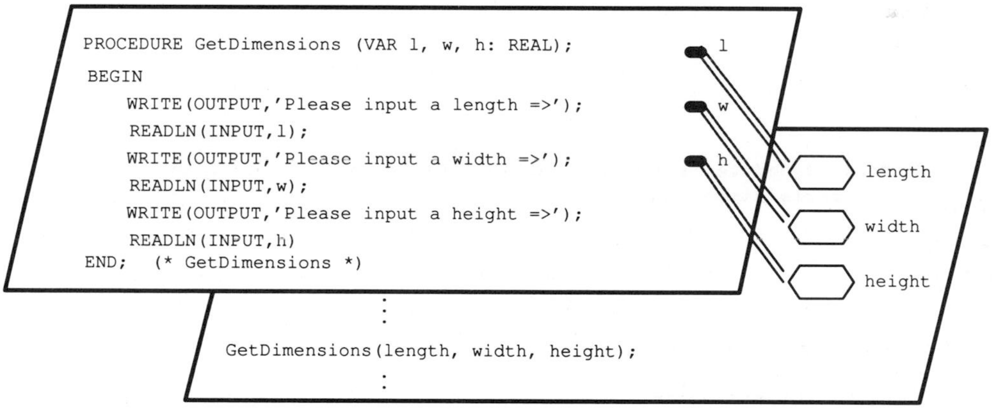

Figure 9-7: GetDimensions with Variable Parameters

The actual parameters are **length**, **width**, and **height**. The formal parameters are labeled **l**, **w**, and **h**. An essential point is that the formal VAR parameters create no new variables. A formal VAR parameter is just an additional name, or alias, for the corresponding actual parameter. To help realize this distinction, compare Figure 9-7 with Figure 9-5.

There are three important points to keep in mind. Formal VAR parameters create no new variable, no new place to store values. Since a formal VAR parameter is just an alias for the actual parameter, changing the value of a formal VAR parameter immediately changes the value of the actual parameter. Consequently, the actual parameter for a VAR parameter must be a VARiable, hence, the name VAR parameter.

Definition 9-6: A *variable parameter*, or *VAR parameter*, communicates information *out of* a subprogram. A VAR parameter is a local *identifier* or alias for storage that is associated with a variable in some other scope.

It is not an arbitrary restriction that actual VAR parameters have to be variables. Although new computer memory cells are allocated to store value parameters, no new memory is allocated to store VAR parameters. Hence, changing a formal VAR parameter must change the actual VAR parameter. If we could have constants as actual VAR parameters, changing the value of a formal VAR parameter would change the value of the constant. Similarly, allowing an arbitrary expression to be an actual VAR parameter would permit changing the value of an expression. It makes no sense to change the value of a constant. Only variables can have values that change. Thus, **actual parameters for VAR parameters must be variables.**

The following points summarize the rules for binding actual parameters and formal variable parameters:

1. There must be the same number of actual parameters in a subprogram call as there are in the formal parameter list of the subprogram declaration.

2. The first actual parameter is bound to the first formal parameter, the second actual parameter is bound to the second formal parameter, and in general the nth actual parameter is bound to the nth formal parameter.

3. An actual VAR parameter must be a **variable of the same type** as the formal VAR parameter.

Table 9-7: Rules for Binding of Actual Parameters and Formal VAR Parameters

With this all in mind, we give a declaration for the procedure **GetDimensions**, complete with a structured comment.

```
PROCEDURE GetDimensions ( VAR l, w, h: REAL );

(* ****************************************************************

 * DESCRIPTION:
        Procedure GetDimensions prompts the user for and returns
        the dimensions of a rectangular solid.

 * METHOD:
        This procedure is simply a WRITE, READLN pair for each of
        the three dimensions.

 * INPUT:
        none

 * OUTPUT:
            l: length dimension
            w: width dimension
            h: height dimension

 **************************************************************** *)

BEGIN
    WRITE(OUTPUT, 'Please input a length => ');
    READLN(INPUT, l);
    WRITE(OUTPUT, 'Please input a width => ');
    READLN(INPUT, w);
    WRITE(OUTPUT, 'Please input a height => ');
    READLN(INPUT, h)
END;     (* GetDimensions *)
```

Programming Example 9-11: GetDimensions Complete with Comment

Note that we have added a new field to our structured subprogram comment. The new field labeled **OUTPUT** indicates information being passed back from a subprogram. It has no connection to output done with the WRITE and WRITELN statements. Our style of structured subprogram comments now has four components, **DESCRIPTION, METHOD, INPUT,** and **OUTPUT.**

Examples of syntactically *invalid calls* to the procedure `GetDimensions` are:

Call	Error
GetDimensions(1, w)	(* number of formal and actual parameters differ *)
GetDimensions(1, w, 2)	(* must be variables not constants *)
GetDimensions(1, w, h, v)	(* number of formal and actual parameters differ *)
GetDimensions(2+5, w, h)	(* must be a variable not an expression *)

Table 9-8: Invalid Calls to `GetDimensions`

Recall that the procedure **GetDimensions** is only one of the two subprograms in our program to determine the volume of a rectangular solid. Now turn your attention to the procedure **ComputeVolume**. It takes the three dimensions as input, computes the volume, and prints the result. Should the three parameters to **ComputeVolume** be value parameters or VAR parameters? The answer depends on whether the information is INPUT (being passed into) or OUTPUT (being passed out of) the subprogram. For the procedure **ComputeVolume**, the information is INPUT, so the parameters are value parameters. Below is the procedure **ComputeVolume**:

```
PROCEDURE ComputeVolume (length, width, height: REAL);

    (* *********************************************************************

     * DESCRIPTION:
            Procedure ComputeVolume computes the volume of a rectangular
            solid from its dimensions and displays the results.

     * METHOD:
            The volume of the rectangular solid is computed as the
            product of its three dimensions.  The volume and each
            of the dimensions are displayed to the user with WRITELNS.

     * INPUT:
            length: length dimension
            width:  width dimension
            height: height dimension

     * OUTPUT:
            none

    ********************************************************************* *)

CONST
    fieldwidth = 8;
    decimals = 2;

VAR
    volume: REAL;

BEGIN
    volume := length * width * height;
    WRITELN(OUTPUT, 'The volume for a rectangular solid with');
    WRITELN(OUTPUT, 'Length = ',length:fieldwidth:decimals);
    WRITELN(OUTPUT, 'Width = ', width:fieldwidth:decimals);
    WRITELN(OUTPUT, 'Height = ',height:fieldwidth:decimals);
    WRITELN(OUTPUT, '  is ', volume:fieldwidth:decimals)
END;     (* ComputeVolume *)
```

Programming Example 9-12: Procedure **ComputeVolume**

Note that the three parameters are listed under the section INPUT of the structured subprogram comment.

With both of the required subprograms completed, our program is done. Programming Example 9-13 depicts the entire program. We have removed the subprogram comments so that the entire program fits on a single page.

```
PROGRAM Volume (INPUT, OUTPUT);

    (* ***********************************************************************

                  Program Volume computes the volume of a rectangular solid.

                  The three dimensions of the solid are determined in the
                  procedure GetDimensions.  Then the volume is computed and
                  displayed in the procedure ComputeVolume.

       *********************************************************************** *)


    VAR
        length,
        width,
        height: REAL;   (* used for illustrative brevity *)


        (***********************************************)


    PROCEDURE GetDimensions (VAR l, w, h: REAL);

    BEGIN
        WRITE(OUTPUT, 'Please input a length => ');
        READLN(INPUT, l);
        WRITE(OUTPUT, 'Please input a width => ');
        READLN(INPUT, w);
        WRITE(OUTPUT, 'Please input a height => ');
        READLN(INPUT, h)
    END;     (* GetDimensions *)


        (***********************************************)


    PROCEDURE ComputeVolume (length, width, height: REAL);

    CONST
        fieldwidth = 8;
        decimals = 2;

    VAR
        volume: REAL;

    BEGIN
        volume := length * width * height;
        WRITELN(OUTPUT, 'The volume for a rectangular solid with');
        WRITELN(OUTPUT, 'Length = ',length:fieldwidth:decimals);
        WRITELN(OUTPUT, 'Width = ', width:fieldwidth:decimals);
        WRITELN(OUTPUT, 'Height = ',height:fieldwidth:decimals);
        WRITELN(OUTPUT, '  is ', volume:fieldwidth:decimals)
    END;     (* ComputeVolume *)


        (***********************************************)


    BEGIN    (* Main Program *)
        GetDimensions(length, width, height);
        ComputeVolume(length, width, height)
    END.     (* Main Program *)
```

Programming Example 9-13: Program **Volume**

9.2.2. A Technique of Ensuring Parameter Passing

Our program to determine the volume of a rectangular solid was reasonably straightforward to design and implement. It was intended to demonstrate the need for parameters as well as an example of each of Pascal's two types of parameter passing. However, the program raises another important related issue.

Our program contains two subprograms: **GetDimensions** and **ComputeVolume**. All information being passed into and out of these procedures is handled with parameters. Note that the program contains three global variables. Recall that a globally declared variable can be accessed anywhere in the program. Although we didn't up-level address the global variables, we could have. For some programmers this temptation is simply too great to resist.

Variables used in the main program must be declared globally. As long as all information communicated into and out of every subprogram is done through parameters, globally declared variables do not present a problem. The fact that globally declared variables can be up-level addressed presents a potential problem. What we would like is a way to declare the variables needed in the main program so they cannot be up-level addressed. This would ensure that all communication between subprograms used parameters. We have a technique to do exactly that.

The technique is as follows: Add one extra procedure. Move all the statements from the main program block to the procedure. Move all the globally declared variables to the procedure. The main program block becomes a single call to this extra parameterless procedure. There are then no global variable declarations. In this way we completely filter out all up-level addressing of global variables by forcing information to be handled by parameters. We normally name this additional procedure **GlobalFilter**, although any unused name will do. We have rewritten the previous program with **GlobalFilter**, as indicated in the following example:

```
PROGRAM Volume (INPUT, OUTPUT);

    (* ***********************************************************************

                Program Volume computes the volume of a rectangular solid.

                The three dimensions of the solid are determined in the
                procedure GetDimensions.  Then the volume is computed and
                displayed in the procedure ComputeVolume.

        ************************************************************************ *)


    PROCEDURE GetDimensions (VAR l, w, h: REAL);

    BEGIN
        WRITE(OUTPUT, 'Please input a length => ');
        READLN(INPUT, l);
        WRITE(OUTPUT, 'Please input a width => ');
        READLN(INPUT, w);
        WRITE(OUTPUT, 'Please input a height => ');
        READLN(INPUT, h)
    END;     (* GetDimensions *)



        (***********************************************)


    PROCEDURE ComputeVolume (length, width, height: REAL);


    CONST
        fieldwidth = 8;
        decimals = 2;

    VAR
        volume: REAL;

    BEGIN
        volume := length * width * height;
        WRITELN(OUTPUT, 'The volume for a rectangular solid with');
        WRITELN(OUTPUT, 'Length = ',length:fieldwidth:decimals);
        WRITELN(OUTPUT, 'Width = ', width:fieldwidth:decimals);
        WRITELN(OUTPUT, 'Height = ',height:fieldwidth:decimals);
        WRITELN(OUTPUT, '  is ', volume:fieldwidth:decimals)
    END;     (* ComputeVolume *)


        (***********************************************)


    PROCEDURE GlobalFilter;

    VAR
        length,
        width,
        height: REAL;

    BEGIN
        GetDimensions(length, width, height);
        ComputeVolume(length, width, height)
    END;     (* GlobalFilter *)


        (* ******************** *)


    BEGIN     (* Main Program *)
        GlobalFilter
    END.     (* Main Program *)
```

Programming Example 9-14: Program **Volume** with **GlobalFilter**

The program contains no globally declared variables. Therefore, there can be no up-level addressing of global variables, intentionally or accidentally. Since the variables are declared locally to the procedure **GlobalFilter**, all communication between subprograms must occur through parameters. In short, this technique enforces parameter passing. We suggest you adopt this technique until you feel comfortable with passing parameters.

9.2.3. Subprogram Comments: Another Tool in the Toolbox

We have been using and strongly advocate structured subprogram comments. A *structured* subprogram comment is a subprogram comment with specific, uniformly present components, regardless of the particular subprogram being described.

You have seen four components of our style of structured subprogram comments. We label them **DESCRIPTION, METHOD, INPUT,** and **OUTPUT.** They refer to a description of *what* the subprogram does, *how* it does it, what information must be passed *into* the subprogram, and what information must be passed *out of* the subprogram.

It is much more important to use *structured* comments than what the particular structure of the comments are. We have developed our style of structured subprogram comments out of years of experience. We believe it to be a good style but recognize that other workable variations exist. For example, if a group of people are working on one program, it is reasonable to add another component explaining who wrote the particular subprogram. If the programming project runs over a long period, it may be useful to add a *history*—information about when the subprogram was written or last modified. Similarly, other components can be added as necessary. Out style reflects the minimum a programmer would need in subprogram comments.

There are at least three benefits to programmers using *structured* subprogram comments. *First, they are easier to write*: Making subprogram comments structured makes the process more systematic, more of a science and less of an art. *Second, they are easier to read*: With uniformity across subprogram comments, the reader knows what to expect and where to find what is needed. *Third, they provide a double check on correct parameter passing*: All information listed under INPUT or OUTPUT should be parameters. Moreover, all parameters listed under both INPUT and OUTPUT or just OUTPUT should be VAR parameters; all parameters listed under only INPUT should be value parameters. This cross check helps the programmer verify that parameters are being passed and are of the correct type (value vs. VAR).

9.2.4. A Style of Declaration

By now, you know quite a bit about procedures, parameter passing, nested declarations, scope of identifiers, global variables, and good programming practice. As you develop as a programmer, things that now seem awkward will become second nature. To help you until you are comfortable with these ideas, Table 9-9 lists the principles of a style of procedure and variable declarations that has proved useful to many programmers. It is an extension of the style presented in the last chapter.

- Define all named constants at the global level.

- Declare all subprograms at the global level.

- Declare all variables local to the scope in which they are used. **All variables referenced in a subprogram should either be declared in the local variable declaration section or in the formal parameter list for that subprogram.**

- Use the procedure **GlobalFilter** to eliminate all global variable declarations, thereby forcing all communication between subprograms to take place through parameters.

Table 9-9: A Style of Declarations

Value and VAR parameters are different and should be used at different times. Value parameters are for passing values *into* a subprogram, and VAR parameters are for communicating information *out of* a subprogram. VAR parameters permit changing variables outside the scope in which they are declared and consequently should only be used when absolutely necessary. The two common uses of VAR parameters are for returning a computed result or values read from the terminal. Most of the time you will need and should use value parameters. **Under no circumstances should you use up-level addressing of global variables rather than parameters to communicate information between subprograms.**

9.2.5. Questions

1. What types of parameter binding are used in Pascal?

2. Why are variable parameters needed?

3. When should value parameters be used?

4. When should variable parameters be used?

5. What is the difference between a formal value parameter declaration and a formal VAR parameter declaration?

6. Which are acceptable actual value parameters?
   a. unnamed constant
   b. named constant
   c. variable
   d. arbitrary expression

7. Which are acceptable actual VAR parameters?
   a. unnamed constant
   b. named constant
   c. variable
   d. arbitrary expression

8. Must all actual VAR parameters always be variables? Justify your answer.

9. What are the rules for binding formal VAR parameters with actual VAR parameters?

10. Does calling a subprogram with value parameters create a new place to store values?

11. Does calling a subprogram with variable parameters create a new place to store values?

12. Why should information be passed into and out of subprograms with parameters?

13. What technique presented in this chapter enforces parameter passing? Describe it.

14. What is a structured subprogram comment?

15. What are the parts of structured subprogram comments presented in this chapter?

16. What are three reasons why programmers should use *structured* subprogram comments?

17. What style of declarations was presented in this chapter?

18. If both a VAR parameter and a value parameter will work, which should you use? Justify your answer.

9.2.6. Exercises

1. What output is generated by the following Pascal program?

```
PROGRAM Example (INPUT, OUTPUT);


PROCEDURE Modify (VAR x: REAL;   y: REAL);

BEGIN
    x := 12.5;
    y := 17.4
END;    (* Modify )


PROCEDURE Start;

VAR
    x, y: REAL;

BEGIN
    x := 42.7;
    y := 23.4;
    WRITELN(OUTPUT, x, y);
    Modify(x, y);
    WRITELN(OUTPUT, x, y)
END;    (* Start *)


BEGIN
    Start
END.
```

2. What output does the following program produce?

```
PROGRAM Show (INPUT, OUTPUT);


PROCEDURE Switch (VAR a, b: INTEGER);

BEGIN
    a := b;
    b := a
END;    (* Switch *)


PROCEDURE Main;

VAR
    x, y: INTEGER;

BEGIN
    x := 10;
    y := 20;
    WRITELN(OUTPUT, x, y);
    Switch(x, y);
    WRITELN(OUTPUT, x, y)
END;    (* Main *)


BEGIN
    Main
END.
```

3. What is the output of the following program?

```
PROGRAM Try (INPUT, OUTPUT);


PROCEDURE Modify (VAR x, y: CHAR);

BEGIN
    x := 'A';
    y := 'Z'
END;    (* Modify *)


PROCEDURE Driver;

VAR
    x, y: CHAR;

BEGIN
    x := 'a';
    y := 'b';
    WRITELN(OUTPUT, x, y);
    Modify(x, y);
    WRITELN(OUTPUT, x, y)
END;    (* Driver *)


BEGIN
    Driver
END.
```

9.3. Chapter Summary

- A parameter permits communication between subprograms.

- Parameters make subprograms more general.

- Pascal has two types of parameters: value parameters and variable parameters.

- A value parameter communicates information into a subprogram.

- Value parameters are defined like and behave like local variables. The difference is that value parameters get an initial value upon subprogram call.

- Formal parameters are declared in the subprogram declaration. Each subprogram has only one formal parameter list.

- Actual parameters appear in the call to the subprogram. There are as many actual parameter lists as there are calls to a subprogram.

- Parameter binding is the association of actual parameters with formal parameters when a subprogram is called.

- Rules for value parameter binding:
    1. There must be the same number of actual parameters in a subprogram call as there are in the formal parameter list of the subprogram declaration.

    2. The first actual parameter is bound to the first formal parameter, the second actual parameter is bound to the second formal parameter, and in general the nth actual parameter is bound to the nth formal parameter.

    3. Actual parameters must be an expression of compatible type with the corresponding formal parameter. (Mentally place an assignment statement between them, *formal := actual*; if it works, the binding is OK.)

- Any expression of the correct type may be used as an actual value parameter.

- Value parameters are always bound in the same way, whether they are constants, variables, or expressions. The actual parameter is evaluated, and the resulting value is copied to the formal parameter.

- The names of the formal and actual parameters have no effect on binding.

- Modifying the value of a value parameter has no effect outside the subprogram in which it is declared, even if the corresponding actual parameter is a variable.

- Subprograms may have any number of parameters.

- Variable parameters communicate information *out of* a subprogram.

- A variable parameter establishes an alias for an existing variable.

- A variable parameter declaration is just like value parameter declaration, except it is preceded by the reserved word VAR.

- The parameter binding associated with VAR parameters is referred to as call-by-reference or call-by-VAR.

- Rules for variable parameter binding:

    1. There must be the same number of actual parameters in a subprogram call as there are in the formal parameter list of the subprogram declaration.

    2. The first actual parameter is bound to the first formal parameter, the second actual parameter is bound to the second formal parameter, and in general the nth actual parameter is bound to the nth formal parameter.

    3. An actual VAR parameter must be a **variable of the same type** as the formal VAR parameter.

- Changing the value of a VAR parameter immediately changes the value of the variable to which it refers.

- There are three cases of parameter binding. (1) For call-by-value parameter passing, new storage is allocated upon a subprogram call, the value of the actual parameter is copied to the new storage, and the storage is deallocated upon subprogram termination. (2) If the resulting value of the formal parameter is copied back to the actual parameter, the binding is called call-by-value-result. (3) If no new storage is allocated, all references to the formal parameter are references to the actual parameter, and the parameter binding is known as call-by-reference.

- The use of parameters rather than up-level addressing simplifies inter-subprogram communication, eliminates the potential of side effects, and simplifies the task of debugging.

- **All communication between subprograms should be by parameters; up-level addressing of global variables should never be used as an alternative.**

9.4. Summary of Style

- A *structured* subprogram comment is a subprogram comment with specific, uniformly present components, regardless of the particular subprogram being described.

- Four components of our style of structured subprogram comments are **DESCRIPTION**, **METHOD**, **INPUT**, and **OUTPUT**. They refer to *what* the subprogram does, *how* it does it, what information must be passed *into* the subprogram, and what information must be passed *out of* the subprogram. **INPUT** denotes value parameters, and **OUTPUT** denotes VAR parameters.

- The use of structured subprogram comments makes writing subprogram comments easier, makes reading them easier, and provides a cross check on parameter passing.

- We have presented a technique to enforce parameter passing. It calls for the addition of one extra procedure, moving all the statements from the main program to the extra subprogram, and making all the global variable declarations local variable declarations in the extra subprogram. Although we can give the extra procedure any desired name, we uniformly call it `GlobalFilter` because it filters out all up-level addressing of global variables.

- The style of declarations proposed in this chapter has been found to work very well, and we hope you adopt it. It is as follows:

  1. Define all named constants at the global level.

  2. Declare all subprograms at the global level.

  3. Declare all variables local to the scope in which they are used. **All variables referenced in a subprogram should either be declared in the local variable declaration section or in the formal parameter list for that subprogram.**

  4. Use the procedure **GlobalFilter** to eliminate all global variable declarations, thereby forcing all communication between subprograms to occur through parameters.

- Variable parameters should be used only when changes to values of parameters must be reflected in the calling routine. Value parameters should be used in all other cases.

- **All communication into and out of a subprogram should be made explicit through use of parameters. Every variable used in a subprogram should either be a local variable or should be passed as a parameter (either value or VAR, appropriately). All variables should be declared in the scope in which they are used.**

9.5. Summary of Terms

- parameter
- value parameter
- formal parameter
- actual parameter
- parameter binding

- variable parameter
- VAR parameter
- call-by-value parameter binding
- call-by-reference parameter binding

- call-by-value-result parameter binding
- global variable
- up-level addressing of variables
- structured subprogram comment

9.6. Chapter Problems

1. Write a procedure that takes two integers as parameter input and writes them and their sum to the terminal.

2. Write a procedure named **swap** that takes two variables of type INTEGER and exchanges their values. *Hint: What kind of parameters does it have?*

3. Write a procedure that prompts for, reads, and returns five integer values from the terminal.

4. Write a procedure that takes five integers and returns their sum and arithmetic mean (average) as parameters.

5. Write a procedure that takes one character and two integers as parameter input. If the character is '+', '-', '*', or '/', perform the corresponding computation on the two integers. For example, if the procedure is named **Evaluate**, the procedure call **Evaluate('+', 2, 5)** might cause the following output:

   ```
   2 + 5 evaluates to 7
   ```

   If the character is not an acceptable operator, perform no computation.
6. Extend the previous procedure to permit modular and integer division.

7. Write a procedure that takes three real numbers as input (the coefficients of a quadratic equation) and returns the two roots of the quadratic equation.

   Hint: For a quadratic equation of the form $ax^2 + bx + c = 0$, *use the quadratic formula*

   $$root = \frac{-b \pm \sqrt{b^2 - 4ac}}{2a}$$

   You may assume that $b^2 - 4ac$ is a nonnegative number.

Chapter 10: Functions

The preceding two chapters were devoted to procedures with no parameters, procedures with value parameters, and procedures with variable parameters. We next turn our attention to the class of subprograms known as *functions*. This subject area is indicated in the following figure:

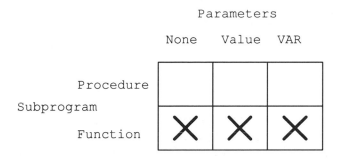

Figure 10-1: Functions

10.1. What Functions Are

Functions, like procedures, are subprograms. Functions must be declared, just as procedures must be declared. Each subprogram is a related sequence of instructions treated as a unit and given a name. Functions, like procedures, may have local declarations and may also have parameters. Procedures and functions are declared in a highly similar manner.

Although procedures and functions are similar and are declared in a very similar fashion, they have a fundamental difference. In Pascal, procedures are a means of writing new *statements*, and functions are a means of writing new *expressions*. A procedure call is always a statement, whereas a function call is always an expression. Since every expression evaluates to some value, every function call must also evaluate to some value. But procedures never evaluate to any value. This is the fundamental difference between the two types of subprograms, and is evident in the following two definitions:

> **Definition 10-1:** A Pascal *procedure* is a user-defined statement.

> **Definition 10-2:** A Pascal *function* is a user-defined expression.

To help distinguish between the two types of subprograms, we find it convenient to view functions in a different way. One way to think of a function is as a machine that takes an *input* and produces an *output*, as illustrated in the following figure:

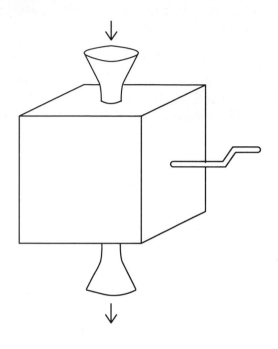

Figure 10-2: Function Machine

In general, a function may have zero or more input values drawn from a collection of valid inputs, and it evaluates to a single output value. Mathematically, the set of valid inputs is known as the *domain* of the function. The function evaluates to a value from a set of possible output values, known as the *range* of the function.

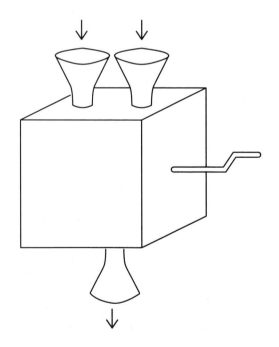

Figure 10-3: Function Machine with Multiple Inputs

Recall our extensive earlier discussion of operators and operands. It turns out that an operator is simply a special type of function, and operands are inputs to the function. For example, the binary division operator (/) is a function that takes two REAL inputs and evaluates to a REAL result. Therefore, the division operator has the type REAL as its domain and type REAL also as its range. The model we used to depict operators is useful for describing functions.

10.2. Predefined Functions

Many commonly needed functions are part of the Pascal *standard library*. Among these *predefined functions* are **SQR** to compute the square of a number, **SQRT** to compute the square root of a number, and **ROUND** to round off numbers. Although a detailed list of all Pascal's predefined functions may be found in Appendix VII beginning on page 545, the following table lists some of Pascal's predefined functions, with their domains and ranges:

Function	Domain	Range	Description
Round	REAL	INTEGER	returns input rounded to nearest INTEGER
Trunc	REAL	INTEGER	returns input truncated to an INTEGER
Odd	INTEGER	BOOLEAN	returns TRUE for odd input, and FALSE otherwise
Sin	REAL	REAL	returns sine of input value
Cos	REAL	REAL	returns cosine of input value
Sqr	INTEGER	INTEGER	returns square of input value[1]
Sqrt	REAL	REAL	returns the square root of the input value

Table 10-1: Some Predefined Pascal Functions

We do not need to declare any of the predefined functions in order to use them. After all, they are *predefined*. The next section discusses how to call functions.

10.3. Calling Functions

A function is called, or invoked, similarly to the way a procedure is called: by specifying the name of the subprogram along with an appropriate actual parameter list. The difference between the two types of subprogram calls is that procedure calls are statements and function calls are expressions. Below are examples of *valid calls* to some of Pascal's predefined functions:

```
IntNum := ROUND(RealNum)                    ordinate := radius * SIN(argument)

IntNum := ROUND(RealNum) MOD 2              abscissa := radius * COS(argument)

IntNum := TRUNC(RealNum)                    WHILE ODD(value) DO
                                                  Process(value)
IntNum := TRUNC(RealNum) DIV IntNum
                                            REPEAT
IF ODD(IntNum)                                    READ(invalue)
        THEN result := SQR(number)          UNTIL NOT(ODD(invalue))
        ELSE result := SQRT(number)
                                            FOR count := 1 TO TRUNC(SQRT(total))
```

Table 10-2: Valid Function Calls

Although each of the previous function calls is part of a Pascal statement, the function calls themselves are used as expressions rather than as statements. A function call evaluates to some value and must be treated as an expression. The following statements are examples of *invalid calls* to some of Pascal's predefined functions:

[1]There is also one that takes a REAL and returns a REAL.

Call	Error
`ROUND`	`(* must be used as expression not statement *)`
`IntNum := ROUND`	`(* missing parameter *)`
`WHILE ROUND(total)`	`(* WHILE needs a BOOLEAN, ROUND returns INTEGER *)`
`IF TRUNC(total)`	`(* IF needs a BOOLEAN, TRUNC returns an INTEGER *)`
`ROUND(total)`	`(* must be used as expression not statement *)`
`IntNum := SQRT(result)`	`(* SQRT returns a REAL not INTEGER *)`
`IF ODD(SQRT(number))`	`(* SQRT returns REAL, ODD requires an INTEGER *)`

Table 10-3: Invalid Function Calls

Function calls must always be used as expressions. Moreover, the type of the expression must be compatible with the type of the function. For example, the predefined function **ROUND** evaluates to an INTEGER value and therefore can never be used as a BOOLEAN expression. Also, input to functions, like input to procedures, is communicated into the subprogram by value parameters. The actual parameters in a function call must match the corresponding formal parameters in number, type, and order.

10.4. Defining New Functions

Although Pascal provides a number of predefined functions in its standard library, the number is in no way exhaustive. Therefore, the programmer may create new functions as necessary. We illustrate the form of a function declaration in the following example:

```
FUNCTION <name> (<parameter-list>): <function-type>;

<constant declarations>

<variable declarations>

<subprogram declarations>

BEGIN
    <statement-1>;
    <statement-2>;
    <statement-3>;
        :
        :
        :
    <statement-N>
END;
```

Programming Example 10-1: Form of Function Declaration

Function declarations are very similar to procedure declarations. Both have a name and a list of statements delimited by a BEGIN-END pair. Both may also have an optional parameter list, as well as optional local constant definitions, variable declarations, and nested subprogram declarations. The reserved word PROCEDURE is replaced with the reserved word FUNCTION. The real difference is that a function declaration contains the declaration of the function's type.

Since functions have a type and evaluate to a value of that type, you may be wondering how the function gets such a value. A Pascal function gets a value by explicitly assigning a value to the name of the function within the body of the function. *One of the statements of a function's body must be the assignment of a value to the name of the function.* To illustrate this point, we give the following declaration for the function **SQR** to compute the square of a number:

```
FUNCTION SQR ( number: REAL ): REAL;

BEGIN
    SQR := number * number
END;    (* SQR *)
```

Programming Example 10-2: Declaration of Function **SQR**

The function to compute the square of a number needs one value as input and returns one value as output. Since both the input and output are of type REAL, the function's domain and range are both type REAL. This is indicated by the actual parameter list declaration and the function's type declaration. The function body simply multiplies the input by itself and assigns the result to the function name. The assignment to the function name gives it its value. Without such an assignment, the function will not contain the computed value. *Every function declaration must contain an assignment to the function name.*

Now, think about the predefined function **Odd**. It takes one INTEGER input and returns a BOOLEAN result. The function's domain is type INTEGER, and its range is type BOOLEAN. Therefore, the declaration must include one INTEGER value parameter, and the function's type is BOOLEAN. Think for a moment how we can determine if an INTEGER is odd or even. The answer lies in whether 2 divides the input evenly or not. For this we can use Pascal's modular division operator MOD. Even numbers have no remainder after division by 2. A number is odd if the result after modular division by 2 is not equal to 0. Therefore, we might define the function **Odd** in the following way:

```
FUNCTION Odd ( number: INTEGER ): BOOLEAN;

BEGIN
    IF (number MOD 2) <> 0
        THEN Odd := TRUE
        ELSE Odd := FALSE
END;    (* Odd *)
```

Programming Example 10-3: A Declaration of Function **Odd**

However, note that the condition is the same type as the function, namely, BOOLEAN. Therefore, we can rewrite the previous function declaration in the following more concise way:

```
FUNCTION Odd ( number: INTEGER ): BOOLEAN;

BEGIN
    Odd := (number MOD 2) <> 0
END;    (* Odd *)
```

Programming Example 10-4: A Better Declaration of Function **Odd**

Both of the previous examples of functions take one input (parameter). Some functions have no parameters. Such functions get their input from the user. The following example illustrates such a function.

```
FUNCTION GetCommand: CHAR;

VAR
    ch: CHAR;

BEGIN
    REPEAT
        WRITE(OUTPUT, 'Please input "y" or "n" => ');
        READLN(INPUT, ch)
    UNTIL (ch = 'y') OR (ch = 'n');
    GetCommand := ch
END;    (* GetCommand *)
```

Programming Example 10-5: Declaration of Function **GetCommand**

The function **GetCommand** has no parameters, yet evaluates to a value of type CHAR. The user is repeatedly prompted until either a "y" or "n" is entered. Once acceptable input is entered by the user, the entered character is returned as the function's value. Note that this function requires input from the user. *All parameterless functions should get some input from the user.* Without input either from parameters or the user, a function will always compute and return the same result. A function that always returns the same value is really a constant. In such cases a named constant should be used instead of a function.

Recall the program to compute the volume of a rectangular solid presented in the last chapter (page 292). In our solution we decomposed the program into two subprograms: **GetDimensions** and **ComputeVolume**. The procedure **GetDimensions** prompts for and reads the dimensions from the user, and the procedure **ComputeVolume** computes the volume and displays the result.   The procedure **ComputeVolume** was declared as follows:

```
PROCEDURE ComputeVolume (length, width, height: REAL);

VAR
    volume: REAL;

BEGIN
    volume := length * width * height;
    WRITELN(OUTPUT, 'The volume for a rectangular solid with');
    WRITELN(OUTPUT, 'Length = ', length:fieldwidth:decimals);
    WRITELN(OUTPUT, 'Width = ', width:fieldwidth:decimals);
    WRITELN(OUTPUT, 'Height = ', height:fieldwidth:decimals);
    WRITELN(OUTPUT, '  is ', volume:fieldwidth:decimals)
END;      (* ComputeVolume *)
```

Programming Example 10-6: Declaration of Procedure **ComputeVolume**

The previous procedure **ComputeVolume** exhibits one feature that is generally regarded as poor programming practice: it mixes calculations with output. Good programming practice dictates that these be in separate subprograms. Therefore, a better design has three subprograms instead of two. They are **GetDimensions**, **ComputeVolume** and **DisplayResults**. **GetDimensions** is as before. **ComputeVolume** now computes the volume and returns the result, and **DisplayResults** actually displays the result.   **ComputeVolume** is a function, and **GetDimensions** and **DisplayResults** are procedures. Each subprogram now has one task. The rewritten program **Volume** is shown in Programming Example 10-7 (page 309).

```
PROGRAM Volume (INPUT, OUTPUT);

    (* ********************************************************************

            Program Volume computes the volume of a rectangular solid.

            The three dimensions of the solid are determined in the
            procedure GetDimensions.  Then the function ComputeVolume
            calculates the volume of the solid.  Finally, the procedure
            DisplayResults displays the results.

       ****************************************************************** *)


PROCEDURE GetDimensions (VAR l, w, h: REAL);

BEGIN
    WRITE(OUTPUT, 'Please input a length => ');
    READLN(INPUT, l);
    WRITE(OUTPUT, 'Please input a width => ');
    READLN(INPUT, w);
    WRITE(OUTPUT, 'Please input a height => ');
    READLN(INPUT, h)
END;    (* GetDimensions *)


FUNCTION ComputeVolume (length, width, height: REAL): REAL;

BEGIN
    ComputeVolume := length * width * height
END;    (* ComputeVolume *)


PROCEDURE DisplayResults (length, width, height: REAL;  volume: REAL);

CONST
    fieldwidth = 8;
    decimals = 2;

BEGIN
    WRITELN(OUTPUT, 'The volume for a rectangular solid with');
    WRITELN(OUTPUT, 'Length = ',length:fieldwidth:decimals);
    WRITELN(OUTPUT, 'Width = ', width:fieldwidth:decimals);
    WRITELN(OUTPUT, 'Height = ',height:fieldwidth:decimals);
    WRITELN(OUTPUT, '  is ', volume:fieldwidth:decimals)
END;    (* DisplayResults *)


PROCEDURE GlobalFilter;

VAR
    length, width, height, volume: REAL;

BEGIN
    GetDimensions(length, width, height);
    volume := ComputeVolume(length, width, height);
    DisplayResults(length, width, height, volume)
END;    (* GlobalFilter *)


BEGIN   (* Main Program *)
   GlobalFilter
END.    (* Main Program *)
```

Programming Example 10-7: Program **Volume** Rewritten with a Function

This program illustrates several important points. First, it shows a program fully decomposed into subprograms. Each subprogram performs a single independent action. Input of values by the user is isolated in **GetDimensions**. Similarly, calculations are done in the function **ComputeVolume**, whereas the procedure **DisplayResults** isolates output from the rest of the program. Also notice the use of parameter passing. All communication between subprograms is done with parameters. The function **ComputeVolume** has three value parameters for its three inputs. Similarly, the procedure

DisplayResults has four value parameters for its four inputs. Since the procedure **GetDimensions** modifies its three parameters, it uses VAR parameters instead of value parameters. Also note the use of a function to return the result of the computation. Finally, note that the procedure **GlobalFilter** sequences the action of the program by the order in which it calls the other subprograms. It illustrates enforcing proper parameter passing. Because program variables are declared here, rather than globally, the only means of inter-subprogram communication is through parameter passing.

Remember that a function call is an expression. Also remember that an actual value parameter is an expression. Hence, we can use a function call as an actual value parameter if the types are compatible. In the last example, we assigned the value of the function call to the variable **volume** and then called the procedure **DisplayResults** with this variable as a parameter. This variable can be eliminated, and the function call may be used as a value parameter itself. The following example illustrates how:

```
PROCEDURE GlobalFilter;

VAR
    length, width, height: REAL;

BEGIN
    GetDimensions(length, width, height);
    DisplayResults(length, width, height, ComputeVolume(length,width,height))
END;     (* GlobalFilter *)
```

Programming Example 10-8: Function Call as Actual Value Parameter

You should be aware that a function call can always be used as an actual value parameter but never as an actual VAR parameter.

10.5. When To Use Functions

There is both confusion and controversy about when to use functions. The confusion arises from the fact that functions are not strictly necessary. They are not necessary in the sense that every program written with the use of functions could be written without the use of functions. Simply put, a function is a subprogram with an output value. Therefore, every Pascal function can be rewritten as a procedure with an extra VAR parameter. To illustrate this point, consider the function **Odd** rewritten as a procedure, as indicated in the following example.

```
FUNCTION Odd (number: INTEGER): BOOLEAN;

BEGIN
    Odd := (number MOD 2) <> 0
END;     (* Odd *)
```

Programming Example 10-9: **Odd** Written as a Function

```
PROCEDURE Odd (number: INTEGER;  VAR IsOdd: BOOLEAN);

BEGIN
    IsOdd := (number MOD 2) <> 0
END;     (* Odd *)
```

Programming Example 10-10: **Odd** Rewritten as a Procedure

By adding a VAR parameter of the same type as the function, any function can be rewritten as a procedure. As another example, consider rewriting the function **ComputeVolume** as a procedure.

```
FUNCTION ComputeVolume (length, width, height: REAL): REAL;

BEGIN
    ComputeVolume := length * width * height
END;     (* ComputeVolume *)
```

Programming Example 10-11: **ComputeVolume** Written as a Function

```
PROCEDURE ComputeVolume (length, width, height: REAL;  VAR volume: REAL);

BEGIN
    volume := length * width * height
END;    (* ComputeVolume *)
```

Programming Example 10-12: `ComputeVolume` Rewritten as a Procedure

So we see that, although functions exist, they are not strictly necessary. But just because they are not strictly necessary, that does not mean you should not use them. Never using functions reflects a poor utilization of all the available programming tools. Functions were included in the programming language Pascal quite intentionally and are intended to be used. However, when to use functions is dictated by style more than anything else.

We believe that any time a subprogram takes input and produces a *single* output, the subprogram should be a function. It is our experience that functions are most useful, most easily debugged, and most easily understood when they are treated as the simple function machine described earlier on page 302.

10.6. When Not to Use Functions

Some people try to avoid using functions altogether, but others feel a function should be used any time a value is to be returned, regardless of how many values are returned. Such use leads to functions such as the following:

```
FUNCTION GetDimensions (VAR length, width: REAL): REAL;

VAR
    height: REAL;

BEGIN
    WRITE(OUTPUT, 'Please input a length => ');
    READLN(INPUT, length);
    WRITE(OUTPUT, 'Please input a width => ');
    READLN(INPUT, width);
    WRITE(OUTPUT, 'Please input a height => ');
    READLN(INPUT, height);
    GetDimensions := height
END;    (* GetDimensions *)
```

Programming Example 10-13: `GetDimensions` as a Function

The previous subprogram has three output values. It returns two outputs by VAR parameters and one as the function value. We believe subprograms that return more than one output value should be written as procedures with a VAR parameter for each of the outputs rather than being written as a function that returns one output value as the function value and the other output values as VAR parameters. We would have written the last subprogram as the following procedure:

```
PROCEDURE GetDimensions (VAR length, width, height: REAL);

BEGIN
    WRITE(OUTPUT, 'Please input a length => ');
    READLN(INPUT, length);
    WRITE(OUTPUT, 'Please input a width => ');
    READLN(INPUT, width);
    WRITE(OUTPUT, 'Please input a height => ');
    READLN(INPUT, height)
END;    (* GetDimensions *)
```

Programming Example 10-14: `GetDimensions` as a Procedure

We have found our style of function usage to be of benefit to many. We encourage you to adopt this style. If you use this style, your functions will always use parameters as input only. This means that a function's parameters will always be value parameters and never VAR parameters. Using VAR parameters permits a subprogram to modify the variables with which it is called. Suppose that a program contained the following fragment:

```
x := 3;
y := Sqr(x);
WRITELN(OUTPUT, x, y)
```

We might expect the output to be the values 3 and 9, since 3 squared is 9. But suppose the output was 9 and 9 or 1 and 9. That would mean that the function **SQR** changed the value of its input. Most people agree that unexpected side effects are a very bad idea!

In general, we do not use functions when more than one value is to be returned. Also, we do not use functions if any of the input values is to be modified. We always use only value parameters with functions. As a consequence of this style, most of our subprograms are procedures, and relatively few are functions.

10.7. Structured Comments for Functions

In the previous two chapters we developed *structured* subprogram comments and demonstrated how they could be used with all procedures. Since functions are also subprograms, we can use the same structure for both types of subprograms. Since a function has an additional output value, we include it under the section labeled **OUTPUT**. The following programming example illustrates this:

```
FUNCTION ComputeVolume (length, width, height: REAL): REAL;

    (* *********************************************************************

     * DESCRIPTION:
             Function ComputeVolume computes the volume of a rectangular
             solid from its dimensions.

     * METHOD:
             The volume of the rectangular solid is computed as the
             product of its three dimensions.

     * INPUT:
             length: length dimension
             width: width dimension
             height: height dimension

     * OUTPUT:
             ComputeVolume: volume of rectangular solid


     ********************************************************************** *)


BEGIN
    ComputeVolume := length * width * height
END;     (* ComputeVolume *)
```

Programming Example 10-15:   Function **ComputeVolume** with Structured Comment

If you adopt the style of function usage advocated in this chapter, the structured comment for each function will always have exactly one item under **OUTPUT** since each function will return exactly one output value.

10.8. Programming with Stubs

The last three chapters have been devoted to the two types of subprograms and the means of communication to, from, and between subprograms. As the size of problems and programs gets larger, the number of subprograms in a program increases accordingly. In such situations the desire to try and run the partially completed program is almost unstoppable. This desire is only natural since the programmer wants to be sure what has already been done is OK before doing a lot more work only to find out that much must be redone or thrown away. It is not only a natural desire but actually good programming practice to test part of a program before the entire program is written.

We advocate the following strategy for implementing larger programs. First, do a top-down design of the entire program, as discussed earlier. Then, implement the subprograms in a top-down design, highest level first, second level second, and so on until all levels are implemented.

Let us elaborate on this strategy a bit further. The first step is to design the entire program completely using the top-down design method. With the program design firmly in hand, we start implementing the program. We first write the main program, which normally consists of calls to the highest-level subprograms. We must then add the declarations for these subprograms. However, rather than write out each subprogram completely, we write only a subprogram shell. The shell has a complete formal parameter list but little more. The subprogram shell does not contain the complete instructions within the subprogram's BEGIN-END block. Normally, the subprogram shell or stub contains only one WRITELN saying that it is is being called. The following example illustrates how this might be done with our previous program to compute the volume of a rectangular solid.

```
PROGRAM Volume (INPUT, OUTPUT);

    (* ********************************************************************

            Program Volume computes the volume of a rectangular solid.

            The three dimensions of the solid are determined in the
            procedure GetDimensions.  Then the function ComputeVolume
            calculates the volume of the solid.  Finally, the procedure
            DisplayResults displays the results.

    ******************************************************************** *)


PROCEDURE GetDimensions (VAR l, w, h: REAL);

BEGIN
    WRITELN(OUTPUT, 'Procedure GetDimensions called')
END;     (* GetDimensions *)


FUNCTION ComputeVolume (length, width, height: REAL): REAL;

BEGIN
    WRITELN(OUTPUT, 'Function ComputeVolume called')
END;     (* ComputeVolume *)


PROCEDURE DisplayResults (length, width, height: REAL;  volume: REAL);

BEGIN
    WRITELN(OUTPUT, 'Procedure DisplayResults called')
END;     (* DisplayResults *)


PROCEDURE GlobalFilter;

VAR
    length, width, height, volume: REAL;

BEGIN
    GetDimensions(length, width, height);
    volume := ComputeVolume(length, width, height);
    DisplayResults(length, width, height, volume)
END;     (* GlobalFilter *)


BEGIN   (* Main Program *)
    GlobalFilter
END.     (* Main Program *)
```

Programming Example 10-16: Program **Volume** with Subprogram Stubs

Having a partially completed program, we can now test it. Testing it should show whether the right subprograms are being called in the right order.

Sometimes, you might wish the stub to display the value of any value parameters. Additionally, you might have functions return some constant to help verify communication between subprograms.

Once we have established that the highest-level subprograms are being called in the desired order and that the communication between them is correct, we then fill out these subprogram stubs completely. In doing so, we add calls to the next-highest level of subprograms. Again, we add subprogram stubs rather than complete subprograms. We then continue the process of testing, filling in existing stubs, and adding new stubs until all stubs have been filled in and no more stubs need to be added. This strategy permits us to test the program continually as it is being implemented. We summarize this strategy in the following table:

Design entire program using top-down design.

Write main program.

Write stubs for all subprograms called in main program.

REPEAT
    Test existing program by running it.
    Fill out existing stubs.
    Add stubs for subprograms that are called but not yet written.
UNTIL all stubs filled out

Table 10-4: Programming with Stubs

The programming practice of writing subprograms first as stubs so that the program can be tested before completing them is known as *programming with stubs*. We have found it to be a good strategy for implementing programs; it is particularly useful if the program has many subprograms. This strategy of implementation goes hand in hand with the top-down design method. We advocate programming with stubs. We will come back to this implementation strategy in later chapters and expand it a bit further.

10.8.1. Questions

1. What are Pascal's two classes of subprograms?

2. What is a function?

3. What is the domain of a function?

4. What is the range of a function?

5. Explain how an operator is related to a function.

6. How are procedure declarations and function declarations alike? How are they different?

7. How are procedure calls and function calls alike? How are they different?

8. What is a predefined subprogram? Give one example of a predefined function in Pascal. What is its domain and range?

9. How can a Pascal function call be used? Can it be used as a statement?

10. Can a programmer create new functions? Explain how.

11. Can a function declaration have parameters? Can it have local declarations?

12. How does a function get a value?

13. Does a function have to have formal parameters? Justify your answer.

14. If a function were to have no parameters, where would it get its input?

15. Can a function call be used as an actual value parameter? Explain.

16. Can a function call be used as an actual VAR parameter? Explain.

17. Are functions strictly necessary? Are there programs that can not be written without functions? Justify your answer.

18. Some programmers try not to use functions, and others try to use them every time any output is returned from a subprogram. What style of function use is advocated in this chapter?

19. If you were writing a subprogram that returned one output, would you use a function or a procedure? Why?

20. If you were writing a subprogram that returned two or more outputs, would you use a function or procedure? Why?

21. If you were writing a subprogram that returned no output, would you use a function or procedure? Why?

22. Can a Pascal function syntactically have VAR parameters?

23. Does our style of function use permit functions to have VAR parameters?

24. What is at least one reason against using functions with VAR parameters?

25. What is a subprogram stub?

26. What does the practice of programming with stubs involve?

27. What is one benefit of using stubs?

10.8.2. Exercises

1. What is wrong with the following function?

```
FUNCTION Test (x: REAL): REAL;

BEGIN
    IF x < 25.0
        THEN x := 0.0
        ELSE x := 100.0;
    WRITELN(OUTPUT, x)
END;    (* Test *)
```

2. What does the following function do?

```
FUNCTION Check: BOOLEAN;

VAR
    ch: CHAR;

BEGIN
    WRITE(OUTPUT, 'Enter a vowel --> ');
    READLN(INPUT, ch);
    IF (ch = 'a') OR (ch = 'e') OR (ch = 'i') OR (ch = 'o') OR (ch = 'u')
        THEN Check := TRUE
END;    (* Check *)
```

3. What is wrong with the following function?

```
FUNCTION GetVal: INTEGER;

BEGIN
    WRITE(OUTPUT, 'Enter an integer --> ');
    READLN(INPUT, GetVal)
END;    (* GetVal *)
```

4. Is the following function valid? If not, why not? If so, what else might be wrong with its style?

```
FUNCTION IsItSmall: BOOLEAN;

VAR
    x: REAL;

BEGIN
    WRITE(OUTPUT, 'Enter a number ');
    READLN(INPUT, x);
    IsItSmall := x < 0
END;    (* IsItSmall *)
```

5. What output does the following program produce?

```
PROGRAM FoolEm (INPUT, OUTPUT);

VAR
    letter: CHAR;


FUNCTION Capital (letter: CHAR): CHAR;

CONST
    CaseDifference = 32;
                        (* difference between upper and lower case in ASCII *)

BEGIN
    IF (letter >= 'a') AND (letter <= 'z')
        THEN Capital := CHAR( ORD(letter) - CaseDifference )
END;    (* Capital *)


BEGIN
    letter := 'e';
    WRITELN(OUTPUT, letter);
    letter := Capital(letter);
    WRITELN(OUTPUT, letter)
END.
```

10.8.3. Problems

1. Write a function **Even** that takes one INTEGER and returns TRUE if the input is even, and FALSE otherwise.

2. Write a function **Abs** that takes an INTEGER and returns its absolute value.

3. Write a BOOLEAN function that takes a REAL and returns TRUE if it is negative, and FALSE otherwise.

4. Write a function **Max** that takes two integer values and returns the larger.

5. Modify the **Max** function so that it is a **Min** funcion instead.

6. Write a function that takes a temperature in degrees Celsius and returns the equivalent temperature in degrees Fahrenheit. Make input and returned values of type REAL.

7. Write a function that takes a temperature in degrees Fahrenheit and returns the equivalent temperature in degrees Celsius. Make input and returned values of type REAL.

8. Write a BOOLEAN function that takes an INTEGER as a parameter and returns TRUE if the integer is prime, and FALSE otherwise.

9. Write a function that takes two integers (beginning and ending page numbers) as parameters and returns the number of pages that are between them (inclusive).
Example: input 2 and 14 returns 13.

10. Write a function **GetDigit** that prompts the user for a digit [0...9] and returns the first valid digit entered. Reprompt if necessary.

11. Write a function that takes a character as a parameter and evaluates to the character unless its input is in lowercase, in which event it evaluates to the uppercase equivalent.

Example: f('a') = 'A', f('A') = 'A', f(';') = ';'

12. Write a BOOLEAN function that asks the user a yes/no question and returns TRUE if the user answers no and FALSE if the user answers yes.

13. Write a BOOLEAN function that takes two REALs and evaluates to TRUE if the first is less than the second and FALSE otherwise.

14. Write a CHARacter-valued function that takes an INTEGER as input and returns the appropriate letter grade. Assume A: 90-100 , B: 80-89, C: 70-79, D: 60-69, F: 59 or less. Return Z if out of range 0-100.

10.9. Chapter Summary

- Pascal has two classes of subprograms: procedures and functions.

- A function may be viewed as a machine that takes one or more inputs and produces an output.

- The set of valid inputs to a function is the function's *domain*.

- The set of possible outputs of a function is the function's *range*.

- An operator is just a function, and operands are just the inputs to the function.

- Functions are declared just like procedures, except they are denoted with the reserved word FUNCTION rather than PROCEDURE, and a type for the function must be declared.

- Functions are called like procedures (by name and with an actual parameter list). However, Pascal function calls are expressions, and procedure calls are statements.

- A predefined subprogram need not be declared to be used. Pascal has a variety of predefined subprograms. See the appendices for a summary of the predefined subprograms in Standard Pascal.

- A Pascal function call may be used *in* a statement but not *as* a statement. All Pascal function calls must be used as expressions.

- A programmer can create new functions.

- A function declaration may have formal parameters. It may also have local declarations.

- A Pascal function gets a value by explicitly assigning a value to the name of the function within the body of the function. *Every function declaration must contain an assignment to the function name.*

- A function declaration is not required to have formal parameters. However, if it has no parameters, input must be gotten from the user.

- A function call can be used as an actual value parameter since any expression is an acceptable value parameter.

- A function call cannot be used as an actual VAR parameter since VAR parameters must always be variables.

- Functions are not strictly necessary. Every program that is written with the use of functions could be written without functions. Every Pascal function can be rewritten as a procedure with an extra VAR parameter.

- A subprogram stub is just an incomplete subprogram (a formal parameter list but little more) that permits the program to be run before its details have been completed.

- *Programming with stubs* refers to implementing programs with the use of stubs. The primary benefit of this strategy is the option to test a program continually during its implementation.

10.10. Summary of Style

- It is considered poor programming practice to mix calculations with either input or output. Normally, each is handled by a separate subprogram.

- Some programmers try not to use functions, and others try to use them every time any output is returned from a subprogram. We advocate using functions only when exactly one output is to be returned. If a subprogram returns more than one or no outputs, we normally use a procedure.

- Pascal functions can syntactically have VAR parameters. However, the style of function use advocated in this chapter uses only value parameters with functions. This prevents unexpected side effects.

- The structured subprogram comments described for procedures also work for functions. If you follow the style of function use advocated in this chapter, the component of the structured function comment labeled **OUTPUT** will always contain exactly one item.

10.11. Summary of Terms

- function
- function call
- function declaration

- function value
- predefined function
- subprogram stub

- domain
- range

10.12. Chapter Problems

1. The standard READ statement does not read BOOLEAN values as input. Write a function that returns a BOOLEAN value corresponding to the user's input of either an 'F' or a 'T'.

2. Extend the previous function so that it also recognizes 'f' and 't'.

3. Modify the previous function so that spaces before the desired input are ignored.

4. Write a function that determines a lottery winner's share, given the total pot and the number of winners. Assume each winner gets an equal share of the pot.

5. Write a function to calculate the euclidean distance between two points (x_1, y_1) and (x_2, y_2). *Hint: the distance is computed as the square root of* $(x_1 - x_2)^2 + (y_1 - y_2)^2$

6. Write a function that takes a date (month and day) and returns the number of the day of the year.

7. Extend the previous function to account for leap year. *Hint: You will need to add another input parameter.*

8. Write a program that takes two arbitrary dates and computes the number of days between them.

9. Write a function that computes interest, given the principal, the interest rate, and the period of investment.

10. Extend the previous function to accommodate an arbitrary number of periods. Use an integer number of periods.

11. *Write a function **UpperCase** that takes a single character as input and returns a character result. If the input is a lowercase character, the result is the uppercase equivalent. Otherwise the result is the unchanged input.

12. *Write a function **LowerCase** that returns the lowercase equivalent of its input character.

13. *Write a program that takes a date and computes which day of the week it falls on.

Chapter 11: Recursive Subprograms

Recursion is a concept that may seem a bit surprising initially because of its ability to solve a seemingly difficult problem relatively easily. Recursion is an interesting and very useful programming tool. Although some programming languages do not support recursion, Standard Pascal does. With a moderate amount of effort you can add recursion to your programming toolbox.

We have yet to see a better introduction to recursion than that provided by David Touretzky.[1] He introduces the topic with a fable. Here is the first part of that fable:

Long, long ago, before the time of computers, there were alchemists who were curious about mathematics. Since these alchemists lacked computers, they used dragons to do their work for them, but the dragons were lazy and bad tempered; the worst ones would sooner burn a man to a crisp than do a single bit of work for him. This is the story of how Martin, an alchemist's apprentice, discovered recursion by outsmarting a lazy dragon.

One day the alchemist for whom Martin worked gave him a list of numbers and told him to go down to the dungeon and ask the dragon if any of them were odd. Martin had never been to the dungeon before. He took a candle down with him and in the far corner found an old dragon, none too friendly looking. Timidly he stepped forward. He did not want to be burned to a crisp.

"What do you want?" grumped the dragon as it eyed Martin suspiciously.

"I have a list of numbers," said Martin, "and I want to know if any of them are odd. Here it is." Martin wrote the list in the dirt with his finger:

(3142 5798 6550 8914)

The dragon was in a disagreeable mood that day. In fact, being a dragon, it always was. "Sorry kid", the dragon said, "I might be willing to tell you if the *first* number is odd, but that is the best I can possibly do. Anything else would be too complicated; probably not worth my trouble."

"But I need to know if *any* number in the list is odd, not just the first number", Martin explained.

"Tough toadstools, kid. I'll only look at the first number of the list. But I'll look at as many of the lists as you'd like if you give them to me one at a time."

Martin thought for a while. There had to be a way around the dragon's orneriness. "How about the first list then?" he asked, pointing to the one he had drawn on the ground:

(3142 5798 6550 8914)

"The first number in that list is not odd," said the dragon.

Then Martin had an idea. He covered the first part of the list with his hand and drew a new left parenthesis, leaving

(5798 6550 8914)

and said, "How about this list?"

The first number in that list is not odd," the dragon replied.

Martin covered some more of the list. "How about this list then?"

(6550 8914)

---

[1]*LISP: A Gentle Introduction to Symbolic Computation*, by David S. Touretzky, copyright (c) 1984, Harper & Row.

"The first number in that list isn't odd either," said the dragon. It looked a little bored, but at least it was cooperating.

"And this one?" asked Martin.

(8914)

"Not odd."

"And this one?"

( )

"That's the empty list," the dragon snorted. "There can't be an odd number in there, because there's *nothing* in there."

"Well," said Martin, "I now know that not one of the numbers in the list the alchemist gave me is odd. They're *all* even."

"I NEVER said that!" bellowed the dragon. "I only told you about the first number in each list you showed me."

"That's true, Dragon. Shall I write down all of the lists you looked at?"

"If you wish," the dragon replied. Martin wrote in the dirt:

(3124 5798 6550 8914)
(5798 6550 8914)
(6550 8914)
(8914)
( )

"Now take the first number of each list," Martin said. "What do you get?"

"3124, 5798, 6550, 8914, and nothing for the last one."

"Don't you see?" Martin asked. "By telling me that the first element of each of those lists wasn't odd, you told me that none of the elements in my original list was odd."

"That's pretty tricky," the dragon said testily. "It looks like you've discovered recursion. But don't ask me what that means—you'll have to figure it out for yourself." And with that it closed its eyes and refused to utter another word.

This fable, although quite cute, contains the essence of recursion. A recursive solution to a problem has two elements: the ability to rephrase problems as simpler problems of the same type, and the solution to the most elemental of the same type of problem. The fable contained both of these elements. The problem was to determine if there are any odd numbers in an entire list of numbers. Martin's solution utilized the dragon's ability to determine if a list with exactly one number contains any odd numbers. His solution also used a somewhat clever way of rephrasing the problem. All recursive solutions exhibit these two elements.

11.1. Recursive Functions

Consider the problem of adding two numbers. Assume we must write a program to add two integers, but we cannot use any looping constructs. Also assume we can only add 1 to or subtract 1 from any value. The only programming features we can use are conditional statements and subprograms. Is it possible to write a program to add two integers with these restrictions? Although you might be thinking no, the answer is yes. A mathematician named Peano [11] actually defined ordinary arithmetic in such terms. This definition of arithmetic, known as Peano's axioms, provides the following example that should help you to understand recursive subprograms.

Can you build a program that is capable of adding two arbitrary nonnegative integers? One reasonable design of such a program might have three modules, one to get two integers from the user, one to actually add the two integers, and one to display the result. You might refer to them as *get integers*, *add two integers*, and *display results*, respectively. This decomposition can be illustrated with the solution tree in Figure 11-1:

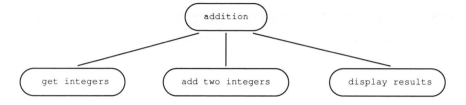

Figure 11-1: Decomposition of the Addition Problem

Although all three subproblems are simple enough to directly implement as Pascal subprograms, we turn our attention to the addition subprogram first and the other two last. We want a subprogram to take two integers as input and return an integer result. We therefore want a function with two value parameters. The two numbers to be added are called **addend** and **augend**, as is illustrated in the following subprogram stub:

```
FUNCTION Add (addend, augend: INTEGER): INTEGER;

BEGIN



END;    (* Add *)
```

Programming Example 11-1: Add Subprogram Stub

The subprogram has two integer value parameters for its two inputs and is an integer function for the output value. If we could use the INTEGER operators fully, we would simply complete the function as follows:

```
FUNCTION Add (addend, augend: INTEGER): INTEGER;

BEGIN

    Add := addend + augend

END;    (* Add *)
```

Programming Example 11-2: Add Using INTEGER + Operator

Recall that the problem statement restricted the use to only adding or subtracting 1. Therefore, we must complete the solution in a different way. Remember that a recursive solution utilizes the solution to the most elemental of the same type of problem. The most elemental addition problem is one in which one of the two numbers is zero. The sum of zero and any other number is always the other number. Therefore, if the **addend** is zero the sum is simply the value of **augend**. This fact is reflected in the following function declaration:

```
FUNCTION Add (addend, augend: INTEGER): INTEGER;

BEGIN
    IF addend = 0
        THEN Add := augend
END;    (* Add *)
```

Programming Example 11-3: Add for the Simplest Case

This previous function works fine if **addend** equals 0. However, it does not work if **addend** has any other value. What we need is an ELSE clause for when the **addend** is not zero. You may gain insight into what to do for the ELSE clause by considering an analogy to the original problem.

Consider the task of adding two integers as analogous to the task of combining two stacks of poker chips. Our first solution represented placing one stack directly on top of the other. Our second solution is that if one stack is empty (0 chips), the combined stack is just the other (nonzero) stack. But what if both are nonzero stacks? In that case we remove one chip from one of the stacks and add it to the other stack. We keep moving one chip at a time until the one stack is gone. At that point both stacks are combined into one.

If **addend** is 0, then the sum of **addend** and **augend** is just **augend**. Otherwise, we reduce **addend** by 1, increase **augend** by 1, and combine **addend-1** with **augend+1**. This is reflected in the following solution:

```
FUNCTION Add (addend, augend : INTEGER): INTEGER;

BEGIN
    IF addend = 0
        THEN Add := augend
        ELSE Add := Add(addend-1, augend+1)
END;    (* Add *);
```

Programming Example 11-4:   Add Written Recursively

Take a close look at the previous function declaration. The function takes two integers as input and returns an integer as output. The body of the function is really quite brief. In fact, the body consists of only one statement. Be sure you understand this one statement!

If the value of **addend** is equal to zero, we have the most elemental type of addition. In this case the sum of **addend** and **augend** is simply the value of **augend**. This is indicated by assigning the value of **augend** as the return value of the function **(Add := augend)**.

If the value of **addend** is not equal to zero, we do not have the simplest case. In such a case, the problem is rephrased. In this case, the sum of addend and augend is the sum of **addend-1** and **augend+1**. This is indicated by another function call **(Add := Add(addend-1, augend+1))**. Note that the function calls itself. Such a function call is called a *recursive* function call.

You might be saying to yourself that it doesn't seem like the function is really computing anything. If the one value is zero, then the problem is simple and the other value is returned. Otherwise, we say the answer is just the sum of an equivalent problem. But this is the beauty of recursion. Solve only the simplest case. Rephrase all other problems as equivalent problems. Eventually the problem is rephrased in terms of the simplest case, and the original problem is solved. In our function **Add**, the value of **addend** is reduced by 1 every function call. Eventually, **addend** will equal zero, and therefore will be rephrased in terms of the simplest case.

Suppose the function **Add** is called with actual parameters *2* and *4* being bound to the formal parameters **addend** and **augend**, respectively. We have added a WRITELN as the first statement of the function **Add** for tracing purposes only.

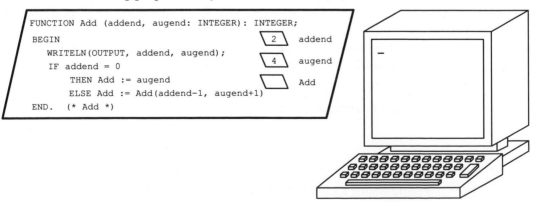

After the WRITELN statement executes, output appears on the terminal screen.

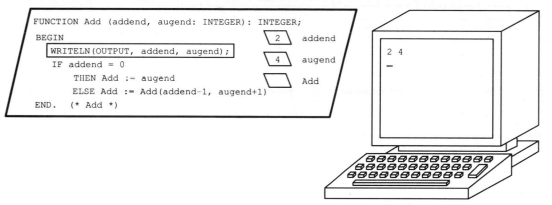

Since the addend is not equal to zero, the function **Add** is called again. This is a recursive function call since it is calling itself. The stack of plates indicates this recursion since the same function is on both plates.

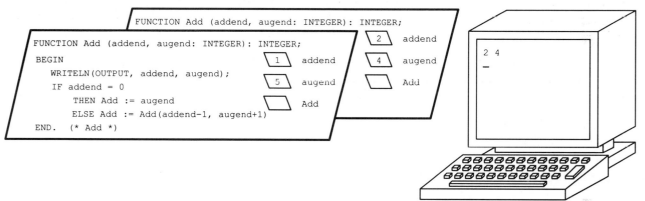

Again the WRITELN sends output to the terminal screen.

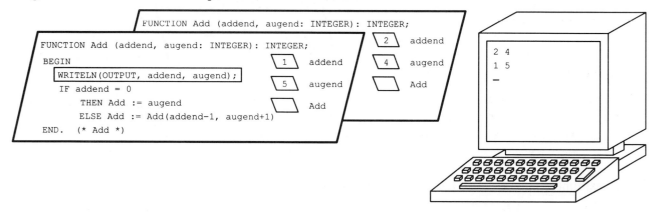

Since **addend** is not equal to zero, the function **Add** is called again, recursively.

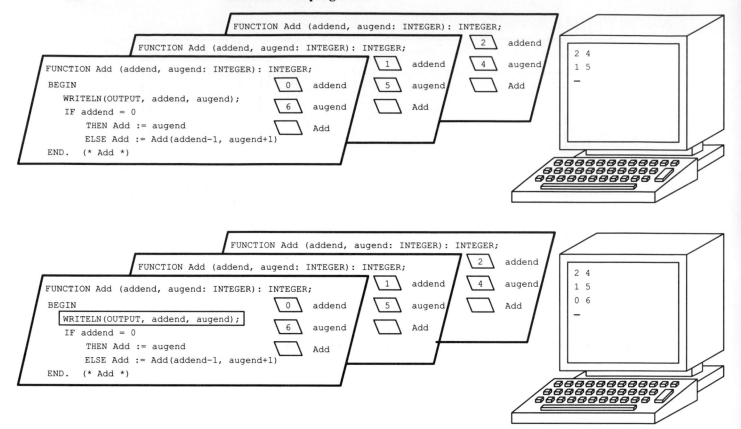

This time **addend** is equal to zero. Therefore, we have the simplest case of addition. The value of the function is simply assigned the value of **augend**, which is 6.

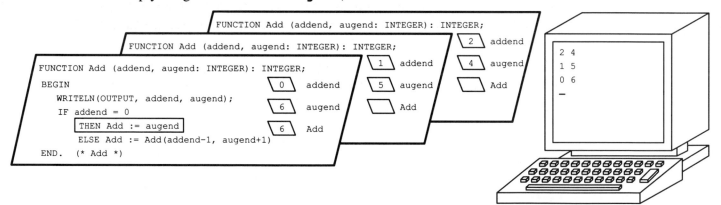

The last function to be called terminates, returning its value, 6.

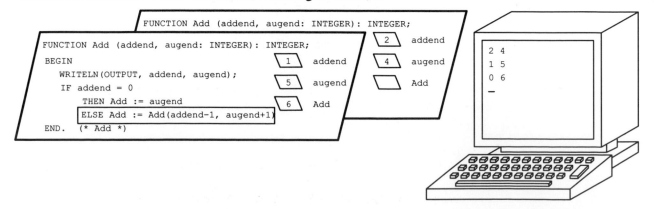

Again the top function terminates, returning its value. And finally, the remaining function terminates.

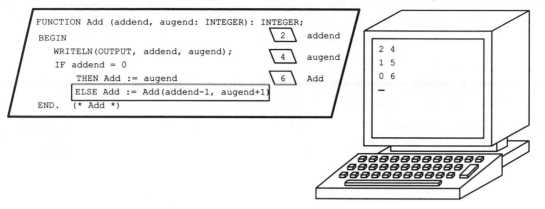

It is important that you understand the action taking place here. A call is made to the function **Add** with **addend** equal to 2 and **augend** equal to 4. Since 2 is not equal to 0, the function **Add** is suspended, and another function is called to add 1 and 5. The function called is also function **Add**. When a function calls itself, it is referred to as a recursive function call. Since 1 is still not equal to 0, the function **Add** is again called. When called to add 0 and 6, the result is just the second value, namely, 6. This result is returned by the function.

Essentially, the problem is rephrased until it is phrased in terms of the simplest case. In the process, the function must call itself every time the problem is rephrased. A subprogram that calls itself is known as a **recursive subprogram**.

Definition 11-1: A *recursive subprogram* is a subprogram that calls itself in its own definition.

To be sure that you understand how this works, rewrite the **Add** function. Move the WRITELN statement so that it follows the IF-THEN-ELSE. Simulate the execution again with actual parameters of 2 and 4. Exactly what is the output of the program?

Now, we should turn our attention to the display module. This module should display both the sum and the **addend** and **augend**. The appropriate Pascal tool to implement this module is the procedure.

```
PROCEDURE Display (addend, augend, sum: INTEGER);

    (* *****************************************************************

    * DESCRIPTION:
            Procedure Display writes to the terminal an addend, an augend
            and their sum.

    * METHOD:
            This procedure takes as input the addend, the augend and their
            sum.  It displays all three on a new line of the terminal with the
            WRITELN statement.  Nothing is computed by this procedure

    * INPUT:
            addend:      addend to be displayed
            augend:      augend to be displayed
            sum:         sum to be displayed

    **************************************************************** *)


BEGIN
    WRITELN(OUTPUT);
    WRITELN(OUTPUT,
      'The sum of ', addend:1, ' and ', augend:1, ' is: ', sum:2)
END     (* Display *);
```

Programming Example 11-5: Procedure **Display**

The procedure **Display** is simpler than the function **Add**, in that it makes no calls to other user-defined procedures or functions. **Display** simply executes the body of the procedure sequentially. The formal parameters of **Display** are value parameters. This is not by accident. Since **Display** must have information on the addend, augend, and their sum, it must have three parameters. Since the values of these parameters are not to change, **call-by-value** parameters are the correct choice.

Finally, consider a module to obtain integers from the user, which we call *get integers*. The following subprogram is a reasonable choice for this module:

```
FUNCTION GetInt: INTEGER;

    (* ********************************************************************

     * DESCRIPTION:
            Procedure GetInt prompts the user for and returns an INTEGER.

     * METHOD:
            The user is prompted for a non-negative integer.  The entered
            value is returned by the function regardless of its sign.

    ******************************************************************** *)


CONST
    prompt = 'Please input a non-negative integer: ';

VAR
    int: INTEGER;


BEGIN
    WRITE(OUTPUT, prompt);
    READLN(INPUT, int);
    GetInt := int
END;     (* GetInt *)
```

Programming Example 11-6:   Function **GetInt**

Again, the function is the best choice. The function interacts with the user, evaluating to an integer. Obviously the function will be called twice to supply the necessary parameters. It turns out that **GetInt** is not the best choice to supply arguments for the function **Add** because the user could type in a negative value for the addend. When a negative actual parameter is bound to the first formal parameter of **Add**, something very bad happens. The parameter **addend** starts out less than 0. When a test for the equality of the parameter and 0 fails, the parameter is decremented. For every pass of this scheme, the addend is decremented, thereby making it more negative and further from zero. Therefore, the parameter addend will never equal 0! This situation is referred to as *infinite recursion* and is to be avoided. A better choice for getting these values is **GoodInt**:

```
FUNCTION GoodInt: INTEGER;

    (* ************************************************************************

     * DESCRIPTION:
             Procedure GetInt prompts the user for and returns an INTEGER.

     * METHOD:
             The user is prompted for a non-negative integer, and reprompted
             until the entered value is greater than or equal to 0, at which
             time the non-negative integer is returned.  Prompting is
             controlled by a REPEAT-UNTIL loop.

    ************************************************************************ *)


CONST
    prompt = 'Please input a non-negative integer: ';

VAR
    int: INTEGER;

BEGIN
    REPEAT
        WRITE(OUTPUT, prompt);
        READLN(INPUT, int)
    UNTIL int >= 0;
    GoodInt := int
END;    (* GoodInt *)
```

Programming Example 11-7: Function **GoodInt**

Notice that the function **GoodInt** ensures that input for **Add** will enable **Add** to terminate. We see that this simple change made the program more robust. The comments correctly reflect this increase in robustness.

The main execution block of this program looks the following way:

```
BEGIN
    addend := GoodInt;
    augend := GoodInt;
    sum := Add(addend, augend);
    Display(addend, augend, sum)
END.  (* Main Program *)
```

Programming Example 11-8: **Addition** Main Program

To understand the program, consider the entire program, including the use of **GlobalFilter**. We have eliminated the comments so that you can see the entire program on a single page:

```
PROGRAM Addition (INPUT, OUTPUT);


FUNCTION GoodInt: INTEGER;

CONST
    prompt = 'Please input a non-negative integer: ';

VAR
    int: INTEGER;

BEGIN
    REPEAT
        WRITE(OUTPUT, prompt);
        READLN(INPUT, int)
    UNTIL int >= 0;
    GoodInt := int
END;     (* GoodInt *)



FUNCTION Add (addend, augend : INTEGER): INTEGER;

BEGIN
    IF addend = 0
        THEN Add := augend
        ELSE Add := Add(addend-1, augend+1)
END;     (* Add *);



PROCEDURE Display (addend, augend, sum: INTEGER);

BEGIN
    WRITELN(OUTPUT);
    WRITELN(OUTPUT,
      'The sum of ', addend:1, ' and ', augend:1, ' is: ', sum:2)
END     (* Display *);



PROCEDURE GlobalFilter;

VAR
    addend, augend, sum: INTEGER;

BEGIN
    addend := GoodInt;
    augend := GoodInt;
    sum := Add(addend, augend);
    Display(addend, augend, sum)
END;     (* GlobalFilter *)



BEGIN
    GlobalFilter
END.  (* Main Program *)
```

Programming Example 11-9: Addition Entire Program

Recall the fable of Martin and the dragon. You now know enough to write a Pascal function that computes Martin's function.

Assume a sequence of integers have been entered by the user. The numbers are separated by spaces and terminated with an end-of-line marker. Write a BOOLEAN function that evaluates to TRUE if one or more of the entered integers is odd and writes FALSE otherwise. If we are at the end of the input, EOLN returns TRUE, and the function should return FALSE. This is indicated in the following function declaration:

```
FUNCTION AnyOddInteger: BOOLEAN;

BEGIN
    IF EOLN(INPUT)
        THEN AnyOddInteger := FALSE


END;      (* AnyOddInteger *)
```

Programming Example 11-10: Function **AnyOddInteger**

What do we do if the INPUT tape contains unread numbers? Essentially we do as the dragon in the fable did. Look only at the first number. Therefore, we must read a number from the input tape. If the number is odd, we know the list contains at least one odd number and must return TRUE as the function value. This is indicated in the following declaration:

```
FUNCTION AnyOddInteger: BOOLEAN;

VAR
    number: INTEGER;

BEGIN
    IF EOLN(INPUT)
        THEN AnyOddInteger := FALSE
        ELSE BEGIN
                READ(INPUT, number);
                IF Odd(number)
                    THEN AnyOddInteger := TRUE

            END
END;      (* AnyOddInteger *)
```

Programming Example 11-11: Function **AnyOddInteger** Nearly Done

If the first number is not odd, we simply call the function on the remaining list. This recursive call is indicated in the following declaration:

```
FUNCTION AnyOddInteger: BOOLEAN;

VAR
    number: INTEGER;

BEGIN
    IF EOLN(INPUT)
        THEN AnyOddInteger := FALSE
        ELSE BEGIN
                READ(INPUT, number);
                IF Odd(number)
                    THEN AnyOddInteger := TRUE
                    ELSE AnyOddInteger := AnyOddInteger
            END
END;      (* AnyOddInteger *)
```

Programming Example 11-12: Function **AnyOddInteger** Done

Notice the ELSE clause in this function declaration. Since the function **AnyOddInteger** calls itself, it is a recursive function.

11.2. Recursive Procedures

Both types of Pascal's subprograms may be recursive; Pascal has recursive procedures as well as recursive functions. A recursive procedure is just a procedure that calls itself. To illustrate recursive procedures, let us consider another example. Assume we want to create a subprogram to print triangles of asterisks in the following form:

```
******
*****
****
***
**
*
```

Figure 11-2: A Triangle of Asterisks

The triangle is simply a collection of rows of asterisks, each row having one fewer asterisks than the one above it. The size of the triangle is simply the number of rows in the triangle.

Consider how we might create a recursive solution to this problem. Recall what is necessary for recursion: a solution to the simplest case and the ability to rephrase a problem as a simpler problem of the same type. The simplest case is a triangle of size 0. In general we can print such a triangle by printing one horizontal line of the triangle and then print another triangle below it, one smaller in size. If we use the **PrintLine** procedure we created earlier, the following procedure will correctly print a triangle of arbitrary size:

```
PROCEDURE PrintTriangle ( size: INTEGER );

BEGIN
    IF size > 0
        THEN BEGIN
                PrintLine(size);
                PrintTriangle(size-1)
            END
END;     (* PrintTriangle *)
```

Programming Example 11-13: Recursive Procedure **PrintTriangle**

Note how brief the procedure **PrintTriangle** is. It is just one IF statement. In order to print a triangle, we simply print one line and then print a triangle one size smaller below it. This illustrates the very essence of recursion, rephrasing the problem as a smaller problem of the same type. Consider a triangle size of 3.

The first illustration shows the initial situation.

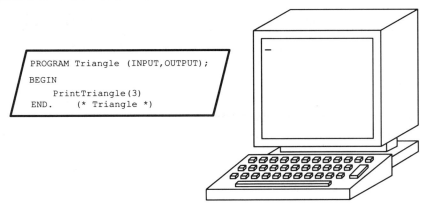

The second illustration shows the procedure **PrintTriangle** being called with a size of 3.

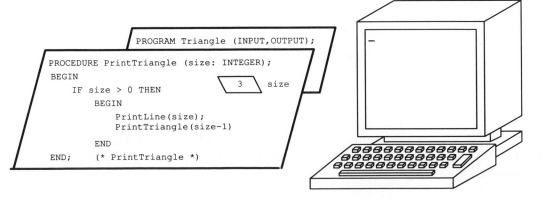

The next illustration shows execution of the conditional statement. The variable **size** has the value 3 and is therefore greater than 0; hence, the procedure **PrintLine** gets called.

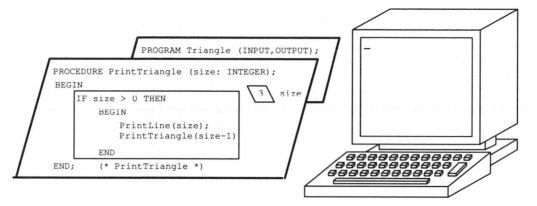

PrintLine is called with a length of 3.

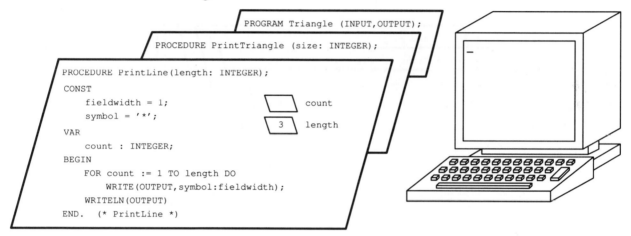

In the interest of brevity, we will not show the entire trace of every step of the procedure **PrintLine**. After procedure **PrintLine** finishes, there is a horizontal line of 3 asterisks written to the output screen.

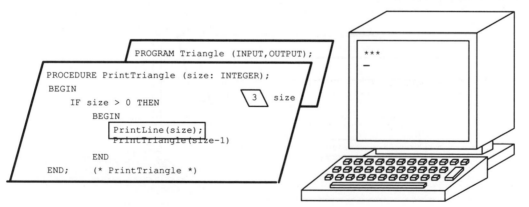

Next the procedure **PrintTriangle** is called with the value 2. Note it is calling itself. Hence it is a recursive procedure. You can see this graphically by the fact that the last two subprograms on the stack are both labeled "PROCEDURE PrintTriangle."

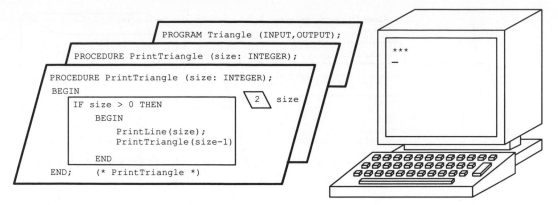

```
PROGRAM Triangle (INPUT,OUTPUT);

    PROCEDURE PrintTriangle (size: INTEGER);

    PROCEDURE PrintTriangle (size: INTEGER);
    BEGIN
        IF size > 0 THEN
            BEGIN
                PrintLine(size);
                PrintTriangle(size-1)
            END
    END;     (* PrintTriangle *)
```

2 size

Since **size** has a value of 2, which is greater than 0, the procedure **PrintLine** is called.

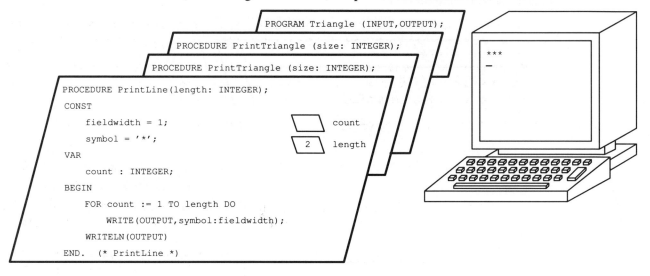

```
PROGRAM Triangle (INPUT,OUTPUT);

    PROCEDURE PrintTriangle (size: INTEGER);

        PROCEDURE PrintTriangle (size: INTEGER);

PROCEDURE PrintLine(length: INTEGER);
CONST
    fieldwidth = 1;
    symbol = '*';
VAR
    count : INTEGER;
BEGIN
    FOR count := 1 TO length DO
        WRITE(OUTPUT,symbol:fieldwidth);
    WRITELN(OUTPUT)
END.    (* PrintLine *)
```

count

2 length

Procedure **PrintLine** is called with the value 2.   After **PrintLine** terminates, there is a line of 2 asterisks on the output screen.

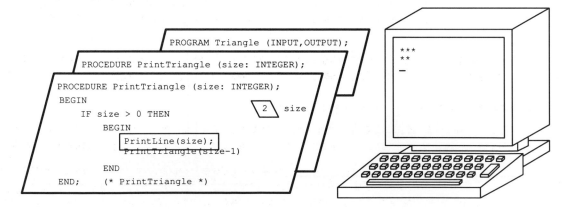

```
PROGRAM Triangle (INPUT,OUTPUT);

    PROCEDURE PrintTriangle (size: INTEGER);

    PROCEDURE PrintTriangle (size: INTEGER);
    BEGIN
        IF size > 0 THEN
            BEGIN
                PrintLine(size);
                PrintTriangle(size-1)
            END
    END;     (* PrintTriangle *)
```

2 size

Next the procedure **PrintTriangle** is called again.   This time it is called with a value of 1.   Note that there are now 3 subprograms on the stack with the name **PrintTriangle**.

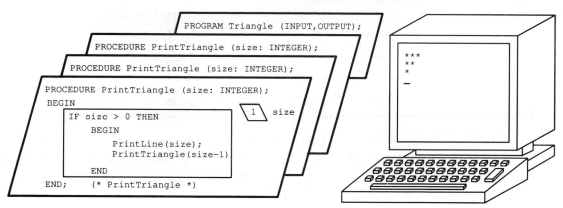

Since the value of **size** is 1, which is still greater than 0, the procedure **PrintLine** is called. It is called with the value 1.

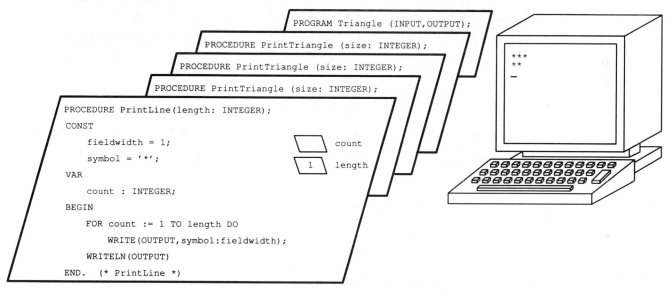

When **PrintLine** terminates, another line has been written on the output screen.

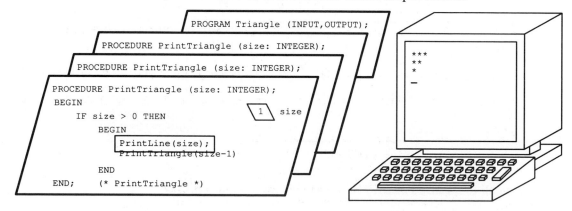

Next the procedure **PrintTriangle** is again called. This time it is called with the value of 0. Note there are four subprograms on the stack with the name **PrintTriangle**.

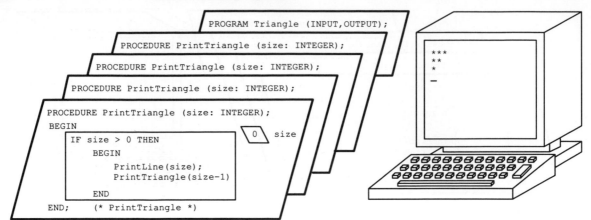

The value of **size** is 0. Since the value of **size** is not greater than 0, the THEN clause is not executed. The procedure call to **PrintTriangle** with value 0 is completed. Note that the next illustration has the last procedure call removed from the stack.

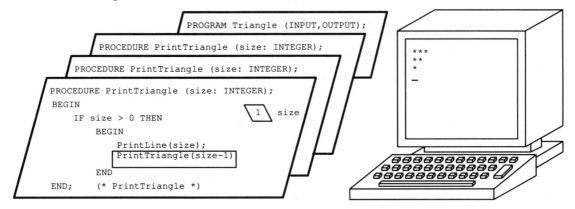

The procedure call to **PrintTriangle** with value 1 is completed.

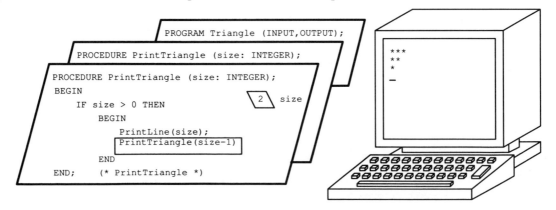

The procedure call to **PrintTriangle** with value 2 is completed.

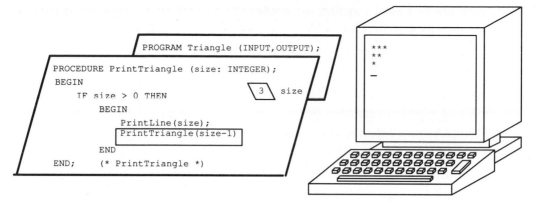

The procedure call to **PrintTriangle** with value 3 is completed.

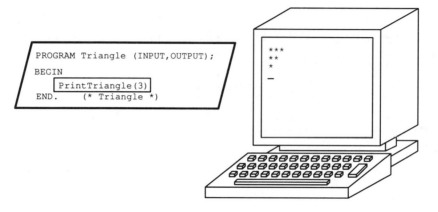

As these illustrations demonstrate, recursive subprograms are simple but elegant. Remember the rules of simplist case and rephrasing. They will serve you well.

11.2.1. Questions

1. What are the two necessary elements of a recursive solution?

2. Briefly describe recursion as a means of solving problems.

3. What is a recursive subprogram?

4. Does Pascal support recursive subprograms? Both recursive functions and recursive procedures?

5. What is infinite recursion?

11.2.2. Exercises

1. We illustrated the function call **Add(2,4)** in a very detailed fashion. What would the output be for the function call **Add(4,2)**?

2. Move the extra WRITELN in the function **Add** to the last statement instead of the first statement. What would the output be for the function call **Add(2,4)**?

3. What would the output be for the modified **Add** function for the call **Add(4,2)**?

11.2.3. Problems

1. The recursive function **Add** shown in this chapter works fine if the addend is nonnegative. If the addend is negative, the result is infinite recursion. Modify the function **Add** to also handle a negative addend. Use only the programming features used thus far.

2. Modify the function for the previous problem so that it handles a negative augend also. What must be changed?

3. Write a recursive Pascal function to subtract one integer from another. Assume both integers are nonnegative.

4. Extend the function in the previous problem to handle negative inputs.

5. Write a function that recursively computes factorials.
   *Note: Factorial(n) = n * Factorial(n-1) and Factorial(1) = 1.*

6. Write a function that recursively computes Fibonacci numbers.
   Note: Fibonacci(n) = Fibonacci(n-1) + Fibonacci(n-2)
   Fibonacci(1) = 1, Fibonacci(2) = 1.

7. * Write a function, **Mult**, that multiplies two nonnegative integers using **Add** as the only primitive. This function should take only two parameters.

8. * Write a function, **Divide**, that divides a larger nonnegative integer by a smaller nonnegative integer. It should use only the previous subtract function and adding or subtracting one.

9. *** Write a recursive procedure to print Pascal's triangle.

11.3. Chapter Summary

- Recursion is a very useful method of problem solving.

- A recursive solution utilizes two elements: the ability to rephrase a problem as simpler problems of the same type, and a solution to the simplest problem of this type.

- Essentially, a recursive solution keeps rephrasing a problem until it is completely phrased in terms of the simplest such problem.

- A recursive subprogram is a subprogram that calls itself in its own definition.

- When a subprogram calls itself without terminating, it is called infinite recursion.

- Although not all programming languages permit recursive subprograms, many do. Standard Pascal does.

- Standard Pascal supports both recursive functions and recursive procedures.

11.4. Summary of Terms

- recursion
- recursive subprogram
- recursive function call
- recursive procedure call
- infinite recursion

UNIT IV: User-Defined Types

Chapter 12: Simple Types

Chapter 13: Structured External Types

Chapter 14: Arrays

Chapter 15: Records and Sets

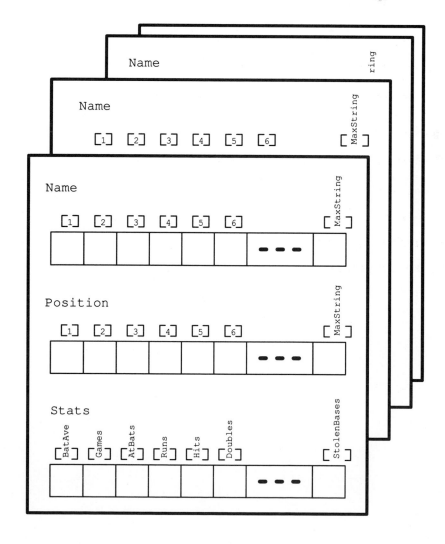

Chapter 12: Simple Types

Thus far, we have seen four Pascal types: INTEGER, REAL, CHAR, and BOOLEAN. However, Pascal has a variety of other types. The following diagram shows thc Pascal types we have reviewed and the ones we will cover in this unit.

The above diagram is similar to the overview maps seen in many parks and tourist areas. Our tour of Pascal's other types will include *enumerated* types and *subrange* types in this chapter, *TEXT* and *FILE* types in the next chapter, *ARRAY* types in the third chapter of this unit, and *RECORD* and *SET* types in the final chapter of this unit. We begin our study of the remainder of Pascal's types with an example.

12.1. The Need for Other Types

The manufacture and sale of automobiles is a very competitive business. Auto manufacturers recognize the need to accommodate consumers' preferences. Among the things that are important to the sale of an automobile is the match between the exterior and interior colors.

One manufacturer offers exterior colors in red, yellow, and blue and interior colors in white, pink, red, orange, yellow, violet, blue, aqua, and black. The manufacturer has used marketing research to determine the color combinations preferred by the driving public. Assume that the public prefers the following color combinations:

Exterior Color	Interior Colors
red	white, black, violet, pink
yellow	orange, black, aqua, white
blue	white, black, aqua, yellow

Table 12-1: Interior/Exterior Color Combinations

The automobile manufacturer needs a little computerized assistance. We must write a BOOLEAN-valued function that takes an exterior color and an interior color as input. The function should return TRUE if the interior color and the exterior color are a desirable color combination; it should return FALSE otherwise.

First, consider this function's declaration. The function declaration has two value parameters: one for the exterior color and one for the interior color. The function's type is BOOLEAN, as indicated in the following declaration:

```
FUNCTION ColorCoordinated (ExteriorColor, InteriorColor: INTEGER): BOOLEAN;

BEGIN

END;    (* ColorCoordinated *)
```

Programming Example 12-1: Declaration of Function `ColorCoordinated`

Notice that the value parameters `InteriorColor` and `ExteriorColor` are declared of type INTEGER. Assuming that we must choose a type from INTEGER, REAL, BOOLEAN, and CHAR, INTEGER seems as good as any. However, it would be better if Pascal had a type for colors.

In order to represent colors as integers, we must establish a correspondence between each color and a distinct integer. For the 9 colors in this problem we choose the integers 1 through 9, as indicated in the following table:

Color	INTEGER
white	1
pink	2
red	3
orange	4
yellow	5
violet	6
blue	7
aqua	8
black	9

Table 12-2: Color/Integer Correspondence

Although each distinct color must correspond to a distinct integer for such a representation to work, the correspondence illustrated above is only one possibility. With a color/INTEGER correspondence established, and a list of acceptable interior/exterior color combinations given, we can now complete the function **ColorCoordinated**. One possible solution is as follows:

```
FUNCTION ColorCoordinated (ExteriorColor, InteriorColor: INTEGER): BOOLEAN;

BEGIN
    ColorCoordinated := FALSE;

    IF ExteriorColor = 3
        THEN
            ColorCoordinated := (InteriorColor = 1) OR
                                (InteriorColor = 9) OR
                                (InteriorColor = 6) OR
                                (InteriorColor = 2);

    IF ExteriorColor = 5
        THEN
            ColorCoordinated := (InteriorColor = 4) OR
                                (InteriorColor = 9) OR
                                (InteriorColor = 8) OR
                                (InteriorColor = 1);

    IF ExteriorColor = 7
        THEN
            ColorCoordinated := (InteriorColor = 1) OR
                                (InteriorColor = 9) OR
                                (InteriorColor = 8) OR
                                (InteriorColor = 5);

END;    (* ColorCoordinated *)
```

Programming Example 12-2: Completed Declaration of Function **ColorCoordinated**

The three IF statements correspond to the three exterior colors in the table of consumer preferences. The very first statement gives the function a value, in case the exterior color parameter is not red, yellow, or blue (3, 5, and 7, respectively).

We know from the acceptable color combinations listed earlier that a car with a red exterior should have either a white, black, violet, or pink interior. Because red is being represented with the number 3, and the colors white, black, violet, and pink are being represented with the numbers 1, 9, 6, and 2, respectively, our first test is phrased:

```
IF ExteriorColor = 3
    THEN
        ColorCoordinated := (InteriorColor = 1) OR
                            (InteriorColor = 9) OR
                            (InteriorColor = 6) OR
                            (InteriorColor = 2);
```

Programming Example 12-3: Color Combination Test Using Integers

If the exterior color is red (3) and the interior color is either white (1), black (9), violet (6), or pink (2), then the function **ColorCoordinated** gets the value TRUE. Note that we must refer back to the color/INTEGER correspondence table in order to understand the function **ColorCoordinated**. It would be easier if we could use the colors' names instead. Then we could write the first color combination test as follows:

```
IF ExteriorColor = red
    THEN
        ColorCoordinated := (InteriorColor = white) OR
                            (InteriorColor = black) OR
                            (InteriorColor = violet) OR
                            (InteriorColor = pink);
```

Programming Example 12-4: Color Combination Test Using Color Names

Forcing the programmer to represent colors as integers puts a burden on the programmer and makes the resulting program much more difficult to read. To do away with the problems of representing colors as integers, we need a separate type to represent colors. If we had such a type, call it **ColorType**, then we could rewrite our previous function as follows:

```
FUNCTION ColorCoordinated (ExteriorColor, InteriorColor: ColorType) : BOOLEAN;

BEGIN
    ColorCoordinated := FALSE;

    IF ExteriorColor = red
        THEN
            ColorCoordinated := (InteriorColor = white) OR
                                (InteriorColor = black) OR
                                (InteriorColor = violet) OR
                                (InteriorColor = pink);

    IF ExteriorColor = yellow
        THEN
            ColorCoordinated := (InteriorColor = orange) OR
                                (InteriorColor = black) OR
                                (InteriorColor = aqua) OR
                                (InteriorColor = white);

    IF ExteriorColor = blue
        THEN
            ColorCoordinated := (InteriorColor = white) OR
                                (InteriorColor = black) OR
                                (InteriorColor = aqua) OR
                                (InteriorColor = yellow)
END;     (* ColorCoordinated *)
```

Programming Example 12-5: Function **ColorCoordinated** Rewritten Without Integers

There is no question that the second version of the function is much easier to read and understand. The problem is that Pascal knows nothing about the type we have called **ColorType** and nothing about the colors red, white, yellow, etc.

For a programming problem that deals with a group of objects, there are three possible ways to represent the objects. There may already exist a type designed to represent the current problem, such as type INTEGER is designed to represent integer numbers. Second, we might use one of the existing types to represent the desired type, even though the existing type was not designed specifically to represent the desired type. An example of this is using the type INTEGER to represent colors. Although the type INTEGER may work just fine for representing ages or salaries, we have already seen that it is pretty poor for colors. Many programming languages provide only these two ways of representing objects. However, Pascal provides a third avenue. Pascal permits the programmer to create new types as needed. A language having this property is said to be **type extensible**. Types created by the programmer are called **user-defined types**.

> **Definition 12-1:** *Type-extensible programming languages* allow the programmer to create new data types.

> **Definition 12-2:** A *user-defined type* is a type that is created by the programmer.

12.2. Defining a New Type

It is relatively easy to create a new type in Pascal. Below is all that is needed to define the type `ColorType`:

```
TYPE
    ColorType = (white, pink, red, orange, yellow, violet, blue, aqua, black);
```

Programming Example 12-6: Definition of Type `ColorType`

The definition of type is probably what you might expect. The reserved word **TYPE** indicates that we are defining a new TYPE, just as the reserved word **CONST** indicates that we are defining a named CONSTant, and the reserved word **VAR** indicates that we are declaring a VARiable. The type-definition includes the name of the type being defined (ColorType), as well as what composes the new type (white, pink, red, etc).

All user-defined types must be defined in a type definition section. In Pascal, the type definition section comes after the constant-definition section and before the variable-declaration section. The following program shell illustrates the location of the type-definition section in Pascal programs.

```
PROGRAM  <program-name> (INPUT, OUTPUT);

    <const-definitions>

    <type-definitions>

    <variable-declarations>

    <procedure and function declarations>


BEGIN
    <statement-1>;
        .
        .
        .
    <statement-n>
END.
```

Programming Example 12-7: Form of a Pascal Program with Type Definitions

As you can see, user-defined types make the language more expressive. With user-defined types, the programmer can represent more clearly both the problem and its solution with the appropriate type definitions. Proper tailoring of user-defined types makes a program very easy to read and understand. An additional benefit is that user-defined types also provide the compiler with much more information. This results in programs that execute more efficiently.

12.3. A Taxonomy of Pascal Types

One of the features that distinguishes Pascal from many of the other high-level programming languages is its approach to types. Pascal makes it easy for the programmer to build types appropriate to the problem at hand. And Pascal is very picky about being sure that types match.

The virtue of user-defined types is that they make a programming language much more powerful. They allow the programmer to define new types that meet the needs of a program. User-defined types allow the programmer to solve problems in a natural way, rather than distorting the problems to fit a predetermined collection of types.

This section is rather technical and precise. We have done this intentionally. It provides a road map for the rest of the unit. There is much material here, and it is unlikely that anyone could assimilate all of it at one reading. You will want to refer back to this section frequently as you study Pascal's types. By the end of the three chapters of this unit, you will have a firm grasp on the material of this section.

Let us first take a look at a formal specification of Pascal types. Recall that BNF is used to describe formally a programming language's features. Here are the BNF definitions for Pascal types:

```
<type definition part> ::= <empty> | TYPE <type definition> ;
        { <type definition> ; }

<type definition> ::= <identifier> = <type>

<type> ::= <simple type> | <structured type> | <pointer type>
```

The first BNF definition states that the type-definition part of a program is optional and, if present, contains the reserved word TYPE, followed by one or more type definitions, each followed with a semicolon. The second BNF definition states that a type definition is an identifier, followed by an equals sign (=), followed by a type. The last BNF states that a type is either a **simple** type, a **structured** type, or a **pointer** type. This unit will cover Pascal's simple types and structured types.

Pascal has a variety of types. One way to categorize those types is according to whether they are *predefined* or *user-defined*. The following figure classifies Pascal's types in this way.

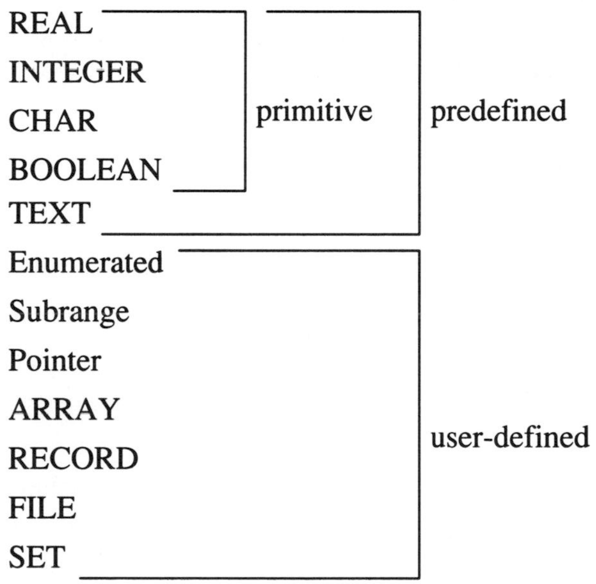

REAL
INTEGER
CHAR   primitive   predefined
BOOLEAN
TEXT

Enumerated
Subrange
Pointer
ARRAY   user-defined
RECORD
FILE
SET

Figure 12-1: Predefined and User-Defined Types

Standard Pascal has five *predefined* types. You have been writing programs using four of them for some time now. We call these four, INTEGER, REAL, CHAR and BOOLEAN, *primitive* types. The fifth predefined type, TEXT, is the subject of the next chapter. Predefined types can be used in Pascal programs without defining them.

Pascal's seven other types are *user-defined* types. All of Pascal's user-defined types must be defined by the programmer before they can be used. We will study two user-defined types, enumerated and subrange types, in this chapter. The FILE type is covered in the next chapter. The ARRAY type is presented in the third chapter of this unit. The types RECORD and SET are presented in the fourth chapter of this unit. The pointer type is covered separately in the next unit.

With as many types as Pascal has, they could be presented in a variety of orders. The following illustration is designed to help you understand why we have categorized Pascal's types the way we have.

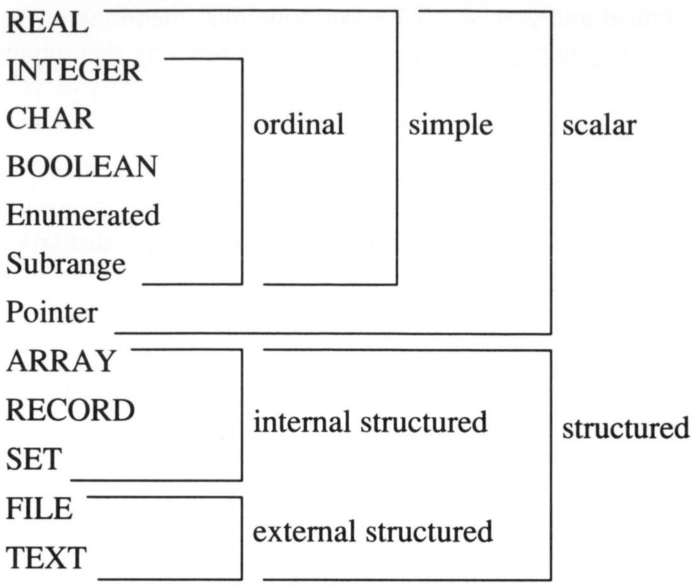

Figure 12-2: Scalar and Structured Types

This figure includes the information in the earlier BNF definition of type. A Pascal type is either a *simple* type, a *structured* type, or a *pointer* type. This figure indicates that Pascal has six simple types and five structured types, in addition to the pointer type.

The difference between simple types and structured types arises from whether the type's values are composed of smaller values. The values of a simple type are not composed of smaller values and therefore cannot be subdivided. The values of a structured type are composed of more than one smaller value and can be subdivided. We contrast these two types with the following definitions:

> **Definition 12-3:** A *simple type* is any Pascal type (other than pointer type) whose values cannot be subdivided into components.

> **Definition 12-4:** A *structured type* is any Pascal type whose values can consist of multiple components.

The pointer type is a special kind of type. However, it is not a structured type. The definition in Standard Pascal treats it differently from simple types. We use the term **scalar** type to include pointer type and all other simple types, as indicated in the following definition:

> **Definition 12-5:** *Scalar type* refers to pointer type and all other *simple* types.

Look back at Figure 12-2 and notice the difference between simple types, scalar types, and structured types. Each of the 12 types listed is either a structured type or a scalar type, but not both. Scalar types include pointer type and all simple types. Understand the differences between simple type, scalar type, and structured type.

A close look at the last figure reveals that structured types may be categorized as either **internal structured types** or **external structured types**. Do you recall from Chapter 1 the Von Neumann model of the computer? This model includes both primary and secondary storage. It turns out that the *internal—external* distinction fits this model exactly. The values of internal structured types reside in primary memory, and the values of external structured types are held in secondary storage. The two following definitions underscore this distinction.

> **Definition 12-6:** *Internal structured types* are structured Pascal types whose values reside in primary memory.

> **Definition 12-7:** *External structured types* are structured Pascal types whose values reside in secondary memory.

12.3.1. Questions

1. What are the three possible ways to represent objects in a programming language such as Pascal?

2. What is a type-extensible programming language?

3. What is a user-defined type?

4. Why would a programmer ever need a type-extensible programming language? Give a specific example.

5. Give at least two reasons for using user-defined types.

6. What is the difference between predefined types and user-defined types?

7. List Standard Pascal's five predefined types and seven user-defined types.

8. What is a simple type?

9. What is a structured type?

10. What is the difference between simple types and structured types?

11. What is a scalar type?

12. What is the difference between scalar types and simple types?

13. Name each of Standard Pascal's six simple types, seven scalar types, and five structured types.

14. What is the difference between an internal structured type and an external structured type?

15. Name Standard Pascal's three internal structured types and two external structured types.

16. We refer to the four predefined simple types in Standard Pascal as *primitive types*. Name these four types.

12.4. Enumerated Types

Recall the example we presented at the beginning of this chapter. That example defined a new type for colors, **ColorType**, as follows:

```
ColorType = (white, pink, red, orange, yellow, violet, blue, aqua, black);
```

Programming Example 12-8: Definition of Type **ColorType**

ColorType is an *enumerated* type. In Pascal it is relatively easy to define enumerated types. We need only list the values of the type within parentheses and separate them by commas. The BNF for Pascal's enumerated types is:

```
<enumerated type> ::= ( <identifier> { , <identifier> } )
```

The values of an enumerated type are the identifiers listed in its type definition. Any valid Pascal identifier can be used, except Pascal's reserved words, such as BEGIN, END, ELSE, and CASE. Let us consider another example of an enumerated type.

Assume that the elections bureau for the Philippines needs some help in correctly counting their election's votes. Suppose that you are to help write a program to tally the votes cast in the election.

For this illustration, we will assume that there is only one position to be filled, that of president. We will also assume there is only one candidate from each of three parties: Democrats, Republicans, and Libertarians. Your initial reaction might be to represent each party with an integer, say, 1 for Democrats, 2 for Republicans, and 3 for Libertarians. However, remember the problems we encountered when we represented colors with the type INTEGER. What we really need is a type to represent votes. An enumerated type works very well for this. The following type is one possible solution:

```
VoteType = (Democrat, Republican, Libertarian);
```

Programming Example 12-9: Definition of Type **VoteType**

Suppose some other programmers have already written part of the needed program. Specifically, suppose there already is a parameterless BOOLEAN function named **MoreVotes**, which returns TRUE if there are any remaining votes to be counted. There also is a parameterless function named **NextVote**, which returns a value of the enumerated type **VoteType** that corresponds to the next vote. The headers for these two functions are as follows:

```
FUNCTION MoreVotes: BOOLEAN;



FUNCTION NextVote: VoteType;
```

Programming Example 12-10: Function Headers for **MoreVotes** and **NextVote**

Your task is to write a procedure to tally the votes. Let us call this procedure **TallyVotes**. This procedure must have three variable parameters, one to return the vote count for the candidate of each of the three parties.

The procedure first initializes all three parameters to zero. Then it counts the votes inside a loop. While there are more votes to be counted, it gets the next vote and increments the appropriate candidate's count. The loop continues until all the votes are tallied. The following program fragment shows how the procedure **TalleyVotes** might look, with the other related definitions:

```
TYPE
    VoteType = (Democrat, Republican, Libertarian);


FUNCTION MoreVotes: BOOLEAN;

BEGIN

END;    (* MoreVotes *)



FUNCTION NextVote: VoteType;

BEGIN

END;    (* NextVote *)



PROCEDURE TallyVotes (VAR DemCount, RepCount, LibCount: INTEGER);

VAR
    vote: VoteType;

BEGIN
    DemCount := 0;        (* initialize count for candidates *)
    RepCount := 0;
    LibCount := 0;

    WHILE MoreVotes DO
        BEGIN
            vote := NextVote;
            CASE vote OF
                Democrat: DemCount := DemCount + 1;
                Republican: RepCount := RepCount + 1;
                Libertarian: LibCount := LibCount + 1
            END    (* CASE *)
        END    (* WHILE *)
END;    (* TallyVotes *)
```

Programming Example 12-11: Procedure **TallyVotes**

The use of the tailormade type **VoteType** makes the procedure **TallyVotes** straightforward. The three counts are initialized to zero. Each vote is taken from the function **NextVote** one at a time. When the vote is Democrat, **DemCount** is incremented; when it is Republican, **RepCount** is incremented; and when it is Libertarian, **LibCount** is incremented. Note that the function **NextVote** is of **VoteType**, the variable **vote** is of **VoteType**, and the CASE statement handles each of the values of **VoteType**.

As a point of style, notice that we chose to suffix the type identifier **VoteType** with the word *Type*. This is not required, but it is a good idea. By referring to our type definitions as *Type*, such as **VoteType** and **ColorType**, we can distinguish type identifiers from other identifiers, such as variable, constant, or subprogram identifiers.

12.4.1. One More Example

Consider another problem based on the days of the week. For representation, we again might try using the primitive type INTEGER, assigning special meaning to seven of the integers, and establishing a correspondence between the days of the week and the seven selected integers. But this leads to the same problems we encountered by representing colors with integers. What happens with the remaining INTEGER values? An INTEGER variable may have many values that do not correspond to any day of the week. Thus, using the INTEGER type for such a problem could lead to confusion. A more reasonable, and a much more readable, approach would be to define a new type specifically for the days of the week. For such problems, an enumerated type works very well. We could create the type by enumerating the days of the week, as indicated in the following type definition:

```
TYPE
    DayOfWeekType = (sunday, monday, tuesday, wednesday, thursday, friday, saturday);
```
Programming Example 12-12:   Definition of **DayOfWeekType**

Having defined the type **DayOfWeekType**, we can declare variables of this new type as indicated in the following variable declarations:

```
VAR
    today, birthday, holiday: DayOfWeekType;
```
Programming Example 12-13:   Declaring Variables of **DayOfWeekType**

With variables of the new type declared, we could use these variables as we would any other variable. The following are examples of the assignment statement:

```
BEGIN
    today := monday;
    birthday := friday;
    dayoff := saturday;
    holiday := birthday
END;
```
Programming Example 12-14:   Using Variables of **DayOfWeekType**

The first three assignment statements each give a variable of type **DayOfWeekType** a value selected from the type definition. The fourth statement assigns the value of the variable **birthday** to the variable **holiday**. In this case, **holiday** would end up with the value *friday*.

12.4.2. Order

Every enumerated type that you define has an explicit ordering associated with the type. The type definition determines the associated ordering. The relative ordering of the elements is exactly the same as their relative positions in the defining enumeration. The first value in the enumeration is also first in the associated ordering. The last value in the defining enumeration is last in the associated order. In general, if a value precedes another value in the defining enumeration, it also precedes it in the associated order. For the type **DayOfWeekType**, *monday* precedes *tuesday*, since *monday* precedes *tuesday* in the enumerated type definition. Similarly, *tuesday* precedes *wednesday*, *wednesday* precedes *thursday*, and *thursday* precedes *friday*; this precedence is due to the order in which we defined the values of the type.

There is an ordering automatically associated with every enumerated type. Although sometimes the ordering is of little interest or importance, many times the associated ordering is very important. Pascal provides several ways to take advantage of the ordering associated with enumerated types, as we will see in the next few pages.

12.4.2.1. Relational Operators

Recall the relational operators presented in Unit II to determine if values were less than or greater than each other. Pascal uses the same binary operators to determine if two values of the same enumerated type precede or follow each other. The following are TRUE for the enumerated type **DayOfWeekType**:

> monday < tuesday
> tuesday < wednesday
> monday < wednesday
> wednesday < saturday
> monday < saturday

Table 12-3: TRUE Relations Among Values of Type **DayOfWeekType**

We can use more than just the *less than* operator. Standard Pascal permits all six relational operators to be used with enumerated types. Therefore, for **DayOfWeekType** the following statements are also TRUE:

> saturday > tuesday
> monday <= wednesday
> thursday <> sunday
> friday >= monday

Table 12-4: Additional TRUE Relations for **DayOfWeekType**

12.4.2.2. Predefined Functions

Often, we are interested in what value precedes a given value in an enumerated type or, alternatively, what value follows a given value in an enumerated type. The functions **PRED** and **SUCC** are predefined in Standard Pascal to provide the *predecessor* and *successor* of a given value of an enumerated type. **PRED** takes a value of an enumerated type and returns the predecessor of the given value. Similarly, **SUCC** takes a value and returns the successor of the given value. Thus, for **DayOfWeekType** the following statements are TRUE:

SUCC(monday) = tuesday	PRED(friday) = thursday
SUCC(tuesday) = wednesday	PRED(thursday) = wednesday
SUCC(wednesday) = thursday	PRED(wednesday) = tuesday

Table 12-5: Example of **PRED** and **SUCC**

The first element of an enumeration has no predecessor, and the last element has no successor. Applying **PRED** to the first element or **SUCC** to the last element typically results in a runtime error.

Standard Pascal does not permit an identifier to be declared more than once within a given scope. In Pascal, identifiers must be declared uniquely. Therefore, an identifier may be an element of only one enumerated type. It is for this reason that there can be only one predecessor and one successor for any element of an enumerated type.

Another quite useful predefined function is the function **ORD**. The function **ORD** takes a value of an enumerated type and returns its ordinal number. Numbering starts with 0 rather than 1. The first element has an ordinal value of 0, the second element has an ordinal value of 1, the third element has an ordinal value of 2, and so on. For **DayOfWeekType**, **ORD** would evaluate as follows:

$$ORD(sunday) = 0$$
$$ORD(monday) = 1$$
$$ORD(tuesday) = 2$$
$$ORD(wednesday) = 3$$
$$ORD(thursday) = 4$$
$$ORD(friday) = 5$$
$$ORD(saturday) = 6$$

Table 12-6: Example Ordinal Values of `DayOfWeekType`

Therefore, an enumerated type with 7 elements would have ordinal values of 0 through 6.

12.4.3. Ordinal Types

We first mentioned **ordinal types** in Unit II. At that time we said three of the four primitive types—INTEGER, BOOLEAN, and CHAR—are ordinal types, but that type REAL is not. All enumerated types also qualify as ordinal types. We will see later in this chapter that all subrange types are also ordinal types. In fact, every simple type is an ordinal type except the type REAL. This can be seen graphically in Figure 12-2 on page 342.

Many people remember ordinal types as all simple types except the type REAL. Others prefer a formal definition. Sit down and take a deep breath, here is the definition of the *ordinal types*.

> **Definition 12-8:** The *ordinal types* are those types whose values can be put into one-to-one correspondence with a subset of the integers.

Recall that earlier in this chapter we created a correspondence table between colors and integers. The previous definition essentially says that for a type to be an *ordinal* type, we must be able to create such a correspondence without running out of integers. However, it is acceptable to have some unused integers. This can be done for the type INTEGER. It can also be done for type BOOLEAN. The two BOOLEAN values can correspond to any two integers, such as 0 and 1, for example. Type CHAR normally has 128 values, so we can establish a correspondence to 128 integers. Similarly, every enumerated type has such a correspondence. We can use the standard function **ORD** to establish such a correspondence.

Because there are infinitely many real numbers between every two integers, there are many more real numbers than there are integers. Hence, there are not enough integers to establish a one-to-one correspondence between integers and real numbers. The conclusion of this is that all of Pascal's simple types are ordinal types except for type REAL.

The predefined function **ORD** can be used with any ordinal type, not just with enumerated types. Similarly, the predefined functions **PRED** and **SUCC** can be used with any ordinal types.

12.4.4. Input and Output of Enumerated Types

Suppose we had a program with a variable declared of type **DayOfWeekType** and wanted the program to write out the value of the variable, call it **day**. We might be tempted to write the following Pascal statement:

```
WRITE(OUTPUT, 'Today is ', day)
```

Programming Example 12-15: Attempted Output of Enumerated Type

Although the previous output statement may seem natural, it will not work. Neither the input nor the output of enumerated types is part of Standard Pascal. This means that READ, READLN, WRITE, and WRITELN cannot be expected to work with enumerated types. Therefore, if we create an enumerated type, we must create the input and output routines to go with it. The last example could be rewritten as:

```
WRITE(OUTPUT, 'Today is ');
WriteDay(day)
```

Programming Example 12-16: Output of Enumerated Type

We would write the procedure **WriteDay** as follows:

```
PROCEDURE WriteDay (day: DayOfWeekType);

BEGIN
    CASE day OF
            monday: WRITE(OUTPUT, 'Monday');
            tuesday: WRITE(OUTPUT, 'Tuesday');
            wednesday: WRITE(OUTPUT, 'Wednesday');
            thursday: WRITE(OUTPUT, 'Thursday');
            friday: WRITE(OUTPUT, 'Friday');
            saturday: WRITE(OUTPUT, 'Saturday');
            sunday: WRITE(OUTPUT, 'Sunday')
    END    (* CASE *)
END;       (* WriteDay *)
```

Programming Example 12-17:   Procedure to Write Enumerated Type **DayOfWeekType**

If we create an enumerated type, we must create the input and output procedures to go with it.

12.4.5. Some Fine Points

12.4.5.1. Looping Through Enumerated Types

We pointed out in Unit II that variables of type REAL cannot be used as a FOR loop index variable because type REAL is not an ordinal type. However, we learned earlier in this chapter that all enumerated types are ordinal types. Therefore, a variable of an enumerated type can be used as a FOR loop index variable. The following are two such examples:

```
FOR today := monday TO friday DO
    WRITELN(OUTPUT, 'Get up and go to work!')


FOR day := sunday TO saturday DO
    process(day)
```

Programming Example 12-18:   Using Enumerated Types with FOR Loops

There are situations where the ability to loop through some or all of the elements of an enumerated type is quite handy.

Similarly, the CASE statement accommodates all ordinal types. It is often useful to use an enumerated type with a CASE statement. The following example illustrates this idea for **DayOfWeekType**:

```
CASE day OF
    friday: WRITELN(OUTPUT, 'T.G.I.F');
    monday: WRITELN(OUTPUT, 'O.S.I.M.');
    saturday, sunday: WRITELN(OUTPUT, 'weekend at last');
    tuesday, wednesday, thursday: WRITELN(OUTPUT, 'business as usual')
END    (* CASE *)
```

Programming Example 12-19:   CASE Statement for an Enumerated Type

12.4.5.2. Predecessor and Successor Functions

We learned earlier in this chapter about the predefined functions **PRED** and **SUCC** to determine the predecessor and successor of any value of an enumerated type. However, both functions can be used with any ordinal types, not just with enumerated types. Therefore, the functions can be used also with the types INTEGER and CHAR. The following examples are TRUE:

SUCC(1) = 2	SUCC('A') = 'B'
SUCC(2) = 3	SUCC('B') = 'C'
PRED(9) = 8	PRED('Z') = 'Y'
PRED(8) = 7	PRED('Y') = 'X'

Table 12-7:   Predecessor and Successor of Types INTEGER and CHAR

Many Pascal programs contain a statement to increment a variable by 1. The following program fragment illustrates this with and without the successor function:

```
count := count + 1;

count := SUCC(count);
```

Programming Example 12-20:   Incrementing an INTEGER Variable

The previous two statements are equivalent. Similarly, the predefined function **PRED** can be used to decrement a variable's value.

12.4.5.3. The Function ORD

We mentioned earlier in this chapter that the predefined function **ORD** establishes a one-to-one correspondence between every enumerated type and a subset of the integers. However, the function **ORD** also works with a value of any ordinal type, not just with enumerated types. For any INTEGER n, **ORD(n)** = **n**. The following are TRUE:

$$ORD(1) = 1$$
$$ORD(2) = 2$$
$$ORD(3) = 3$$

$$ORD(-1) = -1$$
$$ORD(-2) = -2$$
$$ORD(-3) = -3$$

$$ORD(0) = 0$$

Table 12-8:   Ordinal Value of INTEGERS

Since the **ORD** function can be used with any ordinal type, and since the predefined type CHAR is an ordinal type, we can also use the **ORD** function with values of type CHAR. What value do we get when **ORD** is applied to values of type CHAR? Specifically, what is the value of **ORD('A')**? You might be tempted to say, 0 or 1. However, recall that the type CHAR is determined by which character set your computer uses. Therefore, the value returned by **ORD** depends on which character set is used. For the ASCII character set, there are 128 characters with ordinal values of 0 through 127. It turns out that **ORD('A')** = **65**. For CHARacters, there is another predefined function opposite to **ORD**. The standard predefined function **CHR** takes the ordinal value of a character and returns the actual character. **ORD** and **CHR** are inverse functions for the type CHAR. Therefore, **CHR(ORD(ch))** = **ch** for all characters **ch**. For mappings between characters and their ordinal values, see Appendix VIII. You should make a note that the predefined function **CHR** returns a value of type CHAR. Standard Pascal has no predefined function that is the inverse of **ORD** for ordinal types other than CHAR.

12.4.5.4. BOOLEAN Type

The primitive type BOOLEAN may be thought of as an enumerated type with exactly two elements. The following declaration accurately describes how the type BOOLEAN is predefined:

```
TYPE
    BOOLEAN = (FALSE, TRUE);
```

Programming Example 12-21:   BOOLEAN as an Enumerated Type

Since type BOOLEAN is predefined as an enumerated type, it has an associated ordering. We can use the relational operators, as well as the predefined functions **PRED**, **SUCC**, and **ORD**, with BOOLEAN values. Hence, the following are TRUE:

FALSE < TRUE	TRUE > FALSE
PRED(TRUE) = FALSE	SUCC(FALSE) = TRUE
ORD(FALSE) = 0	ORD(TRUE) = 1

Table 12-9:   Expressions Involving BOOLEAN Constants

12.4.6. Questions

1. What is the BNF for Pascal's enumerated type?

2. What is the only restriction on the identifiers used as values of an enumerated type?

3. Do all Pascal enumerated types have an explicit order associated with them? If so, explain how it is determined. If not, explain which enumerated types do not have an ordering.

4. Explain how relational operators can be used to take advantage of the order associated with enumerated types. Can all six of Pascal's relational operators be used with values of an enumerated type?

5. What purpose do the predefined functions **PRED** and **SUCC** serve?

6. Can the predefined functions **PRED** and **SUCC** be used with all enumerated types? Can they be used with all values of every enumerated type? If not, when can they not be used?

7. Describe the purpose of the predefined function **ORD**.

8. What is an ordinal type?

9. Which of Pascal's simple types are of ordinal type?

10. Which of Pascal's simple types are *not* of ordinal type?

11. Does Standard Pascal provide a convenient way to handle input and output of values of an enumerated type? If not, how does a Pascal programmer achieve input and output of enumerated types?

12. Can variables of an enumerated type be used as FOR loop index variables?

13. Can variables of an enumerated type be used as selector expressions of a CASE statement?

14. Can the predefined functions **PRED** and **SUCC** be used with the types INTEGER and CHAR?

15. Can the predefined function **ORD** be used with the types INTEGER and CHAR?

16. Does Standard Pascal have a predefined function that is the inverse of the predefined function **ORD**? If so, does it work for all ordinal types? If such a function exists, but does not work for all ordinal types, name each of the types it will handle.

17. Describe how Pascal's predefined type BOOLEAN is defined in terms of an enumerated-type definition.

12.4.7. Exercises

1. Recall the type **DayOfWeekType** defined earlier in this section. Create a table with four columns and one row for each of the seven values of **DayOfWeekType**. Label the four columns *value*, *ORD(value)*, *PRED(value)*, and *SUCC(value)*. Complete the first column with the seven values of **DayOfWeekType**. Complete each of the other three columns.

2. Given the following type definition, what is the value of each of the Pascal expressions?

```
TYPE
    DirectionType = (north, east, south, west);
```

a. ORD(north)	e. SUCC(north)	i. PRED(north)
b. ORD(east)	f. SUCC(east)	j. PRED(east)
c. ORD(south)	g. SUCC(south)	k. PRED(south)
d. ORD(west)	h. SUCC(west)	l. PRED(west)

3. Define an enumerated type for the four seasons of the year.

4. Define an enumerated type for the months of the year.

5. Define an enumerated type for the three primary colors.

6. Define an enumerated type for the three secondary colors.

7. Is the following a valid Pascal enumerated type? Justify your answer.

```
TYPE
    GradeType = ('A', 'B', 'C', 'D', 'E');
```

8. Define an enumerated type for the four suits of playing cards. Define this type so that the suit hearts has the greatest ordinal value and spades has the smallest ordinal value.

9. Define an enumerated type for weather forecasts. Include at least six different conditions, such as sunny, cloudy, and rainy.

12.5. Subrange Types

The second class of Pascal simple types defined by the user is the **subrange** type. The need for subrange types is quite natural. For example, consider writing a function to prompt the user for a digit (characters '0' through '9' inclusive) and return the entered digit as the function value. The function must reprompt the user if unacceptable input is entered. At this point, you should be able to write such a function. Your solution probably would look something like the following:

```
FUNCTION GetDigit: CHAR;

VAR
    digit: CHAR;

BEGIN
    REPEAT
        WRITE(OUTPUT, 'Please enter a digit => ');
        READLN(INPUT, digit)
    UNTIL ('0' <= digit) AND (digit <= '9');
    GetDigit := digit
END;      (* GetDigit *)
```

Programming Example 12-22: Function `GetDigit`

This solution seems fine. The function `GetDigit` gives the user a graceful prompt, reads the user's input, and returns the input as the function value. The REPEAT-UNTIL loop ensures that the user is prompted until an acceptable digit is entered, thereby ensuring that the function will return a character in the range '0' through '9'.

Think about the function `GetDigit` for a moment. Think about the values it returns. Of all the values of type CHAR, `GetDigit` always returns one of the 10 values '0' through '9'. In situations like this where we are only interested in a portion of a type, we find Pascal's subrange type to be useful. We can define a new type to represent digits, as indicated in the following example:

```
TYPE
    DigitType = '0'..'9';
```

Programming Example 12-23: Subrange `DigitType`

This type definition indicates that `DigitType` is a subset of the type CHARacter containing only the values '0' through '9'. With this type defined, we can rewrite the function `GetDigit` to return a value of `DigitType`:

```
FUNCTION GetDigit: DigitType;

VAR
    digit: CHAR;

BEGIN
    REPEAT
        WRITE(OUTPUT, 'Please enter a digit => ');
        READLN(INPUT, digit)
    UNTIL ('0' <= digit) AND (digit <= '9');
    GetDigit := digit
END;      (* GetDigit *)
```

Programming Example 12-24: Function `GetDigit` of `DigitType`

In general, every type is a set of allowable values that any variable of that type may take on. Additionally, every ordinal type has an ordering associated with it. Subrange types permit the programmer to define a new type that is a subset of some existing ordinal type.

> **Definition 12-9:** A *subrange type* is a subset of an ordinal type. The subrange is specified by its first and last values.

All subrange types are subsets of other ordinal types. It follows that all subrange types are themselves ordinal types. Subrange types use the same ordering associated with the type of which they are a subset. Like all other ordinal types, subrange types also have a first and a last value. A subrange is defined by its first and last values. The BNF for a subrange type is as follows:

`<subrange type> ::= <constant> .. <constant>`

The constants used in a subrange type must be chosen from the same type. Additionally, the first element of a subrange cannot follow the last element in the associated ordering. And finally, you can only define a subrange of an ordinal type. Hence, we cannot have subranges of the type REAL.

Although one could define a subrange of the ordinal type BOOLEAN, in practice we never do this since the subrange of two values would only have one possible value, and a type with only one possible value is of no real use. There are many situations where subranges of the primitive types INTEGER or CHAR are very useful. Since all enumerated types are also ordinal types, we can define a subrange of an enumerated type, such as `DayOfWeekType` defined previously. The following are examples of valid subrange types:

```
TYPE
    LittleLetterType = 'a' .. 'z';      (* subranges of CHAR *)
    BigLetterType = 'A' .. 'Z';
    DigitType = '0' .. '9';

    PositiveInts = 1 .. MAXINT;         (* subranges of INTEGER *)
    NonNegativeInts = 0 .. MAXINT;
    SmallIntType = 1 .. 1000;
    TestScores = 0 .. 100;

    WorkDayType = monday .. friday;     (* subrange of DayOfWeekType*)
```

Programming Example 12-25: Subrange Types

Thus, we may declare variables of these new types:

```
VAR
    LittleLetter: LittleLetterType;
    Digit: DigitType;
    SmallInt: SmallIntType;
    Workday: WorkDayType;
```

Programming Example 12-26: Declaring Variables of Subrange Types

The following examples are valid assignments to variables of these types:

```
LittleLetter := 'r';
SmallInt := 68;
Digit := '7';
Workday := tuesday;
```

Programming Example 12-27: Using Variables of Subrange Types

The following are invalid assignments to variables of these types:

```
smallint := 3500;
littleletter := 'B';
workday := saturday;
digit := 7;
digit := '68';
```

Programming Example 12-28:   Invalid Assignment of Subrange Values

Each subrange type is a subset of some ordinal type, known as the *superior* type. The superior type is either the predefined type INTEGER, the predefined type CHAR, or some user-defined enumerated type. All operators and predefined functions associated with the superior type may be used with any subrange of that type. Therefore, the relational operators, such as <, >, and =, as well as the predefined ordinal type functions **PRED**, **SUCC**, and **ORD**, can all be used with any subrange types.

Because the programmer is permitted to define subranges of ordinal types, the programmer is given greater ability to control the values a variable may take. The programmer may define new types that include only valid values for the problem at hand. This, in turn, takes the burden of range checking off of the programmer. For example, if we are writing a computer program to keep track of students' grades, and we know that every test score is in the range from 0 through 100 inclusive, we can define a subrange of the type INTEGER and know that every variable of the new type will always contain a valid value.

Whereas enumerated types give the programmer a way to create new types, subrange types give the programmer a way to create restricted versions of existing types. We encourage you to define types appropriate to your needs.

12.5.1. Questions

1. What are Pascal's two user-defined simple types?

2. What is a subrange type?

3. Why would a programmer ever want a subrange type? Give a specific example.

4. What does a programmer need to specify to define a Pascal subrange type?

5. What is the BNF of Pascal's subrange types?

6. What are three things Pascal requires in the two constants used in the definition of a subrange type?

7. Are all subrange types ordinal types? Justify your answer.

8. Does Pascal permit subranges of all simple types? Justify your answer.

9. May we define a subrange of the ordinal type BOOLEAN? If so, when would it be useful?

10. May we define a subrange of an enumerated type? If so, can we do so with every enumerated type?

12.5.2. Exercises

1. In this section we gave five examples of invalid assignments to variables of enumerated types. Explain why each was invalid.

2. Define a subrange type for ages. Assume that ages are INTEGERs.

3. Define a subrange type for yearly salaries. Pick your ideal salary as the upper bound of the subrange. *The selected upper bound may not exceed* **MAXINT** *on your system.*

4. Define a subrange to represent the possible grades for this course.

5. Define a subrange for shoe size. Use the type INTEGER as the superior type, ignoring half sizes and width specifications.

6. Define an enumerated type for the twelve months of the year. Define a subrange type of this enumerated type for the season summer.

7. Given the enumerated type defined in the last exercise, define subrange types for each of the remaining three seasons.

8. Define an enumerated type for the six colors comprising the primary and secondary colors. Define two subrange types for the primary colors and secondary colors. *Hint: The enumerated type must be in a particular order for this to work.*

12.6. Chapter Summary

- User-defined types are types created by the programmer.

- Type-extensible programming languages permit user-defined types.

- Pascal's user-defined types are enumerated, subrange, pointer, array, record, file, and set.

- Pascal's predefined types are INTEGER, REAL, BOOLEAN, CHAR, and TEXT.

- Pascal's primitive types are INTEGER, REAL, BOOLEAN, and CHAR.

- Scalar types have only one component.

- Structured types have more than one component.

- Pascal's scalar types are enumerated, subrange, pointer, and all primitive types (INTEGER, REAL BOOLEAN, CHAR).

- Pascal's structured types are ARRAY, RECORD, FILE, SET, and the predefined type TEXT.

- Simple types are all scalar types, except pointer.

- Ordinal types are all simple types, except REAL.

- Internal structured types are ARRAY, RECORD, and SET.

- External structured types are FILE and predefined type TEXT.

- A subrange type is a subset of any ordinal type.

- All simple types are ordinal types, except REAL.

- The predefined function **ORD** returns the ordinal value of an ordinal type. Ordinal values start with 0 rather than with 1.

- The predefined functions **PRED** and **SUCC** return the predecessor and successor, respectively, of an ordinal value.

- The predefined function **CHR** is the inverse of the function **ORD** for the type CHAR. Standard Pascal does not include a predefined function that is the inverse of **ORD** for all ordinal types.

- Any valid identifiers other than reserved words can be used as values of an enumerated type.

- All enumerated type's have an explicit ordering associated with them. The ordering is determined by the order of the values in the types definition.

- Standard Pascal does not provide for input or output of enumerated type values.

- We typically use the suffix *Type* for type identifiers to differentiate them from other identifiers, such as variables and subprograms.

- Pascal permits you to define subranges of any ordinal type.

- You define a subrange type by specifying the first and last element. Both elements must be of the same ordinal type, and the last element may not precede the first in the superior type.

- All operators and predefined functions for a superior type also work for any subrange of the superior type.

12.7. Summary of Terms

- type-extensible programming language
- user-defined type
- predefined type
- primitive type
- scalar type
- structured type

- simple type
- ordinal type
- enumerated type
- subrange type
- superior type
- pointer type

- internal structured type
- external structured type
- **ORD**
- **PRED**
- **SUCC**
- **CHR**

Chapter 13: Structured External Types

In the last chapter we studied Pascal's user-defined simple types: enumerated types and subrange types. The next two types we will study are the class of types known as FILEs and the predefined type TEXT. These two constitute the subject of this chapter. The following illustration indicates where we are currently in our journey through Pascal's types.

There is one point we should make and you should understand before proceeding with this chapter. We present the subject of files as they are defined in Standard Pascal. However, implementations of Pascal files vary widely. In fact, there are probably as many different implementations of Pascal files as there are chapters in this book. For those implementations that adhere to or are reasonably close to adhering to Standard Pascal, this chapter will be of most use. For those implementations that ignore the Standard, this chapter will serve as a guideline. You will need to determine how closely the compiler you are using adheres to the Standard.

13.1. An Overview of Files

Computers store information in units commonly known as *files*. Regardless of whether you are using a personal computer, a mini-computer, or timesharing an even larger computer, you have been using computer files. For example, the programs you have been writing are stored in files.

Pascal, and virtually every other programming language, permits the programmer to manipulate files. File manipulation permits programmers to create dramatically more useful programs. There are several very good reasons why we need computer files:

- Entering information into computers is tedious, time consuming, and prone to error

- Large amounts of information both can be and are reused

- Machine-readable information saves time and money

- Machine-readable information is durable

Entering information into computers is tedious, time consuming, and prone to error.
Think about typing this page of text into a computer. The chances are that you would make at least a few errors in entering just this one page of text. Consider the task of typing every page of this book into a computer. Having done just that, we believe it is impossible to do so without making errors. Sometimes such errors can be disastrous. There is a famous error in copying a FORTRAN program that served as part of the control system for the Mariner spacecraft. Due to an apparently harmless error, the craft failed to orbit Venus as planned, and instead headed off to destruction in the Sun. [1] Entering information into computers is tedious, takes time, and is extremely prone to error.

Large amounts of information can be and are reused.
Government officials and social scientists use the United States Census data to determine growth patterns and to help inform policy makers. These data consist of literally billions of individual pieces of information. Entering the census data into a computer is obviously a very large task. Once the

---

[1] The program should have included something like the loop, `DO i = 1,9`. Unfortunately, the comma was mistyped as a period. The statement read `DO i = 1.9`. FORTRAN ignores all blanks and uses = as the assignment operator. Therefore, the mistyped statement assigned the value 1.9 to the variable with identifier `DOi`. This was indeed a costly mistake!

information is stored in a computer, we certainly do not want to have to enter the information again every time it is needed. If the same data had to be typed in by hand each time it was to be studied, there would be few, if any, studies based on that data.

Machine-readable information saves time and money.

If you store one of your programs in a computer file, you can reuse it as often as you need it. Even if the program is only 50 or 100 lines long, reuse certainly saves you time. The Karel simulator consists of about 10,000 lines of Pascal code. A typical Pascal compiler consists of more that 50,000 lines of code. Suppose that you had to enter each of these lines before executing a program. Even if it could be accurately copied by hand, it is clear that this would be a slow process indeed. The cost of programmer time would be prohibitive, and we would build and execute very few programs. Reusing information stored in computer files clearly saves both time and money.

Machine-readable information is durable.

One really sad fact is that much of the world's great "live" art has vanished because until recently there was no way to record live performances. Thus, we cannot today hear Beethoven play the piano or listen to Bach play the organ. Since the time of Thomas Edison, however, people have begun recording music and visual information (movies). Unfortunately, traditional recordings degenerate over time: vinyl scrapes, tape warps, celluloid becomes brittle. For some time now, it has been possible to synthesize sounds and images from computer-controlled devices. These sounds and images can be indistinguishable from their naturally produced counterparts. Today this technology is being exploited in very high-quality audio systems, the motion-picture industry, military navigation systems, and for archival purposes. Information, whether it be words, data, or sounds, can be stored in computer files and reused (or replayed) as many times as desired.

There is a common thread running through these four areas. *Information can be stored in computers in files. Files are read and written. And, in the process, human error is eliminated. Representation is faithful, despite the passing of time and the use and reuse of the information.*

This chapter provides a model of the Pascal **file**, illustrates file reading and writing, and explains how to develop some commonly used applications.

13.2. Pascal Files

Recall the Turing Machine first presented in Chapter 1. The Turing Machine Tape provides a familiar and accurate model of a computer file. The file is a sequence of cells. The following figure illustrates a file of character values using this model:

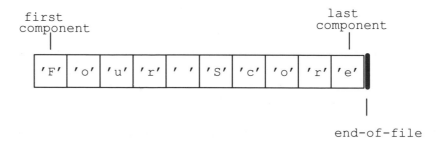

Figure 13-1: File Modeled as a Sequence of Cells

The first component of the file is the left-most cell of the sequence. Consequently, the last component of the file is the right-most cell of the sequence. We denote the end-of-file graphically with a vertical bar after the last component.

Each cell in the illustration holds a character value. For Pascal files, each cell on the tape has the exact same type. We might have a file of INTEGERs, a file of REALs, a file of CHARacters, and so forth. The following figure illustrates a file of REALs and a file of BOOLEANs:

21.2	1.0	−22.01	9.9	5	█

TRUE	TRUE	FALSE	TRUE	FALSE	█

Figure 13-2: File of Various Types

Pascal permits files of any type, as long as every component of the file (i.e. every cell of the Turing Tape) has a value of the same type. Components of any type are permitted, with the exception that Pascal does not support files of files.

The Turing Tape provides a good model of computer files. Files are stored on secondary storage media, such as a disk or magnetic tape. Recall that we said Pascal's structured types have more than one component or value. Therefore, the file is a structured type.

> **Definition 13-1:** A Pascal *file* is a structured type, consisting of a sequence of identically typed components and stored on secondary storage media.

A Pascal file is referred to as a **sequential file** because an element can be accessed only if all the elements preceding it have been accessed. For example, before the third element of a file can be read, the first and second elements of the file must be read. Similarly, before the tenth element can be written to a file, the nine preceding elements must be written to the file.

> **Definition 13-2:** A *sequential file* is a file in which to read (or write) the **n**th component, the **n-1** preceding components must first be read (or written).

The first element in a file is the left-most cell in the sequence; the last element in a file is the right-most cell in the sequence. Another, possibly more intuitive, way to think of the sequential file is to realize that the read head or write head moves along the tape in one direction only, from left to right. Each cell on the tape is read in sequence. To read the third cell on the tape, the first and second cells on the tape must be read.

Some programming languages provide another type of file that can be accessed in any order rather than just sequentially. This type of file is known as a *random-access* file. Standard Pascal does not support random-access files, only sequential files.

The file is accurately modeled as a sequence of elements. Often, when considering a particular file, we are interested in where the read head is positioned. The illustrations graphically denote the read head with a vertical arrow. The element located immediately to the right of the read head is the next element of the file to be read and is referred to as the **current element**.

> **Definition 13-3:** The *current element* is the component of a file immediately to the right of the read head.

In the following illustration, the element immediately to the right of the read head is the fourth element of the file. The fourth element, which happens to be the character 'r', is the current element:

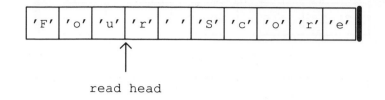

Figure 13-3: The Current Element of a File

Although a Pascal file must have all its components of the same type, Pascal files can have any number of elements. But remember that files are stored on secondary storage media, and such devices have some finite capacity. Therefore, some implementation-dependent limit is placed on file size. For example, you cannot store the current U.S. Census data on a single floppy disk. Similarly, Pascal has no language-required *minimum* number of elements in files. A file may have no elements. A file containing no elements is known as an **empty file**.

Definition 13-4: An *empty file* is a file of no elements.

An empty file is indicated graphically by the end-of-file marker, without any tape cells:

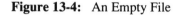

Figure 13-4: An Empty File

13.2.1. Declaring Files

In Pascal, files are structured types defined by the programmer. This fact has several implications. First, variables represent files in Pascal programs. Since all Pascal variables have a type, the programmer normally defines a type for file variables.

Recall that a Pascal file is a sequence of components of the same type. The definition of a file type is the reserved words **FILE OF** followed by the component type. The BNF for a file type is as follows:

```
<file-type> ::= FILE OF <component-type>
```

We can use any valid Pascal type for the component type, except the type file. The following program fragment illustrates the definition of a file type and the declaration of a few file variables:

```
TYPE
    DataFileType = FILE OF CHAR;

VAR
    Chapter1, Chapter2, Index: DataFileType;
```

Programming Example 13-1: Declaring File Variables

The three file variables above are declared as files with component type CHAR. Similarly, we could have declared them with the component type as some other type, such as INTEGER or BOOLEAN. The type CHAR is by far the most common component type for file variables.

13.2.2. The Most Common Files: Text Files

FILE OF CHAR is so common in Pascal programs that Standard Pascal includes the predefined type **TEXT** to denote this particular type of file.

Definition 13-5: The predefined type *TEXT* is a file of characters (FILE OF CHAR).

The following is the way the system defines the type *TEXT*:

```
TYPE
    TEXT = FILE OF CHAR;
```

Programming Example 13-2: Predefinition of Type TEXT

We need not define the type TEXT to use it. The following program fragment illustrates the declaration of file variables of type TEXT:

```
VAR
    Chapter18, resignation, autobiography: TEXT;
```

Programming Example 13-3: File Variables of Type TEXT

Although Standard Pascal permits file variables to be of any component type except file type, in practice most programmers never need files of any type except type TEXT. For this reason, we focus on files of type TEXT in this book.

13.2.3. Peculiarities of Pascal File Variables

There are several differences between Pascal file variables and other Pascal variables. Normally, Pascal variables have no value before a program starts executing, and their values are lost when a program terminates. However, file variables refer to information that can exist both before a program begins and after a program ends.

If a file variable refers to information that exists before or after the Pascal program runs, the file variable must appear in the program heading. Such file variables normally follow the words INPUT and OUTPUT. For example, suppose you are writing a payroll program that has three file variables, **TimeFile**, **RateFile**, and **CheckFile**, which correspond to the file of time worked, the file of hourly rates, and the file to print paychecks, respectively. The program heading would look like the following:

```
PROGRAM Payroll (INPUT, OUTPUT, TimeFile, RateFile, CheckFile);
```

Programming Example 13-4: File Variables in the Program Heading

File variables listed in the program heading are known as *program parameters*. You may recall that we strongly advocated declaring variables local to the subprogram in which they are used. Pascal requires that any file variable listed in the program heading be declared global to the entire program. This differs from other Pascal variables and is counter to the style we advocate. The following program illustrates this language requirement:

```
PROGRAM Payroll (INPUT, OUTPUT, TimeFile, RateFile, CheckFile);

VAR
    TimeFile, RateFile, CheckFile: TEXT;
```

Programming Example 13-5: File Variables Declared Globally

Of course, every subprogram that uses a file variable declared globally to the program should still have the file variable as a parameter to the subprogram.

We said earlier that you should use VAR parameters when a subprogram changes the value of its parameter and use value parameters at all other times. Pascal requires that all file variables be passed as VAR parameters. Pascal prohibits file variables from ever being passed as value parameters. The following table summarizes the peculiarities of Pascal file variables.

- File variables refer to information that can exist both before a program begins and after a program ends.

- If a file variable refers to information that exists before or after the Pascal program runs, the file variable must appear in the program heading.

- Pascal requires that any file variable listed in the program heading be declared globally to the entire program.

- Pascal requires that all file variables be passed as VAR parameters. Pascal prohibits file variables from ever being passed as value parameters.

Table 13-1: Rules for Pascal File Variables

13.2.4. Questions

1. Give at least three good reasons why we need computer files.

2. The Turing Machine Tape provides both a familiar and accurate model of a computer file. Explain how this model can be so used.

3. Computer files are typically stored on what types of media? On what media are files stored in your computer?

4. What is the maximum size a Pascal file can be?

5. What is the maximum size file you can have on your system?

6. Can a Pascal file contain more than one type of component? Explain your answer.

7. Does Standard Pascal support files of files?

8. What does "sequential file" mean?

9. What does "random-access" file mean?

10. What does the "current element" refer to when talking about Pascal files?

11. What is an "empty file"?

12. What is the BNF of a file type?

13. What is the Pascal identifier TEXT?

14. What is the most common type of Pascal file?

15. What are four differences between Pascal file variables and other Pascal variables?

13.2.5. Exercises

1. The following program fragment contains two errors. What are they?

```
PROGRAM UpdateData (INPUT, OUTPUT, InData, OutData, ErrorFile);

TYPE
    DataFileType: FILE OF INTEGER;
    TextFileType: FILE OF TEXT;

VAR
    InData, OutData: DataFileType;
    TempFile: TextFileType;
```

2. The following program fragment contains two errors. What are they?

```
PROGRAM UpdateData (INPUT, OUTPUT, InData, OutData, ErrorFile);

TYPE
    DataFileType: FILE OF INTEGER;

VAR
    InData, OutData: DataFileType;
    ErrorFile,TempFile: Text;

PROCEDURE ProcessData (InData, OutData: DataFileType);

BEGIN

END;     (* ProcessData *)
```

13.3. Reading Files

File variables give programs access to information stored in other computer files. Pascal requires file variables that refer to already existing files to be in the program heading as program parameters. File variables declared as program parameters must be declared globally to the program. In addition to these two requirements, we must also *open* the file for reading before any information can be read from the file. Standard Pascal provides the predefined procedure **RESET** to open a file for reading. The procedure RESET positions the read head before the first element of the file, thereby making the first element the *current element.* The following illustration shows the position of the read head *after* the procedure RESET is called:

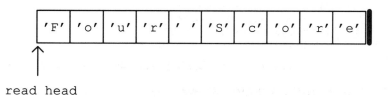

read head

Figure 13-5: File After RESET

In Standard Pascal the procedure RESET has a single parameter, the file variable to be opened for reading. However, there are many nonstandard forms of RESET in use, and there is a strong chance that the system you are using differs from Standard Pascal. You will need to determine how files are opened on the system that you are using. Although some implementations use a different name or different number of parameters for the procedure RESET, they all make the first element the current element.

> **Definition 13-6:** *RESET* is a standard Pascal procedure that takes a file name as a parameter and opens that file for reading. The procedure RESET positions the read head before the first element of the file, thereby making the first element the *current element.*

Once the file is opened, information can be read from it with the standard procedure READ. Up to this point we have always used the READ procedure in the form `READ(INPUT, somevariable)`. To read from a file different from the standard input, we replace the word INPUT with the appropriate file variable. The following program is an example:

```
PROGRAM FileRead (INPUT, OUTPUT, Infile);

VAR
    Infile: TEXT;
    elt: CHAR;

BEGIN
    RESET(Infile);                 (* open file for reading *)
    READ(Infile, elt);             (* read first element of file *)
    READ(Infile, elt)              (* read second element of file *)
END.
```

Programming Example 13-6:   Opening a File and Reading from a File

This example program opens a TEXT file for reading and reads the first two characters from it. To illustrate this example further, consider the following graphical representation:

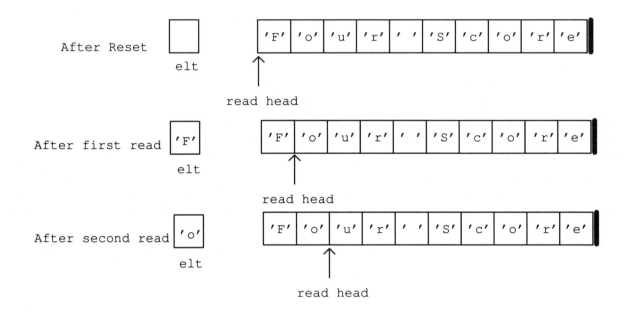

Figure 13-6:   Reading from a TEXT File

13.3.1. Checking for the End-Of-File Marker

Every file has some finite number of components; therefore, every file has an end. We have denoted the end-of-file with a vertical bar after the last element of the file. To enable the programmer to determine when the read head reaches the end-of-file, Standard Pascal provides the predefined function **EOF**. This is a BOOLEAN function that evaluates to TRUE when all components of a file have been read; it evaluates to FALSE if any component has not been read.

The following diagram illustrates the read head at three different points in a file. In the first and second cases, the function EOF returns FALSE; in the third case, the function EOF returns TRUE.

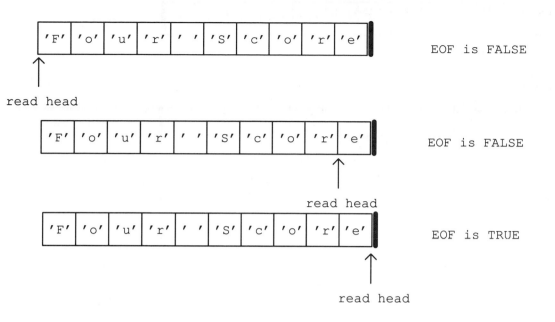

Figure 13-7: Testing a File for EOF

All files have an end, and Pascal programmers can detect the end of the file with the predefined function EOF. Attempting to read from a file once EOF is TRUE for that file is an attempt to read beyond the end of the file. Attempting to read beyond the end of a file normally causes a runtime error. Indeed, the purpose of the function EOF is to provide a way to determine when to stop reading from a file.

> **Definition 13-7:** *EOF* is a standard Pascal function, taking a file variable as a parameter, that evaluates to TRUE only when all components of a file have been read; it evaluates to FALSE at all other times.

13.3.2. Checking for End-Of-Line

Text files (files declared of type TEXT) are sequences of characters. Unlike any other files, text files are organized into *lines*. Each line is terminated with an *end-of-line marker*. Since a text file is a sequence of characters, the end-of-line marker is just a special character chosen to designate that the line is complete. It is not important what particular character is used to denote end-of-line. However, it is important to be able to detect the end-of-line character. Standard Pascal provides the predefined BOOLEAN function EOLN to detect the end-of-line marker. The function returns TRUE only if the next character in a text file is an end-of-line marker; it evaluates to FALSE otherwise.

We denote the end-of-line marker graphically with a cent sign (¢). A text file can, and often does, have more than one end-of-line. Although EOF returns TRUE when the read head is in only one position, EOLN returns TRUE many times (every time the read head is before an end-of-line marker). The following illustration shows the read head in a variety of positions on one file. Pay close attention to where EOLN returns TRUE and where it returns FALSE.

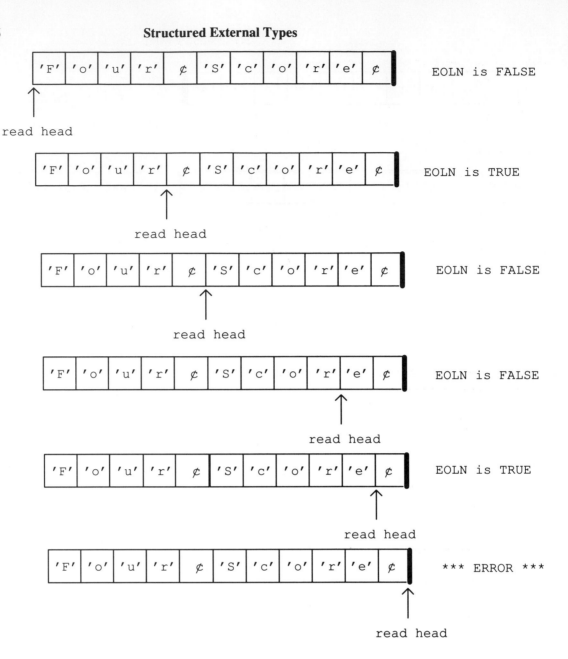

Figure 13-8: Testing a TEXT File for EOLN

We said earlier that a runtime error occurs when one attempts to read from a file after EOF is TRUE for that file. It is also an error in Standard Pascal to call EOLN on a file if EOF is TRUE for that file. The last tape in the previous illustration depicts this situation.

> **Definition 13-8:** *EOLN* is a standard Pascal function, taking a file variable of type TEXT as a parameter, that evaluates to TRUE when the current element of the file is an end-of-line marker.

Only TEXT files contain end-of-line markers. The predefined function EOLN provides the only way to detect them. They are read (i.e. the read head is advanced past an end-of-line marker) with the predefined procedure READLN. Since you have been using the procedure READLN for some time, we will not discuss it in detail again. The following example illustrates READLN used with a file other than standard INPUT:

```
PROGRAM ReadLnExample (INPUT, OUTPUT, Infile);

VAR
    Infile: TEXT;
    elt: CHAR;

BEGIN
    RESET(Infile);              (* open file for reading *)

    READ(Infile, elt);          (* read first char *)
    READLN(Infile, elt);        (* read next char and skip past eoln *)
    READ(Infile, elt);          (* read next char *)
    READLN(Infile, elt)         (* read next char and skip past eoln *)
END.
```

Programming Example 13-7: Reading End-Of-Line Marker with READLN

We further illustrate this example with the following graphic representation:

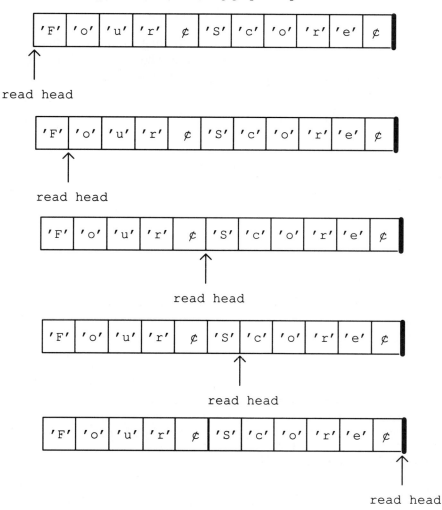

Figure 13-9: Tapes Corresponding to Programming Example 13-7

The end-of-line markers in a text file are detected with the predefined BOOLEAN function EOLN and read with the predefined procedure READLN. If you accidentally (or intentionally) attempt to read an end-of-line marker with the predefined procedure READ (rather than READLN), what value would you expect to be returned? Those implementations conforming to Standard Pascal always return the space character (ASCII character 32) as the end-of-line character, regardless of the particular character used to represent end-of-line. We will see later in this chapter that end-of-line markers are written to text files with the predefined procedure WRITELN.

13.3.3. Looking Ahead: The File Buffer Variable

Every time we use READ or READLN on a file variable, the read head advances and the current element changes. After only a little experience with files, most programmers find they want a way to determine the current element in the file without advancing the read head. Standard Pascal provides a way to do this.

Every file variable has a corresponding variable that contains the value of the next component in the file. This corresponding variable is referred to as a **file buffer variable**. The file buffer variable can be accessed without advancing the read head or changing the file. The file buffer variable is designated by suffixing the file variable with the symbol ^. For example, if **Infile** is a file variable open for reading, then **Infile^** refers to the next component of the file.

The file buffer variable can be of use in a variety of situations. To illustrate one use, consider reading from a text file. Assume the file contains lines of names. However, some lines contain an unknown number of space characters before the name. Here we would like to skip over the blank spaces.

Consider writing a procedure to skip over blank spaces. As long as the next character in the file is a blank space character, we want to read it. This is a case where we need to know what the next component of the file is before reading from the file. The following procedure illustrates how to do this using the file buffer variable:

```
PROCEDURE SkipBlanks (VAR Infile: TEXT);

CONST
    SpaceChar = ' ';

VAR
    garbage: CHAR;

BEGIN
    WHILE (Infile^ = SpaceChar) DO
        READ(Infile, garbage)
END;     (* SkipBlanks *)
```

Programming Example 13-8: Using the File Buffer Variable

The procedure has the file variable **Infile** as a parameter. Recall that file variables always must be passed as VAR parameters. The procedure consists of a single WHILE loop. While the next character in the file is a blank space character **(Infile^ = SpaceChar)**, we read from the file.

You may have noticed that the procedure declares a character variable to read characters into. However, we are never interested in those characters; we only want to advance the read head to the next component. For such situations, Standard Pascal includes a predefined procedure named **GET**, which advances the read head past exactly one component in a file already open for reading. The following procedure is equivalent to our previous version of **SkipBlanks**, except it uses **GET**:

```
PROCEDURE SkipBlanks (VAR Infile: TEXT);

CONST
    SpaceChar = ' ';

BEGIN
    WHILE (Infile^ = SpaceChar) DO
        GET(Infile)
END;     (* SkipBlanks *)
```

Programming Example 13-9: Using the Procedure GET

You will find many uses for both the file buffer variable and the predefined procedure **GET**.

> **Definition 13-9:** The *file buffer variable* contains the value of the next element to be read from the file and is accessed by suffixing the file variable with the ^ symbol.

> **Definition 13-10:** *GET* is a standard Pascal function, taking a file variable opened for reading, that advances the read head past exactly one component of the file.

13.3.4. Counting Lines: Another Application

As one application of what we have learned so far in this chapter, consider writing a function to count the lines in a text file. The function takes the file variable as a parameter. First, the file is opened for reading. Then, each line is read with READLN until we reach the end of the file. Finally, the function value is assigned. The following is one way of writing this function:

```
FUNCTION CountLines (VAR Infile: TEXT): INTEGER;

VAR
    result: INTEGER;

BEGIN
    RESET(Infile);        (* open file for reading *)
    result := 0;

    WHILE NOT(EOF(Infile)) DO
        BEGIN
            READLN(Infile);
            result := result + 1
        END;      (* WHILE *)

    CountLines := result
END;      (* CountLines *)
```

Programming Example 13-10: Function `CountLines`

Although the previous function is relatively simple, it is quite useful. There are a variety of similar functions that are both equally simple and equally useful. Some of them appear as problems in this chapter.

13.3.5. Common Errors

Although some programmers seem to never make certain programming errors, when it comes to files, most programmers have first-hand experience with just about every possible file-related programming error. With this in mind, we summarize some of the most common file errors:

- **File parameters left out of the program heading.**
  Standard Pascal requires all file variables that refer to files existing before or after the program runs to be listed as file parameters in the program heading.

- **Program parameters not declared global to program.**
  Standard Pascal requires that all program parameters be declared as file variables global to the entire program.

- **File not opened for reading.**
  A file must always be opened with the predefined procedure RESET before anything can be read from it.

- **Correct file variable not specified to READ and READLN calls.**
  INPUT refers to the standard input (keyboard). The programmer must specify which file variable is to be used for reading from any other files.

- **File variable not passed as VAR parameter.**
  File variables can never be passed as value parameters.

- **Attempting to read beyond end-of-file.**
  Every file is finite and, therefore, has an end. A runtime error results from attempting to read beyond the end-of-file. The predefined BOOLEAN function EOF returns TRUE when all the elements of a file have been read. Your program should check for end-of-file using EOF *before* reading from a file.

Table 13-2: Common File Errors

With some experience with files, you will become better at detecting and correcting file-related errors.

13.3.6. Questions

1. A file must be opened before information can be read from it. What Standard Pascal procedure opens a file for reading?

2. What is the *current element* after a file has been opened for reading?

3. What predefined procedure can be used to read information from Pascal files? How does one specify which file variable to read from?

4. Every file has some finite number of components and, therefore, has an end. What predefined Pascal function can be used to determine when all the components of a file have been read?

5. What happens if a program attempts to read beyond the end of a file?

6. What is an end-of-line marker?

7. Can all Pascal files contain end-of-line markers? If not, which ones can?

8. What predefined Pascal function can be used to determine if the next file component to be read is an end-of-line marker?

9. What predefined procedure is designed to read end-of-line markers from a Pascal file?

10. Is there any way in Standard Pascal to determine the next component of a file without using the procedures READ or READLN?

11. What is a file buffer variable?

12. Does Standard Pascal provide file buffer variables? If so, how are they indicated in Pascal?

13. Does Standard Pascal have a predefined procedure to advance the read head past one component of a file? If so, what is it named?

14. Name six common errors virtually every programmer encounters when studying file reading.

15. *The following three lines of code can be rewritten as a single procedure call. How?

```
WHILE NOT(EOLN(INFILE)) DO
    get(INFILE);
get(INFILE)
```

13.3.7. Problems

1. Write a procedure **SkipDigits** that takes a TEXT file parameter and moves the read past any digit characters ('0'..'9').

2. Write a procedure **SkipLetters** that takes a TEXT file parameter and moves the read head past any lowercase characters ('a'..'z') or any uppercase characters ('A'..'Z').

3. Write a BOOLEAN function **IsEmptyFile** that takes a TEXT file parameter and returns TRUE if the file is empty and FALSE otherwise.

4. Write a program that counts the number of vowels in a TEXT file and displays the total to the user.

5. A blank line in a TEXT file is indicated by two consecutive end-of-line markers. Write a program that determines the number of blank lines in an arbitrary TEXT file.

6. Write a BOOLEAN function that determines if two files contain the same information. The function should take two TEXT file variables as parameters and return TRUE if the files are the same and FALSE if they are different.

7. Write a Pascal program that compares two TEXT files to determine if they contain the same information. If the files are different, the program should inform the user of the first different character, the number of the line containing the first different character, and the actual line from each of the two files.

13.4. Writing Files

At this point, you have seen everything necessary to create programs that read from files. However, every file must be written before it can be read. This section discusses what you need to know in order to create Pascal programs that write to files.

We learned in the last section that we need to open a file for reading before reading from it. Similarly, we must open a file for writing before writing to it. Standard Pascal includes a predefined procedure to open a file for writing. The procedure is named **REWRITE**. It normally takes one file variable as a parameter. However, like **RESET**, there are many nonstandard forms of **REWRITE**. You will have to check the particular implementation you are using to effectively open files for writing.

Once the procedure **REWRITE** has been called on a file variable, the corresponding file becomes an empty file ready to be written to. For a new file, we would expect the file to start out as an empty file. It is important to realize that the result of **REWRITE** is the same, whether the file existed previously or not. Therefore, calling the procedure **REWRITE** on an existing file destroys any information already in the file. The following illustration depicts this fact:

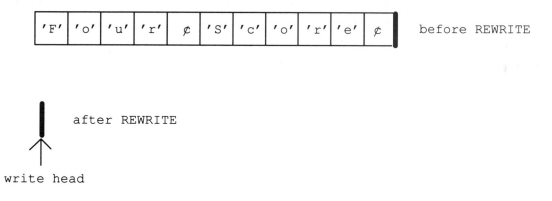

Figure 13-10: Destructive Nature of REWRITE

After calling the procedure **REWRITE**, the write head is always positioned at the start of the file. The programmer must exercise care so existing files do not get erased accidentally.

> **Definition 13-11:** *REWRITE* is a standard Pascal procedure that takes a file name as a parameter and opens that file for writing by setting the write head at the beginning of the file.

Once a file has been opened for writing with the procedure **REWRITE**, information can be written to the file by using the predefined procedure **WRITE**. You have used **WRITE** in the form **WRITE(OUTPUT, somevariable)** many times before. When the word OUTPUT is replaced with a file variable, the output is written to the specified file. The action of the procedure **WRITE** is the same, whether information is being written to the standard OUTPUT or to some other file. Since we have already discussed **WRITE** in detail earlier in this book, we will not repeat that information here.

The surname Miller is said to be the third most common in the United States. The following example procedure opens a file for writing and then writes this surname to the file, one letter at a time:

```
PROCEDURE WriteFile (VAR OutFile: TEXT);

BEGIN
    REWRITE(OutFile);                (* open file for writing *)

    WRITE(OutFile, 'M');
    WRITE(OutFile, 'i');
    WRITE(OutFile, 'l');
    WRITE(OutFile, 'l');
    WRITE(OutFile, 'e');
    WRITE(OutFile, 'r')
END; (* WriteFile *)
```

Programming Example 13-11: Writing to a File

The following illustration depicts the state of the file after calling **REWRITE** and after writing each component to the file.

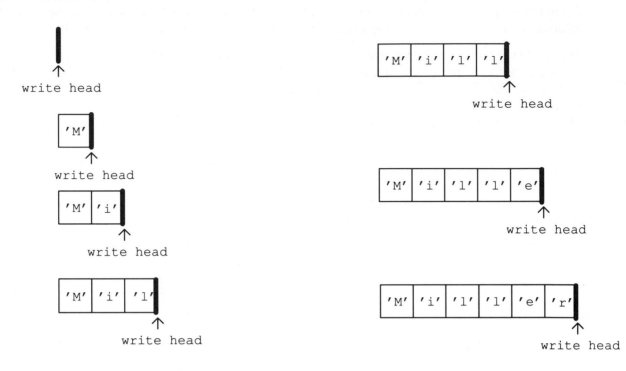

Figure 13-11: Writing to a File

Note that we do not need explicitly to write an end-of-file to the file. Standard Pascal provides the end-of-file automatically.

Additionally, Standard Pascal does not require a program to close the files it has opened. Some implementations of Pascal differ from the Standard on this point and do require files to be closed explicitly. Such implementations provide a predefined procedure to close files. You should determine if the implementation of Pascal you are using requires this.

13.5. Internal Files, External Files, and the Program Heading

When we first described input and output, we used the Turing Machine Tape as a model. We labeled one tape the input tape and another tape the output tape. We said the input tape corresponded to the keyboard and routinely specified the word INPUT in our READ and READLN statements when we wanted to read what the user types. Similarly, we said the output tape corresponded to the output screen and specified the word OUTPUT in our WRITE and WRITELN statements.

In this chapter we learned about files. By replacing the word INPUT with a file variable, we can read from other files. Similarly, by replacing the word OUTPUT with a file variable, we can write to files other than the standard output (terminal screen).

At this point, you might be wondering how the predefined identifiers INPUT and OUTPUT are really defined. INPUT and OUTPUT are just predefined file variables. They are both of the same file type, the most common type—TEXT. The following program fragment indicates how you should consider these identifiers to be defined:

```
VAR
    INPUT, OUTPUT: TEXT;
```

Programming Example 13-12: Declaration of INPUT and OUTPUT

We learned in this chapter that we must call **RESET** on a file before we can read from it, and we must call **REWRITE** on a file before we can write to it. However, we have never called either **RESET** or **REWRITE** on the file variables INPUT and OUTPUT. When a Pascal program starts to execute, it implicitly does a `RESET(INPUT)` and `REWRITE(OUTPUT)`. These *must not be done explicitly by the programmer.*

Files that exist before a program starts executing or after execution has ended are known as **external files**. Files that only exist during the execution of the program are known as **internal files**.

Definition 13-12: *Internal files* exist only during the execution of a program.

Definition 13-13: *External files* exist prior to program execution, after program execution, or both before and after program execution.

All external files must appear as program parameters in the program heading. As a general rule, both INPUT and OUTPUT are always present in the program heading. However, only OUTPUT need always be there. INPUT is needed only if the program takes some user input from the keyboard.

13.5.1. Questions

1. Standard Pascal includes a predefined procedure to open files for writing. What is the name of this procedure, and what parameters does it require?

2. Must a file always be opened for writing before a Pascal program can write to it?

3. What predefined procedure can be used to write all Pascal files?

4. How does a programmer specify which file is to be written to?

5. What does a file contain after the procedure **REWRITE** has been called on it?

6. What does the procedure **REWRITE** do to an already existing file of information?

7. How can a programmer write an end-of-line marker to a TEXT file?

8. Must a program explicitly write an end-of-file to a file being written? If so, how is it done?

9. What is a program parameter?

10. Must all file variables be listed as program parameters?

11. What is the difference between an internal file and an external file?

12. How are internal and external files related to program parameters?

13. What are the predefined Pascal identifiers INPUT and OUTPUT?

14. When and where should your Pascal programs include the following:

        RESET(INPUT);

        REWRITE(OUTPUT);

13.5.2. Problems

1. Create a Pascal procedure **WriteName** that takes a TEXT file variable as a parameter and writes your last name to the file.

2. Extend the procedure from the previous problem so that it writes both your first name and your last name. Write each name on a separate line.

3. Write a procedure **MergeFiles** that takes two file variables as parameters and merges the corresponding files into one file as a third file parameter.

4. Create a Pascal procedure **EmptyFile** that takes a file variable as a parameter and makes the associated file an empty file.

5. *The predefined procedure **REWRITE** obliterates any information already existing in a file. However, there are many times when we want to write new information to a file while keeping the old information. Create a Pascal procedure **AppendFile** that takes a TEXT file variable as a parameter and opens the file for writing so that all information written to the file after calling **AppendFile** is appended to the original information. *Hint: The procedure will need another file variable for a temporary file.*

13.6. Selected Uses of Files

The ability to manipulate files enables a programmer to create dramatically more useful programs. File manipulation is so important that entire books and courses are devoted just to the techniques of creating, updating, and manipulating computer files. In this final section, we will review some selected uses of files

13.6.1. Displaying a Text File

All operating systems provide a program to type, or list, a text file to the screen of a terminal. Suppose we wanted to write our own Pascal procedure to do this same task. We need to open the desired file for reading, then read each character and write it to the user's screen. The following code represents most programmers' first try at such a procedure:

```
PROCEDURE ListFile (VAR Textfile: TEXT);

VAR
    ch: CHAR;


BEGIN
    RESET(Textfile);              (* open file for reading *)

    WHILE NOT(EOF(Textfile)) DO
        BEGIN
            READ(Textfile, ch);
            WRITE(OUTPUT, ch)
        END     (* WHILE *)

END;    (* ListFile *)
```

Programming Example 13-13: Procedure `ListFile`

Does the procedure `ListFile` perform as desired? Think about TEXT files for a moment. Text files can contain end-of-line markers. Since each end-of-line marker is read as a space character, the preceding procedure does not handle end-of-lines correctly. Our procedure does not break lines as they were in the original file. Therefore, we wish to modify the program to write an end-of-line marker when one is detected in the original file. The end-of-line marker is detected with **EOLN**, read with **READLN**, and written with **WRITELN**. The following modified procedure works properly:

```
PROCEDURE ListFile (VAR Textfile: TEXT);

VAR
    ch: CHAR;


BEGIN
    RESET(Textfile);              (* open file for reading *)

    WHILE NOT(EOF(Textfile)) DO
        BEGIN
            IF NOT EOLN(Textfile)
                THEN BEGIN
                        READ(Textfile, ch);
                        WRITE(OUTPUT, ch)
                    END     (* THEN *)
                ELSE BEGIN
                        READLN(Textfile);
                        WRITELN(OUTPUT)
                    END
        END     (* WHILE *)

END;    (* ListFile *)
```

Programming Example 13-14: Corrected Procedure `ListFile`

You should keep in mind that although end-of-line markers are components of a TEXT file, they must be handled differently.

13.6.2. Merging Two Files

Suppose we need to merge two files into one file. Also assume the two initial files consist only of letters of the alphabet and that both files are in alphabetical order. The resulting file is to be in alphabetical order also.

Let us refer to the two initial files as **file1** and **file2** and the resulting file as **MergedFile**. Remember that we do not know the number of letters in either **file1** or **file2**, nor do we know anything else about either file except that they are ordered alphabetically. How would you write a procedure to merge two ordered files into a single ordered file?

We do not know ahead of time which file contains the letter that should be the first letter of the merged file. Therefore, we read the first letter from both files and compare them to determine the first letter of the merged file. We write this letter to the merged file and then read another letter from the file that contained the letter we wrote to the merged file. By comparing the last two letters read from the files, we can determine which letter should be written to the merged file next. We continue this process until one of the files has been exhausted. At that point, we copy the remainder of the unexhausted file to the end of the merged file. The following illustration depicts the first few iterations of this process:

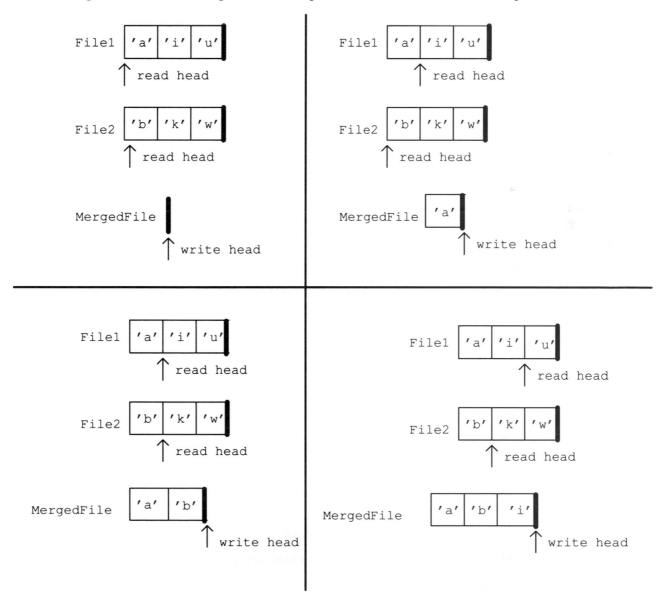

Figure 13-12: Merging Two Ordered Files

Now let us create a Pascal procedure to accomplish this. The procedure has three file parameters for the three files **file1**, **file2**, and **MergedFile**. The procedure first opens the **MergedFile** for writing and the other two files for reading. Next, the first letter of each file is read. We then repeatedly compare the two letters, write the smaller to the merged file, and read another letter from the appropriate file until one of the files is exhausted. Then the remainder of the unexhausted file is copied to the merged file. The following is one way to write such a procedure in Standard Pascal:

```
PROCEDURE MergeTwo (VAR File1, File2, MergedFile: TEXT);

VAR
    Char1, Char2: CHAR;

BEGIN
    RESET(File1);                 (* open for reading *)
    RESET(File2);                 (* open for reading *)

    REWRITE(MergedFile);          (* open for writing *)

    READ(File1, Char1);           (* read first character of each file *)
    READ(File2, Char2);

    REPEAT
        IF Char1 < Char2          (* determine smaller character *)
            THEN BEGIN            (* File1 has smaller character *)
                WRITE(MergedFile, Char1);
                IF NOT EOF(File1) THEN READ(File1, Char1)
            END     (* THEN *)
            ELSE BEGIN            (* File2 has smaller character *)
                WRITE(MergedFile, Char2);
                IF NOT EOF(File2) THEN READ(File2, Char2)
            END
    UNTIL (EOF(File1) OR EOF(File2));   (* one file is exhausted *)

    IF EOF(File1)
        THEN  (* File1 is exhausted, copy rest of File2 *)
            WHILE NOT EOF(File2) DO
                BEGIN
                    READ(File2, Char2);
                    WRITE(MergedFile, Char2)
                END
    ELSE IF EOF(File2)
        THEN (* File2 is exhausted, copy rest of File1 *)
            WHILE NOT EOF(File1) DO
                BEGIN
                    READ(File1, Char1);
                    WRITE(MergedFile, Char1)
                END

END;  (* MergeTwo *)
```

Programming Example 13-15:   Merging Two Alphabetized Files

This particular example illustrates most of the issues in Pascal file manipulation. You should be sure you understand it.

13.7. Chapter Summary

- There are several practical reasons why we need computer files:

    - Entering information into a computer is tedious, time consuming, and prone to error.

    - Large amounts of information both can be and are reused.

    - Machine-readable information saves both time and money

    - Machine-readable information is durable.

- Computer files typically are stored on secondary storage media, such as magnetic tape or disks.

- The Turing Machine Tape provides a familiar and accurate model of a computer file.

- Standard Pascal has no language-specified limit on the size of files.

- All computer files are stored on some media; therefore, they must be finite according to the system-determined limit on size.

- A Pascal file is a sequence of elements, all of the same type.

- Standard Pascal does not support files of files.

- A sequential file is a file in which, to read [write] the nth component, the n-1 preceding components must first be read [written].

- A random-access file is a file in which the components can be accessed in any order.

- Standard Pascal has only sequential files; it does not support random-access files.

- The current element is the component of the file immediately to the right of the file pointer.

- An empty file is a file with no elements.

- The most common type of file is a file of characters.

- Standard Pascal includes a predefined type named TEXT that is for FILE OF CHAR.

- Pascal file variables are different from other variables:
    - File variables refer to information that can exist both before a program begins and after a program ends.

    - If a file variable refers to information that exists before or after the Pascal program runs, the file variable must appear in the program heading.

    - Pascal requires any file variable listed in the program heading to be declared global to the entire program.

    - Pascal requires all file variables to be passed as VAR parameters. Pascal prohibits file variables from ever being passed as value parameters.

- A file must be opened before information can be read from it. Standard Pascal provides the predefined procedure RESET to open files for reading.

- Calling RESET on a file variable makes the first element of the file the current element.

- The predefined procedure READ is used to read information from a file.

- The end-of-file marker can be detected using the predefined BOOLEAN function EOF.

- Attempting to pass the end-of-file normally causes a runtime error.

- Files of type TEXT can also contain end-of-line markers. End-of-line markers are detected with the BOOLEAN function EOLN, read with the procedure READLN, and written with the procedure WRITELN.

- For every file variable there is a file buffer variable. The file buffer variable contains the next component to be read from a file. Standard Pascal indicates the file buffer variable by adding the suffix ^ to the file variable.

- Standard Pascal has a predefined procedure that advances the read head past exactly one component of the file. This procedure is named GET.

- A handful of file-related errors are so common nearly everyone seems to experience them. See table 13-2 on page 369 for a summary.

- Files must be opened for writing before information can be written to them. Standard Pascal provides the predefined procedure **REWRITE** to open files for writing.

- A file is empty immediately after **REWRITE** has been called on it. Any previously existing contents in the file are lost.

- Those files existing before or after a program executes are known as external files. Files that exist only during a program's execution are called internal files.

- All external files are to be listed as program parameters in the program heading.

- The predefined identifiers INPUT and OUTPUT are declared as file variables of type TEXT. INPUT is already open for reading, and OUTPUT is already open for writing. No Pascal program should attempt to open these two files.

13.8. Summary of Terms

- file
- Turing Machine Tape
- sequence
- cell
- sequential file
- random-access file
- current element
- empty file

- FILE OF
- TEXT
- RESET
- current element
- end-of-file
- EOF
- end-of-line
- EOLN

- file buffer variable
- GET
- REWRITE
- INPUT
- OUTPUT
- internal file
- external file
- program parameter

13.9. Chapter Problems

1. Write a program to count the number of characters in an arbitrary TEXT file and display the result to the user.

2. Modify the program in the previous problem so that end-of-line markers are not counted.

3. Using the **SkipBlanks** procedure developed earlier in this chapter, write a program that creates a copy of a TEXT file that is identical to the original file, except that any leading spaces on a line are removed in the copy.

4. Write a program that creates a copy of a TEXT file that is identical to the original file, except that all blank lines are removed.

5. Write a program that creates a copy of a TEXT file that is identical to the original file, except that each line in the copy is preceded by the line number and two blank spaces. Start line numbering with 1.

6. Write a program that takes as input a text file and determines the number of occurrences of each character in the file. You may shorten the summary to show only the number of letters, number of digits, and number of other characters.

7. The lowercase letters ('a'..'z'), the uppercase letters ('A'..'Z'), and the 10 digit characters ('0'..'9') collectively form what are known as the *alpha* characters. Write a procedure named **SkipAlphas** that takes a TEXT file parameter and moves the read head past any alpha characters until the first non-alpha character is encountered.

8. Write a procedure named **SkipNonAlphas** that does just the opposite of **SkipAlphas** in the last problem.

9. Consider a word to be one or more alpha characters. Write a program that determines the number of words in an arbitrary TEXT file. *Hint: You should use the two procedures* **SkipAlphas** *and* **SkipNonAlphas** *from the two previous problems.*

10. Extend the previous program to also determine the length of the longest word in the TEXT file.

11. Extend the previous program to also determine how many words in the TEXT file exceed seven characters.

12. Extend the previous program to also determine the percentage of words in the TEXT file that exceed seven characters.

13. Extend the previous program to determine the average length of all words in the TEXT file.

Chapter 14: Arrays

In the past two chapters of this unit we have reviewed most of the user-defined types. The following illustration indicates where we are currently in our study of Pascal's types:

In the final two chapters of this unit, we will study the three remaining *structured types*, which are known as structured *internal* types. In this chapter we present the **ARRAY**, and in the next chapter we study the **RECORD** and **SET**. These three types, together with those learned in the last two chapters of this unit, not only enable us to solve real-world problems, they help us to solve them better. In addition to learning how to use these types, you will learn how they can make your programs clear, easy to read, and easy to modify.

14.1. The Need for Arrays

Earlier, we created a procedure to help tally the votes cast in an election (Programming Example 12-11 on page 344). The solution was fine for an election involving three candidates, and it is easy to imagine extending this solution to cover elections with more than three candidates. But suppose the election has a very large number of candidates. The parameter list and the CASE statement would grow enormously if we extended our program in the simple way. If the election had fifty candidates instead of three, we would need fifty parameters instead of three. It would be necessary to initialize all fifty variables instead of three. We would also need fifty different clauses in the CASE statement instead of three. If the election had one thousand candidates, the given solution would be totally inappropriate. The procedure would need one thousand parameters, it would take one thousand different statements to initialize the variables, and it would require a one-thousand clause CASE statement to increment the appropriate total.

It would be nice to have some sort of super variable that could hold the counts for all the candidates. What we would like to do for the vote tally problem is group together the counts for all candidates and consider them as a single unit. However, we would still like to be able to pick out or designate the particular value corresponding to the vote count for any particular candidate. This is precisely what **arrays** are designed to do.

The idea for the array came to computer science from mathematics. Mathematicians use objects called vectors. They refer to a particular element of the vector by using a *subscript*. Hence, for a vector named V, they would refer to the elements as V_1, V_2, V_3, and so on. This terminology is often used in talking about arrays and their elements. For example, if vote counts are considered as a single unit called **count**, we could denote individual counts as $\mathbf{count_1}$, $\mathbf{count_2}$, $\mathbf{count_3}$, and so on. The following illustration depicts an array of one thousand vote-count totals:

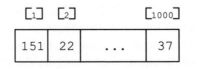

Figure 14-1: Array of 1000 Candidate Vote Totals

Although this illustration does not show all one thousand counts, we can see that candidate 1 has 151 votes, candidate 2 has 22 votes, and the 1000th candidate has 37 votes.

An array is a sequence of values and is, therefore, similar to a file. Every value of an array must be of the same type, just as every value of a file must be of the same type. Arrays differ from files in two distinct ways:

1. Whereas elements of a file must be accessed *sequentially*, elements of an array can be accessed *randomly*.

2. Whereas files are normally held in *secondary memory*, arrays are held in *primary memory*.

14.2. Array Terminology and Declaring Arrays

An array is composed of elements, each of which must have a value of the same type. Standard Pascal permits you to use any defined type as the type for the elements. When we refer to a particular element's value, we use an *index* (sometimes called a subscript) to designate that value. Collectively, they are known as *indices*. The following illustration depicts both the values of an array's elements and the indices used to refer to the values:

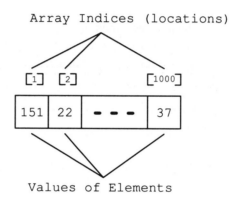

Figure 14-2: Array Terminology

In the previous illustration, the values of the array components are joined as adjacent boxes, and the index for each component appears in brackets.

> **Definition 14-1:** An ***array component value*** is the value of a single component of an array.

> **Definition 14-2:** An ***array index*** designates a particular component of an array.

The vote counts cast in an election can be represented as an array of integers. For one thousand candidates, we can declare such an array in Standard Pascal as follows:

```
TYPE
    ListOfCountsType = ARRAY [1..1000] OF INTEGER;


VAR
    count: ListOfCountsType;
```

Programming Example 14-1: Declaring an Array for Vote Counts

Note that we first define a new type and then declare a variable of that type. The user-defined type **ListOfCountsType** is an ARRAY of INTEGERs. The array has one thousand components, indexed from 1 through 1000. Since the variable **count** is declared of this type, it is an array of one thousand integers. Components of an array variable are indicated by the name of the array followed by the corresponding index in square brackets. For example, the components of the variable **count** are denoted as **count[1]**, **count[2]**, **count[3]**, ... **count[1000]**.

Note how both the type of the component and the indices of the components are specified in the definition of the array. Although Pascal permits any type of component values, as long as they are all of the same type, the index values must be of an *ordinal* type. The component type in this example is the predefined type INTEGER, and the indices are a subrange of INTEGER (1..1000). You can think of the BNF for a Pascal array as follows:

```
<array-type> ::= ARRAY [ <index-type> ] OF <component-type>
```

The index type is any ordinal type, and the component type is any valid type. A few other examples of valid Pascal arrays are as follows:

```
TYPE
    DailyTotalsType = ARRAY [1..365] OF INTEGER;

    AccountBalancesType = ARRAY [1111..9999] OF REAL;

    DivingTimesType = ARRAY [-50..-1] OF REAL;

    TemperatureTotalsType = ARRAY [-75..120] OF INTEGER;
```

Programming Example 14-2: Valid Array Declarations

Note that each of these examples uses a subrange of INTEGER as the index type. The most common index type is a subrange of INTEGER. Although some programming languages permit only positive numbers as array indices, Pascal has no such restriction. Later in this chapter, we will review some other array indices that Pascal also permits.

14.3. Manipulating Arrays and Their Components

Knowing what arrays are and how to declare them in Pascal, we can consider accessing and changing the values held by arrays. Suppose we are interested in monitoring daily temperatures so that we can determine the number of days a particular temperature has been reached. We would probably define an array type with some range of temperatures as the indices. If we are interested in both the high and the low temperatures, we might use the following:

```
CONST
    MinTemp = -20;        (* lowest expected temperature *)
    MaxTemp = 120;        (* highest expected temperature *)

TYPE
    TempTotalsType = ARRAY [MinTemp..MaxTemp] OF INTEGER;

VAR
    LowTemps, HighTemps: TempTotalsType
```

Programming Example 14-3: Daily Temperature Example

We first define a named constant for the minimum and maximum temperatures we expect (**MinTemp** and **MaxTemp**). Next, we define an array type to hold an integer for each of the temperatures in the range **MinTemp..MaxTemp**. Finally, we declare two variables of this type, one for daily low temperatures and one for the daily high temperatures. Individual components of an array can be accessed by specifying both the array name and a valid array index, as indicated in the following example:

```
WRITELN(OUTPUT, HighTemps[100]);

WRITELN(OUTPUT, LowTemps[32]);

IF HighTemps[75] > 0
    WRITELN(OUTPUT, HighTemps[75]);

WRITELN(OUTPUT, 'The high was ', 112, HighTemps[110], ' times.');

WRITELN(OUTPUT, 'The high was ', MaxTemp, HighTemps[MaxTemp], ' times.');

WRITELN(OUTPUT, 'Temperature  HighDays  LowDays');
FOR temp := MinTemp TO MaxTemp DO
    WRITELN(OUTPUT, temp, HighTemps[temp], LowTemps[temp])
```

Programming Example 14-4: Accessing a Component's Value

HighTemps is the array, and **HighTemps[-20]** to **HighTemps[120]** is the range for temperatures—the components of the array. The indices for the array are temperatures, and the value of a component is a number that corresponds to the number of times that temperature has been reached.

The two variables **HighTemps** and **LowTemps** are both array variables. Each is an array of integers indexed from **MinTemp** to **MaxTemp** (-20 to 120). To access a particular array component value, we must specify both the array name and a valid array index.

The number of times the high temperature has reached 100 degrees is specified as **HighTemps[100]**. Since this is an integer value and can be written to the output, it is accessed as the first example indicates: (**WRITELN(OUTPUT, HighTemps[100])**). Similarly, the number of times the low temperature was 32 degrees can be specified as **LowTemps[32]**. Note that we must always specify both the array name and a valid array index for that array.

Since both **HighTemps** and **LowTemps** are arrays of integers, we can use their components as we use any other integer expression. For example, we can use them as integer operands to a relational operator. If we want to perform some action only if the high temperature reached some temperature, say 75 degrees, then we would use an IF statement with an expression using a relational operator and an array component value. Specifically, we would use **IF HighTemps[75] > 0**. Components of an array can be used like other variables, as long as both the array name and a valid array index are specified.

Similarly, the value held by a component can be changed by assigning a value to it. Again, both the variable name and an index must be specified:

```
LowTemps[-18] := 0;

TodaysHigh := 88;
HighTemps[TodaysHigh] := 4;

TodaysLow := 55;
LowTemps[TodaysLow] := LowTemps[TodaysLow] + 1;
```

Programming Example 14-5: Changing a Component's Value

Recall that we normally initialize every variable before using it. To initialize an array variable, every component must be given a value. Since the number of components is known, a FOR loop is normally used, as indicated in the following program fragment:

```
FOR index := MinTemp TO MaxTemp DO
    HighTemps[index] := 0
```

Programming Example 14-6: Initializing an Array Variable

Note that each component must be initialized separately. The following illustration shows how to initialize an array:

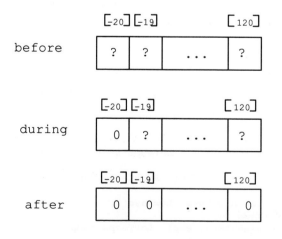

Figure 14-3: Array Initialization

Now that we can access and change the component values of an array, let us turn our attention back to the **TallyVotes** procedure. The revised procedure will take an array variable as a parameter corresponding to the count of votes for each of the candidates rather than 1000 individual variables.

First, the procedure initializes each component value to 0. The remainder of the procedure is close to the way it was before: While there are more votes to be counted, the next vote is read and the appropriate component is incremented. The appropriate count is always a component of the array variable:

```
PROCEDURE TallyVotes (VAR count: ListOfCountsType);

VAR
    vote: INTEGER;


BEGIN
    FOR vote := 1 TO NumberOfCandidates DO
        count[vote] := 0;      (* initialize count for candidates *)

    WHILE MoreVotes DO         (* count votes *)
        BEGIN
            vote := NextVote;
            count[vote] := count[vote] + 1   (* increment appropriate vote count *)
        END      (* WHILE *)
END;      (* TallyVotes *)
```

Programming Example 14-7: `TallyVotes` with an Array Variable

If you compare this **TallyVotes** procedure with its predecessor, you will notice that the rewritten procedure needs only one parameter instead of the one thousand that would be needed if we passed each variable individually. Note that all one thousand counts can be initialized with one statement (the FOR loop). Also, the WHILE loop that tallies the votes is very simple, having only two inner statements. There is no need for a CASE statement at all!

With our first solution, we saw how it was completely inappropriate for a problem size of one thousand. We would never dream of trying the same solution with problem sizes of 10,000, 20,000, or 30,000. But with the second solution, all we need to do is change the value of the named constant **NumberOfCandidates**, and the tallying procedure works correctly without any alteration. This simple example shows the value of arrays. Think of how valuable they are for problems that are complex!

14.4. Some Important Points About Arrays

14.4.1. Random Access

We said earlier that arrays are a lot like files and that both can be thought of as a sequence of elements, with each element of the same type. However, remember the two important distinctions between arrays and files. Files are *sequential* structures, and arrays are *random-access* structures. This means we can access or change any value of an array without having to bother with any of the preceding components, as was required with sequential files. Another difference is that files are typically held in secondary memory, and arrays are always held in primary memory. As a consequence, on most computers, programs can have much larger files than they can have arrays.

14.4.2. Writing an Entire Array

We are used to writing a variable's value by simply using WRITE or WRITELN with the variable of interest. However, array variables must be handled a bit differently. Since an array variable is composed of many values, each value must be written separately, as indicated in the following example:

```
FOR index := 1 TO NumberOfCandidates DO
    WRITELN(OUTPUT, count[index])
```

Programming Example 14-8: Writing an Array

14.4.3. Copying an Entire Array

Suppose we have two array variables called **first** and **second**, both of type **ListOfCountsType**. If we wanted to copy the values from one array to the other, we might create code similar to the following:

```
FOR index := 1 to 1000 DO
    first[index] := second[index]
```

Programming Example 14-9: Copying Arrays One Component at a Time

However, since both variables are of the same type, we can copy all the values in a more convenient way:

```
first := second
```

Programming Example 14-10: Copying Arrays in One Step

For two arrays to be copied in this way, the two array variables must be declared of the same type.

14.4.4. Finding the Maximum Element

Let us return now to our example of counting votes cast in an election. Suppose we wanted to write a procedure to determine the number of votes given to the winning candidate. This is essentially a problem of finding the largest value in an array. The solution is relatively simple: Initialize the current maximum; successively run through all elements in the array, replacing the current maximum with the larger of the element and the current maximum; when all elements have been compared, the current maximum is the desired maximum. Initially, the current maximum must be set to a value less than or equal to the maximum in the array. In this case, zero will work since the maximum cannot be negative. However, either **Minint** or the first element in the array is generally the best choice. The Pascal function to find the maximum would look something like the following:

```
FUNCTION FindMax (count: ListOfCountsType): INTEGER;

VAR
    index, currentmax: INTEGER;


BEGIN
    currentmax := count[1];

    FOR index := 1 to NumberOfCandidates DO
        currentmax := Maximum(count[index], currentmax);

    FindMax := currentmax
END;    (* FindMax *)
```

Programming Example 14-11: Function **FindMax**

where the function **Maximum** is defined as

```
FUNCTION Maximum (first, second: INTEGER): INTEGER;

BEGIN
    IF first > second
        THEN Maximum := first
        ELSE Maximum := second
END;    (* Maximum *)
```

Programming Example 14-12: Function **Maximum**

A similar routine to find the minimum of the array (**FindMin**) can also be written.

Another routine we might want is a function to determine the number of candidates who received a given number of votes. The following function does this:

```
FUNCTION NumberTied (count: ListOfCountsType; DesiredVotes: INTEGER): INTEGER;

VAR
    result: INTEGER;
    index: INTEGER;

BEGIN
    result := 0;

    FOR index := 1 TO NumberOfCandidates DO
        IF (count[index] = DesiredVotes)
            THEN result := result + 1;

    NumberTied := result
END;    (* NumberTied *)
```

Programming Example 14-13: Function **NumberTied**

The number of candidates with the highest number of votes (the number tied for first place) is simply **NumberTied(count, FindMax(count))**. Likewise, the number tied for last place (fewest number of votes) is **NumberTied(count, FindMin(count))**. Determining the minimum value in an array, the maximum value in an array, or the number of occurrences of a particular value in an array are tasks commonly performed on arrays.

14.5. Other Kinds of Array Indexing

Up to this point, every array index type has been a subrange of INTEGERs. However, look closely at the BNF for the array type:

> **<array-type> ::= ARRAY [<index-type>] OF <component-type>**

> **<index-type> ::= <ordinal-type>**

The index type for an array can be any *ordinal* type. This means that we can also use type CHAR, type BOOLEAN, any enumerated type, or a subrange of any of these types. The following are valid array declarations:

```
TYPE
    LetterTotalsType = ARRAY ['a'..'z'] OF INTEGER;

    ColorType = (red, blue, green);
    ColorSelectionsType = ARRAY [ColorType] OF INTEGER;

    DayOfWeekType = (sunday, monday, tuesday, wednesday, thursday, friday, saturday);
    DailyTotalsType = ARRAY [DayOfWeekType] OF REAL;

    WorkWeekTotalsType = ARRAY [monday..friday] OF REAL;
```

Programming Example 14-14: Arrays with Non-INTEGER Indices

The first declaration is an array of INTEGERs indexed with the letters 'a'..'z'. The second example is also an array of INTEGERs, but indexed with the enumerated type **ColorType** (red, blue, and green). The third example is an array of REAL values indexed with the seven days of the week defined by the enumerated type **DayOfWeekType**. The last example is also an array of REAL values, but this time indexed with a subrange of **DayOfWeekType** (specifically, **monday..friday**). Many programming languages permit only integers as array indices. For this reason, Pascal is much richer in user-defined types than most other programming languages. Although Pascal permits a wide variety of array indices, the array itself can be be thought of in the same way, regardless of which indices are used. The following figure shows an array indexed with the characters 'a'..'z':

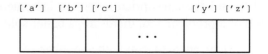

Figure 14-4: Array Indexed by Letters

The following illustration uses the same model of arrays for an array indexed by values of **DayOfWeekType**:

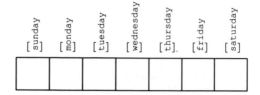

Figure 14-5: Array Indexed by Enumerated Type

To appreciate the usefulness of such array indices, consider this example. Suppose we have a large TEXT file composed only of lowercase letters. Assume that we must analyze the file for character frequencies. Therefore, we must write a Pascal procedure to count the number of occurrences of each character. If we had to use integers as array indices, we might represent the 26 letter counts as indicated in the following type definition:

```
LetterCountsType = ARRAY [1..26] OF INTEGER;
```

Programming Example 14-15: Integer Array Indices

When an 'a' is read, the count for the first element (1) is incremented; when a 'b' is read, the count for (2) is incremented, and so forth. This type of solution requires a correspondence between the 26 letters and 26 integers. Although you can recall easily that 1 means 'a', 2 means 'b', and 3 means 'c', you probably cannot recall the 18th character quite as easily. Although the integers 1..26 will work, we are dealing with letters, and the characters 'a'..'z' are more appropriate array indices. This can be seen in the type definition and procedure to count the letters of the file in Programming Example 14-16 as follows:

```
TYPE
    LetterCountsType = ARRAY ['a'..'z'] OF INTEGER;


PROCEDURE CountCharacters (VAR infile: TEXT;  VAR count: LetterCountsType);

VAR
    ch: CHAR;

BEGIN
    FOR ch := 'a' TO 'z' DO
        count[ch] := 0;          (* initialize count array *)

    RESET(infile);               (* open file for reading *)

    WHILE NOT EOF(infile) DO
        BEGIN
            READ(infile, ch);            (* read next char *)
            count[ch] := count[ch] + 1   (* increment count *)
        END    (* WHILE *)

END;    (* CountCharacters *)
```

Programming Example 14-16: Procedure **CountCharacters**

In this example, the type definition specifies an array of integers indexed by a lowercase letter ('a'..'z'). The procedure is straightforward. It takes two parameters, one for the input file and the other for the array of counts. First, the counts are initialized; second, the file is opened for reading; finally, each character is read from the file and the appropriate count is incremented. Noninteger array indices provide a better representation of a problem and, therefore, a better solution.

As another example, say that we needed to count the number of members of each political party. Although countries with only one political party would not need an array variable for this, assume we will be making computations for a variety of political parties. The following declarations are ones we might use for the political parties in the United States:

```
TYPE
    PartyType = (democrat, republican, independent, libertarian, socialist, communist);

    TallyType = ARRAY [PartyType] OF INTEGER;

VAR
    count : TallyType;
```

Programming Example 14-17:   Array Indexed by Political Party

Array types can be defined according to the following general scheme:

```
TYPE
    IndexSetType = lowbound .. highbound;

    ArrayType = ARRAY [IndexSetType] OF elementtype;
```

Programming Example 14-18:   Generalized Array Definitions

14.6. Arrays of Arrays and Multiple Indexing Sets

Although we have seen that the noninteger array indices of Pascal provide better ways to represent data and, therefore, better programming solutions, there are times when we need additional techniques for representing the problem at hand. For example, say that we decided to write a computer program to play tic-tac-toe. For this program, we need to define a user-defined type to represent the tic-tac-toe board. The following illustration shows such a board:

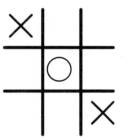

Figure 14-6:   Tic-Tac-Toe Board

Notice that we actually need to represent two types of objects: the board itself and the markers on the board. We could use an enumerated type to represent the markers with three values, say, X, O, and empty. Representing the board is more difficult. We need some structure to hold the nine markers of the board. The desire to use an array to represent the board is predictable and natural. We might define a new type that is an array of markers, containing nine markers. However, what indices do we use? Choosing integer indices 1..9 gives us a representation indicated in the following figure:

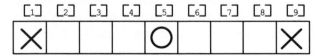

Figure 14-7:   First Try

Although we can establish a correspondence between every row-column pair and an array index 1..9, and use such an array to represent a tic-tac-toe board, it just is not convenient. Another way to think of a tic-tac-toe board is as 3 rows, each row containing 3 markers. The following figure illustrates representing a tic-tac-toe board in this way:

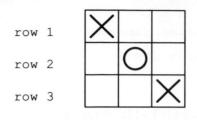

row 1
row 2
row 3

Figure 14-8: Second Try

Therefore, a tic-tac-toe board can be represented as an array 1..3 of rows. Each row, in turn, is an array 1..3 of markers. The board is represented as an array. Each component of this array is also an array. Pascal permits array components to be of any type, including other arrays. The following Pascal type definitions depict this:

```
CONST
    MaxRow = 3;              (* tic-tac-toe board has 3 rows *)

    MaxColumn = 3;          (* tic-tac-toe board has 3 columns *)


TYPE
    MarkerType = (empty, X, O);

    RowType = ARRAY [1..MaxColumn] OF MarkerType;

    BoardType = ARRAY [1..MaxRow] OF RowType;
```
Programming Example 14-19: Tic-Tac-Toe Board as an Array of Arrays

If the variable **board** is declared of **BoardType**, then we can refer to the second row as **board[2]** and the third column of the second row as **board[2][3]**. The procedure to initialize the game board can be written as follows:

```
PROCEDURE InitBoard (VAR board : BoardType);

VAR
    row, column: INTEGER;

BEGIN
    FOR row := 1 TO MaxRow DO
        FOR column := 1 TO MaxColumn DO
            board[row][column] := empty
END;    (* InitBoard *)
```
Programming Example 14-20: Procedure **InitBoard**

Although the array of arrays used here is much superior to a single array indexed from 1 through 9, it is not the best we can do. We really want an array with two dimensions (index sets), one for the row and one for the column. Standard Pascal permits arrays to have as many dimensions as desired, as indicated in the following rewritten representation of a tic-tac-toe board:

```
CONST
    MaxRow = 3;              (* tic-tac-toe board has 3 rows *)

    MaxColumn = 3;          (* tic-tac-toe board has 3 columns *)


TYPE
    MarkerType = (empty, X, O);

    BoardType = ARRAY [1..MaxRow, 1..MaxColumn] OF MarkerType;
```
Programming Example 14-21: Tic-Tac-Toe Board as a Two Dimensional Array

Here is a procedure that will initialize the game board:

```
PROCEDURE InitBoard (VAR board : BoardType);

VAR
    row, column: INTEGER;

BEGIN
    FOR row := 1 TO MaxRow DO
        FOR column := 1 TO MaxColumn DO
            board[row,column] := empty;
END;    (* InitBoard *)
```

Programming Example 14-22: Procedure **InitBoard**

As another example of this type of problem, consider representing a chess board. Again, we need a way to represent both the pieces and the board. We can use an enumerated type for the pieces and a two-dimensional array to represent the board, as indicated:

```
CONST
    MaxRow = 8;          (* chess board has 8 rows *)
    MaxColumns = 8;      (* chess board has 8 columns *)


TYPE
    PieceType = (king, queen, bishop, knight, rook, pawn, empty);

    ChessBoardType = ARRAY [1..MaxRows, 1..MaxColumns] OF PieceType;
```

Programming Example 14-23: Representing a Chess Board

Given the last two examples, you might be thinking that an array of arrays and a two-dimensional array are always equally good representations or that one is always the better representation. It turns out that neither of those assumptions is true.

If an object is represented as a two-dimensional array rather than as an array of arrays, there is no way to specify all elements of exactly one row or one column. However, if we never need to be able to designate just one row or one column at a time, a two-dimensinal array is probably the better choice. An example of when we might want arrays of arrays comes from mathematics. Numbers are often arranged in rows and columns, called a *matrix*, as shown in the following figure.

$$\begin{bmatrix} 5.2 & 3.7 \\ 1.0 & 3.3 \end{bmatrix}$$

Figure 14-9: A Simple Matrix

Although this matrix has only two rows and two columns, matrices can have many rows and columns. Matrices are used very widely because they have mathematical properties that facilitate representing and manipulating many types of information. If we think of a matrix as a collection of rows—commonly called row vectors—we can define a matrix as follows:

```
TYPE
    RowVectorType = ARRAY [1..NumberOfColumns] OF ElementType;

    MatrixType = ARRAY [1..NumberOfRows] OF RowVectorType;

VAR
    matrix: MatrixType;
```

Programming Example 14-24: Declaration of a Matrix

With **matrix** declared this way, we can now refer to the third row as **matrix[3]**. In general, the Nth row can be referred to as **matrix[N]**. Individual elements can still be referred to as **matrix[2][5]**.

We could have defined the matrix to be an array of columns, each column being an array of components; however, once this is done there is no way to refer to just one row. Similarly, if a matrix is defined as an array of rows, there is no way to refer to an entire column. If we instead define the matrix as a two-dimensional array, there is a way to refer to either an entire row or an entire column. The need to do so should determine which representation you use.

The general form of the BNF for an array in Standard Pascal is as follows:

```
<array-type> ::= ARRAY [ <index-type> { , <index-type> } ] OF
                     <component-type>
```

An array can have more than one index set, as long as each set is some ordinal type. The component type of an array can be any valid type—even other arrays—as long as all components have the same type.

14.7. String Variables

A programmer does not need to write very many programs before the need for strings arises. We live in a world full of words, names, and sentences. Although it is true that each of these are composed of characters, we normally are not interested in the individual characters but the words that the characters form. Sequences of characters are referred to as *strings*.

Although there was a lot of debate over whether to include a predefined type for strings in Pascal, Standard Pascal does NOT include such a predefined type. You might be thinking that this was an error. Many Pascal programmers agree. Fortunately, Pascal is a type-extensible programming language, which permits user-defined types. Standard Pascal enables a programmer to create a new type for strings.

We should mention that there are many implementations of Pascal that DO include a predefined type for strings. Some implementations even provide a variety of procedures and functions to use on string variables. However, it is very important that you realize that such features are not part of Standard Pascal. If you are writing a program that you expect to run on a variety of machines with a variety of compilers, we suggest you stay away from such nonstandard features. Even if the implementation of Pascal you are currently using does include predefined string variables and you do decide to use them, you should still learn how to define a type and the associated subprograms for strings.

Since there is both educational and practical value to being able to create and manipulate strings, we will study this subject further. The first step is to define a new type to represent strings. The new type is, not surprisingly, an *array*. The BNF for a string type in Standard Pascal is:

```
<string-array-type> ::= PACKED ARRAY [ <string-index-type> ] OF CHAR
```

```
<string-index-type> ::= 1 .. <string-max>
```

Standard Pascal has three requirements for creating a string type:

1. The component type of the array must be of type CHAR.

2. The index must be a subrange of INTEGER beginning with 1 and ending with an integer larger than 1.

3. The reserved word **ARRAY** must be preceded by the reserved word **PACKED**.

Given these requirements, the following are all valid Pascal string types.

```
CONST
    StringMax = 128;

TYPE
    WordType = PACKED ARRAY [1..10] OF CHAR;

    NameType = PACKED ARRAY [1..25] OF CHAR;

    StringType = PACKED ARRAY [1..128] OF CHAR;

    StringType = PACKED ARRAY [1..StringMax] OF CHAR;

    StringIndexType = 1..StringMax;
    StringType = PACKED ARRAY [StringIndexType] OF CHAR;
```

Programming Example 14-25:   Valid String Type Definitions

However, each of the following are invalid string type definitions in Standard Pascal:

```
TYPE
    WordType = PACKED ARRAY [0..10] OF CHAR;     (* must start with 1 *)

    WordType = ARRAY [1..1] OF CHAR;             (* must end with 2 or more *)

    Letter = 'a'..'z';
    NameType = PACKED ARRAY [1..25] OF Letter;   (* must be of type CHAR *)


    StringIndexType = '1'..'5';
    StringType = PACKED ARRAY [StringIndexType] OF CHAR;
                                        (* must be subrange of INTEGER *)
```

Programming Example 14-26:   Invalid String Type Definitions

These last four type definitions *are* valid array definitions, but they are *not* valid string types.

14.7.1. Initializing String Variables

As with all other variables, we normally give string variables a known value before using them. For string variables, each component is normally set to the space character (ASCII character 32) or, perhaps, the null character (ASCII 0). The following program fragment demonstrates a string type, a string variable, and the initialization of the string variable:

```
CONST
    MaxString = 47;              (* string size *)
    InitChar = ' ';              (* initial string character *)

TYPE
    StringType = ARRAY [1..MaxString] OF CHAR;


PROCEDURE InitString (VAR string: StringType);

VAR
    index: INTEGER;

BEGIN
    FOR index := 1 TO MaxString DO
        string[index] := InitChar
END;    (* InitString *)
```

Programming Example 14-27:   String Initialization

The following illustration depicts the values held by a variable of **StringType** after initialization:

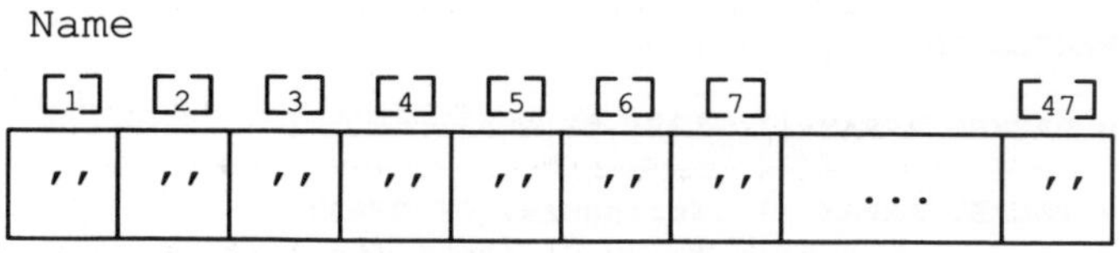

```
Name

[1]    [2]    [3]    [4]    [5]    [6]    [7]                [47]
```

```
┌──────┬──────┬──────┬──────┬──────┬──────┬──────┬──────────┬──────┐
│  ' ' │  ' ' │  ' ' │  ' ' │  ' ' │  ' ' │  ' ' │   ...    │  ' ' │
└──────┴──────┴──────┴──────┴──────┴──────┴──────┴──────────┴──────┘
```

Figure 14-10:   Initialization of a String Variable

14.7.2. Reading String Variables

String variables normally get their values by being read. Sometimes the values are read from the keyboard, and other times they are read from a disk file. The following is a general procedure for reading string values:

```
PROCEDURE ReadString (VAR where: TEXT;  VAR string: StringType);

VAR
    index: INTEGER;

BEGIN
    InitString(string);

    index := 1;
    WHILE NOT(EOLN(where)) AND (index <= MaxString) DO
        BEGIN
            READ(where, string[index]);
            index := index + 1
        END     (* WHILE *)
END;      (* ReadString *)
```

Programming Example 14-28:   Procedure **ReadString**

14.7.3. Writing String Variables

A procedure to write strings is even easier than the procedure for reading strings, since we do not need to be concerned about the end-of-line. The following is a procedure to write strings:

```
PROCEDURE WriteString (VAR where: TEXT;  string: StringType);

VAR
    index: INTEGER;

BEGIN
    FOR index := 1 TO MaxString DO
        WRITE(where, string[index])
END;      (* WriteString *)
```

Programming Example 14-29:   Procedure **WriteString**

Remember Standard Pascal's three requirements for string types. Although Pascal normally requires each element of an array to be output separately, Standard Pascal provides an easier method of outputting variables that meet the requirements of a string type. For variables that meet the three requirements, you can use WRITE or WRITELN with the string variable name rather than using a loop. Thus, **WRITE(where, string)** and **WRITELN(where, string)** are valid in Standard Pascal. Although Pascal permits writing an entire string array using WRITE and WRITELN, Standard Pascal does not permit reading an entire string array at a time.

14.7.4. Comparing String Variables

Comparing strings is relatively straightforward. We simply compare every character of the two strings. If every corresponding character is the same, the strings are equal; otherwise, they are not. The following function illustrates a comparison for string equality:

```
FUNCTION StringsEqual (first, second: StringType): BOOLEAN;

VAR
    index: INTEGER;

BEGIN
    StringsEqual := TRUE;
    FOR index := 1 TO MaxString DO
        IF first[index] <> second[index]
            THEN StringsEqual := FALSE
END;    (* StringEqual *)
```

Programming Example 14-30: Function `StringsEqual`

One of the other things that meeting the three requirements of string type variables provides is an easier way to compare string variables. It is valid in Standard Pascal to simply say `first = second` for two string variables. Meeting the three requirements of string types permits us to use all six relational operators on string variables, not just the = operator. For example, can also use `first < second`. In comparing two string variables, we compare them left-to-right. If every character is the same, then the strings are equivalent. Otherwise, the first different character determines which string variable is less than the other. When two characters differ, one will be of a lesser value. Thus, the string containing the lesser character is smaller than the other string. The order associated with the type CHAR determines the order of string values.

14.8. Questions

1. What is an array?

2. What is a structured type? Is an array a structured type?

3. What is a structured internal type? Is an array a structured internal type?

4. In what ways are arrays and files the same?

5. In what ways are arrays and files different?

6. What is an array index?

7. What is an array-component value?

8. What constraints are placed on array components by Pascal?

9. What constraints are placed on array indices by Pascal?

10. How is an array component specified in Pascal?

11. What is the difference between random-access and sequential-access structures?

12. Are arrays random-access or sequential-access structures?

13. Does Pascal permit negative integers as array indices?

14. Does Pascal permit noninteger values as array indices? If so, specify what types of values can be used as array indices.

15. Must all components of a given array have the same type?

16. Can Pascal arrays have structured types as array components? Can arrays have arrays of other arrays (nested arrays)?

17. Can a Pascal array have more than one dimension?

18. What is the full BNF for an array type definition?

19. Does Standard Pascal have a predefined type for strings?

20. Does the implementation of Pascal you are using have a predefined type for strings? If so, does it also include any procedures and functions to manipulate that type?

21. Does Standard Pascal enable a programmer to define a new type for strings?

22. What is the BNF for a string array in Standard Pascal?

23. What are the three requirements for a string array in Standard Pascal?

24. What two advantages does a **PACKED** ARRAY of CHARacters provide?

14.9. Problems

1. Processing students' exams and grades is a nightmare for many educators. Write a program that accepts an arbitrary number of exam scores, tallies them, and determines the number of exams with each possible score. Assume that the scores range from 0 to 100 in integer values.

2. Extend the previous program so that it displays the highest score, lowest score, and range of actual scores.

3. Extend the previous program to compute the mean of the scores.

4. Extend the previous program to compute the median of the scores.

5. Extend the previous program to compute the mode of the scores.

6. Creating a string package from scratch can be an extremely instructive experience. Implement a simple string package using only what is provided in Standard Pascal. It should include the following:

    - a type **StringType** to represent strings

    - A procedure **ReadString** to read strings

    - A procedure **WriteString** to write strings

    - A function **StringLength** that returns the length of a string

    - A procedure **InitString** that initializes strings to all null characters.

    - All unused elements of the array should be padded with the null character (ASCII 0) at all times.

7. Extend the string package in the previous problem to include a procedure **FillString** that fills a string with a particular character. The procedure has two parameters, one for the string and one for the character.

8. Extend the string package to include a procedure named **ReplaceChar** that replaces one character with another in a specified string. The procedure has three parameters.

9. Extend the string package further to include a function **IsSubString** that takes two strings and determines if the smaller string is a substring of the larger string. If it is, the index of the starting substring should be returned as a function value; otherwise, 0 should be returned. If the smaller string exists in the larger string more than once, return the starting position of the left-most occurrence.

10. The video output display of a computer can be thought of as rows and columns of characters. Define a new type to represent such a display. Define it as a two-dimensional array. Give an alternative type definition as an array of arrays.

14.10. Chapter Summary

- A variable of a *scalar* type has only one value, whereas a variable of a *structured* type has more than one component value.

- A variable of an internal type is stored entirely in primary memory, whereas a variable of an external type is stored in secondary memory, such as a disk.

- Arrays, records, and sets are internal structured types, whereas files are external structured types.

- An array is a structured internal type. Each component of an array has the same type and is referenced by the array name and the array index.

- Arrays differ from files in that arrays are an internal type, whereas files are an external type. Also, arrays are random access rather than sequential access.

- Pascal permits negative integers and noninteger array indices, as long as the array index is of an *ordinal* type.

- Pascal permits arrays of any type, even structured types. Hence, one can have arrays of arrays and arrays of files in Pascal.

- Pascal permits multiple array index sets, instead of just one.

- The BNF for the array type in Pascal is:

      `<array-type> ::= ARRAY [ <index-type> { , <index-type> } ]`
  OF
                      `<component-type>`
  Where index-type is any ordinal type, and component-type is any valid type.

- Standard Pascal does NOT have a predefined type for strings. However, Standard Pascal enables a programmer to create a *user-defined* type for strings.

- Pascal places three requirements on string arrays:
  1. The component type of the array must be type CHAR.
  2. The index must be a subrange of INTEGER beginning with 1 and ending with an integer larger than 1.
  3. The reserved word ARRAY must be preceded by the reserved word **PACKED**.

- The BNF for a string array is:

      `<string-array-type> ::= PACKED ARRAY [ <string-index-type> ]`
               `OF CHAR`

      `<string-index-type> ::= 1 .. <string-max>`

- Although Standard Pascal normally prohibits comparing arrays or writing them out in a single step, string arrays that meet all three requirements can be compared using any of the six relational operators and can be written using WRITE or WRITELN, rather than forcing each character to be written separately.

14.11. Summary of Terms

- structured type
- internal type
- structured internal type
- array
- array component

- array index
- random access
- sequential access
- multiple dimension array

- strings
- ARRAY
- PACKED ARRAY
- string array

Chapter 15: Records and Sets

In the preceding chapter, we reviewed the array and examined how it can be used to solve problems involving large amounts of data. In addition to arrays, Pascal permits the programmer to define two other structured internal types: records and sets. The following diagram illustrates where we are in our tour of types:

In this chapter, we will examine the use of records and sets to develop increasingly sophisticated programs. By the end of this chapter, you will possess the tools necessary to develop an entire range of useful programs capable of managing complex information. In fact, you should be able to write the kinds of programs that are used widely within the world of business. In addition to the examples and problems presented in the text, we encourage you to think about similar programs that are currently in use.

15.1. Records

The physical objects of our world are composed of more primitive substances called *elements*. Although elements are composed of even smaller objects known as protons, neutrons, and electrons, elements cannot be broken down any further using only chemical means.

Each element can be described by a variety of pieces of information. Included in such a description are the number of protons, number of neutrons, number of electrons, the atomic number, the atomic weight, and the atomic symbol. This information is typically summarized in a chart referred to as the *periodic table*. Assume that your help is needed to write a computer program to keep track of this information.

One of the primary concerns for this program is how the information is to be represented. Since you have studied arrays, it seems a natural first avenue to try. We could use an array of integers to represent the number of protons, an array of real numbers to represent the atomic weights, and so on. Essentially, we create six arrays to represent the six pieces of information. Each array is indexed from 1 to the number of known elements, which we assume to be 103. With your knowledge of arrays, you could declare six array variables to represent the chemical information, as indicated in the following program fragment:

```
CONST
    MaxElts = 103;


TYPE
    SymbolType = PACKED ARRAY[1..2] OF CHAR;

    IndexType = 1 .. MaxElts;
    IntegerArrayType = ARRAY [IndexType] OF INTEGER;
    RealArrayType = ARRAY [IndexType] OF REAL;
    SymbolArrayType = ARRAY [IndexType] OF SymbolType;


VAR
    protons, neutrons, electrons, numbers: IntegerArrayType;
    weights: RealArrayType;
    symbols: SymbolArrayType;
```
Programming Example 15-1: Declarations to Represent Chemical Information

Before manipulating this information, we must fill each of the six arrays with the correct data. Assume the needed information already exists in a file for each of the elements from hydrogen (H) through lawrencium (Lr). Once the information is read from the file into the arrays, it can be visualized in the following way:

	[1]	[2]	[3]	[4]	[5]	[6]	[7]		[103]
symbols	H	He	Li	Be	B	C	N	...	Lr

	[1]	[2]	[3]	[4]	[5]	[6]	[7]		[103]
numbers	1	2	3	4	5	6	7	...	103

	[1]	[2]	[3]	[4]	[5]	[6]	[7]		[103]
weights	1.008	4.003	6.9	9.01	10.81	12.01	14.0	...	257.0

	[1]	[2]	[3]	[4]	[5]	[6]	[7]		[103]
protons	1	2	3	4	5	6	7	...	103

	[1]	[2]	[3]	[4]	[5]	[6]	[7]		[103]
electrons	1	2	3	4	5	6	7	...	103

	[1]	[2]	[3]	[4]	[5]	[6]	[7]		[103]
neutrons	0	2	4	5	5	6	7	...	154

Figure 15-1: Parallel Arrays

The first element of the periodic table is described as the first element of each of the six arrays. For example, the number of protons the first element has is **protons[1]**, the number of neutrons the first element has is **neutrons[1]**, the atomic weight of the first element is **weights[1]**, and the symbol for the first element is **symbols[1]**.

Although the six parallel arrays represent the six pieces of information about each element, they violate our sense of how the information *should be* represented. Rather than grouping the atomic weights for all elements together, grouping the symbols for all the elements together, and so on, we intuitively group together all information about a single element. We think of the information about hydrogen forming a cohesive unit, the information about helium forming a cohesive unit, and so on. If we had to represent this information manually, we might put all information about a particular element on 3" by 5" cards, using one card for each element. The 88th element, radium (Ra), could be represented as indicated in the following illustration:

```
symbol  = Ra          protons  = 88


number = 88           electrons = 88


weight  = 226.0       neutrons  = 138
```

Figure 15-2: Index Card of Chemical Information

Pascal provides a type to group information in this fashion. The type is a structured type and is known as the **RECORD**. A record is a collection of named components that can be treated as a single entity. Each component of a record is known as a field and can be accessed separately from the entire record.

15.1.1. Declaring Records

Although arrays and records are collections of components, they are distinctly *different* types. There are two primary differences between them. Although every component of an array has the same base type, components of a record can all be of different types. Although components of an array are referred to by an index (usually an integer), components of a record are referred to by *name*. Therefore, every component of a record declaration must have both a *name* and a *type*. The form of a record definition is as follows:

```
TYPE
   NameOfNewType = RECORD
                     field1: type1;
                     field2: type2;
                     field3: type3;
                          .        .
                          .        .
                          .        .
                     fieldN: typeN
                END;
```

Programming Example 15-2: Form of Record Definition

The name for the field is any valid identifier, and the type of each field is any valid Pascal type. To represent the chemical elements, we can define a new type, a record type, to represent any particular element. The following type definition indicates how to do so:

```
TYPE
     ElementType = RECORD
                     protons: INTEGER;
                     neutrons: INTEGER;
                     electrons: INTEGER;
                     weight: REAL;
                     number: INTEGER;
                     symbol: SymbolType
                  END;
```

Programming Example 15-3: Record Definition for Chemical Element

A variable declared of type **ElementType** can be visualized as follows:

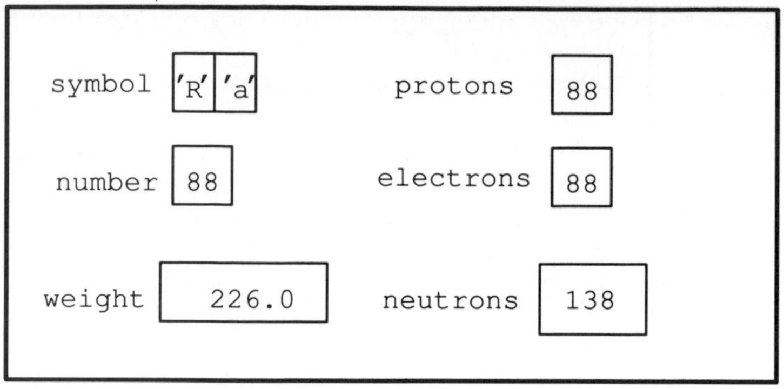

Figure 15-3: Chemical Information as a Pascal Record

Notice that the form of the declaration reinforces the concept of the chemical element as the basic unit of interest. The type declaration actually looks like the illustration of the element written on a 3" by 5" card.

15.1.2. Accessing Record Components

Just as we often wish to refer to individual components of an array, we also often wish to refer to individual components of a record. To do so, we must specify the record variable together with the record field name, just as we must specify both the array variable and the array component index. For example, if we have a variable of **ElementType** named **hydrogen**, we can refer to the weight and number of neutrons as **hydrogen.weight** and **hydrogen.neutrons**, respectively. Note that the name of the record and the name of the field are separated with a period (.). Record fields are variables and can be handled as we normally handle other variables. A few examples are illustrated in the following program fragment:

```
VAR
    chemical: ElementType;

    :
    :
    :
WRITELN(OUTPUT, chemical.weight);

IF chemical.number = 1
    THEN WRITELN(OUTPUT, 'Chemical is hydrogen');

chemical.protons := 88;

chemical.neutrons := 138;

chemical.number := chemical.protons;
```

Programming Example 15-4: Manipulating Fields of a Record

15.1.3. Compact Record Definitions

Although each field of a record can have a completely different type, two or more fields often have the same type. Pascal provides a shorthand way to define records with common types. The names of the fields of the same type are declared together, separated by commas. For the definition of **ElementType**, we could have used the following compact form:

```
TYPE
    ElementType = RECORD
                      protons, neutrons, electrons, number: INTEGER;
                      weight: REAL;
                      symbol: SymbolType
                  END;
```

Programming Example 15-5: Shorthand Record Definition for Chemical Element

Normally, we use the shorthand form of record definitions whenever possible. The BNF for a Pascal record definition can be thought of as:[1]

    \<record-type\> ::= **RECORD \<field-list\> END**

    \<field-list\> ::= **\<record-section\> { ; \<record-section\> }**

    \<record-section\> ::= **\<identifier-list\> : \<type\>**

    \<identifier-list\> ::= **\<identifier\> { , \<identifier\> }**

15.1.4. Collections of Records

At this point we can declare records and access the individual fields of a record. This is very useful for representing the various pieces of information for a chemical element. However, if we wish to represent the 103 known elements, we would need to define 103 variables. A procedure to write out the number of neutrons for each element would have 103 parameters! But this problem should sound familiar. Remember the vote counts for the election with many candidates? We solved that problem by using an array. It follows that we can use an array again for this problem, but this time the components of the array are records. The chemical information for all chemical elements is represented as an *array of records*. The following type definitions illustrate how this can be done:

```
CONST
    MaxElts = 103;


TYPE
    SymbolType = PACKED ARRAY [1..2] OF CHAR;

    ElementType = RECORD
                      protons, neutrons, electrons, number: INTEGER;
                      weight: REAL;
                      symbol: SymbolType
                  END;

    ListOfElementsType = ARRAY [1..MaxElts] OF ElementType;


VAR
    element: ElementType;              (* a single record *)
    ChemList: ListOfElementsType;      (* an array of records *)
```

Programming Example 15-6: Declaring an Array of Records

If we visualize a single record as a 3" by 5" card, we can visualize an array of records as a stack of 3" by 5" cards, as illustrated in Figure 15-4:

---

[1]Since Standard Pascal provides variant records, this BNF description is not quite right. If, after reading the variant records section of this chapter, you would like to see the full BNF for records, see Appendix V.

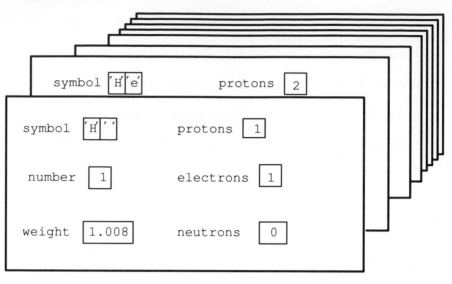

Figure 15-4: Array of Records

This visualization is useful as a model of how to represent information for a variety of different problems. In order to access a particular field of one of the records in the array, we must specify the array name, the index, and the field name. The following examples illustrate this point:

```
ChemList[88].symbol := 'Ra';
ChemList[88].neutrons := 138;
ChemList[103].symbol := 'Lr';
ChemList[2].weight := 4.003
```

Programming Example 15-7: Accessing a Field of an Array of Records

Naturally, we can loop through all the components of an array of records, just as we can loop through any other array. The following program fragment illustrates this:

```
FOR index := 1 TO MaxElts DO
    elements[index].neutrons := 0;


FOR index := 1 TO MaxElts DO
    elements[index].protons := elements[index].electrons
```

Programming Example 15-8: Looping Through an Array of Records

15.1.5. The WITH Statement

When referencing the field of a record, we must always specify the record variable in addition to the the particular field of the record. If we are working with an array of records, we must specify the array name and the array index in addition to the field name. However, if all the fields we are referencing are from the same record of the array, we end up specifying the same array name and the same array index many times. The following program fragment illustrates how this can happen:

```
ChemList[index].protons := 88;
ChemList[index].neutrons := 138;
ChemList[index].electrons := 88;
ChemList[index].symbol := 'Hg';
ChemList[index].weight := 226.0
```

Programming Example 15-9: Repeated Specification of Array Name and Index

Any time we are referencing several fields of the same record, we would like to have to specify the record only once. The Pascal WITH statement is designed to meet this need. When using the WITH statement, you only need to specify the common record variable once. The particular fields of the record are specified in the WITH statment. We can rewrite the previous example using the WITH statement as follows:

```
WITH ChemList[index] DO
    BEGIN
        protons := 88;
        neutrons := 138;
        electrons := 88;
        symbol := 'Hg';
        weight := 226.0
    END
```

Programming Example 15-10: WITH Statement

The WITH statement can help you avoid retyping the same sequence of characters many times. It usually improves readability of the program also.

15.1.6. A Different View of Records

One of the professions finding more uses for computers is the field of music. Assume your help is enlisted to help write a program to synthesize music. One of the first issues you would need to face is how to represent musical notes. The three most important attributes of a musical note are its *pitch*, *timbre*, and *duration*. We could use a Pascal record to represent notes, as indicated in the following type definition:

```
NoteType = RECORD
                pitch: PitchType;
                timbre: TimbreType;
                duration: DurationType
           END;
```

Programming Example 15-11: Type Definition for Musical Notes

Duration refers to how long a note is played. This gives rise to the whole note, half note, etc. The most important durations are enumerated in **DurationType** as follows:

```
DurationType = (sixteenth, eighth, quarter, half, whole):
```

Programming Example 15-12: DurationType

Traditional European music has twelve distinct pitches. Using traditional names (and ignoring all enharmonic equivalents), **PitchType** can be defined as the following enumerated type:

```
PitchType = (aflat, a, asharp, b, c, csharp, d, dsharp, e, f, fsharp, g);
```

Programming Example 15-13: PitchType

Timbre refers to the sound of an instrument. The differing timbres of instruments make a violin, a trumpet, and a piccolo all playing the same pitch sound like a violin and a trumpet and a piccolo. Timbre is how we tell a saxophone from a tuba and a human voice from a piano. A type for timbre might be defined as follows:

```
TimbreType = (string, woodwind, brass, percussion);
```

Programming Example 15-14: TimbreType

We said very early in this book that a type is a set of allowable values. But what about record types? What kind of set of values do they allow? Each field of a record corresponds to a separate type and therefore to a separate dimension. It follows that a record is a cross product of dimensions. More intuitively, the value of a record with three fields corresponds to a point in three-dimensional space. For the record **NoteType** defined earlier, this three-dimensional space can be visualized as in the following figure:

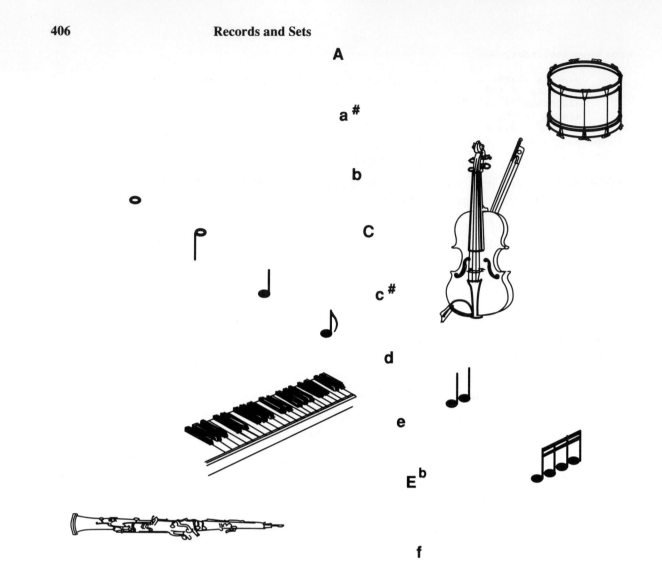

Figure 15-5: Record as a Multidimensioned Space of Values

15.1.7. Questions

1. What is a record type?

2. Why would a programmer need a record type? Give two examples.

3. An array is composed of fields. What two pieces of information must be specified for each field in a record definition?

4. How can individual fields of a record be accessed?

5. Can fields of a record have different types? Do they *have to* have different types?

6. What is the shorthand way of defining a record that has several fields of the same type?

7. What is the BNF for a Pascal record?

8. If a record can be thought of as a 3" x 5" card, how can an array of records be thought of?

9. Can a single field from one record in an array of records be specified? If so, describe how.

10. What is the Pascal WITH statement? When is it useful? Give an example of its use.

15.1.8. Exercises

1. Extend the record definition for chemical elements to include a field for the element's name, such as helium or carbon.

2. Define a Pascal type to represent a student. Choose at least six attributes, such as name or age, for the student. Define any types referenced by fields of the record for StudentType.

3. Define a type for information about textbooks. Some things you might want to include are title, author, publisher, and publication date. Also define any types referenced by the fields of the record.

4. Define a type to represent employees in a company. Include at least five attributes for each employee.

5. The record previously given for musical notes is not very comprehensive. Design a more appropriate record type to include more attributes of notes.

6. Write an electronic card catalog program. The program should permit the user to specify some attribute, such as author, and then search the list of books for any matching books. The information should be represented as an array of records and stored in a file for reuse.

7. Extend the previous program to permit adding new books and removing "misplaced" books.

15.2. Sets

Although sets are very common in mathematics, they are relatively uncommon as a primitive data type in programming languages. Pascal is one of the few widely available high-level programming languages that contains this useful feature. However, we should point out that many implementations of Pascal either severely limit or leave out sets altogether. You should check to see if the implementation of Pascal that you are using has any such constraints.

15.2.1. Set Definition

A set is a collection of objects. The objects of a set are known as members or elements. Mathematicians denote a set by a matching pair of curly braces enclosing the set's members, which are separated by commas. Hence, we would denote a set with four names as {Phil, Lee, Mark, Purvis}. Likewise, we can denote a set of characters as {a, b, c}, and a set of integers as {2, 3, 5, 7}.

There are two important points about sets that you should keep in mind: *Sets have no order*, and *sets have no duplicate members*. Unlike arrays, files, and enumerated types, which have an explicit order associated with them, sets have no order associated with them. Therefore, the set {65, 150, 225} is equivalent to the sets {150, 65, 225} and {225, 65, 150}. Changing the order of the elements does not change the set since we are interested only in the presence or absence of the elements. Similarly, no element can be in a set more than once. An element is either in a set or it is not. If present, it is exactly one member. Again, the focus is on whether or not an element is in a set rather than on its order or frequency.

The number of distinct elements in a set is known as the set's *cardinality*. The sets {Phil, Lee, Purvis} and {9, 65, 150, 225} have cardinalities of 3 and 4, respectively.

15.2.2. Set Operations

There are three operations that can be done on sets. These operations—known as set operations—are *union, difference*, and *intersection*. As you will see in this section, set operations give us a way to create new sets from existing sets. In discussing these three operations, we will use the standard set notation to describe sets. Pascal uses a slightly different notation, which we present at the end of this section.

15.2.2.1. Set Union

Union is the notion of combining several sets into one. We join two sets by combining their elements. The resultant set may not have duplicate members. The symbol ∪ denotes set union.

```
Let s1 = { Phil, Lee, Mark }
    s2 = { Margie, Andrea, Syl }
    s3 = { Mark }
```

```
then
s1 ∪ s2 = { Phil, Lee, Mark, Margie, Andrea, Syl }
s2 ∪ s3 = { Margie, Andrea, Syl, Mark }
```

```
s1 ∪ s3 = { Phil, Lee, Mark } instead of { Phil, Lee, Mark, Mark }
```

15.2.2.2. Set Intersection

Intersection corresponds to the notion of forming a set with the elements common to two sets. The symbol ∩ denotes set intersection.

```
Let s1 = { Phil, Lee, Mark }
    s2 = { Rob, Mark, Wanda, Lee, Purvis }
    s3 = { Phil, Wanda, Purvis }
```

```
then s1 ∩ s2 = { Mark, Lee }
     s1 ∩ s3 = { Phil }
     s2 ∩ s3 = { Wanda, Purvis }
```

15.2.2.3. Set Difference

Set difference describes what is left of one set after removing the elements it has in common with another set. The symbol − normally denotes the difference of two sets. However, we should point out that the symbol \ is also commonly used to denote the set difference operator.

```
Let s1 = { Phil, Lee, Mark }
    s2 = { Phil }
```

```
s1 - s2 = { Lee, Mark }
```

If s1 and s2 are sets, the expression **s1 - s2** is normally read "the set s1 without the elements of set s2." The three set operators described in this section provide a way to create new sets from existing sets. In the next section we present ways to determine information about existing sets.

15.2.3. Set Relations

Since a set is a collection of elements, one of the most obvious things we would like to be able to determine about a set is whether a particular element is a member of that set. There are seven such relations applicable to sets. This section presents these seven set relations, with an example of each.

15.2.3.1. Set Membership

The set membership operator takes one set and one element. The operator returns TRUE only if the element is a member of the set. The set membership operator is normally denoted by the ∈ symbol. The following example demonstrates the set membership operator for a set and two different elements:

```
Let s1 = { Phil, Lee, Mark }
    e1 = Rob
    e2 = Lee
```

```
then
e1 ∈ s1  FALSE
e2 ∈ s1  TRUE
```

15.2.3.2. Subsets and Supersets

When all the elements of one set are members of another set, the smaller set is said to be a *subset* of the larger set. The subset operator is normally denoted by the $\subseteq$ symbol.

```
Let s1 = { Lee, Mark }
    s2 = { Phil, Lee, Mark }
```

then the set s1 is a subset of the set s2, hence, s1 $\subseteq$ s2.

When one set is a *subset* of a larger set, the larger set is said to be a *superset* of the smaller set. Therefore, if s1 and s2 are sets and s1 is a subset of s2, then s2 is a superset of s1. The superset relation is normally denoted with the $\supseteq$ symbol, hence, s2 $\supseteq$ s1. In general, if s and t are sets, and if s $\subseteq$ t, then t $\supseteq$ s.

15.2.3.3. Proper Subsets and Proper Supersets

Consider the three sets defined as follows:

```
Let s1 - { Lee, Mark }
    s2 = { Phil, Lee, Mark }
    s3 = { Lee, Phil, Mark }
```

The set s1 is a subset of s2. The set s1 is also a subset of s3. But what about s2 and s3? Is s2 a subset of s3? Every element of s2 is also a member of s3; therefore, s2 is also a subset of s3. It follows that every set is a subset of itself.

To distinguish those subsets that are smaller than the superset, we use the term *proper subset*. For a subset to be a *proper subset*, there must be at least one element in the superset that is not a member of the subset. Or said another way, a proper subset is a subset with cardinality at least one smaller than the cardinality of the superset. For the previous sets, although both s1 and s2 are subsets of s3, only s1 is a proper subset of s3. The set s2 is not a proper subset of s3. The symbol used to denote a proper subset is $\subset$.

Since every set is a subset of itself, it follows that every set is also a *superset* of itself. The notion of *proper superset* refers to a superset that has at least one element that is not a member of the subset. The symbol used to denote the proper superset relation is $\supset$.

In general, if s and t are sets and s is a proper subset of t, then t is a proper superset of s. This can be stated symbolically as follows: If **s** $\subset$ **t**, then **t** $\supset$ **s**.

15.2.3.4. Set Equality and Inequality

Sets are equal if they contain exactly the same elements. Otherwise, they are unequal. We use the symbols = and $\neq$ for equality and inequality, respectively. If two sets are both subsets of each other, then they are equal. In general, this fact can be stated in the following symbolic way: If s and t are sets, then s = t if and only if s $\subseteq$ t and t $\subseteq$ s; otherwise s $\neq$ t.

15.2.4. The Empty Set and the Universal Set

Consider the following two sets:

```
Let s1 = { Phil, Lee, Mark }
    s2 = { Lee, Phil, Mark }
```

The following are true: s1 is a subset of s2; s2 is a subset of s1. Therefore, s1 and s2 are equivalent sets. This can be stated using set notation: s1 $\subseteq$ s2, s2 $\subseteq$ s1; therefore, s1 = s2. The union of two equal sets is a third equal set. Similarly, the intersection of two equal sets is another equal set. For the two sets s1 and s2, these two facts can be stated symbolically as follows: s1 $\cup$ s2 = s1, and s1 $\cap$ s2 = s1.

But what is s1 $-$ s2? What is left of s1 after removing all the elements of s2? Since s1 and s2 are equivalent, there are no members left. The set that has no members is called the *empty set* and is denoted with the symbol $\varnothing$. In general, the difference of two equal sets is always the empty set. For sets s1 and s2, we denote this by s1 − s2 = ∅. We should probably point out that the empty set is a subset of every set, including itself.

When we speak of sets, we are normally talking about sets of some particular type. For example, we might be talking about sets of integers, sets of characters, or, as in the examples here, sets of names. The set that contains all possible elements of the base type is called the *universal set*.

Having seen the relations between sets and the common set operations, we now turn our attention to sets in the programming language Pascal.

15.2.5. Pascal Sets

Since Pascal can use only the keys found on a keyboard to denote objects and operations on them, Pascal uses slightly different notation to denote sets and operations on them. Pascal sets are delimited with square brackets [ ] instead of curly braces { }, since curly braces are already used in Pascal to delimit comments. To denote set union and set difference, Pascal uses the symbols + and −, respectively. Set intersection is denoted by the symbol * in Pascal. Although all three of these symbols are used to denote other operators, they are reused as set operators, too. In fact, the six relational operators are also reused to denote the six binary set relational operators. The symbols used by Pascal for sets and set operators are summarized in the following table:

Notion	Set Notation	Pascal Symbol
set	{ m1, m2, m3 }	[m1, m2, m3]
union	$\cup$	+
difference	−	−
intersection	$\cap$	*
subset	$\subseteq$	<=
superset	$\supseteq$	>=
proper subset	$\subset$	<
proper superset	$\supset$	>
equality	=	=
inequality	$\neq$	<>
empty set	$\varnothing$	[ ]
membership	$\in$	IN

Table 15-1: Summary of Set Notions and Symbols

Note that the empty set is denoted by empty square brackets [ ], and the set membership operator is denoted by the reserved word **IN**. To illustrate the symbols used by Pascal, we will consider the following examples:

Set Expression	Value	Operation
[Phil, Lee] + [Mark]	[Phil, Lee, Mark]	union
[Phil, Lee, Mark] + [Mark]	[Phil, Lee, Mark]	union
[Phil, Lee, Mark] − [Phil]	[Lee, Mark]	difference
[Phil, Lee, Mark] * [Wanda, Lee]	[Lee]	intersection
[Phil, Lee] <= [Phil, Lee, Mark]	TRUE	subset
[Phil, Lee, Mark] >= [Phil, Lee]	TRUE	superset
[Phil, Lee, Mark] < [Phil, Lee, Mark]	FALSE	proper subset
[Phil, Lee, Mark] <= [Phil, Lee, Mark]	TRUE	subset
[Phil, Lee] <> [Phil, Lee, Mark]	TRUE	inequality
[Phil, Lee] = []	FALSE	equality
Lee IN [Phil, Lee]	TRUE	membership
Mark IN [Phil, Lee]	FALSE	membership

Table 15-2: Pascal Set Expressions

Note that the three set operators and the six set-comparison operators each take exactly two sets as operands. The set-membership operator takes one set and one set element.

15.2.5.1. Defining a Set Type

All members of a particular Pascal set must be of the same type known as the *base type*. In defining a Pascal set type, the base type must always be specified. Pascal set types are defined by using the reserved words **SET OF** followed by the base type of the set. The following type definitions are valid set-type definitions:

```
TYPE
    IntSetType = SET OF INTEGER;

    CharSetType = SET OF CHAR;

    NameType = (Phil, Lee, Mark);
    NameSetType = SET OF NameType;
```

Programming Example 15-15: Pascal Set Type Definitions

The base type of a Pascal set must be an *ordinal* type. Therefore, Pascal permits sets of types INTEGER, CHAR, BOOLEAN, enumerated types, and subrange types. Pascal prohibits sets of REAL or any structured type. Pascal does not permit sets of arrays, sets of records, sets of files, or sets of sets. We should also point out that like everything else implemented on computers, sets must be finite. Although Standard Pascal imposes no limit on the number of elements in a set, every implementation has some finite limit. Check your local implementation for the maximum cardinality permitted.

Any two sets being combined with one of the three set operators or being compared with one of the six set-comparison operators must always have the same base type.

With the previously defined set types, a set variable can be declared, as indicated in the following program fragment:

```
VAR
     CharSet, CommandSet: CharSetType;

     NameSet: NameSetType;
```

Programming Example 15-16: Set Variable Declaration

Similarly, set variables should be given an initial value, like any other variable, as indicated in the following program fragment:

```
CharSet := [ 'a' ];

NameSet := [Lee, Mark];

CommandSet := []
```

Programming Example 15-17: Initializing a Set Variable

15.2.5.2. Example Use of Sets

Consider writing a function to prompt the user for a single-letter command. Assume that valid commands are only the letters 'y' and 'n'. If necessary, the user should be reprompted for a valid response. The following function **GetCommand** illustrates how we have done this in the past:

```
FUNCTION GetCommand: CHAR;

VAR
     response: CHAR;

BEGIN
     REPEAT
         WRITE(OUTPUT, 'Please enter "y" or "n" => ');
         READLN(INPUT, response)
     UNTIL (response = 'y') OR (response = 'n');
     GetCommand := response
END;     (* GetCommand *)
```

Programming Example 15-18: Function **GetCommand**

The user is prompted to enter either a 'y' or an 'n' until an acceptable response has been entered. Once an acceptable command is entered, the function returns it as its value. If uppercase responses were also valid, we might modify the function **GetCommand** in the following way:

```
FUNCTION GetCommand: CHAR;

VAR
     response: CHAR;

BEGIN
     REPEAT
         WRITE(OUTPUT, 'Please enter "y" or "n" => ');
         READLN(INPUT, response)
     UNTIL (response = 'y') OR (response = 'n') OR (response = 'Y') OR (response = 'N');
     GetCommand := response
END;     (* GetCommand *)
```

Programming Example 15-19: Function **GetCommand** Insensitive to Case

As the number of valid commands increases, the attractiveness of this solution becomes less appealing. The important test is to determine whether the entered response is a valid command. We can rephrase this as whether the response is a member of the set of valid commands. The following program fragment is an illustration of the same function rewritten using sets:

```
FUNCTION GetCommand: CHAR;

VAR
    response: CHAR;

BEGIN
    REPEAT
        WRITE(OUTPUT, 'Please enter "y" or "n" => ');
        READLN(INPUT, response)
    UNTIL response IN ['y','n','Y','N'];
    GetCommand := response
END;     (* GetCommand *)
```

Programming Example 15-20: Function **GetCommand** Using Sets

We use the set-membership operator to determine if the entered response is a valid command. As the number of valid commands increases, the usefulness of a set of valid commands increases.

Recall that the base type of a set must always be an ordinal type. There are times when a set corresponds to a subrange of the base type. For these situations, Pascal provides a shorthand notation for specifying sets. As an example, consider a set of characters that includes the ten digit characters '0' through '9'. The following are equivalent sets in Pascal:

```
[ '0', '1', '2', '3', '4', '5', '6', '7', '8', '9' ]

[ '0'..'9' ]
```

Programming Example 15-21: Shorthand Set Notation

A subrange of the set base types is specified, as we specify any other subrange, by specifying the first element and the last element. We should also point out that a set may contain other elements in addition to those specified using the shorthand notation. For example, the set including the 26 lowercase letters in addition to the characters '$' and '%' can be specified as ['a'..'z', '$', '%']. This shorthand notation is quite useful.

15.2.6. Questions

1. What is a set?

2. Is the order of set members distinguished?

3. Can one element be in a set more than once?

4. What are the three set operations that take two sets and result in a new set?

5. What is a subset?

6. What is a superset?

7. What is a proper subset?

8. What is a proper superset?

9. When are two sets equal? When are two sets unequal?

10. What is the empty set?

11. What is a universal set?

12. Does Standard Pascal have sets as a predefined type?

13. What symbols does Pascal use for the following operators:

    a. set union   b. set difference   c. set intersection

14. What symbols does Pascal use for the following set relations:

    a. equal sets   c. subset   e. proper subset

    b. unequal sets   d. superset   f. proper superset

15. What is the set-membership operator?

16. How is the set-membership operator designated in Standard Pascal?

17. How is the empty set designated in Pascal?

18. Describe a valid Pascal set definition.

19. What base types are permitted in Standard Pascal?

20. Does Standard Pascal allow a SET OF REAL? Justify your answer.

21. What is the shorthand notation permitted to designate ranges of values for a set in Pascal?

22. Does the implementation of Pascal that you are using have any nonstandard constraints?

15.2.7. Problems

1. Write a BOOLEAN Pascal function, **IsLowerCase**, that takes one character as input and returns TRUE if the character is a lowercase letter ('a'..'z') and FALSE otherwise. Use Pascal sets.

2. Write a BOOLEAN Pascal function, **IsUpperCase**, that takes one character as input and returns TRUE if the character is an uppercase letter ('A'..'Z') and FALSE otherwise.

3. Write a function, **IsVowel**, that takes a single parameter of type CHAR and returns TRUE if the character is a vowel and FALSE otherwise.

4. Write a BOOLEAN Pascal function, **IsDigit**, that takes one character as input and returns TRUE if the character is a digit ('0'..'9') and FALSE otherwise.

5. Write a Pascal function, **IsValidCommand**, that takes one parameter of type CHAR and returns TRUE if the character is either 'l', 'p', 'q', or 'e' and FALSE otherwise.

6. Extend the function in the preceding question so it takes two parameters, one for the character to validate and one for the set of valid characters.

7. Write a BOOLEAN function, **IsAlpha**, that takes a value of type CHAR as input and returns TRUE if the character is a lowercase letter, uppercase letter, or digit and FALSE otherwise.

8. Write a function, **GetValidCommand**, that takes a set of characters as a parameter, prompts the user for input, and returns as the function value a valid command of type CHAR entered by the user. Reprompt the user if necessary.

9. Extend the function in the preceding question to ensure that if the empty set is the parameter, the function does not get in an infinite loop. Have the function automatically return the null character under these circumstances.

10. Extend the function **GetValidCommand** step further so that the prompt is also a parameter to the function. *Hint: You will need to define a string type.*

11. In the last chapter we saw the procedure **SkipBlanks** that advanced the read head past any blank space characters in a file. Extend this idea to write a procedure **SkipChars** that takes a TEXT file and a set of characters as parameters. The procedure then skips over any characters in the file that are in the set of characters. The procedure should stop when the next character in the file is not in the set. Assume the file has already been opened for reading.

12. *Write an integer-valued function **Card** that takes a set of characters as input and returns the *cardinality* of the set.

13. *The *complement* of a set contains all members of the universal set except those members of the given set. Write a Pascal procedure that determines the complement for any set of characters.

14. ***A *prime* number is any integer larger than one that can be divided evenly only by itself and one. In the third century B.C., a Greek mathematician by the name of Eratosthenes designed an algorithm to determine all prime numbers less than some given number *N*.

We know that no multiple of 2 can be a prime number. Therefore, we can exclude all even numbers larger than 2 from our list of primes. Similarly, we can exclude all multiples of 3 from our list of primes. Eratosthenes' algorithm exploits this idea. The algorithm starts with all integers 2 through N, and then removes multiples of known prime numbers. As an example, consider determining all prime numbers less than 20.

```
start with 2 through N    {2,3,4 5,6,7,8,9,10,11,12,13,14,15,16,17,18,19}

remove multiples of 2     {2,3,5,7,9,11,13,15,17,19}

remove multiples of 3     {2,3,5,7,9,11,13,15,17,19}
```

The next prime number to exclude multiples of is 5. However, notice that we already have taken care of 5*2, 5*3, and 5*4. Therefore, we exclude 5*5, 5*6, 5*7, and so on. But 5*5 is larger than the value of *N* we are using, since here *N* is 20. Therefore, the algorithm can stop throwing away multiples when the square of the number exceeds *N*. Since, 5^2 exceeds 20, we are finished. This algorithm is known as the *sieve of Eratosthenes*. Write a Pascal program that determines all prime numbers smaller than some given number *N*, using Eratosthenes' algorithm. Use sets.

15.3. Solving a Larger Problem: Managing a Baseball Team

The types introduced in this chapter demonstrate that the programming language Pascal is indeed very rich in types. The programmer can create a new type to represent data for any conceivable programming problem. In this section we show how several of these types can be used together to solve a larger real-world problem.

15.3.1. Problem Description

One area in which computers are finding many uses is professional sports. For example, in baseball a computer can be used to store, update, and retrieve statistics on players both accurately and instantly. In addition to the obvious information, such as batting average and number of home runs hit, sports analysts and strategists might be interested in information about a player's offensive performance against left-handed pitchers who throw primarily off-speed breaking pitches, offensive performance with men in scoring position, and a host of other facts. With the help of computers, such information can be readily accessible at one's fingertips. Although we will not develop a comprehensive baseball information-management system here, we will consider writing a computer program that enables a baseball team's manager to store, retrieve, and update a variety of important information about the players.

Consider the information that is a matter of public record: position played, times at bat, hits, batting average, games played, runs scored, doubles, triples, home runs, runs batted in, game winning runs batted in, and stolen bases. The manager needs a computer program that allows him to specify a player and get the relevant statistics, to specify a position and see which players play there, and to update a player's statistics.

15.3.2. Program Design and Representation

When designing such a program, we must consider both what action the program must perform and how the information can be represented. Good programmers do not focus on one without the other. Notice that the problem description gives us a first approximation to both of these!

15.3.2.1. Representing the Information

Consider the data structures that the program will be manipulating. We know that the program is to represent the offensive record of the team's players. This suggests that an appropriate representation is a record for an individual player and an array of these player records for representing the entire team. Notice that we design a data structure by starting with the large pieces rather than the small ones. We focussed on the team and the players rather than considering how the batting average would be represented. The following program fragment illustrates valid Pascal type definitions for the player record and the array for the team, called **PlayerType** and **TeamType**, respectively.

```
TYPE
     TeamType = ARRAY [JerseyType] OF PlayerType;

     JerseyType = MinJersey .. MaxJersey;

     PlayerType = RECORD
                       name: StringType;
                       position: StringType;
                       statistics: OffensiveStatsType
                  END;      (* PlayerType *)
```

Programming Example 15-22: Highest-Level Type Definitions

Notice that we use the jersey numbers of the players as the array indices. Although we do not have to do this, it seems a natural way to refer to the components of the team array. Also notice that the record **PlayerType** has only three fields: one for the player's name, one for the player's position, and one for the player's offensive statistics. Although we could have added fields for every piece of offensive data—such as atbats, runs, and RBIs—we opted to create a separate type to represent the offensive statistics called **OffensiveStatsType**. With this top level of types defined, we can now turn to the next level of types, as defined in the following program fragment:

```
TYPE
     StringType = PACKED ARRAY [1 .. MaxString] OF CHAR;

     OffensiveStatsType = ARRAY [StatCategory] OF REAL;

     StatCategory = (batAve, games, atbats, runs, hits, doubles, triples,
                     homers, rbi, gameWinningRbi, stolenBases);
```

Programming Example 15-23: Next Level of Type Definitions

StringType is defined as a packed array of characters, as you might have expected. Note that all the offensive data statistics are REAL numbers. This allows us to declare an array of REAL to represent this information. If they were not all of the same type, we would have had to use a record. Given this representation of the information, we can visualize it as being organized as illustrated in the following figure:

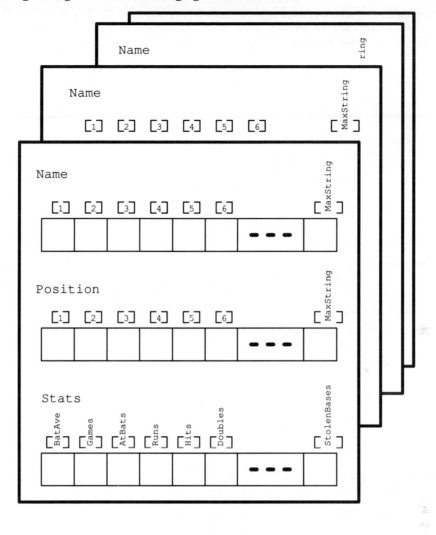

Figure 15-6: `TeamType` Illustrated

Again, each player on the team is represented as a record, and the team is represented as an array of records. The player record has three fields: one for the player's name, one for the player's position, and one for the player's offensive performance information. The name and position fields are, in turn, represented as character strings. The third field is an array of REAL numbers, each component being one statistic.

15.3.2.2. Decomposition into Subprograms

We are now ready to decompose our baseball program into subprograms. If the team information resides in a file, the program's overall action will be as follows: Read team data from a file into the data structure, process the manager's requests on the team data, and write the updated data structure back to a file for reuse. This is indicated in the following program fragment:

```
BEGIN     (* Main Program *)
    GlobalFilter(TeamFile)
END.     (* Main Program *)


PROCEDURE GlobalFilter (datafile: TEXT);
VAR
    team: TeamType;

BEGIN
    ReadTeam(datafile, team);
    ProcessTeam(team);
    WriteTeam(datafile, team);
END;     (* GlobalFilter *)


PROCEDURE ReadTeam (where: TEXT;  VAR team: TeamType);

PROCEDURE WriteTeam  (where: TEXT;  team: TeamType);

PROCEDURE ProcessTeam (VAR team: TeamType);
```

Programming Example 15-24: Highest-Level Subprogram Declarations

Notice that we have used the **GlobalFilter** procedure. Also notice that the procedures are in the order that we used when designing the program rather than in the order in which compilers normally want them to be declared. Keep in mind we are illustrating the design process. The procedure **ProcessTeam** must provide the user with the major capabilities, which can be summarized as follows:

- the ability to specify a player and have his statistics displayed

- the ability to specify a position and see which players play there

- the ability to update a player's statistics

It follows that the procedure **ProcessTeam** is essentially a command loop that calls each of the major functions. The following program example illustrates what we mean.

```
PROCEDURE ProcessTeam (VAR team: TeamType);
VAR
    command: CHAR;

BEGIN
    REPEAT
        command := GetValidCommand;
        CASE command OF
            'D', 'd': DisplayOnePlayer(team);
            'L', 'l': ListPlayersInPosition(team);
            'U', 'u': UpdatePlayerInfo(team);
            'Q', 'q': WRITELN(OUTPUT, 'Quitting')
        END
    UNTIL command IN ['q', 'Q']
END;     (* ProcessTeam *)


PROCEDURE DisplayOnePlayer (team: TeamType);

PROCEDURE ListPlayersInPosition (team: TeamType);

PROCEDURE UpdatePlayerInfo (VAR team: TeamType);
```

Programming Example 15-25: Next-Level Subprogram Declarations

At this point, the most important aspects of the program are mapped out in sufficient detail for us to see how the program can be finished. Combining all the pieces gives us the following program:

```
CONST
    MaxString = 15;                 (* maximum string size *)
    MinJersey = 1;                  (* minimum player jersey number *)
    MaxJersey = 99;                 (* maximum player jersey number *)

TYPE
    StringType = PACKED ARRAY [1 .. MaxString] OF CHAR;

    StatCategory = (batAve, games, atbats, runs, hits, doubles, triples,
                        homers, rbi., gameWinningRbi, stolenBases);

    OffensiveStatsType = ARRAY [StatCategory] OF REAL;

    PlayerType = RECORD
                    name: StringType;
                    position: StringType;
                    statistics: OffensiveStatsType
                END;       (* PlayerType *)

    JerseyType = MinJersey .. MaxJersey;

    TeamType = ARRAY [JerseyType] OF PlayerType;

PROCEDURE ReadTeam (where: TEXT;  VAR team: TeamType);

PROCEDURE WriteTeam  (where: TEXT;  team: TeamType);

PROCEDURE DisplayOnePlayer (team: TeamType);

PROCEDURE ListPlayersInPosition (team: TeamType);

PROCEDURE UpdatePlayerInfo (VAR team: TeamType);


PROCEDURE ProcessTeam (VAR team: TeamType);
VAR
    command: CHAR;

BEGIN
    REPEAT
        command := GetValidCommand;
        CASE command OF
            'D', 'd': DisplayOnePlayer(team);
            'L', 'l': ListPlayersInPosition(team);
            'U', 'u': UpdatePlayerInfo(team);
            'Q', 'q': WRITELN(OUTPUT, 'Quitting')
        END
    UNTIL command IN ['q', 'Q']
END;     (* ProcessTeam *)


PROCEDURE GlobalFilter (datafile: TEXT);
VAR
    team: TeamType;

BEGIN
    ReadTeam(datafile, team);
    ProcessTeam(team);
    WriteTeam(datafile, team);
END;     (* GlobalFilter *)


BEGIN     (* Main Program *)
    GlobalFilter(TeamFile)
END.
```

Programming Example 15-26: Overall Program Design

The program is developed far enough for you to finish it on your own. We will not not expend the pages required to flesh out the program to completion. If you do not feel confident in your ability to complete this program easily, then you should consider it as an exercise.

The program that we have designed to help a manager keep track of baseball players is much smaller and simpler than one that would be of commercial use. For example, in this program a player can play only one position, whereas in reality some people, known as utility players, can play as many as eight different positions. This can, of course, be accommodated, but only at the expense of additional code. You can probably think of other features that might make the program more useful.

This program was designed to illustrate several points. These points can be summarized as follows:

- Programmers must think about how information can be represented in addition how a programming problem can be decomposed.

- A programmer should always have decided on a choice of data structure and program decomposition before sitting down in front of a keyboard to enter the program.

- The top-down design method can be used in defining new types for a program.

15.4. *** Variant Records

In this chapter, we have seen several new classes of types. Together they provide programmers with the tools to create many new types. In fact, it probably appears that the possibilities for new types are limited only by a programmer's imagination.

Assume that you have been enlisted to help develop a package to display some common figures, such as circles, triangles, and rectangles, on computer display devices. One of the issues you need to face in a problem like this is how to represent the figures in terms of the programming language at hand.

A rectangle can be uniquely described by four points. Similarly, a triangle can be specified by three points. Circles are described by a center point and a radius. Given what you have learned in this chapter, you could define a new type to represent each of these. The following program fragment illustrates one way to do so:

```
TYPE
    PointType = RECORD
                    x, y: REAL
                END;


    TriangleType = RECORD
                    point1, point2, point3: PointType
                END;


    RectangleType = RECORD
                    point1, point2, point3, point4: PointType
                END;


    CircleType = RECORD
                    center: PointType;
                    radius: REAL
                END;
```
Programming Example 15-27:   Type Definition of Each Figure

If these three figures are the only three figures we are interested in, we can think of every graphical display as simply a collection of these figures. But consider creating a type to represent a collection of these figures. The natural choice might be an array since we can represent a graphical display as an array of figures. However, every element of the array must be of the same type, and some of the figures are rectangles, some are triangles, and some are circles. In essence, we want the components of the array to be of different types. One solution to this dilemma might be to create one record instead of creating three different record types for the three different figures. We might do that as follows:

```
TYPE
    PointType = RECORD
                    x, y: REAL
                END;


    FigureType = RECORD
                    point1, point2, point3, point4: PointType;
                    center: PointType;
                    radius: REAL
                END;
```

Programming Example 15-28: One Type Definition of **FigureType**

We can then declare an array of **FigureType**. However, for this idea to work, we would also need to store with each figure what kind of figure it is. To accommodate this, we simply add another field to **FigureType**. This is reflected in the following program fragment:

```
TYPE
    PointType = RECORD
                    x, y: REAL
                END;

    KindOfFigureType = (circle, rectangle, triangle)

    FigureType = RECORD
                    kind: KindOfFigureType;
                    point1, point2, point3, point4: PointType;
                    center: PointType;
                    radius: REAL
                END;
```

Programming Example 15-29: **FigureType** as a Record

Now an array of **FigureType** has information stored with each figure to describe what type of figure it is. This enables us to determine which fields are appropriate to access. However, every component of the array will have some unused fields. For example, if the figure is a circle, the 4 points are unused. Similarly, if the figure is a triangle, the **center**, the **radius**, and **point4** are unused. If we have a large number of these records, we can waste a lot of the computer's memory. For many programming languages, there is no alternative to this obvious waste of memory. However, Pascal provides a way to better represent this type of problem, thereby making better use of the computer's memory. What we want is a record that can *vary* according to the type of figure that is being stored (e.g. sometimes a rectangle, sometimes a circle, sometimes a triangle). This is called a *variant record*. The following program fragment illustrates how to define a variant record for this problem:

```
TYPE
    PointType = RECORD
                    x, y: REAL
                END;

    KindOfFigureType = (circle, rectangle, triangle);

    FigureType = RECORD
                    CASE kind: KindOfFigureType OF
                        circle:   (center: PointType; radius: REAL);
                        triangle:  (point1, point2, point3: PointType);
                        rectangle: (point1, point2, point3, point4: PointType)
                END;
```

Programming Example 15-30: **FigureType** as a Variant Record

Notice that in both this definition and the last one we need a field to determine which kind of figure we have. This field is known as the *tag field*. The value of the tag field determines which of the other fields are accessible. For example, if the tag field has the value **circle**, then the fields **center** and **radius** are accessible. If the value of the tag field is **triangle**, a different set of fields is valid.

A variant record can also have fields common to all of the variant types. As an example, suppose that each figure also has a color associated with it. Additionally, each figure has an area. The following program fragment illustrates a variant record that has some *fixed* fields in addition to the *variant* fields:

```
TYPE
    PointType = RECORD
                        x, y: REAL
                   END;


    ColorType = (red, green, blue);

    KindOfFigureType = (circle, rectangle, triangle);

    FigureType = RECORD
                      area: REAL;
                      color: ColorType;
                      CASE kind: KindOfFigureType OF
                            circle:   (center: PointType; radius: REAL);
                            triangle: (point1, point2, point3: PointType);
                            rectangle: (point1, point2, point3, point4: PointType)
                   END;     (* FigureType *)


    PictureType = ARRAY [1..MaxPict] OF FigureType;
```

Programming Example 15-31: Variant Record with Some Fixed Fields

If we define a picture as an array of **FigureType**, then the procedure to display an entire picture simply displays each picture in the array. The following Pascal procedure illustrates how:

```
PROCEDURE DisplayPicture (picture: PictureType);

VAR
    index: INTEGER;

BEGIN
    FOR index := 1 TO MaxPict DO
        DisplayFigure(picture[index])
END;     (* DisplayPicture *)
```

Programming Example 15-32: Procedure **DisplayPicture**

The procedure to display an individual figure must first determine what kind of figure is being displayed. This determination is normally done using a CASE statement. The action clause depends on the tag field of the variant record. The following procedure illustrates this notion:

```
PROCEDURE DisplayFigure (figure: FigureType);

BEGIN
    CASE figure.kind OF
          circle: DrawCircle(figure.circle, figure.radius);
          triangle: DrawTriangle(figure.point1, figure.point2, figure.point3);
          rectangle: DrawRectangle(figure.point1, figure.point2,
                                      figure.point3, figure.point4)
    END
END;     (* DisplayFigure *)
```

Programming Example 15-33: Procedure **DisplayFigure**

We saw earlier how useful the WITH statement can be with a record. The WITH statement can also be used with a variant record. The following programming example is **DisplayFigure** rewritten using the WITH statement.

```
PROCEDURE DisplayFigure (figure: FigureType);

BEGIN
    WITH figure DO
        CASE kind OF
            circle: DrawCircle(circle, radius);
            triangle: DrawTriangle(point1, point2, point3);
            rectangle: DrawRectangle(point1, point2, point3, point4)
        END     (* CASE *)
    END     (* WITH *)
END;     (* DisplayFigure *)
```

Programming Example 15-34: Variant Record and WITH Statement

The WITH statement not only reduces the amount of typing, it also improves the program's readability. We encourage you to make use of the WITH statement whenever possible.

15.5. Chapter Summary

- A record is a collection of named components treated as a single entity. Each component is known as a *field* and has a name and a type.

- Fields of a record are referenced by specifying the record name and the field name.

- Each field of an array *must* have a different name, but each *can* be of a different type.

- Fields of a record with the same type can be declared together in a more compact form.

- The BNF of a Pascal record can be thought of as:

  ```
  <record-type> ::= RECORD <field-list> END

  <field-list> ::= <record-section> { ; <record-section> }

  <record-section> ::= <identifier-list> : <type>

  <identifier-list> ::= <identifier> { , <identifier> }
  ```

- If a subprogram accesses several fields of the same record, the WITH statement can be used to specify the record only once, thereby saving keystrokes and improving the program's readability.

- Pascal permits arrays of any type, even structured types. Hence, one can have arrays of arrays, arrays of records, arrays of sets, and arrays of files.

- If a record is visualized as a 3" by 5" card, an array of records can be visualized as a stack of 3" by 5" cards.

- A *set* is a collection of objects.

- Sets have no order or duplicate members.

- The three operations to form new sets from existing sets are set union, set difference, and set intersection.

- The six relations between two sets are subset, superset, proper subset, proper superset, equality, and inequality.

- The set-membership operator determines if a given element is a member of a particular set.

- The empty set is a set with no members.

- The universal set is a set with all possible members of the base type.

- Pascal sets are a structured internal type.

- The symbols used to denote sets and the set operators are summarized in Table 15-1 on page 410.

- All elements of a Pascal set must have the same base type. Standard Pascal requires the base type of a set to be an ordinal type.

- Standard Pascal provides a useful shorthand way of describing a subrange of values for set members.

- There are times when it useful to be able to define a record type with fields that vary. This type of record is known as a variant record. The fields that vary are known as variant fields. A record can have both fixed fields and variant fields. Which variant fields are accessible is controlled by a field known as the tag field.

15.6. Summary of Terms

- record
- record field
- array of records
- RECORD
- set
- set member
- set union

- set difference
- set intersection
- subset
- superset
- proper subset
- proper superset
- empty set

- universal set
- SET OF
- WITH
- variant record
- variant fields
- fixed fields
- tag field

UNIT V: Modern Programming

Chapter 16: Style

Chapter 17: Dynamic Memory Allocation

Chapter 18: Searching and Sorting

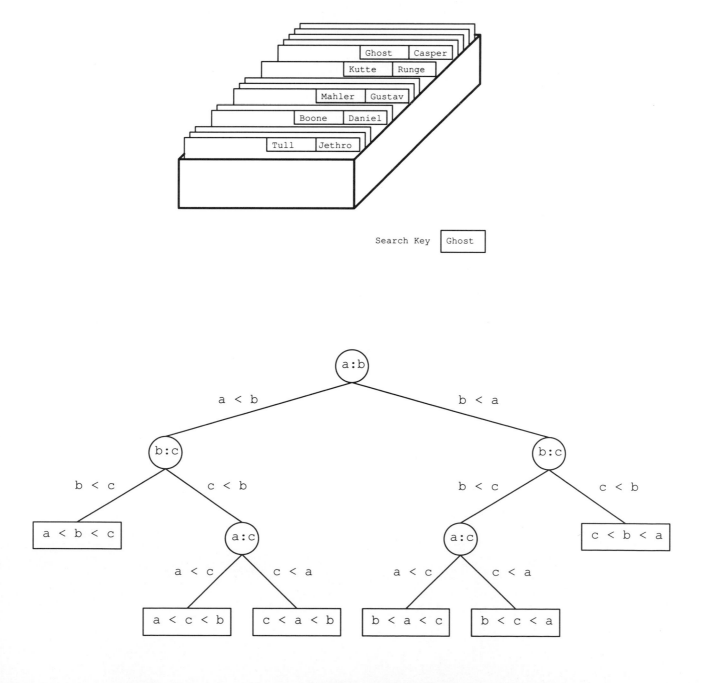

Chapter 16: Style: Writing Better Programs

When we read a good story, we often appreciate the author's writing for more than just catchy phrasing or correct punctuation. A good story works as a whole, with all the pieces fitting together nicely: the characters fit the action, the action fits the setting, and the plot is interesting and believable. A good story does not happen magically; good writers may spend months on short stories and years on novels. They start with ideas, develop an outline, write drafts, read them, and revise them until they get them right. Writing is a process—a series of separate but related activities—that achieves a goal. With this view of writing as a process comes the concept of *style*. Style is control. For example, when critics speak of Hemingway's style or Faulkner's style, they are referring to the way those authors controlled the writing process to achieve particular effects in their fiction.

Just as a good writer controls the process of writing prose or poetry, a good programmer controls the process of writing a computer program. Unlike textbooks on English, many programming textbooks say little or nothing about style. Many of those that do typically discuss the appearance or format of a program. In contrast to that view, we consider programming style to be analogous to writing style: It is a way or method of controlling the entire programming process, from the initial idea to the working program. The programming process includes four separate but related activities:

1. *specification*—what the program should do

2. *design*—how the program is to do what it should do

3. *implementation*—coding the design into a programming language

4. *verification and testing*—ensuring the program does what it should

This chapter will examine each of these four activities in the order in which they are normally carried out. For each activity, we will suggest ways that you can develop a style of programming to make your programs easier to write, easier to use, and easier for other people to read, understand, and modify. If you learn these points and apply them to your programming, you will bypass many of the problems that poor programming practices often create.

16.1. A Style of Program Specification

The first step in creating a computer program is to determine what the program should do. Though this may seem obvious to you, you should try to remember that what is obvious is often overlooked. On many occasions, a programmer has written most of the code for a program before realizing that the program was supposed do something that he or she failed to consider. It is useful to think about developing a computer program as you would think about building a house. If a new house is nearly completed, the building contractor has a real problem if he then finds out that the owner wanted two more bedrooms on the second floor. Analogously, a programmer has a real problem if he or she finds out late in the development that a program should have included additional components.

A computer programmer should always start with a written statement of the problem the program is to solve. If the problem is an assignment for a course, such a problem statement is usually provided. In virtually all other cases, the problem statement must be generated by the programmer or by the person who wants the program written. Based on the problem statement, the programmer then generates what is called a *functional specification*. The specification states exactly what the program will do (its functionality), what input it will take, and what output it will generate. Note that the program specification contains no information on *how* the program works, only information on *what* it does.

Just as building a skyscraper is much more difficult than building a four-room house, building a large computer program is much harder than building a small program. The skyscrapers of programming are called *software systems*, and their builders are called *software engineers*. Just as an architect creates a blueprint before any phase of construction starts, software engineers (architects) prepare a functional specification before starting program construction.

An architect's blueprint is considered good if a builder can build the desired building, given only the information contained in the blueprint. Similarly, a program's functional specification is considered good if a programmer can build a satisfactory program, given only the information contained in the functional specification. A functional specification that neglects required program features is very poor in the same way as a blueprint that fails to mention several rooms of a new building.

We could probably build a dog house without a blueprint, and we could probably write a small program without a functional specification. As the size and complexity of a problem increases, the need for a functional specification increases. Every programming task can be made easier with a good functional specification. You should develop early the habit of creating a specification for *all* of your computer programs before writing them, regardless of their size.

16.1.1. An Example Functional Specification

Consider the program on your computer system that accepts commands from the user to handle such tasks as deleting unwanted files, creating new files, and listing files. Such a program is known as the *monitor*, the *command interpreter*, or the *executive*. Assume we wish to create a simple monitor program. Our first step is to write the functional specification.

The purpose of the program is to do the file-management tasks associated with a monitor. The program must maintain a directory or list of files. Each file has three attributes: name, size (in bytes), and deleted status. Input will be user commands that are confined to single letters. The following are the required commands:

- L   List all files in directory (excluding deleted files)

- D   Delete an existing file

- U   Undelete a deleted file

- C   Create a new file

- P   Print a list of all deleted files in directory

- A   Print a list of ALL files (both deleted and not deleted)

- E   Exits monitor-storing only files that are not marked as deleted

The output is pretty much as you might expect. There must be a confirmation message for each command. For erroneous commands, such as invalid letters, trying to delete a file that does not exist, or trying to undelete a file that is not deleted, an error message must be given. Each of the three listing commands (list, list deleted, list all) must have an appropriate header; it must show each file name and its size on a separate line; and it must give a summary showing the total number of files listed and the total amount of storage (in bytes) for those files.

Note that we have given the program specification in an informal manner. It is more important to be complete than it is to be formal in specifying what a program is to do. Very large programs require a formal functional specification more because of their size and subsequent complexity than anything else. Given the informal specification above, you should be able to write a Pascal program satisfying those requirements. More importantly, this functional specification can be given to several programmers, and each would know *what* the program should do. Although each programmer might implement the program very differently, perhaps even in different programming languages, the resulting programs that conform to the functional specification are functionally equivalent.

16.2. A Style of Program Design

Once the functional specification is completed, the programmer knows *what* the program is to do and can focus on *how* the program is to do it. The wrong way to begin is to sit down at a terminal and start typing in code. If you start this way, you can become bogged down in details and waste a lot of time generating code that you will not be able to use later. You should never allow the details to dictate the design, and that is what can happen if you approach the programming task the wrong way. In Chapter 8 we discussed the right way, *top-down design*.

16.2.1. Top-Down Design

Top-down design is a systematic strategy for solving programming problems. The programmer starts with the overall problem to be solved and decomposes it into smaller problems (subproblems). Each of the subproblems is then decomposed into even smaller subproblems, until all the subproblems are small enough to be solved directly by tasks coded into a programming language. For a more complete discussion of this topic, see section 8.1.3 beginning on page 242, where we give a detailed example for the task of grocery shopping. The following points summarize the benefits of the top-down strategy.

- It moves from the general to the specific, thereby postponing details until last, which permits the programmer to think at the highest level at all times.

- It allows the programmer to modify the design of subprograms without affecting other subprograms since each subprogram is *independent* of others.

- It is a general problem-solving strategy that may be used for problems other than programming problems.

- It yields a hierarchical solution that can be graphically depicted with what we call *solution trees*.

Table 16-1:   Benefits of Top-Down Programming

16.2.2. Example of Program Design

Let us develop an abstract design for the program **Monitor** specified in the previous section. The function of the program is to manage a directory of files. We can decompose this task into the three subtasks of *reading directory information for startup*, *processing user commands on the directory*, and *writing directory information back to storage upon program termination*. This can be graphically depicted with the following solution tree:

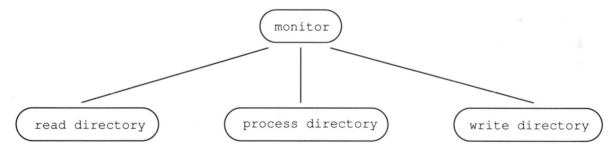

Figure 16-1:   First-Level Decomposition of **Monitor** Program

Both *read directory* and *write directory* are simple enough to be coded directly without any further decomposition. The most complicated module is *process directory*, which should be decomposed further. *Process directory* repeatedly gets a user command and then executes the appropriate command. Therefore, *process directory* may be decomposed into *get command* and one for each of the commands *list*, *delete*, *undelete*, *create*, *list deleted*, and *list all*. This additional level of decomposition is illustrated with the following solution tree:

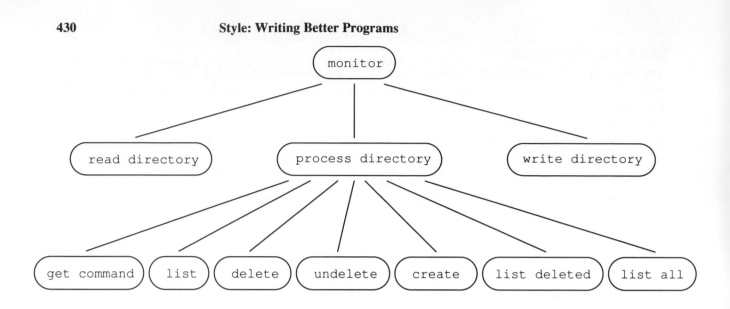

Figure 16-2: Extended Decomposition of **Monitor** Program

Each of the modules under *process directory* are now simple enough to be coded directly into a programming language. We need not decompose the monitor program any further. Note that the first two phases of programming do not involve writing any code. They are essentially planning phases.

16.3. A Style of Program Implementation

After completing the design for the program, the programmer enters the third phase of programming: *implementation*. In this phase, the programmer takes the abstract design and writes the coded program. Note that the selection of a programming language may be postponed until this point. Having selected the programming language, the programmer may start generating code, the phase most people think of when someone says they are programming. Though there is no consensus as to how the implementation phase should be carried out, the method we prefer, advocate, and hope you will adopt is a *top-down* method of refining programs one step at a time: *stepwise refinement*. We highly recommend this method of implementation. The steps are outlined as follows.

1. Start by writing the main program as a sequence of calls to subprograms corresponding to the highest-level subproblems in the solution tree.

2. Add the declarations for each of the subprograms called in the main program. You need not add the entire body for each subprogram declared at this point. You can add only the subprogram shells (stubs), each containing a WRITELN stating which subprogram is called and what input values it requires.

3. Select constants as output for VAR parameters and function values.

4. Run this partial program to verify the correctness of the top level of the design before proceeding.

5. After confirming the design, fill out the body for each of the existing stubs, adding calls to other subprograms.

6. Add the stubs for the additional subprograms.

7. Run the modified partial program.

8. Continue this method of development for each level of the solution tree until all stubs are filled out. Note that you need not fill out *all* existing stubs in each pass; you can fill out as many of them as you are comfortable with.

For the monitor program we have been developing in this chapter, the main program wou[ld] [be] something like the following:

```
BEGIN
    ReadDirectory(directory);
    ProcessDirectory(directory);
    WriteDirectory(directory)
END.
```

Programming Example 16-1:   Main Program of Program `Monitor`

Note how the subprogram calls in the main program correspond to the highest-level subproblems i[n] solution tree.

16.3.1. Declarations

Unit III presented and discussed a style of declarations for constants, variables, and subprograms, [and] Unit IV discussed a style for type definitions. We have found the points stressed in those units to b[e] very useful over the years:

- **All named constants are defined globally to the program** and are, therefore, accessible throughout the program. The same constant should never be defined more than once in a program; it should be defined once globally. The only exception is when some named constant is used by only one subprogram and we wish the constant to be *inaccessible* by all other subprograms. This strategy of keeping information inaccessible from the rest of the program is called *information hiding*. Although information hiding is uncommon in small programs, we have illustrated it with locally defined constants earlier in this text.

- **All user-defined types are defined globally to the program** and are accessible throughout the program. The reasoning behind this is the same as for named constants. Again, the sole exception is for information-hiding purposes. We have never seen a Pascal program in which some named type is used only internally by a single procedure.

- **All subprograms are defined globally to the program.** We discourage nested subprogram declarations. If a subprogram is declared within another subprogram, the nested subprogram may be called only within the scope of the subprogram in which it is declared. Remember that one of the motivations for writing subprograms is reuse, thereby making it unnecessary to duplicate the same code. The sole exception for having a nested subprogram declaration is again *information hiding*. This exception is also uncommon in small programs. Additionally, nested subprograms permit *up-level addressing*, which we also discourage. We only use nested subprograms in this text to illustrate how they work. We never use them in practice, and we urge you not to use them either.

- **All variables are declared local to the subprogram in which they are used.** *Every variable in a procedure should either be a local variable to that procedure or a formal parameter to that procedure. There are no exceptions whatsoever.*

Having already written the main program for **Monitor**, we know we will need a structure to represent a directory of files. We need a user-defined type to hold the list of files and the number of files in the list. We can use a Pascal RECORD for `DirectoryType`, as follows:

```
DirectoryType = RECORD
                  files: FileListType;
                  size: INTEGER
                END;    (* DirectoryType *)
```

Programming Example 16-2: `DirectoryType`

We also need a user-defined type for the list of files. `FileListType` will be an array of files:

```
FileListType = ARRAY [1..MaxFiles] OF FileType;
```

Programming Example 16-3: `FileListType`

Recall that for the purposes of the program **Monitor**, we need a file with three attributes. In Pascal this is a RECORD with three fields, as follows:

```
FileType = RECORD
                name: StringType;
                ByteSize: INTEGER;
                deleted: BOOLEAN
          END;      (* FileType *)
```

Programming Example 16-4: `FileType`

Note that we developed the type definitions in a *top-down* fashion. We defined the largest first, then added the necessary smaller subtypes. We advocate top-down design of user-defined types.

16.3.2. Inter-Module Communication

In Chapter 9, we pointed out the need to communicate information from one subprogram to another subprogram, which we call *inter-module communication*. In Pascal there are exactly two ways to achieve such communication: through *parameters* and *up-level addressing*. A variable may be referenced anywhere within the scope in which it is declared. Therefore, all variables declared in the global scope of a Pascal program may be referenced throughout the entire program. *Up-level addressing* occurs when a variable reference refers to a variable declared in some enclosing scope; that is, the reference and the declaration are in different scopes. You can illustrate up-level addressing by drawing boxes around a program and each of its subprograms as we did in Chapter 8. If you draw a line from the reference to its declaration, the line will cross the boundary of the box if there is up-level addressing.

Up-level addressing of variables should never be permitted. All communication between subprograms should be made explicit through the use of parameters. Nested subprograms allow up-level addressing, so we discourage such nestings. Even if all subprograms are declared globally (no nestings), variables declared globally to a program may still be referenced by up-level addressing. It is for this reason that we also discourage global variable declarations. Remember this rule for variable references and inter-module communication: **Every variable used in a subprogram either must be declared in that subprogram or passed as a formal parameter to that subprogram.** If you follow this rule, your programs will have no up-level addressing; all inter-module communication will be through parameters. You can enforce this rule by declaring all subprograms globally (no nested subprograms) and eliminating all global variables. All global variables and the main program can then be moved to a special subprogram, which we have been calling **`GlobalFilter`**. Some prefer to call this extra procedure **`UpLevelFilter`** since it filters out up-level addressing of variables, the true culprit that we are trying to eliminate.

You may be wondering about file variables. Although it is true that Standard Pascal requires any file variables listed as program parameters to be declared globally to the entire program, it is NOT true that Pascal requires up-level addressing of file variables. File variables should be passed as parameters, like all other variables. The previous rule for inter-module communication should be followed for *all* variables, *including* file variables. All file variables must be passed as VAR parameters; they may not be passed as value parameters. All other variables should be value parameters, except when you want to change the value of the actual parameter.

The use of the procedure **`GlobalFilter`** (or **`UpLevelFilter`**) may be compared to the use of training wheels on a bicycle: At some point you will no longer need them. As you practice the rule stated above, it will soon become second nature. Like the ability to ride a bicycle, the rule is never forgotten once learned.

We introduced functions in a mathematical sense as taking zero or more inputs and returning one result. For this reason, we believe functions should only have value parameters. If we need a subprogram to return three outputs, we use a procedure with three VAR parameters rather than a function with two VAR parameters.

Returning now to the program **`Monitor`**, the first pass at the program looks something like the following:

```
PROGRAM Monitor (INPUT, OUTPUT, data);

VAR
    data: TEXT;



PROCEDURE ReadDirectory (VAR directory: DirectoryType;  VAR infile: TEXT);

BEGIN
END;    (* ReadDirectory *)



PROCEDURE ProcessDirectory (VAR directory: DirectoryType)

BEGIN
END;    (* ProcessDirectory *)



PROCEDURE WriteDirectory (directory: DirectoryType;  VAR outfile: TEXT);

BEGIN
END;    (* WriteDirectory *)



PROCEDURE GlobalFilter (VAR storage: TEXT);

VAR
    directory: DirectoryType;

BEGIN
    ReadDirectory(directory, storage);
    ProcessDirectory(directory);
    WriteDirectory(directory, storage)
END;    (* GlobalFilter *)



BEGIN   (* Main Program *)

    GlobalFilter(data)

END.    (* Main Program *)
```

Programming Example 16-5: Program **Monitor** with Stub Procedures

Note that the main program is one call to **GlobalFilter** with the required file variable. The body of **GlobalFilter** consists of the calls to the three subprograms that correspond to the highest level of program decomposition in our design. The procedure **ReadDirectory** builds the directory structure from permanent storage and has two VAR parameters: the directory structure and the file to read from. The subprogram **ProcessDirectory** processes all the user's commands on the directory structure and has a single VAR parameter. The procedure **WriteDirectory** writes the directory structure back out to permanent storage; it has two parameters, but only the file variable is a VAR. At this stage in the implementation of the program **Monitor**, we might want to add the user-defined types and execute the partially completed program with the stubs.

16.3.3. Comments and Documentation

A computer program is more than a sequence of instructions to be read and executed by a computer. Programs are read by people as well. If a program is executed more than a few times after its completion, it is very likely that someone will want to read the code to repair it, extend it, or to examine it for interest or evaluation. To make your programs easy to read, you should use comments liberally. The comments in a program are ignored by the compiler; they are added only to aid human readers of the program.

Every comment in a program describes some facet of the program. There are three different types of comments in a program, based on *what* they describe: (1) statement comments describing some program statement; (2) subprogram comments describing a subprogram; (3) program comments describing the overall program.

For program comments and subprogram comments, we advocate using *structured comments* with different fields to organize the different information contained in the comment. Our structured subprogram comments contain *what* the subprogram does (DESCRIPTION), *how* the program does it (METHOD), what it requires (INPUT), and what it generates (OUTPUT). Note that all parameters are listed in either INPUT or OUTPUT or both. Value parameters are listed in INPUT but not OUTPUT, and VAR parameters are listed in OUTPUT or both INPUT and OUTPUT.

Program comments at the very least should say *who* wrote the program and *when*, *what* the program does, *how* it does what it does, what *input* it needs, and what *output* it generates.

Statement comments describe some particular statement in the program, typically a statement whose action is not particularly obvious. A statement comment also may describe a variable declaration, a constant definition, or a type definition. We have also used a brief statement comment after each END of a BEGIN-END pair to specify if it is the END of a THEN clause, an ELSE clause, some subprogram, CASE statement, etc.

Here are some principles you can follow for all comments:

- Do not echo the code. The following is an example of a useless comment:

```
total := total + 1        (* this statement adds 1 to total *)
```

- Be sure the code and the comment agree. Never say that code does something in a comment when it does something else. Whenever you change a piece of a program, take care to ensure that the corresponding comments are changed to describe the resulting program accurately.

- Do not use comments to justify bad code. Bad code should be rewritten into good code. Good code usually needs fewer comments.

- All comments describe something, whether it be a subprogram, a statement, or a variable declaration. It should be clear what each comment describes. We normally put the *program comment* at the start of the program, *subprogram comments* at the beginning of each subprogram, and *statement comments* to the right of the statement they describe.

- Comments should not make reading the code difficult. The reader of a program should never be *forced* to read a program's comments. Program comments are to clarify and provide elaboration for the code. The help is to be available when the reader wants it, but someone already familiar with the program may not be interested in reading most of the comments and should not have to do so.

To develop a habit of using these principles, you should start using comments early. Do not wait until the entire program is coded to go back and "make up" comments. The program is fresh in your mind during coding, and comments can help you during implementation and debugging phases. Statement comments should be added when the statement is written, and subprogram comments should be written when the subprogram is written.

Using structured comments helps you to keep your comments organized. You should create structured comments that accommodate the type of programming project you are working on or to satisfy your personal style. The following code illustrates the use of structured comments at all levels of the program.

```
PROGRAM Monitor (INPUT, OUTPUT, data);


    (* ********************************************************************

    * WRITTEN BY:

    * WRITTEN:

    * LANGUAGE:

    * DESCRIPTION:

    * METHOD:

    * INPUT:

    * OUTPUT:

    ******************************************************************** *)


CONST
    MaxFiles = 100;      (* maximum number of files in directory structure *)

TYPE
    FileType = RECORD
                   name: StringType;
                   ByteSize: INTEGER;
                   deleted: BOOLEAN
               END;      (* FileType *)

    FileListType = ARRAY [1..MaxFiles] OF FileType;

    DirectoryType = RECORD
                        files: FileListType;
                        size: INTEGER
                    END;      (* DirectoryType *)


VAR
    data: TEXT;



PROCEDURE ReadDirectory (VAR directory: DirectoryType;  VAR infile: TEXT);


    (* ********************************************************************

    * DESCRIPTION:

    * METHOD:

    * INPUT:

    * OUTPUT:

    ******************************************************************** *)

BEGIN
END;     (* ReadDirectory *)
```

```
PROCEDURE ProcessDirectory (VAR directory: DirectoryType)

   (* *********************************************************************

    * DESCRIPTION:

    * METHOD:

    * INPUT:

    * OUTPUT:

   ********************************************************************** *)

BEGIN
END;    (* ProcessDirectory *)



PROCEDURE WriteDirectory (directory: DirectoryType;  VAR outfile: TEXT);

   (* *********************************************************************

    * DESCRIPTION:

    * METHOD:

    * INPUT:

    * OUTPUT:

   ********************************************************************** *)

BEGIN
END;    (* WriteDirectory *)



PROCEDURE GlobalFilter (VAR storage: TEXT);

VAR
    directory: DirectoryType;

BEGIN
    ReadDirectory(directory, storage);
    ProcessDirectory(directory);
    WriteDirectory(directory, storage)
END;    (* GlobalFilter *)



BEGIN    (* Main Program *)

    GlobalFilter(data)

END.     (* Main Program *)
```

Programming Example 16-6: Program **Monitor** with Stub Procedures and Comment Shells

16.3.4. Efficiency

A topic that comes up sooner or later in all programming courses is *efficiency*. We have purposely said very little about this topic up to this point. The term efficiency is itself a bit vague. Efficiency refers to the consumption of some resource, and normally it is a measure of how the resource is consumed. The two resources normally associated with a computer program are the computer-processing time and the computer memory. However, there is an often overlooked resource: programmer time. When computers used to be very slow and very expensive, computer time and computer memory were much more important than programmer time. Today, computers are much faster and computer memory is much cheaper. It follows that programmer time is a much more important resource today than it was in the past.

Efforts to achieve efficiency try to optimize resources. Trying to optimize the use of one resource almost always costs more of at least one other resource. Therefore, it is imperative to understand the relative costs of programming resources and the tradeoff between savings of one resource and the additional costs in other resources.

Some programmers think efficiency simply means faster programs. Such programmers expend a great deal of effort to make every line of their program, as fast as they can, all in the name of efficiency. Such behavior usually results in programs that are convoluted, difficult to read and understand, more prone to error, and only marginally faster. This kind of programming is characterized by a lack of understanding. We call it the "efficiency hangup." We have avoided discussing efficiency because all too often a beginning programmer can fall prey to efficiency hangup if exposed to the notion of efficiency too early. We advocate the following programming philosophy:

> 1. Make the program simple.
>
> 2. Make sure the program is correct.
>
> 3. *If necessary*, make the program faster.
>
> **Table 16-2:**   A Philosophy of Program Efficiency

All too often, we find programmers eliminating an addition operation here or a subtraction operation there in the name of efficiency. However, if an addition only requires ten microseconds of computer time, the programmer would need to remove 100,000 addition operations from the program to save only one second of CPU time! Computers are quite fast, and they are getting even faster all the time. It typically takes quite a lot of programmer time to save just a little computer time. Resist the temptation to tune your program to save a few seconds of CPU time. Resist the efficiency hangup.

The program should always be correct before you try making it faster. A program that does not work is of no value, regardless of its speed. Besides, anyone can make a program arbitrarily fast if it does not have to work. Correctness is a *must* before speed is considered. Once the program is finished and you know it works, then consider its speed. Quite often the program runs fast enough. If the program must be faster to be acceptable, then—and only then—should you consider ways to make it faster.

In most programs, five to ten percent of the code actually consumes ninety percent or more of the CPU time. So if you want to make a program faster, you should concentrate on that five to ten percent. Unfortunately, programmers are inherently poor at guessing which portion uses the most time. The best way to determine this is by timing your program. Many systems provide a *program profiler* that gives information on how many times each subprogram gets called and how much time each takes. With this information, you can usually determine the target code rather quickly. If you do not have a profiler, you can add timing and counting manually. Most implementations provide access to a system clock (which typically counts in milliseconds) that you can use to time a program and its subprograms.

Once you determine which portion of the program to speed up, study the algorithm used in that portion of the program and try to replace it with a faster algorithm. Once the algorithm has been replaced, time it again. We will say no more about efficiency now, except for a few reminders:

- Do not sacrifice clarity in the name of efficiency.

- Do not sacrifice correctness in the name of efficiency.

- If the program works correctly but it is too slow, then try to make it faster.

- Avoid the efficiency hangup.

16.3.5. Readability

Since people sometimes need to read programs, every programmer should adopt a scheme of program *layout* to make programs easier to read. Just as one can use margins, indentation, and blank lines to make letters, reports, and textbooks more readable, you should also use such things to enhance the readability of your programs. The following is a list of our recommendations to make your programs more readable.

- Put each statement on a separate line.

- Use blank lines to separate things that are logically unrelated.

- Use indentation to show the logical structure of a program. For example, the statements of a subprogram are indented, as are the statements of a BEGIN-END block and the statements of a REPEAT-UNTIL loop. Inconsistent indentation can be worse than none at all.

- Use both uppercase and lowercase characters if available to make identifiers more readable and to emphasize keywords.

- Use redundant parentheses to avoid ambiguity in expressions.

- Use consistent spacing throughout programs. Use the same number of blank lines between each subprogram declaration, the same number of spaces around operators, and the same number of spaces between elements in lists.

The following table summarizes the formatting conventions we have tried to follow throughout this text:

Blank Lines

number before each subprogram declaration	2
number before each subprogram comment	2
number before CONST	1
number before TYPE	1
number before VAR	1
number before subprogram BEGIN	1

New Lines

Put program header statement on a separate line.
Put each subprogram header on a separate line.
Put keywords on separate lines (CONST, TYPE, VAR, BEGIN, END, WHILE).
Put each statement on a separate line.
Put each constant definition on a separate line.
Put each type definition on a separate line.
Put each variable declaration on a separate line.

Spacing

number before program name	1
number before program parameter list	1
number after each program parameter	1
number before each subprogram name	1
number before subprogram formal parameter list	1
number after each formal parameter	1
number after formal parameter type	2
number between each actual parameter	1
number before function type	1
number between operator and operands	1

Indentation

amount for constant definitions	4
amount for type definitions	4
amount for variable declarations	4
amount for BEGIN-END blocks (including main program and subprograms)	4
amount for THEN and ELSE clauses	4
amount for statements in REPEAT-UNTIL loop	4

Table 16-3: Formatting Conventions

Programs that are neat and organized are generally more readable than nonuniform programs. You should strive to create good-looking programs. However, don't wait until the program is finished and then go back to format the program. Keep your program tidy from the time you write the first line of code. It soon will become second nature to do so.

There are programs that format other programs. Such *formatters* take a program as input and generate a formatted program as output. Writing such a program can be very educational, and the resulting program can be very useful. Situations where many programmers work together (software teams) find *pretty printers* or *formatters* extremely useful since all code looks the same and is therefore easier to read.

The following is an example of a poorly formatted program. It is quite difficult to read:

```
PROCEDURE READDIRECTORY(VAR DIRECTORY:DIRECTORYTYPE;VAR FROM:TEXT);
VAR NUMBER:INTEGER;BEGIN INITDIRECTORY(DIRECTORY);RESET(FROM);NUMBER:=0;
WHILE NOT(EOF(FROM)AND(NUMBER<MAXFILES) DO BEGIN NUMBER:=NUMBER+1;WITH
DIRECTORY.FILES[NUMBER] DO BEGIN READNAME(FROM,NAME);READ(FROM,BYTESIZE);
READLN(FROM)END END;DIRECTORY.SIZE:=NUMBER END;
```

Programming Example 16-7: A Poorly Formatted Procedure

Now, consider the exact same program with blank lines, indentation, mixed-case letters, and other features to improve its readability:

```
PROCEDURE ReadDirectory (VAR directory: DirectoryType;  VAR from: TEXT);

VAR
    number: INTEGER;                 (* used to count number of files in directory *)

BEGIN
    InitDirectory(directory);     (* initialize directory structure *)

    RESET(from);                  (* open file for reading *)

    number := 0;                  (* initialize number of files read *)
    WHILE NOT(EOF(from) AND (number < MaxFiles)) DO
        BEGIN
            number := number + 1;
            WITH directory.files[number] DO
                BEGIN
                    ReadName(from, name);
                    READ(from, ByteSize);
                    READLN(from)
                END      (* WITH *)
        END;      (* WHILE *)

    directory.size := number              (* store total number of files read *)
END;      (* ReadDirectory *)
```

Programming Example 16-8: A Well-Formatted Procedure

Which version do you find easier to read?

16.3.6. Understandability

Although good-looking, readable programs are desirable, they still may be difficult to understand. *Understandable* programs are even more desirable. There are several things we can do to make programs easier to understand:

- **Make code simple.** Do not try to be overly clever. Strive for simple, direct programs.

- **Use mnemonic identifier names.** A program that uses cryptic identifier names—such as a, b, and c instead of such names as total, revenues, and profit—are not easy to understand. Every time we see a cryptic identifier, we must translate it to understand what it means in the program. Name your identifiers according to what they represent.

- **Use distinct variable names.** If a procedure has six local variables, **column**, **columns**, **colmn**, **colmns**, **col**, and **cols**, it will be difficult to understand. Avoid using identifiers that differ in only a few characters.

- **Use prefixes and suffixes for identifier names.** We normally use the suffix *Type* for all user-defined types, such as DirectoryType and FileType.

- **Group logically related subprograms.** In languages that support modules or units (e.g. Modula-2), put logically related subprograms together in a separate module. In such languages as Standard Pascal, order the subprograms so that related ones are declared adjacent to one another.

Consider the following procedure declaration:

```
PROCEDURE I1 (VAR I2: I3;  VAR I4: TEXT);

VAR
    I5: INTEGER;

BEGIN
    I6(I2);

    RESET(I4);

    I5 := 0;
    WHILE NOT(EOF(I4) AND (I5 < I7) DO
        BEGIN
            I5 := I5 + 1;
            WITH I2.I8[I5] DO
                BEGIN
                    I9(I4, I10);
                    READ(I4, I11);
                    READLN(I4)
                END
        END;

    I2.I12 := I5
END;
```

Programming Example 16-9: Poorly Chosen Identifiers

Do you understand it? Do you recognize it? It is the procedure **ReadDirectory** from the previous page. We simply replaced all the identifiers with nonmnemonic identifiers (e.g. I1, I2, I3). Picking meaningful identifiers helps others to read and understand your code. A good test of a program's readability is to give the program to a fellow colleague. If the program is not easy for your colleague to read, then it probably is not a readable program.

16.3.7. An Example of Program Implementation

With all of this in mind, consider completing the program **Monitor**. The following example illustrates most of the subroutines refined into actual Pascal code. Although it is not imperative that you study every line of code in this program, you should understand both the design and style employed, note how the points made in this chapter are embodied in this code, and feel comfortable in your ability to create a similar program on your own.

```
PROGRAM Monitor (INPUT, OUTPUT, data);

CONST
    MaxFiles = 100;      (* maximum number of files in directory structure *)

TYPE
    FileType = RECORD
                    name: StringType;
                    ByteSize: INTEGER;
                    deleted: BOOLEAN
               END;    (* FileType *)

    FileListType = ARRAY [1..MaxFiles] OF FileType;

    DirectoryType = RECORD
                        files: FileListType;
                        size: INTEGER
                    END;    (* DirectoryType *)


VAR
    data: TEXT;
```

```
PROCEDURE ReadDirectory (VAR directory: DirectoryType;  VAR from: TEXT);

VAR
    number: INTEGER;              (* used to count number of files in directory *)

BEGIN
    InitDirectory(directory);     (* initialize directory structure *)

    RESET(from);                  (* open file for reading *)

    number := 0;                  (* initialize number of files read *)
    WHILE NOT(EOF(from) AND (number < MaxFiles)) DO
        BEGIN
            number := number + 1;
            WITH directory.files[number] DO
                BEGIN
                    ReadName(from, name);
                    READ(from, ByteSize);
                    READLN(from)
                END       (* WITH *)
        END;      (* WHILE *)

    directory.size := number            (* store total number of files read *)
END;     (* ReadDirectory *)




PROCEDURE WriteDirectory (directory: DirectoryType;  VAR outfile: TEXT);

VAR
    index: INTEGER;

BEGIN
    REWRITE(outfile);    (* open file for writing *)

    FOR index := 1 to directory.size DO
        WITH directory.files[index] DO
            BEGIN
                WriteName(outfile, name);
                WRITE(outfile, ByteSize);
                WRITELN(outfile)
            END     (* WITH *)

END;    (* WriteDirectory *)




FUNCTION GetCommand: CHAR;

CONST
    prompt = 'Monitor>';

VAR
    cmd: CHAR;

BEGIN
    WRITE(OUTPUT, prompt);
    READLN(OUTPUT, cmd);
    GetCommand := cmd
END;     (* GetCommand *)
```

```
PROCEDURE ListAll (directory: DirectoryType);

VAR
    index: INTEGER;
    ByteTotal: INTEGER;

BEGIN
    WRITELN(OUTPUT, 'File      Bytes      Status');

    ByteTotal := 0;
    FOR index := 1 TO directory.size DO
        WITH directory.files[index] DO
            BEGIN
                WriteName(OUTPUT, name);
                WRITE(OUTPUT, ByteSize);
                IF deleted
                    THEN WRITE(OUTPUT, 'DELETED')
                    ELSE WRITE(OUTPUT, 'NOT DELETED');
                WRITELN(OUTPUT);
                ByteTotal := ByteTotal + ByteSize
            END;    (* WITH *)

    WRITELN(OUTPUT, ByteTotal, 'bytes in ', directory.size, 'files.')
END;    (* ListAll *)


PROCEDURE List (directory: DirectoryType);

VAR
    index: INTEGER;
    ByteTotal: INTEGER;

BEGIN
    WRITELN(OUTPUT, 'File      Bytes);

    ByteTotal := 0;
    FOR index := 1 TO directory.size DO
        WITH directory.files[index] DO
            IF NOT(deleted)
                THEN BEGIN
                        WriteName(OUTPUT, name);
                        WRITE(OUTPUT, ByteSize);
                        WRITELN(OUTPUT);
                        ByteTotal := ByteTotal + ByteSize
                    END;    (* THEN *)

    WRITELN(OUTPUT, ByteTotal, 'bytes in ', directory.size, 'files.')
END;    (* List *)


PROCEDURE ListDeleted (directory: DirectoryType);

VAR
    index: INTEGER;
    ByteTotal: INTEGER;

BEGIN
    WRITELN(OUTPUT, 'File      Bytes);

    ByteTotal := 0;
    FOR index := 1 TO directory.size DO
        WITH directory.files[index] DO
            IF deleted
                THEN BEGIN
                        WriteName(OUTPUT, name);
                        WRITE(OUTPUT, ByteSize);
                        WRITELN(OUTPUT);
                        ByteTotal := ByteTotal + ByteSize
                    END;    (* THEN *)

    WRITELN(OUTPUT, ByteTotal, 'bytes in ', directory.size, 'files.')
END;    (* ListDeleted *)
```

```
    PROCEDURE Delete (VAR directory: DirectoryType);

    BEGIN
    END;    (* Delete *)



    PROCEDURE UnDelete (VAR directory: DirectoryType);

    BEGIN
    END;    (* UnDelete *)



    PROCEDURE Create (VAR directory: DirectoryType);

    BEGIN
    END;    (* Create *)



    PROCEDURE Exit;

    BEGIN
    END;    (* Exit *)



    PROCEDURE ProcessDirectory (VAR directory: DirectoryType);
    BEGIN
        REPEAT
            command := GetCommand;

            CASE command OF
                'L', 'l': List(directory);
                'D', 'd': Delete(directory);
                'U', 'u': UnDelete(directory);
                'C', 'c': Create(directory);
                'P', 'p': ListDeleted(directory);
                'A', 'a': ListAll(directory)
                'E', 'e': Exit;
                OTHERS: GiveHelp
            END;      (* CASE *)
        UNTIL (command = 'E') OR (command ='e')
    END;    (* ProcessDirectory *)


    PROCEDURE GlobalFilter (VAR storage: TEXT);

    VAR
        directory: DirectoryType;

    BEGIN
        ReadDirectory(directory, storage);
        ProcessDirectory(directory);
        WriteDirectory(directory, storage)
    END;    (* GlobalFilter *)



    BEGIN    (* Main Program *)

        GlobalFilter(data)

    END.    (* Main Program *)
```

Programming Example 16-10: Program **Monitor** Refined

16.4. A Style of Program Verification

After implementing a program, we are ready enter the final phase of programming, *verification* and *testing*. This phase of program development determines two things: (1) Does the program do everything it is supposed to? and (2) Does the program do everything correctly?

The way to answer the first question is by comparing the program with the functional specification (generated in phase 1) and the original problem statement. As long as you have not forgotten any of the required features during the design or implementation phases, the program should be functionally acceptable. If, however, you neglected to write the directory back out to storage or neglected to provide the ability to list deleted files, you will have an unsatisfactory result.

Answering the second question is much more difficult because a program may appear to work without our knowing whether it will work correctly under all circumstances. There is a way to prove that a program works correctly in all situations. This method is very formal and requires the use of a specialized language known as *predicate calculus*. Because is is difficult (most think it much more difficult than programming), tedious, and time consuming, few people prove their programs to be correct in a formal sense.

The most common way to verify a program is through *testing*. The problem with testing is that the test only tells us if the program works for the particular test data we use. Therefore, to test a program completely, we must give it all possible test data. But if a program requires only one integer, there are infinitely many possible inputs to the program. Even when the possible inputs are finite, there are often too many to try them all. Hence, it usually is impossible in a practical sense to completely test a program. We must settle for a subset of all possible test data. The trick, then, is to pick a reasonable set of test data so that we are reasonably sure that the program works. The following are some suggestions for selecting test data:

- **Test common valid input.** For the **Monitor** program, we would want to pick at least all seven of the valid commands: L, D, U, C, P, A, E.

- **Test fringe or boundary data.** If we were writing a program to test integers to see if they were prime, we should choose 2 as a test case, since it is the smallest prime number. Similarly, we should select the integer 1 since it is on the other side of the boundary. When we have numeric input, it is a good idea to try 1, 0, and −1 as test cases. Also, consider the boundary conditions for data structures, such as zero elements in an array or the maximum allocated.

- **Test clearly invalid data.** For example, in our **Monitor** program, we would want to test some invalid commands, such as x, y, and z. We would also want to try such things as deleting nonexistent files, deleting already deleted files, or creating already existing files. When we have numeric input, we always must try both positive and negative numbers.

Consider a function to determine if an integer is odd or even. An integer is even if there is no remainder when divided by 2; it is odd otherwise. Consider the following Pascal function to determine if inputs are odd or even:

```
FUNCTION Odd (number: INTEGER): BOOLEAN;

BEGIN
    Odd := (number MOD 2) = 1
END;
```

Programming Example 16-11: Function **Odd**

The previous function returns TRUE only if the remainder after division by 2 is 1. For 7, 7 MOD 2 yields 1, so 7 is odd. Similarly, 8 MOD 2 yields 0, so 8 is not odd. It seems to be correct. But what about negative input? −7 MOD 2 yields −1 rather than 1, so the function returns FALSE. But we know that −7 is just as odd as 7. To correct the previous function, we should change it to evaluate negatives:

```
FUNCTION Odd (number: INTEGER): BOOLEAN;

BEGIN
    Odd := (number MOD 2) <> 0
END;
```

Programming Example 16-12: Function **Odd** Corrected

Consider the following function that is designed to return the uppercase equivalent of any character:

```
FUNCTION UpperCase (ch: CHAR): CHAR;

CONST
    CaseDiff = 32;

BEGIN
    IF (ch >= 'a') AND (ch <= 'z')
        THEN UpperCase := CHR(ORD(ch) - CaseDiff)
        ELSE UpperCase := ch
END;     (* UpperCase *)
```

Programming Example 16-13:   Function `UpperCase`

We should try 'a' and 'z' since they are the boundary values. We need only try one value outside the range; we need not try all remaining values, all uppercase, all digits, all punctuation, etc. Often, input falls into two or more classes. If it works for one value in a class, then we need not check any others in the class. Such classes are known as *equivalence classes*. When the input can be so partitioned, we need to select only one item from each class.

The previous function has two equivalence classes: those that are in the range 'a' .. 'z' and those that are not. Hence, we could pick 'd' and 'D' and be sure that if the function works for those two it should work for all character values. We would still test the boundary conditions out of habit.

In Unit II, we learned about loops and loop invariants. The use of loop-invariant assertions helps verify that loops do what we want them to do. You might want to refresh your memory on the subject (see Section 7.4 starting on page 224). Once you determine the invariant for a loop, it is good practice to include the invariant in a comment associated with the particular loop to which it applies.

16.5. Notes on Debugging

In testing your program, you will undoubtedly uncover at least one *bug*. It is natural to find bugs in your programs; in fact, it is unnatural to not find them. Computer programming requires an inordinate amount of attention to detail, and we all let a detail slip past us from time to time. Whereas it is relatively easy to find bugs, it is much more difficult to fix them. We must first identify what is wrong and then determine which portion of the program is causing the bug. Finally, we must determine what to do to remedy the problem.

Most programming systems now provide a *debugger* for debugging programs. Debuggers typically provide the facility to trace a program's execution and the ability to query the values of variables. Some debuggers permit the programmer to have the program stop in certain programmer-selected points and to change the values of varibles. A good debugger is a great tool for helping you to locate and correct bugs. If no debugger is available on your system, you will need to add statements to your program to help you locate bugs. The natural thing is to simply add WRITELN statements to your subprograms to print out input values, key variables, and reminders when a subprogram is called or finished. However, after the bug is located and fixed, we no longer need the debugging output. Instead of just throwing away the debugging WRITELNs, we suggest using conditional debugging statements as indicated in following program fragment:

```
IF debugging
    THEN WRITELN(OUTPUT, debugging information goes here)
```

Programming Example 16-14:   Conditional Debugging Statement

Here, **debugging** is a named constant that is set to TRUE when we are debugging and FALSE when we are finished debugging. Thus, if we later need to debug a subprogram again, we simply change the value of **debugging**, which causes the debugging information to be generated again.

Consider the following example to demonstrate this notion. The two most popular mathematical coordinate systems are the Cartesian (or Rectangular) Coordinate System and the Polar Coordinate System. A point is specified in the Polar Coordinate System by a radius and an angle of inclination. A point is specified in the Cartesian Coordinate System as a pair of numbers known as the ordinate and abscissa (also known as x and y). Assume we must write a subprogram to convert a point in polar coordinates to the more familiar cartesian coordinates. Most people do not know offhand the formula for converting points from one coordinate system to the other. But that should not prevent us from writing a subprogram stub with appropriate debugging information. The following subprogram demonstrates conditional debugging:

```
PROCEDURE PolarToRectangular (radius, angle: REAL;
                             VAR ordinate, abscissa: REAL);

  (* ***********************************************************************

   * DESCRIPTION:
               This subprogram converts a point in Polar Coordinates to
               a point in Rectangular Coordinates.

   * METHOD:

   * INPUT:
               radius:
               angle:

   * OUTPUT:
               ordinate:
               abscissa:

   ****************************************************************** *)


BEGIN
    IF debugging
       THEN BEGIN
               WRITELN(OUTPUT, 'Entering procedure PolarToRectangular');
               WRITELN(OUTPUT, 'radius = ', radius);
               WRITELN(OUTPUT, 'angle = ', angle)
            END;


    (* the real computations will go here once they are understood *)


    IF debugging
       THEN BEGIN
               ordinate := SomeDefaultValue;
               abscissa := SomeOtherDefaultValue;
               WRITELN(OUTPUT, Exiting procedure PolarToRectangular')
            END;

END;     (* PolarToRectangular *)
```

Programming Example 16-15: Using Conditional Debugging

Note that we do not need to know how to translate from polar coordinates to cartesian coordinates to write the stub procedure. We can integrate the preceding stub into a program that needs such a procedure and continue working on the program. The procedure can be fleshed out and refined later, even perhaps by someone else.[1] When the procedure is refined to our satisfaction, we can disable the debugging information by simply setting the constant **debugging** to FALSE. Should we later determine the procedure is not working properly, we need only change the value of the named constant **debugging** to enable our debugging information. We have found this conditional debugging scheme to be very useful. However, we have found a slight variant of this scheme even more useful. Consider the following program fragment:

```
IF ProcDebugging OR PgmDebugging
   THEN WRITELN(OUTPUT, debugging information goes here)
```

Programming Example 16-16: Multiple Condition Debugging Statement

---

[1]For those interested: The ordinate is the product of the radius and the sine of the angle, and the abscissa is the product of the radius and the cosine of the angle.

Note that this statement has a compound condition. There is a named constant for the procedure (**ProcDebugging**) and one for the whole program (**PgmDebugging**). That way we can get the debugging information for just one procedure, or we can get it for all procedures by simply changing the value of the global constant. This variant debugging scheme that employs a multiple condition gives us greater control over the debugging information that is displayed.

Chapter 17: Dynamic Memory Allocation

Up to this point, you have learned a variety of important concepts of programming methodology and style. By solving the exercises and programming problems, you have demonstrated your ability to put your knowledge into practice. You now have the skills to design and implement computer programs that can solve a wide range of problems.

Although the techniques presented in the preceding chapters are very good for solving many programming problems, these techniques are not necessarily the best techniques for *all* problems. The primary reason that the techniques we have learned are not always the best arises from the way computer memory is utilized. Another reason, which tends to be overlooked by many people, concerns making programs more general, easier to use, and easier to understand and extend.

Until now we have assumed that your computer always has *enough* memory. Although computer memory is now relatively cheap and plentiful, every computer has a limited amount of it. It is easy to write a program that requires more memory than your computer has. In fact, there are many programming problems that, when solved using only the techniques learned so far, require more than the available memory. There are other techniques that require substantially less memory that could be used to solve these same programming problems. In this chapter we will review a method of allocating computer memory that will enable you to solve a broad class of programming problems.

17.1. Allocation of Computer Memory

In earlier chapters we developed a model of computer memory to help you visualize and understand the concepts involved. We have suggested thinking of computer memory as a vast collection of mail boxes, with each memory cell having the ability to hold a value. The values of variables are stored in computer memory cells. Therefore, each declared variable uses some of this computer memory. We request computer memory for our programs by declaring variables. For example, if a subprogram has three character variables and an array of integers one hundred elements long, then, when the subprogram are called 103 memory cells to represent these variables is *allocated* to your program. When memory is allocated to a particular subprogram, it is not available to other subprograms. When the subprogram terminates, the memory allocated to it is released and becomes available to represent other variables. This process of releasing memory is referred to as *deallocation*. When a program terminates, all memory that has been allocated to the program is deallocated. This model of computer memory allocation underscores three important points:

1. Computer memory is requested by variable declarations. The more variables declared in a program, the more memory the program needs.

2. The amount of memory required for a particular variable—whether it be an integer, character, record, array of records, or something else—can be determined when the declaration is made. The amount of memory required to represent a variable is known at compile time.

3. Memory for variables declared in this way is allocated and deallocated according to the scope in which the variable is declared. When a subprogram is called, memory cells required for the subprogram's variables are allocated. When a subprogram terminates, memory cells required for the subprogram's variables are deallocated.

Allocating memory in this fashion is known as *static memory allocation*. Variables declared in this way are called *static variables*. All variables declared up to this point have been static variables.

There are definite drawbacks associated with using static variables in real applications programs. For example, recall the program we designed to keep track of statistics on baseball players (Section 15.3). We used a record to represent each player. Fields of the record included name, position, and other statistics. The team of players was in turn represented as an array of records. Indeed, we have found an array of records to be a good way to represent many different kinds of information because we can pick fields of the record that match the attributes of the problem. The drawback is that we are required to specify in advance the possible array indices and, therefore, the number of elements in the array. If we pick the array indices [1..100], then the array holds exactly one hundred records. If the array is declared with array indices [1..1000], then it holds exactly one thousand player records.

If it turns out that there are more players than the size of the array, then the array is unable to accommodate all the players. Some people attempt to avoid this issue by always allocating arrays larger than the biggest problem to be solved. But this strategy just points out another problem with static variables. For example, suppose a programmer declares an index set [1..1000], knowing that no application will require more than one thousand elements. Let us further suppose that only an occasional application needs anywhere near one thousand elements, with most applications needing approximately fifty elements. The program would have enough memory allocated to handle all the applications; however, almost all the applications would waste a lot of memory.

This example demonstrates two very big drawbacks of static variables: (1) If the array is large enough for the problem, it wastes memory because there are some, possibly many, allocated but unused memory cells; (2) regardless of its size, the selected array will not always be large enough because array size is fixed when the program is compiled.

Some programmers try to get around this problem by modifying their program before each execution. They find out the size of the problem to be solved and redeclare the array bounds so that the arrays are just the right size for that problem. There are three major drawbacks to this idea. The first is that we must modify the program for each new application; this leads to a lot of work for the programmer. The second reason is that the programmer must know the size of the problem prior to program execution; sometimes this is impossible. The third reason is that some people who need to use a program are not programmers; such people are not able to modify a program prior to its use, even if they know the problem size.

As we can see from these drawbacks, changing the array bounds is not a workable solution in general. To understand the problem, consider an analogy. Suppose you have worked hard all summer and socked away a respectable portion of your earnings; you decide to reward yourself with a small travel vacation. Because you have deposited your earnings in the local bank, you need to withdraw enough money to pay for your travels. Although you could just empty your entire account, put it in your wallet, and head off on your trip, you remember a television advertisement: Travelers' checks are accepted almost everywhere and are much safer to carry than than cash. Recognizing the merit of travelers' checks, you decide to use them. However, you must decide how much of your bank account to convert to travelers' checks. If you take it all, you will have allocated more than you will probably need. Conversely, you do not want to take too little. Even though you might have some guidelines for how much of your money to allocate to travelers' checks, by picking any fixed amount, you always run the risk of allocating too much or too little.

You visit your bank and explain the allocation problem to a helpful teller who suggests a solution: an automated teller machine (ATM) card for your account. "The ATM card gives you access to the money in your account 24 hours a day in every city that has an automated teller machine in the same ATM network as our bank," says the teller, straightening his bow tie. He hands you a brochure that lists the locations of ATMs in your region of the country, and you discover that there is one in your chosen vacation spot. You apply for and receive your ATM card before taking your vacation.

The situation is a lot like picking array sizes: No matter what size we pick, we always run the risk of allocating too much or too little. We would like to allocate as much as we need. The ATM card solved the funds allocation problem by providing access to the money as it is needed. We need an analogous solution to solve the computer memory allocation problem. We would like to allocate computer memory as it is needed so that we have to request only as much memory as the problem at hand requires. For those people running our baseball statistics program, if information about eight hundred players is needed, then eight hundred records should be allocated; but if information about only twenty players is needed, then only twenty player records should be allocated. The number of player records allocated matches the number of players each user is interested in rather than some arbitrary number.

This process is called *dynamic memory allocation*. Variables allocated in this way are called *dynamic variables*. Many high-level programming languages provide a way to allocate memory dynamically. Pascal also permits dynamic memory allocation.

Although you may not understand the details of dynamic variables in Pascal, you should be able to see that dynamic memory allocation makes much better use of computer memory. You should also be able to understand why a broader range of applications can be handled by a single program using dynamic variables. However, notice that dynamic allocation of memory does not mean that we should not consider the memory requirements of a program. Just as the funds in your bank account are limited, so is the amount of memory in your computer. Although ATM cards make it easier to access funds from your account and dynamic memory allocation provides a better way to allocate computer memory, you can run out of resources in both situations. Neither ATM cards nor dynamic variables create resources; they provide a better way to control the amount of resources you withdraw.

17.1.1. Questions

1. What is the function of computer memory?

2. Describe static memory allocation.

3. What is a static variable?

4. How does a Pascal programmer request computer memory to be allocated for a static variable?

5. When is computer memory allocated for a static variable in a Pascal program?

6. Can it be determined at the time a program is compiled how much computer memory is required to represent any static variable? What about large variables, such as arrays of records?

7. What is dynamic memory allocation?

8. What is a dynamic variable?

9. Why would a programmer ever need dynamic variables?

10. Can we safely ignore the amount of memory our computer has if we always use dynamic variables instead of static variables? Justify your answer.

17.2. Manipulating Dynamic Variables

Having contrasted static memory allocation and dynamic memory allocation and pointing out the need for dynamic variables, we turn our focus to dynamic variables in Pascal. We should point out that the examples in this section are designed to give you the skills for creating and manipulating dynamic variables. The following sections provide examples of using dynamic variables to solve real-world problems.

Recall that we always specify both a *type* and a *name* for every static variable we declare in Pascal. This is possible since we know exactly how many static variables there are when the program is compiled. However, we have no way of knowing how many dynamic variables a program might create. If we do not know how many dynamic variables there are, we cannot specify unique names for each of them. Therefore, the idea is to create a new variable name when we create each new dynamic variable. This, however, is a task that we can leave up to the computer. Therefore, dynamic variables have system-generated names rather than user-specified names.

How do you suppose that the computer generates unique names for each dynamic variable in a program? Recall that we said earlier that every cell of memory has a unique *address*. The computer uses these addresses to refer to its memory cells. Therefore, these addresses are the system-generated unique names. Perhaps this is starting to sound like a leap back to the days of ENIAC, when programmers had to refer to memory cells by their addresses. Programming language designers recognize the problems that occur when programmers are forced to deal with addresses. To avoid these problems, designers provide a special variable to hold these system-generated names. These variables are known as *pointer variables*. A pointer variable holds the system-generated name (address) of a dynamic variable. Therefore, to refer to a dynamic variable, we use the name stored in the corresponding pointer variable.

The scenario for dynamically allocated variables can be summarized as follows. When another variable is needed, the program requests that a dynamic variable be created. When the system creates the dynamic variable, it also creates a unique system-generated variable name. The program then stores the system-generated name in another variable, known as a pointer variable. When we want to refer to a dynamic variable, we use the name stored in the associated pointer variable.

To understand dynamic variables and pointer variables, consider the following type definition.

```
TYPE
    LittleLetterType = 'a'..'z';
```

We have been defining subrange types, such as this subrange of CHAR, for quite a while now. Although you could declare a *static* variable of this subrange type, we want a *dynamic* variable of **LittleLetterType**. Remember that in order to have a dynamic variable, we need a pointer variable to hold the name of the dynamic variable. If the dynamic variable is of type **LittleLetterType**, what type is the pointer variable? Some programming languages have just one type of pointer variable. However, Pascal is heavily typed and, therefore, has more than one pointer type. Pascal denotes a pointer type by the symbol $\uparrow$ followed by the type of the dynamic variable it holds the address of.[1] Therefore, for a dynamic variable of type **LittleLetterType**, the corresponding pointer variable is of type $\uparrow$**LittleLetterType**. These two type definitions appear in the following program fragment:

```
TYPE
    LittleLetterType = 'a'..'z';

    PointerType = ↑LittleLetterType;
```
Programming Example 17-1:   Defining a Pointer Type

Since dynamic variables are unknown at compile time, they are not declared in the variable declaration. However, a pointer variable can be declared at compile time. The following program fragment illustrates a type, a pointer type, and a pointer variable:

```
TYPE
    LittleLetterType = 'a'..'z';

    PointerType = ↑LittleLetterType;


VAR
    p: PointerType;
```
Programming Example 17-2:   Declaring a Pointer Variable

Note that the variable **p** is declared of type **PointerType**. Hence, the variable **p** is of type $\uparrow$**LittleLetterType** rather than of type **LittleLetterType**. Note that there are no static variables of **LittleLetterType**; we create variables of that type dynamically. In order to allocate memory for a variable dynamically, we need a means to request it. Pascal provides the predefined procedure **NEW** for this purpose.

To create a new dynamic variable of **LittleLetterType** and put the system-generated name for the new variable in the pointer variable **p**, we use **NEW(p)**. To illustrate the relationship between a pointer variable and the corresponding dynamic variable, we normally draw an arrow from the pointer variable to the dynamic variable. The following illustration depicts the situation before and after the procedure **NEW** is called:

---

[1]Although we use the uparrow symbol $\uparrow$, many computers use the symbol ^. This symbol is known as the "caret" or "circumflex."

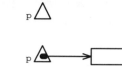

Notice that before the procedure **NEW** is called on the pointer variable **p**, **p** has an unknown value, but after the call to **NEW**, it holds the address of the dynamic variable indicated by the arrow joining the two variables. Also note that the procedure **NEW** is always called on a *pointer variable*. To illustrate the procedure **NEW** further, as well as the common manipulations of pointer variables and dynamic variables, we have prepared a detailed series of illustrations. You should take time to go over these illustrations carefully until you grasp the notions they are intended to demonstrate.

The first illustration shows the declaration of three pointer variables. Note that each is a pointer to a dynamic variable of type CHAR. Initially, all three pointer variables have undefined values:

```
VAR
    p, q, r: ^CHAR;
```

The next illustration shows the creation of a new dynamic variable when the procedure **NEW** is called.

```
NEW(p);

    (* allocate a new variable *)

    (* and put it's name in p *)
```

The next illustration demonstrates the creation of another new dynamic variable. Since the procedure **NEW** is called with the variable **q** as a parameter, the address of the new dynamic variable is placed in **q**.

```
NEW(q);

    (* allocate a new variable *)

    (* and put it's name in q *)
```

At this point, two of the three pointer variables have defined values. However, both of our new *dynamic* variables have *undefined* values. Both dynamic variables can hold a value of type CHAR. How would you give one of the dynamic variables a value? Suppose we wanted to store the CHAR value 'a' in the first dynamic variable. You might be thinking of trying `p := 'a'`. But remember that the variable **p** is a pointer variable, not the dynamic variable. We want to assign the value to the dynamic variable that **p** references. The name of a dynamic variable held by a pointer variable is indicated by following the pointer variable with the symbol ↑. This means that the assignment statement would be `p↑ := 'a'`, as indicated in the following illustration:

```
p^ := 'a'

    (* assign 'a' to dynamic variable *)

    (* whose name is in p *)
```

A pointer variable is meant to hold a *reference* to a dynamic variable. The process of specifying a dynamic variable by a pointer variable is called *dereferencing* the pointer. The symbol ↑ is known as the *dereference operator*. We can assign a character value to the other dynamic variable in a similar way:

```
q^ := 't'

    (* assign 't' to dynamic variable *)

    (* whose name is in q *)
```

Now we are going to create another new dynamic variable. This time the system-generated name will be stored in the pointer variable **r**, as indicated in the following illustration:

```
NEW(r);

    (* allocate a new variable *)

    (* and put it's name in r *)
```

We can copy the value held by one dynamic variable into another dynamic variable. Since we must *dereference* a pointer variable to access a dynamic variable, we must dereference two pointer variables to access the two different dynamic variables. The following illustration indicates how this is done:

```
r^ := q^;

    (* copy the value of the dynamic variable *)

    (* whose name is in q to the dynamic *)

    (* variable whose name is in r *)
```

Just because the value has been copied from one dynamic variable to another, the dynamic variables are in no way bound together. If we change the value of either dynamic variable, it will have no effect on the value held by the other dynamic variable. This is indicated in the following illustration:

```
q^ := 'm';

    (* assign 'm' to the dynamic variable *)

    (* whose name is in q *)
```

Thus, we can change any dynamic variable without affecting any other dynamic variable.

```
r^ := 'b';

    (* assign 'b' to the dynamic variable *)

    (* whose name is in r *)
```

Copying pointer variables is different from copying dynamic variables. Since pointer variables hold the name of a dynamic variable, copying the value from one pointer variable to another pointer variable copies the name of the dynamic variable to the other pointer variable. After the value of one *pointer variable* is copied to another *pointer variable*, both *pointer* variables refer to the same *dynamic* variable. This is depicted in the following illustration:

```
r := q;

    (* copy the name of the dynamic *)

    (* variable in q to r *)
```

Since both pointer variables reference the same dynamic variable, dereferencing either pointer variable specifies the same dynamic variable. Specifically, at this time, both **q↑** and **r↑** point to the same dynamic variable. Notice the dynamic variable holding the value 'b' has no pointer variable referencing it. A dynamic variable with no pointer to it is *inaccessible*. If we called the procedure **NEW** again on one of the pointer variables, we would get another new dynamic variable, as shown in the next illustration:

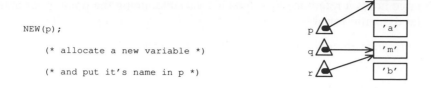

```
NEW(p);

    (* allocate a new variable *)

    (* and put it's name in p *)
```

Note that we now have four dynamic variables but that only two of them have pointers to them. The other two dynamic variables are *inaccessible*. Memory cells allocated for dynamic variables that become inaccessible are known as *garbage*. To *deallocate* dynamic memory cells, Pascal provides the predefined procedure **DISPOSE**. The action of this procedure can be visualized as follows:

```
DISPOSE(p);
```

Note that before the call to **DISPOSE** there are four dynamic variables, but after its call there are only three dynamic variables. The dynamic variable formerly pointed to by the pointer variable **p** is no longer allocated. We should point out that in order to dispose of a dynamic variable, a pointer to the dynamic variable is needed. The predefined procedures **NEW** and **DISPOSE** perform inverse operations. The pointer variable **p** is now *undefined*. There is a special value that pointer variables may hold that indicates the pointer variable currently does not point to a dynamic variable. The special pointer value is **NIL**. We normally indicate the **NIL** pointer with the "ground symbol" indicated in the following illustration:

```
p := NIL;
```

What happens if we dispose of the dynamic variable referenced by **q**?

```
DISPOSE(q);
```

Since both pointer variables **q** and **r** reference the same dynamic variable, disposing of the dynamic variable referenced by **q** also disposes of the dynamic variable referenced by **r**. The pointer variable **r** now contains a reference to a nonexistent dynamic variable. The pointer variable **r** is said to contain a *dangling reference*, or *dangling pointer*. As you might expect, attempting to dereference a dangling pointer will lead to errors.

If you followed these illustrations carefully, you should have the essentials for creating, disposing of, and manipulating dynamic variables. Some of the key points presented in these illustrations are itemized below:

- Dynamic variables are allocated by calls to the predefined procedure **NEW**.

- Dynamic variables are deallocated by calls to the predefined procedure **DISPOSE**.

- Pointer variables hold the name of (address of) a dynamic variable.

- If a pointer variable holds the value **NIL**, it references no dynamic variable.

- Since a pointer variable holds a reference to a dynamic variable, using the pointer variable to specify a particular dynamic variable is called *dereferencing* the pointer variable.

- It is erroneous to dereference an undefined, **NIL**, or dangling pointer.

17.2.1. Questions

1. In declaring a static variable in Pascal, we must specify both a *name* and a *type* for the variable. Since dynamic variables are not declared, how do they get names?

2. What is a system-generated name?

3. How do we store system-generated names?

4. What is a pointer variable?

5. How is a pointer-variable type indicated in Pascal?

6. Is a pointer type a scalar type or a structured type?

7. How is a dynamic variable allocated in Pascal?

8. How is a dynamic variable deallocated in Pascal?

9. How do we refer to a dynamic variable?

10. What symbol is used to dereference a pointer variable?

11. Can a Pascal program access a dynamic variable for which there is no pointer?

12. What are inaccessible dynamic variables called?

13. What special pointer value denotes the fact that a pointer variable references no dynamic variable?

14. Can we call the procedure **NEW** on a pointer variable even if the pointer variable already references a dynamic variable?

15. Is it legal in Standard Pascal to call the procedure **DISPOSE** on a pointer variable with a **NIL** or undefined value?

16. Is it legal in Standard Pascal to dereference a pointer variable with a **NIL** or undefined value?

17. What is a dangling pointer?

18. Is it an acceptable practice to dereference dangling pointers?

17.2.2. Exercises

1. Create a valid Pascal type definition for a pointer to a variable of type INTEGER.

2. Create a valid Pascal variable declaration that declares two pointer variables named **smaller** and **larger**. Both should be pointers to variables of type INTEGER.

3. Write a Pascal program fragment that initializes the two pointer variables in the previous exercise.

4. Write a Pascal program fragment that creates a dynamic variable. The address of the dynamic variable should be placed in the pointer variable **smaller**.

5. Write a Pascal program fragment that creates another dynamic variable but places the address in the pointer variable **larger**.

6. Write the code fragment necessary to give both dynamic variables in the previous example an initial value of 0.

7. Write the Pascal statement that gives the dynamic variable pointed to by **smaller** your favorite negative number.

8. Write the Pascal statement that gives the dynamic variable pointed to by **larger** the value of **MAXINT**.

9. Write a Pascal code fragment that writes out to the screen the values of both dynamic variables you created in the two previous exercises.

10. Write a Pascal code fragment that computes the difference in the values held by the two dynamic variables in the previous exercise and displays the difference as output.

11. Write a Pascal code fragment that exchanges the values of the two dynamic variables in the previous exercise.

12. Write a Pascal code fragment that exchanges the values of the two pointer variables in the previous exercise. *Hint: You need another pointer variable.*

13. *Write a Pascal code fragment that writes out to the screen the values of both *pointer* variables in the previous exercise.

17.3. Dynamically Allocating Record Variables

Recall the program that we designed to keep track of information on players of a baseball team (Section 15.3). We chose to represent an individual player with a record. In turn, the team was represented as an array of records, with each array index corresponding to a player's jersey number. We defined the types in Pascal as follows:

```
TYPE
    TeamType = ARRAY [JerseyType] OF PlayerType;

    JerseyType = MinJersey .. MaxJersey;

    PlayerType = RECORD
                    name: StringType;
                    position: StringType;
                    statistics: OffensiveStatsType
            END;    (* PlayerType *)
```

Programming Example 17-3: Team as an Array of Records

If we define the array index [1..99], then the array has 99 player records. However, if there are only 20 players on the team, then most of the memory allocated for the player records is not needed. Now that we know how to allocate variables dynamically, we can modify our baseball manager program to take advantage of this knowledge. We can modify the array so that it is no longer an array of record variables; instead, it should be an *array of pointer variables*. The pointer variables should hold pointers to player records. We can change the type modifications as indicated in the following program fragment:

```
TYPE
    TeamType = ARRAY [JerseyType] OF PlayerPointerType;

    JerseyType = MinJersey .. MaxJersey;

    PlayerPointerType = ↑PlayerType;

    PlayerType = RECORD
                    name: StringType;
                    position: StringType;
                    statistics: OffensiveStatsType
            END;    (* PlayerType *)
```

Programming Example 17-4: Team as an Array of Pointers to Records

Using this approach to represent a team of baseball players, we now only need to allocate as many player records as there are players. For a team of 20 players, we allocate 20 dynamic record variables. A pointer to each dynamic variable is stored in the array of pointers. Each of the unused components of the array is given the value **NIL**. The procedure to initialize the entire team variable should set each array component to **NIL**, as indicated in the following procedure declaration:

```
PROCEDURE InitTeam (VAR team: TeamType);

VAR
     index: INTEGER;

BEGIN
     FOR index := MinJersey TO MaxJersey DO
          team[index] := NIL

END;     (* InitTeam *)
```

Programming Example 17-5: Procedure `InitTeam`

Modifying a program to use an array of pointers to records instead of using an array of records usually takes very little effort. The most important change is to remember that every record reference no longer just specifies an index of the array; it must *dereference* the array component. For example, we could have refered to a particular player record as `team[JerseyNumber]`, but we must now specify the same record as `team[JerseyNumber]`↑. To see this small but important change, compare the following two procedures to list the entire team:

```
PROCEDURE ListEntireTeam (team: TeamType);

VAR
     index: INTEGER;

BEGIN
     FOR index := MinJersey TO MaxJersey DO
          IF team[index].name <> ''
               THEN WriteOnePlayer(team[index])
END;     (* ListEntireTeam *)



PROCEDURE ListEntireTeam (team: TeamType);

VAR
     index: INTEGER;

BEGIN
     FOR index := MinJersey TO MaxJersey DO
          IF team[index] <> NIL
               THEN WriteOnePlayer(team[index]↑)
END;     (* ListEntireTeam *)
```

Programming Example 17-6: Procedure `ListEntireTeam`

Both procedures use a FOR loop to run through all the elements of the team array. Both procedures check to see if each array component corresponds to a particular player before writing out a player record. The programmer must ensure that a pointer variable holds a valid non-NIL value before dereferencing the pointer variable. It is an error to dereference a **NIL** pointer.

17.3.1. Questions

1. How can an array of records can be replaced with an array of pointers to records?

2. What are the primary modifications that must be made to convert an array of records to an array of pointers?

3. How does an array of pointers use computer memory better than an array of records?

4. Would it be worthwhile to replace an array of integers with an array of pointers to integers? Justify your answer.

5. Although an array of pointers uses computer memory better than an array of records, what is at least one thing about using an array of pointers that is no better and one thing that is worse, from a computer memory standpoint, about using an array of pointers instead of an array of records?

6. Why should we set pointer variables to **NIL** before using them? Give an example explaining when this practice is useful.

7. Is it an error to dereference a pointer variable holding the value **NIL**? Justify your answer.

17.4. Linking Dynamic Variables

In the last section we learned how an array of records can be replaced with an array of pointers to records, thereby allocating only as many records as are needed. Although we need one pointer variable for each dynamic variable, we allocated more pointer variables than we had dynamic variables since every component of the array was a pointer variable. If the total number of pointer variables in the array is small, or if the array indices are some special range of values—such as jersey numbers for array indices—then an array of pointer variables can be the right choice. However, it is not always the right choice. In general, we would like to create new pointer variables only when they are needed. This means that we want pointer variables to be dynamic variables. Dynamic pointer variables can be used to link dynamic variables in a variety of different ways. The most common structure of linked dynamic variables is called the *linked list*.

17.4.1. An Analogy to the Linked List

Imagine that you are a teacher at a pre-school. One of your duties is to monitor the children as they play outside. Remembering the names of all the children is impossible, so you develop a scheme that will help you account for them. Each child can remember his or her own name and point to another child. In this scheme, every child except the last one points to another child. You arrange the pre-schoolers so that two of them will point to the same child. You point at the first child in the chain of pre-schoolers. The last child in the chain does not point at anyone. This notion of linking, or chaining, can be visualized as follows:

Figure 17-1: A Linked List

For our pre-school example, suppose the principal wants to know if your class includes a student named Marvin. You search for Marvin by having the first student, to whom you are pointing, say his name. If this student is not Marvin, you have the student pointed to by this child say his name, and so on. With this method, if Marvin is present, he will eventually say his name. If Marvin is not present, the last student in the chain will say his name, ending the process.

Figure 17-2: Searching A Linked List

Occasionally a new student joins, pre-school and must be added to our linked list. Suppose Nathan comes to class one day, and you have to account for him on the playground. He can be added to the group by a two-step process. You first have the new student, Nathan, point to the child at whom you were pointing (the first student in the list). Next, you point at Nathan. In other words, you add Nathan to the beginning of the chain of children, as illustrated in the following figure:

Figure 17-3: Inserting into a Linked List

Occasionally, a child leaves the pre-school and must be removed from our list. As an example, suppose Marvin is leaving for a military school. You have to keep the remaining students in order, removing only Marvin. To accomplish this, you need only a one-step process. The child who has been pointing at Marvin points to whomever Marvin has been pointing to. The following figure illustrates this:

Figure 17-4: Deleting from a Linked List

Organizing pre-schoolers in such a chained is a good analogy to a linked list because all of the important facts are incorporated. A linked list is a collection of *nodes*. Each node contains some data and a link (or pointer) to the next node. The last node points to no other node. The entire list is represented by a single link to the first node in the list. In our analogy, each student constituted a node. The data were the student's names. The link was each student's arm pointing to the next student. The special pointer to the first node in the list was represented by the teacher pointing to the first student in the chain.

The basic operations on the linked list are *traversal*, *insertion*, and *deletion*. When we searched for Marvin, we traversed the linked list of students. When Nathan was added to the group, we did list insertion. When Marvin was removed from the chain, we did list deletion.

17.4.2. A Linked List in Pascal

In order to implement a linked list in Pascal, we must create types to represent a node and a list. We must also create subprograms to perform the three list operations: traversal, insertion, and deletion. Consider first defining the necessary user-defined types.

17.4.2.1. Defining List and Node Types

A node in a linked list always can be represented as a Pascal record. The record has a field for the data and a field for the link to the next node. For a linked list of names, the data field is the field for the name, and the link field is a pointer variable. A list is simply a pointer to the first node of the list; hence, it is a pointer to a node. The two types for a node and list can be defined as follows:

```
TYPE
    ListType = ↑NodeType;

    NodeType = RECORD
                  name: NameType;
                  tail: ListType
               END;    (* NodeType *)
```

Programming Example 17-7: Type Definitions for `ListType` and `NodeType`

Although you have created user-defined types that are quite a bit more complex than these two types, careful inspection might make you think that something is wrong with the previous example. Specifically, **ListType** is defined as a pointer to **NodeType**, but **NodeType** is defined after—rather than before—**ListType**. In addition to **ListType** being defined as a pointer to **NodeType**, one of the fields of **NodeType** is defined as **ListType**. This example may seem to violate rules of Pascal, in that a variable is referenced before it is defined and because it contains cyclic (or circular) definitions. However, Standard Pascal permits a type to be defined as a pointer to another type not yet defined, as long as the type is defined in the same scope. Similarly, two type definitions can be circular, as long as one of them is a pointer to the other.

17.4.2.2. Empty List

A list with no nodes is called the *empty list*. Given our representation of linked lists, the empty list can be designated by a pointer to **NIL**. You would probably define the empty list as a named constant, as follows:

```
CONST
    EmptyList = NIL;
```

Programming Example 17-8: Empty List as a Named Constant

Unfortunately, the value **NIL** cannot be renamed in Standard Pascal. For this reason, the following function is used to return the empty list:

```
FUNCTION EmptyList: ListType;

BEGIN
    EmptyList := NIL
END;
```

Programming Example 17-9: Empty List as a Function

We define a function **EmptyList** so that we can refer to such a list by name. There are other ways to represent an empty list, but referring to it by name eliminates the need to change more than one spot in the program if we later wish to use a different representation for the empty list. Naturally, we would like a BOOLEAN function to determine if a given list is empty. The following function returns TRUE only if the given list is empty:

```
FUNCTION IsEmpty (list: ListType): BOOLEAN;

BEGIN
    IsEmpty := list = EmptyList
END;       (* IsEmpty *)
```

Programming Example 17-10: Function `IsEmpty`

With definitions in place for nodes, a list, and the empty list, we can now turn our attention to the developing subprograms to create and manipulate lists.

17.4.2.3. Creating the Nodes of a List

Since we are representing each node of a list as a dynamic variable, we must have a subprogram for creating these nodes (allocating these dynamic variables). The predefined procedure **NEW** is used to allocate dynamic variables. Since a pointer to a node is a list, we can create and call procedure **CreateList**, as indicated in the following declaration:

```
PROCEDURE CreateList (VAR list: ListType;  name: NameType);

BEGIN
    NEW(list);
    list↑.name := name;
    list↑.tail := EmptyList
END;       (* CreateList *)
```

Programming Example 17-11: Procedure `CreateList`

This procedure first allocates memory for the new node of the list. Then it copies the name into the new node. Finally, the pointer field is set to the empty list. Having the ability to create nodes for a list, we can turn our attention to inserting into a list.

17.4.2.4. Insertion

A subprogram to insert an object into a linked list would require parameters for the object to be inserted and the list into which it is to be inserted. A procedure to insert a name into a linked list of names can be declared as follows:

The following procedure uses **CreateList** to insert into lists.

```
PROCEDURE InsertName (VAR list: ListType;  name: NameType);

VAR
    NewList: ListType

BEGIN
    IF IsEmpty(list)
        THEN CreateList(list, name)
        ELSE BEGIN
                CreateList(NewList, name);
                NewList↑.tail := list;
                list := NewList
            END
END;      (* InsertName *)
```

Programming Example 17-12: Procedure `InsertName`

Notice that procedure **InsertName** uses the procedure **CreateList**. If a name is to be inserted into an initially empty list, we simply create a new list with one node. Otherwise, we create a new list, put the old list on the tail of the new list, and return a pointer to the new list as the combined list. The following illustration shows this process:

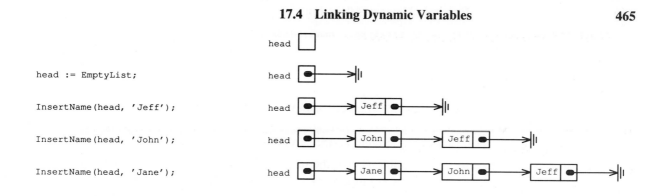

Figure 17-5: Insertion into a Linked List

Note that we represent the empty list with the "ground symbol." Also note that the names are added to the beginning of the list rather than to the tail end of the list. Although a node can be added at any point in the list, we selected the head of the list for the sake of simplicity.

17.4.2.5. Traversal

Once a linked list has been created, we often need to locate a particular item of the list or to write out all the items in the list. In both cases, we must *traverse* the list. Because we have defined a node and a list recursively, traversing a list lends itself to a recursive solution. The following procedure is a recursive way of writing an entire list:

```
PROCEDURE WriteList (list: ListType);

BEGIN
    IF NOT IsEmpty(list)
        THEN BEGIN
                WriteName(list↑.name);
                WriteList(list↑.tail)
             END
END;    (* WriteList *)
```

Programming Example 17-13: Recursive Procedure `WriteList`

If the list is not an empty list, the procedure writes the data (name) of the first node and calls procedure **WriteList** on the tail of the first node. This can be done since the tail of each node is a list. The last node in the list has the empty list as its tail. The recursive calls terminate when the end of the list is reached and all the names in the linked list have been written. The procedure **WriteList** could be written iteratively, as indicated in the following program declaration:

```
PROCEDURE WriteList (list: ListType);

BEGIN
    WHILE NOT IsEmpty(list) DO
        BEGIN
            WriteName(list↑.name);
            list := (list↑.tail)
        END
END;    (* WriteList *)
```

Programming Example 17-14: Iterative Procedure `WriteList`

Although both the iterative and recursive procedures are functionally equivalent, we prefer the recursive solution for this problem.

17.4.2.6. Deletion

Having the ability to traverse a list and insert into a list, we turn our attention to the other list operation: deletion. The procedure to remove a name from a list of names can be written as follows:

```
PROCEDURE DeleteName (VAR list: ListType;   name: NameType);

BEGIN
    IF NOT IsEmpty(list)
        THEN IF (list↑.name = name)
                THEN list := list↑.tail;
                ELSE DeleteName(list↑.tail, name)
END;      (* DeleteName *)
```

Programming Example 17-15: Procedure **DeleteName**

The procedure **DeleteName** takes parameters for the name to be removed and the list from which it is to be removed. If the list is not empty, we compare the name with the first node of the list. If the name of the first node matches the name to be removed, the node is removed; otherwise we call **DeleteName** on the tail of the list. The procedure is recursive. Note that although **DeleteName** removes the desired node, the memory for the removed node is not deallocated. The following figure illustrates the action of the procedure **DeleteName**.

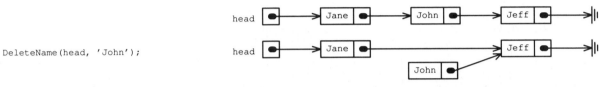

Figure 17-6: Node Deletion Without Deallocation

The node is removed logically—but not physically—from the list because the memory has not been deallocated. Since we no longer have a reference to the dynamic variable, it is *inaccessible*. To avoid the problems of allocated but inaccessible memory, we deallocate the memory of the node to be removed with the predefined procedure **DISPOSE**, as indicated in the following modified procedure:

```
PROCEDURE DeleteName (VAR list: ListType;   name: NameType);

VAR
    garbage: ListType;


BEGIN
    IF NOT IsEmpty(list)
        THEN IF (list↑.name = name)
                THEN BEGIN
                        garbage := list;
                        list := list↑.tail;
                        DISPOSE(garbage)
                     END
                ELSE DeleteName(list↑.tail, name)
END;      (* DeleteName *)
```

Programming Example 17-16: Procedure **DeleteName** with Deallocation

The following illustration shows the effects of the modified procedure.

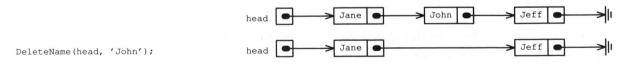

Figure 17-7: Node Deletion with Deallocation

You should make sure that all dynamic variables that are no longer needed get deallocated with **DISPOSE**.

17.4.3. An Implementation of a Linked List in Pascal

Throughout the last section, we discussed a linked list of *names*. Therefore, the data held by each node of the list are names. However, we have not given any details about the names; are they a string array, a record with two string arrays (one for first name and one for last name), or some other representation? We intentionally neglected the data of the nodes to focus on the structure of the list and the operations on the list. The concepts presented in this chapter apply to all lists, regardless of the kind of data they contain. We have used names here only as an example. If we select **NameType** to be the predefined type CHAR, the procedure **WriteName** looks like the following:

```
TYPE
    NameType = CHAR;


PROCEDURE WriteName (name: NameType);

BEGIN
    WRITE(OUTPUT, name:2)
END;     (* WriteName *)
```

Programming Example 17-17: Procedure **WriteName**

By now you have seen how to represent both nodes and linked lists in Pascal. Additionally, you have seen how to create, traverse, insert into, and delete from a linked list. Therefore, you can create a program that puts all of these pieces together, as indicated in the following program example:

```
PROGRAM DemoList (INPUT, OUTPUT);


TYPE
    NameType = CHAR;            (* using a single character for illustrative purposes *)

    ListType = ↑NodeType;

    NodeType = RECORD
                   name: NameType;
                   tail: ListType
               END;     (* NodeType *)



FUNCTION EmptyList: ListType;
FUNCTION IsEmpty (list: ListType): BOOLEAN;

PROCEDURE CreateList (VAR list: ListType;  name: NameType);
PROCEDURE InsertName (VAR list: ListType;  name: NameType);
PROCEDURE DeleteName (VAR list: ListType;  name: NameType);

PROCEDURE WriteName (name: NameType);
PROCEDURE WriteList (list: ListType);



PROCEDURE GlobalFilter;

VAR
    list: ListType;

BEGIN
    list := EmptyList;
    InsertName(list, 'a');
    InsertName(list, 'e');
    InsertName(list, 'i');
    InsertName(list, 'o');
    InsertName(list, 'u');
    WriteList(list);
    DeleteName(list, 'i');
    WriteList(list)
END;     (* GlobalFilter *)



BEGIN    (* Main Program *)
    GlobalFilter
END.
```

Programming Example 17-18: Linked List Program in Pascal

We did not include the complete body for each previous subprogram because they were presented in detail earlier in the chapter. This program illustrates the most important notions of representing and manipulating a linked list. Be sure you understand it.

17.4.4. Replacing an Array of Pointers with a Linked List

We reviewed a program to help manage statistics about baseball players in Section 15.3. At that point, we represented each player as a record and the team as an array of records. Earlier in this chapter, we revised that program using an array of pointers to records rather than an array of records. Now consider representing the team as a linked list of players.

The first modification we must make is to add a pointer variable to every player record so that we can link them together. Since the team is no longer represented as an array, we can no longer use each jersey number as an array index. Therefore, we must also add a field to the player record to store the jersey number. The team now can be represented by a pointer to one player. The modified type definitions are as follows:

```
TYPE
    JerseyType = MinJersey .. MaxJersey;

    PlayerPointerType = ↑PlayerType;

    PlayerType = RECORD
                    jersey: JerseyType;
                    tail: PlayerPointerType;
                    name: StringType;
                    position: StringType;
                    statistics: OffensiveStatsType
                 END;      (* PlayerType *)



    TeamType = PlayerPointerType;
```

Programming Example 17-19: Baseball Team as a Linked List

Prior to this chapter, we used arrays of records frequently, partly because an array of records is a very useful way of representing data but also because we previously had no serious alternative. In this chapter, we have seen how an array of records can be replaced with an array of pointers to records, thereby allocating only the number of records necessary for a particular problem. In the last two sections, we have learned how a linked list can be used instead of an array of pointers, thereby allocating only the number of pointer variables necessary for a particular problem. These three different ways of representing data can be visualized as follows:

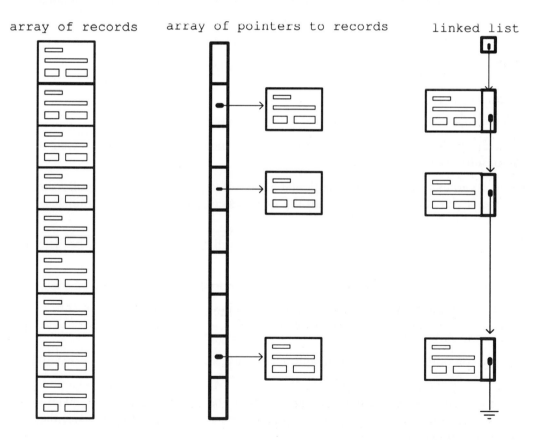

Figure 17-8: An Array of Records, an Array of Pointers to Records, and a Linked List

Although each of these ways of representing data has some advantage over the other two, each also has some disadvantage over the other two. None of these three data representations is always best. Which one is best depends on the circumstances.

Although an array of pointers to records normally allocates fewer records than an array of records, it allocates more pointer variables than a linked list. Although a linked list requires the least number of records and the least number of pointers, it can never access records randomly; it must access them sequentially.

The particular problem you are solving will determine which of the three representations to use. If you need random access to the records, then you must use one of two array representations. The dynamic allocation representations normally are used only when there is not enough memory to support static allocation. If your computer's memory can store 10,000 of the desired records, then it is probably a mistake to implement a linked list to represent just 20 such records. If the maximum number of records needed is either small or known in advance, then we normally use an array of records.

17.4.5. Questions

1. Can pointer variables be dynamic variables? Justify your answer.

2. Why would a programmer want to use a dynamic pointer variable?

3. Can dynamic variables be linked in Pascal? If so, explain how. If not, explain why not.

4. What is the most common structure for linked dynamic variables?

5. What is a linked list?

6. What are the three most common operations performed on a linked list? Describe the action of each.

7. Can every array representation be replaced with a linked list implementation? Justify your answer.

8. What are the benefits of using a linked list instead of an array?

9. What are the drawbacks of using a linked list instead of an array?

17.5. Chapter Summary

- The computer's memory is designed to hold information.

- Declaring variables in a program requests that memory be allocated to your program to hold information.

- For a variable declared in a particular scope, if computer memory is allocated when a scope is activated and is automatically deallocated when the scope terminates, we call it static memory allocation.

- The amount of memory required to represent all static variables can be determined at compile time.

- Dynamic memory allocation uses computer memory for variables as it is needed.

- The number of dynamic variables cannot be determined at compile time.

- Dynamic allocation uses much less memory than static allocation.

- Every computer has a limited amount of memory, and it is possible to exhaust all computer memory by using only dynamic variables.

- Since the user declares static variables, they can be called by the names given to them by the user. However, since dynamic variables are not declared by the user, they have no user-specified names.

- Dynamic variables have system-generated names rather than user-specified names. The system-generated names are the addresses used by the computer.

- A pointer variable is a variable intended to hold the system-generated name of (address of) a dynamic variable.

- A pointer type is indicated in Pascal with the symbol ↑ preceding the type of variable it points to.

- A pointer type is a scalar type rather than a structured type.

- The Pascal predefined procedure **NEW** allocates dynamic variables.

- You should always initialize a dynamic variable as you would any other variable.

- The Pascal predefined procedure **DISPOSE** deallocates dynamic variables.

- To refer to the dynamic variable referenced by a pointer, we must dereference the pointer variable. The pointer dereference operator in Pascal is ↑ after the pointer variable.

- Pascal has a special pointer value that denotes pointing at no dynamic variable. The value is **NIL** and cannot be renamed as another named constant.

- It is not possible to dereference a **NIL** pointer.

- A dynamic variable with no pointer variable referencing it is inaccessible and is referred to as garbage.

- A pointer variable that refers to a dynamic variable that has been deallocated is said to hold a dangling reference or dangling pointer.

- Attempting to dereference dangling or undefined pointers will cause an error.

- An array of records can be replaced with an array of pointers to records. This still provides random access to all elements, but it only allocates as many records as are necessary. The drawback is that it must now store pointers that previously were not required.

- Pointer variables can be either static or dynamic.

- If every dynamic variable has a pointer variable as one of its fields, the dynamic variables can be linked together into structures.

- Although linking dynamic variables can reduce the number of pointer variables necessary, it sacrifices the random access provided by an array.

- The most common structure of linked dynamic variables is the linked list.

- A linked list is a collection of nodes, where each node holds some data and one link to the next node in the list. The list is referenced by a pointer to the first node in the list.

- The three most common operations on a linked list are insertion, deletion, and traversal.

17.6. Summary of Terms

- computer memory
- computer memory allocation
- static memory allocation
- static variable
- dynamic memory allocation
- dynamic variable
- system-generated variable name

- address
- pointer variable
- **NEW**
- reference
- dereferencing
- inaccessible variable
- garbage
- deallocate

- **DISPOSE**
- **NIL**
- dangling reference
- dangling pointer
- array of pointers
- dynamic pointer variable
- linked list
- node

17.7. Chapter Problems

1. Enter program **DemoList** from Programming Example 17-18 on page 468 into your computer and run it. *Note: You will need to add the bodies of the other subprograms.*

2. Modify the previous program so that it inserts your ten favorite characters and then removes three of them. Write the list to the screen after each deletion.

3. Extend the previous program so that names are represented as string arrays with 20 characters. Have it build the list for five of your friends' names.

4. Extend your list of names program to include the function **FindName**, which has two parameters: the list of names and the name to search for. The function should return a pointer to the node containing the desired name or a pointer to **NIL** if the list does not contain the desired name.

5. *Write a procedure **DeleteNode** that takes a list and a pointer to a particular node in the list as parameters. The procedure should remove the node from the list and deallocate the memory for the node. The node that precedes the specified node should point to the node that follows the specified node when the procedure terminates. *Why is the pointer to the first node in the list needed in addition to the pointer to the node to be deleted?*

6. *If you did the preceding problem, you should realize that we often need to know the predecessor of a given node in addition to the successor node. If the node contains only a link to the successor node, we must go back to the beginning of the list and search until we reach the node preceding the node of interest. An alternative is to store two links in every node: a link to the predecessor node and the link to the successor node. A linked list constructed in this fashion is known as a *doubly-linked* list or a *predecessor* list. Write the Pascal definitions for a node, a list, the insert procedure, delete procedure, and traverse procedure for a doubly-linked list.

Chapter 18: Searching and Sorting

Although we earlier stressed the fact that computers can store information, there is nothing unique about the ability to store information: Filing cabinets and cardboard boxes can store information. However, a unique feature of a computer is its ability to search through its store of information and retrieve the right information rapidly. In addition, a computer can arrange its information in any particular order the user chooses. These two actions are referred to as *searching* and *sorting*, respectively. The ability of a computer to search its inventory for a particular piece of information or sort all information according to a particular order *automatically* is what differentiates the computer from the common file cabinet.

Consider the following scenario: On the first day of a new semester your eye is caught by a particularly attractive classmate of the opposite gender. Although you muster up the courage to introduce yourself and make some conversation, you end the school day without the person's phone number. Angry at yourself, you resort to looking through the local phone directory. The directory is alphabetized, which eases your search and allows you to determine quickly that the desired name is missing from your directory. You look at the front cover; the directory is two years old. You remember that your classmate moved to town last week. Things are starting to look bleak. However, technology being what it is, you decide to dial directory assistance. The operator answers and asks for the name of the individual whose number you wish. Almost as soon as you choke out the name, a synthesized voice responds, "The number is ..." followed by the desired number. Fearful of forgetting the number, you immediately dial it. Your classmate answers.

This little scenario illustrates the two notions *sorting* and *searching*. The white pages of the telephone directory are printed in alphabetical order. You can rest assured that a computer was used to *sort* the telephone listings into alphabetical order before the directory was printed. Similarly, you can rest assured that the directory assistance operator used a computer to *search* for the desired number.

Recall that an *algorithm* is a finite sequence of steps that accomplishes a particular task. There are a variety of well-known algorithms for sorting, in addition to several popular algorithms for searching. Certain algorithms work best under certain circumstances. Although the mathematical tools necessary for an exact analysis of algorithms are beyond the scope of this text, an illustrative introduction will be useful for you to develop basic skills in algorithm analysis.

Searching and sorting are both very common problems. It is clearly to the benefit of society to have computers perform these tasks automatically whenever possible. In this chapter, you will learn how to program a computer to search and sort.

18.1. Searching

You are out on the town with some friends and decide to have a pizza and take in a movie. A quick check of the cash on hand determines that you do not have enough money to purchase 30 minutes at the nearest parking meter, much less the evening's entertainment! As luck would have it, one of the group has a 24-hour automatic banking card. You locate an automatic teller, insert the bank card, press the right buttons, and smile as a fistful of dollars appears.

Before presenting the cash to the customer, the automatic teller ran a search on the bank account. Searching for a person's bank account is much like the earlier example of searching for a particular telephone listing. We could enumerate many more similar examples. Using the computer to automate a search is one of the most common uses of computers. In fact, earlier in this book you saw both searching through an array for a particular value and searching through a file for a particular component. Both are examples of computer searches.

There are several notions common to all searches. For example, we normally search through a collection of records for a particular record. The collection of records through which we search is referred to as the **search structure**. Examples of a search structure are a collection of bank account records and a collection of telephone listings.

Definition 18-1: A *search structure* is a collection of records to be searched.

Each record of the search structure is composed of a group of fields. The particular field of each record used to determine if we have found the desired record is known as the **embedded key**. Examples of an embedded key are name, Social Security number, or bank account number. For the same reasons that the Federal Government issues unique Social Security numbers, we will assume throughout our discussion of searching that each record of the search structure has a unique embedded-key value.

Definition 18-2: An *embedded key* is the field of each record that is used to locate the desired record of the search structure.

The particular value we are comparing with each embedded key value is known as the **search key**. Examples of search keys are Social Security numbers and bank account numbers.

Definition 18-3: The *search key* is the particular embedded-key value for which we are searching.

These terms refer to the notions common to all searches. You should commit them to memory. Using this terminology, we can define searching as the process of traversing a *search structure*, comparing the *search key* with the value of the *embedded key* for each record in the search structure.

Suppose we have a small company. One employee of our company has recently distinguished herself, and we would like to reward her with a generous pay raise. Therefore, we must search through our employee records for the record of our hard-working employee. The *search structure* is the collection of employee records, the *embedded key* is the last-name field of each record, and the *search key* is the last name of our distinguished employee (e.g. Ghost for Casper T. Ghost). The following illustration depicts these notions:

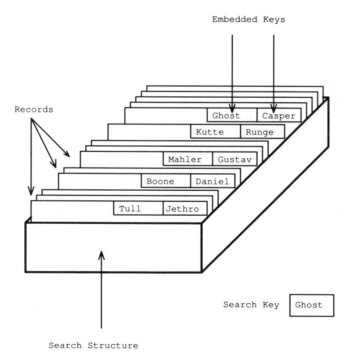

Figure 18-1: Common Search Notions

With an understanding of *what* searching is, we can turn our attention to *how* searching can be done.

18.1.1. Sequential or Linear Search

Although there are a variety of ways to search, the simplest, and probably most obvious, way to search a structure is to begin with the first record of the structure and simply compare the search key with the embedded key. If the embedded key value matches the search key, we have found the appropriate record. Otherwise, we continue by searching the next record in the search structure. Eventually, we will either locate a matching record or run out of records. This method of search is commonly known as *sequential search*. Consider doing a sequential search of the following search structure for Casper Ghost:

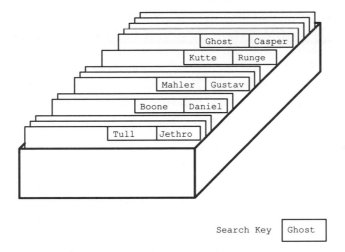

Search Key   Ghost

Figure 18-2: Sequential Search

In the previous example, the first record in our search structure is the employee record of Jethro Tull. Since that is not the record we are searching for, we must examine the next record in the search structure. The employee record of Daniel Boone is the next record, which also is not the record we want. We continue this process until the employee record for Casper Ghost is eventually located.

In discussing and comparing algorithms, it is extremely helpful to see the algorithms written as programming code. However, by using a particular programming language, the details and constraints of the particular programming language often obscure the essential points of the algorithm. To avoid this problem, we use an algorithmic language of a slightly higher level than Pascal that permits us to focus on the essential points and ignore the smaller details. Program fragments expressed in this way are intended to demonstrate a notion rather than to present a program capable of running on a computer. Since such program fragments are never run directly on a computer, they are known as **pseudocode**. Most of the algorithms discussed in this chapter are written in pseudocode. However, you should be able to write them in Pascal so that they execute properly.

> **Definition 18-4:** *Pseudocode* is an abstract form of a program intended to demonstrate an algorithm rather than the implementation of the algorithm in a particular language.

Consider writing a subprogram to perform sequential searching. Assume our search structure is an array of records, **(ARRAY[1..NumberOfElements])**. The subprogram is a function that returns the index of the matching record if one is found and returns 0 otherwise. The following pseudocode illustrates the algorithm for sequential search:

```
FUNCTION SequentialSearch (list: ListType;  SearchKey: KeyType): INTEGER;

BEGIN
    index := 1
    WHILE (index ≤ NumberOfElements) CAND (list[index].EmbeddedKey <> SearchKey)
            index := index + 1

    IF index ≤ NumberOfElements
        THEN RETURN(index)        (* return index of matching record *)
        ELSE RETURN(0)            (* no match *)
END
```

Programming Example 18-1: Sequential Search Pseudocode

The core of this subroutine is the loop. We start with the first record of the search structure. While the embedded key does not match the search key and there are more records to be examined, we simply increment the index. Eventually, we either find the desired record or run out of records. If the value of the index after the loop terminates is less than or equal to the number of elements in the search structure, the function returns it as the index of the desired record. Otherwise, the desired record is not located and 0 is returned.

You may have noticed the loop condition used an operator labeled **CAND**. This was not a typographical error intended to be AND. The CAND operator is short for *Conditional AND* operator. With CAND, the left operand is always evaluated before the right operand, and the right operand is evaluated *only if* the left operand evaluates to TRUE. If the left operand evaluates to FALSE, the expression evaluates to FALSE without evaluating the right operand. The conditional AND operator is commonly used to avoid division by zero or out-of-bounds array indexing. Here, we are avoiding the problem of attempting to access a record when **index** becomes greater than **NumberOfElements**.

Think for a moment about the algorithm for sequential searching. Does its performance depend on how the records of the search structure are ordered? It is important to realize that the sequential searching algorithm will always locate the desired record, regardless of its position, as long as the desired record is in the search structure. However, it is also important to realize that the location of the desired record within the search structure determines how many other records must be examined before the desired record will be located. If we are lucky, the desired record is the first element in the search structure. If we are unlucky, the desired record is the last element in the search structure.

The sequential searching algorithm assumes nothing about the order of the records of the search structure and always works regardless of the order. However, the performance of the sequential searching algorithm is determined by the order of the search structure. There are other searching algorithms that assume the search structure is in a particular order and exploit the order to do a better job of searching.

18.1.2. The Ordered Search

Suppose you needed to find the telephone number of Amy Adams in your local directory. You would probably start with the first page of the telephone directory. If the next entry after Albert Adams is, say, Arthur Adams, you would probably decide that there is no listing for Amy Adams and terminate your search. What allows us to terminate our search without having to examine all the remaining listings in the directory? The directory is alphabetized. If the search structure is arranged in a particular order, the order can be exploited to simplify the search process. Consider searching for Julius Caesar in the search structure in the following figure:

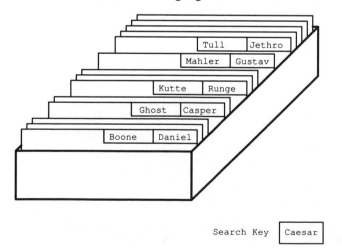

Figure 18-3: Ordered Search

Since the search structure is in alphabetical order, the search can be terminated as soon as we encounter Casper Ghost. We need not examine all the remaining records.

We can rewrite our sequential searching algorithm to exploit an ordered search structure, primarily by changing

`(list[index].EmbeddedKey <> SearchKey)` to `(list[index].EmbeddedKey < SearchKey)`.

The following is pseudocode for an ordered search:

```
FUNCTION OrderedSearch (list: ListType;  SearchKey: KeyType): INTEGER

BEGIN
    index := 1
    WHILE (index ≤ NumberOfElements) CAND (list[index].EmbeddedKey < SearchKey)
            index := index + 1

    IF (index ≤ NumberOfElements) AND (list[index].EmbeddedKey = SearchKey)
        THEN RETURN(index)        (* return index of matching record *)
        ELSE RETURN(0)            (* no match *)
END
```

Programming Example 18-2: Ordered Search Pseudocode

It is fairly easy to see that we can exploit order to improve our first searching algorithm. Can we exploit the order of the search structure further to do an even better job of searching? It turns out we can do a lot better, as we will see in the following sections.

18.1.3. Binary Search

Consider comparing the embedded key value from any record in an ordered search structure with the search key. One of three situations must be true: The embedded key *equals* the search key, the embedded key *precedes* the search key, or the embedded key *follows* the search key. This fact provides the basis for a much better searching algorithm.

If the embedded key equals the search key, we do not need to examine other records of the search structure—we have found the record. If the embedded key precedes the search key, we can forget about the record containing that embedded key. More importantly, we can also forget about all records that precede the given record. Conversely, if the embedded key follows the search key, we can safely forget about both the record containing the embedded key value and all records that follow it.

If the first record we examine is the middle record of the search structure, we will either find the desired record, be in a position to ignore the first half of the structure, or be in a position to ignore the last half of the structure. By looking at only one value, we can reduce the number of records we need to examine by half! This is made possible because the search structure is ordered. This type of searching algorithm is known as *binary search*. The following pseudocode illustrates the algorithm for binary search.

```
FUNCTION BinarySearch (LowerBound, UpperBound: IndexType;
                       SearchKey: KeyType): IndexType

BEGIN
    MidPoint := (LowerBound + UpperBound) DIV 2    (* determine middle position *)

    IF SearchKey = list[MidPoint].EmbeddedKey
        THEN RETURN(MidPoint)                      (* desired record at middle *)
        ELSE IF SearchKey < list[MidPoint].EmbeddedKey

                THEN (* Search first half *)
                    RETURN(BinarySearch(LowerBound, MidPoint-1, SearchKey))

                ELSE (* Search second half *)
                    RETURN(BinarySearch(MidPoint+1, UpperBound, SearchKey))
END
```

Programming Example 18-3: Binary Search Pseudocode

The binary searching algorithm does not require very much code. You should look at it closely to be sure you understand how the algorithm works. The subprogram needs the index of the first and last record of the search structure, as well as the search key. First, the position of the middle record is determined. If the embedded key value of the record in the middle position of the search structure matches the search key, the desired record has been found. Otherwise, we must determine if the search key precedes or follows the embedded key value. If the search key precedes the embedded key, we ignore the second half of the search structure and search only the first half of the search structure. Otherwise, we ignore the first half of the search structure and search only the second half of the search structure. Note that we search the reduced search structure by calling the subprogram itself with reduced bounds. **Binary search is a recursive algorithm.**

To illustrate the binary searching algorithm further, let us apply it in a particular example. The search structure for this example has 15 records, indexed from 1 through 15. The embedded key is a word, and the search structure is ordered according to this embedded key. The search structure is indicated on the left of the illustration, and the passes of the algorithm are indicated on the right:

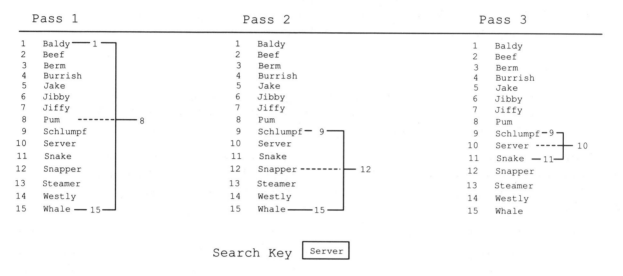

Figure 18-4: Binary Search

We want to determine the index of the record with the embedded key value *Server*. The first pass is to search the entire structure (records [1..15]). The midpoint for the first pass is 8. Since the midpoint embedded key precedes the search key (Pum precedes Server), we reduce the bounds of the search to the range [9..15] for the second pass. The midpoint of the second pass is 12. Since the embedded key at the midpoint follows the search key (Snapper follows Server), we can reduce the bounds of the search to the range [9..13] for the third pass. The midpoint of the third pass is 10. The embedded key for the midpoint matches the search key. Therefore, the algorithm terminates and returns 10 as the index of the matching record of the search structure. The desired record was located in a search structure of 15 records by examining only 3 embedded key values. It turns out that binary search never requires more than 4 record examinations to locate any record in a search structure of 15 records.

18.1.4. Comparing Algorithms

Having seen the three different searching algorithms, *sequential* search, *ordered* search, and *binary* search, you probably formed the opinion that ordered search normally examines fewer records than sequential search and that binary search normally examines fewer records than either of the other two searching algorithms. Although we have said that one algorithm examines more records than another, we have not said how many more. In this section we will look at ways to quantify algorithms so that they can be compared.

18.1.4.1. What We Compare

To compare algorithms, you must understand what it is that you want to compare. Algorithms can be compared in a number of ways. They can be compared on how much memory they use, how much processing time they use, or how many times a particular operation (e.g. addition or multiplication) is required. When considering searching algorithms, we usually are interested in how many records must be examined. Let us assume that this is the criterion with which we wish to compare the three searching algorithms discussed previously.

18.1.4.2. Quantifying Functions

It is natural to expect any searching algorithm to take longer to search a structure of one hundred records than it would to search a structure of ten records. If we select a particular searching algorithm and a particular search key, the size of the search structure then determines the number of records the algorithm will examine. Therefore, the number of records examined is said to be a function of the size of the search structure or, alternatively, a function of the problem size.

It is common in the field of computer science to denote the size of the problem with the symbol N. For a search problem, N is the number of records in the search structure. Therefore, the number of records examined by a searching algorithm is a function of N.

18.1.4.3. Comparative Conditions

If we are lucky with sequential search, the search key is the first record; if we are unlucky, the record is the last one. Therefore, an algorithm's performance can differ dramatically, depending on the conditions under which it is evaluated.

The two different conditions under which algorithms are most commonly evaluated and compared are the *best-case* scenario and the *worst-case* scenario. For the sequential searching algorithm, one record is examined under the best-case scenario, and N records are examined under the worst-case scenario.

There is another set condition under which algorithms are evaluated and compared—the *average-case* scenario. The average-case scenario is rarely as easy to quantify as the best-case scenario or the worst-case scenario. Although the average-case scenario requires a bit more mathematical sophistication, we know it will always lie between the best-case scenario and the worst-case scenario.

Consider the performance of the sequential searching algorithm in the average-case scenario: The search key is equally likely to be matched by any record of the search structure. It requires one record examination to locate the first record, two record examinations to locate the second record, three record examinations to locate the third record, and so on up through N record examinations to locate the last record. The average case requires the average of the numbers 1 through N, which is the sum of the numbers 1 through N divided by N. The sum of 1 through N is N * (N + 1) / 2. Therefore, the average of 1 through N is (N + 1) / 2. Hence, we would expect the sequential searching algorithm to examine (N + 1) / 2 records of a search structure of N records in the average case. As anticipated, the average case [(N + 1) / 2] falls between the best case [1] and the worst case [N].

Although it is possible to express the number of records examined by the sequential searching algorithm as a function of N in all three scenarios using only a very modest amount of mathematical background, most algorithms require more, usually much more. In general, exact analyses are tough. Fortunately, there is an alternative to exact analyses.

18.1.5. Families of Functions

We have said that the amount of a resource required by an algorithm can be expressed as a function of the problem size N. It turns out that mathematical functions can be grouped into families. For example, the functions N, N+1, N+2, 2N, 2N+1, 2N+2, 3N, are all members of the same family of functions known as *linear functions*. They are called linear functions because they are graphed as straight lines. Another important family of functions is known as *logarithmic functions*. The following figure illustrates a linear function and a logarithmic function:

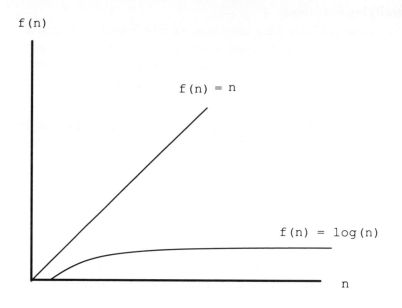

Figure 18-5: Linear and Logarithmic Functions

Notice that a linear function increases in proportion to N, whereas a logarithmic function increases less than proportionately to N.

There are two other families of functions that are of interest to us in analyzing algorithms. They are of the form N^2 and $N*\log(N)$. The following figure illustrates these two families of functions in addition to the linear function family:

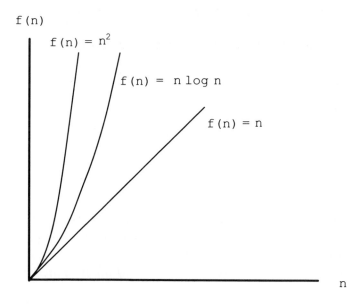

Figure 18-6: N^2 and $N*\text{Log}(N)$ Functions

Note that the $N*\log(N)$ function family increases much faster than proportionately to N. The N^2 function family increases the fastest of all the families.

Some algorithms are not a function of the problem size. These functions are known as constant functions, or simply constants. They are graphed as horizontal lines. The following figure illustrates all five of the families of functions mentioned:

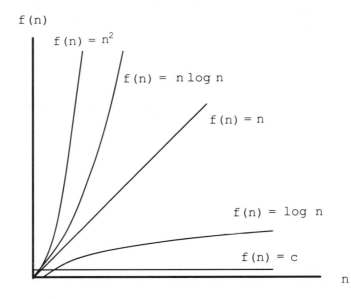

Figure 18-7: Families of Functions

18.1.6. Order Arithmetic and Order Comparisons

We said earlier that determining the precise mathematical function to describe the resources required by a particular algorithm can be quite difficult. As an alternative to determining the exact function, we can determine to what family of functions the function belongs. By focusing on the *family* a function belongs to, we are permitted to ignore all coefficients of a function as well as all terms except the most dominant term of the function. For example, the function $5N^2 + 17$ is reduced to N^2, as is $88N^2 + 7N + 11$—they both belong to the same family of functions. These two functions are said to be order N^2 functions, which are denoted $O(N^2)$. Reducing functions to only their dominant term is known as **order arithmetic**; comparing two functions on the basis of their order is called **order comparison**.

> **Definition 18-5:** *Order arithmetic* considers only a function's dominant term and, therefore, only the function's family.

> **Definition 18-6:** *Order comparison* of functions compares function families.

Determining the family of a function is somewhat easier to understand than the function itself. Although order comparisons are less precise than exact comparison, they are very useful. The "O" indicates "order of" and is sometimes called "big-O" notation.

To help you better appreciate differences between families of functions, we have selected a representative of each family and computed their values for a variety of values of N. These are summarized in the following table:

Values of N

Function	10	100	1,000	1,000,000
constant	1	1	1	1
$\log_2 N$	3.3	6.6	9.9	19.9
N	10	100	1,000	1,000,000
$N \log_2 N$	33	660	9,900	19,900,000
N^2	100	1,000	1,000,000	1,000,000,000,000

Table 18-1: Comparing Function Families over a Range of Values

The linear function (N) increases in proportion to the increase in N, whereas the quadratic function (N^2) increases much faster, and the constant function never increases. The table reveals an important point. As the value of N increases, the importance of the family increases. Look at the last column of the table. The N^2 function family grows much faster than the other function families.

18.1.7. Comparing Searching Algorithms

These points can be used to compare the three search algorithms. We already determined that sequential search requires one record examination in the best case and N record examinations in the worst case. That means the sequential searching algorithm requires a linear function of record examinations in the worst case. It is said to require on the order of N record examinations, which we write as O(N). The binary searching algorithm reduces the number of records to be searched by a factor of 2 with every record examination. Therefore, the binary searching algorithm requires $\log_2 N$ record examinations and is said to be a O(log N) algorithm.

The difference between a searching algorithm of O(N) and one of O(log N) can be seen through an example. Consider searching a structure of 1,000,000 records. The sequential searching algorithm will require 1,000,000 record examinations in the worst case. The binary searching algorithm can always locate the desired record in no more than 20 record examinations! There is quite a difference between twenty and one million. The difference between these two algorithms becomes even more pronounced as N grows even larger. It is very useful to compare the order-of-magnitude differences between the function families to which algorithms belong.

18.1.8. Summary of Searching Algorithms

In the best-case scenario, all three searching algorithms (sequential, ordered, and binary) require only one record examination. The following table illustrates the performance of the search techniques presented in this section:

Algorithm	Search worst	Search average	Insert average	Delete average
sequential	N	N	C	N
ordered	N	N	N	N
binary	log(N)	log(N)	N	N

Table 18-2: Order of Number of Comparisons

It is important to realize that although order arithmetic provides a useful way to compare algorithms, it ignores two important issues: constants and the particular value of N. Both 2N and 2000N are linear functions, but one is 1000 times larger. Although constants are not as important as an order of magnitude, you should not ignore them entirely. They should be considered once a particular family of functions is selected. Order of magnitude is of greatest importance when N becomes large. If N is very small, it is quite possible for an algorithm with a higher order of magnitude to actually perform better than one with a lower order of magnitude.

18.1.9. Questions

1. What is searching?

2. What is a search structure?

3. What is a search key?

4. What is an embedded key?

5. What is pseudocode?

6. What is the Conditional AND operator? When is it useful?

7. Does Standard Pascal have a Conditional AND operator?

8. How does the sequential searching algorithm work?

9. How does the ordered searching algorithm work?

10. How does the binary searching algorithm work?

11. What must be true of the search structure before the binary search algorithm can be used?

12. What is order arithmetic?

13. What is an order comparison of functions?

14. How many record examinations are required by sequential search in the best-case and worst-case scenarios?

15. How many record examinations are required by ordered search under the best-case and worst-case scenarios?

16. How many record examinations are required by binary search under the best-case and worst-case scenarios?

17. When is the order of a function of greatest importance?

18.1.10. Exercises

1. Write a Pascal program that performs a sequential search of an array of integers.

2. Write a Pascal program that performs a sequential search of a singly-linked list.

3. Write a Pascal program that performs a sequential search of a TEXT file that contains one integer per line.

4. Write a Pascal program that performs an ordered search of an array of integers.

5. Write a Pascal program that performs an ordered search of a singly-linked list.

6. Write a Pascal program that performs an ordered search of a TEXT file that contains one integer per line.

7. Write a Pascal program that performs a binary search of an array of integers.

8. Can the binary searching algorithm be implemented to search a Standard Pascal file? If so, write a Pascal program. If not, prove why it cannot.

9. Can the binary searching algorithm be implemented to search a singly-linked list? How about a doubly-linked list? Justify your answers.

10. Does the binary searching algorithm need random access to the elements of a list or just sequential access? Justify your answer.

18.2. Sorting

In the preceding section, we discussed several different searching algorithms. Their performances differed drastically. For example, to search a structure of 1,000,000 records, the sequential searching algorithm requires the examination of all 1,000,000 records in the worst case, whereas binary search never requires examining more than 20 records, regardless of the search key. This dramatic difference is made possible by exploiting the order of the search structure. A consequence is that the binary searching algorithm requires the search structure to be arranged in a particular order. Binary search will not work with an unordered search structure. Arranging a sequence of information in order is called *sorting*. Binary search's need for a ordered search structure provides one of the motivations to study sorting.

Sorting is one of the most studied and best understood phenomena in computer science. There are dozens of general-purpose sorting techniques and many more special-purpose sorting algorithms. In this section, we will present four of the more common general-purpose sorting algorithms and briefly analyze their performance in a variety of situations.

18.2.1. Order, Order!

Ordering is quite prevalent in our everyday lives. It is natural to think of ordering integers numerically from smallest to largest. Similarly, we expect telephone book listings to be ordered alphabetically, just as we expect the index in the back of a book to be sorted alphabetically. Although sorting seems natural and commonplace, the definition for sorting is rather precise and, hence, involves a variety of mathematical notions. Although none of the notions is conceptually difficult, we prefer not to develop each of the notions separately. Instead, we will demonstrate them together using a familiar example. Assume we want to order people according to their heights, from shortest to tallest. The following properties are required:

1. *Comparability:* "That's like comparing apples and oranges" is a saying spoken all too often. However, it indicates the fact that two objects are very different and cannot be compared meaningfully. For example, it is not meaningful to say that "Jim is taller than my favorite song" or "Nathan is shorter than the color pink." For a group of objects to be ordered, we must be able to compare each of the objects in some meaningful way.

2. *Binary Comparisons:* In addition to needing the ability to compare objects, we must always compare exactly two objects at a time. For example, if we are using the comparison relation "is taller than," we need two objects to compare. Thus, it is sensible for someone to say, "Purvis is much taller than Lee." Similarly, it is sensible to compare other features of objects, such as speed: "Phil's mule runs faster than Lee's Edsel." When we compare objects for sorting, we compare exactly two at a time, and we compare them according to the same features.

3. *Unique Comparison Results:* The comparison relation between two objects cannot be contradictory. For example, if a is taller than b, then it cannot also be true than b is taller than a. The result of comparing two unique objects must be unique and noncontradictory.

4. *Transitive Comparison Results:* The comparison relation between objects must be what is called *transitive*. For example, let's use the comparison relation "is taller than" one more time. If Pat is taller than Bill and Bill is taller than Jeff, it follows that Pat is taller than Jeff. This seems quite natural and is known as transitivity. However, not all comparison relations are transitive relations. As a counterexample, consider a favorite pastime for Americans, ranking sports teams. Although for some individuals ordering baseball, basketball, and football teams seems to be more important than anything else, the task cannot be done very well because the property of transitivity does not hold. For example, although the Pittsburgh Steelers defeat the Cleveland Browns with great regularity, and the Browns rub the noses of the Cincinnati Bengals into the astroturf, the Bengals turn right around and beat the Steelers. For a group of objects to be ordered, such as from shortest to tallest, the comparison relation must be transitive.

Without going into a lot of mathematics, we have presented the essential requirements for a group of objects to be ordered. You should commit them to memory so you don't find yourself trying to order a group of objects that cannot be ordered. The most commonly missing essential is a comparison relation that is *transitive*.

18.2.2. Internal and External Sorting

Recall that computers typically have two types of memory: primary memory and secondary memory. These are often called internal memory and external memory, respectively. This difference leads to a distinction known as **internal sorting** and **external sorting**. Whether the objects being sorted are held in primary memory or secondary memory determines this distinction.

> **Definition 18-7:** When all objects being sorted are stored in an internal data structure, we say that we are performing an *internal sort*.

> **Definition 18-8:** When all objects being sorted are stored in an external data structure, we say that we are performing an *external sort*.

It is normally much faster to access information stored in primary memory than secondary memory. However, often we must sort more objects than will fit in our computer's primary memory. In such situations, we must store the objects in secondary memory and sort them there. Because most computers use disks for secondary storage, an external sort is also known as a *disk sort*. Although all four of the sorting algorithms presented in this chapter can be used for internal sorting, one of the algorithms is also particularly useful for external soring.

18.2.3. Insertion Sort

The first sorting algorithm we will consider is called *insertion sort*. Insertion sort generates a sorted list of elements in the following way: Start with an empty list, then insert one element into the list at a time. As each element is inserted into the list, it is placed in a position that keeps the list in order. Since each insertion maintains the sorted order, once all the elements have been inserted, the resulting list is sorted. The following illustration demonstrates the insertion sort algorithm in sorting numbers in increasing order. We assume the unsorted numbers are in **unsorted[1..NumberOfElements]**, and the sorted numbers are to be put in **sorted[1..NumberOfElements]**.

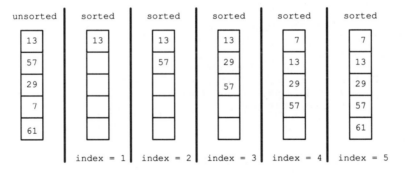

Figure 18-8: Insertion Sort Using Two Lists

First the element 13 is added. A list with just one element is always sorted. We then insert the element 57. The list is still in sorted order. Next, we insert the element 29. Note that 29 is inserted after 13 and before 57 to maintain sorted order. Next, 7 is inserted at the beginning of the list. Finally, 61 is inserted. Note that it is inserted at the end of the list. The resulting list contains all the elements and is in sorted order.

18.2.3.1. Pseudocode

Consider writing a subprogram to perform insertion sort. First, one element from the unsorted list is inserted as the first and only element of the sorted list. Then we repeatedly insert all the remaining elements from the unsorted list into the sorted list, one at a time. Note that the correct position must be determined before the next element can be inserted. The following pseudocode demonstrates the insertion sort algorithm:

```
PROCEDURE InsertionSort (unsorted, sorted)

BEGIN
    sorted[1] := unsorted[1]              (* start with one element *)

    FOR index := 2 to NumberOfElements    (* for each of remaining elements *)
        BEGIN
            inner := index                (* find correct position to insert *)
            WHILE (inner > 1) CAND (unsorted[index] < sorted[inner-1])
                inner := inner - 1

            insert(unsorted[index], sorted, inner)    (*insert at correct position*)
        END
END
```

Programming Example 18-4:   Insertion Sort Pseudocode

Note that the condition for the WHILE loop uses the Conditional AND operator **CAND** introduced earlier. It prevents the expression `inner-1` from referencing an invalid index. Note also that we determine the correct position for the next element to be inserted by starting at the currently last element of the sorted list. That reflects our preference rather than a theoretical requirement. You could rewrite the previous pseudocode to search for the correct position starting from the other end of the list.

We use the subroutine **Insert** to actually insert each value once the correct position has been determined. This subroutine needs the element to be inserted, as well as the position and list it is to be inserted in.

We have described the insertion sort algorithm using two lists, one sorted and one unsorted. However, it is possible do insertion sort using only one list. The following modified pseudocode illustrates how to do so:

```
PROCEDURE InsertionSort (list)

BEGIN
    FOR index := 2 to NumberOfElements
        BEGIN
            inner := index
            WHILE (inner > 1) CAND (list[inner] < list[inner-1])
                BEGIN
                    swap(list[inner], list[inner-1])
                    inner := inner - 1
                END
        END
END
```

Programming Example 18-5:   Insertion Sort with One List

The single-list version is only slightly different. As we search for the correct position for the next element, we move the element along within the list. Eventually, the element comes to rest in the desired position. The following illustration demonstrates this pseudocode:

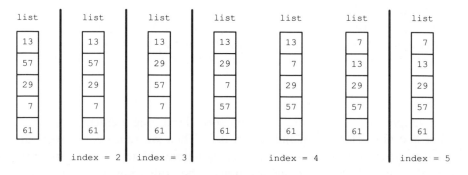

Figure 18-9:   Insertion Sort Using One List

Essentially, the first portion of the list remains sorted, while the unsorted second portion is inserted one element at a time until the entire list is sorted.

18.2.3.2. Analysis

When discussing searching algorithms earlier in this chapter, we analyzed the algorithms so that their performances could be compared. Recall three points we must determine about such analyses: The operation we wish to measure and compare, the conditions under which we wish to analyze the algorithm, and the measurements are normally expressed as a function of the problem size, called **N**.

The two operations most commonly used for sorting algorithms are the number of comparisons and the number of swaps. Let us look at the number of comparisons required by the insertion sort algorithm.

In the best case, each element is compared with only one other element. This means the number of comparisons required is 0 for the first insertion and 1 comparison for of the remaining N-1 insertions. Therefore, in the best case insertion sort requires exactly N-1 comparisons, which is a linear function of N, $O(N)$.

In the worst case, each element is compared with every other element already in the list. The first element requires no comparison. The second element requires one comparison. The third element requires two comparisons, and so on. The Nth element added requires N-1 comparisons. Therefore, the number of comparisons required to sort N elements is the sum $(0 + 1 + 2 + 3 + ... + (N-1))$. This sum equals $N(N-1)/2$ comparisons, which is equivalent to $N^2/2 - N/2$. Therefore, in the worst case, insertion sort requires $O(N^2)$ comparisons!

Remember the function families discussed earlier in this chapter. The N^2 family was the most expensive family of functions mentioned. Therefore, under the worst-case scenario, as the number of elements to be sorted (N) increases, the number of comparisons required by the insertion sort algorithm becomes extremely large. For sorting a large number of objects (large values of N), insertion sort can require a prohibitively large number of comparisons. We will see some sorting algorithms later in this chapter that perform better than insertion sort for large values of N.

18.2.4. Bubble Sort

If you had to create an algorithm for sorting, chances are very good that you would create an algorithm either the same as or very similar to the algorithm known as *bubble sort*. Although you might have picked a different name for the algorithm, and although it is known by several names, the next sorting algorithm we look at is very common.

The idea behind bubble sort is quite simple. The first element is compared to the second element; if they are out of order, they are exchanged. Next the second element is compared to the third element; if they are out of order, they are exchanged. Next the third and fourth elements are compared and exchanged if necessary. This idea continues with the fourth and fifth elements, then fifth and sixth elements, and so on through the last element of the list. If we are sorting into increasing order, then the largest element "bubbles up" in the last position of the list. By making a second pass over the list, the second largest element will "bubble up" in the second from last position. By making additional such passes over the list, each element will bubble up in the correct position, and the list will be in sorted order. This gives rise to the name *bubble sort*.

18.2.4.1. Pseudocode

The code for the bubble sort algorithm is shorter and simpler than the other algorithms presented in this chapter, as the following pseudocode shows:

```
PROCEDURE BubbleSort (list)

BEGIN
    FOR outer := 1 TO NumberOfElements
        FOR inner := 1 TO NumberOfElements-1
            IF list[inner] > list[inner+1]
                THEN Exchange(list[inner], list[inner+1])
END
```

Programming Example 18-6: Simplest Bubble Sort

Two *adjacent* elements are compared. If they are out of order, they are exchanged. The algorithm uses two loops. The inner loop controls which two elements are being compared, and the outer loop controls the number of passes over the list. Note that the inner loop passes over every element in the list, regardless of how many sorted values have already bubbled up at the end of the list. We can improve the previous algorithm in the way indicated in the following pseudocode:

```
PROCEDURE BubbleSort (list)

BEGIN
    FOR outer := NumberOfElements DOWNTO 1
        FOR inner := 1 TO outer-1
            IF list[inner] > list[inner+1]
                THEN Exchange(list[inner], list[inner+1])
END
```

Programming Example 18-7:   Bubble Sort Pseudocode

This small change permits the inner loop to stop when it has reached the sorted values already bubbled up at the end of the list. Note that at the center of the algorithm is the operation **Exchange**. It is for this reason that some people refer to *bubble sort* as *exchange sort*.

The following illustration demonstrates the bubble sort algorithm for a particular example:

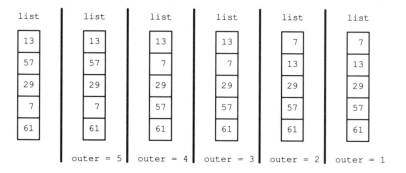

Figure 18-10:   Bubble Sort

Notice that after the first pass, the largest value is in the last position. After the second pass, the second-largest value is in the second-to-last position, and so on until all values are in the correct positions.

18.2.4.2. Analysis

Again, let us analyze the number of comparisons required by this algorithm. Each iteration of the inner loop requires exactly one comparison. Therefore, the number of comparisons required by bubble sort is the same in the best case, worst case and average case. Therefore, the inner loop will require `outer-1` comparisons for each iteration of the outer loop. For sorting N elements, the outer loop will execute N iterations. Therefore, the number of comparisons required by the bubble sort algorithm is the sum: $(0 + 1 + 2 + 3 + ... + (N-1))$. This sum equals $N(N-1)/2$ comparisons, which is equivalent to $N^2/2 - N/2$. Therefore, in the best case, worst case, and average case, bubble sort requires $O(N^2)$ comparisons.

18.2.5. Selection Sort

Consider the following strategy for sorting a list of numbers in increasing order. We first find the smallest element of the list and remove it from the list. We then find the smallest element in the remaining list, which is the second-smallest element of the original list. Next, we again select and remove the smallest element from the list. This time we have the third-smallest element of the original list. We continue this process until we have selected every element of the original list. Note that each pass over the list selects the next-smallest element in the original list. The elements selected in this fashion are ordered from smallest to largest, thereby giving rise to the name *selection sort*. The following illustration demonstrates selection sort with a particular example:

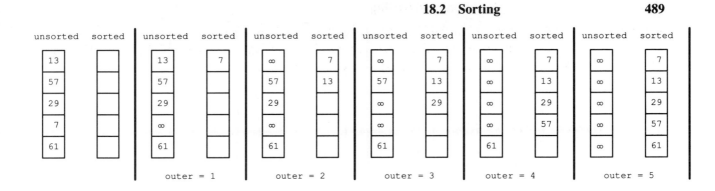

Figure 18-11: Selection Sort with Two Lists

18.2.5.1. Pseudocode

The following pseudocode starts with the unsorted list in **unsorted[1..NumberOfElements]** and builds the sorted list in **sorted[1..NumberOfElements]** through selection:

```
PROCEDURE SelectionSort (unsorted, sorted)

BEGIN
    FOR outer := 1 TO NumberOfElements
    BEGIN
        CurrentMin := unsorted[1]
        CurrentMinPosition := 1

        FOR inner := 1 TO NumberOfElements        (* find minimum value *)
            IF unsorted[inner] < CurrentMin
                THEN BEGIN
                        CurrentMin := unsorted[inner]
                        CurrentMinPosition := inner
                    END

        sorted[outer] := CurrentMin               (* copy min to sorted list *)
        unsorted[CurrentMinPosition] := +∞        (* remove min from unsorted list *)
    END
END
```

Programming Example 18-8: Selection Sort Pseudocode

The inner loop selects the minimum of the remaining elements, and the outer list controls how many elements are selected. As with insertion sort, selection sort can be done using only one list instead of two. The following modified code illustrates how this is done:

```
PROCEDURE SelectionSort (list)

BEGIN
    FOR outer := 1 TO NumberOfElements
    BEGIN
        CurrentMin := list[outer]
        CurrentMinPosition := outer

        FOR inner := outer+1 TO NumberOfElements
            IF list[inner] < CurrentMin
                THEN BEGIN
                        CurrentMin := list[inner]
                        CurrentMinPosition := inner
                    END

        swap(list[outer], list[CurrentMinPosition])
    END
END
```

Programming Example 18-9: Selection Sort with One List

The single-list selection sort is more commonly used since it requires only half as much memory for list storage and does fewer comparisons than its two-list counterpart. The following illustration demonstrates the single-list selection sort algorithm:

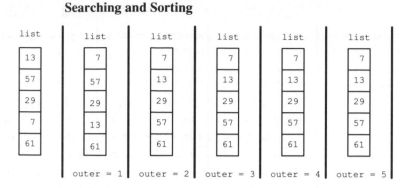

Figure 18-12: Selection Sort with One List

18.2.5.2. Analysis

Let us analyze the number of comparisons of both versions of selection sort. For the original two-list version of selection sort, there is exactly one comparison for each iteration of the inner loop, regardless of whether it is the best-case, worst-case, or average-case scenario. The way we have it written here, the inner loop requires N comparisons, and the outer loop executes N times. Therefore, the two-list version of selection requires N^2 or $O(N^2)$ comparisons in the best case, worst case, and average case.

For the single-list version of selection sort, there is again exactly one comparison for each iteration of the inner loop, regardless of whether it is the best-case, worst-case, or average-case scenario. The inner loop requires N-1 comparisons the first pass, N-2 comparisons the second pass, N-3 comparisons the third pass, and so on. Therefore, the number of comparisons required by the single-list algorithm is the sum: (N-1) + (N-2) + (N-3) + ... + 1, which equals N(N-1)/2. Although the single-list version only requires half as many comparisons as the two-list version, both variants of selection sort require $O(N^2)$ comparisons in both the best-case, worst-case, and average-case scenarios. The next sorting algorithm we look at requires far fewer comparisons.

18.2.6. Merge Sort

Consider the task of merging two sorted lists into another, single sorted list. As an example, consider merging the following two sorted lists of numbers:

        list 1 = {21, 43, 47, 51}

        list 2 = {16, 18, 22, 27, 33, 59}

Since both lists are sorted from smallest to largest, we need only compare the first element of each list to determine the first element of the resultant list. Specifically, since 16 is smaller than 21, 16 will be the first element of the merged list. This captures the essence of merging two sorted lists. Compare the smallest element of each list, remove the smaller of the two, and add it to the end of the merged list. Eventually, one of the lists is exhausted, and the remainder of the other list can be appended onto the end of the merged list. Merging the two sorted lists yields the following list:

        resultant ordered list = {16, 18, 21, 22, 27, 33, 43, 47, 51, 59}

It is actually quite easy to merge two sorted lists into a single sorted list. However, in sorting we normally start with one *unsorted* list rather than with two already-sorted ones. For this idea to be generally useful, we need an easy way to get two already-sorted lists from one unsorted list. If we think about it in the right way, this isn't a very hard problem either.

Instead of thinking of one unsorted list of N elements, think of it as N lists of one element each. Any list with just one element is by definition already sorted. Therefore, every sorting problem starts with N *already-sorted* lists.

To merge N lists of one element each, we first merge pairs of lists into N/2 lists, each having two elements. We then merge pairs of lists again, resulting in N/4 lists, each having four elements.

Eventually, we have two lists, each with N/2 elements. We then merge the two lists into one list of N elements. The resulting list is sorted. We end up with a sorted list by merging already-sorted lists. The following illustration demonstrates the merging process for N equal to sixteen.

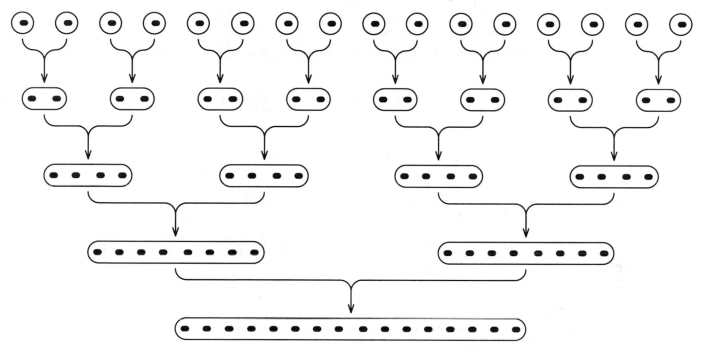

Figure 18-13: Abstract Merge Sort

The merge sort algorithm seeks to sort a list by merging two sorted lists. The algorithm for merge sorting is recursive, as indicated in the following pseudocode:

```
FUNCTION Sort (list: ListType): ListType

BEGIN
    IF length(list) = 1
        THEN RETURN(list)
        ELSE BEGIN
                middle := length div 2
                RETURN( Merge( Sort(list[1..middle]), Sort(list[middle+1..length]) ))
            END
END
```

Programming Example 18-10: Merge Sort Pseudocode

Pseudocode for merging is as follows:

```
FUNCTION Merge (firstlist, secondlist): ListType

BEGIN
    WHILE NotEmpty(firstlist) AND NotEmpty(secondlist) DO
        BEGIN
            compare the smallest element of each list

            remove the smaller of the two from the sorted list
            and add it to result list
        END

    add any remaining segment of the original list to the new list
END
```

Programming Example 18-11: Merging Pseudocode

To illustrate the merge sort algorithm further, we demonstrate it on the values shown in the following diagram:

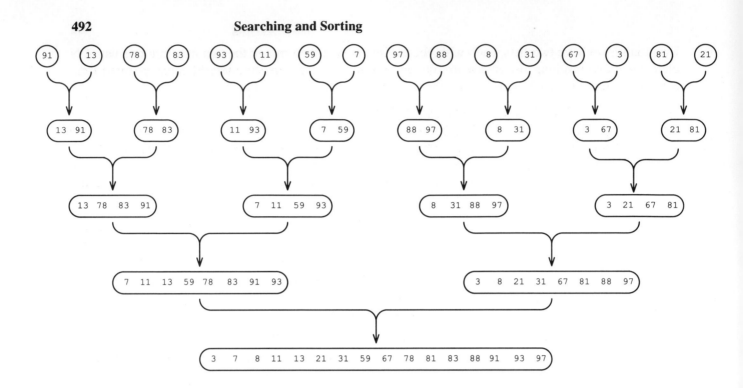

Figure 18-14: Merge Sort with Actual Values

This diagram illustrates sorting sixteen elements by merging sixteen lists of one element into one list of sixteen elements. Work through the illustration from beginning to end so that you are sure to understand it.

18.2.6.1. Analysis

Consider the number of comparisons required by the merge sort algorithm. To merge two sorted lists into one sorted list of N elements requires N-1 comparisons in the worst case. Therefore, the very last merge of merge sort requires not more than N-1 comparisons. To merge two sorted lists into one sorted list of size N/2 elements requires N/2 - 1 comparisons in the worst case. The next-to-last merging step has two such merges; hence, it means 2(N/2 - 1) or N - 2 comparisons. The same logic can be used to show that the previous step in the merge sort process requires 4(N/4 - 1 or N - 4 comparisons in the worst case. Therefore, the number of comparisons required by the entire merge sort process is the sum: (N-1) + (N-2) + (N-4) + (N-8) + ... + (N-N). If we are not interested in the exact number of comparisons, we could simply round each term in the sum up to N. Our analysis would consequently compute a higher number of comparisons than the algorithm really requires. If we ignore this consequence for a moment, we have a sum of terms, each no larger than N. But how many terms are in the sum?

The first level of merging deals with lists with one element. The second level of merging deals with lists of two elements. The third level of merging deals with lists of four elements. The fourth level of merging deals with lists of eight elements. The size of the lists double at each level of the merging process. It follows that for **L** levels and **N** elements, $2^L = N$. Therefore, $L = \log_2 N$. We have a sum of $\log_2 N$ terms, each no larger than N. This sum is no larger than $N * \log_2 N$. Therefore, the merge sort algorithm requires no more than O(N * log N) comparisons in the worst case!

The three other sorting algorithms presented in this chapter all required $O(N^2)$ comparisons in the worst case. Merge sort corresponds to a different function family. Merge sort is said to be an *order of magnitude* better than the other sorting algorithms presented. For large sorting problems (large values of N), merge sort is far superior to the other sorting algorithms presented.

Since we need only concern ourselves with the currently smallest value of the two lists being merged, merge sort needs only two values in primary memory at one time. All other values can reside on secondary storage. Therefore, merge sort can be used for external sorting if necessary.

The illustrations for merge sort all used lists with sizes that were a convenient power of two. We picked such sizes so the illustration would work out nicely. However, we should point out that merge sort works just fine for all other sizes.

18.2.7. A Lower Bound on Comparison-Based Sorting

At this point, you should feel comfortable with the idea of sorting. You know what the problem is and have at your disposal at least four different algorithms to solve the problem. Did you notice that central to each of those four algorithms is the notion of comparing elements to one another? In all cases, we used comparisons to gain information about the elements to be sorted. Hence, all four of these sorting algorithms are *comparison-based* sorting algorithms.

When we analyzed each algorithm, we focused on the number of comparisons required under a variety of scenarios. While some of the algorithms required $O(N^2)$ comparisons in some cases, we saw that insertion sort only requires $O(N)$ comparisons in the best case, while merge sort requires only $O(N*\log(N))$ comparisons under any scenario. You might be wondering if there are even better comparison-based sorting algorithms. It turns out that no comparison-based sorting algorithm can require fewer than $O(N*\log(N))$ comparisons under *all* scenarios.

Consider the problem of sorting three elements named *a*, *b*, and *c*. We use a tree known as a *decision tree* to model the decision process. The two elements being compared appear in the circular nodes. The outcome of each comparison is indicated along the arcs of the tree.

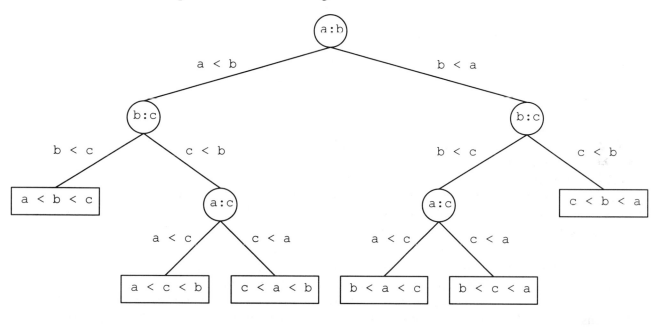

Figure 18-15:   Decision Tree for Sorting Three Elements

The decision tree indicates that we first compare the elements *a* and *b*. The left arc from that node indicates that comparison tells us *a* < *b*, while the right arc from the same node indicates that comparison tells us *b* < *a*. Each leaf node (indicated by a box) corresponds to a possible arrangement of the elements. For N elements there are N! (N factorial) permutations. Therefore, the decision tree has N! leaf nodes. A binary tree of height *h* has at most 2^h leaves. Therefore, a binary tree with N! leaves has at least a height of $\log_2(N!)$. Since each level of the tree has a comparison, all comparison-based sorts on some input require $O(\log(N!))$ comparisons. Stirling's formula tells us that $N! = (N/e)^N$. Knowing this we can determine that $\log(N!) = \log((N/e)^N)$, which is equivalent to $N(\log(N) - \log(e))$. This can, in turn, be simplified to $N*\log(N) - 1.4N$. But this expression is $O(N*\log(N))$. Thus, we may state the following fact: **All comparison-based sorting algorithms must sometimes require $O(N*\log(N))$ comparisons.** We suggest that you commit this fact to memory.

18.2.8. Selecting the Best Sorting Algorithm

Given several sorting algorithms from which to choose, we must make a decision as to which algorithm is the best. Since every comparison-based sort must require $O(N*\log(N))$ comparisons under some scenario, and since the merge sort algorithm requires $O(N*\log(N))$ comparisons under all scenarios, you might be tempted to choose merge sort as the best sort. Unfortunately, there is no sorting algorithm that performs the best in all situations. Which sorting algorithm performs best on a given sorting problem is determined by the problem itself. We can give you some guidelines to help you determine which algorithm to select for a given problem:

- *What is the problem size (N)?*
  Recall that, as the value of N increases, the difference between function families becomes more pronounced. For large values of N, an $O(N*\log(N))$ algorithm will perform much better than an $O(N^2)$ algorithm.

- *Will it be an internal or external sort?*
  Although computer memory is getting cheaper all the time, every computer still has a finite amount of it. If all the elements to be sorted cannot fit in primary memory, then an external sorting algorithm, such as merge sort, must be used.

- *How large are the records to be sorted?*
  Most of the analyses for sorting algorithms focuses on the number of comparisons required. The other important operation involved in sorting is exchanges, or swaps, of elements. The number of exchanges varies from one algorithm to another, as well as for a given algorithm under different scenarios. Sometimes the cost of exchanges is more important than the cost of comparisons. For example, if the records being sorted are very large, exchanges become very expensive, and the deciding factor can be the number of exchanges required.

- *Are the data nearly sorted already?*
  Many times, the data to be sorted are not really in random order. There are times when the data are nearly sorted already. We have mentioned that the performance of a sorting algorithm can vary dramatically, depending under what conditions it runs. For example, although insertion sort requires $O(N^2)$ comparisons under the worst-case scenario, it only requires $O(N)$ comparisons under the best-case scenario. Remember that $O(N)$ is better than both $O(N^2)$ and $O(N*\log(N))$. If we know the data to be sorted are nearly sorted already, we can select a sorting algorithm to exploit that fact.

- *Is code simplicity a bigger factor than performance?*
  There are times when we need a sorting algorithm, and its performance is of no great consequence. Say that we are writing several programs to demonstrate a debugger, a pretty printer, or some other programming aid. In such situations, we usually are interested in the system being demonstrated rather than in the performance of the sorting algorithm. Similarly, say that we need to sort 100 numbers only once. We will never need to sort them again and, therefore, never need the program again. Here we should use the simplest algorithm, such as bubble sort. It simply is not worth our while to get merge sort implemented for this type of sorting problem.

Table 18-3: Some Guidelines for Selecting a Sorting Algorithm

You should try to find out as much as possible about the data to be sorted before choosing a sorting algorithm. If you know absolutely nothing about the data you will be sorting, use what you consider to be the simplest sort. In such situations, we typically choose the three-line algorithm for bubble sort. We can always replace bubble sort with another sorting algorithm if necessary.

The following Table summarizes the order of magnitude of number of comparisons required by the sorting algorithms already studied:

Algorithm	Best Case	Worst Case	Average Case
Insertion	N	N^2	N^2
Bubble (exchange)	N^2	N^2	N^2
Selection	N^2	N^2	N^2
Merge	$N*\log(N)$	$N*\log(N)$	$N*\log(N)$

Table 18-4: Order of Comparisons Required by Sorting Algorithms

Sorting is one of the fundamental problems in computer science, and consequently it is one of the best-studied problems in this field. The definitive work on the subject is Volume III of Donald Knuth's *Art of Computer Programming* [8]. However, Knuth's treatise is very mathematical and somewhat difficult to read. Another useful source is *Design and Analysis of Computer Algorithms* by Aho, Hopcroft, and Uhlman [1].

18.2.9. Questions

1. What is sorting?

2. What is at least one reason why we would want to sort items?

3. What are four requirements that must be met before a collection of items can be sorted?

4. What is internal sorting? What is external sorting? What is the difference between internal sorting and external sorting?

5. What is a disk sort?

6. What is the central notion of insertion sort? Describe the insertion sort algorithm.

7. How many comparisons are required by insertion sort in the best-case, worst-case, and average-case scenarios?

8. What is the central notion of bubble sort? Describe the bubble sort algorithm.

9. How many comparisons are required by bubble sort in the best-case, worst-case, and average-case scenarios?

10. Why is bubble sort sometimes called exchange sort?

11. What is the central notion of selection sort? Describe the selection sort algorithm.

12. How many comparison are required by selection sort in the best-case, worst-case, and average-case scenarios?

13. What is the central notion of merge sort? Describe the merge sort algorithm.

14. How many comparisons are required by merge sort in the best-case, worst-case, and average-case scenarios?

15. What is comparison-based sorting?

16. Which of the sorting algorithms presented in this chapter are comparison-based algorithms?

17. What is the "best" sorting algorithm?

18. What are at least five questions you should try to answer about the data to be sorted before choosing a sorting algorithm? Explain why each question can be important.

18.2.10. Problems

1. Write a Pascal program that implements bubble sort to sort integers in increasing order.

2. Write a Pascal program that implements bubble sort to sort integers in decreasing order.

3. Write a Pascal program that implements two-list selection sort to sort integers in increasing order.

4. Write a Pascal program that implements one-list selection sort to sort integers in increasing order.

5. Write a Pascal program that implements selection sort to sort integers in decreasing order.

6. Write a Pascal program that implements two-list insertion sort to sort integers in increasing order.

7. Write a Pascal program that implements one-list insertion sort to sort integers in increasing order.

8. Write a Pascal program that implements insertion sort to sort integers in decreasing order.

9. What are the number of exchanges required under the worst-case scenario for bubble sort, selection sort, and insertion sort?

10. What are the number of exchanges required under the best-case scenario for bubble sort, selection sort, and insertion sort?

11. Write a Pascal program to perform external sort on a TEXT file containing one integer per line.

12. There are times when the data to be sorted contain duplicates. Consider executing a sorting algorithm on a list of data that is already sorted and contains two or more duplicates. Of course, the sorting algorithm yields a sorted list; however, it may or may not exchange some of the duplicates. If the algorithm makes no exchanges among the duplicates in the sorted list, the algorithm is considered *stable*. Which of the following sorting algorithms are stable?

    a. Bubble sort

    b. Insertion sort

    c. Selection sort

    d. Merge sort

18.3. Chapter Summary

- Searching refers to the process of locating a particular piece of information in a collection of data.

- A search structure is a collection of records to be searched.

- An embedded key is the field of each record that is used to locate the desired record of the search structure.

- The search key is the particular embedded key value for which we are searching.

- Pseudocode is an abstract form of a program intended to demonstrate an algorithm rather than to be run on a computer.

- The conditional AND operator is equivalent to the AND operator, except the left operand is always evaluated first and the right operand is evaluated only if the left operand is TRUE. It is useful to avoid index out-of-bounds problems as well as division-by-zero problems.

- The sequential searching algorithm assumes nothing about the order of the search structure. It simply examines each record in the search structure until the desired record is found or the search structure is exhausted.

- The ordered searching algorithm assumes the search structure is ordered. Unlike sequential search, ordered search terminates if a record is encountered that follows the desired record.

- The binary searching algorithm looks at the middle element of an ordered search structure. If the element does not match the search key, half of the records can be ignored safely. The process is continued with the remaining element until the desired elements is found or no elements remain.

- Binary search needs random access to the elements to be searched. Therefore, sequential search structures, such as linked lists and sequential files, prohibit binary search.

- The number of records examined by a searching algorithm is a function of the size of the search structure (N).

- Order arithmetic ignores all but the dominant term of a function.

- Order comparison refers to comparing only the families to which functions belong.

- The family of a function is more important as the number of items increases.

- The number of comparisons required by the three searching algorithms presented in this chapter are summarized in Table 18-2 on page 482.

- Sorting refers to the process of arranging data in order.

- Binary search requires the search structure to be ordered (sorted). This is only one of many needs for sorting.

- Before a collection of data can be sorted, every two elements must be comparable with the same binary relation. The relation must return unique and noncontradictory results as well as being transitive.

- If the data being sorted are all stored in primary memory, the sort is called an internal sort. If the the data are stored in secondary memory, the sort is called an external sort.

- Disk sort is another name for external sort.

- Insertion sort starts with an empty list and inserts one element into the list at a time while maintaining a sorted list at each stage of the insertion.

- Bubble sort compares *adjacent* elements and exchanges them if they are out of relative order.

- Selection sort determines the smallest element in a list and then determines the smallest element from the remaining elements in the list until all elements in the list have been selected.

- Merge sort sorts a list of N elements by breaking the list up into N lists of one element each and then merging these N sorted lists into one sorted list.

- All four sorting algorithms presented in this chapter can be used as an internal sort, but only merge sort can be used as an external sort.

- An algorithm that sorts a list of elements by comparing the elements is called comparison-based sorting.

- All comparison-based sorting algorithms must require $O(N*\log(N))$ comparisons under some scenario.

- The number of comparisons required by each sorting algorithm presented in this chapter is summarized in Table 18-4 on page 495.

- No sorting algorithm performs best under all scenarios. We summarized some guidelines for choosing a sorting algorithm in Table 18-3 on page 494. You should always try to find out as much as possible about the data to be sorted before selecting an algorithm.

18.4. Summary of Terms

• algorithm	• sequential search	• family of functions
• searching	• linear search	• order arithmetic
• search structure	• ordered search	• order comparisons
• embedded key	• binary search	• order of magnitude
• search key	• pseudocode	• N

- O(N)
- O(log N)
- O(N^2)
- O(N*log(N))
- ordered
- sorting

- transitivity
- internal sort
- external sort
- disk sort
- insertion sort

- bubble sort
- selection sort
- merge sort
- exchange sort
- comparison-based sorting

Appendix I: Karel Reserved Words and Special Symbols

Primitive Instructions

move

turnleft

pickbeeper

putbeeper

turnoff

Conditional Tests

front-is-clear	front-is-blocked
left-is-clear	left-is-blocked
right-is-clear	right-is-blocked
facing-north	not-facing-north
facing-south	not-facing-south
facing-east	not-facing-east
facing-west	not-facing-west
next-to-a-beeper	not-next-to-a-beeper
any-beepers-in-beeper-bag	no-beepers-in-beeper-bag

Reserved Words

AS	END-OF-EXECUTION
BEGIN	END-OF-PROGRAM
BEGINNING-OF-EXECUTION	IF
BEGINNING-OF-PROGRAM	ITERATE
DEFINE-NEW-INSTRUCTION	THEN
ELSE	TIMES
END	WHILE

Appendix II: Karel Syntax—BNF

We use a special language to formally describe the languages Karel and Pascal. The language we use is known as Backus-Naur Form (BNF). The particular version we use has a few more special symbols than the original BNF and is referred to as *extended BNF*.

Each BNF definition is called a *production*. The object being defined appears to the left of the *production symbol* ::=, and its definition appears to the right of the production symbol. The names of objects are enclosed in angle brackets <>. Square brackets [] enclose objects that may be included 0 or 1 times. Curly brackets {} enclose objects that may be repeated 0 or more times. The vertical bar | separates alternative objects, either of which is valid. Reserved words and special symbols appear in boldface type.

```
<program> ::= BEGINNING-OF-PROGRAM { <new-instruction definition> }
        BEGINNING-OF-EXECUTION { <instruction> } END-OF-EXECUTION
        END-OF-PROGRAM

<new-instruction definition> ::= DEFINE-NEW-INSTRUCTION <new name> AS
        <instruction> ;

<new name> ::= <identifier>

<instruction> ::= <primitive instruction> | <block> |
        <conditional instruction> | <repetitive instruction> | <new name>

<primitive instruction> ::=
        move | turnleft | pickbeeper | putbeeper | turnoff

<block> ::= BEGIN <instruction> { ; <instruction> } END

<conditional instruction> ::= IF <test> THEN <instruction>
        | IF <test> THEN <instruction> ELSE <instruction>

<repetitive instruction> ::= WHILE <test> DO <instruction>
        | ITERATE <positive integer> TIMES <instruction>
```

Appendix III: Karel Syntax—Bubble Diagrams

1. program

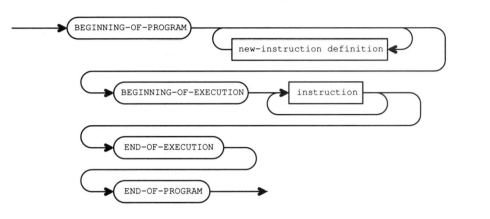

2. new instruction definition

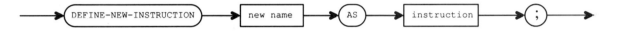

3. new name

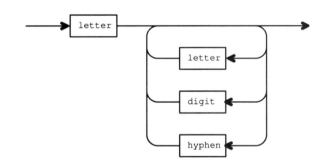

4. letter

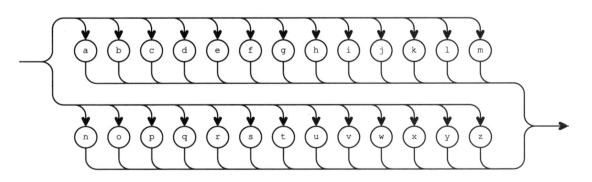

5. digit

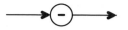

6. hyphen

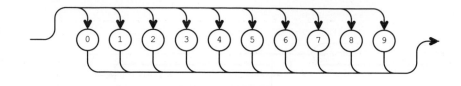

7. instruction

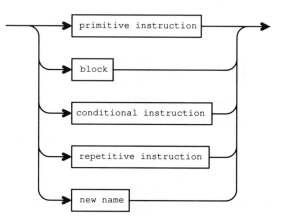

8. primitive instruction

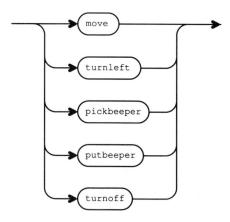

9. block

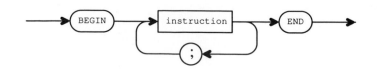

10. conditional instruction

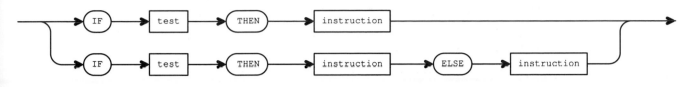

11. repetitive instruction

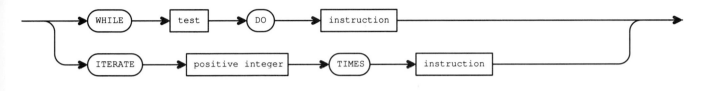

12. test

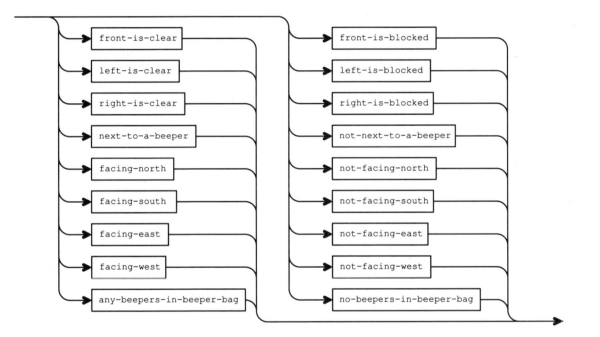

13. positive integer

Appendix IV: Pascal Reserved Words and Special Symbols

Reserved Words

AND	ARRAY	BEGIN	CASE	CONST
DIV	DO	DOWNTO	ELSE	END
FILE	FOR	FUNCTION	GOTO	IF
IN	LABEL	MOD	NIL	NOT
OF	OR	PACKED	PROCEDURE	PROGRAM
RECORD	REPEAT	SET	THEN	TO
TYPE	UNTIL	VAR	WHILE	WITH

Special Symbols

+	arithmetic plus, set union
–	arithmetic subtract, set difference
*	arithmetic multiplication, set intersection
/	arithmetic division
=	equal
<>	not equal
<=	less than or equal, subset
>=	greater than or equal, superset
<	less than, proper subset
>	greater than, proper superset
:=	assignment operator
;	statement separator
,	element separator for variable declarations and parameter lists
:	delimiter for variable declaration type and function type
'	delimit character constants and literal strings
.	decimal point, record selector, and program terminator
..	subrange specifier
{ }	comment delimiters
(* *)	comment delimiters
% \	comment delimiters (albeit archaic)
( )	parameter list delimiters, nested expression delimiters
[ ]	array subscript list delimiters, set delimiters
↑	pointer type denoter, dereference operator

Appendix V: Pascal Syntax—BNF

This appendix gives a formal description of the syntax of the language Pascal. A brief description of Backus-Naur Form (BNF) appears in Appendix II. A more detailed explanation of BNF can be found in Chapter 4 starting on page 117.

Although there are many different programming languages called Pascal, we describe the language defined as ISO Standard Pascal that was subsequently approved by the American National Standards Institute (ANSI) and the Institute of Electrical and Electronics Engineers (IEEE) [2]. Since the ISO Standard provides for two versions of Pascal, known as Level 0 and Level 1, we describe both versions. There are only two BNF productions that differ from Level 0 to Level 1. These two productions have their production symbols underlined for emphasis.

```
<actual-parameter> ::= <expression> | <variable-access> |
        <procedure-identifier> | <function-identifier>

<actual-parameter-list> ::= ( <actual-parameter> { , <actual-parameter> } )

<adding-operator> ::= + | - \ OR

<apostrophe-image> ::=   "

<array-type> ::= ARRAY [ <index-type> { , <index-type> }
        ] OF <component-type>

<array-variable> ::=  <variable-access>

<assignment-statement> ::=
        <variable-access> | <function-identifier> := <expression>

<base-type> ::=  <ordinal-type>

<block> ::=  <label-declaration-part> <constant-definition-part>
        <type-definition-part> <variable-declaration-part>
        <procedure-and-function-declaration-part> <statement-part>

<boolean-expression> ::=  <expression>

<bound-identifier> ::=  <identifier>

<buffer-variable> ::=  <file-variable> ^

<case-constant> ::=  <constant>

<case-constant-list> ::=  <case-constant> { , <case-constant> }

<case-index> ::=  <expression>

<case-list-element> ::=  <case-constant-list> : <statement>

<case-statement> ::=  CASE <case-index> OF <case-list-element>
        { ; <case-list-element> } [ ; ] END

<character-string> ::=  ' <string-element> { <string-element> } '

<component-type> ::=  <type-denoter>

<component-variable> ::=  <indexed-variable> | <field-designator>

<compound-statement> ::=  BEGIN <statement-sequence> END
```

```
<conditional-statement> ::= <if-statement> | <case-statement>

<conformant-array-parameter-specification> ::=
          <value-conformant-array-specification> |
          <variable-conformant-array-specification>

<conformant-array-schema> ::=  <packed-conformant-array-schema> |
          <unpacked-conformant-array-schema>

<constant> ::=  [ <sign> ] <unsigned-number> |
          <constant-identifier> | <character-string>

<constant-definition> ::=  <identifier> = <constant>

<constant-definition-part> ::=
          [ CONST <constant-definition> ; { <constant-definition> ; } ]

<constant-identifier> ::=  <identifier>

<control-variable> ::=  <entire-variable>

<digit> ::=  0 | 1 | 2 | 3 | 4 | 5 | 6 | 7 | 8 | 9

<digit-sequence> ::= <digit> { <digit> }

<directive> ::= <letter> { <letter> | <digit> }

<domain-type> ::= <type-identifier>

<else-part> ::= ELSE <statement>

<empty-statement> ::=

<entire-variable> ::=  <variable-identifier>

<enumerated-type> ::=  ( <identifier-list> )

<expression> ::=
          <simple-expression> [ <relational-operator> <simple-expression> ]

<factor> ::=  <variable-access> | <unsigned-constant> |
          <function-designator> | <set-constructor> |
          ( <expression> ) | NOT <factor>

<factor> ::=  <bound-identifier>

<field-designator> ::=  <record-variable> . <field-specifier> |
          <field-designator-identifier>

<field-designator-identifier> ::=  <identifier>

<field-identifier> ::=  <identifier>

<field-list> ::=  [ <fixed-part> [ ; <variant-part> ] |
          <variant-part> [ ; ] ]

<field-specifier> ::=  <field-identifier>

<file-type> ::=  FILE OF <component-type>

<file-variable> ::=  <variable-access>
```

```
<final-value> ::=  <expression>

<fixed-part> ::=  <record-section> { ; <record-section> }

<for-statement> ::=  FOR <control-variable> := <initial-value>
          TO | DOWNTO <final-value> DO <statement>

<formal-parameter-list> ::= ( <formal-parameter-section> { ;
          <formal-parameter-section> } )


<formal-parameter-section> ::=  <value-parameter-specification> |
          <variable-parameter-specification> |
          <procedural-parameter-specification> |
          <functional-parameter-specification>

<formal-parameter-section> ::=
          <conformant-array-parameter-specification>

<fractional-part> ::=  <digit-sequence>

<function-block> ::=  <block>

<function-declaration> ::=  <function-heading> ; <directive> |
          <function-identification> ; <function-block> | <function-heading>
          ; <function-block>

<function-designator> ::=
          <function-identifier> [ <actual-parameter-list> ]

<function-heading> ::=
          FUNCTION <identifier> [ <formal-parameter-list> ] : <result-type>

<function-identification> ::=  FUNCTION <function-identifier>


<function-identifier> ::=  <identifier>

<functional-parameter-specification> ::=  <function-heading>

<goto-statement> ::=  GOTO <label>

<identified-variable> ::=  <pointer-variable> ^

<identifier> ::=  <letter> { <letter> | <digit> }

<identifier-list> ::=  <identifier> { , <identifier> }

<if-statement> ::=
          IF <boolean-expression> THEN <statement> [ <else-part> ]

<index-expression> ::=  <expression>

<index-type> ::=  <ordinal-type>

<index-type-specification> ::=
          <identifier> .. <identifier> : <ordinal-type-identifier>


<indexed-variable> ::=  <array-variable> [ <index-expression>
          { , <index-expression> } ]
```

```
<initial-value> ::= <expression>

<label>::= <digit-sequence>

<label-declaration-part> ::= [ LABEL <label> { , <label> } ; ]

<letter> ::= A | B | C | D | E | F | G | H | I | J | K | L | M |
             N | O | P | Q | R | S | T | U | V | W | X | Y | Z

<member-designator> ::= <expression> { .. <expression> }

<multiplying-operator> ::= * | / | DIV | MOD | AND

<new-ordinal-type> ::= <enumerated-type> | <subrange-type>

<new-pointer-type> ::= ^ <domain-type>

<new-structured-type> ::= [ PACKED ] <unpacked-structured-type>

<new-type> ::=
        <new-ordinal-type> | <new-structured-type> | <new-pointer-type>

<ordinal-type> ::= <new-ordinal-type> | <ordinal-type-identifier>

<ordinal-type-identifier> ::= <type-identifier>

<packed-conformant-array-schema> ::= PACKED ARRAY [
        <index-type-specification> ] OF <type-identifier>

<pointer-type> ::= <new-pointer-type> | <pointer-type-identifier>

<pointer-type-identifier> ::= <type-identifier>

<pointer-variable> ::= <variable-access>

<procedural-parameter-specification> ::= <procedure-heading>

<procedure-and-function-declaration-part> ::= { <procedure-declaration> |
        <function-declaration> ; }

<procedure-block> ::= <block>

<procedure-declaration> ::= <procedure-heading> ; <directive> |
        <procedure-identification> ; <procedure-block> |
        <procedure-heading> ; <procedure-block>

<procedure-heading> ::=
        PROCEDURE <identifier> [ <formal-parameter-list> ]


<procedure-identification> ::= PROCEDURE <procedure-identifier>

<procedure-identifier> ::= <identifier>


<procedure-statement> ::= <procedure-identifier>
        [ <actual-parameter-list> ] |
        <read-parameter-list> | <readln-parameter-list> |
        <write-parameter-list> | <writeln-parameter-list>

<program> ::= <program-heading> ; <program-block> .
```

```
<program-block> ::=  <block>

<program-heading> ::=  PROGRAM <identifier> [ ( <program-parameters> ) ]

<program-parameters> ::=  <identifier-list>

<read-parameter-list> ::=
        ( [ <file-variable> , ] <variable-access> { , <variable-access> } )

<readln-parameter-list> ::=
        [ ( <file-variable> | <variable-access> { , <variable-access> } ) ]

<real-type-identifier> ::= <type-identifier>

<record-section> ::=  <identifier-list> : <type-denoter>

<record-type> ::= RECORD <field-list> END

<record-variable> ::= <variable-access>

<record-variable-list> ::= <record-variable> { , <record-variable> }

<relational-operator> ::=  = | <> | < | > | <= | >= | IN

<repeat-statement> ::=
        REPEAT <statement-sequence> UNTIL <boolean-expression>

<repetitive-statement> ::=
        <repeat-statement> | <while-statement> | <for-statement>

<result-type> ::= <simple-type-identifier> | <pointer-type-identifier>

<scale-factor> ::= <signed-integer>

<set-constructor> ::=
        [ [ <member-designator> { , <member-designator> } ] ]

<set-type> ::= SET OF <base-type>

<sign> ::= + | -

<signed-integer> ::= [ <sign> ] <unsigned-integer>

<signed-number> ::= <signed-integer> | <signed-real>

<signed-real> ::=  [ <sign> ] <unsigned-real>

<simple-expression> ::=  [ <sign> ] <term> { <adding-operator> <term> }

<simple-statement> ::=  <empty-statement> | <assignment-statement> |
        <procedure-statement> | <goto-statement>

<simple-type> ::= <ordinal-type> | <real-type-identifier>

<simple-type-identifier> ::=  <type-identifier>

<special-symbol> ::= + | - | * | / | = | < | > | [ | ] | . | , |
        : | ; | ^ | ( | ) | <> | <= | >= | := | .. | <word-symbol>

<statement> ::= [ <label> : ] <simple-statement> | <structured-statement>

<statement-part> ::=  <compound-statement>
```

```
<statement-sequence> ::=  <statement> { ; <statement> }

<string-character> ::= <one-of-a-set-of-implementation-defined-characters>

<string-element> ::=  <apostrophe-image> | <string-character>

<structured-statement> ::=  <compound-statement> | <conditional-statement> |
          <repetitive-statement> | <with-statement>

<structured-type> ::= <new-structured-type> | <structured-type-identifier>

<structured-type-identifier> ::= <type-identifier>

<subrange-type> ::= <constant> .. <constant>

<tag-field> ::= <identifier>

<tag-type> ::= <ordinal-type-identifier>

<term> ::=  <factor> { <multiplying-operator> <factor> }

<type-definition> ::=  <identifier> = <type-denoter>

<type-definition-part> ::= [ TYPE <type-definition> ;
          { <type-definition> ; } ]

<type-denoter> ::=  <type-identifier> | <new-type>

<type-identifier> ::= <identifier>

<unpacked-conformant-array-schema> ::=
          ARRAY [ <index-type-specification> { ;
          <index-type-specification> } ] OF <type-identifier> |
          <conformant-array-schema>

<unpacked-structured-type> ::= <array-type> | <record-type> |
          <set-type> | <file-type>

<unsigned-constant> ::=  <unsigned-number> | <character-string> |
          <constant-identifier> | NIL

<unsigned-integer> ::=  <digit-sequence>

<unsigned-number> ::=  <unsigned-integer> | <unsigned-real>

<unsigned-real> ::=  <unsigned-integer> . <fractional-part> [ E
          <scale-factor> ] | <unsigned-integer> E <scale-factor>

<value-conformant-array-specification> ::=
          <identifier-list> : <conformant-array-schema>

<value-parameter-specification> ::=
          <identifier-list> : <type-identifier>

<variable-access> ::= <entire-variable> | <component-variable> |
          <identified-variable> | <buffer-variable>

<variable-conformant-array-specification> ::=
          VAR <identifier-list> : <conformant-array-schema>

<variable-declaration> ::=  <identifier-list> : <type-denoter>
```

```
<variable-declaration-part> ::=  [ VAR <variable-declaration> ;
        { <variable-declaration> ; } ]

<variable-identifier> ::=  <identifier>

<variable-parameter-specification> ::=
        VAR <identifier-list> : <type-identifier>

<variant> ::= <case-constant-list> : ( <field-list> )

<variant-part> ::=
        CASE <variant-selector> OF <variant> { ; <variant> }

<variant-selector> ::= [ <tag-field> : ] <tag-type>

<while-statement> ::=  WHILE <boolean-expression> DO <statement>

<with-statement> ::=  WITH <record-variable-list> DO <statement>

<word-symbol> ::=  PROGRAM | LABEL | CONST | TYPE |
        PROCEDURE | FUNCTION | VAR | BEGIN | END | DIV | MOD |
        AND | NOT | OR | IN | ARRAY | FILE | RECORD | SET | PACKED |
        CASE | OF | FOR | TO | DOWNTO | DO | IF | THEN | ELSE |
        REPEAT | UNTIL | WHILE | WITH | GOTO | NIL

<write-parameter> ::=
        <expression> [ : <expression> [ : <expression> ] ]

<write-parameter-list> ::=
        ( [ <file-variable> , ] <write-parameter> { , <write-parameter> } )

<writeln-parameter-list> ::=
        [ ( <file-variable> | <write-parameter> { , <write-parameter> } ) ]
```

Appendix VI: Pascal Syntax—Bubble Diagrams

The following syntax diagrams are the graphical equivalent to the BNF definitions given in Appendix V.

1. actual parameter

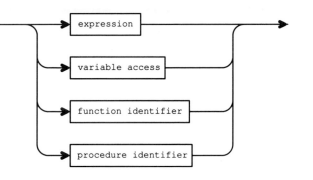

2. actual parameter list

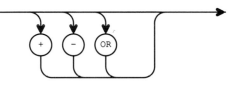

3. adding operator

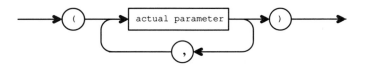

4. apostrophe image

5. array type

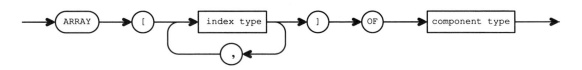

6. array variable

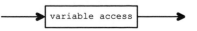

7. assignment statement

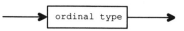

8. base type

9. block

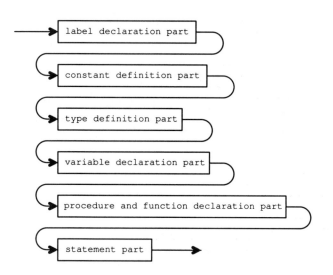

10. boolean expression

11. bound identifier

identifier

12. buffer variable

13. case constant

14. case constant list

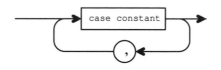

15. case index

16. case list element

17. case statement

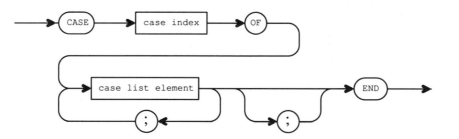

18. character string

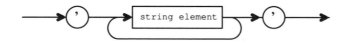

19. component type

20. component variable

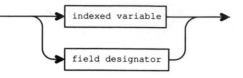

21. compound statement

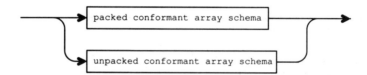

22. conditional statement

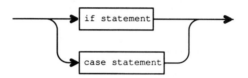

23. conformant array parameter specification

24. conformant array schema

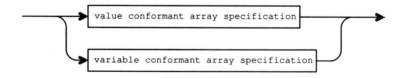

25. constant

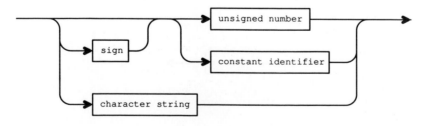

26. constant definition

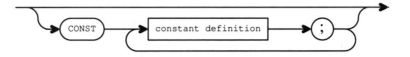

27. constant definition part

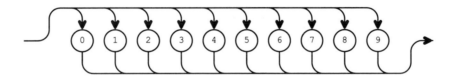

28. constant identifier

29. control variable

30. digit

31. digit sequence

32. directive

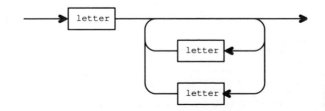

33. domain type

34. else part

35. empty statement

36. entire variable

37. enumerated type

38. expression

39. <u>factor</u>

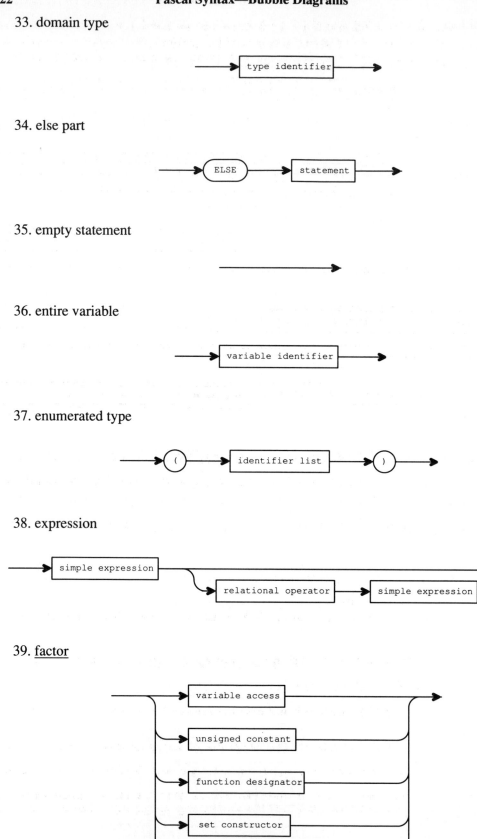

40. <u>factor</u>

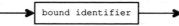

41. field designator

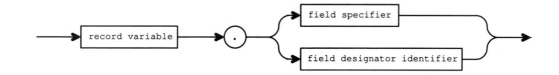

42. field designator identifier

43. field identifier

44. field list

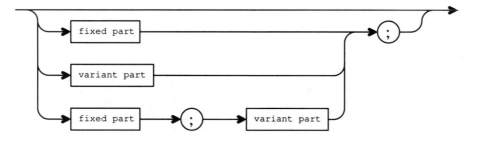

45. field specifier

46. file type

47. file variable

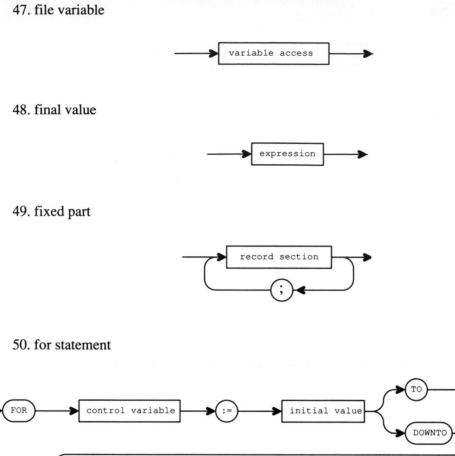

48. final value

49. fixed part

50. for statement

51. formal parameter list

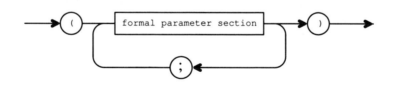

52. <u>formal</u> <u>parameter</u> <u>section</u>

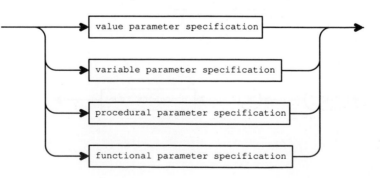

53. <u>formal</u> <u>parameter</u> <u>section</u>

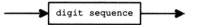

54. fractional part

55. function block

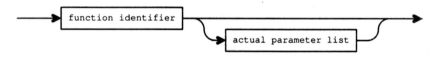

56. function declaration

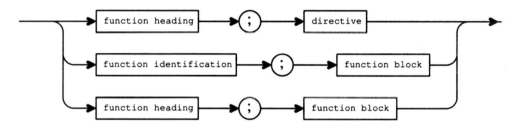

57. function designator

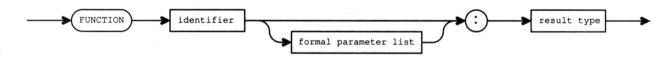

58. function heading

59. function identification

60. function identifier

61. functional parameter specification

62. goto statement

63. identified variable

64. identifier

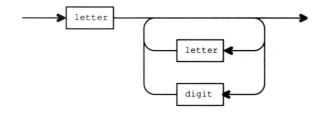

65. identifier list

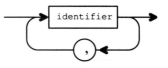

66. if statement

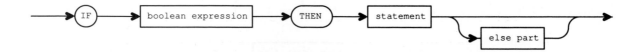

67. index expression

68. index type

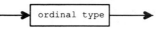

69. index type specification

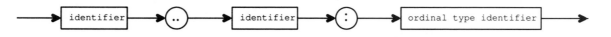

70. indexed variable

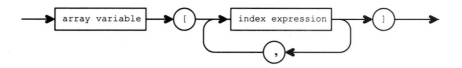

71. initial value

72. label

73. label declaration part

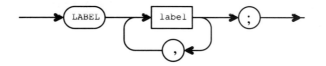

74. letter

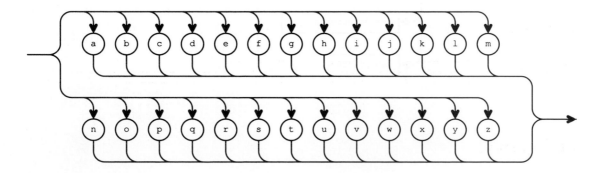

75. member designator

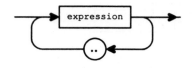

76. multiplying operator

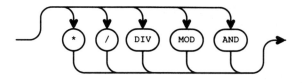

77. new ordinal type

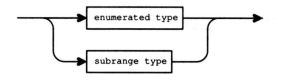

78. new pointer type

79. new structured type

80. new type

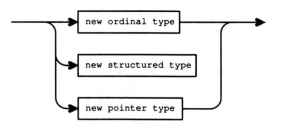

81. ordinal type

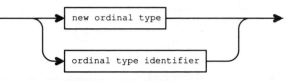

82. ordinal type identifier

83. packed conformant array schema

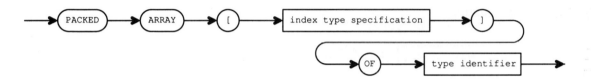

84. pointer type

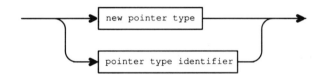

85. pointer type identifier

86. pointer variable

87. procedural parameter specification

88. procedure and function declaration part

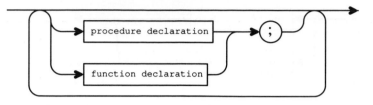

89. procedure block

90. procedure declaration

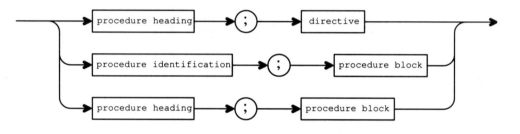

91. procedure heading

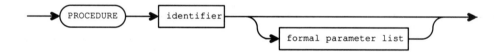

92. procedure identification

93. procedure identifier

94. procedure statement

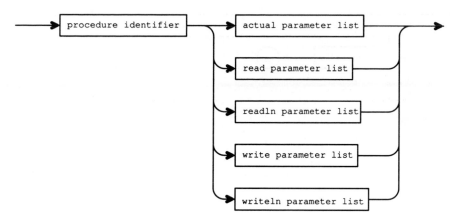

95. program

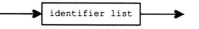

96. program block

97. program heading

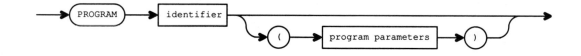

98. program parameters

99. read parameter list

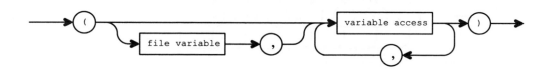

100. readln parameter list

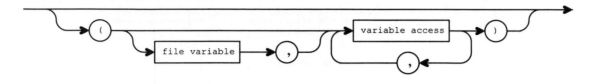

101. real type identifier

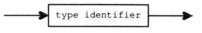

102. record section

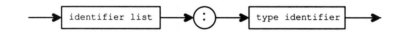

103. record type

104. record variable

105. record variable list

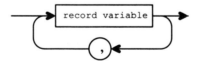

106. relational operator

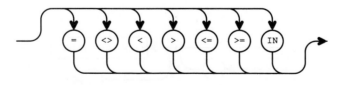

107. repeat statement

108. repetitive statement

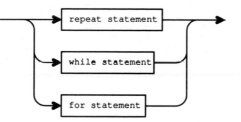

109. result type

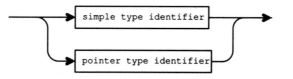

110. scale factor

111. set constructor

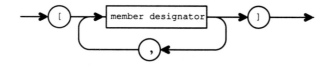

112. set type

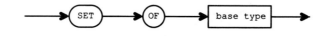

113. sign

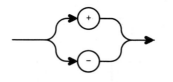

114. signed integer

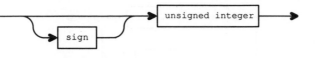

115. signed number

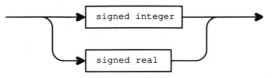

116. signed real

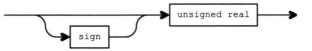

117. simple expression

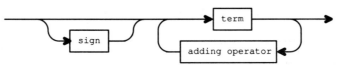

118. simple statement

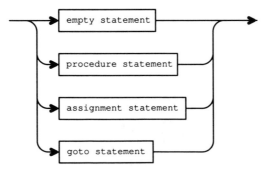

119. simple type

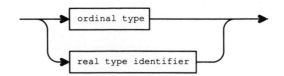

120. simple type identifier

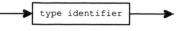

121. special symbol

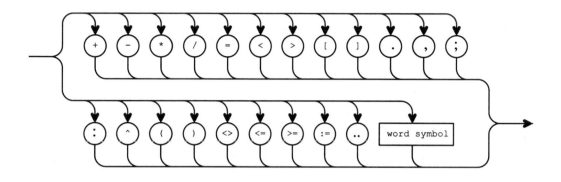

122. statement

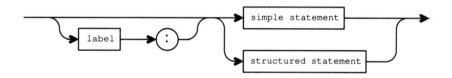

123. statement part

124. statement sequence

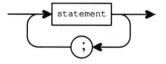

125. string character

126. string element

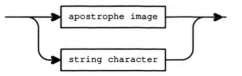

127. structured statement

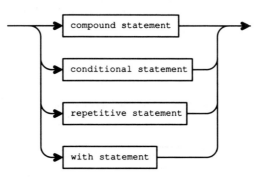

128. structured type

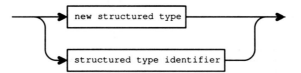

129. structured type identifier

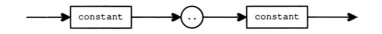

130. subrange type

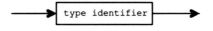

131. tag field

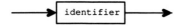

132. tag type

133. term

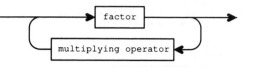

134. type definition

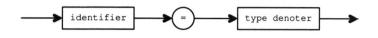

135. type definition part

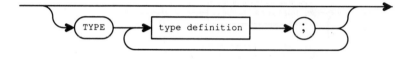

136. type denoter

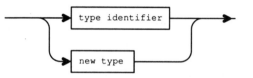

137. type identifier

138. unpacked conformant array schema

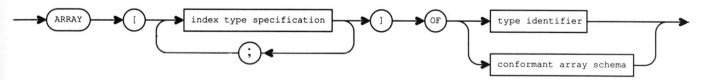

139. unpacked structured type

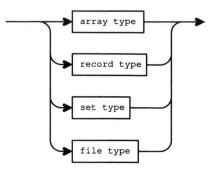

140. unsigned constant

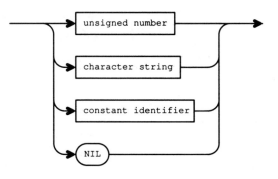

141. unsigned integer

142. unsigned number

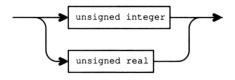

143. unsigned real

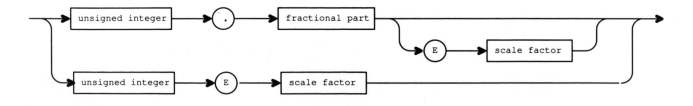

144. value conformant array specification

145. value parameter specification

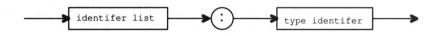

146. variable access

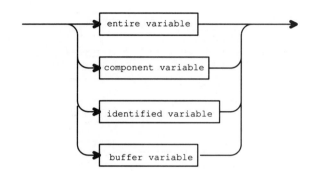

147. variable conformant array specification

148. variable declaration

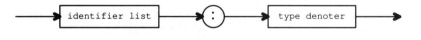

149. variable declaration part

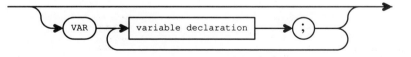

150. variable identifier

151. variable parameter specification

152. variant

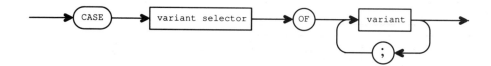

153. variant part

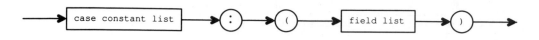

154. variant selector

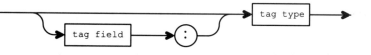

155. while statement

156. with statement

157. word symbol

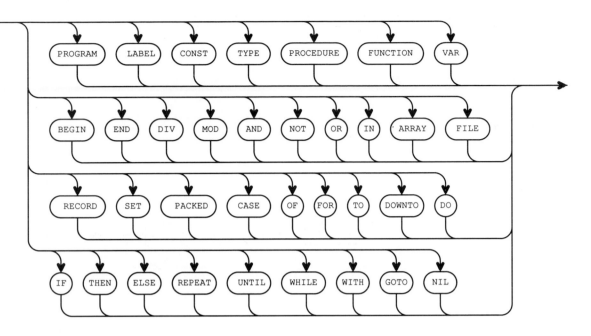

158. write parameter

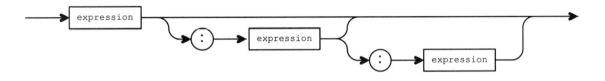

159. write parameter list

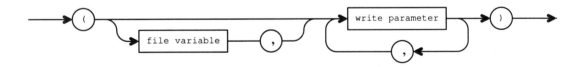

160. writeln parameter list

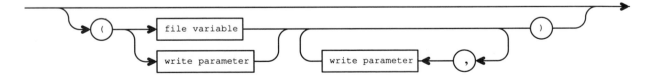

Appendix VII: Pascal Library Routines

Arithmetic Functions

```
FUNCTION Sin ( r: REAL ): REAL;

FUNCTION Cos ( r: REAL ): REAL;

FUNCTION Exp ( r: REAL ): REAL;

FUNCTION Ln ( r: REAL ): REAL;

FUNCTION Sqrt ( r: REAL ): REAL;

FUNCTION ArcTan ( r: REAL ): REAL;

FUNCTION Sqr ( x: integerorreal ): sametypeasx;

FUNCTION Abs ( x: integerorreal ): sametypeasx;
```

Type Transfer Functions

```
FUNCTION Trunc ( r: REAL): INTEGER;

FUNCTION Round ( r: REAL ): INTEGER;

FUNCTION Odd( i: INTEGER ): BOOLEAN;

FUNCTION Chr ( i: INTEGER ): CHAR;
```

Ordinal Functions

```
FUNCTION Ord ( x: anyordinaltype ): INTEGER;

FUNCTION Pred ( x: anyordinaltype ): sametypeasx

FUNCTION Succ ( x: anyordinaltype ): sametypeasx
```

File Handling Routines

```
PROCEDURE Read ( VAR f: anyfiletype;  VAR r: readparameter );

PROCEDURE ReadLn ( VAR f: anyfiletype;  VAR r: readparameter );

PROCEDURE Write ( VAR f: anyfiletype;  w: writeparameter );

PROCEDURE WriteLn ( VAR f: anyfiletype;  w: writeparameter );
```

```
PROCEDURE Reset ( VAR f: anyfiletype );

PROCEDURE Rewrite ( VAR f: anyfiletype );

FUNCTION EOF ( f: anyfiletype ): BOOLEAN;

FUNCTION EOLN ( f: TEXT ): BOOLEAN;

PROCEDURE Get ( VAR f: anyfiletype );

PROCEDURE Put ( VAR f: anyfiletype );

PROCEDURE Page ( VAR f: TEXT );
```

Dynamic Storage Allocation Procedures

```
PROCEDURE New ( p: anypointertype );

PROCEDURE Dispose ( p: anypointertype );
```

Packing and Unpacking Procedures

```
PROCEDURE Pack ( u: unpackedarray;
                 i: index;
                 VAR p: packedarray );

PROCEDURE Unpack ( VAR u: unpackedarray;
                   i: index;
                   p: packedarray );
```

Appendix VIII: Character Sets

Pascal supplies standard functions to manipulate characters and their ordinal values. The character set most commonly used with Pascal is known as the American Standard Code for Information Interchange (ASCII). Below we illustrate the ASCII character set and two other popular character sets known as EBCDIC and CDC character sets.[1] To use the tables below, first locate the desired character in the table. The decimal value of the character is obtained by adding the number associated with the row and column in which it resides.

ASCII Character Set

	0	1	2	3	4	5	6	7	8	9	10	11	12	13	14	15
0	^@	^A	^B	^C	^D	^E	^F	^G	^H	^I	^J	^K	^L	^M	^N	^O
16	^P	^Q	^R	^S	^T	^U	^V	^W	^X	^Y	^Z	^[	^\	^]	^^	^_
32		!	"	#	$	%	&	'	(	)	*	+	,	-	.	/
48	0	1	2	3	4	5	6	7	8	9	:	;	<	=	>	?
64	@	A	B	C	D	E	F	G	H	I	J	K	L	M	N	O
80	P	Q	R	S	T	U	V	W	X	Y	Z	[	\	]	^	_
96	`	a	b	c	d	e	f	g	h	i	j	k	l	m	n	o
112	p	q	r	s	t	u	v	w	x	y	z	{	|	}	~	

ASCII 32 is the space character; ASCII 0 is the null character; ASCII 127 is the DEL key.

EBCDIC Character Set

	0	1	2	3	4	5	6	7	8	9	10	11	12	13	14	15
0																
16																
32																
48																
64												.	<	(	+	|
80	&											!	$	*	)	;
96	-	/										^	,	%	_	>	?
112												:	#	@	'	=	"
128		a	b	c	d	e	f	g	h	i						
144		j	k	l	m	n	o	p	q	r						
160		s	t	u	v	w	x	y	z							
176		\	{	}	[	]										
192		A	B	C	D	E	F	G	H	I						
208		J	K	L	M	N	O	P	Q	R						
224			S	T	U	V	W	X	Y	Z						
240	0	1	2	3	4	5	6	7	8	9						

EBCDIC 0-63 and 250-255 are control characters.

CDC Character Set

	0	1	2	3	4	5	6	7	8	9	10	11	12	13	14	15
0	:	A	B	C	D	E	F	G	H	I	J	K	L	M	N	O
16	P	Q	R	S	T	U	V	W	X	Y	Z	0	1	2	3	4
32	5	6	7	8	9	+	-	*	/	(	)	$	=		,	.
48	≡	[	]	%	≠		∨	∧	↑	↓	<	>	≤	≥	¬	;

---

[1]EBCDIC is an abbreviation for Expanded Binary Coded Decimal Interchange Code while CDC is an abbreviation for Control Data Corporation.

References

[1]   Aho, Alfred & Hopcroft, John & Ullman, Jeffrey.
        The Design and Analysis of Computer Algorithms.
        Addison-Wesley Publishing Company, 1974.

[2]   Cooper, Doug.
        Standard Pascal User Reference Manual.
        W. W. Norton & Company, Inc., 1983.

[3]   Dijkstra, E. W.
        Notes on Structured Programming.
        Structured Programming.
        Academic Press, 1972.

[4]   Goldstine, Herman H.
        The Computer from Pascal to Von Neumann.
        Princeton University Press, 1972.

[5]   Gries, David.
        The Science of Programming.
        Springer-Verlag, 1981.

[6]   Hilbert, David.
        Principles of Mathematical Logic.
        Chelsea Publishing Company, 1950.

[7]   Jensen, Kathleen & Wirth, Niklaus.
        Pascal User Manual and Report.
        Springer-Verlag, 1975.

[8]   Knuth, Donald E.
        The Art of Computer Programming: *Sorting and Searching.*
        Addison-Wesley Publishing Company, 1973.

[9]   Newell, Allen & Simon, Herbert.
        Human Problem Solving.
        Prentice-Hall, 1972.

[10]   Papert, Seymour.
        Mindstorms: Children, Computers, and Powerful Ideas.
        Basic Books, 1980.

[11]   Peano, Giuseppe & Kennedy, Hubert.
        Selected Works of Giuseppe Peano.
        University of Toronto Press, 1973.

[12]   Turing, Alan M.
        Computing Machinery and Intelligence, Mind.
        McGraw-Hill, 1963.

[13]   Von Neumann, John.
        The Computer and the Brain.
        Yale University Press, 1958.

Index of Figures

Index of Tables

Index of Programming Examples

Index of Terms